ISLAM in Sub-Saharan Africa

A Partially Annotated Guide

Compiled by Samir M. Zoghby
African Section

Library of Congress Washington 1978

Library of Congress Cataloging in Publication Data

Zoghby, Samir M
Islam in sub-Saharan Africa.

Includes index.
1. Islam—Africa, sub-Saharan—Bibliography.
2. Africa, sub-Saharan—History—Bibliography. I. Title.
Z7835.M6Z63 [BP64.A1] 297'.0967 76-7050
ISBN 0-8444-0183-8

For sale by the Superintendent of Documents, U.S. Government Printing Office,
Washington, D.C. 20402
Stock Number 030-001-00068-1

Contents

Preface

Islam is a dynamic and growing religion in Africa, where it has alternately passed through militant and peaceful phases. The evolutionary phase of the Ghana Empire, in which Muslim traders played a major political role, was followed by the militant Almoravid era of the 11th century. A peaceful stage of Islamization under the influence of traders who settled in both the East and the West and spread the Message of the Prophet was followed by the Jihad movements of the 19th century. In the 20th century, Islam has become an important political variable. Throughout these various changes, Islam has shown its plasticity and ability to adapt to the African milieu, becoming in the process a truly indigenous faith.

This partially annotated bibliography presents a selection of books and periodical articles pertaining to Islam in sub-Saharan Africa. North Africa has been omitted because responsibility for the northern tier of the continent belongs to the Near East Section of the Orientalia Division rather than to the African Section and also because of the wealth of similar guides to reference material dealing with Islam in the North.

The main criterion in selecting items was whether Islam and Muslim populations are the central focus and major theme of a given work. Included are works dealing with the Islamization of the sub-Saharan zone; Muslim populations and their social, political, and religious structure; the impact of Islam and Arabic culture on the converted peoples; the resistance of Muslim leaders and reformers to European imperial designs; and the role of Islam as a major variable in political relations between Muslim states in the 20th century.

The most difficult decisions in the selection process related to works on the impact of Arabs and the Arabic language as carriers of Islam; a number of such peripheral items have been included, however, because they provide an understanding of the many and complex facets of Arabo-Islamic culture. Excluded from the compilation are unpublished doctoral dissertations.[1]

Entries are arranged by historical periods, with each chronological grouping divided by four broad regions of Africa. These in turn are subdivided by subject.

Susan Knoke Rishworth, a former staff member of the African Section, compiled the entries relating to papers on Islam read at annual meetings of the African Studies Association and those dealing with African fictional writing reflecting a Muslim milieu and influence. H. Dwight Beers prepared the glossary.

December 1974 was the terminal date for adding entries and bibliographic information.

Samir M. Zoghby
African Section
General Reference and
Bibliography Division
Reference Department

1. For information on doctoral dissertations, see: *American & Canadian Doctoral Dissertations & Master's Thesis on Africa, 1886–1974,* compiled by Michael Sims and Alfred Kagan (Waltham, Mass., African Studies Association [c1976] 365 p. Z3501.S5); *American Doctoral Dissertations on the Arab World, 1883–1974,* compiled by George D. Selim, Near East Section, Orientalia Division (Washington, Library of Congress; for sale by the Supt. of Docs., U.S. Govt. Print. Off., 1976. xviii, 173 p. Z3013.S43 1976); *Dissertations in History; an Index to Dissertations Completed in History Departments of United States and Canadian Universities,* compiled by Warren F. Kuehl ([Lexington] University of Kentucky Press, 1965–[72] 2 v. Z6201.K8) covering the period 1873–June 1970, and *Doctoral Dissertations in History,* v. 1+ Jan./June 1976+ ([Washington] semiannual. Z6205.D6) plus earlier compilations of the American Historical Association, Institutional Services Program.

Key to Location Symbols

CSt-H
: Stanford University, Hoover Institution on War, Revolution, and Peace, Stanford, Calif.

CU
: University of California, Berkeley, Calif.

CtHC
: Hartford Seminary Foundation, Hartford, Conn.

CtY
: Yale University, New Haven, Conn.

CtY-D
: Yale University, Divinity School, New Haven, Conn.

DHU
: Howard University, Washington, D.C.

DLC
: Library of Congress, Washington, D.C.

DLC-LL
: Library of Congress, Law Library, Washington, D.C.

DLC-Micro
: Library of Congress, Microform Reading Room, Washington, D.C.

ICU
: University of Chicago, Chicago, Ill.

IEN
: Northwestern University, Evanston, Ill.

IU
: University of Illinois, Urbana, Ill.

MBA
: American Academy of Arts and Sciences, Boston, Mass.

MBU
: Boston University, Boston, Mass.

MH
: Harvard University, Cambridge, Mass.

MH-P
: Harvard University, Peabody Museum, Cambridge, Mass.

MiEM
: Michigan State University, East Lansing, Mich.

MiU
: University of Michigan, Ann Arbor, Mich.

MnU
: University of Minnesota, Minneapolis, Minn.

NN
: New York Public Library, New York, N. Y.

NN-Sc
: New York Public Library, Schomburg Collection, New York, N. Y.

NNC
: Columbia University, New York, N. Y.

NjPT
: Princeton Theological Seminary, Princeton, N.J.

WU
: University of Wisconsin, Madison, Wisc.

Key to Periodical Abbreviations

A & A
L'Afrique et l'Asie. [Paris] DT1.A85

BCAOF
Comité d'études historiques et scientifiques de l'Afrique Occidentale française. Bulletin. Paris. DT521.C6

BIFAN
Institut fondamental d'Afrique noire. Bulletin. Dakar. DT1.I5123

BSOAS
London. University. *School of Oriental and African studies*. Bulletin. [London] PJ3.L6

CEA
Cahiers d'études africaines. Paris. DT1.C3

JAH
Journal of African history. [London, New York] DT1.J65

JHSN
Historical Society of Nigeria. Journal. [Ibadan] DT515.A2H5

JOSAF
Société des africanistes, Paris. Journal. Paris. DT1.S65

MW
The Muslim world. Hartford. DS36.M7

NA
Notes africaines. [Dakar] DT1.I513

RMM
Revue du monde musulman. Paris, E. Leroux. DS36.R4

SNR
Sudan notes and records. Khartoum. DT118.S85

TNR
Tanzania notes and records. Dar es Salaam. DT436.T3

Key to Sources

ASA Program
African Studies Association, *15th, Philadelphia, 1972*. [Program. Waltham, Mass., Brandeis University, 1972?] 52 p. DLC

Brasseur
Brasseur, Paule. Bibliographie générale du Mali (anciens Soudan français et Haut-Sénégal-Niger) Dakar, IFAN, 1964. 461 p. (Institut français d'Afrique Noire. Catalogues et documents, 16) Z3711.B7

Col. Off. Lib. Cat.
Gt. Brit. *Colonial Office. Library*. Catalogue of the Colonial Office Library, London. Boston, G. K. Hall, 1964. 15 v. Z921.L388

Col. Off. Lib. Cat. Suppl.
———First supplement. Boston, G. K. Hall, 1967. 894 p. Z921.L388 Suppl.

Gaskiya
Gaskiya Corporation, Zaria. Gaskiya catalogue 1970. 12 p. DLC

I.A.I. Cat.
International African Institute. *Library*. Cumulative bibliography of African studies. Boston, G. K. Hall, 1973. 2 v. Z3509.I57

Ita
Ita, Nduntuei O. Bibliography of Nigeria; a survey of anthropological and linguistic writings from the earliest times to 1966. London, F. Cass [1971] xxxv, 271 p. Z3597.I8

Jahn
Jahn, Janheinz, *and* Claus P. Dressler. Bibliography of creative African writing. Millwood, N.Y., Kraus-Thompson Organization, 1973. xl, 446 p. Z3508.L5J28 1973

Joucla
Joucla, Edmond A. Bibliographie de l 'Afrique occidentale française. Par E. Joucla, avec la collaboration des services du gouvernement général de l 'Afrique occidentale française et pour le Dahomey de M. Maupoil, administrateur des colonies. Paris, Société d'éditions géographiques, maritimes et coloniales, 1937. 704 p. (Bibliographie générale des colonies françaises) Z3711.J68 1937

London. Univ. Inst. of Educ. Cat.
London. University. *Institute of Education*. Catalogue of the collection of education in tropical areas. Boston, G. K. Hall, 1964. 3 v. Z5819.L648

Marcus
Marcus, Harold G. The modern history of Ethiopia and the Horn of Africa: a select and annotated bibliography. Stanford, Calif., Hoover Institution Press [1972] xxii, 641 p. (Hoover Institution bibliographical series, 56) Z3521.M35

Rishworth
Rishworth, Susan K. Spanish-speaking Africa; a guide to official publications. Washington, D.C., Library of Congress, 1973. 66 p. Z2689.R57

Royal Comm. Soc. Cat.
Royal Commonwealth Society. *Library*. Subject catalogue of the Library of the Royal Empire Society, formerly Royal Colonial Institute, by Evans Lewin. v. 1. The British Empire generally, and Africa. [London] 1930. 582, cxxiii p. Z7164.C7R82, v. 1

Africa, General

ARCHIVAL MATERIAL

1
Brockelmann, Carl. Geschichte der arabischen Litteratur. 2. den supplementbänden angrepasste aufl. Leiden, E. J. Brill, 1943–49. 2 v. PJ7510.B7 1943
——— ——— Erster-[dritter] supplementband. Leiden, E. J. Brill, 1937–42. 3 v.
PJ7510.B7 Suppl.

2
——— Tarīkh al-Adab al-ʻArabī [History of Arabic literature] Transl. by ʻAbd al-Ḥalīm al-Najjār. Cairo, Dār al-Maʻārif, 1962+
Z7052.B862 Orien Arab
At head of title: Jāmiʻat al-duwal al-ʻArabīyah.
Translation of *Geschichte der arabischen Litteratur.*
L.C. has v. 1–3.

3
Huisman, A. J. W. Les manuscrits arabes dans le monde. Une bibliographie des catalogues. Leiden, E. J. Brill, 1967. 100 p. Z6605.A6H8

4
Ibrāhīm, ʻAbd al-Laṭīf. Min al-wathāʼiq al-ʻArabīyah, dirāsāt fī al-kutub wa al-maktabāt al-Islāmīyah. [From Arab documents, studies in Islamic books and libraries] [Cairo, Dār wa maṭābiʻ al-shaʻb, 1962] 1 v. (various pagings) illus., facsims., plates. Z8.E412 Orien Arab
Though related to Egypt, these studies on Arab libraries and book production reflect an organization and attitude toward books prevalent in the whole Islamic world, including sub-Saharan Africa.

5
Lewicki, Tadeusz. Źródła Arabskie do dziejów Afryki na Południe od Sahary. [Arabic sources for the history of Africa south of the Sahara] Etnografia polska, tom 9, 1965: 221–293.
GN585.P6E8, v. 9
Investigation of the external Arabic sources on the region, from al-Fazārī at the end of the eighth century to such 19th-century writers as ʻUmar al-Tūnisī.

6
London. University. *School of Oriental and African Studies. Library.* Index Islamicus, 1906–1955; a catalogue of articles on Islamic subjects in periodicals and other collective publications, compiled by J. D. Pearson, librarian. Cambridge, Eng., W. Heffer [1958] xxxvi, 897 p. Z7835.M6L6
——— ——— Supplement. 1956–60+ 4 v. Cambridge, Eng., W. Heffer. Z7835.M6L62
Compiler 1956+ : J.D. Pearson.

7
Monteil, Vincent. Les manuscrits historiques arabo-africains. pt 1–3. BIFAN, t. 27, juil./oct. 1965: 531–542; t. 28, juil./oct. 1966: 668–675; t. 29, juil./oct. 1967: 599–603. DT1.I5123, v. 27, 28, 29
A most useful bibliographic essay by the former director of IFAN on manuscripts using Arabic script. The regions covered include Ghana, Nigeria, East Africa, Mauritania, Senegal, Niger, Mali, Guinea, Ivory Coast, and Upper Volta. The material surveyed includes documents in Arabic, constituting the bulk of the works, Hausa, Swahili, Fulfulde, and a few in Mamprule, Akan, and Dyula. A mine of information.

8
al-Munajjid, Ṣalāḥ al-Dīn. Qawā ʻid fahrasat al-Makhṭuṭāt al-ʻArabīyah. [Rules for the indexing of Arabic manuscripts] Beirut, Dār al-Kitāb al-jadīd, 1973. 79 p. DLC

9
Sow, Alfâ Ibrâhîm. Inventaire du Fonds Amadou-Hampâté Bâ, répertorié à Abidjan en 1969. Paris, C. Klincksieck, Université de Paris X, Laboratoire d'éthnologie et de sociologie comparative, 1970. 85 p. Z6616.B23S68
Inventory of the holdings (865 items) of the eminent Fulbe scholar, grouped by the following categories: general, literature, history, linguistics, religion, symbolism and astrology, geomancy and magic, and ethnology The citation provides the title of the piece, its author, pagination, and language.

10
Tetuán. *al-Maktabah al-ʻĀmmah.* Catálogo de materias (obras relativas al Islam y Africa) de la Biblioteca General del Protectorado; redactado por Guillermo Guastavino Gallent, Director de Archivos y

Bibliotecas del Protectorado. Tetuán, Editora Marroquí, 1952. 608 p. Z965.T45

11

Vajda, Georges. Index général des manuscrits arabes musulmans de la Bibliothèque nationale de Paris. Paris, Éditions du Centre national de la recherche scientifique, 1953. 743 p. (Publications de l'Institut de recherche et d'histoire des textes, 4) Z6621.P22A6 1953

12

Vatican. *Bibliotheca vaticana.* Elenco dei manuscritti arabi islamici della Biblioteca vaticana: vaticani, barberiani, borgiani, rossiani. Città del Vaticano, Biblioteca apostolica vaticana, 1935. xxix, 347, 41* p. ([Vatican. Biblioteca vaticana] Studi e testi. 67) Z6621.R78A6

At head of title: Giorgio Levi della Vida.

"Opere bio-bibliografiche e pubblicazioni periodiche": p. [xix]-xx; "Cataloghi di manuscritti": p. xxi–xxvi.

13

Yusuf Kamal, *Prince.* Monumenta cartographica Africae et Aegypti. [Le Caire] 1926–51. 5 v. in 16. illus., plates, port., maps (part fold., part col.), diagrs., facsims. (part col.) G2445.Y8

Vol. 1 has added t.p. in Arabic.

An encyclopedic compilation of maps and geographical descriptions of African regions. The texts are in the original language with a French translation, printed in black with the geographical names printed in red. A unique aid to scholarship, produced with great technical skill.

14

———Quelques éclaircissements épars sur mes Monumenta cartographica Africae et Aegypti. Leiden, Imprimés pour l'auteur par E. J. Brill, 1935. 216 p. GA1341.Y84

BIOGRAPHY

15

'Abd al-Nabī, 'Abd al-Ḥamīd. al-Qādah al-Ifrīqīyūn. [African leaders] [Cairo, al-Dār al-qawmīyah lil-ṭibā'ah wa-al-nashr, 1964] 153 p. ports. (Madhāhib wa shakhṣīyat, 96) DT18.A6 Orien Arab

Biographies of a number of African leaders.

16

Badawī, 'Abduh. Shakhsīyāt Ifrīqīyah, [African personalities] [Cairo] Wizārat al-Thaqāfah wa-al-Irshād al-Qawmī, al-Idārah al-'Āmmah lil-Thaqāfah [1963?] 167 p. illus. DT18.B3

Biographies of 35 black leaders.

17

Ḥasan, Muḥammad 'Abd al-Ghanī. al-Sharīf al-Idrīsī, Ashhar jughrāfiy al-'Arab wa-al-Islām. [Al-Sharīf al-Idrīsī, the most famous geographer of the Arabs and Islam] [Cairo] al-Hay'ah al-'Āmmah lil-ta'līf wa-al-nashr, 1971. 239 p. (A'lām al-'Arab, 97) G93.I432H33 Orien Arab

18

Mughal, Munir Ahmad. Hadrat Bilal. Islamic literature, v. 15, July 1969: 43–48. BP1.I68, v. 15

Short biography of Bilāl, the black muezzin of the Prophet Muḥammad, who was one of the first converts to Islam.

19

Muḥsin, Ḥasan 'Abd al-Samī'. Ibn Baṭṭūṭah al-raḥḥālah; wa kayfa ṣawwara al-mujtama' al-Islāmī fī 'aṣrihi. [Ibn Battutah the traveler; and how he described the Islamic society of his era] Cairo, al-Majlis al-a'lā lil-shu'ūn al-Islāmīyah, 1965. 114 p. (Dirāsāt fī al-Islām, no. 48)

BP20.D5, no. 48 Orien Arab

General introduction to the travels of Ibn Baṭṭūṭah during the 14th century. Muḥsin provides a biographical sketch, a synopsis of Ibn Baṭṭuṭah's travels from Tangiers, including a visit to the Sudan, and commentary on his description of the Islamic society he observed.

20

al-Munajjid, Ṣalāḥ al-Dīn. A'lām al-tārīkh wa-al-jughrāfīyah 'ind al-'Arab. [Outstanding Arab historians and geographers] Beirut, Mu'assasat al-turāth al-'Arabī, 1959+ DS222.8.M8

L.C. has v. 1. One of a series by Ṣalāḥ al-Dīn al-Munajjid. Contents: pt. 1. al-Balādhurī, Yāqūt, Ibn Khāliqān. —pt. 2. al-Muqaddasī, al-Ḥumaydī, Ibn 'Asākir. —pt. 3. Abū al-Fidā', Ibn al-Athīr, al-Dhahabī.

21

Mus'ad, Muṣṭafā Muḥammad. al-Ḥasan ibn Muḥammad al-Wazzān (Liyū al-Ifrīqī). [Leo Africanus] *In* Jāmi'at al-Qāhirah fī al-Kharṭūm. Majallah, m. 1, 1970: 41–66. DLC

Biography of Leo Africanus and description of the 15 "kingdoms" he visited: "Wālātā, Ghinyā, Mālī, Tumbuktū, Gāgaw (Ghāw), Gūbir, Aghādīs, Kānu, Katsinā, Zagzag, Zamfarā, Wangarā, Bornū, Gāgawā, al-Nūbah."

22
Qāsim, Jamāl Zakariyā. Kitāb waṣf Ifrīqiyā wa tārīkhihā lil Ḥasan ibn Muḥammad al-Wazzān; al-Musammā bi-Liyūn al-Ifrīqī. [The Book of the description of Africa and its history by Hasan ibn Muhammad al-Wazzan; known as Leo Africanus] *In* Cairo. Jāmi'at 'Ayn Shams. *Kulliyat al-Ādāb.* Ḥawliyyāt, m. 11, 1968: 279–306.
AS693.C36, v. 11 Orien Arab
Study of Leo Africanus and his magnum opus as an example of Arab writings on Africa.

23
Stafford, A. O. Antar, the Arabian Negro warrior, poet and hero. Journal of Negro history, v. 1, Apr. 1916: 151–162. E185.J86, v. 1
'Antar ibn Shaddād al-'Absī (d. ca. 615) was the son of Zubaydah, an Ethiopian woman taken prisoner by his father in a tribal raid. Stafford, citing a number of authorities, shows the prominent place occupied by a black poet in the pantheon of Arab literary figures.

CHRISTIAN MISSIONS

24
al-Azam, Yusuf. Christian missionary onslaught in Africa. Islamic literature, v. 14, Dec. 1969: 57–59.
BP1.I68, v. 14
Brief appeal to the Muslim community for help against the danger of Christianity in Africa. al-Azam cites statistical data to back his call for Muslims to resist the "machinations of Christian missions which are out to damage Islam and demoralize Muslims in Africa."

25
Blyden, Edward W. The Koran in Africa. *In* African Society. Journal, v. 4, Jan. 1905: 157–171. DT1.R62, v. 4
Empathic examination of Islam in Africa and its influence manifested by the veneration for the Holy Koran and the diffusion of Arabic. Blyden points out the problems facing Christian missionaries, concluding: "What is needed is not only the *preaching,* but the *acts* of the Apostles."

26
Bonet-Maury, Gaston. L'islamisme et le christianisme en Afrique. Paris, Hachette, 1906. 299 p. fold. map. BP65.A4B6

27
Breetveld, Jim. Islam reaches for Africa. Catholic digest, v. 28, Dec. 1963: 32–36. BX801.C34, v. 28

28
Filesi, Teobaldo. Esordi del colonialismo e azione della chiesa. Africa, anno 20, giugno 1965: 143–162; anno 20, sett. 1965: 269–293; anno 20, dic. 1965: 370–403. DT1.A843, v. 20

29
Küsters, P. M. Der Islam als afrikanische Macht und Gefahr. Hochland, 35. Jahrg., Mai 1937/38: 112–119. AP30.H67, v. 35

30
Putney, Ethel W. Islam in pagan Africa. MW, v. 8, Apr. 1918: 162–167. DS36.M7, v. 8
Beginning with a review of Johannes du Plessis' *Thrice Through the Dark Continent* (London, Longmans, Green, 1917. DT351.D85), Miss Putney warns the world of missions of the dangers of Islam in "pagan Africa." She attempts to explain the reasons for the success of Muslim proselytization and urges a more energetic Christianization campaign.

31
Rogers, Joel A. The Negro's experience of Christianity and Islam. Review of nations, no. 6, Jan./Mar. 1928: 69–81. AP4.R38, 1928

32
Roome, W. J. W. The border marches of Islam from the Red Sea to the Gulf of Guinea. MW, v. 10, July 1920: 220–240. DS36.M7, v. 10
Harping on the theme of the Arab/Muslim slave trader—"the Moslem is by instinct and religion an oppressor and slaver"—Roome presents the missionary view on the advance of Islam and how the latter "raises hopes by a hollow prestige and leaves its victims with a false idea of God, that frustrates the work of the Christian missionary, coming with the Story of Redeeming Love."

33
———"The dead weight of Islam" in Equatorial and Southern Africa. MW, v. 4, July 1914: 273–290. DS36.M7, v. 4

34
———"The dead weight of Islam" in Western and Eastern Sudan. MW, v. 4, Apr. 1914: 120–136.
DS36.M7, v. 4

35
Silberman, Leo. The challenge of Islam in Africa: I. Christian century, v. 76, Mar. 25, 1959: 356–358. BR1.C45, v. 76

36
———The challenge to missions in Africa: II. Christian century, v. 76, Apr. 13, 1959: 387–388. BR1.C45, v. 76

37
Simon, Gottfried. Islam and backward races. MW, v. 2, Oct. 1912: 387–404. DS36.M7, v. 2

Dr. Simon bemoans the "rapid expansion of Islam" in East, Central, and West Africa and shows the impact of Islamization on the populations of these areas. In his conclusion Simon reflects the general feeling of missionaries of the era when he says: "We cannot . . . quietly look on while Islam makes its triumphant progress among the backward races. It means we are exposing them to brutal violence. Let us see to it that Christian missions have a free hand both as regards means and workers; they alone can undertake the difficult task of educating these people, for they alone know what educative love is, they alone have acquired their wisdom, and their educative wisdom withal, where we can gain it best of all, from the Word of Him Who is moulding all the nations upon earth, at the feet of the Crucified Savior, Who gave Himself in love for mankind."

38
Sossidi, Elef. Gott in Afrika. Die Islamische und die Christliche mission in der neuen afrikanische gesellschaft. Frankfürter Hefte, 20. Jahrg., Feb. 1965: 108–114. AP30.F555, v. 20

39
Zwemer, Samuel M. The influence of animism on Islam; an account of popular superstitions. New York, Macmillan Co., 1920. 246 p. front., illus., plates. BP175.A6Z8

"This volume contains the A. C. Thompson lectures for 1918–1919 delivered on the Hartford Seminary Foundation and at Princeton Theological Seminary in a course of lectures on missions." *See also* 418.

40
———Mohammed or Christ; an account of the rapid spread of Islam in all parts of the globe, the methods employed to obtain proselytes, its immense press, its strongholds, and suggested means to be adopted to counteract the evil. New York, Fleming H. Revell Co. [1915?] [17]–292 p. front., illus., plates, facsims. BP172.Z8

Collection of articles by the then editor of the *Muslim World,* stressing the importance and magnitude of the Islamic threat and proposals to put a stop to the spread of Islam.

CITIES

41
Abbās, Muḥammad Jalāl. Tumbuktū. *In* Cairo. al-Jāmi‘ al-Azhar. Majallat al-Azhar, m. 36, Apr. 1965: 1078–1085. BP1.C3, v. 36 Orien Arab

A short history of the "port of the desert" and its vicissitudes, from its foundation to the independence of Mali. ‘Abbās closes with the statement that Timbuktu is the only city in the world that, in the words of al-Sa‘dī, "was not spoiled by the worship of idols, and none but the Merciful was bowed to on its spot."

42
Badawī, ‘Abduh. Mudun Ifrīqīyah. [African cities] [Cairo, al-Dār al-qawmīyah lil-ṭibā‘ah wa-al-nashr, 1963] 241 p. (Min al-Sharq wa-al-Gharb, 75) DT12.2.B3 Orien Arab

Free verse presentation of 14 African cities in a radio program style.

43
Davidson, Basil. The lost cities of Africa. Boston, Little, Brown [1959] 366 p. illus. DT25.D3 1959a

London edition (Gollancz) has title: *Old Africa Rediscovered* (DT25.D3 1969).

44
The Islamic city: A colloquium [held at All Souls College, June 28–July 2, 1965] published under the auspices of the Near Eastern History Group, Oxford, and the Near East Centre, University of Pennsylvania. Oxford, Cassiere; [Philadelphia] University of Pennsylvania Press, 1970. 222 p. 11 plates, illus., maps, plans. (Papers on Islamic history, no. 1) D199.3.I789

Papers delivered at a meeting organized by the Near Eastern History Group, Oxford. English and French.

45
Lapidus, Ira M. Muslim cities in the later Middle Ages. Cambridge, Harvard University Press, 1967. xiv, 307 p. maps. (Harvard Middle Eastern studies, 11) JS61.L3

46
Silla, Ousmane. Villes historiques de l'Afrique Saharo-Soudanaise. Revue française d'études politiques africaines, no 29, mai 1968: 25–38. DT1.R4, 1968

Descriptions of five cities, namely, Kumbi Ṣāliḥ, Awdaghost, Gao, Jenne, and Timbuktu.

46a
Tanga, L. Note bibliographique sur les villes de l'Afrique noire avant 1850. Études congolaises, v. 10, mai/juin, 1967: 112–122. DT658.E8, v. 10

EDUCATION

47
'Abbās, Muḥammad Jalāl. al-Ta'līm al-Islāmī fī Ifrīqiyā: Dawr al-Nash'ah wa-l-izdihār; Dawr al-nash'ah wa-l-izdihār, 'aṣr al-turuq al-ṣufīyah; dawr al-nash'ah wa-l-izdihār; Hāḍiruhu wa mustaqbaluhu. [Muslim education in Africa: the beginnings and flourishing; the beginnings and flourishing, the era of Sufi orders; the beginnings and flourishing; its present and future] *In* Cairo. al-Jāmi' al-Azhar. Majallat al-Azhar, m. 37, Sept. 1965: 196–200; m. 37, Jan. 1966: 421–426; m. 38, Aug. 1966: 358–364; m. 39, Feb. 1968: 779–783. BP1.C3, v. 37–39, Orien Arab

A thorough study of Muslim education in Africa from its beginnings to the post-independence period. The first part describes the introduction of Muslim education, the programs, educators, and levels of achievement, and its zenith under the great Islamic medieval empires. The second part shows the collapse of the great Western empires and the Portuguese crusades on the East coast, a period which witnessed a revival of animism. In this chaotic situation the Sufi orders emerged as a zealot reaction, thus saving Islam in its African "times of troubles." Sufism maintained Muslim education from the 17th to the 19th century.

The colonial period and the Europeans' perennial conflict with Islam and Muslim education are studied in the third part. 'Abbās argues that the European authorities encouraged missionary activities surreptitiously as well as blatantly, as when Britain supported such rival Muslim sects as the Aḥmadīyah after the Christian missions failed. Islam and Muslim education emerged weakened and shaken, to be given a new lease on life by the revivalist and reformist trend initiated by the Salafīyah movement of Shaykh Muḥammad 'Abduh of Egypt. The reaction of the colonial powers was to stress the differences among the sects and urge a confrontation, such as the riots in Bamako in 1957, between the reformists and Sufi traditionalists. The fourth part examines the legacy of the colonial era and the necessity to reform Muslim education to make it relevant to the modern needs of African states. The author calls upon the Azhar to contribute to the rejuvenation of Muslim education in Africa.

48
'Azzūz, Ibrāhīm, *and* 'Abd al-Fattāḥ Shalabī. Kayfa Tuṣali. [How to pray] Keifa tusali. [Cairo] Maktabat al-Wa'y al-'Arabī [1967]. 39 p. col. illus. BP183.3.A9 Orien Arab

Detailed presentation on the preliminaries and procedures of the Muslim prayer, geared to young French-speaking Muslims.

49
Barnes, Leonard C. Shall Islam rule Africa? [a paper read before the Baptist Ministers' Conference of Boston and vicinity]. Boston [1890]. 32 p. CtY

50
Conference on Muslim Education, *Dar es Salaam, 1958*. Proceedings of the Conference on Muslim Education on 20th-22nd November 1958. [Nairobi, Govt. Printer, 1959] 40 p. DLC

51
Dodge, Bayard. Al-Azhar; a millennium of Muslim learning. Washington, Middle East Institute, 1961. 239 p. illus. LG511.C45D6

52
———Muslim education in medieval times. Washington, Middle East Institute, 1962. 119 p. LA99.D6

A thorough description of the Islamic educational system. Dealing essentially with the Middle East, the study also records Muslim education as it was probably followed in the Sudanic area.

53
el-Garh, M. S. The philosophical basis of Islamic education in Africa. West African journal of education, v. 15, Feb. 1971: 8–20. L81.W4, v. 15

After sketching the development of education in the Muslim world and Africa, the author concludes that "in the end 'Islamic education' would have to mean, not just—as it has meant for centuries prior to modern times—education in the religion of Islam, but education—without any qualifications—of the Muslim masses all over the world."

54
Goody, John R. Literacy in traditional societies, edited by Jack Goody. Cambridge [Eng.] Cambridge University Press, 1968. 347 p. LC149.G6

55
Hiskett, Mervyn. Problems of religious education in Muslim communities in Africa. Overseas education, v. 32, Oct. 1960: 117–126. LC2601.O8, v. 32

56
Histoire universelle des missions catholiques d'aprés la conception originale de J. L. Françoisprimo. Publiée sous la direction de S. Delacroix. Paris, Grund [1956–59] 4 v. illus., col. plates, ports., maps (part fold., part col.), diagrs., facsims.
BV2100.H45

57
Muḥammad 'Abd al-Raḥīm Ghunaymah. Tārīkh al-Jāmi'āt al-Islāmīyah al-Kubrā [History of the great Islamic universities] Tetouan, Dār al-ṭibā'ah al-Maghribīyah, 1953. 330 (i.e. 332) p. LA99.M8
At head of title: Ma'had mawlāy al-Ḥasan.

58
Qurrā'ah, Sanīyah. Tārīkh al-Azhar fī alf 'ām. [The history of the Azhar [University] during the past one thousand years] [Cairo] 1968. 462 p. illus., ports. LG511.C45Q7
At head of title: Maktab al-ṣaḥāfah al-duwalī lil-ṣaḥāfah wa-al-nashr yuqaddim.

59
Rajab, Manṣūr 'Alī. al-Azhar bayna al-māḍī wa-al-ḥāḍir. [The Azhar [University] between past and present] [Cairo] Maṭba'at al-maqtaṭaf wa-al-muqattam, 1946. 88 p. LG511.C45R2

60
Shalabī, Aḥmad. History of Muslim education. Beirut, Dar el-Kashshāf, 1954. 16, 266 p. plates, map, facsims., plan. LA99.S5
Thesis—Cambridge University.
General introduction to education in the Muslim world. Traditional Muslim educational systems in sub-Saharan Africa were often patterned on the Arab model with regional variations and adjustments.

61
Signaté, Ibrahima. Education, Koran à l'écoute de la voix des anciens. Jeune Afrique, no 304, 6 nov. 1966: 60–62. DLC

62
Strelcyn, Stefan. Jak pisali i jak pisza mieszkancy Afryki. [How have written and how write now the peoples of Africa] Kontynenty, Nr 8, 1964: 34–35.
G464.K685, v. 8

63
Totah, Khalil A. The contribution of the Arabs to education. New York, Teachers College, Columbia University, 1926. 105 p. (Teachers College, Columbia University. Contributions to education, no. 231) LA99.T6 1926a
Although not touching upon Africa south of the Sahara, this dissertation examines Arab education during the Middle Ages in the Muslim world, of which regions of Africa have been an integral part. Relies heavily on Arabic primary sources.

64
al-Zayyāt, Aḥmad Ḥasan. Makkinū lil-Azhar fī Ifrīqīyā al-jadīdah. [Consolidate the Azhar in the new Africa] *In* Cairo. al-Jāmi' al-Azhar. Majallat al-Azhar, m. 32, Dec. 1960: 661–664.
BP1.C3, v. 32
The editor of the review urges the government to support the Azhar University in Africa. "The Azhar in Cairo and the Kaaba in Mecca are the two words which embody the meaning of Islam in the mind of the Muslim African, who turns to the Holy Mosque in search of its belief and to the Holy Azhar in search of its jurisprudence." The Foreign Students' City of the Azhar includes about 3,000 students from Africa and Asia. The author feels that it is not enough and suggests that "the state should make it possible for the Azhar [to carry its message] in this virgin land by providing it with funds and backing it with its influence to make it possible for the Azhar to achieve through Truth and Good what France had hoped to accomplish through Evil and Wrongdoing."

HISTORY

65
'Abd al-Qādir, Ḥāmid. al-Islām, ẓuhūruhu wa-intishāruhu fī al-'ālam. [Islam, its rise and propagation in the world] al-Ṭab'ah 2. muzayyadah wa-munaqqaḥah. [Cairo] Maktabat nahḍat Miṣr [1964] 320 p. BP50.A2 Orien Arab

66
Abdul Basit. Problems confronting Islam and Muslims in Africa. Islamic literature, v. 14, July 1968: 25–35. BP1.I68, v. 14
Islam in Africa, according to the author, has been slowed by "Christian onslaught and Muslim complacency." He urges Muslims to contribute to the education of their coreligionists in Africa and to the dispatch of missionaries. He believes that Islam is bound to triumph over Christianity not only because "it is the True Religion of the Creator" but also "because Christianity is linked to colonialism and racism, and is not capable of solving its own problems."

67
Abū al-'Arab Muḥammad ibn Aḥmad al-Tamīmī. Tabaqāt 'Ulamā' Ifrīqīyah wa-Tūnis. [Classes of the erudites of Ifriqiyah and Tunis] Edited by 'Alī al-Shābī [and] Na'īm Ḥasan al-Yāfī. [Tunis] al-Dār al-Tūnisīyah lil-nashr, 1968. 318 p. (Nafā'is al-makhṭūṭāt) DT269.T8A3

68
Abulfeda, 1273–1331. Géographie d'Aboulféda; traduite de l'arabe en français, et accompagné de notes et d'éclaircissements par m. Reinaud. Paris, Imprimerie nationale, 1848–83. 2 v. in 3. 3 fold. maps. G93.A15

Vol. 2, pt. 2, translated by Stanislas Guyard.

One of the early translations of *Taqwīm al-Buldān,* the major work by the prince of Hama province in Syria during the tumultuous Mameluke period. The 28-page section dealing with *Bilād al-Sūdān* covers Somalia, Ethiopia, and the Sudanic belt. The cities mentioned by Abū al-Fidā include "La capitale du Takrour, Berysa, Gana, Koukou, Djadjé, Sofala, Mâtan, Djymy, Zeghaoua, Dendema, Saharta, Bedje, Djarmy, Vefat, Hadyé, Dongola, Garfouné, Zeyla, Marka, and Macdaschou."

69
Adams, William Y. Ethnohistory and Islamic tradition in Africa. Ethnohistory, v. 16, fall 1969: 277–288. E51.E8, v. 16

Participation in the Islamic tradition requires historical validation. Such validation in Africa generally takes the form of migration legends or of family genealogies. Both are examined in terms of their effect on the ethnohistory of the region.—(Abstract supplied, modified)

70
African perspectives; papers in the history, politics and economics of Africa presented to Thomas Hodgkin. Edited by Christopher Allen and R. W. Johnson. Cambridge [Eng.] Cambridge University Press, 1970. xx, 438 p. illus., map, port. DT4.A33

Festschrift offered to Thomas Hodgkin on the occasion of his 60th birthday. The guiding principle in the selection made from the large number of essays presented was that they should reflect Hodgkin's own major concerns and interest and represent the several generations of Africanists he influenced. Partial contents: J. O. Hunwick, Notes on a Late Fifteenth Century Document Concerning 'al-Takrur'.—Ivor Wilks and P. Ferguson, In Vindication of Sidi al-Hajj 'Abd al-Salam Shabayni.—Jean Suret-Canale, Touba in Guinea; Holy Place of Islam.—J. Holden, The Samorian Impact on Buna: an Essay in Methodology.—J. Goody, Reform, Renewal and Resistance: a Mahdi in Northern Ghana.—Donal Cruise O'Brien, The Saints and the Squire; Personality and Social Forces in the Development of a Religious Brotherhood.

71
Ahmad, Mubarak. Islam in Africa. Rabwah, 1962. MH

72
Ahmad, S. Maqbool, *comp.* Islam in Africa and the Near East. Allahabad, Abbas Manzil Library [1955?] MiEM

73
Akademiia nauk SSSR. *Institut etnografii.* Drevnie i srednievekovye istochniki po etnografii i istorii narodov Afriki iuzhnee Sakhary. [Ancient and medieval sources on the ethnography and history of the peoples of Africa south of the Sahara] [Podgotovka tekstov i perevody L. E. Kubbelia i V. V. Matveeva. Otvestvennye redaktory V. I. Beliaev i D. A. Ol'derogge] Leningrad, Izd-vo Akademii nauk SSSR. [Leningradskoe otd-nie] 1960–65. 4 v. tables. DT1.A6

Each vol. has a special t.p.

Encyclopedic compilation of Arabic writings on sub-Saharan Africa.

74
Alexandre, Pierre. L'Afrique noire et l'expansion de l'Islam. Monde non-chrétien, t. 36, 1955: 315–334. NjPT

75
Anene, Joseph C., *and* Godfrey N. Brown, *eds.* Africa in the nineteenth and twentieth centuries. [Ibadan] Ibadan University Press, 1966. xviii, 555 p. illus., maps. DT28.A8 1966

Partial contents: J. O. Hunwick, The Nineteenth Century Jihads.—Joseph C. Anene, The Omani Empire and Its Impact on East African Societies.

76
Arnold, *Sir* Thomas W. The preaching of Islam; a history of the propagation of the Muslim faith. Lahore, Sh. Muhammad Ashraf, 1961. 508 p. BP170.3.A7 1961

First published in 1896.

Reprint of a major work on Muslim missions. Chapter 11 deals with the spread of Islam in Africa, from the conversion of the Berbers to Islam in Cape Coast "colony."

77
Atterbury, Anson P. Islam in Africa: Its effects—religious, ethical, and social—upon the people of the country. New York, Negro Universities Press, 1969. xxvi, 208 p. BP64.A1A84 1969

Reprint of the 1899 ed.

Atterbury provides interesting insight into the misconceptions prevalent in 1899 regarding Islam in Africa. In his concluding paragraph he affirms that "the great solution of the problem, the true civilisation of Africa, will be accomplished by Commerce and Christianity."

78
Azam, A. P. L'Islam en Afrique noire. Revue des troupes coloniales, no 286, mars 1947: 35–47. UA709.A6T7, 1947

The history of Islam in West and East Africa, the rise of the various empires, and Islam's revival under the Tukulor. The final section deals with the present situation in the continent. The author ends his essay with the prediction: "Peut-être dans l'humanité de demain, y aura-t-il place pour une Afrique Noire Musulmane et il semble que, pour la voir apparaître, il faille concentrer nos regards sur la région du nord de la Nigéria."

79
———. Les limites de l'Islam africain. A&A, no [1], 1948: 16–30. DT1.A85, 1948

Islam spread into Africa through various channels. Azam analyzes the routes of penetration, the centers of resistance, and the areas of Islamic diffusion. He stresses the two types of Islamization: that of the ruling aristocracy resulting in a restricted conversion, and that of the masses through the religious fraternities which anchor Islam in the state regardless of political changes.

80
Bâ, Amadou-Hampâté. L'Islam et l'Afrique noire. *In* Colloque sur la contribution des religions à l'expression culturelle de la personalité africaine, *Abidjan, Ivory Coast, 1961.* Colloque sur les religions, Abidjan, 5–12 1961. Paris, Présence africaine [1962] p. 101–118. BL2400.C6 1961

81
Bachelet, Michel. Systèmes fonciers et réformes agraires en Afrique noire. Paris, Librairie générale de droit et de jurisprudence, 1968. xxiv, 679 p. illus., tables. HD963.B33

Includes: Animisme, Islam et Christianisme—la rencontre de trois mondes qui s'ignorent; L'influence de l'Islam ou l'essai d'une colonisation dans l'ordre du spirituel.

82
Badawī, ʻAbduh. Maʻa ḥarakat al-Islām fī Ifrīqīyah; dirāsah min khilāl al-duwal al-latī qāmat qabl al-Istiʻmār. [With the movement of Islam in Africa; study through the pre-colonial states] [Cairo] al-Hay'ah al-Miṣrīyah al-ʻāmmah lil-ta'līf wa-al-nashr, 1970. 191 p. BP64.A1B3 Orien Arab

Starting with the Rustumites of Tahert and concluding with the Tukulors under the leadership of Shaykh ʻUmar ibn Idrīs, Islam was a prime mover and initiator of change before the colonial period in North Africa and the Sahel. Badawī analyzes the era and divides it into three main currents—the Sunni, Shi'ite, and Kharijite—and describes the various states that developed under their aegis.

83
al-Balādhurī, Aḥmad ibn Yaḥyā. Anonyme arabische Chronik, Band IX: vermuthlich das Buch der Verwandtschaft und Geschichte der Adeligen, von Abulhasan Ahmed ben Jahja Gabir ben Dawud Elbeladori Elbagdadi. Aus der arabischen Handschrift der Königl. Bibliothek zu Berlin, Petermann II 633, autographirt und hrsg. von W. Ahlwardt. Greifswald, 1883. xxvii, 448 p. DS234.B2 1883

Added t.p.: al-Juz' al-ḥādī ʻashar min tārīkh muṣannaf majhūl wa huwa laʻallahu Kitāb ansāb al-ashrāf wa-akhbārihim li-Abī al-Ḥasan Aḥmad ibn Yaḥyā ibn Jābir ibn Dā'ūd al-Balādhurī al-Baghdādī.

84
———. Futūḥ al-Buldān. [The conquest of countries] Taṣnīf Abī al-ʻAbbās Aḥmad ibn Yaḥyā ibn Jābir al-Balādhurī al-Baghdādī, Ḥaqqaqahu wa-sharahahu wa-ʻallaqa ʻalā hawāshīhi wa-qaddama lahu ʻAbd Allāh Anīs al-Ṭabbāʻ [wa] ʻUmar Anīs al-Ṭabbāʻ. [Beirut] Dār al-Nashr lil-Jāmiʻiyīn 1957 [i.e. 1958] 768 p. DS234.B22 1958

85
Barth, Heinrich. Travels and discoveries in North and Central Africa: being a journal of an expedition undertaken under the auspices of H. B. M.'s government, in the years 1849–1855. Centenary ed. London, F. Cass [1965] 3 v. illus., fold. col. maps. Imprint covered by label: New York, Barnes & Noble. "First published . . . in 1857." DT351.B273 1965

Heinrich Barth's magnum opus is a mine of information on the Sahel region. His knowledge of Arabic and his disguise allowed him to enter into contact with otherwise unapproachable groups. He has thoroughly and meticulously noted, copied, and commented on what he saw during his voyage.

86
Besrascoli, P. Cirillo. Islam africano. Nigrizia, anno 83, luglio-agosto 1965: 14–20. BV3500.A43, v. 83

87
Bessa, Carlos G. Incidências do Islamismo no Ultramar Português. Ultramar, ano 5, no. 20, 1965: 5–35. JV4201.M62, v. 5

Description of Islam in the Portuguese territories in Africa. Discussed are the geographical distribution, doctrinal concepts, sects, fraternities, and the Islamic renaissance and its links with the nationalism of the Third World.

88
Bibliotheca geographorum Arabicorum, editit M. J. de Goeje. Lugduni Batavorum, E. J. Brill, 1870–94. 8 v. maps (part col.) G93.B52 Orien Arab

Contents:

1. al-Iṣṭakhrī, Abū Isḥāq Ibrāhīm ibn Muḥammad al-Fārisī, known as al-Karkhī. Kitāb Masālik al-Mamālik.

2. Ibn Ḥawqal, Abū Qāsim. Kitāb ṣūrat al-ard.

3. al-Muqaddasī, Shams al-Dīn Abū ʻAbd Allāh Muḥammad ibn Aḥmad ibn Abī-Bakr al-Bannāʼ al-Shāmī, known as Bishārī. Kitāb aḥsan al-taqāsīm fī maʻrifat al-aqālīm.

4. Indices, Glossarium et Addenda et Emendanda ad part I–III.

5. Ibn al-Faqīh, Abū Bakr Aḥmad ibn Muḥammad al-Hamadhānī. Mukhtār kitāb al-buldān.

6. Ibn Khuradādhbih, Abū Qāsim ʻUbayd Allāh ibn ʻAbd Allāh. Kitāb al-masālik wa-al-mamālik.

7. Ibn Rustah, Abū ʻAlī Aḥmad ibn ʻUmar. Kitāb al-aʻlāq al-nafīsah.

al-Yaʻqūbī, Aḥmad ibn Abī Yaʻqūb ibn Wadhīd al-kātib. Kitāb al-buldān.

8. al-Masʻūdi. Abū al-Ḥasan ʻAli ibn al-Ḥusayn ibn ʻAlī. Kitāb al-tanbīh wa-al-ishrāf.

89
Blyden, Edward W. Christianity, Islam and the Negro race; with an introduction by Christopher Fyfe. Edinburgh, University Press, 1967. xvii, ix, 407 p. (African heritage books, 1) DT4.B54 1967

Collected essays by Blyden, who visited Egypt and Palestine in 1815 and was impressed by Muslim unity there. Though he never converted to Islam, he advocated the spread of Islam in the continent and consequently incurred the wrath of Christian missionaries.

90
Boer, Harry R. A brief history of Islam, a Christian interpretation. Ibadan, Daystar Press [1968] 121 p. geneal. table. DS38.3.B6

91
Boni, Nazi. Histoire synthéthique de l'Afrique résistante; les réactions des peuples africains face aux influences éxtérieures. Paris, Présence africaine, 1971. 310 p. illus. DT532.B6

Stressing the fact that Africa must rewrite its history, Nazi Boni states in his introduction, "Voici nos mobiles: Pour nous, cette oeuvre est un acte de foi une tentative de rétablissement de la vérité si souvent travestie, un essai d'objectivité, non de neutralité, car personne ne reste indifférent devant l'histoire de sa patrie . . . ." In the first section the author looks at the early and medieval relations of Africa with the outside world, starting with the Phoenicians and the advance of Islam. However, the major part of his work deals with the confrontation between Africa and European colonialism and the resistance efforts of leaders in Senegal, Mauritania, the Masina, Upper Volta. He closes with Almamy Samory's struggle against French encroachments.

92
Borattav, P. N. Les noirs dans le folklore turc et le folklore des noirs de Turquie. JOSAF, t. 28, fasc. 1–2, 1958: 7–23. DT1.S65, v. 28

Brief note on blacks in Turkey and description of the roles they played in Turkish rituals and festivities.

93
Boston University. *African Studies Center.* Papers on Africa. v. 1+ 1964+ Boston, Boston University Press. DT1.B6

Volume 4, *Western African History,* was edited by Daniel F. McCall, published for the African Studies Center of Boston University, and issued as a Praeger Special Studies in International Politics and Public Affairs. Partial contents: Daniel F. McCall, Exegesis of a Mahram.—Martin A. Klein, The Moslem Revolution in Nineteenth Century Senegambia.—Lucy Behrman, The Islamization of the Wolof by the End of the Nineteenth Century.

Volume 5, *Aspects of West African Islam,* was edited by Daniel F. McCall and Norman R. Bennett. It includes: Daniel F. McCall, Islamization of the Western and Central Sudan in the Eleventh Century.—Nehemia Levtzion, Patterns of Islamization in West Africa.—Ann Pardo, The Songhay Empire Under Sonni Ali and Askia Muhammad: a Study in Comparisons and Contrasts.—Bradford G. Martin, A Muslim Political Tract From Northern Nigeria: Muhammad Bello's Usul al-Siyasa.—Richard Hull, The Impact of the Fulani *Jihad* on Interstate Relations in the Central Sudan Katsina Emirates: a Case Study.—Lucie G. Colvin, The Commerce of Hausaland, 1780–1833.—Louis Brenner, The Northern African Trading Community in the Nineteenth-Century Central Sudan.—Joseph P. Smaldone, The Firearms Trade in the Central Sudan in the Nineteenth Century.—Allan Meyers, Slavery in the Hausa Fulani Emirates.—Lucy Behrman, French Muslim Policy and the Senegalese Brotherhoods.—Alfred G. Gerteiny, Islamic Influences on Politics in Mauritania.—Lyndon Harries, Women in African Islamic Literature.

L.C. has v. 1–5.

94

Brelvi, Mahmud. Islam in Africa. Lahore, Institute of Islamic Culture [1964] xxxvi, 657 p. illus., maps, ports. BP64.A1B7

General study of Islam in the African continent by a former director of External Affairs of the Mu'tamar al-Islāmī [Islamic Conference], located in Cairo.

95

The Cambridge history of Islam; edited by P. M. Holt, Ann K. S. Lambton [and] Bernard Lewis. Cambridge [Eng.] Cambridge University Press, 1970. 2 v. illus., maps. DS35.6.C3

Contents: v. 1. The Central Islamic Lands.—v. 2. The Further Islamic Lands, Islamic Society and Civilization.

96

Cardaire, Marcel P. Contribution à l'étude de l'Islam noir. *In* Institut français d'Afrique noire. *Centre Cameroun, Douala.* Mémorandum, 2 [1949]: 1–119. DT1.I512, v. 2

Entire issue devoted to this study.

After introducing the causes of Islamic unity and the characteristics of African animism, Cardaire investigates the two-pronged invasion of Africa by Islam, ". . . alors que l'Islam envahissait le pays noir à partir du Moghreb occidental et du Sénégal, véhiculé par des caravaniers du Sahara et les Foulbé du Fouta Toro, un autre courant islamique, parti d'Egypte et rattaché directement au Yemen, s'étendait sur le Soudan Oriental et atteignait le Tchad." The author then develops the theme of the Fulbe Jihad, the Senussia movement, "l'Islam noir et la conquête européenne," and in a final chapter the expansion of Islam and its close contacts with the world centers of Islamic learning. He closes on a political note reflecting his main interest: "L'Angleterre espère ainsi, et il ne semble que cet espoir soit déçu un jour prochain, exercer un controle sévère de l'évolution présente et à venir de l'Islam noir et des répercussions possibles de cette évolution sur les grands événements politiques mondiaux."

97

———. L'Islam et le terroir africain; études soudaniennes. [Koulouba, Imprimerie du Gouvernement, 1954] 168 p. fold. maps. BP64.A1C3

Africans, according to Cardaire, are faced with three alternatives, namely, materialism, Christianity, and Islam. He believes that "L'Islam Noir est tiraillé selon deux tendances. La première pousse les croyants à rechercher au fond d'eux-mêmes, au fond de leur puits, de quoi soutenir et enrichir leur foi, la seconde les invite à recevoir un dogme et des rites qui les attachent à un monde étranger, et qui les y attachent indissolublement, car c'est à une fusion culturelle qu'ils seront finalement poussés." Describing the "spiritual void" of traditional Africa, he presents the "Muslim solution" and the confrontation of Reformist versus traditional Islam. Reformist Islam, in its "traders" and "clerics" aspects, seems suspicious to Cardaire because of its links with the Azhar University in Cairo and its Arab political overtones. The reaction of the Westernized African Muslims who are "appelés à jouer un rôle important dans le refus des idées orientales" and the "Clerical Counter-Reformation" movement started in 1952 represent the tendencies opposed to a pro-Arab Islam.

98

Carpenter, G. W. The role of Christianity and Islam in contemporary Africa. *In* Haines, C. C., *ed.* Africa today. New York, Greenwood Press, 1968 [c1955] p. 90–113. DT5.H25 1968

99

Cattenoz, Henri G. Tables de concordance des ères chrétiennes et hégiriennes. Casablanca, Editions techniques nord-africaines, 1952. 1 v. (unpaged) CE59.C3

100

Chailley, Marcel, *and others.* Notes et documents sur l'Islam en Afrique noire. Paris, J. Peyronnet, 1962. 194 p. illus., maps. (Université de Paris. Centre de hautes études administratives sur l'Afrique et l'Asie modernes. Recherches et documents. Sér. Afrique noire, 1) DLC-Micro 40846

101
Cherbonneau, M. A. Les géographes arabes au Moyen Age. Revue de géographie, t. 8, jan./juin 1881: 81–92; 169–180; 268–278. G1.R43, v. 8

102
Comhaire, Jean. Some notes on Africans in Muslim history. MW, v. 46, Oct. 1956: 336–344.
DS36.M7, v. 46

Providing an overview of the role of Africans in Islam, Comhaire studies "the receptivity of Muslim societies to individuals of African descent and culture and the place of these immigrants in their new communities." He delineates the contribution of Africans in Mecca; under the Umayyads and Abbasids; in North Africa, Spain, and Sicily; Iran and India; under the Ottoman Empire; in modern Arabia and India; and modern Morocco. Comhaire also investigates their contributions in sectarianism and scholarship.

103
Constantin, F., *and* C. Coulon. Le développement des relations entre l'Afrique noire et le monde arabe en 1972. L'Année africaine 1972: 280–296. tables. DT30.A56, 1972

Investigation of Arab-African relations and the role of Islam as a catalyst.

104
Cornevin, Robert. Histoire des peuples de l'Afrique noire. 3. ed. Paris, Berger-Levrault, 1963 [c1960] 715 p. illus., geneal. tables, maps, ports. [Monde d'outre-mer. Série: Histoire) DT352.C6 1963

105
Davidson, Basil. Africa: history of a continent; with photographs by Werner Forman. Rev. ed. London, New York, Spring Books, 1972. 320 p. illus. (some col.), facsims., maps, plan.
DT20.D28 1972b

Published in 1968 and 1969 under the title *Africa in History: Themes and Outlines.*

Profusely illustrated and well-presented essay that includes large sections pertaining to Muslim influences.

106
Davidson, Basil, *ed.* The African past; chronicles from antiquity to modern times. Boston, Little, Brown [1964] 392 p. DT20.D3

Using a selection culled from the "chronicles and records of chiefs and kings, travelers and merchant-adventurers, poets and pirates and priests, soldiers and men of learning," Davidson provides a history of Africa—including the impact of Islam—as seen from the inside and by its early visitors.

107
De Graft-Johnson, John C. African glory; the story of vanished Negro civilization. London, Watts [1954] 209 p. illus. DT22.D4 1954

108
Delafosse, Maurice. The Negroes of Africa; history and culture. Translated from the French by F. Fligelman. Port Washington, N.Y., Kennikat Press [1968, c 1931] 313 p. maps. (Kennikat Press series in Negro culture and history) GN645.D44 1968

A translation of the author's *Les noirs de l'Afrique,* published in 1922 (DT15.D4); *Civilisations négro-africaines,* published in 1925; and part of *Les nègres,* published in 1927.

Includes three chapters dealing in part with the history of Islam and Muslim states. Most valuable as an attitudinal study of writers on Africa at the turn of the century.

109
Deluz-Chiva, Ariane. Anthropologie, histoire et historiographie. Kyklos, v. 17, fasc. 4, 1965: 1–12.
H1.A15, v. 17

110
al-Dhahabī, Muḥammad ibn Aḥmad. Kitāb duwal al-Islām fī al Tārīkh. [Book on Islamic states in history] Hyderabad, Maṭba'at jam'iyat dā'irat al-ma'ārif al-'uthmānīyah, 1364–1365 [1944/45–45/46] 2 v. DS234.D5

111
Dimashqî, Shems el-din al- Quid Schems Eddin el-Dimashqi geographus de Africa cognitum habuerit. Thesim Parisii, Georges Carre & C. Naud, 1897.
DHU

112
Di Soleb, M. L'Islam nell'Africa subsahariana. Affari esteri, anno 5, genn. 1970: 46–53.
D839.E812, v. 5

113
Doi, A. R. I. The Arab concept of Ifriqiya and the planting of Islam in Africa. Africa quarterly, v. 12, Oct./Dec. 1972: 202–214. DT1.A216, v. 12

114
Dos Santos, Eduardo. Religiões do ultramar Português. *In* Portugal. *Agencia Geral do Ultramar.* Boletim geral do Ultramar, ano 43, Maio 1967: 113–176. JV4201.A33, v. 43

Includes a brief note on Islam.

115
Durello, Gaetano. La battaglia dell'Islam. Nigrizia, anno 84, sett. 1966: 11–14. BV3500.A43, v. 84

116
Einzig, Paul. Primitive money in its ethnological, historical and economic aspects. London, Eyre & Spottiswoode [1949] 517 p. HG235.E35

117
Evliyā [Çelebi] *efendi,* Narrative of travels in Europe, Asia, and Africa, in the seventeenth century. Translated from the Turkish by the Ritter Joseph von Hammer. London, Printed for the Oriental Translation Fund of Great Britain and Ireland; sold by Parbury, Allen, 1834–50. 2 v. in 3. (Oriental Translation Fund. Publications) PJ408.O6

No more published.

Evilya Çelebi is a Turkish traveler who lived in the 17th century and wrote a Baedeker describing the various regions he visited.

118
Fage, J. D. An atlas of African history. [London] E. Arnold [1958] 64 p. 62 maps.
G2446.S1F5 1958 G&M

The first atlas of this kind. The set of maps begins with Roman Africa in the fifth century, followed by the penetration of Islam into Africa, the vagaries of North African politics, and the ebb and flow of the various African empires. The last part covers the European penetration of the continent, beginning with the Portuguese maritime expansion in the 15th century, followed by the "exploration" movement (1788–1900), and culminating with the scramble for Africa.

119
Freeman-Grenville, G. S. P. Chronology of African history. London, Oxford University Press. xxii, 312 p. DT17.F73

120
Frobenius, Leo. The voice of Africa; being an account of the travels of the German Inner African Exploration Expedition in the years 1910–1912. New York, B. Blom [1968] 2 v. (682 p.) illus., maps. DT351.F853 1968

Reprint of the 1913 ed.

Translation of *Und Afrika sprach.*

121
Froelich, Jean-Claude. L'Egypte et les peuples noirs. Orient, 9. année, 4. trimestre, 1965: 13–38.
DS1.O44, v. 9

122
——— Essai sur l'islamisation de l'Afrique noire. *In* L'Afrique islamique. [Lausanne, Théophile Grin] 1966. p. 171–245. (Le monde religieux. Nouv. sér., v. 29) BP64.A1A3

Concise essay on the Islamization of the continent south of the Sahara, divided into three major sections. "Old Islam" includes the Berber phase in the West and the Arab in the East. "Recent Islam" covers the Fulbe jihad period and the colonial era, as well as the agents of Muslim penetration, namely, warriors, traders, and monarchs. The last, "Modern Islam," analyzes the various religious sects and reform movements, with emphasis on former French Africa.

123
———Islam 1965. *In* Académie des sciences d'outre-mer. Comptes-rendus mensuels des séances, t. 25, mars 1965: 111–127.
JV1802.A314, v. 25

124
———Les musulmans d'Afrique noire. Paris, Editions de l'Orante [1962] 406 p. (Lumière et nations) BP64.A4S8

Froelich's book represents the tail end of what may be labeled "Administration scholarship," continuing the tradition of the Delafosses and the Martys. In the first part he presents a historical narrative of the advent of Berber Islam in the western part of Africa and Arab Islam in the east, concluding with a section on the impact of colonialism on the spread of Islam. The second part of the study relates the characteristics—as seen by the author—of black Islam. The third and last part looks at Islam in the contemporary world.

125
———Les musulmans d'Afrique noire en 1965. Revue militaire générale, t. 8, oct. 1965: 295–311.
U2.R48, v. 8

126
———Relationships between Islam in Africa north and south of the Sahara. African forum, v. 3, fall 1967/winter 1968: 44–57. DT1.A225, v. 3

Analysis of the role and nature of Islam in Africa south of the Sahara and the historical contacts between the two shores of the great desert. Islam came to East Africa through Arab efforts and was marred by the slave trade, while West Africa was introduced to Islam primarily by the Berbers, who were mainly interested in trade relations after the Almoravid episode. Froelich claims that Islam in West Africa is "profoundly traditional, mystical and naive," whereas in the eastern part it is "more learned and tolerant." The colonial period witnessed the development of Islam leading to the very active role played by the Arab states through the medium of Islam.

127
Fulayjah, Aḥmad Najm al-Dīn, *and* Yusrā 'Abd al-Rāziq al-Jawharī. Ifrīqiyah. [Africa] [Cairo, Dār al-Ma'ārif] 1967. 2 v. maps, ports. (al-Maktabah al-Jughrāfīyah) DT4.F8 Orien Arab
Vol. 1 pertains to sub-Saharan Africa.

128
Gautier, Emile-Félix. Les deux centres d'influences méditerranéennes qui rendent intelligible l'Afrique occidentale. *In* Association de géographes français. Bulletin, no 71/72, juil./oct. 1933: 109–111. G11.A8 1933

129
———Le passé de l'Afrique du Nord; les siècles obscurs. Nouv. éd. Paris, Payot [1964, c1952] 432 p. (Petite bibliothèque Payot, 67) DT194.G3 1964
Previously published under the title *L'Islamisation de l'Afrique du Nord.*

130
Ghoraba, Hammouda. Islam and slavery. Islamic quarterly, v. 2, Oct. 1955: 153–159. D198.I8, v. 2

131
Hama, Boubou. Kotia-Nima, rencontre avec l'Europe. [Paris] Présence africaine, 1969. 3 v. DT547.6.H3A3

132
Hamidullah, M. L'Afrique découvre l'Amérique avant Christophe Colomb. Présence africaine, no 17/18, fév./mai 1958: 173–183. GN645.P74, 1958

133
Hartmann, Johann M. Edrisii Africa. Editio altera. Gottingae, Svmtibvs J. C. Dieterich, 1796. 530 p. G93.I43H3 1796

134
Ḥasan, Ḥasan Ibrāhīm. Intishār al-Islām fī al-qārah al-Ifrīqīyah. [The spread of Islam on the African continent] al-ṭab'ah 2. Cairo, Maktabat al-nahḍah al-Miṣriyah, 1963. 248 p. maps. BP64.A1H37 1963

135
———Masālik al-Islām ilā al-qārah al-Ifrīqīyah. [The paths of Islam into the African continent] *In* Cairo. al-Jāmi' al-Azhar. Majallat al-Azhar, m. 34, Oct. 1962: 287–297. BP1.C3, v. 34 Orien Arab
Ḥasan, who teaches Islamic civilization at the University of Rabat, investigates the Islamization of Africa. After reviewing the importance of the continent, the major cities on both sides of the Sahara, and the trails of the trans-Saharan trade, he investigates three paths followed by Islam into Africa: from Yemen and Hadramawt to the East African coast; from Nubia and Dongola after the Islamization of Egypt; and from North and West Africa under the initial leadership of the Almoravids.

136
———Tārīkh al-Islām al-siyāsī wa-al-dīnī wa-al-thaqāfī wa-al-ijtimā'ī. [The political, religious, cultural and social history of Islam] al-ṭab'ah 3. Cairo, Maktabat al-nahḍah al-Miṣrīyah, 1961–1967. 4 v. DS35.6.H37 Orien Arab

137
Ḥasan, Muḥammad Muṣṭafā. al-Ish'ā' al-'Arabī fī Ifrīqiyā [The Arab diffusion in Africa] [Cairo, al-Dār al-qawmīyah lil-ṭibā'ah wa-al-nashr, 1960] 54 p. (Kutub siyāsīyah, 191) DLC

138
Hazard, Harry W. Atlas of Islamic history. Maps executed by H. Lester Cooke, Jr., and J. McA. Smiley. [Princeton] Princeton University Press, 1951. 49 p. col. maps. (Princeton oriental studies, v. 12) PJ25.P7, v. 12 1951

139
Historic de l'Islam au 16ᵉ siècle, programme africain et malgache . . . 5ᵉ lycées et collèges. Paris, Nathan, 1966. 256 p. illus., col. plates. (Collection du Centre africain de recherches et d'action pédagogiques) D103.H5

140
Hodgkin, Thomas L. Muslims south of the Sahara. Current history, v. 32, June 1957: 345–348. D410.C82, v. 32

141
Holas, Bohumil. L'Afrique noire. [Paris] Bloud & Gay [1964] 115 p. illus., fold. map. (Religion du monde) BL2400.H6
Short introduction to religion in Africa. Islam is briefly presented under the following subheadings: Expansion de l'Islam en Afrique; Les confréries religieuses; Vue panoramique; Ouest-Est; Le marabout; Les pratiques; Influences et

compromis. Holas believes that "accéder à l'Islam constitue donc pour un Africain de la tradition à la fois une formule plus ample de vie intérieure et une visible promotion sociale avec toutes les implications pratiques que cela compte."

142
Houdas, Octave V. L'Islamisme. Nouv. éd. Paris, E. Leroux, 1908. 288 p. 4BP–47

143
Hushaymah, 'Abd Allāh. Fī Ifrīqiyā al-Sawdā'. [In black Africa] Beirut, al-Matba' ah al-Kāthūlīkīyah [1962] 150 p. (al-'Ālam wa-al-'aṣr)
DT352.H87 Orien Arab

144
Huwaydī, Yaḥyā. Tārīkh falsafat al-Islām fī al-qārah al-Ifrīqīyah. [The history of the philosophy of Islam in the African continent] Cairo, Maktabat al-nahḍah al-Miṣrīyah, 1965 [i.e. 1966]+
BP64.A1H8
L.C. has pt. 1: Fī al-Shimāl al-Ifrīqī.

145
Ibn al-'Imād, 'Abd al-Ḥayy ibn Aḥmad. Shadhārāt al-dhahab fī akhbār man dhahab. [Fragments of gold about he who traveled] 'An nuskhat al-muṣannaf al-mahfūḍhah fī Dār al-Kutub al-Miṣrīyah, ma'a muqābalat ba'ḍaha bi-nuskhatayn fī al-Dār ayḍan, wa-ba'ḍaha bi-nuskhat al-Amīr 'Abd al-Qādir al-Jazā'irī. Cairo, Maktabat al-Qudsī, 1350–1951 [1931/32–32/33] 8 v. facsim.
DS234.I116

146
Ibrāhīm, Muḥammad 'Abd al-Fattāh. Afrīqīyah . . . al-arḍ wa-al-nās, ma'a al-'ināyah bi-simāt wa-mu'aththirat ba'ḍ al-ṭawābi' al-thaqāfīyah al-Ifrīqīyah. [Africa . . . the land and the people, with special reference to the characteristics and influences of some African cultural traits] Cairo, Maktabat al-Anjlū-al-Miṣrīyah [1964] 244 p. illus., maps. DT20.I195

147
———Ifrīqīyah, min al-Sinighāl ilā nahr jūbā, ṣafaḥāt min al-tārīkh al-Ifrīqī. [Africa, from the Senegal to the Juba river, pages of African history] Cairo, Maktabat al-Anjlū-al-Miṣrīyah [date of introduction: 1961] 303 p. illus., maps. DT20.I2

148
'Ilbi, Aḥmad. Thawrat al-'Abīd fī al-Baṣrah. [The slave revolt in Basra] al-Ṭarīq, m. 29, Feb. 1970: 93–112. DLC

Starting with a critique of a dissertation by Alexandre Popovic entitled "Ālī Ibn Sa'īd and the Slave Revolt in Basrah" (Sorbonne. Doctorat d'état, 1965), the author analyzes the revolt of the Zanj (A.D. 869–883) within a Marxist framework and sees the movement as a manifestation of a class struggle in Islam.

149
al-Imbābī, 'Abd al-Wāḥid. al-Islām fī Afrīqiyā. [Islam in Africa] [Cairo] al-Majlis al-a'lā lil-shu'ūn al-Islāmīyah, wizārat al-awqāf, 1962. 63 p. illus. (Kutub Islāmīyah, 13) DLC

150
International African Seminar. *5th Zaria, Nigeria, 1964.* Islam in tropical Africa: studies presented and discussed at the fifth International African Seminar, Ahmadu Bello University, Zaria, January 1964; edited with an introduction by I. M. Lewis, foreword by Daryll Forde. London, Published for the International African Institute by Oxford University Press, 1966. 470 p. maps. DS38.I5 1964

After a substantial introduction (125 p.) by the editor, the following represent the major contributions presented at the Zaria meeting: J. Spencer Trimingham, The Phases of Islamic Expansion and Islamic Zones in Africa; Yusuf Fadl Hasan, The Penetration of Islam in the Eastern Sudan; Jean-Claude Froelich, Essai sur les causes et méthodes de l'islamisation de l'Afrique de l'Ouest du XIe siècle au XXe siècle; P. Ceulemans, Introduction de l'influence de l'Islam au Congo; George Shepperson, The Jumbe of Kota Kota and Some Aspects of the History of Islam in British Central Africa; R. C. Stevenson, Some Aspects of the Spread of Islam in the Nuba Mountains (*see also* 1399); P. T. W. Baxter, Acceptance and Rejection of Islam Among the Boran of the Northern Frontier District of Kenya; I. M. Lewis, Conformity and Contrast in Somali Islam; P. J. A. Rigby, Sociological Factors in the Contact of the Gogo of Central Tanzania with Islam; J. O. Hunwick, Religion and State in the Songhay Empire, 1464–1591; Ivor Wilks, The Position of Muslims in Metropolitan Ashanti in the Early Nineteenth Century; Vincent Monteil, Lat-Dyor, Damel du Kayor (1842-86) et l'islamisation des Wolofs du Sénégal; Elliott P. Skinner, Islam in Mossi Society; Peter Lienhardt, A Controversy Over Islamic Customs in Kilwa Kivinje, Tanzania; D. J. Stenning, Cattle Values and Islamic Values in a Pastoral Population; Pierre F. Lacroix, L'Islam peul de l'Adamawa; M. G. Smith, The Jihad of Shehu Dan Fodio: Some Problems; Saburi Biobaku and Muhammad al-Hajj, The Sudanese Mahdiyya and the Niger-Chad Region; Thomas Hodgkin, The Islamic Literary Tradition in Ghana. *See also* 1399.

151
International Congress of African Historians, *University College, Dar es Salaam, 1965.* Emerging themes of African history: proceedings of the International Congress of African Historians held at University College, Dar es Salaam, October 1965; T. O. Ranger, editor. London, Heinemann Educational [1969] xxii, 230 p. DT19.I59 1965a

Partial contents: Osman Sid Ahmed Ismail, The Historiographical Tradition of African Islam.—Tadeuz Lewicki, External Arabic Sources for the History of Africa to the South of the Sahara.—Nehemia Levtzion, Reflections on Muslim Historiography in Africa.—B. Kamian, Can We Enrich Current Historiography by Drawing on the Traditional and Islamic Past?

152
Irving, T. B. West African Islam. Islamic literature, v. 15, May 1969: 53–63. BP1.I68 v. 15

Historical investigation of Islam south of the Sahara. Irving begins with the Almoravids' conquest of Ghana in the 11th century and closes with the problems facing 20th-century Islam in Africa.

153
al-'Iryān, Muḥammad Sa'īd. al-'Arab . . .la Khristūf Kūlumbūs! [The Arabs . . .not Christopher Columbus!] al-Ṭab'ah 2. Cairo, Dār al-Ma'ārif, 1962. 158 p. illus. (Maktabat sindibād, silsilat al-riḥlāt) PJ7838.R9A88

154
Ismael, Tareq Y. Islam in sub-Saharan Africa. Current history, v. 56, Mar. 1969: 146–150. D410.C82, v. 56

155
———Religion and UAR African policy. Journal of modern African studies, v. 6, 1968: 49–57. map. DT1.J68, v. 6

Islam binds all Muslims, wherever they are, into the Muslim community. The United Arab Republic, because of its traditional leading position in the Muslim world, developed a foreign policy for Africa where Islam was one of its principal levers. Ismael, who has written his dissertation on UAR policy in Africa, gives a historical analysis of the vicissitudes of the UAR in African politics, using Islam as a major variable. *See also* 157.

156
———The United Arab Republic in Africa. Canadian journal of African studies, v. 2, autumn 1968: 175–194. DLC

Substantial analysis of the role of the UAR in Africa. The Nile question and relations with the Sudan have been an integral part of Egyptian history for centuries. With the revolution, President Nasser extended Egypt's role in Africa and provided support for the nationalist movement, participated in the Bandung Conference, and helped with the creation of the Casablanca Group in 1961. The initial phase gave way eventually to a more realistic approach of establishing good relations with the largest possible number of African states and stressing the similarities, rather than differences, between the two cultures.

157
———The U.A.R. in Africa; Egypt's policy under Nasser. Evanston, Ill., Northwestern University Press, 1971. xiv, 258 p. map. DT82.5.A3718

Based on the author's dissertation.

158
Issawi, Charles. Arab geography and the circumnavigation of Africa. Osiris, v. 10, 1952: 117–128. Q1.O7, v. 10

159
al-Jāḥiẓ, 'Amr ibn Baḥr. Fakhr al-Sūdān 'alā al-Bīḍān. [Superiority of blacks over whites] *In* Rasā'il al-Jāḥiẓ. [al-Jāḥiẓ's letters] Edited by 'Abd al-Salām Muḥammad Hārūn. Cairo, Maktabat al-Khanjā, 1964. p. 177–226. (Maktabat al-Jāḥiẓ) PJ7745.J3R3 1964, v. 1

Referring to this work, Charles Pellat has said: "This title might suggest that Jahiz, who was probably of African origin, was a racialist, intent on disparaging the white race to which the Arabs belong. He certainly displays a good deal of gusto in recounting the glories of his own race, quoting as object-lessons famous figures from Arab history and expatiating on the civilization of the Indians (whom he regards akin to the Negro peoples). But, in fact, this work is placed here because it is really a work of anthropology. The author devotes much space to his theory that the skin colour of the Negroes is the result solely of soil and climate" (introduction, *'Amr ibn Baḥr al-Jāḥiẓ. The Life and Works of Jāḥiẓ,* ed. by Charles Pellat, tr. from the French by D. H. Hawkes (London, Routledge and Kegan Paul [1969]), PJ7745.J3A26 1969b). *See also* 242.

160
Jaulin, R. Sur l'Islam noir. La Table ronde, no 126, juin 1958: 102–111. AP20.T3, 1958

161
Jeffreys, M. D. W. Arabs introduce African exotic plants: the banana and cotton plant. Islamic review, v. 44 Nov. 1956: 31–33. BP1.I7, v. 44

162
———Pre-Columbian navigation in the Atlantic; presumptive evidence of trans-Atlantic voyages of the Arabs. Islamic review, v. 44, Oct. 1956: 37–39. BP1.I7, v. 44

Basing his assertions on medieval sources, Jeffreys suggests that the maps in possession of Columbus were prepared by Arab sailors who "brought back the information of islands in the Atlantic and of a continent, Brazil, Antillia, and beyond."

163
Jiddawi, Abdurrahim Mohamed. Extracts from an Arab account book, 1840–54. TNR, no. 31, July 1951: 25–31. DT436.T3, 1951

164
al-Jiddāwī, Muṣṭafā. Dirāsah jadīdah 'an al-riqq fī al tārīkh wa-fī al-Islām. [A new study on slavery in history and in Islam] [Alexandria? 1963] HT861.J45

L.C. has pt. 1.

165
Johnston, James H. The Mohammedan slave trade. Journal of Negro history, v. 13, Oct. 1928: 478–491. E185.J86, v. 13

Review of the role of slaves in Muslim history, including slaves from Europe, Asia, and Africa.

166
Kāmil, 'Abd al-'Azīz 'Abd al-Qādir. Islam and the race question. [Paris] Unesco [1970] 65 p. (United Nations Educational, Scientific and Cultural Organization. [Document] SHC.70/IX.6/A) (The Race question and modern thought) AS4.U8A15 SHC.70/9.6/A

Also issued in Arabic (BP190.5.R3K35 Orien Arab).

167
———al-'Urūbah wa-al-Ḥaḍārāt al-Ifrīqīyah fī mandhūr jadīd. [Arabism and African civilizations in a new perspective]. *In* Cairo. Ma'had al-buḥūth wa-al-dirāsāt al-'Arabīyah. Majallah, no. 3, Mar. 1972: 221–260. DS36.M22, no. 3 Orien Arab

Kāmil explodes the myth of the division of Africa into North and South of the Sahara, and shows the deep and ancient roots linking the two shores of the Sahara. The concept of Africa as an indivisable unit has been adopted by both Unesco and the Organization of African Unity.

168
———Wajhat al-Islām fī al-qārah al-Ifrīqīyah. [Aspects of Islam in the African continent] al-Siyāsah al-duwalīyah, v. 2, Jan. 1966: 94–111. D839.S55, v. 2 Orien Arab

Introducing his essay by stating that "this study attempts to get the pulse of Islam in Africa," Kāmil looks at the channels and routes into Africa followed by Islam, examines its present limits, and hypothesizes about the future, in which he sees Islam growing in tropical Africa in clusters gravitating around a number of cores rather than following a linear path of development as it did in the past.

169
Kanouté, Dembo. Tradition orale: histoire de l'Afrique authentique. Traduite par Tidiane Sanogho et Ibrahima Diallo. [Dakar, Impricap, 1972] illus. DT476.K36, v. 1

L.C. has v. 1.

170
King, Noel Q. Christian and Muslim in Africa. New York, Harper & Row [1971] xiv, 153 p. BR1360.K55 1971

171
Klemp, Egon. Africa on maps dating from the twelfth to the eighteenth century. Africa auf Karten des 12. bis 18. Jahrhunderts. [Seventy-seven photo copies from European map collections. Editor and author, on behalf of the Deutsche Staatsbibliothek, Berlin: Egon Klemp] [Leipzig] Edition Leipzig [1968] 77 maps (part col.) G2445.K6 1968 G&M Vault

Text: 57 p. inserted in pocket.
Issued in slip-case.

172
Kritzeck, James, *and* William H. Lewis, *eds.* Islam in Africa. Contributors: J. Spencer Trimingham [and others] New York, Van Nostrand-Reinhold Co. [1969] 339 p. maps. BK64.A1K7

Contents: J. Spencer Trimingham, The Expansion of Islam.—J. N. D. Anderson, The Legal Tradition.—Norbert Tapiéro, Evolving Social Patterns.—Vincent Monteil, Marabouts.—S. S. Richardson, Social Legal Reform.—Humphrey J. Fisher, Separatism in West Africa.—Hatim Amiji, The Asian Minority.—William H. Lewis, Nationalism and Modernism.—Norman Daniel, The Sudan.—Martin Lowenkopf, Uganda.—Frank Schildnecht, Tanzania.—Harm de Blij, South Africa.—Crawford Young, The Congo.—Pierre Alexandre, Cameroun.—John A. Ballard, Equatorial Africa.—Mervyn Hiskett, Northern Nigeria.—Nehemia Levtzion, Coastal West Africa.—Alfred G. Gerteiny, Mauritania.

173

Labique, Henri. Les fondements de l'Africanité; ou, Négritude et Arabité. *In* Cairo. Institut dominicain d'études orientales. Mélanges, no 9, 1967: 251–270. PJ9.C3, 1967

Annotated excerpts from the speech given by President Senghor at Cairo University during his visit to Egypt (Feb. 11–18, 1967). The gist of the speech is summarized in his definition of *Africanité,* namely, "la symbiose complémentaire des valeurs de l'*Arabisme* et des valeurs de la *Négritude.*"

174

Labouret, Henri, *ed.* Livre renfermant la généalogie des diverses tribus noires du Soudan et l'histoire des rois après Mahomet. *In* Académie des sciences coloniales. Annales. Paris, 1929. p. 189–225. DLC-Micro 04038 JV1802.A314, v. 3

Manuscript by Mamadu Aïssa Kaba Diakata on the history of the Sudan. The document was written at the request of the Commandant de Cercle of Nioro in 1891. A reviewer in *Revue de l'histoire des colonies françaises* (v. 18, janv./fév. 1903, p. 99. JV1801.R4) states, "Le général Archinard l'a offert à l'Académie comme un document curieux, montrant ce que les indigènes instruits pensaient de leur passé, plutôt que comme un précis d'histoire."

175

La Roncière, Charles G. M. B. de. Bruges et la découverte de l'Afrique au Moyen-Age. Bruges, Imprimerie Vve L. De Plancke, 1924. 12 p. 4G.362

176

———Communications sur la cartographie du Sahara et du Niger dans les planispheres du Moyen-Age. *In* Académie des inscriptions et belles lettres. Comptes rendus des séances. mars/avril, 1922. Paris, 1922. p. 87–88. AS162.P315, 1922

177

———La découverte de l'Afrique au moyen âge, cartographes et explorateurs. [Le Caire, Société royale de géographie d'Egypte, 1924–27] 3 v. plates, col. port., maps (part fold.) double facsim. (Mémoires de la Société royale de géographie d'Egypte. t. V–VI, XIII) DT3.L3

Date on cover, v. 1: 1925.

178

———Nègres et négriers. 7. ed. Paris, Editions des Portiques [c1933] 2 p.l., [7]–254, [2] p. front., plates. NN

179

Le Grip, A. L'avenir de l'Islam en Afrique noire. A&A, no 10, 2. trimestre, 1950: 5–20. DT1.A85, 1950

Islam in black Africa has come under many influences. The fraternities, the Arab League, the Ahmadi movement, as well as the attitudes of the colonial government are important factors, according to Le Grip. He concludes that the future of Islam in sub-Saharan Africa will be determined by its attitudes toward and the solutions it will offer to the problems of modernization.

180

Leo Africanus, Joannes. Description de l'Afrique. Nouv. éd. traduite de l'italien par A. Epaulard et annoté par A. Epaulard [et al.] Paris, Adrien-Maisonneuve, 1956. 2 v. (629 p.) illus., plates, maps (part fold., 1 col.) facsims. (Publications de l'Institut des hautes études marocaines, no 61) DT7.L55

Translation of *Della descrittione dell'Africa e delle cose notabili che ivi sono,* which was edited on the basis of the author's original text (probably written in Italian) by G. B. Ramusio and first published in Venice in 1550.

181

———The history and description of Africa and of the notable things therein contained, written by al-Hassan ibn Mohammed al-Wezaz [sic], al-Fasi, a Moor, baptised as Giovanni Leone, but better known as Leo Africanus. Done into English in the year 1600 by John Pory, and now edited, with an introduction and notes, by Robert Brown. New York, B. Franklin [1963?] 3 v. (1119 p.) 4 fold. maps. (Works issued by the Hakluyt Society, 1st ser., no. 92–94) G161.H22, no. 92–94

Reprint of the 1896 ed. published by the Hakluyt Society.

182
Levtzion, Nehemia. Ha-Islam be-Afrika: Be'ayot merkaziyot le-meḥkar ve-hora'ah. [Islam in Africa: Some central issues for research and teaching] Ha-Mizraḥ he-ḥadash, kerakh 17, mispar 1/2: 1–17. DS41.M56 Hebr
Includes a 6-page bibliography on Islam in Africa and an English summary (p. I–III).

183
———Oral traditions and Arabic documents in the Muslim historiography of Africa. Paper presented to the International Congress of Africanists, Second Session, December 11–20, 1967. Dakar, Senegal. 15 p. DLC

184
Lewicki, Tadeusz. Arabic external sources for the history of Africa to the south of the Sahara [Translated by Marianna Abrahamowicz] Wrodwa, Zakłao Naródowy im Ossolinskich, 1969. 102p. maps. DLC
See also 151.

185
———Ze studiów nad geografia historyczna Afriki. Królestwo organa map Eurpejskich XIV–XVI w. [Research on the historical geography of Africa. The kingdom of Organa according to European maps from the 14th and 15th centuries] Przeglad Orientalistyczny, nr 3 (75), 1970: 183–198. PJ9.P7, 1970

186
Lewis, William H. Islam, a rising tide in tropical Africa. Review of politics, v. 19, Oct. 1957: 446–461. JA1.R4, v. 19

187
Lubis, Mohammad Arief. Perkembangan Islam di Afrika (ketjuali keliling Lautan Tengah) dari dahulu sampai sekarang. [The development of Islam in Africa (with the exception of the Near East) from the past to the present] Djakarta, Azam [1964] 79 p. illus., maps, ports.
BP64.A1L8 Orien Indo

188
Lyautey, Pierre. L'empire colonial français. Paris, Les Editions de France, c1931. 540 p. (La Troisième république, 1870 à nos jours. [v. 14])
JV1811.L9

189
Mahmud, Faruq. Jāgrata Musalima Āphrikā. [Rising Muslim Africa] Dacca, Islāmia Lāibreri, 1966. 268 p. col. illus., maps. DT21.M29
In Bengali.

190
Maḥmūd, Ḥasan Aḥmad, *and* Aḥmad Ibrāhīm al-Sharīf. al-'Ālam al-Islāmī fī al-'aṣr al-'Abbāsī. [The Islamic world during the Abbassid period] [Cairo] Dār al-fikr al-'Arabī [1966] map. DS236.M3
L.C. has v. 1.

191
Majīd, 'Abd al-Mun'im. al-Aṭlas al-tārīkhī lil-'ālam al-Islāmī fī al-'uṣūr al-wusṭā. [Historical atlas of the Islamic world during the Middle Ages] al-ṭab'ah 2., [Cairo] Dār al-fikr al-'Arabī, 1967. 36 p. maps (16 fold.) G1786.S1M3 1967 G&M

192
Malḥas, Luṭfī. al-Lughah al-'Arabīyah wa-al-dīn al-Islāmī aḥāṭā Ifrīqiyā bi-hālah 'Arabīyah Islāmīyah. [The Arabic Language and Islam have surrounded Africa with an Arabic Islamic aureole] al-Wa'y al-Islāmī, m. 8, Nov. 6, 1972: 52–55.
BP1.W3, v. 5

193
al-Maqrīzī, Aḥmad ibn 'Alī. Kitāb ighāthat al-ummah bi-kashf al-ghummah. [Book on the salvation of the nation by the lifting of grief] Edited by Muḥammad Muṣṭafā Ziyādah [and] Jamāl al-Dīn al-Shayyāl. Ṭab'ah 2. munaqqaḥah. Cairo, Lajnat al-ta'līf wa-al-tar-jamah wa-al-nashr, 1957. 92 p. facsims. (*His* Maktabat al-Maqrīzī al-saghīrah, 4)
DT96.M217 1957

194
Mármol Carvajal, Luis del. L'Afriqve de Marmol, de la tradvction de Nicolas Perrot, sieur d'Ablancvrt. Divisée en trois volvmes, et enrichie des cartes géographiques de M. Sanson. Avec l'Histoire des chérifs, traduite de l'espagnol de Diégo Torrés, par le duc d'Angoulesme le père. Rev. et retouchée par P. R. a. Paris, L. Billaine, 1667. 3 v. 28 fold. maps. DT7.M35
From Mármol Caravajal's "Descripción general de Africa," Granada & Malaga, 1573–99; translation left unfinished by Perrot d'Ablancourt, completed by Olivier Patru, and edited by Pierre Richelet, avocat.

195
Martin, Alfred G. P. Quatre siècles d'histoire marocaine, au Sahara de 1504 à 1902, au Maroc de 1894 à 1912, d'après archives et documentations indigènes. Paris, F. Alcan, 1923. xv, [1], 591 p.
DT314.M3

The first part of the treatise deals with the Moroccan impact on the Sahara and the ramifications of a politico-religious influence and presence in the Great Desert.

196
al-Marzūqī, Aḥmad ibn Muḥammad. Kitāb al-azminah wa-al-amkinah. [The book of times and places] Hyderabad al-Dakn, maṭba'at majlis dā'irat al-Ma'ārif, 1332 [1914] 2 v. PJ6680.M3 1914

197
Masry, Youssef el. The Arab role in Africa [by] Jacques Baulin. Baltimore, Penguin Books [1962] 143 p. maps. (Penguin African library, AP6)
DT176.M34

An investigation of the interplay between Africa north and south of the Sahara by an Arabic-speaking Muslim French journalist. He analyzes the efforts made by the Arab states in general and Egypt in particular to influence, through the channel of Islam, sub-Saharan politics.

198
Massignon, Louis. Causes et modes de la propagation de l'Islam parmi les populations païennes de l'Afrique. *In* Convegno di scienze morali e storiche, *8th, Rome.* [Atti] 1938. Rome, Reale accademia d'Italia, 1939. p. 663–669.
AS222.R5353, 1938

199
———Elements arabes et foyers d'arabisation; leur rôle dans le monde musulman actuel. RMM, t. 57, 1. section, 1924: 1–157. DS36.R4, v. 57

200
al-Mas'ūdī. Murūj al-dhahab wa-ma'ādin al-jawhar. [The meadows of gold and the metals of essence] Edited by Yūsuf As'ad Dāghir. Beirut, Dār al-Andalus [1965–66] 4 v.
D17.M29 1965 Orien Arab

Includes indexes.

201
———Les prairies d'or. Texte et traduction par C. Barbier de Meynard et Pavet de Courteille. Paris, Impr. impériale, 1861–1917. 9 v. (Collection d'ouvrages orientaux publiée par la Société asiatique) D17.M322 Orien Arab

At head of title: Société asiatique. Maçoudi.

Vols. 1, 5–9, 1861–71; v. 2–4, "Deuxième tirage," 1914–17.

Vols. 2, 4, 6–9 have imprint: Paris, Imprimerie nationale.

Vols. 4–9 edited and translated by Barbier de Meynard alone.

202
Matip, Benjamin. Heurts et malheurs des rapports Europe-Afrique noire dans l'histoire moderne, du 15e siècle au 18e siècle. [Paris] La Nef de Paris éditions [1959] 124 p. port., map. DT353.M3

203
Matveev, V. V. Records of early Arab authors on Bantu peoples ("Muluk al-Zinj," i.e. "Kings of Zinjs," according to Arabic sources of the 9th-10th centuries) *In* International Congress of Anthropological and Ethnological Sciences, 7th, Moscow, 1964. v. 9; 1970. Moscow, Nauka. p. 244–249.
GN3.I39 1964r

204
Mauny, Raymond. Navigations arabes anonymes aux Canaries au XIIe siècle. NA, no 106, avril 1965: 61. DT1.I513, 1965

205
———Notes sur les "Grands voyages de Léon l'Africain." Hespéris, t. 41, 3.–4. trimestre, 1954: 379–394. DT181.H4, v. 41

Critical study of the travels of Ḥasan ibn Muḥammad al-Wazzān al-Fāsī al-Zayyāt, better known as Leo Africanus. Corroborating the data meticulously culled from the writings of the wandering Leo, Mauny shows that "Léon doit être considéré, aprés Ibn Battouta, mais bien des siècles avant les grands voyageurs de la fin du XVIIIe et du début du XIXe, comme l'un des premiers explorateurs de l'intérieur de l'Afrique."

206
———Les siècles obscurs de l'Afrique noire; histoire et archéologie. [Paris] Fayard [1971] 314 p. illus. (Resurrection du passé) DT352.65.M38

207
Mayer, Leo A. Bibliography of Moslem numismatics, India excepted. 2d, considerably enl. ed. London, Royal Asiatic Society, 1954. 283 p. (Oriental Translation Fund [London. Publications, new ser.] v. 35) PJ408.O6, n.s., v. 35

208
Mazaheri, Ali Akbar. La vie quotidienne des Musulmans au Moyen Age, Xe au XIIIe siéle. [Paris] Hachette [c1951] 319 p. illus. (La Vie quotidienne)
BP163.M384

Drawing on a thorough knowledge of the sources, Mazaheri sketches, with a sure hand, the day-to-day existence of Muslims during the medieval period. His description is also valid for the sub-Saharan Islamized areas.

209
Meyer, A. J. Israel and the Arabs in Africa. The Harvard review, v. 1, spring 1963: 10–17. AS36.H23, v. 1

210
Mendelsohn, Jack. God, Allah, and Juju; religion in Africa today. New York, Nelson [1962] 245 p. BR1430.M4

Includes a chapter on Islam in sub-Saharan Africa.

211
Molla, C. F. Some aspects of Islam in Africa south of the Sahara. International review of missions, v. 56, Oct. 1967: 459–468. BV2351.I6, v. 56

A Christian missionary in Cameroon, Molla analyzes the sociological and religious causes for the success of Islam in sub-Saharan Africa.

212
Monteil, Vincent. L'Islam noir. 2e edition, revue, corrigée et augmentée. Paris, Éditions du Seuil, 1971. 418 p. illus., plates, fold. map. (Collection Esprit. Frontière ouverte) BP64.A4S83 1971

Monteil knows Africa viscerally, and his book shows this empathic knowledge of things African, thus redeeming the cavalier organization of the work.

213
Mubarak Ahmad, Mirza. Islam in Africa. Rabwah, Pakistan, Ahmadiyya Muslim Foreign Missions Office [introd. 1962] 41 p. BP64.A1M8

Translation of a paper by the Secretary of the Ahmadiyya Muslim Foreign Missions read at the annual gathering of the Ahmadiyya Movement at Rabwah in Western Pakistan. In his introduction the deputy delegate for missions says: "It is a brief statement, as of necessity it had to be. But it is packed with solid material on five aspects of the question: (a) the impact of Christian missionary activities, aided and abetted as it was by the political power of the western nations with colonies, protectorates, or empires in Africa; (b) Christian hopes of winning the entire continent in a short time for the Cross, expressed buoyantly in the press; (c) the part played by Christians in the creation and development of the Slave Trade; (d) the impact of Ahmadiyya missionary endeavour in Africa; (e) and the rolling back of the Christian tide, that now western observers themselves freely concede that their dream of the emergence of a Christian Africa, was no more than a delusion, and Islam seemed destined to be the religion of the African peoples for the future."

214
Muḥammad, Muḥammad ʻAwad. al-Shuʻūb wa-al-sulālāt al-Ifrīqīyah. [The African peoples and races] [Cairo] al-Dār al-Miṣrīyah lil-ta'līf wa-al-tarjamah [1965] 357 p. illus., maps (1 fold.) (Silsilat dirāsāt Ifrīqīyah, 1) DT15.M8

215
Muslim on the march. The Christian century, v. 71, Sept. 8, 1954: 1063–1064. BR1.C45, v. 71

216
al-Muusawy, Muhammad Mahdi, *tr.* Historia ya Islam. [History of Islam] Dar es Salaam, Biala Muslim Mission of Tanzania [1971] 48 p. (Jalada la Kwanza) DLC

In Swahili.

217
Norris, H. T. Saharan myth and saga. Oxford, Clarendon Press, 1972. xv, 240, [6] p. illus. PJ8390.S2N58

218
Now this is true peace; an interesting book of comparative study of Christianity and Islam. Mombasa, Bilal Muslim Mission of Kenya [1973?] 29 p. DLC

219
Ogunsheye, F. Adetowun. Maps of Africa—1500–1800 (A bibliographic survey). Nigerian geographical journal, v. 7, June 1964: 34–42. DT515.A2N5, v. 7

220
Ohly, Rajmund, *and* Janina Markiewcz. Czarny Islam [Black Islam]. Euhemer, Rok 9, Nr 1 (44), 1965: 3–21. BL9.P6E8, 1965

Comprehensive article on Islam in sub-Saharan Africa. Translated in JPRS 33496.

221
Onibonoje, G. O. Africa from the rise of Islam to the end of the slave trade. [Rev. Ibadan Nigeria Onibon-Oje Press, 1965] 169 p. illus., maps, ports. (*His* History book 2) DT22.O53 1965

School text.

222
Ouane, Ibrahima Mamadou. L'Islam et la civilisation française. [Avignon] Presses universelles [1957] 44 p. BP64.A4F7

In introducing the booklet, Marguerite and Gabriel Schoel-Langlois, Lauréats de l'Académie française, state: "Souhaitons que les autorités françaises ne négligent pas l'atout majeur que peut representer pour elles, cet écrivain profondément attaché à la double culture arabe et française, et dont le voeu le plus cher est que le Soudan, berceau de civilisations, et l'Afrique, deviennent un terrain d'entente entre trois continents, ainsi qu'il est lui-même le symbole vivant de l'harmonie qui peut et doit exister entre la France et l'Islam." Ouane presents a brief historical narrative on the spread of Islam in the Sudanic belt. The last chapter suggests that "libre au wahabiste d'exalter en notre temps de linitypes ses pieuses et paresseuses calligraphies, d'épouiller rageusement les néologismes arabo-berbères et de raffiner sur le concept de l'Unique. Mais le temps est aux machines et au baccalauréat latin-sciences," and recommends closer Franco-African collaboration for the greater benefit of Africa.

223

Pageard, Robert. Contribution à la chronologie de l'Ouest Africain suivie d'une traduction des tables chronologiques de Barth. JOSAF, t. 32, fasc. 1, 1962: 91–177. DT1.S65, v. 32

Periodization and chronology are two thorny problems facing Africanists. Pageard, in this lengthy and thorough review, examines two major sources, namely, Maurice Delafosse and Heinrich Barth reporting on the history of West Africa. The author divides his chronology into exact dates, doubtful dates of Ghana, Mali, and Songhay, as well as dating problems of dynastic genealogies.

224

Papers on the Manding. Carleton T. Hodge, *ed.* Bloomington, Indiana University [distributed for U.S. and Canada: Humanities Press, New York, 1971] 307 p. illus. (Indiana University publications. African series, v. 3) DT474.5.P36

The African Seminar of the African Studies Program of Indiana University focused, in the spring of 1969, on the Mandingo people of West Africa. The following papers represent "nearly all of the seminar lectures": David Dalby, Introduction: Distribution and Nomenclature of the Manding People and Their Language; Charles S. Bird, Oral Art in the Mande; Daniel F. McCall, The Cultural Map and Time-Profile of the Mande-Speaking Peoples; Nicholas S. Hopkins, Mandinka Social Organization; Labelle Prussin, Sudanese Architecture and the Mande; Bradford G. Martin, al-Hajj 'Umar Tall, Samori Ture, and Their Forerunners; Robert R. Griffeth, The Dyula Impact on the Peoples of the West Volta Region; William B. Cohen, The French Colonial Service in French West Africa; Charlotte A. Quinn, Mandingo States in Nineteenth Century Gambia; Frances A. Leary, The Role of Mandinka in the Islamization of the Casamance, 1850–1901; Peter M. Weil, Political Structure and Process Among the Gambia Mandinka: the Village Parapolitical System; Barbara Lewis, The Dioula in the Ivory Coast.

225

Park, Mungo. The journal of a mission to the interior of Africa in the year 1805. Together with other documents, official and private relating to the same mission. To which is prefixed an account of the life of Mr. Park. Philadelphia, Published by Edward Earle. William Fry, printer, 1815. 302 p. illus. DT356.P3 1815

226

———Travels in the interior districts of Africa. New York, Arno Press, 1971. 372 p. illus., fold. maps, port. (Physician travelers) DT356.P3 1971

Reprint of the 1799 ed.

227

Pedrals, D. Pierre de. L'Islam de l'ouest et du centre africains français. Revue politique et parlementaire, t. 48, nov. 1946: 163–170. H3.R4, v. 48

228

Peerbhai, Adam. Islam, remedy to world distress. Durban, Islamic Institute [1969] [28] p. BP173.75.P4

229

Planhol, Xavier de. Les fondements géographiques de l'histoire de l'Islam. Paris, Flammarion, 1968. 443 p. illus., maps. (Nouvelle bibliothèque scientifique) DS39.P54

A history of the land of Islam and a study of the impact of the Muslims on the territories they permeated and conquered. The role of the pastoral nomads in the spread of the religion is analyzed in a section on Africa south of the Sahara. The two major carriers were the Fulbe and the urban trading communities, thereby reproducing the original pattern of Arabian Islam as an urban religion diffused mainly by nomads in a setting where peasants played only a marginal role.

230

———The world of Islam. Le monde islamique; essai de géographie religieuse. Ithaca, N.Y., Cornell University Press [1959] 142 p. BP163.P533

A study of the impact of geography on the history of Islam. With a profusion of examples, in which Africa is well represented, the author analyzes urban Islam, Muslim attitudes toward exploitation of the soil, the groupings and modes of life derived from Islam, and the geographic factors in the expansion of Islam.

231
Pommerel, Jean. L'Islam africain; chez ceux qui guettent. Nouv. éd. Paris, Fontemoing [1910?] 370 p. IEN

232
Popovic, Alexandre. Quelques renseignements inédits concernant "le maître des Zanǧ" 'Alī b. Muḥammad. Arabica, t. 12, juin 1965: 175–187. PJ6001.A7, v. 12

233
Principaux ouvrages de M. Delafosse. Outre-mer, v. 1, 1929: 411–413. NN

234
al-Qalqashandī, Aḥmad ibn 'Alī. Ṣubḥ al-A'shā fī ṣinā'at al-inshā'. [The morn of the night-blind in the making of composition] [Cairo] al-Mu'assasah al-Miṣrīyah al-'Āmmah lil-ta'līf wa-al-tarjamah wa-al-ṭibā'ah wa-al-nashr [1964] 14 v. (Turāthunā) **AE2.Q3 1964 Orien Arab**

235
al-Rāfi'ī, 'Abd al-Raḥmān *and* Sa'īd 'Abd al-Fattāḥ 'Āshūr. Miṣr fī al-'uṣūr al-wusṭā min al-fatḥ al-'Arabī ḥattā al-Ghazw al-'Uthmānī. [Egypt during the Middle Ages from the Arab conquest to the Ottoman invasion] Cairo, Dār al-nahḍah al-'Arabīyah, 1970. 582 p. DT95.R3

236
al-Ramādī, Jamāl al-Dīn. Ifrīqiyā al-Jadīdah wa al-Islām. [The new Africa and Islam] Cairo. al-Jāmi' al-Azhar. Majallat al-Azhar, m. 32, Aug./Sept. 1960: 315–318. BP1.C3, v. 32

Short country-by-country study of Islam in modern Africa, including discussion of the Mali Federation, Togo, Congo, Cameroon, and Somalia. al-Ramādī concludes: "But these countries are still in dire need of the guidance of Islam [manifested by] the sending of missions to spread religion and develop the true teachings in order to get people out of the darkness and into the light."

237
Riyāḍ, Zāhir. Kanīsat al-Iskandarīyah fī Ifrīqiyā. [The Alexandria Church in Africa] [Cairo] 1962. 215 p. illus. BX133.2.R5

Historical investigation of the ties that linked the Coptic Church of Alexandria to Ethiopia. The dependency of the former was severed only in 1952 when the Egyptian Coptic Patriarch no longer appointed the head of the Ethiopian Coptic Church, who was elected by the Synod of Ethiopian bishops.

238
Rivlin, Benjamin. The "Africanness" of North Africa. African forum, v. 3, fall 1967/winter 1968: 2–14. DT1.A225, v. 3

"Is North Africa *really* African?" is the theme of this study in African relations. After summarizing the pros and cons of the issue, Rivlin concludes that the matter is still a complex open question needing further research to arrive at a clear definition of "Africanness."

239
Rondot, Pierre. L'Islam et les musulmans d'aujourd'hui. De Dakar à Djakarta. L'Islam en devenir. Paris, Éditions de l'Orante, 1960. 250 p. **BP161.2.R64**

Includes a section on "L'Islam noir."

240
Roolvink, Roelof. Historical atlas of the Muslim peoples. [Compiled by R. Roolvink, with the collaboration of Saleh A. el Ali, Hussain Monés, and Mohd. Salim. With a foreword by H. A. R. Gibb] Amsterdam, Djambatan, 1957. 40 p. of col. maps. G1786.S1R6 1957 G&M

241
Rosenthal, Franz. A history of Muslim historiography. 2d rev. ed. Leiden, E. J. Brill, 1968. 656 p. D198.2.R67 1968

242
Rotter, Gernot. Die Stellung des Negers in der islamisch-arabischen Gesellschaft bis zum XVI. Jahrundert. Bonn, 1967. 192 p. DS59.N4R67

Inaug. Diss.—Bonn.

See also 159.

243
Roux, Jean P. L'Islam en Occident, Europe-Afrique; l'Europe et l'Islam: guerre, conversions, contacts culturels et influences idéologiques, l'Islam en Europe, au Maghreb et en Afrique noire. Paris, Payot, 1959. 304 p. (Bibliothèque historique) CB251.R64

244
al-Sakhāwī, Muḥammad ibn 'Abd al-Raḥmān. al-Ḍaw' al-lāmi' li-ahl al-qarn al-tāsi'. [The bright light

for the people of the 9th century] Beirut, Dār maktabat al-ḥayāt [1966] 12 v. in 6. DS37.3.S212
Photo-offset of the Cairo ed. of 1934–36.

245
———Kitāb al-ṭibr al-masbūk fī dhayl al-sulūk. [Book of the cast gold, being a supplement to al-Sulūk] Cairo, Maktabat al-Kulliyāt al-Azharīyah [1972] 431 p. DT96.7.S23 1972 Orien Arab
Reprint of the 1879 ed.
A continuation of al-Maqrizi's *al-Sulūk li-ma'rifat duwal al-mulūk* [Ways to Know the Kingdoms].

246
al-Sāmir, Fayṣal. Thawrat al-Zanj. [The Zunj revolt] Baghdad, Dār al-Qāri', 1954. 165 p. fold. map. (Manshurāt Dār al-qāri', 2) DS76.S3

247
Samkange, Stanlake J. T. African saga: a brief introduction to African history. Nashville, Abington Press [c1971] 222 p. DT20.S15

248
Schacht, Joseph. The legacy of Islam. Edited by Joseph Schacht with C. E. Bosworth. 2d ed. Oxford, Clarendon Press [1974] xiv, 530 p. illus., plates. DS36.85.S3
Includes a section on sub-Saharan Africa by Ioan M. Lewis, p. 105–116.

249
Sell, E. Islam in Africa. MW, v. 1, Apr. 1911: 136–146. DS36.M7, v. 1

250
Shalabī, Aḥmad. al-Tārīkh al-Islāmī wa-al-Ḥaḍārah al-Islāmīyah; dirāsah taḥlīlīyah lil-tārīkh al-Islāmī wa-al-ḥaḍārah al-Islāmīyah fi jamī' al-'uṣūr wa jamī' al-anḥā'. [Islamic history and civilization; analytical study of Islamic history and civilization in all periods in all the world] Cairo, Maktabat al-nahḍah al-Miṣrīyah, 1964+ illus. DS35.7.S32 Orien Arab
L.C. has v. 1–6.
Vol. 6 is entitled *al-Islām wa-al-duwal al-Islāmīyah janūb al-Ṣaḥarā' mundhu dakhalahā al-Islām ḥattā al-ān.* [Islam and Islamic States South of the Sahara From Their Conversion to Islam to the Present].

251
al-Shayyāl, Jamāl al-Dīn. Tārīkh Miṣr al-Islāmīyah. [History of Islamic Egypt] Dār al-Ma'ārif, 1967. 2 v. illus. (al-Maktabah al-Tārīkhīyah) DT95.5.S46 Orien Arab

252
Sheppard, R. Burton. Islamic Africa. New York, Methodist Book Concern [c1914] 127 p. illus. BP65.A4S5
Alarmist description of Islam in Africa by a Methodist missionary. In his concluding paragraph, Sheppard suggests that "if Islam is an enemy of civilization, a forerunner of political trouble; if it is an enemy of the home and degrading to womanhood; if it results in fanaticism, and is detrimental to moral growth and spiritual thought, certainly its defeat in Africa is necessary for the greatest future of the black man."

253
Shiḥātah, 'Alī. al-Riqq baynanā wa-bayna Amrīkā. [Slavery between us and America] Damascus, Dar al-Fikr al-Islāmī [1958] 135 p. E185.61.S55

254
Sík, Endre. The history of Africa. [Translated by Sándor Simon] Budapest, Akadémiai Kiadó, 1966+ illus., maps (part col.), ports. DT351.S4713
L.C. has v. 1–2.
Major history of the continent with a Marxist interpretation.

255
Strong, Tracy. A pilgrimage into the world of Islam. Geneva, World Alliance of Young Mens Christian Associations [n.d.] 143 p. DS39.S79
Report on a world tour of inspection of YMCA organizations by the executive director of the World Alliance.

256
Sukarno, *Pres. Indonesia.* Islam must fight colonialism. Inaugural address by President Sukarno, African-Asian Islamic Conference Bandung, 6th March 1965. [Djakarta, Govt. Print. Off., 1965] 10 p. DLC

257
al-Ṭabarī. Tārīkh al-Umam wa-al-Mulūk [History of nations and kings] [by] Abī Ja'far Muḥammad ibn Jarīr al-Ṭabarī. Beirut, Dār al-qāmūs al-ḥadīth lil-ṭibā'ah wa-al-nashr [1968?] 13 v. in 6. D17.T215
Reprint of the edition published in Cairo, 1336 A.H.
Known also under title: Tārīkh al-rusul wa-al-mulūk [History of Apostles and Kings].
Vol. 12 contains text of 'Arīb's *Ṣilat Tārīkh al-Ṭabarī*; v. 13, al-Ṭabarī's *al-Muntakhab min zayl al-muzayyal.*

258
Ternaux-Compans, Henri. Bibliothèque asiatique et africaine, ou catalogue des ouvrages relatifs à l'Asie et à l'Afrique qui ont paru depuis la découverte de l'imprimerie jusqu'en 1700. [Réimpression de l'édition Paris 1841]. Amsterdam, B. R. Grüner, 1968. 350 p. Z3002.T32 1968

259
Thābit, Muḥammad. Jawlah fī rubū' Ifrīqīyah bayna Miṣr wa-ra's al-Rajā' al-Ṣāliḥ, min mushāhadāt sā'iḥ miṣrī. [Voyage in the land of Africa between Egypt and the Cape of Good Hope; impressions of an Egyptian tourist] al-Ṭab'ah 3. [Cairo] Maktabat al-Nahḍah al-Miṣrīyah, 1948. 240 p. illus., maps. DT12.T5 1948

260
Three forgotten wars: Moslem/Negroid incompatibility in Africa. *In* Africa Institute. Bulletin, v. 8, Apr. 1970: 103–111. DT1.A2146, v. 8

261
Toynbee, Arnold J. Between Niger and Nile. London, Oxford University Press, 1965. 133 p. DT165.2.T6

Though this is essentially a series of impressions of Egypt, Morocco, Nigeria, the Sudan, Ethiopia, and Libya, Toynbee raises the important question of negritude and Arabism within the context of African unity.

262
Trimingham, J. Spencer. Islam in tropical Africa: the contemporary situation. Middle East Forum, v. 42, winter 1966: 13–22. DS41.M45, v. 42

263
al-Tūnisī, Muḥammad ibn 'Umar. Tashḥīdh al-adhhān bi-sīrat bilād al-'Arab wa-al-Sūdān. [The whetting of minds with the story of Arab countries and the Sudan] Edited by Khalīl Maḥmūd 'Asākir [and] Muṣṭafā Muḥammad Mus'ad. Reviewed by Muḥammad Muṣṭafā Ziyādah. Cairo, al-Dār al-Miṣrīyah lil-ta'līf wa-al-tarjamah, 1965. 477 p. illus., maps (3 fold.) (Turāthunā) DT135.D2T8 1965

See also 1381, 1409.

264
al-'Ubūdī, Muḥammad ibn Nāṣir. Fī Ifrīqīyah al-khaḍrā', Mushāhadāt wa-inṭiba'āt wa-aḥādīth 'an al-Islām wa-al-Muslimīn. [In green Africa; views, impressions, and conversations about Islam and Muslims] [Beirut, Dar al-Thaqāfah] 1968. 779 p. maps. DT12.2.U28

265
'Ulabī, Aḥmad Suhayl. Thawrat al-zunj wa-qā'iduha 'Alī ibn Muḥammad, 255–270 A.H./869–883 A.D. [The Zunj revolt and its leader Ali ibn Muhammad, 255–270 A.H./869–883 A.D.] Beirut, Dar Maktabat al-Ḥayāt [1961] 139 p. DS76.U4 Orien Arab

At head of title: Min al-Thawrāt al-Ijtimā'īyah fī al-Islām.

Added t.p.: Révolte des Zanj et son chef Ali-ben-Mohamed, 255–270 H.—869–883 ap. J.C., par Ahmad S. Olabi.

266
von Sivers, Peter. Comparative analysis of Islamic resistance in Africa in the 19th century.

Source: ASA, Program, 15th, 1972.

267
Welch, Galbraith. Africa before they came; the continent, north, south, east, and west, preceding the colonial powers. New York, Morrow, 1965. 395 p. illus. DT25.W4

268
Wiedner, Donald L. A history of Africa south of the Sahara. New York, Random House [1962] 578 p. illus. DT352.W48

269
Williams, John A., *comp.* Themes of Islamic civilization. Berkeley, University of California Press, 1971. 382 p. BP20.W53

Includes a selection of articles on Mahdism in Africa.

270
Willis, John R. Historiography of Islam in Africa: the last decade (1960–1970). African studies review, v. 14, Dec. 1971: 403–424. DT1.A2293, v. 14

271
Wilmeth, Roscoe. Islamic penetration in the sub-Saharan area. *In* Michigan Academy of Sciences, Arts, and Letters. Papers. v. 48; 1962. Ann Arbor, Mich., 1963. p. 443–467. Q11.M56, v. 48

Includes a chart showing population density and percentage of Muslims in each state.

272
Yaḥyā ibn Abī Bakr, Abū Zakariyā. Chronique d'Abou Zakaria, pub. pour la première fois, tr. et commentée par Emile Masqueray. Alger, Impr. de l'Association ouvrière V. Allaud, 1878. 410 p. (Livres des Beni Mzab) BP195.K4Y3

Relates the history of the Banū Mzāb, who played a major role as trade intermediaries in the Sahara and in West and North Africa.

273
al-Ya'qūbī, Aḥmad ibn Abī Ya'qūb. Les pays. Tr. par Gaston Wiet. Le Caire, 1937. xxxi, 291 p. geneal. table. (Publications de l'Institut français d'archéologie orientale. Textes et traductions d'auteurs orientaux, t. 1) G93.Y174 1937

al-Ya'qūbī wrote his compendium about A.D. 890. He includes a section on the kingdoms of the Berbers and the "Afāriq."

274
Yāqūt ibn 'Abd Allāh al-Ḥamawī. Kitāb mu'jam al-buldān. [Geographic dictionary] Teheran, 1965. 6 v. (Manshūrāt Maktabat al-Asadī, no. 7)
G93.Y192 Orien Arab

Added t.p.: Jacut's Geographisches Wörterbuch, aus den Handschriften zu Berlin, St. Petersburg und Paris auf Kosten der Deutchen Morgen ländischen Gesellschaft hrsg. von Ferdinand Wüstenfeld.

Photo-offset reproduction of the edition published in Leipzig, 1866–73.

275
Zakī, 'Abd al-Raḥmān. al-Islām wa-al-Muslimūn, majmū'at muḥāḍarāt ulqiyat fī ma'had al-dirāsāt al-Islāmīyah. [Islam and Muslims; a series of lectures presented at the Institute of Islamic Studies] Cairo, Maṭba'at Yūsif [1965] 2 v. maps. BP64.A1Z3

Part 1 deals with East Africa, while part 2 encompasses West Africa.

After examining Islam of the medieval period in both West and East Africa, Zakī describes the various kingdoms and empires from Ghana to Samory's in the West, and Ethiopia, Nubia, Somalia, and the coastal region in the East. Of special interest is a section entitled "Arabic Sources for Islamic History in West Africa."

276
———al-Muslimūn fī al-'Ālam al-yawm [Muslims in today's world] [Cairo] Maktabat al-nahḍah al-Miṣrīyah, 1958–60. 5 v. in 2. illus., maps. BP60.Z3

Parts 1 and 2 deal with Muslim Africa.

277
Zambaur, Eduard K. M. von. Manuel de généalogie et de chronologie pour l'histoire de l'Islam, avec 20 tableaux généalogiques hors texte et 5 cartes. Hanovre, H. Lafaire, 1927. 388 p. portfolio of 5 maps, 20 geneal. tables (part col.)
DS223.Z3

278
Zaqlamah, Anwar. Miṣr al-Kubrā; Ifrīqiyā lil-Ifrīqīyīn. Cairo, Maktabat al-anjlū al-Miṣrīyah, 1955. 158 p. DLC

The author attempts to show that a large part of Eastern and Central Africa—including the Sudan, Uganda, and parts of Zaïre—were once part of an Egyptian empire. He tries to justify such an entity on political, economic, and other grounds.

279
Zimová, Nadĕžda. Osmanští a Cerná Afrika. [Ottoman Turks in black Africa] Novy Orient, roč, čis. 3, 1968: 70–71. DS1.N6, 1968

280
Ziyādah, Muḥammad Muṣṭafā. al-Mu'arikhūn fī Miṣr fī al-qarn al-khāmis 'ashar al-mīlādī/al-qarn al-tāsi' al-hijrī. [Historians in Egypt during the 15th century A.D./9th century A.H.] Cairo, Lajnat al-Ta'līf wa al-tarjamah wa-al-nashr, 1949. 111 p.
DT76.8.Z5

281
Zoghby, Samir M. Blacks and Arabs: past and present. A current bibliography on African affairs, v. 3, May 1970: 5–22. Z3501.C87, v. 3

Investigation of a once awkward and troubled relationship that is being transcended in the common interest of a still crystallizing Third World.

282
———Medieval West Africa, 1965–1968. pt. 1–2. A current bibliography on African affairs, new ser., v. 2, Apr. 1969: 5–18; v. 2, May 1969: 5–14.
Z3501.C87, n.s., v. 2

283
Zwemer, Samuel M. Islam in Africa. MW, v. 15, July 1925: 217–222. DS36.M7, v. 15

Editorial on Islam in Africa and the urgency of stemming the tide of the Prophet's message. In conclusion, Zwemer quotes President Coolidge: "As the Christian nations have assumed the responsibility for bringing this new and higher civilisation in touch with all peoples so they must recognize their responsibility to press on and on in their task of enlightenment, education, spiritualization, Christianizing. There can be no hesitancy; no cessation of effort."

LANGUAGES & LINGUISTICS

284
'Abbās, Muḥammad Jalāl. al-Lughah al-'Arabīyah fī Ifrīqiyā. [The Arabic language in Africa] Cairo. al-Jāmi' al-Azhar. Majallat al-Azhar, m. 33, Sept. 1961: 463–467. BP1.C3, v. 33 Orien Arab

Arabic spread in Africa through the migration of Arab tribes, the Islamization of parts of the continent, and the Arab role in commerce, with the result that Arabic became a trade language. The author examines the borrowing of Arabic terms in such African languages as Swahili, Wolof, Mandingo, and Hausa, describes the opposition of the colonial powers to Arabic, and shows how indigenous and European languages were used to stymie the development of Arabic. He proposes that Arabic be adopted as the language of the continent and concludes that "the Arabic language is the most important means of achieving cultural independence after political independence, as it is the only way to arrive at a complete understanding among the countries of the continent after it had brought about a rapprochement in the political and international fields, and that a great African language is more deserving than any foreign language to bring about unity and cultural cooperation on a continental basis."

285
Blanc, Haim. Arabic. *In* Sebeok, Thomas A., *ed.* Current trends in linguistics. The Hague, Mouton, 1971. p. 501–509. P25.S4

Review of the state of research on the varieties of Arabic used in Western, Central, and Eastern Africa. Includes a 4-page bibliography.

286
Greenberg, Joseph H. The decipherment of the "Ben Ali Diary," a preliminary report. Journal of Negro history, v. 25, July 1940: 372–375. E185.J86, v. 25

Analysis of an Arabic manuscript sent in 1937 to Northwestern University for translation. The 13-page document was written by a Muslim slave brought to Georgia in the early 19th century. Greenberg believes it to be excerpts from the *Risālah* of Abū Muḥammad 'Abd Allāh ibn Abī Zayd al-Qayrawānī.

287
Lebeuf, Jean-Pierre. L'écriture verticale des caractères arabes et latins dans l'Afrique subsaharienne. NA, no 88, oct. 1960: 126–127. DT1.I513, 1960

Arabic script has been used in Fulfulde, Hausa, Kanuri, Kotoko, Malagasy, Swahili, and Yoruba. Lebeuf reports on an example he discovered in which Arabic letters are used in an unorthodox vertical manner.

288
Monteil, Vincent. Sur l'arabisation des langues négro-africaines. Genève-Afrique/Geneva-Africa, v. 2, no 1, 1963: 12–20. DT1.G44, v. 2

289
N'Diaye, Aïssatou. Sur la transcription des vocables africains par Ibn Baththutah. NA, no 38, avril 1948: 26–27; no 41, janv. 1949: 31. DT1.I513, 1948, 1949

290
Paris-Teynac, E. J. Essai sur le Koufique ancien dit koufique carré. BIFAN, t. 21, juil./oct. 1959: 501–543. illus. DT1.I5123, v. 21

Kufic script, as its name indicates, originated in al-Kufah (Iraq) and became popular in the Sudanic belt after it spread in North Africa. After presenting the historical development of the script, the author shows how it was used in traditional Muslim calligraphy and decorative arts as a substitute for the representation of human forms prohibited by the Prophet Muḥammad. Profusely illustrated. Extensive bibliography.

291
Rizvi, S. Saeed Akhtar *Maulana*. "Zenj": its first known use in Arabic literature. Azania, v. 2, 1967: 200–201. DT365.3.A94, v. 2

292
Wansbrough, John. Africa and the Arab geographers. *In* Dalby, David, *ed.* Language and history in Africa: a volume of collected papers presented to the London Seminar on Language and History in Africa (held at the School of Oriental and African Studies, 1967–69). London, Cass, 1970. p. 89–101. illus., maps. PL8003.D3

The author examines the problems of Arabic sources pertaining to Africa and notes six terms that have puzzled scholars using these sources: "sāḥil, jubb, sūsīyāt, karāzī, ka'bar, and zanj."

LAW

293
Afrika-Instituut (*Netherlands*). The future of customary law in Africa. L'avenir du droit coutumier

en Afrique. Symposium-colloque, Amsterdam, 1955. Organized by the Afrika Instituut, Studiecentrum, Leiden, in collaboration with the Royal Tropical Institute, Amsterdam. Leiden, Universitaire Pers Leiden, 1956. xvii, 305 p. DLC–LL

294
Anderson, James N. D. The adaptation of Muslim law in sub-Saharan Africa. *In* Kuper, Hilda, *and* Leo Kuper, *eds.* African law: adaptation and development. Berkeley, University of California Press, 1965. p. 149–164. DLC–LL

295
———Colonial law in tropical Africa: the conflict between English, Islamic and customary law. Indiana law journal, v. 35, summer 1960: 433–442. DLC–LL

Investigation of the problems arising out of the coexistence and interaction of the three legal systems in tropical Africa.

296
———Comments with reference to the Muslim community. East African law journal, v. 5, Mar./June 1969: 5–20. DLC–LL

Entire issue is devoted to the Republic of Kenya's reports on the law of marriage and divorce succession, known as the Spry Commission Report and the Slade Commission Report.

297
———Islamic law in Africa. London, H. M. Stationery Off., 1954. 409 p. (Colonial research publication no. 16) JV33.G7A52, no. 16

"This survey covers the work of six months in Africa, three of them spent on a rapid tour of Tanganyika, Nyasaland, Uganda, British Somaliland and the Colony and Protectorate of Aden, and the other three on similar visits to Nigeria, the Gold Coast, the Gambia and Sierra Leone. . . . it is hoped . . . that this Survey will provide a reasonably accurate and comprehensive account of the application of Islamic law throughout the territories concerned and will at least furnish a framework into which detailed studies of more limited aspects of a vast subject may conveniently be fitted."

298
———Islamic law in African colonies. Corona, v. 3, July 1951: 262–266. JV1001.C77, v. 3

Status report and discussion of the administrative problems regarding the application of Islamic law in the former British colonies of East Africa.

299
———Relationship between Islamic and customary law in Africa. Journal of African administration, v. 12, Oct. 1960: 228–234. JQ1881.A1J6, v. 12

Looking at the legal system as applied in Africa as a whole, Anderson analyzes the relationship between the two systems and the ensuing symbiotic results. He suggests that "the question inevitably arises, therefore, whether it is preferable to regard Islamic law as a variety of native law and custom, or as a distinct system. On the one hand purists may protest, and have protested, that it is not at all suitable to regard a law which was very highly developed in Arabia, Spain and North Africa as the indigenous customary law of African tribes today. Yet it is eminently convenient from a practical point of view, to apply Islamic law in a country like Nigeria under the comprehensive umbrella of native law and custom, since this allows for an infinite number of gradations between a fairly strict application of Islamic law in strongly Muslim areas, an application of purely pagan customary law in entirely pagan areas, and any variety of amalgam in the area in between."

300
Anderson, James N. D., *and* Norman J. Coulson. Islamic law in contemporary cultural change. Saeculum, Bd. 18, Heft 1–2, 1967: 13–92. D2.S3, v. 18

Includes a section on "Islamic Systems of Law in East and West Africa."

301
Froelich, Jean-Claude. Droit musulman et droit coutumier. *In* Poirier, Jean. Études de droit africain et de droit malgache [par] M. Allot [*et al.*] [Paris, Éditions Cujas, 1965] p. 361–389. DLC–LL

302
Maudoodi, Syed Abul 'Ala, *Mawlana.* Rights of non-Muslims in Islamic state. Translated and edited by Khurshid Ahmad. Lahore, Islamic Publications, 1961. 28 p. DLC–LL

Review of rights of Dhimmi in an Islamic state.

303
N'dir, Mohamadou Lamine. Réflexions sur le mariage et le divorce en pays musulman. Afrique documents, no 83, 6. cahier, 1965: 251–258. DT1.A479, 1965

Lecture delivered by the deputy public prosecutor of the Senegal Court of Appeals on the legislative problems related to marriage and divorce in a society that encompasses many religions.

304
Ouane, Ibrahima Mamadou. La pratique du droit musulman. [Andrézieux, Loire, Impr. moderne, 1958] 43 p. illus. DLC–LL

305
———Le principe du droit musulman. [Avignon] Presses universelles [1957] 91 p. illus. DLC–LL

306
Schacht, Joseph. An introduction to Islamic law. Oxford, Clarendon Press, 1964. 304 p. DLC–LL

307
Wallis, C. Braithwaite. Influence of Islam on African native law. [pts.] 1–2. MW, v. 11, Apr. 1921: 145–168; July 1921: 296–308
DS36.M7, v. 11

Conversion to Islam dictates the adoption of the Shari'a, or Muslim jurisprudence, which often clashes with traditional social systems. Wallis reviews the conflicts between Fanti law and the Malikite rite on marriage and between Temne inheritance law and Islamic law. He also discusses Fulbe Islam and its methods of proselytizing.

LITERATURE

308
Badian, Seydou Kouyate. Sous l'orage: Kany. Paris, Présence africaine, 1963. 155 p. DLC

309
Basset, René M. J. Contes populaires d'Afrique. [nouv. ed.] Paris, G.-P. Maisonneuve et Larose, 1969. 457 p. (Les littératures populaires de toutes les nations, t. 47) GR350.B33 1969

310
Crouzat, Henri. Azizah de Niamkoko. Paris, Presses de la cité [1959] 415 p. IEN

311
Diop, Birago. Contes et lavanes [Paris] Présence africaine [1963] 255 p. (Collection Contes africains)
PQ2664.I66C6

312
Diop, Ousmane Socé. Contes et légendes d'Afrique noire. Couverture et dessins de Samba Ousso. Paris, Nouvelles éditions latines [1962] 154 p. illus.
PQ3989.D56C6

313
Fall, Malick. La plaie. Paris, A. Michel, 1967. 253 p.
PQ2666.A45P55

314
al-Fītūrī, Muḥammad. Ifrīqiyā: Aghānī, 'Āshiq min, Idhkurīnī yā. Shi'r Muḥammad al-Fītūrī. [Africa: Songs, Lover from, Remember me O, Poetry by Muhammad al-Fituri] Beirut, Dār maktabat al-hayāt [1967] 320 p. illus., port. (Aghānī Ifrīqiyā. [Songs from Africa]) PJ7824.I8A7

al-Faytūrī is a Sudanese poet with a grandfather from Bahr el-Ghazal and an Egyptain mother. He grew up in Alexandria, Egypt, where his father was intimately linked with the Sufi fraternities, whose ceremonies Muḥammad attended, and where he became alienated from a city which faced, in all respects, the Mediterranean Sea. This alienation is the seed of his Africa-oriented poetry. One of his significant poems, *Anā Zunjī* [I Am Black], was translated by Ḥalīm al-Dab' in *3000 Years of Black Poetry; an Anthology* (edited by Alan Lomax and Raoul Abdoul; New York, Dodd, Mead [1970] 261 p. PN6109.7.L6)

315
Knappert, Jan. The figure of the Prophet Muhammed according to the popular literature of the Islamic peoples. Swahili, new ser., v. 1, pt. 3, 1967: 24–31. PL8701.E2, n.s., v. 1

316
Kourouma, Ahmadou. Les soleils des indépendances. Paris, Éditions du Seuil [1970] 207 p.
PQ3989.2.K58S6

317
Lagneau-Kesteloot, Lilyan. Les écrivains noirs de langue française: naissance d'une littérature. 3. éd. Bruxelles, Université libre de Bruxelles, Institut de sociologie, 1967. 343 p. tables. (Études africaines) Q3897.L3 1967

318
Ouologuem, Yambo. Le devoir de violence, roman. Paris, Éditions du Seuil, 1968. 208 p.
PQ3989.2.O8D4

Translated as *Bound to Violence* (PZ4.O925Bo3).

319
Ousmane, Sembene. Les bouts de bois de Dieu: Banty Mam Yall. [Paris] Le Livre contemporain [1960] 381 p. PQ3989.O8B6

A novel. Translated as *God's Bits of Wood* (PZ4.O935Go3).

320
———Vehi-Ciosane; ou, Blanche-Genèse. Suivi du Mandat. [Paris] Présence africaine [1972, c1966] 190 p. PQ3989.O8V4 1972

Translated as *The Money-order; With White Genesis* (PZ4.O935Mo).

321
———Voltaïque la noie de . . . Nouvelle. Paris, Présence africaine [1971] 215 p. PQ3989.O8V6

322
Sadji, Abdoulaye. Maïmouna, roman. Paris, Présence africaine [1958] 251 p. PQ3989.2.S2M3

323
Salīm, Maḥmūd Rizq. 'Asr ṣalāṭīn al-Mamālīk wa-nitājuhu al-'ilmī wa-al-adabī. [The era of the Mameluke sultans and its scientific and literary contributions] [Cairo] Maktabat al-ādāb, 1947–65. 4 pts. in 8 v. PJ8206.S3

Vol. 6 published by Wizārat al-Thaqāfah wa-al-Irshād al-Qawmī, al-Idārah al-'Āmmah lil-Thaqāfah.

324
Syad, William J. F. Khamsine, poèmes. Paris, Présence africaine [1959] 70 p. 4PQ Fr. 4616

325
Tiendréogo, Yambo. L'hyène va à la Mecque. Visages d'Afrique, 1. année, sept. 1967: 22. NX589.6.U6V55, v. 1.

METALLURGY

326
Cline, Walter B. Mining and metallurgy in Negro Africa. Menasha, Wisc., George Banta Pub. Co., 1937. 155 p. illus. (incl. maps) (General series in anthropology, no. 5) GN4.G4, no. 5

Technical discussion of the problems of metal production, including iron, copper, gold, and silver.

327
Diop, Louis-Marie. Métallurgie traditionnelle et âge du fer en Afrique. BIFAN, t. 30, janv. 1968: 10–38. DT1.I5123, v. 30

328
Dunlop, D. M. Sources of gold and silver in Islam according to al-Ahdani (10th century A.D.). Studia Islamica, v. 8, 1957: 29–49. BP1.S8, v. 8

329
Gautier, Emile-Félix. L'or du Soudan dans l'histoire. Annales d'histoire économique et sociale, t. 7, 1935: 113–123. HB3.A5, v. 7

330
Huard, Paul. Nouvelle contribution à l'étude du fer au Sahara et au Tchad. BIFAN, t. 26, juil./oct. 1964: 297–396. DT1.I5123, v. 26

The diffusion of iron use in North Africa, the Sahara, and the Chad area is thoroughly discussed by Huard, who has studied it for a number of years. On the basis of 600 documents examined, he concludes that iron reached the region south of the Sahara between 3 B.C. and A.D. 4, starting from Meroë and reaching the Tibesti region. For the Chad area, Huard leaves the matter unsettled until further study.

331
Lewicki, Tadeusz. Les écrivains arabes du Moyen-Age au sujet des mines de pierres précieuses et des pierres fines en territoire africain et de leur exploration. Africana bulletin, v. 7, 1967: 49–68. DT19.9.P6A65, v. 7

From a thorough reading and examination of Arabic sources, Lewicki has drawn a history of precious and semiprecious stones in the medieval period in Africa. He divides his study into nine sections, each dealing with one stone.

332
Mauny, Raymond. Essai sur l'histoire des métaux en Afrique occidentale. BIFAN, t. 14, avril 1952: 545–594. Q89.I5, v. 14

Mauny traces the history of metals in West Africa. Drawing on Arabic sources, archeological remains, and oral traditions, he studies the origins of gold, silver, copper, iron, and tin, showing the patterns of influences and the diffusion of metal in the region. He concludes by reminding prehistorians of the immensity of the task still unfinished. Substantial bibliography.

POLITICS

333
Abu-Lughod, Ibrahim. The Islamic factor in African politics. Orbis, v. 8, summer 1964: 425–444. D839.O68, v. 8

Noting that "one out of three Africans is a Muslim," the author discusses the importance of Islam as a political force. Analyzing the introduction of Islam in Africa and the political struggle for independence, he concludes that "while Islam and its civilisation might thus play a unifying role among groups of states that share this common ground, by the same token it might impede an overall Pan-African movement should this ever become a serious possibility."

334
Beling, Willard A. North African vision of black Africa: social and economic aspects. Maghreb digest, v. 4, Jan. 1966: 6–17. DT181.M34, v. 4

"Following independence, the Maghreb sought to re-orient the ties it had hitherto with Europe. Nationalism still prevailed, of course, and colonialism was also very real in their memories. Turning to the Middle East as a substitute for their former relations with Europe, they found that it was a broken reed. But when they turned to Africa, the Maghreb again faced disillusionment.

Recognizing their situation finally for what it is, the Maghreb has gradually returned to face this reality. Thus, despite the threat that close ties with Europe imply, the Maghreb is now in the process of re-orienting itself in this direction. In the opinion of the author, Africanism reached its peak some time ago in North Africa and is definitely on the wane."—(Author's conclusion)

335
Carles, Fernand. La France et l'Islam en Afrique occidentale. Contribution à l'étude de la politique coloniale dans l'Afrique française. Toulouse, V. Rivière, 1915. 214 p. DT532.C3

Thèse—Toulouse.

336
Catta, E. Etats arabes d'Afrique du Nord et Tiers-Monde africain noir. Revue française d'études politiques africaines, no 1, janv. 1966: 71–87. DT1.R4, 1966

337
Deluz, Ariane. Reflexions sur la fonction politique chez des islamisés et des animistes. L'homme, t. 13, janv./juin 1973: 83–96. GN1.H68, v. 13

338
Diara, Agadem L. Islam and Pan-Africanism. [Detroit, Agascha Productions, 1973] 95 p. BP62.N4D5

339
Faugère, Armand P. De la propagande musulmane en Afrique et dans les Indes. Paris, 1851. MH

340
Froelich, Jean-Claude. Pan-Islamisme en Afrique noire. Etudes, nov. 1969: 514–526. AP20.E8, 1969

341
el-Gamal, Shawki. Influence of Egypt in Africa. Paper presented to the International Congress of Africanists, third session, Dec. 9–19, 1973. Addis Ababa. 13 p. DLC

342
Ganiage, Jean. L'Expansion coloniale de la France sous la Troisième République, 1871–1914. Avec la collaboration de Daniel Hémery. Paris, Payot, 1968. 434 p. illus., maps. (Bibliothèque historique) JV1817.G3

343
Gann, Lewis. Colonialism in Africa; 1870–1960: edited by L. H. Gann and Peter Duignan. London, Cambridge University Press, 1969–71. 3 v. (Hoover Institution publications) DT31.G35

344
Gaudefroy-Demombynes, Maurice. Les institutions musulmanes. 3 éd. Paris, Flammarion [1946] 221 p. (Bibliothèque de philosophie scientifique) BP163.G3 1946

345
Gonçalves, José J. O mundo árabico-islâmico e o ultramar português. 2. ed. [Lisboa] Junta de Investigaçoes do Ultramar, Centro de Estudos Politicos e Sociais, 1962. 354 p. illus., facsims. (Estudos de ciências politicas e sociais, no. 10) BP52.G6 1962

346
Ḥamdān, Jamāl. al-Islām fī Ifrīqiya; dirāsah siyāsīyah. [Islam in Africa; a political study] al-Majallah, no. 83, Nov. 1963: 27–33. AP95.A6M25-1963 Orien Arab

"At the time when the victorious continent is moving and exploding with the political revolution, and when religion becomes, per force, a political factor with its danger and weight, we look in vain for a general and objective study of Islam in Africa as a political power." In an attempt to fill the void, Ḥamdān presents the geography of Islam in the continent, investigates the impact of the Muslim faith and its geopolitical strength, and estimates future possible and potential trends, drawing the "plausible and inescapable religious policies." He divides the continent into Islamic countries, semi-Islamic countries, and countries with Islamic minorities. In the third category, including countries such as those of coastal West Africa, Islam is advancing with giant steps. Ḥamdān suggests that the division of Africa into north and south of the Sahara is nothing but the creation of imperialism. He concludes, "Everything indicates that Islam is the religion of the future in the continent of the future."

347
Heikal, Muhammad Hassanein. Israel in Africa; Israel's two main objectives in Africa. The Islamic review, v. 54, June 1966: 24–26. BP1.I7, v. 54

348
Heintzen, H. The role of Islam in the era of nationalism. *In* Georgetown Colloquium on Africa. *1st, Georgetown University, 1961*. New forces in Africa. Edited by William H. Lewis. Washington, Public Affairs Press [1962] p. 42–50.
DT30.G4 1961

349
Hodgkin, Thomas L. Islam, history and politics. (Review article) Journal of modern African studies, v. 1, Mar. 1963: 91–98. DT1.J68, v. 1

350
———Mahdisme, messianisme, et marxisme dans le contexte africain. Présence africaine, no 74, 2. trimestre, 1970: 128–153. GN645.P74, 1970

351
Hoskins, Halford L. Africa's Arab fringe. Current history, v. 50, Mar. 1966: 136–141.
D410.C82, v. 50

352
al-'Imarī, Aḥmad Suwaylim. al-Ifrīqīyūn wa-al-'Arab. [Africans and Arabs] Cairo, Maktabat al-Anjlū-al-Miṣrīyah, 1967. 246 p. DT31.I4

353
Itey, R. Die Araber und Schwarz Afrika. Internationales Afrika forum, Jahr 1., Nov. 1967: 557–560. DLC

354
Junayd, 'Abd al-Mun'im. La République Arabe Unie "Egypte" dans l'unité arabe et l'unité africaine. Cairo, Dār al-Kitāb al-Arabi, 1968. 339 p. map. (al-Maktabah al-'Arabīyah, 78. al-ta'līf, 52. al-'Ulūm al-siyāsīyah, 2) DT82.5.A7J85
At head of title: al-Jumhūrīyah al-'Arabīyah al-Muttaḥidah. Wizārat al-Thaqāfah.

355
Lacouture, Jean. La politique nasserienne en Afrique. Revue de défense nationale, t. 20, mai 1964: 846–853. D410.R45, v. 20

356
Le Grip, A. Le Mahdisme en Afrique noire. A&A, no 18, 2. trimestre, 1952: 3–16. DT1.A85, 1952
A religious revolt calling for a return to the original purity of Islam, Mahdism acquired during the colonial period a political anti-imperialistic character. In the East, revolts against foreigners were led by Muḥammad ibn 'Abd Allāh in the Sudan and by Muḥammad ibn 'Abd Allāh Ḥasan, called "Mad Mullah" by the European colonialist press, in Somalia. In the West, a plethora of "Mahdiou"—from Senegal with Mohamadu, known as Wiyaru (1828), to Cameroon with Amagobdo Konara (1939)—appeared and attempted to defend their land and religion against the onslaught of colonialism with varying degrees of success.

357
McKay, Vernon. The impact of Islam on relations among the new African states. *In* Proctor, Jesse Harris, *ed.* Islam and international relations. New York, Praeger [1965] p. 158–193. BP173.5.P7
An analysis of the role of Islam as an instrument of foreign policy by the then director of the African Program of Johns Hopkins University's School of Advanced International Studies. Contrasting the official attitude—secular, democratic, and social—of most states with the cultural affinities of the masses in the Muslim world, the author concludes that Islam is not a useful instrument of foreign policy. Of note in the Sudanic belt is the dichotomy between a Muslim population in the north and a Christian and/or animist population in the south, in such states as Nigeria, Cameroon, Chad, and the Sudan.

358
Marais, Benjamin J. Islam: political factor in Africa. *In* Africa Institute. Bulletin, v. 9, Mar. 1971: 51–64. DT1.A2146, v. 9
Explorations of the political implications of Islamic states after they became independent.

359
Marchand, J. La République Arabe Unie et le mythe de l'Afrique noire. Revue de défense nationale, v. 22, déc. 1966: 2001–2013. D410.R45, v. 22
Impressions about the evolution, since 1960, of Egyptian politics towards Africa.

360
Mazrui, Ali A. Africa and the Egyptians' four circles. African affairs, v. 63, Apr. 1964: 129–141.
DT1.R62, v. 63

361
———Islam, political leadership and economic radicalism in Africa. Comparative studies in society and history, v. 9, Apr. 1967: 274–291.
H1.C73, v. 9

Mazrui begins by asking the question, "How conservative a force is Islam in Africa?" He suggests that a radicalized Islam could be an ally of the revolutionary commitment in Africa but that this is checked by the fact that "Islam, under certain conditions, has the propensity to produce both rebellious leaders and submissive followers." Intertwined with these two factors is the defensive attitude of Islam towards Christianity, which is considered by many Africans to be connected with capitalist imperialism.

362
Megahed, Horeya T. The empires of Western Sudan; a political analysis. African studies review, v. 1, 1972: 23–41. DLC

Political structures from the Ghana Empire to al-Ḥājj 'Umar's state shared a number of characteristics, according to Miss Megahed: conquest states, centralization of authority, and the political role of Islam. She also suggests that the legacy of these large-scale political systems is population dispersion, a stratified social structure, the vital importance of trade, and the development of an urban civilization.

363
Mwamba, Zuberi. Egypt's contribution to Africa's liberation: 1952–1970. Paper presented at the 16th annual meeting of the African Studies Association, Syracuse, N.Y., 1973. DLC-Micro 03782

Collation of the original: 17 p.

364
Nasser, Gamal Abdel, *Pres. United Arab Republic.* On Africa. Cairo [1966] 48 p. DT30.N282

At head of title: Ministry of National Guidance, Information Administration. Cover title: Africa From the Speeches of President Gamal Abdel Nasser.

Translation of *Ifrīqiyā, min aqwāl al-ra'īs* (DT30.N2822 Orien Arab). *See also* his *On the Road to African Unity; the Fourth Summit Conference, November 5, 1966* (DT30.U49).

365
Proctor, Jesse H., *ed.* Islam and international relations. New York, Praeger [1965] 221 p. map. BP173.5.P7

Papers read at a meeting held at Duke University in June 1963. The topics include a comparison of religion and politics in Christianity and Islam, the appeal of communism to Islamic peoples, the impact of Islam on relations among the new African states, and pan-Islam in the modern world. The paper by Vernon McKay (*see* 357) deals with the role of Islam as a factor in the relations between Muslim states north and south of the Sahara.

366
Revue française d'études politiques africaines, no 27, mars 1968. DT1.R4, 1968

Entire issue is devoted to Arabs and Africa. Partial contents: Jean-Claude Froelich, Les arabes en Afrique de l'est.—Hubert Michel, La politique africaine des états du Maghreb.—André Pautard, Le Maghreb et les états d'Afrique noire.

367
Rifā'ī, 'Abd al-'Azīz. Taṭawwur al-'ilāqāt al-'Arabīyah al-Ifrīqīyah. [The evolution of Arab-African relations] [Cairo, al-Dār al-qawmīyah lil-ṭibā'ah wa-al-nashr, 1963?] 46 p. (Kutub qawmīyah, 237) DS63.R28

368
Rondot, Pierre. L'Egypte et le continent noir. Revue des troupes coloniales, no 285, fév. 1947: 62–72. UA709.A6T7, 1947

Rondot, who at the time of writing was Commandant, discusses the idea that "quoiqu 'en pensent les géographes, il n'est pas sûr que l'Egypte soit en Afrique." After a description of modern Egypt he concludes, "Nation islamique. Etat oriental moderne, associée plus ou moins rétive de la puissance britannique, tels demeurent les traits essentiels de l'Egypte, telles sont les conditions de l'influence qu'elle peut exercer, ou qui peut s'exercer à travers elle, dans le continent africain."

369
Rosenthal, Erwin I. J. Islam in the modern national state. Cambridge [Eng.] Cambridge University Press, 1965. xxi, 416 p. BP173.6.R6

370
Schildkrout, Enid. Islamization and political incorporation among urban immigrants. Source: ASA, Program, 15th, 1972.

371
Sengor, Léopold Sédar, *Prés. Senegal.* Les fondements de l'africanité; ou négritude et arabité. [Paris] Présence africaine [1967?] 108 p. DT15.S47

"Conference . . . prononcée à l'Université du Caire, le . . . 16 février, 1967."

Analysis of the long relationship between blacks and Arabs by one of the most eminent proponents of negritude.

372
Sharif, Kamil. The importance of the African peoples to the Arabs in particular and Muslims in general: The tactics of Israel, some suggestions. The Islamic review, v. 53, June 1965: 24–26, 29. BP1.I7, v. 53

373
al-Sharqāwī, Maḥmūd. al-Islām wa-l-lughah al-ʻArabīyah fī mustaqbal Ifrīqiyā al-jadīdah. [Islam and the Arabic language in the future of the new Africa] *In* Cairo. al-Jāmiʻ al-Azhar. Majallat al-Azhar, m. 33, Dec. 1961: 818–827. BP1.C3, v. 33

In spite of their efforts and the means at their disposal to cut Africa from its Arab sources, the author says, the former colonial powers, the United States, and Israel have failed in their endeavor. He sees clear indications in many African countries of a renewal of Islamo-Arabic influence and the Islamization of its masses.

374
Smith, Robert. Peace and palaver: international relations in pre-colonial West Africa. JAH, v. 14, no. 4, 1973: 599–621. DT1.J65, v. 14

International relations during this period were conducted according to customary law affected to some degree by two major external influences, namely Islam and Western European culture. The first part deals with Islam and the innovations it introduced, such as the contribution of literacy and the distinction in international law and practice between Muslims and non-Muslims.

375
Trimingham, J. Spencer. Islam and secular nationalism in Africa. MW, v. 56, Oct. 1966: 305–307. DS36.M7, v. 56

376
ʻŪdah, ʻAbd al-Malik. al-Siyāsah wa-al-ḥukm fī Ifrīqiyā. [Politics and power in Africa] [Cairo] Maktabat al-Anjlū-al-Miṣrīyah, 1959. 575 p. DLC

377
Vermont, René. Le Moyen Orient et l'Afrique. Revue de défense nationale, v. 22, janv. 1966: 79–93. D410.R45, v. 22

Analysis of Arab-African relations within the context of the Arab-Israeli conflict.

378
Wagner, Ewald. Political and religious authorities. Paper presented to the International Congress of Africanists, third session, Dec. 9–19, 1973. Addis Ababa. 7 p. DLC

SECTS

379
Ahmad, Bashruddin Mahmud, *Hazrat Mirza.* Le mouvement Ahmadiyya dans l'Islam [Port Louis?] Ahmadia Association of Mauritius [1964] 84 p. BP195.A5A334

An abridgment of the author's *Ahmadiyyat.*

History of the Ahmadi movement and introduction to its interpretation of Islam, by one of its eminent leaders.

380
André, Pierre J. Contribution à l'étude des confréries religieuses musulmanes. Alger, La Maison des livres [1956] 368 p. BP189.2.A5

Chapter 7 deals with religious fraternities in former French Africa (p. 119–135).

381
Depont, Octave, *and* Xavier Coppolani. Les confréries religieuses musulmanes. Alger, A. Jourdan, 1897. 576 p. illus., plates (part col.), ports., facsims. BP189.2.D4

——— ———Carte de l'Algérie, l'Afrique, l'Asie & la Turquie d'Europe; domaine géographique des confréries religieuses musulmanes. Alger, A. Jourdan, 1898. col. map 99 x 131 cm. fold. to 29 × 20 cm. BP189.2.D4 Atlas

Scales vary.

382
Froelich, Jean-Claude. L'importance et l'influence de l'Islam, du Christianisme et des sectes en Afrique noire. Europe-France-outre-mer, no 396, 1963: 36–40. illus. JV1801.E65, 1963

383
———Sectes musulmanes et civilisations négro-africaines. Le mois en Afrique; revue française d'études politiques africaines, t. 1, mai 1966: 98–105. DT1.R4, v. 1

384
Rinn, Louis M. Marabouts et Khouan. Etude sur l'Islam en Algérie. Avec une carte indiquant la marche, la situation et l'importance des ordres religieux musulmans. Alger, A. Jourdan, 1884. 552 p. map. BP65.A5R5

Map wanting.

Although dealing with Islam in Algeria, Rinn's work is of great use in tracing to North Africa the origin of a number of fraternities that played a major role in the development of sub-Saharan Islam.

385
Shukrī, Muḥammad Fu'ād. al-Sanūsīyah. [The Senussi movement] [Cairo] Dār al-fikr al-'Arabī, 1948. 424 p. facsims. BP189.7.S4S5

386
Spillmann, Georges. Esquisse d'histoire religieuse du Maroc; confréries et zaouïas [par] Georges Drague. Paris, J. Peyronnet [1951] 332 p. geneal. tables (part fold.) (Cahiers de l'Afrique et l'Asie, 2) BP64.M6S6

Useful in tracing the history of some of the fraternities that spread south of the Sahara.

387
Trimingham, J. Spencer. The Sufi orders in Islam. Oxford, Clarendon Press, 1971. 333 p. 4 fold. plates, geneal. tables. BP189.T7

Introduction to the history of the Sufi orders, their formation, organization, and rituals, as well as their role in the Islamic society and the problems they are facing in the modern world.

388
Ziadeh, Nicola A. Sanusiyah: a study of a revivalist movement in Islam. Leiden, E. J. Brill, 1958. 148 p. BP187.7.S4Z5

SOCIETY & CULTURE

389
al-'Abbādī, 'Abd al-Ḥamīd. al-Islām wa-al-mushkilah al-'unṣurīyah. [Islam and the racial question] Bayrūt, Dār al-'ilm lil-malāyīn [1969] 112 p. BP190.5.R3A2 Orien Arab

390
'Abbās, Muḥammad Jalāl. Islam and African thought. *In* Cairo. al-Jāmi' al-Azhar. Majallat al-Azhar, m. 40, Feb. 1969: 14–16; v. 41, Apr. 1969: 14–16. BP1.C3, v. 40–41 Orien Arab

Islam and traditional African religions share basic beliefs in one Supreme Being, the world of spirits and angels, and an afterlife. 'Abbās, who is general secretary of the Cairo-based Society of African Culture, strives to show that "Islam had been intellectually accepted and spiritually welcomed by Africans and that it was not enforced or based on blind or material incitements."

391
———al-Islām wa-al-mu'taqadāt al-Ifrīqīyah. [Islam and African beliefs] al-Hady al-Islāmī, m. 5, May 1966: 28–32. BP1.H33, v. 5 Orien Arab

Refuting the suggestion by some missionaries and orientalists that Islam spread in Africa because of its appeal "to the world and its pleasures, to polygamy, which found a response in the hearts of the Africans, and that it [Islam] developed as widely as it did because Africans gathered around in *Zikr* ceremonies and by the beating of the tambourine," the author suggests that Islam spread and developed because of three basic African beliefs, namely the belief in a supreme being, in afterlife, and in the existence of benevolent and malefic spirits. *See also* 390.

392
Ahmed, Jamal M. Islam in the context of contemporary socio-religious thought in Africa. *In* Philosophy Symposium, American University of Beirut, 1967. God and man in contemporary Islamic thought; proceedings of the Philosophy Symposium held at the American University of Beirut, February 6–10, 1967. Edited with an introd. by Charles Malik. [Beirut, American University of Beirut] 1972. 100, 208 p. (American University of Beirut Centennial publications) p. 16–47. BP165.P48 1967

After a survey of African socioreligious thought, Jamāl Aḥmad concludes that "the African is a pragmatist and looks on religion as a force in his pursuit for a system of government, for an order out of the multiplicity of its individual countries, for new forms of culture, that preserve, as much as anything can be preserved in the face of Euro-american cultural deluge, his mores and sensibilities, yet help him grow into economic and political manhood, with as few growing pains as possible. That is the African bondage, the point where all meet, Muslim, Christian and the millions who are not adherent to either yet."

393
Baumann, Hermann. Les peuples et les civilisations de l'Afrique. Suivi de Les langues et l'éducation [par] D. Westermann. Traduction française de L. Homburger. Préf. de Théodore Monod. Paris, Payot, 1970. 605 p. illus. (Bibliothèque scientifique) DT14.B38 1970

394
Beltran, Luis. O Islã, a cultural e a lingua arabes na Africa negra. Afro-Asia, no. 8/9, 1969: 41–49. DLC

395
Berque, Jacques. Islam et socialisme. *In* Brussels. University libre de Bruxelles. *Institut de sociologie.* Revue, no 2/3, 1967: 199–216. H13.B728, 1967

396
Cohen, Ronald, *and* David Spain. Feminism, divorce, and the role of women in Africa. Paper presented at the 8th annual meeting of the African Studies Association, Philadelphia, 1965.
DLC-Micro 03782

Collation of the original: 17 p.

397
Colloque sur la contribution des religions à l'expression culturelle de la personnalité africaine, *Abidjan, Ivory Coast, 1961.* Colloque sur les religions, Abidjan, 5/12 avril 1961. Paris, Présence africaine [1962] 240 p. BL2400.C6 1961

398
Conference on the Maintenance and Transmission of Islamic Culture in Tropical Africa, Boston University, 1973. [Papers of a conference held at the African Studies Center, Boston University, April 27–28, 1973. Boston, 1973] 16 papers in 1 v.
IEN

Papers arranged alphabetically by author.

399
Dahal, Muhammad H. Comment accomplir le Hajj (pèlerinage à la Mecque). [Port Louis? Islamic Circle, 1971?] 18 p. DLC

A how-to pamphlet on performance of the pilgrimage to Mecca.

400
Delafosse, Maurice. L'Islam et les sociétés noires de l'Afrique. *In* Comité de l'Afrique française. Renseignements coloniaux, 1922: 321–333.

Source: Brasseur 1773.

401
Delange, Jacqueline. L'art peul. CEA, v. 4, 1. Cahier, 1963: 5–13. DT1.C3, v. 4

The nomadic Fulbe, constantly on the move searching for grazing grounds, has kept his material goods to a minimum. He has channeled his main artistic expression into polished speech, a refined etiquette and poetry, music and singing. The author, attached to the Musée de l'Homme in Paris, studies the various artistic manifestations of the still enigmatic Fulbe.

402
Desanti, Dominique. Le conflit des cultures et l'aventure ambigüe. African arts/Arts d'Afrique, v. 1, winter 1968: 60–61; 106; 109–110.
NX587.A6, v. 1

403
Fisher, Allan G. B., *and* J. Humphrey Fisher. Slavery and Muslim society in Africa: the institution in Saharan and Sudanic Africa, and the trans-Saharan trade. London, C. Hurst, 1970. 182 p. illus., maps. HT1381.F54 1970

Reacting against the restriction of studies on slavery to the trans-Atlantic slave trade, the authors state that "this book attempts somewhat to redress the balance, by exploring a little the trans-Saharan trade, and rather more the domestic demand in the heart of Africa." Looking at the role of slavery in African Muslim society, they investigate the size of the slave populations, slave status and religion, and exports and marketings; focusing on the domestic scene, they examine the slaves in the family, slaves at work, slaves and the state, and slaves as currency.

403a
Fisher, Humphrey J. Prayer and military activity in the history of Muslim Africa south of the Sahara. JAH, v. 12, no. 3, 1971: 391–406. DT1.J65

In the Islamic history of tropical Africa, prayer has often played an important, sometimes even a decisive, part. The functions of prayer may be ceremonial, instrumental (directed to the achievement of specific objectives), and disciplinary. In the military context the two latter are particularly significant. The discipline of Muslim prayer is strict and has sometimes underpinned military discipline.

The various stages of an hypothetical military campaign are traced, with specific historical examples of instrumental and disciplinary prayer at each stage. Preliminary prayer, often for ultimate success, might prepare the way. . . . There is no doubt of the considerable practical significance of these forms of prayer. An almost unparalleled discipline was achieved; the morale of the troops was greatly enhanced; the anxieties and fears of the enemy were stimulated; and many heroic gestures took their part in the sagas from which men in later generations may draw their inspiration, this leading in turn to renewed practical endeavour.—(Abstract supplied, modified)

404
———Religious toleration in black Africa. Patterns of prejudices, v. 8, May/June 1974: 23–28.
DS145.P34, v. 8

405
Froelich, Jean-Claude. Islam et culture arabe en Afrique au sud du Sahara. Le mois en Afrique; revue française d'études politiques africaines, t. 1, janv. 1966: 54–70. DT1.R4, v. 1

406
———Problèmes actuels de l'Islam en Afrique noire. Communautés et continents, t. 57, avril/juin 1965: 35–47. JV1801.N6, v. 57

Froelich sees black Islam confronted by reformist Orthodox Islam, Christianity, Marxism, and the Ahmadi and Bahai faiths and groping for a way to modernize and harmonize itself with the realities of the 20th century.

407
Galwash, Ahmad. Civilising influence of Arabs in Africa. *In* Cairo. al-Jam'iyah al-Miṣrīyah lil-'ulūm al-siyāsīyah. al-Majallah al-Miṣrīyah lil-'ulūm al-siyāsīyah, al-'adad 55, Oct. 1965: 13–25. JA26.M2, 1965 Orien Arab

After an extensive enumeration of Arab contributions to Western civilization, Galwash quotes at length from Bosworth Smith's *Mohammed and Mohammedanism* to show Islam's contribution to the well-being of Africans.

408
Gardet, Louis. La cité musulmane; vie sociale et politique. Paris, J. Vrin, 1954. 404 p. (Etudes musulmanes, 1) HT147.A2G3

A third edition was published in 1969.

409
———L'Islam, religion et communauté. Paris, Desclée de Brouwer, 1967. 496 p. (Bibliothèque française de philosophie) BP161.2.G28

410
Gouilly, Alphonse. Le pèlerinage à la Mecque. Revue juridique et politique; indépendance et coopération, t. 18, janv./mars 1964: 99–106. DLC-LL

411
Hartmann, M. Islam and culture in Africa. MW, v. 1, [Oct.?] 1911: 373–380. DS36.M7, v. 1

412
Hussain, Sheikh Munir. Some facts about Muslim population in Africa. Islamic literature, v. 15, June 1969: 5–13. BP1.I68, v. 15

Introduced as "a dirge on the woefully sad state of affairs of Muslims in Africa," this presentation suggests that "Muslims constitute an overwhelming majority in most of the African states, but they are ruled by non-Muslim minorities."

413
Lewis, Bernard. Race and color in Islam. New York, Harper & Row [1971] 103 p. illus. (Harper torchbooks, TB1590) BP190.5.R3L48

Based on a lecture published in *Encounter*, August 1970.

Well-documented essay attempting to show that Islam is not free of racial discrimination. Citing A. J. Toynbee and Malcolm X in his introductory remarks, Lewis claims that Islam is prejudiced toward blacks, asking in conclusion, "If, as we have tried to demonstrate, the traditional picture of a society free from racial discrimination is a false one, how then did this picture appear?" His explanation is that "the myth of Muslim freedom from racial prejudice seems to have arisen in the circle of Christian missionaries in Africa in the nineteenth century, who sought some explanation of the failure of their missions as contrasted with the success of Islam, despite every advantage of power, wealth, and (as they saw it) truth."

414
Lewis, Herbert S. The origins of African kingdoms. CEA, v. 6, 3. cahier, 1966: 402–407. DT1.C3, v. 6

414a
Mahmud, Hasan Ahmad. al-Islam wa-al-thaqāfah al-'Arabīyah fī Ifrīqīyah. [Islam and Arab culture in Africa] Cairo, Dār al-nahḍah al-'Arabīyah [1963]+ maps. BP64.A1M3 Orien Arab

L.C. has v. 1.

415
Monteil, Vincent. Un cas d'économie ostentatoire: les griots d'Afrique noire. Economies et sociétés, v. 2, avril 1968: 773–791. MH

416
La Mosquée, signe de l'unité islamique. Afrique nouvelle, t. 16, no 868, 27 mars 1964: 19–20. AP27.A58, v. 16

417
Muḥammad, Maḥmūd Sa'īd. Islam condemns racial discrimination. Translated by Ahmad Kamil Metwalli. Rev. by Shawki Sukkary. [Cairo, Supreme Council for Islamic Affairs, 1963] 67 p. (Studies in Islam series, no. 7) BP20.S7, no. 7

418
Nalder, L. F. The influence of animism on Islam. SNR, v. 9, July 1926: 75–88. DT118.S85, v. 9

Extensive review of *The Influence of Animism on Islam* by Samuel M. Zwemer who analyzes animistic practices that have been adopted by Islam (*see* 39).

419
N'Diaye, Jean Pierre. Elites africaines et culture occidentale, assimilation ou résistance? Paris, Présence africaine, 1969. 219 p. DT14.N34

Includes a section on "L'Animisme négro-africain et l'Islam."

420
Niehoff, Arthur, *and* Juanita Niehoff. The influence of religion on socio-economic development. International development review, v. 3, June 1966: 6–12. HC60.I546, v. 3

On the basis of a study of 203 case histories of induced socio-economic change we can say the following: The process of economic development on a local level is influenced significantly by two aspects of religion, its beliefs and its leaders.

. . . religious beliefs can be classified as a very minor hindrance to modernizing change and religious leadership can be powerfully positive or negative insofar as such leaders are actively included in planning and implementation of change projects or are opposed or ignored.—(Abstract supplied, modified)

421
Northern Africa: Islam and modernization; papers on the theme of Islamization, modernization, nationalism and independence presented and discussed at a symposium arranged by the African Studies Association of the United Kingdom on the occasion of its annual general meeting, 14 September, 1971; edited with introduction by Michael Brett. London, Cass, 1973. 177 p. BP64.A1N67 1973

Partial contents: Peter M. Holt, The Islamization of the Nilotic Sudan.—Humphrey J. Fisher, Hassebu: Islamic Healing in Black Africa.—R. S. O. O'Fahey, Saints and Sulṭans: The Role of Muslim Holy Men in the Keira Sultanate of Dar Fur.—Mervyn Hiskett, The Development of Islam in Hausaland.—Richard Gray, Some Aspects of Islam in the Southern Sudan During the Turkiya.—G. N. Anderson, Sudanese Nationalism and the Independence of the Sudan.

422
P. A. Petite critèriologie pour une sociologie de l'Islam négro-africain. A&A, no 44, 4. trimestre, 1958: 42–50. DT1.A85, 1958

423
Reid, Inez S. Arab Africa and black Africa: Prospects for unity; a bibliographic essay. African forum, v. 3, fall 1967/winter 1968: 82–91. DT1.A225, v. 3

Short bibliographic essay on a relationship which is only now getting the attention it deserves.

424
Renaud, H. P. J. La noix de cola dans la matière médicale arabe. Hespéris, t. 9, 1. trimestre, 1928: 43–57. DT181.H4, v. 9

While the kola nut became known in the western world only with the 19th century, Arab medical science knew of it as early as the 15th century as shown in the writings of 'Abd al-Razzāq al-Jazayrī. Renaud provides a historical analysis of Arab knowledge of the medicinal fruit.

425
Rodinson, Maxime. Islam et capitalisme. Paris, Editions du Seuil, 1966. 304 p. BP173.75.R6

A theoretical analysis of the relationship between Islam and capitalism by a student of Marxism who has also been studying the sociology of Islam for more than 30 years. Though not dealing specifically with Islam in Africa, this work provides a useful frame of reference for the study of the effect of Islam in the development of a trade mentality and outlook among the Islamized populations of Africa.

426
Rondot, Pierre. Le réformisme musulman à la recherche de son deuxième souffle. A&A, no 72, 4. trimestre 1965: 37–42. DT1.A85, 1965

427
Sanneh, Lamin. Amulets and Muslim orthodoxy; one Christian's venture into primal religious spirituality. International review of missions, v. 63, Oct. 1974: 515–529. BV2351.I6, v. 63

428
al-Shahāwī, Ibrāhīm Disūqī. al-Ḥisbah fī al-Islām. [The Accounting & Control Office in Islam] Cairo, Maktabat dār al-'Urūbah [1962] 174 p. JS7435.S47

429
Snouck Hurgronje, C. L'Islam et le problème des races. RMM, v. 50, juil. 1922: 1–27. DS36.R4

430
Syracuse University. *Libraries.* Islam in Africa; a bibliography of reference and general books in the Bird Library. Compiled by Samia A. Salem. [Syracuse, N.Y.] 1972. 11 leaves. CtY

431
Trimingham, J. Spencer. The influence of Islam upon Africa. New York, Praeger [1968] 159 p.

maps (Arab background series) BP64.A1T7

Investigation of the impact of Islam on the social structures and conceptualization of reality in Africa.

432
Tubiana, Marie-José. Implications économiques et politiques du renoncement à l'exogamie en faveur de mariage avec la fille de l'oncle. Paper presented to the International Congress of Africanists, third session, Dec. 9–19, 1973. Addis Ababa. 10 p. DLC

433
Von Grunebaum, Gustave E. Medieval Islam; a study in cultural orientation. 2d ed. Chicago, University of Chicago Press [1953] 378 p. maps (on lining papers) (An Oriental Institute essay) D199.3.V64 1953

434
———Modern Islam; the search for cultural identity. Berkeley, University of California Press, 1962. 303 p. DS57.V6

Articles by the author which have appeared previously in various publications.

435
———Unity and variety in Muslim civilization. Edited by Gustave E. von Grunebaum, with papers by Armand Abel [and others. Chicago] University of Chicago Press [1955] 385 p. illus., map (on lining paper) (Comparative studies of culture and civilization) DS38.V6

436
Yusuf, Ahmed Beitallah. A preliminary survey of the Islamic hadj: its overall meaning, and sociological implications with reference to Africa. Paper presented to the 16th annual meeting of the African Studies Association, Syracuse, N.Y., 1973. DLC-Micro 03782

Collation of the original: 19 p.

THEOLOGY

437
Abdul Haye, Muhammad. L'ABC de religion. [Port Louis, Ile Maurice, Impr. Idéale, 1969] 84 p. (Publications de la série 'Al-Hasanaat') DLC

438
Abedi, Kaluta Amri. Uongofu wa tafsiri ya Kurani tukufu, na husuda ya Sh. Abdulla Saleh: upinzani umejibiwa. [The correctness of the translation of the Glorious Koran, the spite of Sh. Abdulla Saleh: answer to his criticism] [Nairobi] Chama cha Ahmadiyya katika Afrika Mashariki, 1967. 100 p. BP105.5.S9A4534 1967

Text in Swahili.

439
Gardet, Louis, *and* M. M. Anawati. Introduction à la théologie musulmane; essai de théologie comparée. Paris. J. Vrin, 1948. 543 p. (Études de philosophie médiévale, 37) BP161.G32

This work on theology provides a basis for comparison when analyzing the development of African Islam. Includes an index of Arabic philosophical terms as well as a substantive bibliography.

440
Hemani, G. H. An understanding of Islam. Dar es Salaam, 1966. 14 p.

Source: Dar es Salaam lib. bull. no. 86.

441
Ingur, Ahmad Said. Talimouddine ou livret d'instruction religieuse; kitabutdaawate (Doahs). [Port Louis, Impr. Idéale, n.d.] 63 p. DLC

Series of questions and answers on Islam followed by 15 du'ā' [invocations] from the *Hadīth of al-Bukhārī*, as well as 40 invocations from the Koran.

442
al-Muusawy, Muhammad Mahdi, *trans.* Mwenge wa haki; majadiliano kati ya Khalifa Mamun ar-Rashid na wanachuani arobaini. [The torch of truth; a discussion between the Caliph Ma'mun al-Rashid and forty ulemas] Dar es Salaam, Bilal Muslim Mission of Tanzania [1971] 40 p. DLC

Text in Swahili.

443
———Kitabu cha sala. [Book of prayer] Dar es Salaam, Bilal Muslim Mission [1972, c1967] 100 p. BP184.3.M88

Text in Swahili.

444
———Kitabu cha saumu. [Book of fasting] Dar es Salaam, Bilal Muslim Mission [1971, c1967] 56 p. BP186.4.M88

Text in Swahili.

445
Saheb, Badre Alam. Guide sur le hadj; pèlerinage; ou le vrai compagnon du Hadjee. [Traduit de l'anglais] [Port-Louis, Ile Maurice] 1968. 74 p. DLC

446
Siddiqui, Mohammad Abdul Aleem. Catéchisme de l'Islam (hanafite) 3. éd. Port Louis, Ile Maurice, Librairie Eshack Abdullatif, 1955, 78 p.
BP45.S514 1955
Translation of *A Short Catechism of Islam.*

TRADE

447
Bohannan, Paul, *and* George Dalton, *eds.* Markets in Africa. [Evanston, Ill.] Northwestern University Press [1962] 762 p. maps, diagrs., tables. (Northwestern University [Evanston, Ill.] African studies, no. 9) HF5475.A42S73

448
Braudel, Fernand. Monnaies et civilisations; de l'or du Soudan à l'argent d'Amérique. Annales; économies, sociétés, civilisations, t. 1, janv./mars 1946: 9–22. AP20.A58, v. 1
Braudel regards gold and silver as the primary motivators of trade and civilizations. He investigates their role in the Sudanic, European, Mediterranean, and American commercial networks.

449
Brunschvig, R. Coup d'oeil sur l'histoire des foires à travers l'Islam. *In* Société Jean Bodin pour l'histoire comparative des institutions. Recueil, t. 5; 1953. Brussels. p. 43–75. H13.S622, v. 5

450
Charbonneau, R. Les Libano-Syriens en Afrique noire. Revue française d'études politiques africaines, no 26, fév. 1968: 56–71. DT1.R4, 1968

451
Guignes, M. de. Observations générales sur le commerce et les liaisons des peuples de l'intérieur de l'Afrique, soit entre eux, soit avec ceux de la Barbarie, de l'Egypte et de l'Arabie, etc. Journal des sçavans, juil. 1791: 393–401. MBA

452
al-Jāḥiẓ, 'Amr ibn Baḥr. Kitāb al-tabaṣṣur bi-al-tijārah. [Book of reflection on trade] Edited by Ḥasan Ḥusnī 'Abd al-Wahāb. [Beirut] Dār al-kitāb al-jadīd, 1966. 55 p. HF351.J3 Orien Arab

453
Labouret, Henri. L'échange et le commerce dans les archipels du Pacifique et en Afrique tropicale. *In* Lacour-Gayet, Jacques, *ed.* Histoire du commerce. v. 3. Paris, Spid, 1953. p. 9–125.
HF352.L3, v. 3

454
Lelong, M. H. La route du kola. Revue de géographie humaine et d'ethnologie, t. 1, oct. 1948/oct. 1949: 35–40. GN1.R54, v. 1

455
———Traité des monnaies musulmanes, tr. de l'arabe de Makrizi par A. I. Silvestre de Sacy. Paris, Fuchs, an V (1797). 89 p. HG247.M2
Translation of *Shudhūr al-'uqūd fī dhikr al-nuqūd* [Fragments of Necklaces About Monies]. *See also* 684.

456
Marcus, Louis. Essai sur le commerce que les Anciens faisaient de l'or avec le Soudan. Journal asiatique, t. 3, mars 1829: 202–224; t. 3, avril 1829: 275–292; t. 3, mai 1829: 355–366. PJ4.J5, v. 3

457
Mathew, G. Some reflections on African trade routes. Ghana. University, Legon. *Institute of African Studies.* Research review, v. 3, no. 3, 1967: 63–71.
DT1.G48, v. 3

458
Monod, Théodore. Nouvelles observations sur la technique du long-cours chamelier. NA, no 104, oct. 1964: 124–127. DT1.I513, 1964

459
Scherer, Hermann. Histoire du commerce de toutes les nations, depuis les temps anciens jusqu'à nos jours. Tr. de l'allemand, avec l'autorisation de l'auteur, par MM. Henri Rechelot [and] Charles Vogel. Avec des notes par les traducteurs et une préface par M. Henri Richelot. Paris, Capelle, 1857. 2 v. HF352.S32

460
Thomas, Benjamin E. Trade routes of Algeria and the Sahara. Berkeley, University of California Press, 1957. 165–287 p. illus., maps (University of California publications in geography, v. 8, no. 3)
G58.C3, v. 8, no. 3
HE185.Z7A4

461
Walz, Terence. Notes on the organization of the African trade in Cairo, 1800–1850. Annales islamologiques, v. 11, 1972: 263–286. BP1.A65, v. 11
"Volume dédié à la mémoire de Gaston Wiet."

900–1600

GENERAL

462
Hansberry, W. Leo. Ancient Kush, Old Aethiopia, and the Balad es Sudan. Journal of Human relations, v. 8, no. 3/4, 1960: 357. H1.J55, v. 8

463
Heyd, Wilhelm von. Histoire du commerce du Levant au moyen-âge. Edition française refondue et considérablement augmentée par l'auteur, publiée sous le patronage de la Société de l'Orient latin, par Furcy Raynaud. Leipzig, O. Harrassowitz, 1885–86. 2 v. HF404.H6

464
Inayatullah, Sh. Bibliophilism in medieval Islam. Islamic culture, v. 12, Apr. 1938: 155–169. DS36.I74, v. 12

465
Kobishchakov, I͡Urii Mikhailovich. Media for communicating geographical information in pre-colonial Africa. Paper presented to the International Congress of Africanists, second session, Dec. 11–20, 1967. Dakar. Senegal. 18 p. DLC

466
Tritton, Arthur S. Materials on Muslim education in the Middle ages. London, Luzac, 1957. 209 p. LA99.T7

Introduction to the development of Muslim education from the beginning to the introduction of modern methods. It deals with the Muslim world in general and includes information on the scholastic life, institutions, curricula, books, and other facets of education.

467
Lewicki, Tadeusz. Dzieje Afryki od czasów najdawniejszych do XIV w.; wybrane zagadnienia. [Facts about Africa from oldest times to the 14th century; selected writings] [Skrypt. Warszawa] 1963. 242 p. fold. maps (Wydawnictwa Uniwersytetu Warszawskiego) DT25.L4

At head of title: Uniwersytet Warszawski. Studium Afrykanistyczne.

Roads & Itineraries

468
Benjamin ben Jonah, *of Tudela, 12th cent.* The itinerary of Benjamin of Tudela; critical text, translation and commentary by Marcus Nathan Adler. London, H. Frowde, 1907. 2 pt. in 1 v. front. (fold. map), 7 facsim. (1 fold.) G370.B473

From Heluan "thence people travel in caravans a journey of fifty days through the great desert called Sahara, to the land of Zawilah, which is Havilah in the land of Gana" whence "they bring gold, and all kind of jewels."

469
Hess, R. L. The itinerary of Benjamin of Tudela: a 12th century Jewish description of north-east Africa. JAH, v. 6, no. 1, 1965: 15–24. DT1.J65, v. 6

470
Mauny, Raymond. Un itinéraire transsaharien du Moyen âge. Bulletin de liaison saharienne, no 13, juin 1953: 31–41. DT331.B83, 1953

471
Shaw, W. B. K. Darb el Arba'in; the forty days' road. SNR, v. 12, pt. 1, 1929: 63–72. plates. DT118.S85, v. 12

Description of the "forty-day trail" that goes from Asyūṭ, through Khargā, Selima, Bīr Natrūm, and ends in Kobbe some 35 miles northwest of el-Fasher in the western part of Sudan. This route has been used since antiquity and is the one used by Leo Africanus in 1513 to travel from Walātāh to Cairo.

472
Wilks, Ivor. A medieval trade-route from the Niger to the Gulf of Guinea. JAH, v. 3, no. 2, 1962: 337–341. DT1.J65, v. 3

CENTRAL REGION

History

473
Brunschvig, R. Un texte arabe du IXe siècle intéressant le Fezzan. Revue africaine, no 89, 1. trimestre, 1945: 21–25. DT271.R4, 1945

474
Lhote, Henri. Découverte des ruines de Tadeliza ancienne résidence des sultans de l'Aïr. NA, no 137, janv. 1973: 9–16. illus. DT1.521.C6, 1973

Around A.D. 1405, the Kel Aïr were ruled temporarily from Tadeliza. Armed with his knowledge of the Aïr Tuareg and the region and thoroughly familiar with the oral traditions and Arabic written sources concerning the city, Lhote located and described the ruins near the village of Irezren Meloudnin, about 20 kilometers north of Agadez. Carbon 14 examinations of two samples, however, gave two dates, namely 1440 and 1230, which led Lhote to conclude his article on a note of puzzlement about the latter date.

475
Palmer, *Sir* Herbert R. The Central Sahara and Sudan in the twelfth century. *In* African Society. Journal, v. 28, July 1929: 368–378.
DT1.R62, v. 28

476
———A Muslim divine of the Sudan in the 15th century. Africa, v. 3, Apr. 1930: 203–216.
PL8000.I6, v. 3

Translation of an Arab chronicle reporting the reign of a Sultan of Bornu, 'Ali ibn Dunama (Gaji Dunamami), who, according to Barth's chronological table, ruled from 1472 to 1504. Palmer introduces the translation with a critical analysis of the events covered by the chronicle.

477
———The origin of the name Bornu. *In* African Society. Journal, v. 28, Oct. 1928: 36–42.
DT1.R62, v. 28

478
Pâques, Viviana. Origines et caractères du pouvoir royal au Baguirmi. JOSAF, t. 37, fasc. 2, 1967: 183–214. illus. DT1.S65, v. 37

Bagirmi, located east of Lake Chad, was constantly at war with its two neighbors, Waday and Kanem-Bornu. Investigating the origin and nature of the royal authority in the kingdom, Pâques presents the history of Bagirmi as expressed in the people's oral traditions and some written documents. The Arab origin, the stages of the migration, and the various traditions of origins are studied in addition to the cosmology of the Bagirmi. Several dynastic lists are appended.

EASTERN REGION

History

479
'Ābdīn, 'Abd al-Majīd. Some general aspects of the Arabization of the Sudan. SNR, v. 40, 1959: 48–74.
DT118.S85, v. 40

Arabization of the Sudan began with the "peace treaty" signed by 'Abd Allāh ibn Sa'd ibn Abī Ṣarḥ with the Nubians in 651–2. In addition to tracing Arab migrations, 'Ābdīn deals with the role of the Ja'lī-Dongolāwī group in the diffusion of educational Islamic culture. He concludes with a discussion of the Sufi-Faqīh [Jurist] conflict and the great popularity of the Sufi religious order. Arabic text, with English translation by Fawzi F. Gadallah, edited by G. N. Sanderson.

480
———Tārīkh al-Thaqāfah al-'Arabīyah fī al-Sūdān mundhu nash'atihā ilā al-'aṣr al-ḥadīth; al-dīn, al-ijtimā', al-adab. [History of Arabic culture in the Sudan since its inception to the modern period; religion, society, and literature] Cairo, Maktabat al-Khanjā, 1953. 368 p. DT121.A62 Orien Arab

'Ābidīn looks at the development of Arabic culture—religion, social life, and literature—in the Sudan and discusses Arabic prose and poetry in some detail. Islamic education and cultural life in the Sudan from the 16th century to the modern era are also studied.

A second edition published in 1967 is held by NjP.

481
al-Adawi, I. A. Description of the Sudan by Muslim geographers and travelers. SNR, v. 35, Dec. 1954: 5–16. DT118.S85, v. 35

The Nile has been a link between the Sudan and Egypt since time immemorial. al-Adawi reviews the various geographers and travelers who described the Sudan and its contacts with its northern neighbor, including al-Mas'ūdī, al-Aswānī, Yāqūt, al-Idrīsī, al-Bakrī, al-'Umarī, and Ibn Baṭṭūṭah.

482
Aḥmad ibn Mājid al-Sa'dī. Thalāth azhār fī ma'rifat al-biḥār. [Three flowers on the knowledge of the seas] by Aḥmad ibn Mājid, Mallāḥ Fāskū dī Jāmā [pilot of Vasco da Gama] Edited and published by Teodor Adamovich Shumovskiĭ. Translated and commented on by Muḥammad Munīr Mursī. Cairo, Ālam al-Kutub [1969] 237 p. 1 illus., map.
VK801.A3618 Orien Arab

"Mutarjammah 'an al-nuskhah al-maṭbū'ah bi-maṭba'at al-majma' al-'ilmī lil-Ittiḥād al-Sufyītī, Mūskū-Līnīnjrād 1957, naqlan 'an al-nuskhah al-'Arabīyah al-farīdah al-mawjūdah bi-maktabat ma'had al-istishrāq al-tābi' lil-majma'." [Translated from the text printed at the press of the Academy of Science of the USSR, Moscow-Leningrad, 1957, copied from the only Arabic text located in the library of the Oriental Institute of the Academy]

Text of and commentary on a poem on nautical science by Vasco da Gama's pilot (1462–1498).

See also the Portuguese translation (VK801.A3617 1960) and the Russian translation (VK801.A37).

483

Arkell, Anthony J. The medieval history of Darfur in its relation to other cultures and to the Nilotic Sudan. SNR, v. 40, 1959: 44–47.

DT118.S85, v. 40

484

al-Biyalī, 'Uthmān Sayyid Aḥmad Ismā'īl. 'As-Sudan' and 'Bilad as-Sudan' in early and medieval Arabic writing. *In* Khartoum. Jāmi'at al-Qāhirah fī-al-Kharṭūm. Majallat Jāmi'at al-Qāhirah fī-al-Kharṭūm, v. 3, 1972: 33–48. DLC

"Regionalization in history, like periodization, can be a matter of convenience or a matter of convention. It can also be a matter of purpose. Projection is not uncommon amongst students of history. For how often do we, unaware, reflect attitudes of our own culture to other cultures without regard to time and place. . . . It is essential that terms like the ones under consideration, which have linguistic, ethnological as well as geographical connotations, are taken in their proper context, their intended application and their historical perspective." Thus, al-Biyali looks at the two terms as used by both modern scholars and medieval Arab authors who range from al-Jāhiz (d. 868) to Ibn Khaldūn (d. 1405).

485

Cerulli, Enrico. Il Sultanato della Scioa nel secolo XIII secondo un nuovo documento storico. Rassegna si studi Ethiopici, anno 1, 1941: 5–42.

DT371.R3, v. 1

486

Devic, L. Marcel. Le pays des Zendjs ou la côte orientale d'Afrique au Moyen-Age géographie, moeurs, productions, animaux légendaires d'aprés les écrivains arabes. Paris, Hachette, 1883. 280 p.

DT365.D49

487

Elles, R. J. The Kingdom of Tegali. SNR, v. 18, pt. 1, 1935: 1–36. geneal. tables, map.

DT118.S85, v. 18

The Kingdom of Tegali was founded in 1530 by Muḥammad al-Ja'lī, who came from the north, and his dynasty was still reigning at the time Elles wrote this article. Tegali, located near Rashad southwest of El-Obeid, was under the jurisdiction of kings who once ruled supreme over the Eastern Nuba mountains from the Abū Ḥabl in the north to Talodi in the south. In this narrative, based on oral traditions, Elles presents the story of the founding of the dynasty, its zenith during the latter part of the 19th century, its clash with the Mahdist movement, and its problems with the Condominium Government.

488

Flury, S. The Kufic inscriptions of Kisimkazi Mosque, Zanzibar, 500 H. (A.D. 1107). *In* Royal Asiatic Society. *London.* Journal, 2d quarter, Apr. 1922: 257–264. AS122.L72, 1922

489

Freeman-Grenville, G. S. P. Coinage in East Africa before Portuguese times. The numismatic chronicle, 6. ser., v. 17, 1957: 151–179.

CJ1.N6, 6. s., v. 17

490

———Ibn Batuta's visit to East Africa A.D. 1332: a translation. Uganda journal, v. 19, Mar. 1955: 1–6.

DT434.U2U3, v. 19

491

———The medieval history of the coast of Tanganyika, with special reference to recent archaelogical discoveries. Berlin, Akademie-Verlag, 1962. 238 p. illus., geneal. tables, 3 maps (in pocket) (Deutsche Akademie der Wissenschaften zu Berlin. Institut für Orientforschung. Veröffentlichung Nr. 55) DT444.F7 1962a

492

———The times of ignorance: a review of pre-Islamic and early settlement on the East African coast. *In* Posnansky, Merrick, *ed.* Discovering Africa's past. Kampala, Uganda Museum, 1959. p. 4–17. (Uganda Museum occasional paper 4) DLC

Drawing on archeological remains in addition to Arabic sources, such as the *Sunnah Kilāwīyah* (ca. 1520) and *Kitāb al-Zunūj* (*see also* 1243), the author observes that the material for the history of the coast from the first to the 13th century is rather "meagre and often tenuous."

492a
Giamberardini, Gabriele, *ed.* I viaggatori Francis-cani attraverso la Nubia del 1689 al 1710. *In* Studia orientalia Christiana. Collectanea, no 8, 1963: 361–437. BX130.578, 1963

493
Ḥaṣan, Yūsuf Faḍl. The Arabs and the Sudan; from the seventh to the early sixteenth century. Edinburgh, Edinburgh University Press [1967] 298 p. 4 plates (incl. map), diagrs. DT108.1.H3

The Sudan, not unlike Mauritania, is a bridge between Africa north and south of the Sahara. The slow Arab penetration into the Sudan and the ultimate Arabization and Islamization of its northern part took place between the seventh and the early 16th centuries. In this thorough study, Yūsūf Faḍl Ḥaṣan analyzes the confrontation with Christian Nubia and the Beja country and the process of Islamization which now pervades all aspects of the life of northern Sudan. Annexed is a valuable "Survey of the Major Sources of the History of the Sudan in the Middle Ages," which includes a chronological study of literary sources and Sudanese traditions. Extensive bibliography.

494
———Muqaddimah fī tārīkh al-mamālik al-Islāmīyah fī al-Sūdān al-Sharqī, 1450–1821. [Introduction to the history of the Islamic states in the Eastern Sudan, 1450–1821]. [Cairo] Ma'had al-buḥūth wa-al-dirāsāt al-'Arabīyah, qism al-buḥūth wa-al-dirāsāt al-tārīkhīyah wa-al-jughrāfīyah. 1971. 157 p. DT108.1.H33

495
Hilmī, 'Abd al-'Azīz 'Abd al-Ḥaqq. Ṭalā'i' al-thaqāfah al-'Arabīyah fī al-Sūdān. [Aspects of Arab culture in the Sudan]. Cairo. al-Jāmi' al-Azhar. Majallat al-Azhar, m. 38, Apr. 1966: 31–35; v. 38, May 1966: 152–157.
BP1.C3, v. 38 Orien Arab

Arabic culture developed in the Sudan only toward the 17th century, due to historical factors and geographical barriers. Hence the Sudan did not share in the golden age of Arab civilization which flourished in Damascus, Cairo, Baghdad, and Fès. The migration of such Arab tribes as the Rabī'ah and Banī Hilāl, which began in the 8th century, however, was the major factor in its Arabization and the development of its Arabic culture.

496
Kāmil, 'Abd al-'Azīz. al-'Arab fī Ifrīqīyah, fī al-Muḥīṭ al-Hindī; min al-Janūb al-'Arabī; min al-Yaman; qiṣat al-riyāḥ al-mawsimīyah; (al-baḥth mawṣūl). [Arabs in Africa, in the Indian Ocean; from the Arab [Peninsula] south; from Yemen; the story of the seasonal winds; (to be continued)] al-Risālah, m. 22, June 3, 1965: 20–23; m. 22, June 10, 1965: 14–17; m. 22, June 17, 1965: 18–21; m. 22, June 24, 1965: 21–24.
AP95.A6R5, v. 22 Orien Arab

In this incomplete essay, Kamil studies contacts between the Arabs and the populations of the east coast of Africa. Dhows have traveled from the coast to the Arabian Peninsula since the dawn of time, though because of the trade winds Sofala was the southernmost point of contact for many years. The author reviews contacts between Oman, southern Arabia, Yemen, and the African coast as well as the conflicts between Arabs and Romans, including the Roman expedition of 24 B.C. which Strabo had joined. The last part of the essay examines the increased Greek interest in the trade winds and how the Arab sailors told fantastic tales—such as Sindbad the Sailor—to keep the Greeks from venturing into the Indian Ocean.

497
Kilhefner, Donald W. The Christian kingdoms of the Sudan, 500–1500. The Africanist, v. 1, June 1967: 1–13. DLC

498
Małecka, A. La côte orientale de l'Afrique au Moyen Age d'après le Kitab ar-Rawd al-Mi'tar de al-Himyārī (XVe siècle) Folia orientalia, t. 4, 1962: 331–339. PJ9.F6, v. 4

Excerpts in Arabic from *Kitab al-Rawd al-Mi'ṭār fī Akhbār al-Aqṭār* (1461), by Ibn 'Abd al-Mun'im al-Himyārī, describing the coast of east Africa during the medieval period. Places mentioned include "al-Bans[?], Dahgwâtah, Dindamah, Ṣayûnah, Malindi, Mombasa, and Waq-Waq."

499
Mhina, J. E. F. A review of the Kilwa chronicle from 1300–1520 A.D. Kenya education journal, v. 6, Sept. 1965: 19–21. DLC

500
Mus'ad, Muṣṭafā Muḥammad. *ed.* al-Maktabah al-Sūdānīyah al-'Arabīyah, majmū'at al-nuṣūṣ wa-al-wathā'iq al-'Arabīyah al-khāṣah bi-tārīkh al-Sūdān fi al-'uṣūr al-wusṭā. [The Sudano-Arabic library, collection of Arabic texts and documents pertaining to the history of the Sudan during the Middle Ages] [Cairo, Dār al-Ittiḥād al-'Arabī lil-ṭibā'ah] 1972. 452 p. DLC

Added t.p.: Bibliothèque soudano-arabe. Recueil de textes et de documents arabe[s] relatifs à l'histoire du Soudan au moyen-âge.

501
Oded, Arye. Islam in Uganda: Islamization through a centralized state in pre-colonial Africa. New York, Wiley [1974] 381 p. illus. BP64.U3503
"A Halsted Press book."

502
Paul, A. Aidhab: a medieval Red Sea port. SNR, v. 36, June 1955: 64–70. illus. DT118.S85, v. 36
A short history of the Venice of the Red Sea. During the medieval period, Aydhab was considered by Arab writers one of the best ports of the Middle East. Today all that remains are "a confused mass of mounds, a half buried cistern or two, extensive cemeteries and, scattered everywhere, fragments of glass, pottery and celadon."

503
Riyāḍ, Zāhir. al-Islām fī Ityūbyā fī al-'uṣūr al-wusṭā; ma'a al-ihtimām bi-wajh khāṣ bi-'ilāqat al-Muslimīn bi-al-Masīḥiyīn. [Islam in Ethiopia during the Middle Ages; with special emphasis on relations between Muslims and Christians] Cairo, Dār al-Ma'rifah [1964] 303 p. BP64.E8R5 Orien Arab
Dr. Riyād has been involved with Ethiopian studies since 1934 when he was teaching history in Ethiopian secondary schools. His knowledge of Amharic and Italian as well as his use of Arabic sources put him in an advantageous position to present the history of a long and dynamic relationship between Islam and Ethiopia. The text of the Prophet Muhammad's letter to the Negus is appended.

504
———Ittijāhāt Miṣr al-Ifrīqīyah fi al-'uṣūr al-wusṭā. [African trends of Egypt during the Middle Ages *In* Cairo. Jāmi'at al-Qāhirah. Kulliyat al-ādāb. Majallat Kulliyat al-ādāb, m. 20, May 1958: 65–80. AS693.C25, v. 20 Orien Arab
"The early development of civilization in Egypt and her position in this part of Africa, made it imperative for her, since the dawn of time, to play an African role." With this introduction, Riyad provides an overview of Egypt's role in Africa, including the impact of the Coptic Church in Nubia and Ethiopia, the exodus of Egyptian populations during such periods of instability as the Abbasid era, the clashes with the south and the slave trade during the Tulunid, Ikhshidid, Fatimid, and Mameluke reigns, the influence of Egypt on both North Africa and West Africa through the trans-Saharan trade and the pilgrimage of such rulers as Kankū Mūsā and Askiya Muḥammad. Riyad concludes with a note on the role of the Azhar as a religious university and the various riwāqāt, or hostels, for the students of various nationalities.

505
Royal chronicle of Abyssinia. The glorious victories of 'Āmda Ṣeyon, king of Ethiopia. Translated and edited by G. W. B. Huntingford. Oxford, Clarendon Press, 1965. 142 p. illus., facsim., 3 maps (1 fold.) (The Oxford library of African literature) DT383.R67
See also 510.

505a
Schneider, Madeleine. Stêles funéraires arabes de Qiha. Annales d'Ethiopie, t. 7, 1967: 107–122. DT379.A6, v. 7
Investigation of 12 funerary stelae discovered in Quiha in the Tigre district. The Kufic Arabic style suggests a date between 1000 and 1154 which antedates, according to the author, the known Arab presence in Ethiopia by about five centuries.

506
Sergew Hable Selassie. Ancient and medieval Ethiopian history to 1270. Addis Ababa [Printed by United Printers] 1972. 370 p. illus. DT383.S46

507
Shinnie, P. L., *and* M. Shinnie. New light on medieval Nubia. JAH, v. 6, no. 3, 1965: 263–273. DT1.J65, v. 6

508
Taddesse Tamrat. Islam and trade in Ethiopia ca. 900–1332. *In* Universities of East Africa Social Science Conference. Annual conference proceedings. v. 3; 1970. Dar es Salaam, Provisional Council for the Social Sciences in East Africa, 1970. p. 76–87 [i.e. 1–10] H29.A46U5 1970, v. 3

509
el-Tahtawy, Hussein. Die Ausfuhrgüter der ostafrikanischen Küste im Mittelalter. Nach zeitgenössischen Berichten islamischer Autoren. Ein Beitrag zur Geschichte des afrikan. Wien, Verlag Notring, 1972. 353 p. (Dissertationen der Universität Wien, 67) HF3895.T33 1972

Originally presented as the author's thesis, Vienna, 1970.

510
Ullendorf, E. The glorious victories of 'Amda Seyon, king of Ethiopia. BSOAS, v. 29, pt. 3, 1966: 600–611. PJ3.L6

Chronicle of the victories of 'Āmda Ṣeyon (1314–1344) against the Muslim sultanates in the Horn region, such as Adal, Harar, Ifat, Dawara, Bali, and Hadya. Ullendorf suggests amendments to G. W. B. Huntingford's translation of the chronicle (*see* 505).

511
Vel'gus, V. O srednevekovykh Kitaĭskikh izvestiíàkh ob Afrike i nekotorykh voprosakh ikh izucheniíà. [Medieval Chinese relations on Africa and some problems related to their study] *In* Akademiíà nauk SSSR. *Institut etnografii.* Trudy. Novaíà seriíà, t. 90. Moskva, 1966. (Afrikanskii etnograficheskii sbornik, 6) p. 84–103. GN2.A2142, v. 90

English summary.

512
———Strany Mo-lin' i Bo-sa-lo (Lao-bo-sa) v srednevekovykh Kitaiskikh izvestiíàkh ob Afrike. [The countries of Mo-lin and Bo-sa-lo (Lao-bo-sa) in medieval Chinese works on Africa] *In* Akademiíà nauk SSSR. *Institut etnografii.* Trudy. Novaíà seriíà, t. 90. Moskva, 1966. (Afrikanskii etnograficheskii sbornik, 6) p. 104–121. GN2.A2142, v. 90

English summary.

512a
Velozo, Francisco J. Portugal e los Árabes da costa oriental de Africa. *In* Sociedade de geografia de Lisboa. Boletim, N. 7/9 e 10/12, Julho/Set. e Out./Dez. 1965: 229–235. G27.S5, 1965

513
Zaborski, Andrzej. Notes on the medieval history of Beja tribes. Folia orientalia, v. 7, 1965: 289–307. PJ9.F6, v. 7

The Beja tribes, located in Upper Egypt, Sudan, and Eritrea, have been likened to the Meju and Blemyes. The first reliable information, however, on Arab contacts with the Beja is provided by Ibn 'Abd al-Ḥakam, who related the story of the expedition led against Nubia by 'Abd Allah ibn Sa'd ibn Abī Ṣarḥ A.D. 651–52. Zaborski traces the history of the Beja according to accounts by Ibn Ḥawqal, al-Maqrīzī, al-Ṭabarī, and al-Ya'qūbī, in addition to that of Ibn 'Abd al-Ḥakam.

WESTERN REGION

Biography

514
Beckingham, C. F. Le pèlerinage et la mort de Sakoura, roi de Mali. BIFAN, t. 16, juil./oct. 1954: 390–391. DT1.I5123, v. 16

It was long believed that Tadjoura, the city where Sakoura the usurper of the Mali throne was assassinated about 1300 on his return from pilgrimage, is located in the territory of the Afars and Issas. Beckingham, puzzled by the strange itinerary, searched for and found a likely Tadjoura on the Mediterranean coast 20 kilometers east of Tripoli, Libya. This new location of the city fits better in the pilgrimage route that was probably followed by Sakoura.

See also BSOAS, v. 25, pt. 2, 1953: 391–392 (PJ3.L6).

515
Bertol, Roland. Sundiata: the epic of the Lion King, retold. Illustrated by Gregorio Prestopino. New York, Crowell [1970] 81 p. illus. PZ8.1.B4194Su

The story of the Mali emperor, directed to a juvenile audience.

516
Cepollaro, Armando. La figura di Sundiata Keita nella tradizione orale e nei documenti scritti. Africa, anno 22, guigno 1967: 171–197. DT1.A843, v. 22

In this study—to be considered as the introduction to a bigger work, for which the author continues to amplify his documentation—Dr. Cepollaro attempts a review of the oral and written sources containing information on Sundiata, the legendary founder of historic Mali according to the Sudanese tradition. In particular, the author underlines the importance of the historico-legendary narratives forming the bulk of the inexhaustible heritage of African oral tradition; a tradition to be accepted as living history, with all the dangers and traps it implies, because it alone can integrate the scanty and largely inadequate information supplied by medieval written texts, mainly due to Arab geographers and travellers or to islamized local chronists. As a sequel to this review, the author reports some "versions" of historico-legendary narratives obtained from the very mouth of traditionists and translated into French by French or African scholars between 1913 and 1960, his aim being to exemplify the discrepancies and variations between the different versions."—(Abstract supplied)

517
Cissoko, Sékéné Mody. Quel est le nom du plus grand empereur du Mali: Kankan Moussa ou Kankou Moussa? NA, no 124, oct. 1969: 113–114. DT1.I513, 1969

518
Diabate, Massa Makam. Presentation du Sunjata faasa-version originale de KELA. Etudes maliennes, no 1, 1970: 71–77. DLC

The famous epic song of praise of Sundiata Keita, in translation.

519
Ḥammūsh, 'Abd al-Ḥaqq. Ibn Tāshfīn. Casablanca, Dar al-kitāb [196–] 95 p. maps. DP103.H34

520
Humblot, P. Episodes de la légende de Soundiata. NA, no 52, oct. 1951: 111–113. DT1.I513, 1951

521
Kake, Baba Ibrahima. Un grand érudit de la Nigritie au XVIe siècle: Ahmed Baba le Tombouctien. Présence africaine, no 60, 4., trimestre 1966: 34–45. GN645.P74, no. 60

Aḥmad Bābā al-Tumbuqtī is described by Kake as the epitome of the black-Arab-Berber culture and civilization.

522
Monteil, Vincent. L'oeuvre d'Idrissi. BIFAN, t. 1, oct. 1939: 837–857. Q89.I5, v. 1

Three-part bibliographical essay on Abū 'Abd Allāh Muḥammad al-Idrīsī (1100–1166) by the former director of IFAN when he was a young lieutenant in the French Army. The first section notes the sources for excerpts from al-Idrīsī's *Geography;* the second lists important dates in his life and approximate dates for his writings. The third part is a general bibliography of works dealing with the Arab geographer.

523
Niane, Djibril Tamsir. Le problème de Soundiata. NA, no 88, oct. 1960: 123–126. DT1.I513, 1960

Mali became a great empire under Sundiata. The life of this charismatic leader is so intertwined with legendary feats that it is difficult to separate the man from the myth. Niane, studying various oral traditions and comparing them with the genealogical list of Ibn Khaldūn, tries to bring some order to the chaotic record of Sundiata's reign (1230–50).

524
———Soundjata; ou, l'épopée mandingue. 3. éd. Paris, Présence africaine [1971, c1960] 153 p. maps. DT532.2.N5 1971

"L'épopée de Soundjata vue par un griot du village de Diéliba Koro (Siguiri)."

525
Norris, H. T. New evidence on the life of Abdullah B. Yasin and the origins of the Almoravid movement. JAH, v. 12, no. 1971: 255–268. DT1.J65, v. 12

The Qāḍī 'Iyāḍ in his biography of 'Abdullāh b. Yāsīn confirms many details in al-Bakrī's record of the rise of the Almoravids. His account differs in a few important respects, and furnishes new information which is valuable in reassessing the life of 'Abdullāh b. Yāsīn. Since no insular *ribāṭ* is mentioned, its historicity is increasingly suspect, and in the light of Maghribī cosmological ideas it is better regarded as a myth, and not as a historical fact. This text is the earliest surviving one to mention the *Dār al-Murābiṭīn* of Wajjāj b. Zalwī al-Lamṭī.—(Abstract supplied)

526
———Ṣanhājah scholars of Timbuctoo. BSOAS, v. 30, pt. 3, 1967: 635–640. PJ3.L6, v. 30

Norris suggests that the essentially Ṣanhājah and Saharan origin of the medieval Sudan scholars—descendants of Muḥammad Aqīt ibn 'Umar ibn 'Alī ibn Yaḥyā al-Ṣanhājī—is "sometimes underrated." He traces, painstakingly, the origins of this intellectual elite of Wadan and Timbuktu.

527
Pageard, Robert. Soundiata Keita and the oral tradition. Présence africaine, nouv. sér., no 36, 1. trimestre 1961: 51–70. GN645.P74, n.s., 1961

528
Sidibé, Mamby. Soundiata Keita, héros historique et légendaire, empereur du Manding. NA, no 82, avril 1959: 41–50. DT1.I513, 1959

Study of Sundiata based on oral traditions and the Keita genealogies on the occasion of the creation of Mali in 1959.

529
Skalníková, Olga. Griots: West African chroniclers. New Orient, v. 4, Feb. 1965: 25–26. DS1.N43, v. 4

530
Smith, H. F. C. A note on Muhammad al-Maghili. *In* Historical Society of Nigeria. Bulletin of news, v. 7, Dec. 1962. IEN

531
Vidal, J. La légende officielle de Soundiata fondateur de l'Empire Manding. BCAOF, t. 7, avril/juin 1924: 317–328. DT521.C6, v. 7

The Sundiata Keita epic, as reported by an "administrateur en chef des colonies," was recorded by Vidal in Kangaba from the official griots of the former Mandingo dynasty.

Cities

531a
Berchem, Van. Note [sur les inscriptions arabes estampée par M. de Gironcourt dans la boucle du Niger] *In* Académie des inscriptions et belles-lettres. Compte rendus. mars/avril 1913. Paris, 1913. p. 150–152. AS162.P315, 1913

Commentaries on the report of de Gironcourt concerning the Arabic inscriptions on funerary stelae from Bentia providing more exact dates than those previously accepted. *See also* 534a, 541, 541a.

532
Bonnel de Mézières, A. Découverte de l'emplacement de Tirekka. *In* France. *Comité des travaux historiques et scientifiques.* Bulletin, t. 29, 1914: 132–135. G11.F8, v. 29

Report on the discovery of Tirekka, an important town in the Niger Bend region along the caravan route from Kumbi Ṣālih to Es-Souk. The city was mentioned by al-Bakrī.

533
———Recherches de l'emplacement de Ghana (fouilles à Koumbi et à Settah), et sur le site de Tekrour. *In* Académie des inscriptions et des belles-lettres. Mémoire, t. 13, 1. partie, 1920: 227–273.

Source: Brasseur 2219.

534
Brouin, Georges. Du nouveau au sujet de la question de Takedda. NA, no 47, juil. 1950: 90–91. DT1.I513, 1950

The search for the copper-producing city visited by Ibn Baṭṭūṭah in 1354. Brouin believes that the city was located at Azelik, northeast of Teguidda-N-Tessemt, though the mine was not located at the time (1950).

534a
Un "Corpus" des inscriptions lithiques du Niger. Revue de l'histoire des colonies françaises, t. 4, 3. trimestre, 1916: 239–244. JV1801.R4, v. 4

In 1908 de Gironcourt discovered—130 kilometers downstream from Gao, near Bentia—a Muslim cemetery with tombstones carrying Arabic inscriptions. In a second expedition, he compiled a corpus of these inscriptions. *See also* 531a, 541, 541a.

535
Delafosse, Maurice. Le Gâna et le Mali et l'emplacement de leurs capitales. BCAOF, t. 9, juil./sept. 1924: 479–542. DT521.C6, v. 9

Analytical summation of research concerning the capitals of the Ghana and Mali empires. Delafosse draws together, corrects, and weaves the various conclusions of the time (1924) into a meaningful narrative.

536
———La question de Ghana et la Mission Bonnel de Mézières. *In* Comité d'études historiques et scientifiques de l'Afrique occidentale française. Annuaire et mémoire. 1916 [Paris?, 191–?] p. 40–61.

Source: Joucla 4006.

537
Filipowiak, Władysław. Contribution aux recherches sur la capitale du royaume de Mali à l'époque du haut Moyen-Age (Afrique occidentale). Archaeologia Polona, t. 10, 1968: 217–232. GN845.P7A75, v. 10

The search for Niani, the capital of the Mali Empire, was undertaken by a joint expedition including the historians of the Institut de recherches et de documentation of Conakry and a Polish archeological team. In this article, Filipowiak sums up the result of the search in Niani on the Sankarani River, thought to be the site referred to by Ibn Baṭṭūṭah.

538
———Expéditions archéologique polono-guinéenne à Niani (Guinée). Africana bulletin, v. 4, 1966: 116–127. DT19.9.P6A65, v. 4

Short report of a joint expedition to the site of Niani, capital of the Mali empire. The team consisted of S. Jasnosz, Archaeological Museum of Poznań; W. Filipowiak, Western Pomerania Museum of Szczecin; and Djibril T. Niane, representing the Institut national de recherches et de documentation of Conakry. Full report in Polish in *Materialow zachodnio-pomorskie,* t. 14, 1970: 575–648 (DD491.P745M3).

539
——Sredniowieczna stolica Mali w swietle zródel pisanych, ustnych i archeologicznych, na tle zaplecza gospodarczopolitycznego. La capitale moyen-âgeuse du Mali à la lumière des sources écrites, orales et des trouvailles archéologiques, de l'arrière pays économiques et des conditions politiques. Materiały zachodnio-pomorskie, t. 13, 1969: 541–573. DD491.P745M3, v. 13

540
Gaillard, M. Niani, ancienne capitale de l'empire mandingue. BCAOF, t. 6, oct./déc. 1923: 620–630. DT521.C6, v. 6

Report on a follow-up expedition in search of the capital of the Mali empire. The author concludes that none of the four locations he investigated was Niani.

541
Gironcourt, G. de. Les inscriptions de la nécropole de Bentia (avec extraits d'une notes de M. Houdas) *In* Académie des inscriptions et des belles-letters. Comptes rendus, fév./mars 1911. Paris, 1911. p. 198–206. AS162.P315, 1911

See also France. Comité des travaux historiques et scientifiques. Bulletin de la section de géographie, v. 29, 1914: 1–39 (G11.F8, v. 29).

541a
——Les inscriptions lithiques du Niger et de l'Adrar. *In* Missions de Gironcourt, Documents scientifiques, 293–356.

Source: Brasseur, 2256.

Description des nécropoles (avec leurs inscriptions) du Niger en amont de Gao, de L'Adrar des Iforas et du Tilemsi, de Gao et de sa région. Sépultures des nécropoles isolées entre Gao et Bentia. Extrait du répertoire déposé au Corpus des inscriptions à l'Académie des Inscriptions et Belles-Lettres.—(Abstract supplied)

541b
Hodgkin, Thomas L. A Tombouctou au Moyen Age, le livre était le plus prospère des commerces. United Nations Educational, Scientific and Cultural Organization. Le courrier, v. 12, no 10, 1959: 26–27. illus. AS4.U8A23, v. 12

542
Hugot, Henri J. Deuxième mission à l'île de Tidra (Mauritanie), 27 janvier-4 mars 1966. BIFAN, t. 28, juil./oct. 1966: 1019–1023. DT1.I5123, v. 28

Report of an elaborate mission to Tidra. Hugot states that there are no cemeteries or ancient inscriptions going back to the Almoravid episode, although zoological, botanical, and geological data show that life could have been sustained on the island. Another discovery was a shallow passage, used by the Awlād Bū Sbā, who now occupy the island, which confirms the statement of Ibn Khaldūn. Hugot's provisional conclusion is that Ibn Yāsīn probably did not establish his Ribāṭ as buildings and mosques, since no building stone is available on the island, but founded it as a nomadic, military, temporary settlement.

543
——Mission à l'île de Tidra. BIFAN, t. 28, janv./avril 1966: 555–564. DT1.I5123, v. 28

Report on Hugot's first mission to the island of Tidra, north of Mimghar in Mauritania, trying to locate the site of the Ribāt of Ibn Yāsīn, as reported by Ibn Khaldun and other writers. On this trip Hugot verified that the island can be reached by foot at low tide and discovered a tombstone with Arabic inscriptions. *See also* 542 for the report on his second mission.

544
Hunwick, J. O. The mid-fourteenth century capital of Mali. JAH, v. 14, no. 2, 1973: 195–208. DT1.J65, v. 14

For over a century scholars have been attempting to locate the area and the actual site of the capital of the Mali empire in its period of greatness. Since the 1920's attention has been focused on an area near the Sankarani river, a tributary entering the Niger from the south, upstream from Bamako.

A close reading of the few descriptions we have of the capital of Mali, and in particular of the route taken by Ibn Baṭṭūṭa, who visited the capital in 1352, suggests that the city lay on the left bank of the river Niger somewhere between Segu and Bamako. This is in fact a logical site for the capital of an empire whose tributaries lay mainly in the savannah and Sahel belts, and in whose armies cavalry played a significant role. For this reason, among others, the recent hypothesis of Claude Meillassoux, suggesting a location for the capital south of the River Falémé (and perhaps also the River Gambia), seems doubtful. The proper name for the capital is also discussed.—(Abstract supplied, modified)

545
Ibn Ṣaghīr. Chronique sur les Imams Rostemides en Tahert. Published by A. De Motylinski. *In* International Congress of Orientalists. *14th,*

Algiers, 1905. Actes; Section 3: Langues Musulmanes. Paris, Ernest Leroux, 1908. p. 3–132.
PJ20.A73, 1905

546
Kalck, Pierre. Pour une localisation du royaume de Gaoga. JAH, v. 13, no. 4, 1972: 529–548.
DT1.J65, v. 13

Le terme Gaoga, qui figure fréquemment au centre des cartes anciennes de l'Afrique, se retrouve dans un seul texte, la 'description de l'Afrique', du diplomate marocain, Léon l'Africain, publiée en italien en 1550 par Ramusio. Relevant de fréquentes confusions avec la ville de Gao sur le Niger, certains africanistes en tirent la conclusion hâtive que le voyage de Léon se serait limité aux pays du Niger. Selon eux, le reste des notes ne ferait que reproduire des récits de caravaniers, plus ou moins fantaisistes. Pierre Kalck, ancien administrateur français, auteur d'une thèse de doctorat ès lettres sur l'histoire des régions qu'il a administrées, estime au contraire que le voyage de Léon du Bornou en Egypte fut bien effectué et qu'il a existé un Etat du nom de Gaoga, semblable aux grandes entités politiques africaines de l'époque. . . . Citant la découverte par Arkell, à Aïn Fara et à Ouri dans le Darfour, de vestiges nubiens chrétiens, Kalck estime que c'est dans cette région montagneuse qui constituait l'ancien Gaoga que se trouve la solution de bien des énigmes de l'histoire de l'Afrique Centrale. Le texte de Léon, aussi bref soit-il, apparaît comme un premier fil conducteur.—(Abstract supplied, modified)

547
Laforgue, Pierre. Notes sur Aoudaghost, ancienne capitale des Berbères Lemtouna (Mauritanie saharienne). BIFAN, t. 2, janv./avril 1940: 217–236.
Q89.I5, v. 2

One of the many landmarks leading to the discovery of the famous Berber outpost.

548
Lessard, Jean-Michel. Sijilmassa: la ville et ses relations commerciales au 11e siècle d'après el-Bakri. Hespéris-Tamuda, v. 10, fasc. 1/2, 1969: 5–36. maps. DT301.H45, v.10

549
Lhote, Henri. Recherches sur Takedda, ville décrite par le voyageur arabe Ibn Battouta et située en Aïr. BIFAN, t. 34, juil. 1972: 429–470. illus.
DT1.I5123, v. 34

In an attempt to settle once and for all the location of Ibn Baṭṭūṭah's city of Takedda, Lhote visited Teguidda-N-Tagaït, Teguidda-N-Adrar, Azelik, Aouzam, Marandet, and Teguidda-N-Tessemt, all located in the vicinity of Agadez. He believes the historic city of Teguidda-N-Tessemt to be the site of a salt and not a copper mine as generally accepted. Lhote examines Ibn Baṭṭūṭah's text, explains it in terms of his new discoveries, and concludes that "la description de Takedda correspond en tous points à celle de Teguidda-n-Tesemt et il suffit pour cela de changer un seul mot. . . ."

550
———Sur l'emplacement de la ville de Tademekka, antique capitale des Berbères soudanais. NA, no 51, juil. 1951: 65–69. DT1.I513, 1951

Basing his argument on historical records, excavations, oral traditions, and aerial photography, Lhote identifies the Tademekka of Ibn Ḥawqal and al-Bakrī as the town Es-Souk, whose ruins are located 300 kilometers northeast of Gao. The original town as destroyed in 1640 in the struggle between the Tademekket and the Ioulliminden.

551
Lombard, J., *and* Raymond Mauny. Azelick et la question de Takedda. NA, no 64, oct. 1954: 99–100. DT1.I513, 1954

Another milestone in locating the site of the famous copper mine visited by Ibn Baṭṭūṭah in 1353. After weighing the evidence, the authors conclude that Azelik in Northern Mali is probably Ibn Baṭṭūtah's Takedda.

552
Masson-Détourbet, A. Terres cuites de Mopti (Soudan). NA, no 60, oct. 1953: 100–102. illus.
DT1.I513, 1953

553
Mauny, Raymond. Découverte d'un atelier de fonte du cuivre à Marandet (Niger). NA, no 58, avril 1953: 33–35. DT1.I513, 1953

The Marandā of Arab writers from al-Ya'qūbī to al-Idrīsī is believed to be present-day Marandet, 90 kilometers south of Agadez in Niger. The description of the ruins there, provided by Lieutenant Prautois after a visit to the site, indicates that it was a center of copper smelting during the 14th century.

554
———Etat actuel de la question de Ghana. BIFAN, t. 13, avril 1951: 463–475. map.
Q89.I5, v. 13

Interpretive essay based on the archeological

discoveries of 1949 in Kumbi Ṣāliḥ. Mauny, who has been intimately involved with the problem, gives the historical background of the question and discusses the location of the capital of the Ghana Empire. He also attempts to date the site. Bibliography.

555
———Niches murales de la maison fouillée à Koumbi Saleh (Ghana). NA, no 46, avril 1950: 34–35. illus. DT1.I513, 1950

Note on the architectural motifs of a house dug out at Kumbi Ṣāliḥ. Mauny points out the similarity with houses in Tichit and other Mauritanian cities.

556
———Notes d'histoire et d'archéologie sur Azougui, Chinguetti et Ouadane. BIFAN, t. 16, janv./avril 1955: 142–152. illus. DT1.I5123, v. 16

Description of three Mauritanian cities which played a major role in the medieval period. Azougui, north of Atar, holds the remains of an Almoravid fort still not investigated in 1955; Chinguetti—the old Shinqīṭ—with its qsar and mosque; and Wadan, whose founding, according to some traditions, goes back to the 12th century. Diagrams and photographs.

557
———Les ruines de Tegdaoust et la question d'Aoudaghost. NA, no 48, oct. 1950: 107–109. DT1.I513, 1950

The excavations done by Mauny and aerial photography suggest that the ruins of the city of Awdaghost, first mentioned by al-Ya'qūbī in 872, are located in Tegdaoust in Mauritania.

558
McCall, Daniel F. The traditions of the founding of Sijilmassa and Ghana. *In* Historical Society of Ghana. Transactions. v. 5; 1961. Legon, 1961. p. 3–32. DT510.A1H55, v. 5

559
Mercier, E. Sildilmassa selon des auteurs arabes. Revue africaine, no 63, mai 1867: 233–242; no 64, juil. 1867: 274–284. DT271.R4, 1867

560
Monod, Théodore. Une découverte au Soudan. NA, no 2, 1940: 2. MH–P

Among the links to an Islamic past in the Songhay Empire are the tombstones discovered by Governor Chambon in 1939 in a cemetery at Sané, located about six kilometers from Gao and presented by Monod to the attention of the academic world. *See also* 569a.

561
———Découvertes archéologiques à Gao. NA, no 12, 1941: 9–10. MH–P

Refers to the Sané stelae.

562
———Encore les stèles de Gao. NA, no 12, 1941: 2. MH–P

563
———Nouvelle remarques sur Teghaza. BIFAN, t. 2, janv./avril 1940: 248–250. illus. Q89.I5, v. 2

Brief report of preliminary archeological digs in the Saharan salt mine.

564
Monteil, Charles V. L'île de'Aoulil d'Idrisi. NA, no 48, oct. 1950: 128–130. DT1.I513, 1950

An attempt to locate the island of Awlīl cited in al-Idrīsī. Monteil believed it to be the village of Busar [from the word *assar,* meaning "tree" in Zenaga Berber] now called Char, in the vicinity of Saint Louis in Senegal.

565
———Le site de Goundiourou. BCAOF, t. 11, oct./déc. 1928: 647–653. DT521.C6, v. 11

An exercise in African history combining archeology, Arabic manuscripts, and cartography in an effort to locate the site of the city of Goundiourou, once a center of Muslim learning visited by al-Bakrī.

566
Montrat, M. Notice sur l'emplacement de la capitale du Mali. NA, no 79, juil. 1958: 90–92. DT1.I513, 1958

Memorandum written in 1931 on the location of the capital of the Mali empire. Montrat, relying on oral traditions, holds that Niani, which was believed to be the capital, was in fact a suburb of the seat of the Mandingo rulers.

567
Niani. Ancienne capitale de l'empire du Mali. Recherches africaines; études guinéennes, nouv. sér., no 1, janv./mars 1969: 168–177. DT543.A3R4, n.s., 1969

Report of the first mission of the Guinea and Polish archeological team to Niani (1965) to collect oral traditions and information and undertake a general study of the site. The report concludes that

Niani is definitely the capital of Sundiata Keita, emperor of the Mali Empire.

568
La Question de ghana et la mission Bonnel de Mèzière. *In* Comité d'études historiques et scientifiques de l'Afrique occidentale française. Annales et mémoires, t. 1, 1916: 40–61. MnU

569
Roy, *Lt.* Vestiges de Takedda, ancienne capitale des Igdalen, centre minier et caravanier de l'Aïr au XVIe siècle. NA, no 29, janv. 1949: 5–7.
DT1.I513, 1949

569a
Sauvaget, J. Les épitaphes royales de Gao. al-Andalus, v. 14, no. 1, 1949: 123–142. illus.
DP102.A6, v. 14

A recognized Arabist, Sauvaget presents translations of 10 stelae with commentaries. He contends that some of the tombstones were carved during the 12th century at Almeira in Muslim Spain. *See also* 560.

570
Scarisbrick, J. J., *and* P. L. Carter. An expedition to Wangara. Ghana notes and queries, no. 1, Jan./Apr. 1961: 4–5. DLC

Brief report on an expedition in the Wangara region "to be identified with the quadrilateral formed by the Upper Niger, the Upper Senegal, the Tinkisso and the Faleme rivers" in search of the source of the gold which played such a major role in 13th-century European trade.

571
Terrasse, Henri. Note sur les ruines de Sijilmassa. *In* Fédération des sociétés savantes de l'Afrique du Nord. *2d Congress, Tlemcen, 1936.* Deuxième congrès de la Fédération des sociétés savantes de l'Afrique du Nord, Tlemcen, 14–17 avril 1936. v. 2; 1936. Alger, 1936. p. 581–589. illus.
DT271.R4 1936

572
Thomassey, Paul. Notes sur la géographie de l'habitat et la région de Koumbi Saleh. BIFAN, t. 13, avril 1951: 476–486. Q89.I5, v. 13

Brief study of the geography and population of the region of Kumbi Ṣāliḥ. Provides an insight into the situation when the city was the capital of the Ghana Empire.

573
Thomassey, Paul, *and* Raymond Mauny. Campagne de fouilles à Koumbi Saleh. BIFAN, t. 13, avril 1951: 438–462. illus., map. Q89.I5, v. 13

Report on the archeological digs performed at Kumbi Ṣāliḥ in 1949 by two members of IFAN. The report includes a general description of the city and various sites as well as line drawings of artifacts retrieved. Aerial photography was used to obtain a general idea of the sites.

574
———Campagne de fouilles de 1950 à Koumbi Saleh (Ghana?). BIFAN, t. 18, janv./avril 1956: 117–140. DT1.I5123, v. 18

Report of archeological excavations undertaken in 1950 at Kumbi Ṣāliḥ, which the authors tend to believe is the merchants' city described by al-Bakrī. The evidence found in four houses and the large amount of artifacts collected show the site to be an Arab medieval town inhabited by North African and other Arab traders, corroborating the description of al-Bakrī.

575
Vidal, J. Le mystère de Ghana. BCAOF, t. 6, juil./sept. 1923: 512–524. DT521.C6, v. 6

Synopsis of research done by the author concerning the location of the capital of the Ghana Empire. His main sources are Ibn Ḥawqal, al-Bakrī, al-Idrīsī, Ibn Saʿīd, and Yāqūt, as well as Soninke oral traditions and the archeological findings of Bonnel de Mézières. Vidal concludes that there is no hope of finding the remains of a city called Ghana.

576
———Un problème historique africain: le véritable emplacement de Mali. BCAOF, t. 6, oct./déc. 1923: 606–619. DT521.C6, v. 6

Report of an archeological expedition to Niani in search of the capital of the Mali Empire. Although the author was unable to complete his investigation, he suspects that Niani was the imperial capital.

577
———Un problème historique africain au sujet de l'emplacement de Mali (ou Melli) capitale de l'ancien empire mandingue. BCAOF, t. 6, avril/juin 1923: 251–268. DT521.C6, v. 6

Another element of the elaborate search for the capital of the Mali Empire. Mainly based on Ibn Baṭṭūṭah.

577a
Viré, Marie-Madeleine. Notes sur trois épitaphes royales de Gao. BIFAN, t. 20, juil./oct. 1958: 368–376. DT1.I5123, v. 20
Information on three tombstones from Gao with Arabic inscriptions. Description of the stelae and reproduction in modern Arabic characters of the Kufic inscriptions.

577b
———Stèles funéraires musulmanes soudano-sahariennes. BIFAN, t. 21, juil./août 1959: 459–500. illus. DT1.I5123, v. 21
After a short description of three tombstones from the Gao region, Mme Viré gives extensive general coverage of Muslim cemeteries in the Sudanic belt. The main sites discussed include el-Kreib, Kumbi-Ṣāliḥ, Timbuktu, Gao-Sané, and Bentia. The inscriptions of about 25 stelae are reproduced in modern Arabic script and both Kufic and naskhi scripts. *See also* 569a.

578
Widal, Georges. L'île d'Arguin. BCAOF, t. 5, janv./mars 1922: 114–127. DT521.C6, v. 5

History

579
al-'Abbādī, Aḥmad Mukhtār. al-Ṣafahāt al-ūlā min tārīkh al-Murābiṭīn. [The early pages in the history of the Almoravids] *In* Alexandria, Egypt. Jāmi'at al-Iskandarīyah. Kulliyat al-ādāb. Majallat Kuliyyat al-ādāb, m. 21, 1967: 47–79. AS693.A86, v. 21
After discussing the often unflattering image of the Almoravids projected by both Arab and western historians, al-'Abbādī relates the historical development of Almoravid hegemony according to an anonymous work entitled *Kitāb zikr ba'ḍ a'yān Fās fī al-qadīm* [Books About Some Notables of Fés in the Past].

580
'Abd al-Wāḥid al-Marrākushī. al-Mu'jib fī talkhīṣ akhbār al-Maghrib; min ladin fatḥ al-Andalus ilā ākhir 'aṣr al-Muwahhidīn ma'a mā yattaṣil bi-tārīkh hadhihi al-fatrah min akhbār al-qurrā' wa-a'yān al-kuttāb. [The inspiror of wonder in summing up the chronicle of the Maghreb from the conquest of Andalusia to the end of the Almohad era including the chronicles of the readers and notable writers involved in the history of this period] Edited by Muḥammad Sa'īd al-'Iryān. Cairo, 1963. 494 p. (al-Jumhūrīyah al-'Arābīyah al-Muttahidah. al-Majlis al-a'lā lil-shu'ūn al-Islāmīyah. Lajnat iḥyā' al-tirāth al-Islāmī. al-Kitāb 3.)
DT199.A63 1963 Orien Arab
Includes references to sub-Saharan Africa.

581
Ahmed ibn Fartua. History of the first twelve years of the reign of Mai Idris Alooma of Bornu (1571–1583) by his Imam, Ahmed ibn Fartua; together with the "Diwan of the Sultans of Bornu" and "Girgam" of the Magumi, translated from the Arabic with introduction and notes by H. R. Palmer. Lagos, Printed by the Govt. Printer, 1926. 121 p. incl. geneal. table, fold. map. DT515.A65
The Arabic manuscript of this document was located by Heinrich Barth at Kukawa, then capital of the Kanembu rulers of Bornu, about 1853. The work relates the various military campaigns undertaken between 1571 and 1853 and provides a fairly accurate picture of the life of an African kingdom during the 16th century.

582
'Allām, 'Abd Allāh 'Alī. al-Da'wah al-Muwaḥḥadīyah. [The Almohad call] Cairo, Dār al-Ma'rifah [1964] 406 p. (Jāmi'at al-Rabāṭ – Risālat al-mājīstīr) DT199.A8 Orien Arab
Rejecting the common contention that Ibn Tumart (d. ca. 1129) was "a seeker of a state, and not the propagator of a faith" when he established the Almohad state, 'Allām presents a detailed analysis of Ibn Tumart showing that his was a reformist and intellectual mission rather than a strictly political endeavor. 'Allām also explores the vagaries of the Almohad state and its impact. The text of a number of letters by the reformist is appended.

583
Bâ, Amadou-Hampâté, *and* G. Dieterlen. Les fresques d'époque bovidienne du Tassili N'Ajjer et les traditions des Peul: hypothèse d'interprétation. JOSAF, t. 36, fasc. 2, 1966. illus. DT1.S65, v. 36
Hypothesis regarding the relationship between wall paintings of the Tassili in southern Algeria and Fulbe initiation rites proposed by Hampâté Bâ, the eminent Malian scholar.

584
al-Bakrī, Abū 'Ubayd 'Abd Allāh ibn 'Abd al-'Azīz. Description de l'Afrique septentrionale, par Abou-Obeïd el-Bekri. Texte arabe revu sur quatre manuscrits et publié sous les auspices de M. le maréchal comte Randon, par le b[on] de Slane. Paris, Librairie d'Amérique et d'Orient Adrien-Maisonneuve, 1965. 20, 212 p. DT188.B3 1965

Reproduction of the 1911 edition, Algiers.

al-Bakrī, whose family ruled a principality in Andalusia, settled in Cordoba where he received a solid education and entered, in 1064, the service of the emir of Almeira. His wide knowledge of contemporary literature and contacts with various traders, if not agents, make his description of the Sudan reliable although he himself did not travel across the Sahara. *See also* the 1964 edition (DT188.B3 1964).

585

Béraud-Villars, Jean M. E. L'empire de Gaô, un état soudanais aux XVe et XVIe siècles. Paris, Plon [1942] 214 p. illus. maps (part fold.) DT551.B4

Historical narrative on the Songhay Empire from its beginning to the French occupation. The author warns the reader that the story "will show a world which will shock our patterns of thought," namely, an organized, well administered state with large cities, a commercial class, a learned aristocracy, and an army led by knights.

586

Blyden, Edward Wilmot. West Africa before Europe, and other addresses, delivered in England in 1901 and 1903. London, C. M. Philips, 1905. 158 p. front. (port.) DT471.B5

Includes the author's article "Islam in the Western Soudan," reprinted from *Journal of African Society,* October 1902.

587

Bosch Vilá, Jacinto. Los Almorávides. *In* Historia de Murrueacas. t. 5. Tetuán, Editora Marrogui, 1956. 405 p. maps.

Source: Rishworth, 345.

588

Castries, Henri de. La conquête du Soudan par el Mansour. Hespéris, t. 3, 4. trimestre, 1923: 433–489. DT301.H45, v. 3

Juder, a young renegade from Las Cuevas brought up in the palace of Aḥmad al-Manṣūr, headed a commando of 2,500 musketeers and defeated the Songhay army at Tondibi in 1591. The two sources used by Castries are a letter from Mawlāy Aḥmad al-Manṣūr to the sherifs and notables of Fès announcing the success of the expedition and an anonymous Spanish contemporary description of the invasion, probably by an agent of the Spanish court residing in Marrakech. Included are the texts of the two manuscripts with translation, as well as information on the number of troops involved in the operation.

589

Cissoko, Sékéné Mody. Histoire de l'Afrique occidentale . . . [de la 6e à la terminale.] Paris, Présence africaine, 1966+ v. illus. (part col.) DT471.C59

L.C. has v. 1.

Deals at length with the western Sudanic empires. Reflects the new curricula and focuses of interest of the new African schools of national history.

590

Clair, Andrée. Le fabuleux empire du Mali. Illus. de Tall Papa Ibra. Paris, Présence africaine [1959] unpaged. illus. DT532.2.C55

The story of the great West African empire, tailored to a juvenile audience.

591

Cooley, William D. The Negroland of the Arabs examined and explained; or, An inquiry into the early history and geography of Central Africa. 2d ed., with a bibliographical introduction by John Ralph Willis. London, Cass, 1966. xxvi, 148 p. plates, maps, tables. DT356.C77 1966a

First published in 1841.

A welcome reprint of a classic in medieval African history. Cooley brings together essentially all the available information on the Sudanic belt. His knowledge of Arabic allows him to draw on Arabic sources and look at the trade relations between North Africa and the Sudan as a continuum unobstructed by the Sahara. Some of his hypotheses are outmoded, but his narrative still provides a wealth of information.

592

Crone, Gerald R., *ed. and tr.* The voyages of Cadamosto and other documents on western Africa in the second half of the fifteenth century. London, Printed for the Hakluyt Society, 1937. 159 p. fold. front., 2 fold. maps. (Works issued by the Hakluyt Society. Second series, no. LXXX) G161.H2 2d ser., no 80

Includes the "Letter of Antoine Malfante from Tuat, 1447."

593

Davidson, Basil. Songhay—end of an epoch (Empires of old Africa, 5). West African review, v. 33, Aug. 1962: 22–27. illus. DT491.W47, v. 33

594

Davies, Oliver. West Africa before the Europeans: archaeology and prehistory. London, Methuen,

1967. 364 p. illus., 24 plates, maps, tables, diagrs. (Methuen's handbook of archaeology) DT471.D34

595

Dutel, *Lt.* Comparaison entre une généalogie sonrai de tradition orale et la généalogie des Askias de Gao donnée par les sources historiques. NA, no 25, 1945: 22–23. DT1.I513, 1945

596

Fage, J. D. Ancient Ghana: a review of the evidence. Historical Society of Ghana. Transactions, v. 3, 1957–1958: 77–98. DT510.A1H55, v. 3

597

Hallam, W. K. R. The Bayajida legend in Hausa folklore. JAH, v. 7, no. 1, 1966: 47–80. DT1.J65, v. 7

598

Hama, Boubou. L'empire Songhay, ses ethnies, ses légendes et ses personnages historiques. [Paris] P. J. Oswald [1974] 176 p. (Poésie/prose africaine, 8) DT551.42.H35

599

Huici Miranda, Ambrosio. Un fragmento de Ibn Idari sobre los Almorávides. Hespéris-Tamuda, t. 2, fasc. 1, 1961: 43–111. DT301.H45, v. 2

600

———Las luchas del Cid Campeador con los Almorávides y el enigma de su hijo, Giego. Hespéris-Tamuda, t. 6, 1965: 79–114. DT301.H45, v. 6

601

Ibn 'Abd al-Ḥakam. Conquête de l'Afrique du nord et de l'Espagne (Futûh' Ifrîqiya wa'l-Andalus), texte arabe et traduction française, avec une introduction et des notes, par Albert Gateau. Alger, Editions Carbonel, 1942. 163 p. (Bibliothèque arabe-française [v. 2]) DT173.I23

Arabic and French on opposite pages.

Fifth part of the author's *Futūḥ Miṣr wa-al-Maghrib.*

602

———Futūḥ Ifrīqiyā wa-al-Andalus. [The conquest of Ifriqiya and Andalusia] Edited by 'Abd Allāh Anīs al-Ṭabbā'. Beirut, Maktabat al-madrasah wa-Dār al-kitāb al-Lubnānī lil-ṭibā'ah wa-al-nashr, 1964. 109 p. DT173.I2 1964

603

[Ibn Abī Zar' al-Fāsī, 'Ali ibn 'Abd Allāh] [Roudh el-Kartas. Histoire des souverains du Maghreb (Espagne et Maroc) et annales de la ville de Fès. Traduit de l'arabe par A. Beaumier. Paris, Impr. impériale, 1860] 576 p. DT319.I174

L.C. copy imperfect: p. [i]-xi, including t.p., wanting. Title supplied from *Catalogue général* of the Bibliothèque nationale, Paris.

Translation of *al-Anīs al-muṭrib bi-rawḍ al-qirṭās fī akhbār mulūk al-Maghrib wa-tārīkh madīnat Fās* by 'Ali ibn 'Abd Allāh ibn Abī Zar' al-Fāsī (cf. Brockelmann, *Geschichte der arabischen Litteratur,* 2. aufl., v. 2, p. 312). In some manuscripts it is ascribed to an otherwise unknown Ṣāliḥ ibn 'Abd al-Ḥalīm al-Gharnaṭī. *See also* the Arabic version edited by Muḥammad al-Hāshimī al-Filālī (Rabat, Sharikat al-nashr al-Maghribīyah, 1355/1936. DT319.I168 1936 Orien Arab).

604

Ibn Baṭṭūṭah. Riḥlat Ibn Baṭṭuṭah al-musammāh Tuḥfat al-nuẓẓār fī gharā'ib al-amṣār wa-'ajā'ib al-asfār. [The voyage of Ibn Baṭṭūṭah called the gem of the viewers on strange metropoleis and wondrous travels] [Verified and corrected according to a number of complete copies with the approval of a committee of scholars] Cairo, al-Maktabah al-tijārīyah al-kubrā, 1964. 2 v. in 1. G370.I2 1964

605

———Textes et documents relatifs à l'histoire de l'Afrique; extraits tirés des *Voyages d'Ibn Baṭṭrēṭa.* Traduction annotée [par] R. Mauny [et al.] Dakar, 1966. 86 p. fold. map, plates. (Université de Dakar. Publications de la Faculté des lettres et sciences humaines. Histoire, no 9) DT7.I45 1966

See also his *Voyages d'Ibn Battûta,* translated by C. Dufrēmy and B. R. Sanguinetti (G490.I18).

Translation of excerpts of Ibn Baṭṭūṭah's travels to West and East Africa. The merit of this volume stems from the fact that it was produced by a team effort that brought together Arabists and Africanists. The result is a lucid translation with a wealth of annotations explaining the background and origin of terms used and names.

606

———Travels in Asia and Africa, 1325–1354. Translated and selected by H. A. R. Gibb, with an introduction and notes. New York, A. M. Kelley [1969] 398 p. illus., maps. (The Broadway travellers) G490.I2 1969

Reprint of the 1929 ed.

Translation of *Tuḥfat al-nuẓẓār.*

607
Ibn Faḍl Allāh al-'Umarī, Aḥmad ibn Yaḥyā. Masālik al-abṣār fī mamālik al-amṣār. [The paths of sight into the kingdoms of the civilized world] Traduit et annoté, avec une introduction, par Gaudefroy-Demombynes. I. L'Afrique moin l'Egypte. Paris, P. Geuthner, 1927. 282 p. maps. (Bibliothèque des géographes arabes, t. 2)
VK800.B5, v. 2

No more published?

Although dealing with North Africa, this is useful for the study of the Mali Empire. The original work, dated 1337, provides invaluable information on the pilgrimage of Kanku Mūsā. Includes some passages from al-Qalqashandī.

608
———Masālik al-abṣār fī mamālik al-amṣār. [The paths of sight into the kingdoms of the civilized world] Edited by Aḥmad Zakī. Cairo, Dār al-Kutub al-Miṣrīyah, 1924+ (Iḥyā' al-ādāb al-'Arabīyah) G93.I27 Orien Arab

L.C. has v. 1.

609
Ibn Hawqal, Abu al-Qasim Muhammad. Description de l'Afrique. Traduction de Slane. Journal asiatique, 3. sér., t. 13, fév. 1842: 153–196; mars 1842: 209–258. PJ4.J5, 3d ser., v. 13

610
———Configuration de la terre (Kitab surat al-ard) [par] Ibn Hauqal. Introduction et traduction, avec index, par J. H. Kramers et G. Wiet. Beyrouth, Commission internationale pour la traduction des chefs-d'oeuvre, 1964 [i.e. 1965.] 2 v. (550 p.) maps (part fold.) (Collection UNESCO d'oeuvres représentatives. Série arabe)
G93.I32214 1965

Translation of *Kitāb Ṣūrat al-arḍ,* the author's revision of his own work originally entitled *Kitab al-Masalik wa-al-mamalik* and published by de Goeje in 1873.

Translated from the text as edited by Kramers (Leiden, 1938–39).

611
———Kitāb al-masālik wa-al-mamālik. [The book of roads and kingdoms] Leiden, Brill, 1872 [i.e. 1873] 406, xxi p. (Bibliotheca geographorum Arabicorum, pars 2) G93.I29

Added t.p.: Viae et regna, descriptio ditionis Moslemicae, auctore Abu'l-Kásim ibn Haukal, editit M. J. de Goeje.

Indexes, glossary, addenda, and emendanda to this volume are included in part 4 of the series.

612
Ibn 'Idhārī, *al-Marrākushī.* al-Bayān al-mughrib fī akhbār al-Maghrib wa-al-Andalus. [The utmost elucidation on the news of the Maghreb and Andalusia] Edited by G. S. Colin and E. Lévi-Provençal. Beirut, Dar al-thaqafah [1967] 4 v.
DT173.I262 Orien Arab

613
———Histoire de l'Afrique du Nord et de l'Espagne musulmane, intitulée *Kitāb al-bayān al-mughrib,* et fragments de la chronique de 'Arīb. Nouv. éd. publiée d'aprés l'éd. de 1848–1851 de R. Dozy et de nouveaux manuscrits, par G. S. Colin & É. Lévi-Provençal. Leiden, E. J. Brill, 1948–51. 2 v.
DT173.I26

Added t.p.: Kitāb al-Bayān al-Mughrib fī akhbār al-Andalus wa-al-Maghrib, li-ibn 'Idhārī al-Marrākushī.

Vol. 3 of this text was published by Lévi-Provençal under title: *al-Bayān al-mugrib: tome troisième, histoire de l'Espagne musulmane au XIème siècle* (Paris, 1930).

The fragments of 'Arib's history were not included in this edition.

Contents.—t. 1. Histoire de l'Afrique du Nord de la conquête au xie siècle.—t. 2. Histoire de l'Espagne musulmane de la conquête au xie siècle.

614
Ibn Khaldūn. Histoire des Berbères et des dynasties musulmanes de l'Afrique septentrionale. Traduite de l'arabe par le baron de Slane. Nouv. éd. publiée sous la direction de Paul Casa nova, et suivie d'une bibliographie d'Ibn Khaldoun. Paris, P. Geuthner, 1925–56. 4 v. geneal. tables. DT199.I24

"Tome quatrième, suivi de la table géographique et de l'index général des quatre tomes, publié par Henri Pérès."

A translation of part 4 of the second book and the whole of the third book of *Kitāb al-'ibar.*

615
Ibn Khurradādhbih, 'Ubayd Allāh ibn 'Abd Allāh. Le livre des routes et des provinces. Edité par C. Barbier de Meynard. Journal asiatique, 6. sér., t. 5, janv./fév. 1865: 1–127; 446–527.
PJ4.J5, 6th ser., v. 5.

616
al-Idrisi. Description de l'Afrique et de l'Espagne [par] Abou-'Abdallah Moh. Edrisi. Texte arabe,

publié pour la première fois d'après les manuscrits de Paris et d'Oxford, avec une traduction, des notes et un glossaire par Reinhart P. A. Dozy et Michaël J. de Goeje. [Réimpression de l'édition Leiden 1866.] Amsterdam, Oriental Press, 1969. 1 v. (various pagings) DT7.I43 1969

Added t.p.: Ṣifat al-Maghrib wa-arḍ al-Sūdān wa-al-Andalus, ma'khūdhah min kitāb Nuzhat al-mushtāq fī-ikhtirāq al-āfāq, ta'līf al-Sharīf al-Idrīsī.

617

———Géographie d'Edrisi. Tr. de l'arabe en français d'après deux manuscrits de la Bibliothèque du roi et accompagnée de notes, par P. Amédée Jaubert. Paris, Impr. royale, 1836–40. 2 v. fold. maps. (Société de Géographie, Paris. Recueil de voyages et de mémoires, 5–6) G161.S67 t. 5–6

Title also in Arabic.

618

Ismā'īl, 'Abbās Hilmī. Min Riḥlāt al-Hajj fī al-'Uṣūr al-Wusṭā. [On pilgrimage in the Middle Ages] *In* Cairo. al-Jāmi' al-Azhar. Majallat al-Azhar, m. 37, Feb. 1966: 508–511. BP1.C3, v. 37 Orien Arab

Though not directly related to sub-Saharan Africa, this essay on a medieval pilgrimage route during the 12th century describes the itinerary of Ibn Jubayr al-Andalusī and the bureaucratic procedure he encountered on his voyage from Granada to the holy places via Cairo. These procedures were probably also followed by African pilgrims. It is interesting to note that the pilgrimage was used by the Ayyubids as a forum to organize Islamdom against the Crusaders settled in Arab lands.

619

al-Iṣṭakhrī. al-Masālik wa-al-mamālik. [Roads and states] By Isḥaq Ibrāhīm ibn Muḥammad al-Fārisī al-Iṣṭakhri, known as al-Karkhī. [Edited by Muḥammad Jābir 'Abd al-'Āl al-Ḥīnī. Reviewed by Shafīq Ghurbāl] [Cairo, Dār al-qalam] 1961. 214 p. facsims. (Turāthunā) G93.I8 Orien Arab

620

Jaubert, Amédée. Relation de Ghanat et des coutumes de ses habitants, traduit littéralement de l'arabe. *In* Société de géographie, *Paris*. Recueil de voyages et de mémoires, t. 2, 1825: 1–14. G161.S67, v. 2

621

Kāmil, Muṣtafā Muḥammad. al-Sharīf al-Idrīsī wa atharuhu fī al-jughrāfīyah. [The Sherif al-Idrisi and his impact on geography] Cairo, al-Majlis al-a'lā lil-shu'ūn al-Islāmīyah, 1964. 80 p. (Kutub Islāmīyah, no. 40) BP20.K8, no. 40 Orien Arab

al-Idrīsī was one of the great names in medieval geography. Kāmil begins with a general discussion of Arab geography and its main luminaries, then relates the life and works of this Ceutan who lived at the court of Roger, the Norman king of Sicily. The third part of the work is a briefly annotated bibliography of his works, and the last chapter, dealing with his impact on the new science of geography, includes a section on al-Idrīsī's connection with the discovery of America.

622

Kitāb al-istibṣār fī 'ajā'ib al-amṣār; waṣf Makkah wa-al-Madīnah wa-Miṣr wa-bilād al-Maghrib. Li-kātib Marrākushi min kuttāb al-qarn al-sādis al-hijrī (12 A.D.). [Book of reflection on the marvels of countries; description of Mecca and Medina, Egypt and North Africa by a Moroccan writer of the 6th century A.H. (12 A.D.)] Edited and translated by Sa'd Zaghlūl 'Abd al-Ḥamīd. Alexandria, 1958. 252, 90 p. (Jāmi at al-Iskandarīyah, Kulliyat al-ādāb, 'al-matbū' raqm 10) DT163.K5 Orien Arab

Added t.p.: Kitāb al-istibṣār fī 'ajā'ib al-amṣār; description de la Mekke et de Médine, de l'Egypte et de l'Afrique septentrionale par un écrivain marocain du VIe siècle de l'hégire (XIIe s. J.C.). Texte arabe annoté, publié avec une traduction de la partie relative aux lieux saints et à l'Egypte, par Saad Zaghloul Abdel-Hamid.

623

Kubbel', Lev Evgen'evich. Histoire de la vallée du Niger Supérieur et Moyen du VIIIe au XVIe siècle: quelques reflexions sur le découpage chronologique. Notes et documents voltaïques, t. 1, juil./sept. 1968: 13–28. DLC

In this study of periodization of Ghana, Mali, and Songhay, Kubbel' suggests that "l'application à l'étude de ce problème des principes de périodisation élaborés par la théorie du matérialisme historiques nous permet de considerer ces structures étatiques comme trois étapes successives de l'évolution économique et sociale de la région en question. Pour un chercheur partageant ces principes, le niveau du développement des forces productrices et des rapports de production dans une société donnée est le facteur déterminant de l'évolution de celle-ci."

624

La Roncière, Charles de. De Paris à Tombouctou au temps de Louis XI. Revue des deux mondes, t. 93, 1. fév. 1923: 653–675. AP20.R3, v. 93

625
———Découverte d'une relation de voyage datée du Touat et décrivant en 1447 le bassin du Niger. *In* France. Comité des travaux historiques et scientifiques. Bulletin, t. 33, 1918: 3–28.
G11.F8, v. 33

626
Levtzion, Nehemia. Ancient Ghana and Mali. London, Methuen, 1973. 283 p. 2 maps. (Studies in African history, 7) DT532.15.L48 1973

627
———Muslims and chiefs in West Africa: a study of Islam in the Middle Volta Basin in the precolonial period. Oxford, Clarendon Press, 1968. 228 p. 2 maps. (Oxford studies in African affairs)
BP64.A4W36

Levtzion spent 11 months (September 1963–July 1964) visiting "over a hundred Muslim communities" in Ghana, Togo, Upper Volta, and Dahomey, gathering traditional evidence for his study on the Islamization of the Middle Volta Basin. He writes, "The present study deals with the history of social groups (the Muslim communities) of different ethnic origins (but mainly Mande and Hausa) in several separate political units (Gonja, Chokossi, Dagomba, Mamprusi, Wa, as well as Mossi, Borgu, Kotokoli, and Ashanti) over a period of more than four centuries (from the fifteenth to the nineteenth centuries)." He analyzes trade patterns including the Mande and Hausa trade as well as the trading town of Salaga; "Islam in the Middle Volta States," namely Gonja, Dagomba, Mamprusi, and Islam in the country of the stateless peoples; and "patterns of Islamization" in Mossi, Borgu, Kotokoli, and Ashanti. An extensive bibliography.

628
———The thirteenth and fourteenth century kings of Mali. JAH, v. 4, no. 3, 1963: 341–353.
DT1.J65, v. 4

629
Lewicki, Tadeusz. L'Afrique Noire dans le *Kitāb al-Masālik wa' l-mamālik* d'Abū 'Ubayd al-Bakrī (XIe s.) Africana bulletin, t. 2, 1965: 9–14.
DT19.9.P6A65, v. 2

al-Bakrī, who never visited the Sahara or West Africa, relied upon previous works and personal contacts with people who visited the area to compile his opus magnum. Lewicki considers al-Bakrī's description of these two regions "la meilleure et la plus complète de toutes celles que nous possédons sur les pays africains au Sud du Sahara."

630
———Un état soudanais médieval inconnu: le royaume de Zafun(u). CEA, v. 11, 4. cahier, 1971: 501–525. DT1.C3, v. 11

With the breakup of the Ghana Empire under the Almoravids in 1076, various political units regained their independence. Zafun, according to Lewicki, is one of these entities. Meticulously examining Yāqūt's *Mu'jam al-Buldān* and other Arabic sources, the author reconstructs, locates, and narrates the history of this little-known Sudanic state.

631
Lhote, Henri. Contribution à l'étude des touaregs soudanais. Pt. 1–2. BIFAN, t. 17, juil./oct. 1955: 334–370; t. 18, juil./oct. 1956: 391–407.
DT1.I5123, v. 17–18

Investigation of the role played by the Sudanic Tuareg during the Mali and Songhay empires. Lhote lived among the nomadic tribes of the Sahara for a considerable time and studied Arab writers such as al-Bakrī and al-Idrīsī. He critically analyzes the origins of the Saghmâra and Maghcharen tribes; the expeditions of Askia Muhammad in the Aïr region; the confusion between the two terms *Takedda* and *Tademekka,* referring to the medieval city whose location is disputed by many writers; the limits of the Mali Empire; the route from Gao to Cairo via the Aïr complex; the Tuareg of the Timbuktu region; and the Songhay in the Adrar des Iforas.

632
Maḥmūd, Ḥasan Aḥmad. al-Marḥalah al-Ifrīqīyah min tārīkh al-Murābiṭūn. [The African phase in the history of the Almoravids] *In* Cairo. al-Jam'īyah al-Miṣrīyah lil-dirāsāt al-tārīkhīyah. al-Majallah al-tārīkhīyah al-Miṣrīyah, m. 12, 1964–1965: 111–118. DT77.J28, v. 12 Orien Arab

The nomadic Tuareg—Lemtah, Lamtuna, and Juddālah—moved along the fringes of the southern Sahara, where they came in contact with the black populations of the Savanna such as the Wolof, Songhay, and Mandingo. Maḥmūd suggests that the Islamization of the Tuareg in the 10th century led to the creation of the Almoravid movement and the eventual conversion of the Sudanic belt to Islam. He draws a parallel between the action of the Seljuk in the east and that of the Almoravids to the west of the Muslim world.

633
Małowist, Marian. The social and economic stability of the Western Sudan in the Middle Ages. Past and

present, no. 33, Apr. 1966: 3–15. D1.P37, 1966
Investigation of the Western Sudan during the 14th and 15th centuries and the sources for their economic and commercial prosperity.

634
———Wielkie państwa Sudanu Zachodniego w późnym średniowieczu. [The great states of the Western Sudan during the early Middle Ages] Warszawa, Państwowe Wydawn. Naukowe, 1964. 460 p. map. DT532.2.M3
Table of contents also in French.

635
al-Maqrīzī, Aḥmad ibn 'Alī. Description des races noires *and* Pèlerinage des sultans du Tekrour (1306–1442). *In* Aḥmad ibn Yaḥyā Ibn Faḍl Allāh al-'Umarī. Masālik al-abṣār fī mamālik al-amṣār. [The paths of sight into the kingdoms of the civilized world] Traduit et annoté, avec une introduction, par Gaudefroy-Demombynes. I. L'Afrique moins l'Egypte. Paris, P. Geuthner, 1927. p. 85–93. VK8000.B5, v. 2

636
Mauny, Raymond. L'Ouest africain chez les géographes arabes du Moyen Age. *In* International West African Conference. Comptes rendus. v. 2; 1945. Dakar, 1951. p. 502–508. DT471.I58, 1945
Report on Arab knowledge about West Africa during the medieval period. Starting with Ibn Munabbih in the seventh century, Mauny cites a number of Arab geographers who wrote about the area, concluding with Leo Africanus in the 15th century.

637
Meillassoux, Claude. L'itinéraire d'Ibn Battuta de Walata à Mali. JAH, v. 13, no. 3, 1972: 389–395. DT1.J65, v. 13

638
———Recherche de Tarikhs sur l'histoire du Hodh et de l'ancien empire de Ghana. no 109, janv. 1966: 30. DT1.I513, 1966
Request for information on two *Tarikh* by Shaykh Sīdī Mukhtār al-Kuntī, pertaining to the history of the Hodh region in Mauritania and the Ghana Empire. The two documents, as reported by an informant, are "Rissalatt Raoud fi Anassab Ahaly alhaod" [Risālat al-rawḍ fī ansāb ahālī al-Ḥawḍ] and "Alkalani" [al-Kalām(?)]. Meillassoux states that 'Alī ūld Sīdī Yaḥyā, a marabout from Walātah, is the presumed owner of the manuscripts.

639
Monod, Théodore. A propos d'un document concernant la conquête du Soudan par le Pacha Djouder (1591). *In* Académie royale des sciences d'outre-mer. Bulletin des séances. Nouv. sér., v. 10, 1964: 770–791. JV2802.A3, n.s., v. 10
Translation of, and commentaries on, a report about the Juder expedition, found by the author at the Hunt Botanical Library in Pittsburgh. Monod has discovered that the text is extracted from al-Ifrānī's *Nuzhat al-Ḥādī* and provides parallel citations to show the similarity (*see* 863).

640
Monteil, Charles V. Les empires du Mali (Etude d'histoire et de sociologie soudanaises). BCAOF, t. 12, juil./déc. 1929: 291–448. DT521.C6, v. 12
Substantial history of the Mali empires using a multidisciplinary approach. Called "a revision of Delafosse's synthesis" by the author, it is based on oral traditions, early and recent Arab and European writers, ethnography, and linguistics.
Reprint published in 1968 by Maisonneuve and Larose (DT532.2.M6).

641
———Les "Ghana" des géographes arabes et des européens. Hespéris, t. 38, 3./4. trimestres, 1951: 441–452. DT181.H4, v. 38

642
———L'oeuvre des étrangers dans l'empire soudanais du Mali. Revue des études islamiques, t. 2, 2. cahier, 1929: 227–235. BP1.R53, v. 2

643
Monteil, Vincent. Al Bakrî (Cordoue 1068). Routier de l'Afrique blanche et noire du nord-ouest. BIFAN, t. 30, janv. 1968: 39–116. DT1.I5123, v. 30
New translation of 16 chapters of *Kitāb al-Masālik wa al-Mamālik* (1068) by Abū 'Ubayd 'Abd Allāh Ibn 'Abd al-'Azīz Ibn Muḥammad Ibn Ayyūb al-Bakrī. With the valuable collaboration of two Mauritanian scholars—Mokhtar ould Hamidoun and Mūḥammad Ūld Mawlūd Ūld Dāddah—Monteil used the Arabic Manuscript 17 Bd-PSS/902 of the British Museum pertaining to the various itineraries, to which he added copious notes and commentaries based on his vast African experience.

644
———Introduction aux voyages d'Ibn Baṭṭûṭa (1325–53). BIFAN, t. 30, avril 1968: 444–462. DT1.I5123, v. 30

A sympathetic study of Ibn Baṭṭūṭah, as seen through his writings and travel descriptions.

645
Moraes Farias, Paulo F. de. The Almoravids: some questions concerning the character of the movement during the periods of closest contact with the Western Sudan. BIFAN, t. 29, juil./oct. 1967: 794–878. illus., maps. DT1.I5123, v. 29

A critical examination of medieval Arabic sources dealing with the Almoravid movement. The study attempts to apply the concepts of warfare as described by Ibn Khaldūn in his *Muqaddimah,* or *Prolegomena,* to the investigation of the movement started by Ibn Yāsīn. Also included are a discussion of the island of Tidra in Mauritania as the site of the Almoravid Ribat and a study of Mauritanian oral traditions and written medieval sources, from Morocco and Andalusia, on the historicity of Imām al-Ḥaḍramī, a companion of the Almoravid leader Abū Bakr Ibn ʻUmar.

646
al-Munajjid, Ṣalāḥ al-Dīn, *ed.* Mamlakat Mālī ʻind al-Jughrafiyīn al-Muslimīn. [The Mali kingdom as seen by Arab geographers] Beirut, Dār al-Kitāb al-jadīd. 1963+ 1 v. fold. map (inserted), port. NjP

Cover title: L'empire du Mali vu par les géographes musulmans.

647
N'Diaye, Amadou. Assoka; ou, Les derniers jours de Koumbi. Dakar, Nouvelles editions africaines, c1973. 181 p. PQ3989.2.N43A9

Historical novel.

648
Niane, Djibril Tamsir. Mythes, légendes et sources orales dans l'oeuvre de Mahmoûd Kâti. Recherches africaines; études guinéennes, nouv. sér. no 1/4, janv./déc. 1964: 36–42. DT543.A3R4, n.s., 1964

Relates the attempts of al-Kaʻtī to create an Arab or Hebrew ancestry for black leaders and the myth of the genesis of the peoples of the Western Sudan that was used to justify the socio-political organization of the Sudan in the 16th century.

649
———Recherches sur l'empire du Mali au Moyen-Age. Recherches africaines; études guinéennes, nouv. sér., no 1, janv./mars 1960: 17–36. DT543.A3R4, n.s., 1960

Sundiata Keita expanded the authority of the Mali Empire from the forest to the desert and from the ocean to east of the Niger River. Consequently, legend has obscured the man and Niane has been endeavoring diligently to separate the wheat from the chaff. He says, "Pour Soundjata, il est nécessaire de faire le départ toutefois entre légendes et récits des traditionalistes; à les comparer on voit la part d'éxagération d'un côté et de l'autre par moment, un souci de vérité qui est tout à l'honneur de la caste des griots." Drawing on oral traditions and Arab authors he presents the biography of the victor of Kirina and describes the Malian society during his reign.

650
———Recherches sur l'Empire du Mali au Moyen Age. Diplôme d'études supérieures soutenu à la Faculté des lettres de Bordeaux. [Conakry] République de Guinée, Ministère de l'information et du tourisme, 1962. 70 p. geneal. tables, map. (Mémoire de l'Institut national de recherches et de documentation, no 2) H35.G93 no. 2

"Le présent volume de mémoires réunit une suite d'études sur l'Empire du Mali, publié dans notre revue 'Recherches africaines' no 1–4/59, no 1/60, no 2/60."

"Mise en place des populations de la Haute Guinée (Diplôme complémentaires aux recherches sur l'Empire du Mali)": p. [57]–70.

651
Ol'derogge, Dimitriĭ A. Zapadniĭ Sudan v XV-XIX vv. [Western Sudan in the 15th-19th centuries] *In* Akademii͡a nauk SSSR *Institut etnografii.* Trudy. Novai͡a serii͡a, t. 53. Moskva, 1960. p. 1–266. illus. GN2.A2142, v. 53

652
Palausi, G. Un projet d'hydraulique fluviale soudanaise au XVe siècle: le canal de Soni-Ali. NA, no 78, avril 1958: 47–49. DT1.I513, 1958

In his *Tārīkh al-Sūdān,* al-Saʻdī mentions a canal leaving Ra's al-Mā' (at the western end of Lake Faguibine) and going northwest towards Walātah. Palausi, after studying the terrain, climate, and aerial photographs, concludes that Sonni Ali tried to cut a channel in an area covered by marshes.

653
Palmer, *Sir* Herbert R. The kingdom of Gaòga of Leo Africanus. *In* African Society. Journal, v. 29, Apr. 1930: 280–284; v. 29, July 1930: 350–369. DT1.R62, v. 29

654
Péhaut, Yves. L'Ouest africain au moyen âge. Les cahiers d'outre-mer, v. 15, oct./déc. 1962: 407–414. G1.C15, v. 15

Review article on Raymond Mauny's major work on medieval West Africa (*see* 1954).

655
Pérès, Henri. Relations entre le Tafilelt et le Soudan à travers le Sahara du XIIe au XIVe siècle. *In* Mélanges de géographie et d'orientalisme offerts à E.-F. Gautier, professeur honoraire à la Faculté des lettres d'Alger. Tours, Arrault, 1937. p. 410–414. G62.M4

Excerpts from, and comments on, the *Riḥlah* of Ibn Ḥammūyah al-Sarahsī and other writings about the attempts of the governors of Sijilmāsah and the rulers of Ghana to iron out difficulties and create a favorable climate for the development of trade contacts.

656
Person, Yves. Le Moyen Niger au XVe siècle d'après les documents européens. NA, no 78, avril 1958: 45–47. DT1.I513, 1958

The history of the Sudan is reported by a number of Arab writers. There is, however, a dearth of European sources on the Niger during the 15th century. Drawing on Cá da Mosto, Malfante, Diego Gomez, and others, Person attempts to locate the cities mentioned and traces historical developments at the end of the Mande Empire.

657
Quatremère. Notice d'un manuscrit arabe contenant la description de l'Afrique. *In* Notices et extraits des manuscrits de la Bibliothèque du roi et autres bibliothèques, t. 12, 1. partie; Paris. 1831. p. 437–667. Z6620.F8P2, 1831

Comments on and translation of a manuscript missing its first pages and conclusion. It appears to be an incomplete version of al-Bakrī's *Description de l'Afrique septentrionale* (*see* 584).

658
Semonin, Paul. The Almoravid movement in the Western Sudan; a review of the evidence. *In* Historical Society of Ghana. Transactions. v. 7, pt. 1; Legon, 1964. p. 42–59. DT510.A1H55, v. 7

Using the words of Ambrosio Huici Miranda on *Kitāb al-Bayān al-Mughrib fī Akhbār al-Maghrib wa-al-Andalus* by Ibn 'Idhārī (1312), Semonin reviews the sources for the history of the Almoravid movement during its Saharan phase.

659
Shelton, Austin S. The problem of griot interpretation and the actual causes of war in Sondjata. Présence africaine, nouv. sér., no 66, 2. trimestre 1968: 145–152. GN645.P74, 1968

The estimation of griot repertories as valid sources of historical information has fluctuated greatly. Shelton reviews the various authorities and examines the case of the Kouyaté griots of the Keita branch in their reports of Sundiata Keita's reign.

660
Shu'ayrah, Muḥammad 'Abd al-Hādī. al-Murābiṭūn, tārīkhuhum al-siyāsī, 430–539 A.H. [The Almoravids, their political history, 430–539 A.H.] [Cairo] Maktabat al-Qāhirah al-ḥadīthah [1969] 166 p. maps. DT199.S55

661
Slane, W. MacGukin de. Conquête du Soudan par les Marocains en l'an 999 (1590 de J.-C.) Récits extrait de l'ouvrage d'un historien arabe. Revue africaine, t. 1, no 1, 1856: 287–298. DT271.R4, 1856

Excerpts from a work by Aḥmad Bābā al-Tinbuqtī on the conquest of the Sudan by Juder. Of note is the comment on Aḥmad Bābā (p. 296–297), which reveals the contempt of some French scholars of the 1850's for sub-Saharan erudites.

662
Stępniewska, Barbara. Rola pielgrzymzk z Sudanu Zachodniego do Mekki w XIII/XVI v. [Le rôle des pèlerinages du Soudan occidentale à la Mecque au XIIIe et au XVIe s.] Przeglad historyczny, t. 60, zecz. 2, 1969: 257–269. DK401.P915, v. 60

French summary supplied.

663
———Rozpowszechnianie sie islamu w Sudanie Zachodnim od XII do XVI wieku. [The spread of Islam in the western Sudan from the 12th to the 16th century] Wrocław, Zakład Narodowy im. Ossolińskich, 1972. 119 p. BP64.S8S73

At head of title: Polska Akademia Nauk. Instytut Historii.

Summary in French.

664
Ṭarkhān, Ibrāhīm 'Alī. Dawlat Mālī al-Islāmīyah; Dirāsāt fī al-tārīkh al-qawmī al-Ifrīqī. [The Islamic state of Mali; studies in African national history] [Cairo] al-Hay'ah al-Miṣrīyah al-'Āmmah lil-kitāb, 1973. 213 p. illus. DT532.2.T37

665
———Dirāsāt fī al-Tārīkh al-qawmī al-Ifrīqī: Qiyām imbirātūrīyat Mālī al-Islāmīyah. [Studies in African national history: The rise of the Islamic empire of Mali] *In* Khartoum. Jāmi'at al-Qāhirah fī-al-Khartūm. Majallat Jāmi'at al-Qāhirah fī-al-Khartūm, v. 1, 1970: 1–40 DLC

Before relating the history of the Mali Empire in great detail, Professor Ṭarkhān devotes part of his article to the sources of African history for this period. He lists oral traditions; Greek and Roman sources; Islamic Arabic sources, which he divides into writings of Muslims foreign to the area and indigenous Muslim writers; European sources; and archeological discoveries. The problem of identifying African names cited in Arabic sources is also noted.

666
———Ghānah fī al-'Uṣūr al-Wusṭā. [Ghana in the Middle Ages] *In* Cairo. al-Jam'īyah al-Miṣrīyah lil-dirāsāt al-tārīkhīyah. al-Majallah al-tārīkhīyah al-Miṣrīyah, v. 13, 1965: 25–89.
DT77.J28, v. 13 Orien Arab

Substantial study of the Ghana Empire, including both an historical narrative and a detailed description of the social, political, and commercial structures of the state. In a final section, Ṭarkhān provides his interpretations as to why Nkrumah's Ghana adopted the name of the medieval empire.

667
———Imbirātūrīyat Ghānah al-Islāmīyah. [The Muslim empire of Ghana] [Cairo] al-Hay'ah al-Miṣrīyah al-'Āmmah lil-ta'līf wa-al-nashr, 1970. 106 p. illus., maps (al-Maktabah al-'Arabīyah, 105. al-Ta'līf, 70. al-Tārīkh, 9.) DT532.15.T37

At head of title: al-Jumhūrīyah al-'Arabīyah al-Muttaḥidah. Wizārat al-Thaqāfah.

668
Tarverdova, Ekaterina Astvatsaturovna. Rasprostranenie islama v Zapadnoĭ Afrike, XI–XVI vv. [The diffusion of Islam in West Africa, 11th-16th century] Moskva, Nauka; Glav. red. bostochnoi lit-ry, 1967. 85, [3] p. BP64.A4W37

At head of title: Akademiiâ nauk SSSR. Institut Afriki E. A. Tarverdova.

669
Triaud, Jean-Louis, Islam et sociétés soudanaises au Moyen âge; étude historique. Paris, Collège de France, Laboratoire d'anthropologie sociale, 1973. 238 p. maps (part fold.) (Recherches voltaïques, 16) DT553.U7A26, no. 16
BP64.A1

670
———Quelques remarques sur l'Islamisation du Mali des origines à 1300. BIFAN, t. 30, oct. 1968: 1329–1352. DT1.I5123, v. 30

A reevaluation of the beginnings of Islam in the Mali Empire. Triaud argues that a thorough reading of Arabic sources and new translations of medieval writings show that the first pilgrimage of a Mali sovereign, between 1260 and 1277, established a solid link between the Muslim world and Mali, based on common interests of religion and trade.

671
Tucci, Raffaele di. Nuovi documenti e notizie sul genovese Antonio Malfante il primo viagiatore europeo nell'Africa occidentale (1447). *In* Società geografica italiana, *Rome.* Bolletino, anno 11, marzo 1934: 179–210. G17.S67, v. 11

672
Vuillet, J. Essai d'interpretation des traditions legendaires sur les origines des vieux empires soudanais. Académie des sciences coloniales. Comptes rendus des séances mensuels, t. 10, avril 1950: 268–287. DLC Micro: 04038

673
el-Wakkad, Mahmoud. Qissatu Salaga Tarikhu Gonja: the story of Salaga and the history of Gonja. Ghana notes and queries, no. 3, Sept./Dec. 1961: 8–31; no. 4, Jan./June 1962: 6–25.
DT510.A1H553, 1961

Text and translation of "a composite work consisting of: an account of the campaigns of Japka (*Tarikhu Gonja*); and a history of Salaga (*Qissatu Salga*)," reporting the history of northern Ghana as reflected in the city of Salaga and the kingdom of Gonja.

674
Wilks, Ivor. A note on the chronology, and origins, of the Gonja kings. Ghana notes and queries, no. 8, Jan. 1966: 26–28. DLC

Mandingo influence in Gonja, northern Ghana, is better known since the location of *Aṣl al-Wanghariyyīn,* by 'Abd al-Raḥmān ibn Muḥammad ibn Ibrāhīm ibn Muḥammad Qithīmah al-Wangharī, written in Kano in 1650–51. Bringing together available information, Wilks compiled a list of Gonja kings as well as data on the origins of the dynasty.

675
Wingfield, R. J. The story of Old Ghana, Melle & Songhai. Cambridge [Eng.] Cambridge University Press, 1957. 59 p. DT471.W75

676
Zakī, 'Abd al-Raḥmān. Imbirāṭūrīyah Ifrīqīyah fī al-'aṣr al-wasīt. [An African empire in the Middle Ages] al-Majallah, no. 47, Oct. 1960: 42–48. AP95.A6M25, 1960 Orien Arab

Description of Ghana drawn from Arabic sources such as al-Idrīsī, Maḥmūd Ka'tī, Ibn Ḥawqal, Ibn Khaldūn, and al-Bakrī. Zakī also outlines the rise of the Almoravid movement, its clash with Ghana, and the Islamization of the Sudanic belt.

677
Ziadeh, Nicola A. Ruwwād al-Sharq al-'Arabī fī al-'Uṣūr al-Wusṭā. [Explorers of the Arab East in the Middle Ages] [Cairo?] 1943. 230 p. DS46.Z5

"Hadīyat al-Muqtaṭaf al-Sanawīyah [Annual Present of the Muqtataf]."

Languages & Linguistics

678
Delafosse, Maurice. Mots soudanais du Moyen-Age. *In* Société de linguistique de Paris. Mémoire, t. 18, 4. fasc., 1913: 281–288. P12.S45, v. 18

679
Kaké, Ibrahima Baba. Glossaire critique des expressions géographiques concernant le pays des noirs d'aprés les sources de langue arabe du milieu du VIIIe à la fin du XIIIe siècle. Paris, Présence africaine, 1965. 165 p. illus. IEN

680
Lewicki, Tadeuz. A propos du nom de l'oasis de Koufra chez les géographes arabes du XIe et du XIIe siècle. JAH, v. 6, no. 3, 1965: 295–306. DT1.J65, v. 6

681
Mauny, Raymond. Découverte à Gao d'un fragment de poterie émaillée du moyen-âge musulman. Hespéris, t. 39, 3./4. trimestres, 1952: 514–516. illus. DT181.H4, v. 39

Note on the discovery of an enameled pottery fragment found at Sané. Mauny believes that it could be of Spanish origin dating back to the 12th century.

681a
Terrasse, Henri. Sur des tessons de poterie vernissée et peinte trouvés à Teghaza. BCAOF, t. 21, oct./déc. 1938: 520–523. illus. DT521.C6, v. 21

Illustrated article on pottery fragments found at Teghaza, the medieval salt mine near Araouane. The author suggests that these remains might have come from Fès and date from the 16th and 17th centuries, coinciding with the Moroccan Saadian presence at the "coaling station" of the Sahara.

Numismatics

682
Daaku, K. Yeboa. Pre-European currencies of West Africa and Western Sudan. Ghana notes and queries, no. 2, May-Aug. 1961: 12–14. DLC

683
Latruffe, J. Au sujet d'une pièce d'or millenaire trouvée à Gao. NA, no 60, oct. 1953: 102–103. DT1.I513, 1953

Gao was a major trade center during the medieval period. Latruffe reports on a golden dinar found in Old Gao and probably minted in Sijilmāsah under the Fatimite al-Mu'izz lidīn-Illāh between 952 and 975.

684
al-Maqrīzī, Aḥmad ibn 'Alī. al-Nuqūd al-Islāmīyah al-musammā bi-shudhūr al-'uqūd fī zikr al-nuqūd. [Islamic coins called fragments of necklaces about monies] Edited with additions by Muḥammad al-Sayyid 'Alī Baḥr al-'ulūm. al-Ṭab'ah 5. al-Najaf, al-maktabah al-Ḥaydarīyah, 1967. 318 p. CJ3421.M3 1967 Orien Arab

685
Mauny, Raymond. Monnaies anciennes d'Afrique Occidentale. NA, no 42, avril 1949: 60–61. DT1.I513, 1949

Politics

686
Bell, Nawal Marcos. The age of Mansa Musa of Mali: problems in succession and chronology. The International journal of African history, v. 5, no. 2, 1972: 221–234. DLC

686a
Bovill, E. W. Mohammed el Maghili. *In* African Society. Journal, v. 34, Jan. 1935: 27–31.

DT1.R62, v. 34

Brief note on the discovery and first translation of al-Maghīlī's *Tāj al-dīn fīmā yajib 'alā al-mūlūk*, better known as *The Obligations of Princes.*

687

Cissoko, Sékéné Mody. The century of Kankou Moussa. Présence africaine, no 52, oct./déc. 1964: 94–103. GN645.P74, 1964

Description of social, political, and economic structures under the Malian ruler.

688

Diagne, Pathé. Pouvoir politique traditionnel en Afrique occidentale, essai su les institutions politiques précoloniales. Paris, Présence africaine, 1965. 295 p. maps. DT471.D5

689

Diop, Cheikh Anta. L'Afrique noire pré-coloniale; étude comparée des systemes politiques et sociaux de l'Europe et de l'Afrique noire, de l'antiquité à la formation des états modernes. Paris, Présence africaine [1960] 213 p. illus. (part col.), maps. (Collection Présence africaine) DT25.D5

690

Egwuonwu, Alex N. Islamic influences on the ancient Sudanese empires. The African historian, v. 1, March 1965: 25–30. DLC

691

Lloyd, P. C. The political development of West African kingdoms: review article. JAH, v. 9, no. 2, 1968: 319–329. DT1.J65, v. 9

691a

M'Baye, Ravane, *al-Hajj, trans.* and *ed.* Un aperçu de l'Islam songhay ou réponses d'Al-Maghîlî aux questions posées par Askia El-Hadj Muhammad, Empereur de Gao. BIFAN, t. 34, avril 1972: 237–267. DT1.I5123, v. 34

When Askiya Muḥammad (1493–1528) usurped, the Songhay throne, he relied upon the ulemas for his support and, consequently, during his reign Islam gained a greater position than under Sonni 'Alī. Muḥammad ibn 'Abd al-Karīm al-Maghīlī, who visited Gao (1497–1502), advised Muḥammad on the proper Muslim way to govern the empire. In this translation of two manuscripts located in the Fonds Brévié (Cahiers no 22–23), he answers seven questions forwarded by the Songhay monarch. These queries range from an opinion on Sonni 'Alī to succession systems according to the Shari'a.

692

Ol'derogge, Dimitriĭ A. Die Geselschaftserdnung Songhais in 15. und 16. Jahrhundert. *In* Lukas, Johannes, *ed.* Afrikanische Studien. Berlin, Akademie-Verlag, 1955. (Deutsche Akademie des Wissenschaften zu Berlin. Institut für Orientforschung veröffentlichung Nr 26) p. 243–251. illus. PL8003.L8

693

Sharevskaia, b. I. O kharaktere vlasti vozhdei i narodov tropicheskoi Afriki v dokolonial'nyi period. [Characteristics of the authority of the chief among peoples of tropical Africa in the pre-colonial period] Sovetskaîa etnografiîa, 1, 1962: 67–71. GN1.S65, 1962

Tables of contents and summaries also in French.

694

Tymowski, Michał. Les domaines des princes du Songhay (Soudan occidental). Comparaison avec la grande propriété foncière en Europe au début de l'époque féodale. Annales; économies, sociétés, civilisations, 25. année, nov./déc. 1970: 1637–1658. AP20.A58, v. 25

Sects

695

Lewicki, Tadeuz. Les commerçants Ibadites nord-africains dans le Soudan au Moyen-Âge. *In* International Congress of Anthropological and Ethnological Sciences, *7th, Moscow, 1964.* VII [i.e. Sed'moĭ] Mezhdunarodnyĭ kongress anthropologischeskikh i etnografischeskikh nauk, Moskva (3–10 Avg. 1964) [Trudi] Moscow, Nauk (1968–71), v. 2, 1963: 35–38. GN3.I39 1964r

Professor Lewicki, of the University of Krakow, has studied extensively the Ibadi sect of the Saharan oases. In this investigation based on Arabic documents, he examines in great detail relations between the Berber Ibadi state of Tahert (present-day Tiaret, southeast of Algiers) and the kingdoms of the Western Sudan during the eighth and ninth centuries. He suggests that Ibadi traders started trading with Ghana, under the Rustumite dynasty, as early as the eighth century.

696

———L'état nord africain de Tahert et ses relations avec le Soudan occidental à la fin du VIIIe et au IXe siècle. CEA, v. 2, 4. cahier, 1962: 513–535. DT1.C3, v. 2

697
———Quelques extraits inédits relatifs aux voyages des commerçants et des missionnaires ibadites nord-africains au pays du Soudan occidental au Moyen-Âge. Folia Orientalia, t. 2, pts. 1–2, 1960: 1–28. PJ9.F6, v. 2

Excerpts of Ibadi literature (11th and 12th centuries) of medieval West Africa. Professor Lewicki examines three works on the relations of Ibadi traders with the Sudanie region: *Kitā al-Sīrah wa-Akhbār al-a'immah,* by Abū Zakarīya Yaḥya ibn Abī Bakr al-Warjalāni, *Kitab al-Siyar* by Abū al-Rabi Sulaymān ibn 'Abd al-Salām al-Wisyānī, and the anonymous *Siyar al-Mashāyikh.*

698
———Un royaume ibadite peu connu: l'Etat des Banu Massala (IXe s.). Rocznik Orientalistyczny, t. 31, zesz. 2, 1968: 7–14. PJ9.R6, v. 31

English summary in *Africana Bulletin,* v. 12, 1970: 98–99 (DT199.P6A65).

699
———Traits d'histoire du commerce transsaharien. Marchands et missionnaires ibadites en [sic] Soudan occidental et central au cours des VIII–XII siècles. Etnografia polska, t. 8, no. 2, 1964: 291–311. GN585.P6E8, v. 8

Using Ibadi sources, Lewicki probes into trade relations between members of the sect and Central and Western Sudan. He discusses the following problems: relations between Tahert, capital of the Rustumite imams, with the Western Sudan (end of the eighth to early ninth century); information on North African Ibadi traders' activities in Ghana and Awdaghost (10th-11th century); trade relations with Tadmekka; and trade relations between Ibadis from Tripolitania and the Fezzan with Kanem (ninth-10th century).

700
Mu'ammar, 'Alī Yaḥyā. al-Ibāḍīyah fī Mawkib al-tārīkh. [The Ibadi movement in the procession of history] Cairo, Maktabat wahbah [1964] 2 v. in 3. BP195.I3M8 Orien Arab

Society & Culture

701
Cherbonneau, M. A. Essai sur la littérature arabe au Soudan, d'après le Tekmilet ed-dibadj d'Ahmed-Baba le Tombouctien. Paris, 1866.

Source: Joucla 333.

702
Kamian, Bakari. L'Afrique occidentale précoloniale et le fait urbain. Présence africaine, no 22, oct./nov. 1958: 76–80. GN645.P74, 1958

703
Kubbel', Lev Evgen'evich. On the history of social relations in the West Sudan in the 8th to the 16th centuries. *In* Africa in Soviet studies. Moscow, Nauka Pub. House, Central Dept. of Oriental Literature, 1968. p. 109–128. DT19.9.R9A63

704
Lewicki, Tadeuz. Animal husbandry among medieval agricultural people of Western and Middle Sudan (according to Arab sources). Acta ethnographica, t. 14, 1965: 165–178. GN1.A25, v. 14

705
———Pożywienie ludności zachodniej Afryki w Sredniowieczu Według źródeł Arabskich. [West African food in the Middle Ages according to Arab sources]. Etnografia Polska, t. 7, 1963: 31–191. GN585.P6E8, v. 7

706
———West African food in the Middle Ages: according to Arabic sources. With the assistance of Marion Johnson. London, Cambridge University Press, 1974. xv, 262 p. map. TX360.A3L4913

Translation from the Polish by Marianne Abrahamowicz.

707
Modat, *Colonel.* La société berbère mauritanienne à la fin du XIe siècle. BCAOF, t. 4, oct./déc. 1921: 659–666. DT521.C6, v. 4

708
Stępniewska, Barbara. Portée sociale de l'Islam au Soudan Occidental, aux XIVe-XVIe s. Africana bulletin, t. 14, 1971: 35–58. DT19.9.P6A65, v. 14

Studying the impact of Islam on the societies of the 14th and 15th centuries, the author looks at a number of variables such as commerce, handicrafts, agriculture, and religion and attempts to determine how Islam permeated them. With the rise of an indigenous class of marabouts, animistic practices were integrated in a flexible Islam, resulting in a symbiotic relationship between the two faiths.

Trade

709
Brett, Michael. Ifriqiya as a market for Saharan trade from the tenth to the twelfth century A.D. JAH, v. 10, no. 3, 1969: 347–364. DT1.J65, v. 10

Ever since Ibn Khaldūn stated that the Arab tribes of Banū Hilāl and Sulaym had fallen on North Africa "like a swarm of locusts," the common belief has been that Ifrīqiyah—eastern Maghreb—succumbed to anarchy and poverty from 1050 onward. In a well-constructed essay, Brett refutes the idea, suggesting that nomadic activity was symptomatic rather than causative of the turmoil.

710
Levtzion, Nehemia. Ibn Ḥawqal, the cheque, and Awdaghost. JAH, v. 9, no. 2, 1968: 223–233. DT1.J65, v. 9

Ibn Ḥawqal is considered by most scholars as a reliable authority on the Western Sudan, as he is reported to have visited Awdaghost. Levtzion probes into the Arab traveler's writings—including the reference to a check for 42,000 dinars—and "casts some doubts" on Ibn Ḥawqal's visit to the Mauritanian trade center, also questioning the source, whether north or south of the Sahara, of Ibn Ḥawqal's information.

711
Lombard, M. Les bases monétaires d'une suprématie économique. L'or musulman du VIIe au XIe siècle. Annales; économies, sociétés, civilisations, 2. année, avril/juin 1947: 143–160.

712
Małowist, Marian. Le commerce d'or et d'esclaves au Soudan occidental. Africana bulletin, t. 4, 1966: 49–72. DT19.9.P6A65, v. 4

Gold and slaves were two of the major "items" of the trans-Saharan trade during the medieval period. Małowist outlines the role played by both in the economies of the Western Sudan, Europe, and the Middle East. This thorough essay is part of chapter 2 of *Wielkie państwa Sudanu Zachodniego w późnym średniowieczu* [The Great States of the Western Sudan During the Early Middle Ages] published in Warsaw in 1964 and, to our knowledge, not yet translated (*see* 634).

713
———Quelques observations sur le commerce de l'or dans le Soudan occidental au Moyen-Âge. Annales; économies, sociétés, civilisations, 25. année, nov./déc. 1970: 1630–1637. AP20.A58, v. 25

714
Meillassoux, Claude. Le commerce précolonial et le développement de l'esclavage à Gūbu du Sahel (Mali). L'homme et la société, no 15, janv. fév. mars 1970: 147–158. HM3.H6, 1970

See also 2420.

715
———L'économie des échanges précoloniaux en pays gouro. CEA, v. 3, 4. cahier, 1963: 551–576. DT1.C3, v. 3

716
Tymowski, Michał. Le Niger, voie de communication des grands états du Soudan occidental jusqu'à la fin du XVIe siècle. Africana bulletin, t. 6, 1967: 73–95. DT19.9.P6A65, v. 6

The Niger River played a major role in the empires of the Western Sudan. As a link between the various urban centers and a channel for transportation, the Niger was an instrument of economic and political cohesion. Tymowski reviews the social, trade, and military structures which developed along the river and were sustained by it.

1600–1850

CENTRAL REGION

History

717
Carniaux, M. Le mariage chez les nomades du Bahr el-Ghazal (Tchad). Encyclopédie mensuelle d'outre-mer, t. 4, fév. 1954: 68–69.
JV1801.E5, v. 4

718
Davidson, Basil. From Kanem to Bornu (Empires of Old Africa, 6). West African review, v. 33, Sept. 1962: 20–24, 59. DT491.W47, v. 33

719
Derendinger, *Colonel.* Traduction d'un texte baghirmien. JOSAF, t. 2, fasc. 2, 1932: 147–151.
DT1.S65, v. 2

Transliteration and word-by-word translation of a Baguirmi text on the origins of the Baguirmi Empire, established in the 16th century and subjugated by the Waday in 1808.

720
Ellison, David. A Turk in Bornu. Did Evliya Celebi, the Turkish traveler, ever reach Bornu? Nigeria magazine, no. 11, Apr. 1969: 399–400.
DT515.N47, 1969

Detective work concerning the possibility that the author of the *Siyāhat-nāme* could have visited Bornu. Ellison, using the list of "useful words" of Çelebi, offers a tentative answer to the question. *See also* 844.

721
Fọlayan, Kọla. Tripoli-Bornu political relations, 1817–1825. JHSN, v. 4, June 1971: 463–476.
DT515.A2H5, v. 4

Refuting a statement by A. Adu Boahen that the rulers of Tripoli and Bornu were "on very intimate terms," Fọlayan illustrates the fluctuations of Tripoli-Bornu relations, suggesting that "rather, beneath the facade of a seeming cordiality, there was, between Tripoli and Bornu in this period, the reality of an atmosphere charged with fear, distrust, tension, diplomatic rumpus, secret military preparations, and all the ingredients that would go together to make for a state of belligerency."

722
Hornemann, Friedrich K. The journal of Frederick Horneman's travels, from Cairo to Mourzouk, the capital of the kingdom of Fezzan, in Africa, in the years 1797–8. London, G. and W. Nicol, 1802. 195 (i.e. 196) p. 3 maps (2 fold.) incl. front.
DT219.H79

723
La Roncière, Charles de. Une histoire de Bornou au XVIIe siècle par un chirurgien français captif à Tripoli. Revue de l'histoire des colonies françaises, t. 7, 3. trimestre, 1919: 73–77. JV1801.R4, v. 7

Excerpts of a "relation" about Bornu by a French marine surgeon taken prisoner in 1668. He was assigned to the Pasha 'Uthmān of Tripoli where he wrote "l'histoire chronologique du royaume de Tripoly" (Bibliothèque nationale, MS Franc. 12220, fol. 87 Ve) and a "discours historique de l'estat du royaume de Borno" (fol. 317) in which he describes what he saw and heard about Bornu in the Pasha's palace. He reports that Muhammad, the pasha of Tripoli, in 1636 had sent a group of young European renegades to the Bornu court "avec des mousquets et des cimeterres incrustés de pierreries."

724
Lavers, John E. Islam in the Bornu caliphate: a survey [1500–1800] Odū, no. 5, Apr. 1971: 27–53.
DT515.A2O32, 1971

725
Martin, Bradford G. Kanem, Bornu and the Fazzan: notes on the political history of a trade route. JAH, v. 10, no. 1, 1969: 15–27.
DT1.J65, v. 10

726
———Maî Idrîs of Bornu and the Ottoman Turks, 1576–78. International journal of Middle Eastern studies, v. 3, Oct. 1972: 470–490. DLC

Information on relations between the Ottoman Empire and kingdoms south of the Sahara, such as Kanem and later Bornu, is still sketchy. Having investigated both Turkish and Arabic sources, Martin has based this history of the contacts primarily on sources reproduced here: two versions of a letter of the Porte to Maī Idrīs of Bornu written in the conservative Mameluke style, and a document in Turkish containing instructions from the Porte addressed to the Beylerbeyi of Tunis, found in the *Defter-i-ahkâm-i-mühimme-i-Divân-i-hümâyun* [Register of Important Decrees of the Imperial Divan].

727
Mohammadou, Eldridge. Introduction historique à l'étude des sociétés du Nord-Cameroun. Abbia, no 12/13, mars/juin 1966: 233–271. AP9.A24, 1966
The colonial phase of African history is only one of the various acculturation periods which the continent experienced. In this study, based on his research in oral traditions, Mohammadou attempts to determine the nature, direction, and magnitude of social change brought about by the Fulbe in northern Cameroon. He then analyzes the history, society, and political entities which developed in the area before the colonial period.

728
Mouchet, J. Note sur la conversion à l'Islamisme, en 1715, de la tribu Wandala. *In* Société d'études camerounaises. Bulletin, no 15–16, Sept./Dec. 1946: 105–108. DT561.S6, 1946
Oral tradition on the conversion of the Wandala tribe in northern Cameroon as related to Mouchet by Liman Umate, Imam of the Sultan. According to that tradition, the Wandala became Muslim about 1715 with the conversion of "May Bukar Haji" at the hand of "Mohaman Guro," the ancestor of Liman Umate.

729
Palmer, *Sir* Herbert R. Two Sudanese manuscripts of the seventeenth century. BSOAS, v. 5, pt. 3, 1939: 541–560. PJ3.L6, v. 5
Translation of two manuscripts from Bornu. The first is an account of Mai 'Ali ibn al-Ḥājj 'Umar's court at N'gazaragamu, and the second—of which a facsimile is given—is a mahram by Mai Dunama ibn 'Alī dated 1694.

730
———Sudanese memoirs: being translations of a number of Arabic manuscripts relating to the Central and Western Sudan. London, Cass, 1967. 3 v. in 1 [373 p. various pagings] 7 plates (incl. 2 fold.), illus., geneal. tables, maps. (Cass library of African studies. General studies, no. 47) DT108.A1P3 1967
First edition originally published in three volumes, Lagos, 1928.
Translation of about 70 manuscripts concerning the history of the Sudanic belt that were brought together early in the 20th century by an administrator and scholar empathically interested in the area he administered.

731
Rodinson, Maxime, *and* J. P. Lebeuf. L'origine et les souverains du Mandara. BIFAN, t. 18, janv./avril 1956: 227–255. DT1.I5123, v. 18
Text, translation of, and commentaries on two Arabic manuscripts from the Chad region on the origins of the sultans of Mandara. The text appeared originally in H. R. Palmer's *Sudanese Memoirs* under the title "Mandara Chronicle." Appended is a genealogical list of rulers and a substantial bibliography.

EASTERN REGION

Cities

732
Gray, *Sir* John M. A French account of Kilwa at the end of the 18th century. TNR, no. 63, Sept. 1964: 224–228. DT436.T3, 1964

733
Kirkman, James S. The arab city of Gedi; excavations at the great mosque, architecture and finds. [London] Oxford University Press, 1954. 197 p. illus. DT434.E2K5
At head of title: Royal National Parks of Kenya. Gedi National Park.

734
———Gedi, the palace. The Hague, Mouton, 1963. 80, [20] p. illus., 16 plates. (Studies in African history, 1) DT434.E29G4

735
———The great pillars of Malindi and Manbrui. Oriental art, n.s., v. 4, 1958: 55–67. N8.O75, n.s., v. 4

736
———The history of the coast of East Africa up to 1700. *In* M. Posnansky, *ed.* Prelude to East African history. London, Oxford University Press, 1966. p. 105–124. DT25.E15 1962a

737
Knappert, Jan. The chronicle of Mombasa. Swahili, no. 34, pt. 2, 1964: 21–27. PL8701.E2, 1964

History

738
'Abd al-Jalīl, al-Shāṭir Busaylī. Tārīkh wa-Ḥaḍārāt al-Sūdān al-Sharqī wa-al-Awsaṭ min al-qarn al sābi' 'ashar ilā al-qarn al-tāsi' 'ashar lil mīlād. [History and civilizations of Eastern and Central Sudan from the 17th to the 19th century, A.D.] [Cairo] al-Hay'ah al-Miṣrīyah al-'āmah lil-kitāb, 1972. 515 p. maps. (al-Maktabah al-'Arabīyah, 120)
DT108.1.A58 Orien Arab

This study analyzes political and social developments in the Central Nile Basin. 'Abd al-Jalīl draws on Arabic as well as European sources to present an all-encompassing picture of the region under consideration.

739
'Abd al-Majīd, Amīn 'Abd al-Majīd. al-Tarbiyah fī al-Sūdān min awwal al-qarn al-sādis 'ashar ilā nihāyat al-qarn al-thāmin 'ashar wa al-usus al-nafsīyah wa-al-ijtimā'īyah al-latī qāmat 'alayhā. [Education in the Sudan from the beginning of the sixth century to the end of the 18th century and its psychological and social bases] Cairo, al-Maṭba'ah al-Amīrīyah, 1949. 3 v. DLC

740
Abir, Mordechai. Ethiopia: the era of the princes; the challenge of Islam and re-unification of the Christian Empire, 1769–1855. New York, Praeger [1968] 208 p. illus., maps. DT384.A55 1968

History of the confrontation between Islam and Christianity and the consolidation, with the rise of the Shoa Kingdom, of the Christian Empire under Teodros.

741
Abū al-Rūs, Khālid. Riwāyat kharāb sūbā. [Khartoum, al-Majlis al-qawmī li-ri'āyat al-ādāb wa-al-funūn, 1971] 76 p. port. DLC

Modern Arabic play in Sudanese dialect verse form, based on historical anecdotes concerning disputes between Arabs and Nubians during the early 16th century.

742
Aḥmad, Ḥasab Allāh Muḥammad. Qiṣṣat al-ḥaḍārah fī al-Sūdān; al-fatrah min 3400 q.m. ilā 1900 mīlādīyah. [The story of civilization in the Sudan; the period from 3400 B.C. to 1900 A.D.] [Cairo, Dār yūlyū lil-tarjamah wa-al-nashr, 1966] 402 p. map, plates. DT108.A498 Orien Arab

Aḥmad, a founding member of the Society for the Renaissance of Sudanese History (1964) while a student at the Azhar University, wrote this general history of the Sudan. Of interest is the part on Islam and its impact on the political and social life of the area.

743
Arkell, Anthony J. A history of the Sudan: from the earliest times to 1821. With a foreword by Harold MacMichael. [2d ed., rev., London] University of London, Athlone Press, 1961. 252 p. illus. DT108.1.A7 1961

744
Basset, René M. J., *ed.* Histoire de la conquête de l'Abyssinie (XVIe siècle) par Chihab ed-Din Ahmed ben 'Abd el-Qâder surnommé Arab-Faqih. Paris, E. Leroux, 1897. 504 p. (Publications de l'Ecole des lettres d'Alger. Bulletin de correspondance africaine, v. 20, fasc. 1 and 2) AS651.A6, v. 20

Translation of *The History of the Conquest of Ethiopia* by Shihāb al-Dīn Aḥmad ibn 'Abd al-Qādir Salīm, also known as 'Arab Faqīh. *See also* 766.

745
Berg, Fred J. The Swahili community of Mombasa, 1500–1900. JAH, v. 9, no. 1, 1968: 35–56.
DT1.J65, v. 9

746
Cerulli, Enrico. Gli Emiri di Harar dal secolo XVI alla conquista Egiziana, 1875. Rassegna di studi Etiopici, anno 2., 1942: 3–20. DT371.R3, v. 2

747
———L'Islam di ieri e di oggi. Roma, Istituto per l'Oriente, 1971. 497 p. plates (Pubblicazioni dell'Istituto per l'Oriente, n. 64) BP64.E8C47

In French or Italian.

One section of this general study of Islam is "Islam in Ethiopia" (p. 99–395), including the following articles: Islam in East Africa; Ethiopian Islam; Arabic Documents for the History of Ethiopia; The Sultan of the Shoa in the 13th Century According to a New Historical Document; Amharic Songs of the Muslims of Abyssinia; Medieval Ethiopia in Some Excerpts of Arab Writings; Harar, Muslim Center in Ethiopia; The Sidamo and the Muslim State of Bali; The Emirs of Harar From the 16th Century to the Egyptian Conquest

(1875) (*see also* 746); The End of the Harar Emirate According to New Historical Documents.
Another essay in a section on "Islam in Persia" deals with Persian arts and techniques in East Africa (p. 457–469).

748
Chittick, H. Neville. The early history of Kilwa Kivinje. Azania, v. 4, 1969: 153–159.
DT365.3.A94, v. 4
Translation of the "Chronicle of the Coastal City" from C. Velten's *Prosa und Poesie der Suaheli* (p. 253–264).

749
———Two traditions about the early history of Kilwa. Azania, v. 3, 1968: 197–200.
DT365.3.A94, v. 3
Report on oral traditions regarding the beginnings of Kilwa.

750
Coupland, *Sir* Reginald. East Africa and its invaders, from the earliest times to the death of Seyyid Said in 1856. New York, Russell & Russell, 1965. 584 p. maps. DT365.C58 1965
First published in 1938.

751
Ferry, Robert. Quelques hypothèses sur les origines des conquêtes musulmanes en Abyssinie au XVIe siècle. CEA, v. 2, 1. cahier, 1961: 24–36.
DT1.C3, v. 2

752
Foster, William, *comp.* The Red Sea and adjacent countries at the close of the seventeenth century as described by Joseph Pitts, William Daniel, and Charles J. Poncet. Nendeln, Liechtenstein, Kraus Reprint, 1967. 192 p. 2 facsims., 2 maps (1 fold.), fold. plate. (Work issued by the Hakluyt Society, 2d ser., no. 100 G161.H23, 2d ser., no. 100
Reprint of the 1949 edition.

753
Freeman-Grenville, G. S. P., *comp.* The East African coast; select documents from the first to the earlier nineteenth century. Oxford, Clarendon Press, 1962. 314 p. DT365.F7

754
Froelich, J. C. Les Arabes en Afrique de l'Est. Revue francaise d'études politiques africaines, no 27, mars 1968: 26–71. DT1.R4, 1968

755
Garlake, Peter S. The early Islamic architecture of the East African coast. Nairobi, London, Published for the Institute by Oxford University Press, 1966. 207 p. 12 plates, plans, tables, diagrs. (British Institute of History and Archaeology in East Africa. Memoir no. 1) NA1597.E2G3

756
Gray, *Sir* John M. The British in Mombasa, 1824–1826, being the history of Captain Owen's protectorate. London, New York, Macmillan, 1957. 216 p. illus., maps. (Kenya History Society. Transactions, v. 1) DT421.K43, v. 1

757
———History of Zanzibar, from the Middle Ages to 1856. London, Oxford University Press, 1962. 314 p. illus. DT435.G7

758
———The recovery of Kilwa by the Arabs in 1785. TNR, no. 62, Mar. 1964: 20–26. DT436.T3, 1964

759
Haight, Mabel V. J. European powers and South-east Africa: a study of international relations on the South-East coast of Africa, 1796–1856. Rev. ed., London, Routledge & K. Paul, 1967. 368 p. front., maps, tables. DT365.H3 1967

760
al-Ḥamawī, Muḥammad Yāsīn. al-Malāḥ al-ʻArabī Aḥmad ibn Mājid, nāḥiyah majīdah min al-thaqāfah al-baḥrīyah al-ʻArabīyah. [The Arab sailor Ahmad ibn Majid; glorious facets of Arab maritime culture] [Damascus] Maktab al-nashr al-ʻArabī [1947] 39 p. illus. D198.4.A5H3 Orien Arab

761
History of East Africa; the early period. Edited by Roland Oliver and Gervase Mathew. Nairobi, Oxford University Press, 1967 [c1963] 211 p. illus., maps. DT365.H552
"A reprint of the first six chapters of *History of East Africa,* volume I . . . published in 1963."

762
Mondain, G. L'histoire des tribus de l'Imoro au XVIIe siècle d'après un manuscrit historique arabico-malgache. Paris, E. Leroux, 1910. 230 p. (Publications de la Faculté des lettres d'Alger. Bulletin de correspondence africaine, v. 43) AS651.A6, v. 43

763
———Islam in Madagascar. MW, v. 3, July 1913: 257–261. DS36.M7, v. 3
Arabs visited the "Great Isle" as early as the seventh century, followed by a second wave at the beginning of the 18th century. Mondain briefly relates the struggle in the first era between the kingdom of Antalaotra and the Sakalava and the establishment of the kingdom of Boina. He also shows the relative Islamization of the Sakalava.

764
———Note historique sur les manuscrits arabo-malgaches. *In* Académie malgache. Bulletin, v. 30, nouv. sér., 1951–52: 161–166.
DT4H9.M21A35, n.s., v. 30

765
Mus'ad, Muṣṭafā Muḥammad. The downfall of the Christian Nubian kingdoms. SNR, v. 40, 1959: 124–128. DT118.S85, v. 40
The Nubian kingdoms of Nobatia, Maqurra, and Alwa were converted to Christianity A.D. 580. In this short essay, Mus'ad analyzes the downfall of Maqurra and Alwa in the face of Islam's sweep up the Nile during the Mameluke period in Egypt and shows the interaction between Muslim Egypt and the Fung kingdom on one hand and Christian Nubia and Ethiopia on the other.

766
Nerazzini, Cesare, *ed.* La conquista musulmana dell'Etiopia nel secolo XVI. Traduzione d'un manoscritto arabo. Roma, Forzani e c., 1891. 174 p. fold. map. DT384.N44
Translation of *The History of the Conquest of Ethiopia* by Shihāb al-Dīn Aḥmad ibn 'Abd al-Qādir Salīm, also known as 'Arab Faqīh. *See also* 744.

767
Riyāḍ, Zāhir. al-Rawābiṭ bayn al-Ḥabashah wa Miṣr. [Relations between Ethiopia and Egypt] al-Majallah, no. 2, Feb. 1957: 105–108.
AP95.A6M25, 1957 Orien Arab
After analyzing the conflict between the two countries and their supporters. Riyad reviews the conversion of Negus Susenyos (1607–32) to Catholicism, the failure of his policy, and his return to the Coptic Church as background to the cordial relations between Egypt and the Coptic Church since the fourth century.

768
Said-Ruete, Rudolph. Said bin Sultan (1791–1856), ruler of Oman and Zanzibar: his place in the history of Arabia and East Africa. With a foreword by Major-Gen. Sir Percy Cox. London, Alexander-Ouseley [1929] 200 p. front. (port.), plates, facsim., fold. map. DS247.O6S3
First published in 1929.

769
Strandes, Justus. The Portuguese period in East Africa. Translated from the German by Jean F. Wallwork. Edited with topographical notes by J. S. Kirkman. [2d ed.] Nairobi, East African Literature Bureau [1968] 325 p. 4 illus.
DT365.65.S753 1968
Translation of *Die Portugiesenzeit von Deutsch- und Englisch-Ostafrika.*

770
Strelcyn, Stefan. Les chapitres concernant les plantes d'un lexique arabe-éthiopien du XVIe. Rocznik Orientalistyczny, t. 31, zesz. 1, 1968: 7–28.
PJ9.R6, v. 31

771
Trimingham, John S. Islam in East Africa. Oxford, Clarendon Press, 1964. 198 p. maps. BP64.A4E27
According to Trimingham, "The history of Islam in East Africa belongs more to the history of the Indian Ocean than to African history. . . . The history of the interior does not become relevant until the nineteenth century when Islamic penetration began." The study is divided into the following chapters: Historical Background; Features of East African Islam; Islamic Organization; Popular Religion; The Cycle of Personal Life; Islamic Society; The Muslim in an Era of Change. In his conclusion, the author looks at "Islam within the context of the changing Africa of today" to "see what has been the effect of the transforming force of secular civilization upon the Swahili of the coastal civilization and Muslims of recent Islamization." Appended is a glossary-index of Swahili and Arabic words. *See also* his *Islam in East Africa; the Report of a Survey Undertaken in 1961* ([London] published for the World Council of Churches Commission on World Mission and Evangelism by Edinburgh House Press, 1962. 47 p. BP64.A4E28).

Trade

772
Abir, Mordechai. Caravan trade and history in the northern parts of East Africa. Paideuma, v. 14, 1968: 103–120. CB3.3, v. 14

A further exploration of the theory that Islam followed the expansion of trade. Abir traces the development of commercial links with the hinterland of the East Coast, describing the latter's close association with the trade systems of the Indian Ocean and southern Arabia.

773
Chanaiwa, D. Politics and long-distance trade in the Mwene Mutapa Empire during the sixteenth century. International journal of historical studies, v. 5, no. 3, 1972: 424–435. DT1.A226, v. 5

774
Nicholls, Christine S. The Swahili coast; politics, diplomacy and trade on the East African littoral, 1798–1856. New York, Africana Publications Corporation [1971] 419 p. illus. DT432.N5 1971b

775
Pankhurst, Richard K. P. An introduction to the economic history of Ethiopia, from early times to 1800. [London] Lalibela House; distributed by Sidgwick and Johnson, 1961. 454 p. illus. HC591.A3P25

Includes a section on the rise of Islam and other references to trade relations with the Muslim east and north.

SOUTHERN REGION

History

776
Price, T. The "Arabs" of the Zambezi. MW, v. 44, Jan. 1954: 31–37. DS36.M7, v. 44

Goncalo da Silveira, a Jesuit missionary, visited Monomatapa in 1560, where he met Muslim traders involved in the gold and ivory trade. The Boers in their northward treks came across these "Islamic Kaffirs." Remnants of these groups are found among the Shona, and the Amwenye have the vaguest recollection of their peregrinations and show remnants of a Muslim origin.

WESTERN REGION

Archival Material

777
Bivar, A. D. H. Arabic documents of Northern Nigeria. BSOAS, v. 22, pt. 2, 1959: 324–349. illus. PJ3.L6, v. 22

Introduction to the wealth of Arabic material located in Northern Nigeria. Bivar, expressing his deep concern for the preservation of manuscripts, describes three classes of documents: "a. correspondence of the Kanemi Shaikhs (Shehus) of Bornu, and tributary states; b. correspondence of the Fulani Sultanate of Sokoto; c. correspondence of foreign, i.e. non-Nigerian, powers, including that relating to the Sudanese Mahdiya."

778
Bivar, A. D. H., *and* Mervyn Hiskett. The Arabic literature of Nigeria to 1804: a provisional account. BSOAS, v. 25, pt. 1, 1962: 104–148. PJ3.L6, v. 25

"The purpose of this essay is to provide a convenient introduction to the Arabic literature composed in Nigeria and the immediate adjoining areas in the period before the commencement of the Fulani *Jihād*." The authors then present a well-footnoted list of authors, closing with al-Hājj Jibrīl ibn 'Umar, the renowned teacher of Shehu Usuman dan Fodyo.

The beginnings of the extant literature: Abū 'Abd Allāh Muḥammad ibn 'Abd al-Karīm ibn Muḥammad al-Maghīlī al-Tilimsānī, Muḥammad ibn Aḥmad ibn Abī Muḥammad al-Tāzakhtī, known as Aida-Aḥmad, Makhlūf ibn 'Alī ibn Ṣālih al-Bilbālī, Al-'Āqib ibn 'Abd Allāh al-Anṣamunī al-Massūfī, Al-Imām Aḥmad ibn Fartuwa al-Barnāwī, and Shams al-Dīn al-Najīb ibn Muḥammad al-Takiddāwī al-Anṣamunī.

The 17th century: Muḥammad al-Kashināwī, known as Ibn al-Sabbāgh (Hausa: Dan Marina), Abū 'Abd Allāh Muḥammad ibn Masānih ibn Ghumahu ibn Muḥammad ibn 'Abd Allāh ibn Nūḥ al-Barnāwī al-Kashināwī (Hausa: Dan Masanih), Shaykh al-Shuyūkh al-Bakrī, 'Abd Allāh Thīkah (elsewhere Shikatu) al-Fallātī al-Baghāwī, and Abū Bakr al-Bārikum, called Ibn Ājurrum. The 18th century, the forerunners of the Fulani *Jihād*: Al-Imām Muḥammad ibn al-Hājj 'Abd al-Raḥmān al-Barnāwī, Muḥdammad ibn Muḥammad al-Fullani al-Kashināwī, al-Ṭāhir ibn Ibrāhīm al-Fallātī, Ramaḍān ibn Aḥmad, and al-Hājj Jibrīl ibn 'Umar.

Also included is the text and translation of the controversial *Shurb al-Zulāl.*

779
Chin, Sheng-pao. Hsi lun yu kuan Ao-ssu-man Tan Fu-ti-ao han Fu-lan-ni sheng chan chih ying wen chi shu. [Note on English literature on Usuman Dan Fodio and the Fulani jihad] Fei-chou yen chiu/African studies, no. 2, Jan. 1973: 62–70. DLC

780
Deverdun, G. Un nouveau manuscrit des Masālik al-Abṣār d'Ibn Fadl-Allāh al-'Umarī. Hespéris, t. 41, 3./4. trim. 1954: 475–478. DT181.H4, v. 41
A note on the discovery of a new manuscript of al-'Umarī at the Ibn Ghāzī Library of Meknès. Until then, according to the author, the only available copy of *al-Masālik* was the one in the library of the Shaykh al-Islam of Tunis entitled *Wasf Ifrīqīyā wa-al-Andalus.*

781
Fisher, Humphrey J. Three further manuscripts of 'Abdallah b. Fudi's Tazyin al-waraqat. *In* Ibadan, Nigeria. University. *Centre of Arabic Documentation.* Research bulletin, v. 5, July 1969: 47–56. DT352.4.I2a, v. 5

782
Ghana. University, Legon. *Institute of African Studies.* Report on Arabic documents, organised by the Institute of African Studies and held at Akuafo Hall, University of Ghana, Feb. 26th and 27th, 1965. Legon, 1965. 25 p. Z3502.G5 1965

783
Gill, J. Withers. Short history of Salaga, translated from Hausa. Accra, Govt. Printer, 1924. 16 p.
Source: I.A.I. Cat., p. 525.

784
Hunwick, J. O. Arabic manuscript material bearing on the history of the Western Sudan. *In* Historical Society of Nigeria. Bulletin of news, v. 7, 1962: supplement. IEN

785
Jeffreys, M. D. W. Two Arabic documents, Diyyâ s-Sultan and Tazyin al-Waraqat. Africa studies, v. 9, June 1950: 77–85. facsims. DT751.A4, v. 9

786
Kendsdale, W. E. N. The Arabic manuscript collection of the library of the University College of Ibadan, Nigeria. WALA news, v. 2, June 1955: 21–22. Z674.W25, v. 2

787
———A catalogue of the Arabic manuscripts preserved in the University Library, Ibadan, Nigeria. [Ibadan] Ibadan University Library, 1955–1958. 3 v. in 1. IEN

788
———Field notes on the Arabic literature of the Western Sudan. *In* Royal Asiatic Society. Journal, 1955, pt. 3/4: 162–168; 1956, pt. 1/2: 78–80; 1958, pt. 1/2: 53–57. AS122.L72, 1955, 1956, 1958

789
Last, D. Murray. Arabic manuscripts in the National Archives, Kaduna. *In* Ibadan, Nigeria. University. *Centre of Arabic Documentation.* Research bulletin, v. 2, July 1966: 1–10 [In continuation] DT352.4.12a, v. 2

790
———Arabic source material and historiography in Sokoto to 1864: an outline. *In* Ibadan, Nigeria. University. *Centre of Arabic Documentation.* Research bulletin, v. 1, July 1965: 3–19. DT352.4.I2a, v. 1

791
———National Archives Kaduna: manuscripts of West African authorship. *In* Ibadan, Nigeria. University. *Centre of Arabic Documentation.* Research bulletin, v. 3, Jan. 1967: 1–15. DT352.I2a, v. 3

792
———Northern Nigeria manuscript books in Ahmadu Bello University: a report. JHSN, v. 8, July 1965: 4–7. DT515.A2H5, v. 8

793
Mahmud, Khalil. The Arabic collection of Ibadan University Library. Libri, v. 14, no. 2, 1964: 97–107. Z671.L74, v. 14
Appended is a list of "recent writing concerning or in part based upon the Arabic manuscripts in the Ibadan University Library."

794
Smith, H. F. C. An old manuscript from Timbuktu. *In* Historical Society of Nigeria. Bulletin of news, v. 4, Mar. 1960. DLC

795
Waniko, Samuel Sidali. A descriptive catalogue of the early Lugard-Sultan of Sokoto correspondence, including a description of 131 Arabic letters found in Sokoto in 1903. [Kaduna, National Archives] 24 p.
Source: Ita, 55.

796
Whitting, C. E. J. Extracts from an Arabic history of Sokoto. African Affairs, v. 47, July 1948: 160–169. DT1.R62, v. 47

Extracts from a new translation of a history of Sokoto by al-Hājj Saʿīd. The text, printed as an addendum to *Tadhkirat al-Nisyān* published in 1899 by Houdas and Benoîst, covers the period of Muhammad Bello, ʿAtīqu, and ʿAliyyu. "It presents a graphic account of life in these days of sporadic revolt of the old Hausa states against the new Fulani power." *See also* 918.

797

———The unprinted indigenous literature of Northern Nigeria. *In* Royal Asiatic Society. Journal, pt. 1/2, 1943. p. 23–26. AS122.L72, 1943

List of 99 titles by 37 authors from northern Nigeria including Usuman dan Fodyo and other religious figures.

Biography

798

Ali, Mastafa *Malam.* Umar ibn Abu Bakar Garbai el-Amin el-Kanemi, Shehu of Bornu; the profile of the Shehu of Bornu. [Maiduguri, Military Governor's Office, Public Relations Section, 1968] Zaria, Printed by the Gaskiya Corporation. MBU

799

Batrān, ʿAbd al-ʿAzīz ʿAbd Allāh. A contribution to the biography of Shaikh Muhammad ibn ʿAbd-al-Karīm ibn Muhammad (ʿUmar-aʿMar) al-Maghīlī, al-Tilimsānī. JAH, v. 14, no. 3, 1973: 381–394. DT1.J65, v. 14

Few African scholars have had such an impact on both North and West Africa as al-Maghīlī (d. 1503/4 or 1505/6). This biographical sketch begins by assessing his part in the theological debate preceding the persecution of the Jewish community at Touat (conventionally dated to 1492), which was largely instigated by him, and relates it to his unsuccessful campaign against the Banú-Waṭṭāṣ, whom he opposed because of their incapacity to check the growth of Christian power and Jewish influence in Morocco. After his failure against the Banū-Waṭṭāṣ, al-Maghīlī went to the western Sudan, where in Air, Takidda, Kano, Katsina, and Gao he exerted a more peaceful and scholastic influence as a great renovator of Islam. The death of his son at Touat led him to return there about 1503, and to resume his active campaigning against the Jews and their influence until his death a year or two later.—(Abstract supplied, modified)

800

Callcott, George H. Omar ibn Seid, a slave, who wrote an autobiography in Arabic. Journal of Negro history, v. 39, Jan. 1954: 58–62. E185.J86, v. 39

Umar ibn Saʿid was a Fulbe brought to Charleston in 1807. Using excerpts from the biography, Callcott relates the life of "Uncle Moreau" in Fayetteville, N.C., and his conversion to Christianity into the Presbyterian Church.

801

Demaison, André. Le pacha de Tombouctou. Paris, A. Fayard [c1927] 284 p. PQ2607.E385P3 1927

Fictionalized version of the life of Juder, the renegade who led the Moroccan expedition against the Songhay Empire.

802

Doi, A. R. I. The Shehu ʿUthman Dan Fodio (1754–1817); the great Nigerian African *Mujahid* and *Mujaddid.* The Islamic review and Arab affairs, v. 58, May 1970: 12–15. BP1.I7, v. 58

In conclusion the biographer states, "The *Jihád* of the Sheḥú ʿUthmán certainly proved a revolutionary movement. It succeeded in breaking down local and ethnic loyalties, substituting a cosmopolitan loyalty which transcended the boundary of kith and kin. As an Islamic empire, the Sharíʿah Law was applied rigorously as the basis of political administration. This undoubtedly ensured a social, legal and religious revolution in Northern Nigeria. By the time of the Shehu's death in 1817 C.E., the *Jihád* had *created,* out of the disunited Hausa states, perhaps the largest Islamic empire ever known in the history of Nigeria. It had by so doing, accomplished the first step towards the unification of Nigeria."

803

Duboc, F. Samory le sanglant. Paris, S.F.E.L.T., 1947. 205 p. maps.

Source: Brasseur, 4854.

Un des premiers ouvrage d'ensemble publiés sur Samori. Peu intéressant.—(Abstract supplied)

804

Hiskett, Mervyn. The 'Song of the Shaihu's Miracles': A Hausa hagiography from Sokoto. African language studies, v. 12, 1971: 71–107. PL8003.A34, v. 12

805
———The sword of truth; the life and times of the Shehu Usuman dan Fodio. New York, Oxford University Press, 1973. 194 p. illus., maps. DT515.9.F8H57

"This study is one in a series of short biographies of distinguished Black Americans and Black Africans, prepared under the editorship of Professor Hollis R. Lynch of Columbia University."

Biography of the founder of the Sokoto Fulani Caliphate by a scholar eminently qualified to undertake it because of his knowledge of Hausa and Arabic, historical research, and residence in the area.

806
Hunwick, J. O. Further light on Ahmad Bābā al-Tinbuktī. *In* Ibadan, Nigeria. University. *Centre of Arabic Documentation.* Research bulletin, v. 2, July 1966: 19–31. DT352.4.I2a, v. 2

807
———A new source for the biography of Aḥmad Bābā al-Tinbuktī (1556–1627). BSOAS, v. 27, no. 3, 1964: 568–593. PJ3.L6, v. 27

Text and translation of an excerpt on the life of the Timbuktu scholar. Hunwick, who has undertaken considerable research on the man, states, "The biography of Aḥmad Bābā presented here is extracted from a work as yet unpublished, the biographical dictionary *Fatḥ al-Shakūr fī ma'rifat a'yān 'ulamā' al-Takrūr* [The Introduction of the Thankful on Knowing the Eminent Learned Men of the Takrur] written in 1214/1799–1800 by . . . al-Ṭālib Muḥammad b. Abī Bakr al-Ṣiddīq, who died on 22 Dhu'l-Hijja 1219/24 March 1805." Appended is a chronology of Ahmad Baba's writings.

808
el-Masri, Fathi Hasan. The life of Shehu Usuman Dan Fodio before the Jihad. JHSN, v. 2, Dec. 1963 [Nov. 1964]: 435–448. DT515.A2H5, v. 2

Biography of the Fulbe reformer before his Jihad. Al-Maṣrī recounts the origins of the family, his youth and education, the teachers who influenced him, his travels, and the beginnings of the movement leading to the armed revolt.

809
el-Masri, Fathi Hasan, *and others.* Sifufin Shehu: an autobiography and character study of Uthman B. Fudi in verse. *In* Ibadan, Nigeria. University. *Centre of Arabic Documentation.* Research bulletin, v. 2, Jan. 1966: 1–36. DT352.I2a, v. 2

Text and translation with annotations by F. H. el-Masri, R. A. Adeleye, J. O. Hunwick, and I. A. Mukoshy of a poem written originally in Fulfulde by the Shehu, but of which only a Hausa translation in Ajami script remains. A transliteration of the text is provided with substantial annotations. The work draws parallels between the lives of the Shehu, the Prophet Mohammad, and the expected Mahdi.

810
Milsome, John R. Usuman dan Fodio; great leader and reformer. Ibadan, Oxford University Press, 1968. 56 p. illus. (Makers of Nigeria) DT515.9.F8M54

An introduction for children to the Sokoto leader.

811
———El Kanemi, the saviour of Bornu. Ibadan, Oxford University Press, 1968. 40 p. illus. (Makers of Nigeria) DT515.9.B6M54 1968

Biography of Muḥammad al-Amīn al-Kānimī (1778–1835), the Bornu leader, written for children.

812
Mohammadou Aliou Tyam. La vie d'el Hadj Omar, qacida en poular; transcription, traduction, notes et glossaires par Henri Gaden. Paris, Institut d'ethnologie, 1935. 288 p. facsim. (Université de Paris. Travaux et mémoires de l'Institut d'ethnologie, XX1) PL8184.M6

813
Mus'ad, Muṣṭafā Muḥammad. al-Ṭā'ifah al-Tijānīyah. [The Tijani Sect] Khartoum. Jāmi'at al-Qāhirah fī-al-Kharṭūm. Majallat Jāmi'at al-Qāhirah fī-al-Kharṭūm, m. 1, 1970: 67–100. DLC

Biography of the founder of the Tījānīyah sect, al-Sayyid Abū al-'Abbās Aḥmad ibn Muḥammad ibn al-Mukhtār ibn Sālim al-Tījānī (1737–1815), and his religious itinerary. The development of the sect is then analyzed in terms of the interaction of its leaders and the political vagaries of the region.

814
Niane, Djibril Tamsir. Koly Tenguella et le Tekrour. Recherches africaines; études guinéenes, nouv. sér., no 1, janv./mars 1969: 58–68. DT543.A3R4, n.s., 1969

Study of a Tekrur leader of the 16th century whose role and dates are uncertain. Niane, working with written material and especially with oral traditions, has provided better guidelines for further studies on Koly Tenguella.

815
———A propos de Koli Tenguella. Recherches africaines; études guinéennes, nouv. sér., no 4, oct./déc. 1960: 33–36. DT543.A3R4, n.s., 1960
Brief clarification on Koly Tenguella. Niane says that "la lumière n'est point completement faîte sur le héros Dénianké."

816
Norris, H. T. Znāga Islam during the seventeenth and eighteenth centuries. BSOAS, v. 32, pt. 3, 1969: 496–526. PJ3.L6, v. 32
History of Zanāghah Islam during the 17th and 18th centuries as reflected in the lives of Nāṣir al-Dīn (d. 1674?), the head of a zāwiyah and leader of the Moors in the Shurbubba war, and his follower, Muḥammad al-Yadālī (d. 1166). Norris concludes, "Thus the Zwāya hero of Muḥammad al-Yadālī has become a national hero. His Znāga background, his *jihād,* and war with the 'Arabs' are now regarded objectively as part of an historical process. Mauritanian nationalism is seen to be foreshadowed in his shortlived *umma* which embraced all races and which sought to build up a new community in the coastal *sāḥil* where some believed centuries earlier the Almoravid 'Abdullah b. Yāsīn had established his prophetic *ribāṭ*." Appended is a list of the major works of Muḥammad al-Yadālī and a brief note on Walīd al-Muṣṭafā ibn Khālunā al-Daymānī (d. 1797), "the most famous pupil of al-Yadālī."

817
Ol'derogge, Dimitriĭ A. Osman Dan Fodio une seine bedentunge. *In* International Congress of Orientalists. *24th, Munich, 1957.* Verhandlungen: 731–735. PJ20.A73, 1957

818
Smith, H. F. C. The death of Shehu Muhammad al-Aminu al-Kanemi. *In* Historical Society of Nigeria. Bulletin of news, v. 6, Sept. 1961. IEN

819
———A seventeenth-century writer of Katsina. *In* Historical Society of Nigeria. Bulletin of news, v. 6, 1961: supplement. IEN

819a
Wesley, Charles H. The life and history of Abou Bakr Sadiki, alias Edward Doulan. Journal of Negro history, v. 21, Jan. 1936: 52–55. E185.J86, v. 21
Dr. Wesley, of Howard University, discovered the manuscript by Abū Bakr al-Ṣiddīq "at the bottom of an old box of slavery and anti-slavery materials at the office of the Anti-Slavery Society, Dennison House, London." Abū Bakr, born in Timbuktu and brought up in Jenne, was taken prisoner and sold on the coast at "Dago." He wrote his autobiography in Kingston, Jamaica, in 1834.

Cities

820
Hervé, H. Niani, ex-capitale de l'empire manding. NA, no 82, avril 1959: 50–55. DT1.I513, no. 82

821
Marc-Schrader, Lucien. Tombouctou et le traffic saharien. La revue de Paris, t. 19, 15 mars 1912: 369–390. AP20.R268, v. 19

822
Mauny, Raymond. Notes d'archéologie au sujet de Gao. BIFAN, t. 13, juil. 1951: 837–852. Q89.I5, v. 13
Gao, the capital of the Askiya dynasty, witnessed many changes. Mauny presents the historical background of the city as described by various Arab writers from al-Khuwarāzmī (c. 833) to Leo Africanus (16th century) and European travelers from Malfante (1447) to Barth (1854). He also studies the archeological remains of the old city and its various cemeteries and concludes with a request for more digs.

823
Robert, Serge. Fouilles archéologiques sur le site présumé d'Aoudaghost (1961–1968). Folia Orientalia, t. 12, 1970: 261–278. illus. PJ9.F6, v. 12
Report on seven archeological missions to Tegdaoust, in the Noudache canyon of the Rkiz Mountains in eastern Mauritania, in search of the elusive Awdaghost of medieval Arab chroniclers. However, the goal of these digs is no longer restricted to locating Awdaghost but encompasses the history of the whole sub-Saharan area.

824
Sadoux. Sur l'emplacement présumé de la casbah marocaine de Koulen (ou Koulani) (1591–1593) BCAOF, oct./déc. 1922: 585–589. DT521.C6, 1922
Investigation of a hill named Borokoulenia, located on the Niger River between Gaya and Niamey. The author, struck by the topography of the site and having read *Tārīkh al Sūdān* (chapter 21), suggests that it is the location of a fort named Kulani which was built by Maḥmūd Zarqūn, successor of Juder.

History

825
'Abd Allāh ibn Muḥammad, *Emir of Gwandu.* Tazyīn al-waraqāt. Edited with a translation and introductory study of the author's life and times by M. Hiskett. [Ibadan, Nigeria] Ibadan University Press, 1963. 144 p. facsims., geneal. table, fold. map. DT515.9.S6A2

Text and translation of the history of Usuman dan Fodyo's Sokoto empire written by his brother Abdullahi. The translation and commentary were undertaken by the former vice principal of the School of Arabic Studies in Kano, Nigeria, a well-known scholar in the field of Islamic studies in sub-Saharan Africa.

825a
Ajayi, J. F. Ade, *and* Michael Crowder, *eds.* History of West Africa. New York, Columbia University Press, 1972– 2 v. illus. DT475.A77

"The aim of the editors of the two volume *History of West Africa* is to provide a lucid, scholarly and authoritative synthesis of West African history that can serve as a basic university textbook, as a work of reference for teachers, and a general background for all those interested in West African studies." The following articles in volume 1 are relevant to Islam in the continent: Nehemia Levtzion, The Early States of the Western Sudan to 1500; H. F. C. Smith, The Early States of the Central Sudan; John Hunwick, Songhay, Bornu and Hausaland in the Sixteenth Century; John R. Willis, The Western Sudan from the Moroccan Invasion (1591) to the Death of al-Mukhtar al-Kunti (1811); R. A. Adeleye, Hausaland and Bornu 1600–1800.

826
Arnett, E. J. Gazetteer of Zaria province. London, 1920. Cst-H

827
———A Hausa chronicle. *In* African Society. Journal, v. 9, Jan. 1910: 161–167. DT1.R62, v. 9

Translation of the *Daura Makas Sariki,* a short chronicle reporting the origins and rulers of Daura. The record includes a list of kings before and after Islam.

828
———The rise of the Sokoto Fulani. Kano, 1922. IEN

829
Balogun, Ismail A. B. The penetration of Islam into Nigeria. [Khartoum] University of Khartoum, Sudan Research Unit [1969] 32 leaves. (University of Khartoum. Sudan Research Unit. African studies seminar paper no. 7). BP64.N49B3

"Islam entered Nigeria from two directions: from the North into Kanem-Bornu . . . and from the West into Hausaland. . . ." Balogun delineates the spread of Islam in Nigeria from the 11th century to the present, using as his sources Muslim historians and geographers who have traveled in the region, Muslims of Western Sudanese origin, Muslims in the Central Sudan itself, Fulbe writers, and Yoruba Muslims.

830
Barry, Boubacar. La guerre des marabouts dans la région du fleuve Sénégal de 1673 à 1677. BIFAN, t. 33, juil. 1971: 564–589. DT1.I5123, v. 33

831
———Le royaume du Waalo. Le Sénégal avant la conquête. Paris, François Maspéro, 1972. 395 p. DT549.9.W34B37

The history of the Waalo from 1658 to 1859 provides an interesting case of the internal dynamics of an African state closely involved in the Atlantic and trans-Saharan trades. The introduction by Samir Amin includes a periodization scheme based on Marxist concepts of history.

832
Boahen, A. Adu. Britain, the Sahara, and the Western Sudan, 1788–1861. Oxford, Clarendon Press, 1964. 268 p. maps (part fold.) (Oxford studies in African affairs) DT356.B57

833
Bocar, Cissé. L'Origine des Armas vivant en amont de Tombouctou. NA, no 66, avril 1955: 40–41. DT1.I513, 1955

Oral tradition on the history of the Armas of Gentou, a small village on the Niger near Timbuktu. The Armas are reported to be the descendants of the Moroccan troops of Juder, the Spanish renegade who conquered the Askiya Empire.

834
Boisboissel, Y. de. Une expédition militaire transsaharienne au XVIe siècle du Maroc au Niger: la colonne Djouder (1561). Revue internationale d'histoire militaire, no 17, 1956: 123–134. D25.R4, 1956

835
Bovill, E. W. The Moorish invasion of the Sudan. *In* African Society. Journal, v. 26, Apr. 1927: 245–262; v. 26, July 1927: 380–387; v. 27, Oct. 1927: 47–56. DT1.R62, v. 26–27

Narrative of Juder's invasion and its results based on Delafosse, de Castries, and the two *Tarikh.* Cites also letters from Englishmen in Morocco reporting on the influx of gold from the Sudan.

836
Brigaud, Félix. histoire traditionnelle du Sénégal. *In* Institut français d'Afrique noire. *Centre Sénégal-Mauritanie, Saint Louis, Sénégal.* Connaissance du Sénégal. Saint Louis du Sénégal, 1962. 331 p. fold. map, profiles. (Etudes sénégalaises, fasc. 9, no 9) DT549.I53

The legitimacy of oral tradition as a source of African history was not firmly established when Brigaud wrote his book as his preface shows:

La réticence des chercheurs de parchemins devant une tradition purement orale ne peut empêcher qu'un peuple n'ait son histoire relatant ses origines et ses migrations, ses heurs et ses malheurs. Cètte histoire, certes, n'a été ni papyrusisée ni granitisée, si l'on nous permet ces néologismes, mais elle est restée imprimée dans le cerveau humain, archive vivante, dont la défaillance entraînait, il n'y a pas si longtemps, pour certains griots, la mort.

Il faut, comme toujours, manier les documents oraux avec prudence. Il convient de laisser à l'incertain ce qui appartient à l'incertain. Il y aurait plus que de l'outre-cuidance à torturer les données recueillies pour en tirer une chronologie douteuse ou une affirmation hasardeuse. Le prisme de l'historien doit décomposer mais non dévier.

Présenter l'histoire du Sénégal telle qu'elle est vue par ses enfants, avec ses variantes et ses légendes, cela nous a semblé honnête. Nous en avons cherché la trame, et, ce faisant, avons laissé la broderie quand elle était belle.

837
Brue, André. Voyages du Sieur André Brue au long des côtes occidentales d'Afrique. *In* [Prévost, Antoine F., *called* Prévost d'Exiles] *ed.* Histoire générale des voyages. v. 3. La Haye, 1747. p. 267–456. plates, maps. G160.P94, v. 3

838
Brun, J. P. Notes sur le *Tarikh-el-Fettach.* Anthropos, t. 9, 1914: 590–596. GN1.A7, v. 9

839
Burdon, J. A. The Fulani Emirates of Northern Nigeria. The Geographical journal, v. 24, Dec. 1904: 636–651. G7.R91, v. 24

Description of the emirates by a former Resident of the Sokoto Province.

840
———Sokoto history; tables of dates and genealogy. *In* African Society. Journal, v. 6, July 1907: 367–374. DT1.R62, v. 6

841
Carnochan, J. The coming of the Fulani: a Bachama tradition. BSOAS, v. 30, pt. 3, 1967: 622–637. PJ3.L6, v. 30

Text and translation of an oral tradition in Bachama—a language spoken in northeastern Nigeria and adjacent parts of Cameroon—reporting the arrival of the Fulbe to Gobirland, an area covering parts of northern Nigeria and Niger.

842
Chailley, Marcel. Histoire de l'Afrique occidentale, 1638–1959. Paris, Berger-Levrault, 1968. 581 p. maps, plates. (Monde d'outre-mer. Série: Histoire) DT532.C48

843
Chronique d'Agadés. Trans. Yves F. M. A. Urvoy. JOSAF, t. 4, fasc. 2, 1934: 145–177. DT1.S65, v. 4

Translation of eight Arabic manuscripts found in the archives of the sultans of Aïr living in Agadez. The documents include a history of the dynasty, the origin of the sultanate, a list of Gobir black sultans, the memoirs of a man named Abū Bakr, born in 1657, and the conflicts of the "Sandals, Kel-Gress and Kel Oui" Tuareg tribes.

844
Ciecierska-Chłopowa, Teresa. Extraits de fragments du *Siyāhat-nāme* d'Evliyā Čelebi concernant l'Afrique noire. Folia orientalia, t. 6, 1964: 239–243. PJ9.F6, v. 6

Short excerpts in Turkish and French from Çelebi's *Travel Report,* pertaining to Bornu and the Hausa Bokwai.

845
Cissoko, Sekéné-Mody. Famines et épidémies à Tombouctou et dans la boucle du Niger du XVIe au XVIIIe siècle. BIFAN, t. 30, juil. 1968: 806–821. DT1.I5123, v. 30

Two factors have led to the demographic decline

in West Africa, namely the slave trade on a continental scale and natural disasters such as drought, locusts, floods, and epidemics. In this detailed examination, Cissoko has tried to tackle quantification, one of the most complex problems of West African history. Painstakingly he has gleaned from Arabic and other available sources information on the incidence of diseases and famines in the Niger bend region from the 16th to the 18th century, and their implications concerning social and political developments.

846
Colvin, Lucie. Islam and the state of Kajor: a case of successful resistance to Jihad.
Source: ASA, Program, 15th, 1972.

847
Conton, William F. West Africa in history. Revised new ed. London, Allen & Unwin, 1966. 2 v. maps, table. DT471.C65
Introductory work. The first volume deals with the pre-European period; the second begins at 1800.

848
Coutouly, François de. Hakoundé Fouta. Au coeur du Fouta. BCAOF [v. 27?] 1918: 563. MH

849
Crozals, J. de. Peuhls et Foulahs. Revue de géographie, t. 10, janv./juin 1882: 106–124; t. 11, juil./déc. 1882: 321–338. G1.R43, v. 10, 11

850
Davidson, Basil. A history of West Africa 1000–1800. In collaboration with F. K. Buah and the advice of J. F. Ade Ajayi. New expanded ed. London, Longmans, 1967 [i.e. 1968] 320 p. illus., facsims., maps, plans, ports. (The Growth of African civilisation) DT476.D33 1968
First published in 1965 under title: *West Africa 1000–1800.*

851
Delafosse, Maurice. De l'animisme nègre et sa résistance à l'islamisation en Afrique occidentale. RMM, t. 49, mars 1922: 121–163. DS36.R4, v. 49

852
———Les relations du Maroc avec le Soudan à travers les âges. Hespéris, v. 4, 2. trimestre, 1924: 153–174. DT181.H4, v. 4

853
Diallo, Thierno. Origine et migration des Peuls avant le XIXe siècle. *In* L'Afrique; philosophie, littérature, histoire. Paris, Presses universitaires de France. 1972. p. 121–181. (Université de Dakar. Annales de la Faculté des lettres et sciences humaines, 2) DT4.A36
The origins of the Fulbe have baffled students of Africa for a long time. Some have suggested a Malayan, Jewish, Hyksos, Roman, Gaul, Gypsy, or Vietnamese origin, while others have even hinted that they come from Brittany! Using a multidisciplinary approach, Diallo focuses on two problems, namely their origins and their migrations. He concludes that "la question peule, tant sur le plan de l'origine que sur celui des migrations, demeure encore obscure. . . . En définitive, il apparaît ainsi que le problème peul—malgré toutes les tentatives, et elles ont été nombreuse depuis un siècle et demi,—demeure un de ceux qui attendent encore une solution."

854
Dupuis, Joseph. Journal of a residence in Ashantee. 2d ed. edited with notes and an introduction by W. E. F. Ward. London, Cass, 1966. [520] p. plates (incl. maps) DT507.D94 1966
First published in 1824.

855
Fernandes, Valentim. Description de la côte d'Afrique de Ceuta au Sénégal, par Valentim Fernandes (1506–1507) Paris, Larose, 1938. 214 p. illus., fold. map. (Publications du Comité d'études historiques et scientifiques de l'Afrique occidentale française, sér. A, no 6) DT524.F42
Names of editors, P. de Cenival and Th. Monod, at head of title.
Portuguese and French on opposite pages.
From the "Descripçam de Cepta por sua costa de Mauritania e Ethiopia," which occupies folios 45–140 of a manuscript in the Bayerische Staatsbibliothek, Munich, designated Codex monacensis hispanicus 27, and entitled in Peutinger's hand: De insulis et peregrinatione Lusitanorum.
See also the 1951 edition, edited by Theodore Monod, A. Taxeira da Mota, and Raymond Mauny (DT526.F45, no. 11).

856
Habraszewski, Tomsz. Kanuri—language—and people in the "Travel-Book" (Siyahetname) of Evliya Çelebi. Africana bulletin, t. 6, 1967: 59–66. DT19.9.P6A65, v. 6
This 17th-century Turkish traveler paid particu-

lar attention to the languages spoken in the areas he visited and provided word lists and "useful phrases." Habraszewski reviews Kanuri word lists and compares Çelebi's transliteration system with those of various other European travelers.

857
Haillot, Jean. Sur la géomancie et ses aspects africains. BCAOF, t. 19, janv./mars, 1936: 131–139. DT521.C6, v. 19

858
al-Hajj, Muhammad. A seventeenth century chronicle on the origins and missionaries activities of the Wangarawa. Kano studies, v. 1, pt. 4, 1968: 7–16. DLC

Wangara, the land of gold, has intrigued people ever since mentioned by al-Idrisi in the 12th century. The Wangarawa, the Dyula branch of the Mande, carried Islam wherever they traded. Muhammad al-Hajj, who teaches at Abdullahi Bayero College in Kano, presents the text and translation of the chronicle *Waraqah maktūbah fīha aṣl al-Wanqarīyyin al-muntasibīn lil-Shaykh* [A Leaf Relating the Origin of the Wangara, Followers of the Shaykh], dated 1650/1651 and relating their history, voyages to Kano, and missionary activities in the region.

859
Hernandes-Pachero, F. Panorama historico-geografico de la epoca de Leon el Africano. *In* Spain. *Consejo de Investigationes Cientificas. Instituto de Estudios Africanos.* Archivos, año 7, set. 1954: 13–31. DT1.S75, v. 7

859a
Hopewell, James F. Muslim penetration into French Guinea, Sierra Leone, and Liberia before 1850. Ann Arbor, Mich., University Microfilms [1958] Micro AC–1 no. 58–3231

Microfilm copy (positive) of typescript.

Collation of the original: iii, 180 leaves, maps, tables.

Thesis—Columbia University.

860
Houdas, Oscar V. Protestation des habitants de Kano contre les attaques au sultan Mohammed-Bello, roi du Sokoto. *In* Homenaje á D. Francisco Codera en su jubilación del profesorado; estudios de erudición oriental con una introducción de D. Eduardo Saavedra. Zaragoza, M. Escar, 1904. p. 121–131. PJ26.C7

Text and translation of a letter written by the learned men of Kano to Muḥammad Bello, Sultan of Sokoto, complaining about his treatment of the Muslim community of that city.

861
Hunwick, J. O. Ahmad Baba and the Moroccan invasion of the Sudan, 1591. JHSN, v. 2, Dec. 1962: 311–328. DT515.A2H5, v. 2

862
Ibn Raḥḥāl, Muḥammad, *trans.* Le Soudan au XVIe siècle, traduit de l'original arabe par M'hammed ben Rahhal. *In* Société de géographie et d'archéologie de la Province d'Oran. Bulletin, t. 7, 1887: 320–331. DT298.O8S622, v. 7

863
al-Ifrānī, Muḥammad al-Saghīr ibn Muḥammad. Nuzhat al-ḥādī bi-akhbār mulūk al-qarn al-ḥādī. [The voyage of the camel driver concerning the news of the 11th century kings] [Fés, n.d.] 276 p. DT321.I35 Orien Arab

Lithographed.

History of Morocco and its rulers by a 17th-century author.

863a
Ismāʿīl Ḥāmid, *ed. and tr.* Chroniques de la Mauritanie sénégalaises. Nacer Eddine. Texte arabe, traduction et notice. Paris, E. Leroux, 1911. 2 p. l., 271 p., 4 l., [104]p. fold. geneal. tables. DT553.M217

History of Mauritania based on five Arabic manuscripts: *Risālat al-Shaykh Sayyid Muḥammad ibn Sulaymān ilā Ḥākim al-Tarārizah* [Letter of al-Shaykh Sayyid Muḥammad ibn Sulaymān to the Governor of the Trarza], *Amr al-Wālī Nāṣir al-Dīn* [History of the Holy Nāṣir al-Dīn], *Kitāb Shiyam al-Zawāyā* [Book of the Dispositions of the Zawāyā], *Kitāb al-Ansāb* [Book of Origins, i.e. genealogies], and *Risālat al-Shaykh Saʿd Abīhi ilā Ḥākim al-Tarārizah* [Letter of Shaykh Saʿd Abīhi to the Governor of the Trarza]. The compilation merges the manuscripts into one narrative describing the geography, history, and social structure of Mauritania from the 17th to the 20th century. Both the Arabic texts and translations of the five documents are appended.

864
Jannequin [Claude] Voyage en Libye, particulièrement au royaume de Sénégal, sur le fleuve Niger. *In* Walckener, Charles A., *baron.* Collection des relations de voyage par mer et par terre,

en différentes parties de l'Afrique, depuis 1400 jusqu'à nos jours. v. 2. Paris, 1842. p. 328–348. DT1.W16, v. 2

865
Johnston, Hugh A. S. The Fulani Empire of Sokoto. London, Ibadan [etc], Oxford University Press, 1967. 312 p. 18 plates (incl. 6 maps), diagrs. (West African history series) DT515.9.F8J63

866
Khan, Sarwat. Islam in West Africa. Islamic review, July 1952: 12–19. BP1.I7, 1952

867
Kubbel', Lev Evgen'evich. Origin of statehood in Western Sudan. Paper presented to the International Congress of Africanists, Second Session, Dec. 11–20, 1967. Dakar, Senegal. 13 p. DLC

868
Kup, A. P. A history of Sierra Leone, 1400–1787. Cambridge [Eng.] Cambridge University Press, 1961. 211 p. DT516.K8

869
Labat, Jean-Baptiste. Nouvelle relation de l'Afrique occidentale: contenant une description exacte du Sénegal & des païs situés entre le Cap-Blanc & la rivière de Sierra Leone, jusqu'à plus de 300 lieuës en avant dans les terres. L'histoire naturelle de ces païs, les differentes nations qui y sont répanduës, leurs religions & leurs moeurs. Avec l'etat ancien et present des compagnies qui y font le commerce. Ouvrage enrichi de quantité de cartes, de plans, & de figures en taille-douce. Paris, Chez G. Cavalier, 1728. 4 v. in 2. plates (part fold.), fold. maps, fold. plans. DT471.L12

870
Last, D. Murray. Aspects of administration and dissent in Hausaland, 1800–1968. Africa, v. 40, Oct. 1970: 345–357. PL8000.I6, v. 40

871
———A note on the attitudes to the supernatural in the Sokoto Jihad. JHSN, v. 4, Dec. 1967: 3–14. DT515.A2H5, v. 4

"In this paper, I want to move to the irrational aspect of the community's world, not only to emphasize the important part the irrational played in the jihad but also, in passing, to raise the problem of how to treat the supernatural events reported."

872
———The Sokoto Caliphate. [New York] Humanities Press [1967] 280 p. illus., 5 geneal. tables (fold. in pocket), maps, ports. (Ibadan history series) DT515.9.F8L3 1967b

Based on author's thesis, University of Ibadan.

A comprehensive study of the Sokoto Empire during the 19th century and the jihad of Usuman dan Fodyo. Making ample use of contemporary Arabic sources, the author describes the Sokoto community and its administration according to the tenets of the Shari'a. He analyzes the establishment of Dār al-Islām from 1754 to 1817 and its maintenance from 1817 to 1903, as well as the organization of the wizirate. A chapter on sources provides a thorough introduction to the material used. Includes also an extensive bibliography on works in Arabic.

873
———A solution to the problems of dynastic chronology in 19th century Zaria and Kano. JHSN, v. 3, Dec. 1966: 461–469. DT515.A2H5, v. 3

874
Last, D. Murray, *and* M. A. al-Hajj. Attempts at defining a Muslim in 19th century Hausaland and Bornu. JHSN, v. 3, Dec. 1965: 231–240. DT515.A2H5, v. 3

Islam developed in the Hausa and Bornu regions during about five centuries. At the beginning of the 19th century, many animistic practices had infiltrated the orthodoxy of Islam. The jihad movement is seen as a reaction against the dilution of Islamic dogmata and principles and a return to pristine Meccan Islam.

875
Le Châtelier, Alfred. l'Islam dans l'Afrique occidentale. Paris, G. Steinheil, 1899. 376 p. illus. BP64.A4L4

After an extensive introduction on the geography of the area and its peoples, the author looks at the Islamization of the region and investigates the various religious sects, such as the Tijani and Qadiri. Of interest is the last chapter, "The Future of Sudanic Islam," where Le Châtelier advocates a thorough knowledge of sub-Saharan Islam for use in furthering French interests.

876
Légende de la dispersion des Kusa (épopée soniñke) par Claude Meillassoux, Lassana Doucouré [et] Diaowé Simagha. Dakar, I.F.A.N., 1967. 133 p. (Initiations et études africaines, 22) PL8686.8.L4

At head of title: Université de Dakar. Institut fondamental d'Afrique noire. Narrated by Diaowé Simagha. Transcribed by Lassana Doucouré.

Text of the legend in French and Soninké.

877
Lévi-Provençal, Evariste. Un document inédit sur l'éxpédition Sa'dide au Soudan. Arabica; revue d'études arabes, t. 2, janv. 1955: 89–96. PJ6001.A7, v. 2

Having defeated Askiya Isḥāq II at Tondibi (1591), Juder was later accused of laxity and replaced as commander of the Moroccan forces by another renegade, Maḥmud Zarqūn, who adopted a more militant policy. In examining the legados of the Arabic collections of the Escorial, Lévi-Provençal discovered a letter from Zarqūn to the qadi of Timbuktu, 'Umar ibn Maḥmūd, inquiring about the rebellion and the qadi's role in it. Included are the Arabic text and its French translation.

878
Levtzion, Nehemia. The long march of Islam in the Western Sudan. *In* Oliver, Roland A. The middle age of African history. London, Oxford University Press, 1967. p. 13–18. maps. DT20.O39

879
———Maḥmūd Ka'ti fut-il l'auteur de Ta'rikh al-Fattāsh. BIFAN, t. 33, oct. 1971: 665–674. DT1.I5123, v. 33

Final conclusions of a longer study (*see* 880) on the *Tārīkh al-Fattāsh.* According to Levtzion, the work was written in its present form by Ibn al-Murkhtār, husband of al-Ka'tī's granddaughter. *See also* Ibadan, Nigeria. University. *Centre of Arabic Documentation.* Research bulletin, v. 6, Dec. 1970: 1–12. (DT352.4.I2a).

880
———A seventeenth-century chronicle by Ibn al-Mukhtār: a critical study of *Ta'rīkh al-fattāsh.* BSOAS, v. 34, pt. 3, 1971: 571–593. PJ3.L6, v. 34

Levtzion suggests, after a close investigation of *Tārīkh al-Fattāsh,* that Maḥmūd Ka'tī did not author the chronicle, including the first part generally attributed to him. He believes the work to be that of Ibn al-Mukhtār, who lived in the second half of the 17th century, and not the joint effort of three generations of writers.

881
Lhote, Henri. Léon l'Africain et le Sahara. Encyclopédie mensuelle d'outre-mer, t. 5, fasc. 56, 1955: 149–152. JV1801.E5, v. 5

882
Lighton, G. Islam in the Western and Central Sudan. MW, v. 26, July 1936: 253–273. DS36.M7, v. 26

883
Lintingre, Pierre. Le pachalik du Soudan. Afrique documents, no 84, 1. cahier 1966: 49–53. DT1.A479, 1966

Lintingre asks the rhetorical question as to the future of Africa had the renegade Pasha "Ammar el-Feta," who ruled in 1598 and returned to the Sudan in 1608 with 400 fusiliers, established a Christian kingdom in the Sudan.

884
Ly, Madina. Quelques remarques sur le Tarikh el-Fettach. BIFAN, t. 34, juil. 1972: 471–493. DT1.I5123, v. 34

After discussing the questions of chronology regarding the author of the work, Ly concludes, "Nous voyons que le problème du *Tarikh el-Fettach* est loin d'être résolu . . . ." He believes that the work was written by three distinct persons, and that its historical value depends on whether the writers were eye witnesses or mere compilers. *See also* 879, 880.

885
Macintyre, J. L. Islam in Northern Nigeria. MW, v. 2, April 1912: 144–151. DS36.M7, v. 2

"What effect has Islam had on those tribes in Northern Nigeria which have come under its sway, and how far is it responsible for the degree of civilisation to which they have attained?" In attempting to answer this question, Macintyre concentrates on the Nupe, who were relatively recent converts to Islam. After listing all the "evils" brought about by Islam, he concludes that the impact of Islam on the Nupe was negative. Macintyre also says of the struggle in Northern Nigeria between Islam and Christianity, "Even on purely political grounds one cannot but have grave doubts of the wisdom of thus helping to consolidate and extend the Mohammedan power in this recently conquered protectorate, when it is an open secret that many of the Mohammedan ruling class would be only too glad to be rid of the British altogether."

886
Maḥmūd K't ibn al-Mutawakkil K't. Tārīkh al-Fattāsh fī akhbār al-buldān wa-al-juyūsh wa-akābir al-nās. [The history of the searcher on the chronicle of countries, armies and eminent poeple] by Maḥmūd Ka't ibn al-Ḥājj al-Mutawakkil Ka't al-

Karmanī al-Tinbuqtī al-Wa'karī. Paris, Adrien-Maisonneuve, 1964. 186 p. (Documents arabes relatifs à l'histoire du Soudan) (Collection U.N.E.S.C.O. d'oeuvres représentatives. Série africaine) (Publications de l'École des slangues orientales vivantes, 5. sér., v. 9) DT532.2.M2714 1964

Added t.p.: Tarikh el-fettach fi akhbâr el-bouldân oua-l-djouyoûch oua-akâbir en-nâs, par Mahmoûd Kâti ben al-Hadj el-Moutaouakkel Kâti.

With, as issued, the author's *Tarikh el-fettach*, traduction française (Paris, 1964).

Reprint of the 1913 ed. *See also* his *Tarikh el-fettach, ou la Chronique du chercheur* (DT551.M214).

Tārīkh al-Fattāsh and *Tārīkh al-Sūdān* (*see* 912a) are considered invaluable guides to medieval West Africa, without which our knowledge of the Sudanic kingdoms would be greatly reduced.

887

Marty, Paul. Relation d'un pèlerinage à la Mecque par un marabout peul en 1794–1795. RMM, t. 43, fév. 1921: 228–235. DS36.R4, v. 43

On November 9, 1794, Birahima, son of Alfa Guidado, a Fulbe marabout, left Oualata for Mecca via the Tuat, Siwah, and Cairo. He reached the Holy City on June 25, 1795, where he acquired the much-sought title of hajj. The logbook of Birahima's journey was found by Marty, who provides this translation.

888

———Tableau historique des Cheikh Sidia. BCAOF, t. 4, janv./mars 1921: 76–95. DT521.C6, v. 4

Translation of a traditional history of the tribes of Mauritania according to Shaykh Sīdiyā ūld al-Mukhtār ūld al-Haybah and Aḥmadū ūld Aḥmad ūld Sīd Amīn ūld Aḥmad al-Amīn ūld Alfarā Aḥmad. The period covered extends from before the arrival of the Lamtah tribes during the 11th century to the end of the 19th century.

889

Matthews, John, *R.N.* A voyage to the River Sierra-Leone, containing an account of the trade and productions of the country and of the civil and religious customs and manners of the people, by John Matthews during his residence in that country in the years 1785, 1786 and 1787, with an additional letter on the African slave trade. London, Cass, 1966. 183 p. front. (fold. map), plate. DT516.2.M3 1966

Originally published in London, 1791.

890

Mauny, Raymond, L'éxpédition marocaine d'Ouadane (Mauritanie) vers 1543–1544. BIFAN, v. 11, janv./avril 1949: 129–140. Q89.I5, v. 11

Mauny reconstructs the first Moroccan expedition toward Timbuktu, which presaged the disastrous expedition of 1585; the third, which led to the occupation of Teghaza in that same year; and the fourth under Juder in 1591, which ended with the collapse of the Songhay Empire. A useful table of both Moroccan and Songhay dynasties is appended.

891

Mischlich, A. Contributions to the history of the Hausa states. With introduction by J. Lippert. *In* African Society. Journal, v. 4, July 1905: 455–479. DT1.R62, v. 4

The first account reports the conversion to Islam of Bornu and the Hausa states, and the second includes information on Kano, Katsina, Gobir, Kebbi, Zaria, and Bauchi.

892

Monod, Théodore. Rabelais et le Mali. NA, no 82, avril 1959: 37. DT1.I513, 1959

Short note, in a special issue devoted to Mali, on a mention of "Melli" in *Gargantua and Pantagruel* by François Rabelais (1542).

893

Monteil, Charles V. Notes sur le Tarikh es-Soudan. BIFAN, t. 27, juil./oct. 1965: 479–530. DT1.I5123, v. 27

Edited by Vincent Monteil, these notes are annotations and corrections by the author on his personal copy of *Tārīkh al-Sūdān.* The 778 corrections were made during a residence in Jenne and with the help of its local learned men.

894

Moreira, J. M. Os Fulas de Guiné portuguesa na panorâmica geral do mundo fula. Boletim cultural da Guiné portuguesa, v. 19, jul. 1964: 289–327. DT613.B6, v. 19

Summary of the views regarding the origins of the Fulbe. Moreira combines the writings of French and German writers with oral traditions to investigate the Fulbe of Guinea-Bissau.

895

Muhammad Bello, *Sultan of Sokoto.* Infaku'l maisuri. Edited from local mss. by C. E. J. Whitting and the staff of the School of Arabic Studies, Kano. London, Luzac, 1951. 212 p.

DT515.65.M8 Orien Arab

Arabic text has title Infāq al-maysūr fī tārīkh bilād al-Takrūr, reproduced from handwritten copy.

896

Muḥammad ibn al-Ḥājj Ibrāhīm, *al-Zarhūnī.* La Rihla du marabout de Tasaft. Notes sur l'histoire de l'Atlas, texte arabe du XVIIIe siècle traduit et annoté par le colonel Justinard. Paris, Geuthner, 1940. 212 p. fold. map. (Documents d'histoire et de géographie marocaines, publications de la Section historique du Maroc [5]) DT308.M813

Title also in Arabic.

Translation of *Rihlat al-wāfid fī akhbār hijrat al-wālid* [The Voyage of the Envoy Concerning the Emigration of the Father to the City].

897

Notice sur un Maure de Tombouctou. *In* Société de géographie, *Paris,* Bulletin, t. 9, 1828: 268–270, 282–283. G11.S4, v. 9

Note on a Fulbe from Timbo, in present-day Guinea, who was taken as a slave, lived 39 years in the United States, and returned to settle in Liberia.

898

Nwabara, Samuel N. The Fulani conquest and rule of the Hausa kingdom of Northern Nigeria (1804–1900). JOSAF, t. 33, fasc. 2, 1963: 231–241. DT1.S65, v. 33

A Fulbe-centered interpretation of the Fulbe conquest of Northern Nigeria by Usuman dan Fodyo.

899 (not used)

900

Nwosu, B. E. The economic effects of the jihad in West Africa. The African historian, v. 1, Mar. 1963: 17–18. DLC

901

Ozor, O. N., *and* Segun Adesina. Reflections on the Fulani Jihad of 1804. The African historian, v. 1, Mar. 1964: 32–39. DLC

902

Pachero Pereira, Duarte. Esmeraldo de situ orbis. Translated and edited by George H. T. Kimble. Nendeln, Liechtenstein, Kraus Reprint, 1967. 193 p. illus., facsim., maps (part fold.) (Works issued by the Hakluyt Society, 2d ser., no. 79) G7161.H23 2d ser., no. 79

Reprint of the 1937 ed.

903

Pageard, Robert. La marche orientale du Mali (Ségou-Djenné) en 1644, d'aprés le Tarikh es-Soudan. JOSAF, t. 31, fasc. 1, 1961: 73–81. DT1.S65, v. 31

Critical analysis of the description in *Tārīkh al-Sūdān* of the region between the Niger and the Bani rivers in present-day Mali. Al-Sa'dī, who lived in Jenne from 1629 to 1643, acquired a certain influence as mediator and ambassador between the local chiefs and the Moroccan Pashas of Timbuktu. Pageard retraces a voyage by the Muslim scholar from Sibila, near Sansanding, to Jenne via Bina, not far from San.

904

Palmer, *Sir* H. Richmond. Western Sudan history; being the Raudhât'ul afkâri. *In* African Society. Journal, v. 15, Apr. 1916: 261–273. DT1.R62, v. 15

Translation of Muhammad Bello's *Rawḍat al-Afkār.*

905

Pianel, Georges. Les préliminaires de la conquête du Soudan par Maulāy Aḥmad al-Manṣūr (d'aprés trois documents inédits). Hespéris, t. 40, 1./2. trimestres, 1953: 186–194. DT181.H4, v. 40

Aḥmad al-Manṣūr, king of Morocco known as al-Dhahabī (The Golden One), was determined to conquer the southern sources of gold, and he sent a now-famous letter to Isḥaq II, the Songhay ruler, regarding the mine of Teghaza. Included here are two fragments of another letter sent by the Moroccan king to the same ruler.

906

Pilkington, Frederick. Islam in Nigeria. The contemporary review, no. 1099, July 1957: 41–46. AP4.C7, 1957

907

Rainero, R. La bataille de Tondibi (1591) et la conquête marocaine de l'empire songhay. Genève-Afrique, v. 5, no 2, 1966: 217–247. DLC

One of the latest investigations of the battle of Tondibi and the defeat of the Songhay empire in 1591. Rainero, who teaches history at the University of Genoa, has consulted the majority of sources on the event, a list of which he has appended, and provides a clear picture of this major battle in African history. *See also Africa,* anno 21, marzo 1966: 23–53.

908
Rançon, André. Le Bondon: étude de géographie et d'histoire soudanienne de 1681 à nos jours. *In* Société de géographie commerciale de Bordeaux. Bulletin, t. 17, 1894: 188–210.
DLC-Micro 38304

909
Riad, Mohamed. The Jukun: an example of African migrations in the 16th century. BIFAN, t. 22, juil-oct. 1960: 476–485. DT1.I5123, v. 22

The 16th century witnessed a series of upheavals and migrations in the savanna belt south of the Sahara. The Jukun, now located in the vicinity of the Benue River, are analyzed as a case in point. Looking at their cultural traits, Riad believes them to have come from Darfur in Eastern Sudan where they were probably pushed west by the Arab tribes of the Sudan.

910
Ritchie, Carson I. A. Deux textes sur le Sénégal. BIFAN, t. 30, janv. 1968: 289–353.
DT1.I5123, v. 30

Study of two manuscripts located at the Bibliothèque municipale of Dieppe (index no. 66), presumably written by Louis Moreau de Chambonneau, an administrator and explorer of Senegal in the 17th century. The first book, "Traité de l'origine des Nègres du Sénégal Coste d'Afrique, de leurs pays, relligions, coutumes et moeurs," describes the area, its people, and their religion (Islam) and way of life. The second, "l'Histoire de Toubenau ou changement de souverains, et reformes de relligion desdits Nègres, depuiz 1673 son origine jusques en la présente année 1677," recounts the story of a Muslim Moorish reformist crusade against the rulers of Djolof, and Cape Verde in 1673 and the French intervention in the conflict.

911
Robert, Serge, *and* **Denise Robert.** Douze années de recherches archéologiques en République Islamique de Mauritanie. *In* L'Afrique; philosophie, littérature, histoire. Paris, Presses universitaires de France, 1972: 195–231. illus. (Université de Dakar. Annales de la Faculté des lettres et sciences humaines, 2) DT4.A36

Substantial report on archeological digging in Mauritania. Serge Robert, who teaches medieval history at the University of Dakar, has undertaken digs in Tegdaoust, Kumbi Ṣāliḥ, and various Saharan trails.

912
Roger, Jacques-François, *baron.* Résultats des questions adressées au nommé Mbouia, marabou maure, de Tischit, et à un nègre de Walet. *In* Société de géographie, *Paris.* Recueil de voyages et de mémoires, t. 2, 1825: 51–62.
G161.S67, v. 2

Baron Roger was "Commandant pour le Roi, au Sénégal." He reports on his conversation with a man from Tîchît in Mauritania about travel conditions in West Africa.

912a
al-Saʻdī, ʻAbd al-Raḥmān ibn ʻAbd Allāh. Tarikh es-Soudan. Texte arabe édité et traduit par O. Houdas avec la collaboration de Edm. Benoîst. Paris, Adrien-Maisonneuve, 1964. 2 v. in 1 (xix, 540, 333 p.) (Documents arabes relatifs à l'histoire du Soudan) [(Collection U.N.E.S.C.O. d'oeuvres representatives. Série africaine) (Publications de l'Ecole des langues orientales vivantes. 4. sér., v. 12–13) DT532.2.S2142

Reprint of the edition published in 1898–1900.

A major source on the history of the Sudanic Kingdoms of West Africa. *See also* 886.

913
Smith, H. F. C. Arabic manuscript material bearing on the history of the Western Sudan: a list (published in the 1950's) of books written by the Khalifa Muhammad Bello. *In* Historical Society of Nigeria. Bulletin of news, v. 3, Mar. 1959: supplement, 1–4. IEN

914
———The dynastic chronology of Fulani Zaria. JHSN, v. 2, Dec. 1961: 277–285.
DT515.A2H5, v. 2

915
———The Fulani empire of Sokoto. JHSN, v. 4, June 1969: 615–619. DT515.A2H5, v. 4

916
———Some considerations relating to the formation of states in Hausaland. JHSN, v. 5, Dec. 1970: 329–346. DT515.A2H5, v. 5

In his final paragraph Smith states, "Our provisional conclusion in this matter, therefore, is that state-like political organizations emerged in Hausaland as the result of conditions favouring the foundation and development of *Birnin*-type settlements. And it is to these conditions that research must be directed, rather than the pursuit of the phantom of the strange invader, the *héros civilisateur* from the east with his superior culture. Political institutions, like the other institutions of human culture, are devised and developed because they offer solutions to the problems which arise for mankind out of the conditions in which it has to live; and this is no doubt to be remembered of Nigeria at the present time with all its problems of state-development, just as it is applicable to ancient Hausaland."

917
———Some notes on the history of Zazzau under the Hausa kings. *In* Mortimer, M. J., *ed.* Zaria and its region; a Nigerian savanna city and its environs. Zaria, Dept. of Geography, Ahmadu Bello University, 1970. p. 82–101. (Ahmadu Bello University. Dept. of Geography. Occasional paper, no. 4) DLC

918
Tadhkirat al-nisyān fī akhbār mulūk al-Sūdān. [The reminder about the rulers of the Sudan] *French and Arabic*. Tedzkiret en-nisiān fi akhbār molouk es-Soudān. Suivi de l'Histoire de Sokoto] Traduction française, [texte arabe édité] par O. Houdas. [Avec la collaboration d'Edmond Benoist. Nouv. éd. Paris, Librairie d'Amérique et d'Orient, 1966. 420, 234 p. (Documents arabes relatifs à l'histoire du Soudan) (Publications de l'Ecole des langues orientales vivantes, 4. sér., v. 20) DT108.05.A2T3

Includes text and translation of a fragment entitled by the translator Tarikh Sukutu and attributed to "Hadj-Sa'id."

"Reproduction photographique de l'édition originale datée de 1913–1914."

The *Tadhkitarah* constitues a complement to the two *Tarikh* as it deals with the vicissitudes of the Moroccan presence in Timbuktu after the defeat of the Songhay Empire.

919
Tapiero, Norbert. Le grand Shaykh Peul Uthmân Ibn Fûdî (Othman Dan Fodio, mort en 1232 H.-1816–17 J.C.) et certaines sources de son Islâm doctrinal. Revue des études islamiques, t. 31, 1. cahier, 1963: 49–88. BP1.R53, v. 31

Tapiero presents the Fulbe and their golden age under Usuman dan Fodyo and the fall of Sokoto to the troops of Sir J. Lugard in 1904. Then he examines the writings of the Shehu and provides information on nine of Shehu's works in manuscript form located in the Bibliothèque nationale.

920
Tauxier, Louis. Chronologie des rois Bambaras. Outre-mer, v. 2, 1930: 119–130. NN

921
Teixeira da Mota, Avelino. Un document nouveau pour l'histoire des Peuls au Sénégal pendant le XVe et XVIe siècle. Boletim cultural da Guiné Portuguesa, v. 24, out. 1969: 781–860. DT613.B6, v. 24

922
———Nota sobra a história dos Fulas—Coli Tenguêla e a chegada dos primeiros Fulas ao Futa-Jalom. *In* International West African Conference. *2nd, Bissau, 1947*. Trabalhos. v. 5; 1947. Lisboa, 1952. p. 53–69. DT471.I58, 1947

At head of title: [Portugal] Ministério das Colónias. Junta de Investigações Colónias.

Proceedings issued without title.

Various languages.

923
Tonkin, T. J. Muhammadanism in the Western Sudan. *In* African Society. Journal, v. 3, Jan. 1904: 123–141. DT1.R62, v. 4

Historical analysis on the Islamization of West Africa. Tonkin concludes that Islam "is destined to remain the active religious factor" there in spite of Christian missionary efforts.

924
Tracy, Joseph. Colonization and missions. A historical examination of the state of society in western Africa, as formed by paganism and Muhammedanism, the slave trade, and piracy, and of the remedial influence of colonization and missions. By Joseph Tracy, secretary of the Massachusetts Colonization Society. Published by the Board of Managers. 5th ed., rev. and enl. Boston, Press of T. R. Marvin, 1846. 40 p. E448.T77

925
Trimingham, John S. A history of Islam in West Africa. London, New York, Published for the University of Glasgow by the Oxford University Press, 1962. 262 p. maps, tables. (Glasgow University publications) BP64.A4W38

Trimingham writes in his preface: "This book provides the historical background to my study of *Islam in West Africa* (Clarendon Press, 1962; *see* 2057). The history of the penetration of a religious culture is essential as a means towards understanding its present-day manifestations. . . . The two books are, therefore, complementary to each

)ther." Divided into the following chapters: The Expansion of Islam in North Africa, Sahara and Sudan; West Sudan States; Central Sudan States; Islamic Stagnation and Pagan Reaction; The Recrudescence of Islam in the Nineteenth Century: Western Sudan; The Central Sudan in the Nineteenth Century; West Africa Under European Rule.

Included also are chronological tables for the dynasties of the region.

926

Waldman, Marylin R. The Fulani *Jihad*: a reassessment. JAH, v. 6, no. 3, 1965: 333–355.
DT1.J65, v. 6

Analysis of the approach of Usuman dan Fodyo to the religious reform movement. When a peaceful reform of the social and religious structures failed, he was reluctantly forced to abandon it for a militant attitude culminating in the jihad.

927

———A note on the ethnic interpretation of the Fulani *jihād*. Africa (London), v. 36, July 1966: 286–291. PL8000.I6, v. 36

Rejecting the view that the jihad is basically the attempt of one ethnic group to dominate another, Waldman suggests that "the characteristics often attributed to the Fulani before the jihad and thus said to be responsible for it—a sense of ethnic superiority and even hostility to the Hausa, an ethnic consciousness of an alien authority in Hausa society, and an ability to rule superior to that of the Hausa—were not in fact significant traits of the Fulani before the jihad and therefore cannot be said to have caused it." As Hausa and Fulbe became more mixed through intermarriage, the "pseudo-ethnic" distinctions acquired greater significance in the distinction between rulers and ruled.

928

Wilks, Ivor. A note on the early spread of Islam in Dagomba. *In* Historical Society of Ghana. Transactions. v. 8; 1965. Legon, 1965. 87–98.
DT510.A1H55, v. 8

929

Zakī, 'Abd al-Raḥmān. Ḥaḍārāt wa imbirātūrīyat fī gharbī Ifrīqiyah. [Civilizations and empires in West Africa] al-Majallah, no. 11, Sept. 1957: 70–78.
AP95.A6M25, 1957

After a brief introduction describing the populations, languages, major cities, and political status of West Africa, the author reviews the empires of Ghana, Mali, Songhay, and Bornu.

930

———Ḥarakat al-Iṣlāḥ al-dīnī fī Gharb Ifrīqiyā. [The religious reform movement in West Africa] *In* Madrid. Ma'had al-dirāsāt al-Islāmīyah. Ṣaḥīfah, v. 13, 1965–1966: 139–160.
DP103.M32, v. 13

Zakī outlines the reform movement that began in the 15th century with 'Abd al-Karīm al-Maghīlī and Jalāl al-Dīn al-Suyūṭī. He gives three reasons for the Islamic awakening that swept West Africa, namely, the religious revival among the Berbers and the Kuntah Arabs, the development of religious fraternities, especially the Qadiri and Tijani sects, and, more important, the wave of political reformers and the numerous jihad, from Karamoko Alfa in the Fouta Djallon to the Shehu of Sokoto. Zakī suggests that the establishment of these Islamic states brought about an era of stability and good government in which democratic institutions were developing, only to be ended by the colonial onslaught. He closes with an appeal to Muslim scholars to work on the Arabic manuscripts awaiting editing, translating, and publishing.

931

———Tārīkh al-Duwal al-Islāmīyah al-Sūdānīyah bi-Ifrīqiyā al-Gharbīyah. [History of the Sudanic Islamic States of West Africa] Cairo, al-Mu'assassah al-'Arabīyah al-Ḥadithah, 1961. 246 p. maps. (al-Alf Kitāb, 384) DT471.Z3

Languages & Linguistics

932

Brunton, Henry. A grammar and vocabulary of the Susoo language. 2d ed. London, Frank Cass, 1969. 136 p. DLC

Reprint of the 1802 ed.

933

Hunwick, J. O. Studies in the Tārīkh al-Fattāsh (I): Its authors and textual history. *In* Ibadan, Nigeria. University. *Centre of Arabic Documentation.* Research bulletin, v. 5, Dec. 1969: 57–65. DT352.4.I2a, v. 5

934

———The term 'Zanj' and its derivatives in a West African chronicle. *In* Language and history in Africa: a volume of collected papers presented to the London Seminar on Language and History in Africa (held at the School of Oriental and African Studies, 1967–69); edited by David Dalby. London, Cass, 1970. p. 102–108. PL8003.L3

Investigation of the term *zanj* cited in *Tārīkh al-Fattāsh.* The Zanj were one of 24 servile castes of the rulers of Mali.

935
Monod, Théodore. Sur les inscriptions arabes peintes de Tim-m-Missao, Sahara Central. JOSAF, t. 8, fasc. 1, 1938: 83–95. DT1.S65, v. 8

Reproduction and translation of Arabic rock inscriptions located at Tim-m-Missao in the Tassili-n-Adrar. The Kufic characters, as well as oral traditions referring to the *Ṣaḥābah* [Companions of the Prophet], led some scholars to date them to the seventh and eighth centuries. This early date is contested by Monod, who believes that they are of "relative antiquity."

936
Roger, Jacques-François, *baron.* Recherches philosophiques sur la langue ouolofe, suivies d'un vocabulaire abrégé français-ouolof. Paris, Dondey-Dupré père et fils, 1829. 175 p. PL8785.R6

937
Skinner, A. Neil. The origin of the name "Hausa." Africa, v. 38, July 1968: 253–257. PL8000.I6, v. 38

Hausa has appeared in written sources since the 16th century. Skinner suggests a close relationship with Songhay from whom the Hausaphone peoples wrested their independence in the 16th century—a period of stress for the Hausa and one during which they might have developed a separate identity in opposition to the Songhay. Through analysis of loan words, Skinner suggests a Songhay origin of the word *Hausa.*

Literature

938
Dubié, Paul, *ed.* 'El- Omda,' poème sur la médecine maure par Aoufa Ould Abou Bekrin (1780–1850). BIFAN, t. 5, no. 1/4, 1943: 38–66. Q89.I5, v. 5

939
Mombéyâ, Tierno Mouhammadou-Samba. Le filon du bonheur éternel. Edité par Alfâ Ibrâhîm Sow. Paris, A. Colin [1971] 200 p. (Classiques africains, 10) PL8184.M63M3

Added cover title: Ma'din al-sa'ādah. Ghūfird Malāl [Oogirde Malal].

Includes text in Fulah [sic], reproduced from ms. in Arabic script and in romanized form as well as translation into French.

Religious poem in Fouta Djallon Fulfulde by a Tierno of the Diallo clan (ca. 1765–ca. 1850). Sow considers this work on fiqh as "le plus remarquable produit que les lettrés du XIXe siècle mirent à la portée des masses populaires pour diffuser, en leur sein, la connaissance exacte de la religion musulmane que l'enseignement traditionnel en langue arabe ne pouvait leur dispenser."

940
Muḥammad al-Mukhtār Ould Bah. Introduction à la poésie mauritanienne (1650–1900). Arabica, t. 18, fév. 1971: 1–48. PJ6001.A7, v. 18

Introduction to Mauritanian poetry and its various genres from the time poetry was composed according to set norms and Moorish social structures were consolidated, to the beginning of the colonial era that deeply altered these structures and hence their artistic manifestations.

Politics

941
Aschwanden, Irene. Organisation und strategie der Fulbe Armee von Macina im 19. Jahrhundert. Bern, Herbert Lang; Frankfurt/M., Peter Lang, 1972. 152 p. illus. (Europäische Hochschulschriften. Reihe 19: Ethnologie/Kulturanthropologie. Abteilung B: Völk-erkunde, Nr 1) DT551.42.A8 1972

Originally presented as the author's thesis.

942
Bivar, A. D. H. The *Wathīqat ahl al-Sūdān*: a manifesto of the Fulani *jihād.* JAH, v. 2, no. 2, 1961: 235–243. DT1.J65, v. 2

Text, translation of, and commentary on an important Sokoto manuscript written by Shaykh Usuman dan Fodyo. The document under study is a copy of the original text.

943
Cissoko, Sékéné-Mody. Les princes exclus du pouvoir royal (Mansaya) dans les royaumes du Khasso (XVIII–XIXe s.). BIFAN, t. 35, janv. 1973: 46–56 DT1.I5123, v. 35

944
———La royauté (Mansaya) chez les Mandingues occidentaux, d'après leurs traditions orales. BIFAN t. 31, avril 1969: 325–338. DT1.I5123, v. 31

Study of the Mandingo monarchy structure as reported by oral traditions gathered in Kangaba.

945
Coifman, Victoria B. Wolof political and social organization until the 19th century. Paper presented at the 8th annual meeting of the African Studies Association, Philadelphia, 1965.
DLC-Micro 03782
Collation of the original: 11 p.

946
Doi, A. R. I. Political role of Islam in West Africa (with special reference to 'Uthman Dan Fodio's Jihad). The Islamic review and Arab affairs, v. 58, Feb. 1970: 37–40. BP1.I7, v. 58
"The purpose of the present study is to consider the role of religion in political resurgences, and some of the ways by which religion contributed to the development of various reformists movements in Islam in West Africa." After investigating the history of the Sokoto Jihad, Doi concludes, "The *Jihād* of Shehú 'Uthman certainly proved a revolutionary movement. It succeeded in breaking down local and ethnic loyalties, substituting a cosmopolitan loyalty, which transcended the boundary of kith and kin. As an Islamic empire the *Sharī'ah* law was applied rigorously as the basis of political administration. This undoubtedly ensured a social, legal and religious revolution in Northern Nigeria. By the time of Shehú's death in 1817 C.E., the *Jihád* had created, out of the disunited Hausa states, perhaps the largest Islamic empire ever known in the history of Nigeria. It had, by so doing, accomplished the first step towards the Unification of Nigeria." *See also* Africa Quarterly (New Delhi), v. 7, Jan./Mar. 1968: 335–342.

947
al-Hajj, Muhammad. The Fulani concept of Jihād; Shehu Uthmnān dān Fodio. Odu, no. 1, July 1964: 45–58. DT515.A2U32, v. 1
Many causes have been suggested for the jihad of Usumam dan Fodyo. After comparing the classical concept of jihad with that of the Fulbe, al-Hajj proposes that the jihad of Shaykh Usuman was "primarily a religious conflict between the Fulani who had a long-standing tradition of Islam, and the indigenous Hausa who were only 'nominal Muslims' or half-Islamized."

948
Hiskett, Mervyn. An Islamic tradition of reform in the Western Sudan from the sixteenth to the eighteenth century. BSAOS, v. 25, pt. 3, 1962: 577–596. PJ3.L6, v. 25
Drawing on three works by Shehu Usuman dan Fodyo—*Sirāj al-Ikhwān* [The Torch of the Brothers], *Bayān al-Bida' al-Shayṭānīyah* [The Devil's Innovations], and *Naṣā'iḥ al-Ummah al-Islāmīyah* [Advice of the Islamic Community]—Hiskett traces "the development of a tradition of reform, which, having remote origins in the Almoravid movement of the eleventh century A.D. achieved literary expression in the Muslim empire of Songhay, at the beginning of the sixteenth century, and which continued in the Habe kingdoms almost three centuries later. They also illustrate the continuity of social custom in the Sudan over this period."

949
———*Kitab al-farq*: a work on the Habe kingdoms attributed to Uthman dan Fodio. BSOAS, v. 23, pt. 3, 1960: 558–579. PJ3.L6, v. 23
Text, translation of, and commentaries on *Kitāb al-Farq bayn wilāyāt ahl al-Islām wa bayn wilāyāt ahl al-kufr* [Book on the Differences Between the States of Islam and the States of the Unbelievers]. Hiskett concludes that "the Shehu's theory of government was based on late Abbasid sources for the *Sharī'a,* and much of it is clearly apologetic . . . . It is clear that the Shehu conceived the Fulani empire as a microcosm of the ideal Islamic polity of the Abbasid jurists, evolved retrospectively to justify the political realities of their day."

950
Mas-Latrie, Louis de, *comte, ed.* Traités de paix et de commerce et documents divers concernants les relations des chrétiens avec les Arabes de l'Afrique septentrionale au Moyen âge, recueillis par l'ordre de l'Empereur et publiés avec une introduction historique. New York, B. Franklin [1964] 2 v. (Burt Franklin research and source works series, 63)
JX122.M3 1964
Reprint of the edition originally published in Paris, 1865–68.
Provides valuable information on trade relations between Europe and North Africa, the gateway for most of the goods coming from the Sudanic belt.

951
Mémoire adressé à M. le Ministre de la Marine et des Colonies par les négotiants, marchands, détaillants et habitants indigènes de Saint-Louis. Bordeaux, 1842.
Source: Joucla, 7098.

952
Ol'derogge, Dimitriĭ A. Fiodalizm v Zapodnom Sudane v. 16–19 vv. [Feudalism in the Western Sudan during the 16th-19th century] Sovetskaia etnografiia, 4, 1957: 91–102. GN1.S65, 1957
Tables of contents also in French; summaries in French.

953
Zeys, E. Esclavage et guerre sainte. Consultation adressée aux gens du Touat par un érudit nègre, cadi de Timboctou au XVIIe siècle. *In* Réunion d'études algériennes. Bulletin, v. 2, 1900: 125–151; 166–189.

Source: Brasseur, 3019.

Résumé de la conquête marocaine. Ahmed Baba, chef moral de la résistance aux Marocains. Interné à Marrakech jusqu'à la mort d'El Mansour (1603), il retourne alors à Tombouctou. Exposé de la controverse au sujet de l'esclavage entre les habitants du Touat et Ahmed Baba. L'auteur justifie la position de l'Islam et conclut à la nécessité de son implantation dans le continent noir.—[Abstract supplied]

Society & Culture

954
Boulnois, Jean, *and* Boubou Hama. L'empire de Gao; histoire, coutumes et magie des Sonraï. Paris, Librairie d'Amérique et d'Orient, 1954. 182 p. illus. DT551.B6

Recalling the contributions of Heinrich Barth, Félix Dubois, Maurice Delafosse, and the various *Tarikh,* to the history of Songhay, the authors note that they will look at the empire from an ethnographic viewpoint, using local documents to present the beliefs and customs of the Middle Niger Songhay.

955
Cissoko, Sékéné Mody. L'humanisme sur les bords du Niger au XVIe siècle. Présence africaine, nouv. sér., t. 21, no 1, 1964: 81–89. GN645.P74, v. 21

The 16th century witnessed the culmination of Sudanic civilization on the Niger Bend. Cissoko describes the religious and academic life in Timbuktu and the other centers of learning.

956
———L'intelligentsia de Tombouctou aux XVe et XVIe siècles. BIFAN, t. 31, oct. 1969: 927–952. DT1.I5123, v. 31

957
Féral, G. A propos de cotonnades. NA, no 57, janv. 1953: 16. DT1.I513, 1953

Short comment on the term "Chiqquet" reported by Charles Monteil (*see* 962). The word is an Arabic one, *Shiqqah,* referring originally to a piece of woven cloth used as currency and later to cambric cotton.

958
Hess, Andrew. Social change on the Northwestern African frontiers and Islam in the 16th century.

Source: ASA, Program, 15th, 1972.

959
Hiskett, Mervyn. Materials relating to the state of learning among the Fulani before their Jihad. BSOAS, v. 19, pt. 3, 1957: 551–578. PJ3.L3, v. 19

960
Kourouma, K. En glanant dans La Courbe. NA, no 62, avril 1954: 63. DT1.I513, 1954

Comment on an excerpt about the fast of Ramadan in Gorée from *Premier voyage fait à la Coste d'Afrique en 1685* by La Courbe.

961
Last, D. Murray. Aspects of the Caliph Bello's social policy. Kano studies, no 2, July 1966: 56–59. DLC

Muḥammad Bello had the difficult task of implementing the principles of religious reform and the jihad into practical socio-political structures. Last shows that "for the first time Islam became the undisputed established faith of the state, and a uniform and elaborate code of law was enforced throughout; peace was maintained over areas which had never known unity before, and with peace came increasing prosperity through trade and agriculture. Lastly, the integration on a large scale of Fulani and Hausa into one Muslim society was begun."

962
Monteil, Charles V. Le coton chez les noirs. BCAOF, t. 9, oct./déc. 1926: 585–684. DT521.C6, v. 9

Part of this paper studies the historical diffusion of cotton cultivation. Monteil traces its various phases, using Arab, Portuguese, and French sources.

963
Ogunbiyi, I. A. The position of Muslim women as stated by 'Uthmān b. Fūdī. Odù, no. 2, Oct. 1969: 43–60. DT515.A2O32, 1969

964
Palmer, *Sir* Herbert R. An early Fulani conception of Islam. *In* African Society. Journal, v. 13, July 1914: 407–414; v. 14, Oct. 1914: 53–59; v. 14, Jan. 1915: 185–192. DT1.R62, v. 13–14

This is apparently the first translation of Usuman dan Fodyo's *Tanbīh al-Ikhwān.* Palmer points out that "perhaps the chief interest of the work is that it shows most clearly the conception the Fulanis themselves had of their State."

965
Prouteaux, Maurice. Une éclipse de Lune chez les Dioulas de Bondoukou. L'Anthropologie, t. 29, no 3/4, 1918–1919: 337–340. GN1.A68, v. 29

966
Suret-Canale, Jean. Essai sur la signification sociale et historique des hégémonies peules (XVIIe–XIXe siècles). Recherches africaines; études guinéennes, nouv. sér., no 1, janv./mars 1969: 5–29.
DT543.A3R4, 1969

At the beginning of the 17th century, the trans-Saharan trade, cornerstone of the Sudanic empires, was being replaced by the coastal slave trade. In this Marxist interpretation, Suret-Canale sees the rise of Fulbe hegemonies as an attempt to forge political entities based on Islamic reform, yet not strong enough to withstand European expansion and too early to rely upon a national resistance. He concludes: "C'est la colonisation elle-même qui devait créer par un retour vengeur de l'histoire . . . les conditions de leur unité et de leur emancipation."

967
Tarverdova, Ekaterina Astvatsaturovna. Rasprostranenie islama v Zapodnoĭ Afrike. [Diffusion of Islam in West Africa, 11th-16th century] Moscow, Nauka, Glav. red. Bostochnoi lit-ry, 1967. 85 p.
BP64.A4W37

At head of title: Akademiiâ Nauk SSSR. Institut Afriki. E. A. Tarverdova.

968
Villemur, J. Découverte d'un sabre droit marocain ancien prés de Taoudeni. NA, no 68, oct. 1955: 98. DT1.I513, 1955

Report on the discovery of a 17th-century sword in the region of Taoudenni (Ksar Smeïdi) in northern Mali. The sword probably belonged to the pashas of Timbuktu, who still maintained tenuous relations with Morocco.

Theology

969
Balogun, Ismail A. B. *Features of the Ihya' al-Sunnah wa-ikhmād al-Bid'a* of 'Uthma, b. Fodiye. *In* Ibadan, Nigeria. University. *Centre of Arabic Documentation.* Research bulletin, v. 6, Dec. 1970: 13–41.
DT352.4.I2a, v. 6

Content analysis of what is considered one of the major works of the Sultan of Sokoto.

970
Fūdī, 'Abd Allāh ibn Muḥammad. Kifāyat al-Ḍu'afā' al-Sūdān, tafsīr al-Qur'ān al-Karīm. [That which suffice the irresolute blacks [in], the exegesis of the Holy Koran] Beirut, Dār al-nashr al-'Arabīyah [196 ?] 2 v. in 1. BP130.4.F8

Vol. 2 has title: Kifāyat Ḍu'afā' al-Sūdān fī bayān tafsīr al-Qur'ān [That Which Suffice the Irresolute Ones Among the Blacks in Explaining the Exegesis of the Koran].

Known also under title: Kifāyat ahl al-Imān fī bayān tafsīr al-Qur'ān. [That Which Suffice the Believers in Explaining the Exegesis of the Koran].

Abridgment of the author's *Ḍiyā' al-ta'wīl fī ma'ānī al-tanzīl.* [Lights on Interpreting the Meaning of the Given Word].

971
al-Hajj, Muhammad A. The thirteenth century in Muslim eschatology: Mahdist expectations in the Sokoto caliphate. *In* Ibadan, Nigeria. University. *Centre of Arabic Documentation.* Research bulletin, v. 3, July 1967: 100–115. DT352.4.I2a, v. 3

972
Martin, Bradford G. Unbelief in the Western Sudan: Uthman dan Fodio's *Ta'līm al-ikhwān.* Middle Eastern studies, v. 4, Oct. 1967: 50–97.
DS41.M535, v. 4

Text and translation of a work by Usuman dan Fodyo called *Ta'līm al-ikhwān bi-al-umūr al-latī kaffarnā bihā mulūk al-Sūdān al-ladhīn kānū min ahl hadhihi al-buldān* [Instruction to the Brethrens in Those Matters in Which We Have Designated the Kings of the Sudan as Unbelievers, Who Were From Among the People of This Land] completed in December 1813. According to Martin, it is "chiefly concerned with the double question of unbelief (*Kufr*), and the practice of branding others as unbelievers (*Takfīr*)."

973
Tapiéro, Norbert. A propos d'un manuscrit arabe, d'origine soudanaise, déposé à la Bibliothèque Nationale, Paris. *In* Ibadan, Nigeria. University. *Centre of Arabic Documentation.* Research bulletin, v. 4, Dec. 1968: 26–40. DT352.4.I2a, v. 4

Comments on *Shams al-ikhwān yastaḍī'ūna bihi fī uṣūl al-adyān* [The Sun of the Brothers From Which to Seek Enlightment on the Bases of Religions] of Usuman dan Fodyo.

Trade

974
Bovill, E. W. The golden trade of the Moors. 2d ed. revised and with additional material by Robin Hallett. London, New York, Oxford University Press, 1968. 293 p. 11 plates, illus., maps. DT356.B6 1968

New edition of the classic *Caravans of the Old Sahara* published in 1933. Bovill examines the sub-Saharan trade from antiquity to the modern era in this thoroughly researched, well-written book.

975
Curtin, Philip D. The lure of Bambuk gold. JAH, v. 14, no. 4, 1973: 623–631. DT1.J65, v. 14

976
Emerit, M. Les liaisons terrestres entre le Soudan et l'Afrique du Nord au XVIIIe et au début du XIXe siècle. *In* Algiers (city). Université. *Institut de recherches sahariennes.* Travaux, t. 2, 1. semestre, 1954: 29–47. DT331.A4, v. 2

977
Jobson, Richard. The golden trade; or, A discovery of the River Gambra, and the golden trade of the Aethiopians, with a new introduction by Walter Rodney. London, Dawsons of Pall Mall, 1968. 209 p. (Colonial history series) DT509.J63 1968

First published in 1623.

978
Nicolas, François-J. Le Bouracan ou Bougran, tissu soudanais du Moyen Age. Anthropos, t. 53, fasc. 1/2, 1958: 265–268 GN1.A7, v. 53

1850–1960

CENTRAL REGION

Biography

979
Bivar, A. D. H. Rabāḥ ibn Faḍlullāh—The autograph of a despot. Nigeria magazine, no. 68, Mar. 1961: 83–88. DT515.N47, 1961

Rabāḥ, called the "African Napoleon" by his biographer Max von Oppenheim, was reported by the French administrator Gentil to be illiterate. Bivar believes that this claim can now be refuted by the discovery of Rabāḥ's autograph on an Arabic manuscript, *Kitāb al-Shifā' fī Ta'rīf al-Muṣṭafā* by Abū al-Faḍl 'Iyyād ibn Mūsā (A.D. 1083–1149, 476–544 A.H.). The manuscript once belonged to Shehu Hashimi, ruler of Bornu.

980
Dujarric, Gaston. La vie du Sultan Rabah; les français au Tchad. Paris, J. André, 1902. 146 p. DT551.D87

981
Hallam, W. K. R. The itinerary of Rabih Fadl Allah, 1879–1893. BIFAN, t. 30, janv. 1968: 165–181. DT1.I5123, v. 30

A report on the peregrinations of Rabāḥ ibn Faḍl Allāh, the slave trader who built an empire between Lake Chad and Jabal Marra in the Sudan. Hallam has methodically reconstructed the itinerary from the time of Sulaymān Wād Zubayr's arrest in July 1879 to Rabāḥ's defeat and death at Kousseri (later called Fort Foureau) by the combined forces of the Lamy, Gentil, and Loalland missions.

982
——— Rabeh: The tyrant of Bornu. Nigeria magazine, no. 86, Sept. 1965: 164–175. illus. DT515.N47, 1965

983
Paré, Isaac. Un artiste camerounais peu connu: Ibrahim Njoya. Abbia, no 6, août 1964: 173–185. illus. AP9.A24, 1964

Ibrahim Njoya (1896–1962) was a Muslim painter, sculptor, and decorator who expressed the artistic traditions of his Bamun ancestors. Paré presents the artist's life and works, with reproductions of a selection of his paintings inspired by oral traditions.

984
Verbeken, Auguste. Msiri, roi du Garenganze; l'homme rouge du Katanga. Bruxelles, L. Cuypers, 1956. 262 p. DT665.K3V38

Cities

985
Bakari [Yaya], *Modibbo.* Histoire des sultans de Maroua. Abbia, no 3, sept. 1963: 77–92. AP9.A24, 1963

A translation and annotation by J. C. Zeltner of a chronicle of the sultans of Maroua, covering the period 1740–1943. The text relates the arrival of the Fulbe and their conquest of the original Giziga in the Maroua Plain and closes with the election of Muḥammad al-Ṭāhir as sultan on May 23, 1943. A genealogy and a tentative chronology are included.

986
Bassoro, Mal Hammadou. Un manuscrit peul sur l'histoire de Garoua. Abbia, no 8, 1965: 45–75. AP9.A24, 1965

Transliteration and translation by Eldridge Mohammadou of an oral tradition of the Fulbe of Garoua in northern Cameroon. Written down in 1964, it tells the genealogy of the laamibe and the major events since 1801, when the first laamido reached the Benue River.

987
Lebeuf, Annie M.-D. Boum Massénia, capitale de l'ancien royaume du Baguirmi. JOSAF, t. 37, fasc. 2, 1967: 215–244. DT1.S65, v. 37

Boum Massénia, the capital of the Bagirmi kingdom, was established during the 15th or 16th century. It was abandoned and burned in 1898 by Sultan Gaorang when Rabāḥ threatened the city. Lebeuf, who has been working in Chad for a number of years, describes the old and the new city according to both archeological research and the description of the area by Heinrich Barth. She also reports the traditional origins of the capital and closes with an interpretative essay reflecting the Barma cosmology and its conception of space as evidenced in the ruins of Boum Massénia.

988
Lebeuf, Jean-Pierre, *and* Maxime Rodinson. Les mosquées de Fort-Lamy (A.O.F.). BIFAN, t. 14, juil. 1952: 970–974. Q89.I5, v. 14

Text and translation of an Arabic language list of "places of worship" in Fort-Lamy. According to this list, compiled by a Kanuri learned man named al-Hajj Umar, there are 38 "mosques" in Fort-Lamy.

989
Thier, Franz M. de. Singhitini, la Stanleyville musulmane. Bruxelles, Centre pour l'étude des problèmes du monde musulman contemporain [1963] 107 p. illus., map. (Correspondance d'Orient, no 6) HC498.C6, no. 6

Historical narrative of the city of Kisangani, formerly Stanleyville, then Singhitini. The city, built about 1877 by Arab traders, soon became a major Arab center for trade. The author traces the symbiotic relationship which developed between the Belgians and the Arabs, best illustrated by Stanley and Tippu Tip, and ended with the defeat of the Arabs' troops in 1894. The second part of the study is about the Muslim community in what became Stanleyville: its religious life, its legal system, and the political implications of Islam which the Belgian authorities were determined to curtail.

History

990
Abbo [Mo]Hamadou, Jean-Pierre Lebeuf, *and* Maxime Rodinson. Coutumes du Mandara. BIFAN, t. 11, juil./oct. 1949: 471–490. Q89.I5, v. 11

Arabic text with French translation, describing the titles and functions of the high officials of the court of Mandara, located in northern Cameroon. A list of Arabic terms given special meanings and words foreign to the Arabic language is appended.

991
Abbo, Mohammadou, *and* Eldridge Mohammadou. Un nouveau manuscrit arabe sur l'histoire du Mandara. Revue camerounaise d'histoire; Cameroon historical review, no 1, oct. 1971: 130–169. charts. DLC

Text, translation, and commentary on an Arabic manuscript on the Mandara kingdom in northern Cameroon. This document is the sixth published manuscript on the history of the state and was lent to Mohammadou by Sultan Ḥamīdū 'Umar. Included are two dynastic chronologies and a comparative list of nine dynastic tables drawn from available documents.

992
Abel, Armand. Les musulmans noirs du Maniema. Avec des contributions du chef Salumu (Rumonge) [et al.] Bruxelles, Publications du Centre pour l'étude des problèmes du monde musulman contemporain [1960] 160 p. illus. (Correspondance d'Orient, no 2) HC498.C6 no. 2

993
———Traduction de documents arabes concernant le Bahr-el-Ghazal (1893–1894); note presentée par M. Georges Smets. *In* Académie royale des sciences coloniales. Bulletin des séances, t. 25, no 5, 1954: 1385–1409. JV2802.A3, v. 25

Texts and translations of 11 letters written by various political leaders of the Bahr-el-Ghazal region during the period 1893–94. Includes commentaries by Abel.

994
Abemba, Bulaimu. Pouvoir politique traditionnel et Islam au Congo oriental. *In* Centre d'étude et de documentation africaines. Cahiers, sér. 4, 2, 1971: 1–43. DT1.C45, 1971

Analysis of the influence of Islam on the traditional political life and social structure of the eastern part of present-day Zaïre from the 1840's to the 1950's.

995
Abubakar, S. The establishment of Fulbe authority in the Upper Benue basin, 1809–47. Savanna, v. 1, June 1972: 67–80. DLC

Investigates how the Fulbe in the region south of the Chad basin waged a jihad against their non-Fulbe overlords and founded the emirate of Fombina, also known as Adamawa, with its capital at Yola.

996
Alexandre, Pierre. Le facteur islamique dans l'histoire d'un état du Moyen-Congo [Togo] A&A, no 65, 1964: 26–30. DT1.A85, 1964

The kingdom of Kotokoli is located in Central Togo near Sokode. Alexandre divides the Islamization of this group into six phases covering precolonial as well as colonial periods. He concludes with a question regarding the role of Islam as a factor of national cohesion after the introduction, in 1945, of Western political structures.

997
Arbaumont, J. d'. Organisation politique au Tibesti; une convention entre Arna et Tonagra. BIFAN, t. 18, janv./avril 1956: 148–155.
DT1.I5123, v. 18

Translation of a convention between the Arna and Tonagra groups in the Tibesti providing information on customary law and the political structure of the area.

998
Braukämper, Ulrich. Der Einfluss des Islam auf die Geschichte und Kulturentwicklung Adamauas. Abriss e. afrikan. Kulturwandels. Mit 4 Ktn. Wiesbaden, F. Steiner, 1970. 223 p. map. (Studien zur Kulturkunde, Bd. 26) BP64.N5A63

"Veröffentlichungen des Frobenius-Instituts an der Johann Wolfgang Goethe-Universität zu Frankfurt/Main."

Originally presented as the author's thesis, Cologne.

Summary in English.

999
Ceulemans, P. La question arabe et le Congo, 1883-1892. [Bruxelles, 1959] 296 p. maps. (Académie royale des sciences coloniales. Classe des sciences morales et politiques. Mémoires in 8°. Nouv. sér., t. 22, fasc. 1) DT641.A27, n.s., v. 22

A detailed study of the Arab role in the Congo (1883–92) by a Belgian missionary of the De Scheut Order. Concentrating his analysis on the humanitarian, political, and economic aspects, he outlines the first contacts with the Arabs at Stanley Falls, the role of Tippu Tip in the Emin Pasha Relief Expedition, the Congress of Berlin, the attempt and failure of collaborating with Arab leaders on the political and economic levels, and the conflict leading to the collapse of the Arab presence in the Congo. Includes an extensive bibliography.

1000
Comhaire, Jean. Notes sur les musulmans de Léopoldville. Zaïre, v. 2, mars 1948: 303–304.
DT641.Z3, v. 2

Brief note on the approximately 100 Muslims of Leopoldville in 1948, who consisted mainly of "Senegalese" and "Hausa." Included is a list of occupations.

1001
Cookey, S. J. S. Tippu Tib and the decline of the Congo Arabs. Tarikh, v. 1, Nov. 1965: 58–69.
DLC

1002
Duisberg, Adolf von. Zur geschichte der Sultanate Bornu und Wándala (Mandara). Anthropos, v. 22, janv./avr. 1927: 187–196. GN1.A7, v. 22

1003
East, Rupert M. Stories of old Adamawa: a collection of historical texts in the Adamawa dialect of Fulani, with a translation and notes. Farnborough (Hants.), Gregg, 1967. 143 p. plate, map.
PL8184.A2E3

Parallel Fulfulde and English text.

Facsimile reprint of first edition, Lagos, London, West African Publicity Ltd., for the Translation Bureau, Zaria, 1934.

1004
Hagenbucher, Frank. Notes sur les Bilala du Fitri. France. O.R.S.T.O.M. Cahiers. Sér. sciences humaines, v. 5, no 4, 1968: 39–76. illus., map.
DT521.C3, v. 5

1005
Hinde, Sidney L. The fall of the Congo Arabs. New York, Negro Universities Press [1969] 308 p. map (1 fold.), ports. DT655.H5 1969

Reprint of the 1897 ed.

1006
Hirschberg, W. Die stammtafel der Bamum-könige. Archiv für völkerkunde, Bd. 17/18, 1962/1963: 48–58. fig., plate. GR1.A59, v. 17/18

1007
Horowitz, Michael M. Ba Karim: an account of Rabeh's wars. African historical studies, v. 3, no. 2, 1970: 391–402. DT1.A226, v. 3

1008
Huard, Paul, *and* P. Bacquie. Un établissement islamique dans le désert tchadien: Ouogayi. BIFAN, t. 26, janv./avril 1964: 1–20.
DT1.I5123, v. 26

1009
Hugot, Pierre. Entre l'Afrique blanche et l'Afrique noire: le Tchad. Le mois en afrique; revue française d'études politiques africaines, no 1, janv. 1966: 43–53. DT1.R4, 1966

1010
———Le Tchad. Paris, Nouvelles Editions latines [1965] 155 p. illus., map, port. (Survol du monde) DT546.H8

1011
Jeffreys, M. D. W. Some notes on the Fulani of Bamenda in West Cameroon. Abbia, no 14/15, juil./déc. 1966: 127–134. AP9.A24, 1966

1012
Kelinguen, Y. Renaissance d'un sultanat dans l'Afrique centrale française: Le Ouaddai. A&A, no 13, 1. trimestre, 1951: 36–40. DT1.A85, 1951

1013
Kirk-Greene, Anthony H. M. Adamawa past and present: an historical approach to the development of a northern Cameroons province. London, Reprinted for the International African Institute by Dawsons, 1969. 230 p. fold. plate, geneal. table, maps. DT515.A3K5 1969

1014
Labouret, Henri. Les sultans peuls de l'Adamawa. Togo-Cameroun, avril/juil. 1935: 88–109. HC557.T6T6, 1935

1015
Lacroix, Pierre-Francis. Matériaux pour servir à l'histoire des Peul de l'Adamawa. (A suivre). *In* Institut français d'Afrique noire. *Centre du Cameroun.* Etudes camerounaises, t. 5, sept./déc. 1952: 3–61. DT561.I5, v. 5

History of the Adamawa Fulbe from their legendary origins to the period of the French administration. Lacroix investigates political developments in the Adamawa and the Fulbe contacts with the European powers until just before World War II. The article apparently was never completed.

1016
Lebeuf, Jean-Paul, *and* Maxime Rodinson. Généalogie royales des villes Kotoko (Goulfeil, Kousseri, Makari). *In* Institut français d'Afrique noire. *Centre du Cameroun.* Etudes camerounaises, t. 1, sept./déc. 1948: 31–46. DT561.I5, v. 1

Text, translation, and analysis of three dynastic lists from cities in northern Cameroon on the origins of the Kotoko.

1017
Lecoste, Baudoin. La religion des arabisés. Bulletin de jurisprudence des tribunaux indigènes du Ruanda-Urundi, v. 18, juil./août 1950: 310–317. DLC–LL

1018
Le Rouvreur, Albert. Sahéliens et sahariens du Tchad. Paris, Berger-Levrault, 1962. 467 p. illus. (L'Homme d'outre-mer, nouv. sér., no 5) DT546.442.L4

On cover: Sahariens et sahéliens.

1019
Macleod, Olive. Chiefs and cities of Central Africa, across Lake Chad by way of British, French, and German territories. Edinburgh and London, W. Blackwood and Sons, 1912. 322 p. front., illus., plates, 3 maps (1 fold. in pocket), ports., facsim. DT356.M16

1020
Malcolm, L. W. G. Islam in the Cameroons, West Africa. African Society. Journal, v. 21, Oct. 1921: 35–46. map. DT1.R62, v. 21

Investigation of the factors related to the spread of Islam in the Cameroons.

1021
Martin, Henri. Le pays Bamum et le sultan Njoya. *In* Institut français d'Afrique noire. *Centre du Cameroun.* Etudes camerounaises, t. 4, sept./déc. 1951: 5–40. DT561.I5, v. 4

General introduction to the history of the Bamum of Cameroun with emphasis on the reign of Sultan Njoya (1888–1923) and his achievements.

1022
Migeod, Frederick, W. H. Arab origins at Garun Gabbas. Man, v. 23, June 1923: 92–93. GN1.M25, v. 23

Investigation of the claim by peoples located west of Lake Chad to an Arabian, and chiefly Yemenite, origin.

1023
Mohammadou, Eldridge. L'Histoire de Tibati, chefferie Foulbé du Cameroun. Yaoundé [Cameroon], Editions Abbia, 1965. 72 p. illus., maps, ports. DT570.M6

A history of Tibati, a Fulbe chieftaincy of the Adamawa region in the Cameroon, based essentially on oral traditions patiently put together by a senior researcher of the Centre fédéral linguistique et culturel of Yaounde. Mohammadou, a Fulbe himself, has drawn on the traditions held by the elders of the region and reconstructed from a mosaic of sources the history of one region.

1024
———L'histoire des Lamidats Foulbé de Tchamba et Tibati. Abbia, no 6, août 1964: 15–158. AP9.A24, 1964

Exhaustive study of the Fulbe "lamidats" of Tchamba and Tibati in northern Cameroon. Mohammadou, who has studied the northern region in depth through archival materials as well as recorded oral traditions, presents an inside view of these emirates from the end of the 18th century to the present. Included are three major texts in Fulfulde—chronologies of the Tchamba and Tibati laamibe and their genealogies.

1025
Mveng, Engelbert. Histoire du Cameroun. Paris, Présence africaine [1963] 533 p. illus., maps.
DT572.M9

Includes a section on the Muslim north.

1026
Njeuma, Martin Z. Adamawa and Mahdism: The career of Hayatu ibn Sai'd in Adamawa, 1878–1898. JAH, v. 12, no. 1, 1971: 61–77.
DT1.J65, v. 12

Njeuma, head of the history department at the University of Yaounde, wrote his doctoral dissertation on "The Rise and Fall of Fulani Rule in Adamawa, 1809–1901." In this article he proposes to "examine the efforts of Hayatu ibn Sai'd, great grandson of Uthman dan Fodio, to transform latent feelings of expectations of the Mahdi in the Sokoto empire into a positive movement linked to the Sudanese Mahdiyya in the late nineteenth century."

1027
Njoya, *Sultan of the Bamun.* Histoire et coutumes des Bamum, rédigées sous la direction du Sultan Njoya. Traduction du pasteur Henri Martin. [Dakar] 1952. 271 p. 5 facsims. (Mémoires de l'Institut français d'Afrique noire, Centre du Cameroun. Série: Populations, no 5) DT570.N574

1028
Njoya, Idrissou Mborou. Le sultanat du pays Bamoun, et son origine. Société d'études camerounaises. Bulletin, v. 1, déc. 1935: 63–64.
DT561.S6, 1935

The present ruler, one of the sons of Sultan Njoya, writing on the origins of the dynasty and its early political structure.

1029
Palmer, *Sir* Herbert H. A Bornu Mahram and the pre-Tunjur rulers of Wadai. SNR, v. 5, Dec. 1922: 197–199. DT118.S85, v. 5

"A mahram in Bornu was a charter of privilege and exemption from taxation and other obligations to the *mês* (kings) of Kanem and Bornu." Palmer presents the contents of a Mahram from the 12th century and puts it in historical context.

1030
Paré, Isaac. Les allemands à Foumban. Abbia, no 12/13, mars/juin 1966: 211–231. AP9.A24, 1966

1031
Pety de Thozée, Charles T. L'Islamisme au Congo. Bruxelles, 1910. IUC

1032
Poux-Cransac, Germaine. Tage Rabebe, chanson de Rabah, recueillie et commentée par l'auteur. JOSAF, t. 7, fasc. 2, 1937: 173–188.
DT1.S65, v. 7

Text, translation, and music of a poem praising Rabāḥ and relating his struggle against Gentil and Lamy.

1033
Prins, P. L'Islam et les musulmans étrangers dans les sultanats de Haut Oubangui. *In* L'Afrique française; bulletin du Comité de l'Afrique française et du Comité du Maroc. Renseignements coloniaux et documents, 1907: 136–142, 162–173.
DLC-Micro 03878

1034
Rodinson, Maxime. Généalogie royale de Logone-Birni (Cameroun). *In* Institut français d'Afrique noire. *Centre du Cameroun.* Etudes camerounaises, t. 3, mars/juin 1950: 75–82. DT561.I5, v. 3

Text, translation, and commentaries on a manuscript list of the sultans of Logone-Birni in northern Cameroon. The manuscript was provided by sultan Ma'rūf III, and the script shows Maghrebi influences. A well-known Arabist, Rodinson confesses that the translation is only tentative as "la syntaxe en est d'une incorrection extrême." Annexed is a genealogical chart. *See also* 1050.

1035
Roome, W. J. W. Islam on the Congo. MW, v. 6, July 1916: 282–290. DS36.M7, v. 6

Short essay on Islam in the Congo and the problems encountered by Christian missionaries.

1036
Ṣaqr, 'Atīyah. al-Islām fī al-Kūnghū. [Islam in the Congo] Cairo. al-Jāmi' al-Azhar. Majallat al-Azhar, m. 32, Nov. 1960: 596–600. BP1.C3, v. 32

Citing a lecture delivered in Cairo by Stanley on January 20, 1890, in which he admits prior Arab knowledge of the Congo region, Ṣaqr describes the introduction of Islam in the area and how Islam played a major role in the wars of resistance against European encroachments. He notes three Muslim leaders: Zubayr Pasha in the Upper Nile region (1856–75), Rabāḥ ibn Faḍl Allāh in the Chad basin (1877–1900), and "Hajj 'Umar Tall, who organized an army of Muslims from Gabon . . . in the Congo region, and fought the Animists and spread the call of Islam until his death in 1865." He also mentions Tippu Tip who helped a number of explorers, including Livingstone and Stanley. The Muslims of the Congo, according to Ṣaqr, are concentrated around "Kazunghu" [Kasongo?], speak Swahili, and "are in dire need of guidance towards the true religion." Ṣaqr urges the government to provide religious education to Congolese students who would then be sent back to proselytize among their own people rather than send foreign Muslim missionaries.

1037

Tarverdova, Eraterina Astvatsaturovna. Role of Senussites on monitoring caravan trade of peoples of Chad Basin with the countries of North Africa in the second half of the 19th century. Paper presented to the International Congress of Africanists, second session, Dec. 11–20, 1967. Dakar, Senegal. 10 p. DLC

1038

Thomas, Frederick C., Jr. The Juhaina Arabs of Chad. The Middle East journal, v. 13, spring 1959: 143–155. DS1.M5, v. 13

1039

Tubiana, Marie-José. Un document inédit sur les sultans de Wadday. CEA, v. 2, 2. cahier, 1960: 49–112. maps. DT1.C3, v. 2

Investigation of two versions of a history of the Wadāy ruling dynasty during the last 300 years. The texts are critically studied with ample annotations. From these a "probable succession list of Waddāy" is drawn up and compared with those of the author of the manuscript and of Muhammamad ibn 'Umar al-Tūnisī (who visited Waday 1810–11), Heinrich Barth, Gustav Nachtigal, Charles-André Julien, and Henri Carbou. Included are a genealogy of the sultans, maps, an annotated bibliography, and an index of names.

1040

Urvoy, Yves F. M. A. Essai de bibliographie des populations du Soudan central (Niger français, Nord de la Nigeria anglaise). BCAOF, v. 19, avril/sept. 1936: 243–333. DT521.C6, v. 19

Extensive bibliography on Central Sudan, essentially Niger, northern Cameroon, and parts of Chad. The work is arranged by periods and ethnic and linguistic groups. The periods include antiquity, the Middle Ages, the modern period (1500–1800), the 19th century, European occupation (1885–1900), and the contemporary period (from 1936). These divisions are subdivided into regional sections: Songhay-Djerma, Bariba, Hausa, Fulbe, Bornu, Tuareg, and Tubu. The major languages covered are Hausa, Fulfulde, Kanuri, and Songhay.

1041

——— Histoire des populations du Soudan central (Colonie du Niger). Paris, Larose, 1936. 350 p. maps, plates. (Publications du Comité d'études historiques et scientifiques de l'Afrique occidentale française, sér. A, no 5) DT547.U7

A study of the Central Sudan, a region encompassing Bilma, Maiduguri, Zaria, Yelwa, and Gao, and including the Aïr complex, from the 15th century to the French occupation. The historical narrative, by a French administrator who traveled extensively in the area, is based on oral traditions, local Arabic manuscripts, and general writings by Arab travelers and geographers, as well as Heinrich Barth's *Travels.*

1042

Vischer, *Sir* Hanns. Across the Sahara from Tripoli to Bornu. London, E. Arnold, 1910. 308 p. front., illus., plates, fold. map. DT333.V6

1043

Vivien, A. Essai de concordance de cinq tables généalogiques du Baguirmi (Tchad). JOSAF, t. 37, fasc. 1, 1967: 25–33. DT1.S65, v. 37

Preliminary comparison of five chronological lists on the history of Bagirmi in present-day Chad. The lists are by Escayrace de Lauture (1855), based on a tradition reported by a relative of the Sultan of Bagirmi, and by Barth, Nachtigal, Lanier, and Devallée. Appended are six genealogies.

1044

Vossart, J. Histoire du Sultanat du Mandara. *In* Institut français d'Afrique noire. *Centre du Cameroun.* Etudes camerounaises, t. 4, 1953: 19–52. DT561.I5, v. 5

A thorough investigation of the history of the Mandara sultanate of northern Cameroon. The study is divided into three major sections: description of the area, its early history, and the dynasties before and after Islam.

1045
Westermann, Diedrich. Die verbreitung des Islams, in Togo und Kamerun, bearbeitet von Diedrich Westermann; mit beiträgen von Eugen Mittwoch. Berlin, D. Reimer (E. Vohsen) 1914. 90 p.
BP65.T6W4
"Sonderabdruck ams 'Die Welt des Islams.' "

1046
Young, Crawford. L'Islam au Congo. Etudes congolaise, v. 10, sept./oct. 1967: 14–31.
DT658.E8, v. 10
Islam penetrated the Congo via the east in the 19th century. Young reports that the Islamic community centered initially around the Lualaba valley. Isolated from the rest of the country and discriminated against by the colonial authorities, the Muslims lived a secluded life, developing a particular form of Shi'ite Islam. He suggests that they did not participate in the nationalist movement.

1047
———Materials for the study of Islam in the Congo. Cahiers économiques et sociaux, v. 4, déc. 1966: 461–464. JQ3601.A2C3, v. 4

1048
Zeltner, J.-C. Histoire des sultans de Maroua, par le Modibbo Bakari. Traduit de l'arabe et annoté par J.-C. Zeltner. Abbia, no 3, sept. 1963: 77–92.
AP9.A24, 1963
Translation of and commentary on a history of the Fulbe dynasties that ruled Maroua, in northern Cameroon, starting with the arrival of the Fulbe nomads, who settled among the Giziga populations and ending with the reign of Muḥammad al-Ṭāhir, who ascended the throne in 1943. Modibbo Bakari Yaya, a scholar from Maroua, was still active and a fount of knowledge for researchers in 1971.

1049
———L'installation des Arabes au sud du lac Tchad. Abbia, no 16, mars 1967: 129–153.
AP9.A24, 1967
Excerpts on the settlement of Arabs south of Lake Chad from the author's forthcoming book, *Histoire des Arabes sur les rives du lac Tchad.* Zeltner divides the settlers into two major groups. One group, the Ghawalme, "came by way of the steppes and the desert using camels; the other group, consisting of the Salamat, Hemmadiyet, and Bari Sayd," followed a more southerly route and were essentially pastoral, having exchanged the camel for cattle. In addition to written sources, the author has relied upon oral traditions which he collected between 1949 and 1964.

1050
———Notes relatives à l'histoire du Nord-Cameroun. *In* Institut français d'Afrique noire. *Centre du Cameroun.* Etudes camerounaises, t. 4, 1953.
DT561.I5, v. 4
Report on two documents on the history of Cameroon, "le premier, A, a été recueilli à Logone-Birni, de la bouche des anciens que le Sultan MAROUF s'est aimablement prêté à réunir en 1949. Il est précédé d'un manuscrit A donnant la liste des sultans de Logone. Ce manuscrit arabe à l'origine, a été mis en français par le Sultan MAROUF. L'original arabe n'a pu être retrouvé. Le second B, est un manuscrit arabe dû à l'obligeance du Lamido de Maroua, MUHAMMAD AT TAHER. Le texte en a été établi en 1944, lorsqu'à son accession au Lamidat, MUHAMMAD AT TAHER voulut rédiger les traditions fulbé dont un incendie venait de faire disparaître les témoignages écrits." Includes a number of genealogies. *See also* 1034.

Languages & Linguistics

1051
Delafosse, Maurice. Naissance et évolution d'un système d'écriture de création contemporaine. Revue d'ethnographie et des traditions populaires, v. 3, 1. trimestre, 1922: 11–36. illus. GN1.R53, v. 3
One of the first studies on the writing system developed by Sultan Njoya, ruler of the Bamun of western Cameroon.

1052
Dugast, I. La langue secrète du Sultan Njoya. *In* Institut français d'Afrique noire. *Centre du Cameroun.* Etudes camerounaises, t. 3, sept./déc. 1950: 231–260. DT561.I5, v. 3
Analysis of the secret palace language developed by the eclectic Sultan Njoya (1888–1923).

1053
Hosten, Ph. Origine du nom "Maniema." Académie des sciences d'outre-mer. Bulletin des séances, v. 11, no 6, 1965: 1387–1392. illus.
JV2802.A3, v. 11

1054
Jeffreys, M. D. W. L'Origine du nom "Fulani". Société d'études camerounaises. Bulletin, v. 5, nov. 1944: 5–24. DT561.S6, v. 5
Elaborate essay on the origins of the term "Fulani."

1055
Lacroix, Pierre-Francis. Remarques sur les emprunts lexicaux étrangers dans le peul de l'Adamawa. *In* International Congress of Anthropological and Ehtnological Sciences, *7th, Moscow, 1964.* VII [i.e. Sed'moĭ] Mezhdunarodnyĭ kongress antropologischeskikh i etnografischeskikh nauk, Moskva [3–10 Avg. 1964 [Trudi] v. 9, 1970. Moskva, Nauk [1968–71] p. 146–151.
GN3.I39 1964r

1056
Lebeuf, Jean-Pierre. Dessin et écriture chez les Fali. Abbia, no 16, mars 1967: 25–40. AP9.A24, 1967

Literature

1057
Amadu, *Malum.* Amadu's bundle: Fulani tales of love and djinns. Collected by Gulla Kell and translated into English by Ronald Moody. London, Heinemann Educational, 1972. 88 p. (African writers series, 118) (An H.E.B. paperback)
PZ4.A4813 Am
Collection of stories, fairy tales, riddles, and songs dictated by Malum Amadu, a Fulbe from Yola.

1058
Clair, Andrée. Eau ficelée et ficelle de fumée; contes recueillis au Tchad et au Cameroun par l'auteur. Dessins de Ragataya. Paris, Editions La Farandole [1957] 22 p. 4PZ840

1059
Lacroix, Pierre-Francis, *ed. and tr.* Poésie peule de l'Adamawa. [Paris] Julliard [1965] 2 v. (645 p.) (Classiques africains 3–4) PL8184.A2L3
Poems in Fulfulde with French translations on facing pages.

1060
Mayssal, Henriette. Aspects de la poésie Guider. Abbia, no 17/18, juin/sept., 1967: 69–91.
AP9.A24, 1967
Transliteration and translation of two Guider (northern Cameroon) poems illustrating the themes of love and war.

1061
Mohamadou, Eldridge. Contes et poèmes foulbé de la Bénoué, Nord-Cameroun, présentés par Eldridge Mohamadou et Henriette Mayssal. Yaoundé, Editions Abbia, 1965. 84 p. illus. PL8184.A2M6
French and Fulfulde.

1062
———Contes Foulbé de la Bénoué. Abbia, no 9/10, juil./août 1965: 11–46. AP9.A24, 1965
Six translated and annotated tales in Fulfulde.

1063
———Introduction à la littérature peule du Nord-Cameroun. Abbia, no 3, sept. 1963: 66–72.
AP9.A24, 1963
The author makes the distinction between the Mallum'en (from *Mu'allim* in Arabic) or Koranic teachers and the modiɓɓo (from *Mu'abbib* in Arabic) or court scribe and learned man, and he divides poetry and prose into its various component parts. Included is a hymn to Usuman dan Fodyo in Fulfulde with English and French translations.

1064
Patterson, John R. Kanuri songs. With a translation and introductory note by J. R. Patterson . . . and a preface by His Honour H. R. Palmer . . . [Lagos] Printed by the Government Printer, 1926] 31 p.
PL8361.Z77 1926
GB8.N4

1065
Seid, Joseph Brahim. Un enfant du Tchad, récit. Paris, Sagerep, l'Afrique actuelle, 1967. 112 p.
PQ3989.2.S4E5

1066
———Au Tchad sous les étoiles. [Paris] Présence africaine [1962] 101 p. GR360.C45S4
Collections of legends and chronicles from the lake region, including a short tradition on the Wadai sultanate and another on its ruler, Sultan Sabun.

1067
Tubiana, Marie-José, *ed.* Contes Zaghawa; trente-sept contes et deux légendes recueillis au Tchad. Paris, Les Quatre Jeudis [1962, c1961] 206 p. illus. GR360.Z27T8

Politics

1068
Anciaux, L. Le problème musulman dans l'Afrique belge. [Bruxelles, G. van Camenhout, 1949] 81 p. (Institut royal colonial belge. Section des sciences morales et politiques. Mémoires. t. 18, fasc. 2) NN

1069
Boyle, C. Vicars. Historical notes on the Yola Fulani. African Society. Journal, v. 10, Oct. 1910: 73–92. DT1.R62, v. 10

Yola, located near the northeastern Nigerian border, was the capital of the Adamawa outpost of the Sokoto empire. Boyle, who was Assistant Resident in Northern Nigeria, reports on the origins and political development of the Yola Fulbe.

1070
Forget, D. A. L'Islam et le christianisme dans l'Afrique centrale. Paris, Librairie Fischbacher, 1900. 103 p. fold. map. DLC-Micro 13803 BP

1071
Hafkins, Nancy J. Sheikhs, slaves and sovereignty: Politics in 19th century Northern Mozambique. Paper presented at the 14th annual meeting of the African Studies Association, Denver, Colo., 1971. DLC-Micro 03782

Collation of the original: 21 p.

1072
Kirk-Greene, Anthony H. M. The British consulate at Lake Chad: A forgotten treaty with the Sheikh of Bornu. African affairs, v. 58, Oct. 1959: 334–339. DT1.R62, v. 58

1073
Le Cornec, Jacques. Histoire politique du Tchad, de 1900 à 1962. Préf. de Léo Hamon. Paris, Librairie générale de droit et de jurisprudence, 1963. 374 p. illus., maps. (Bibliothèque constitutionelle et de science politique, t. 4) DT546.48.L4

Society & Culture

1074
Abel, Armand. Ein fund aus der Kongolesischen Ostprovinz: eine zeitgenössische Ernennungsurkunde für einen quadritischen khalifa. Internationales Afrika forum, Jahr 3, 7/8, 1967: 387–392. DLC

1075
Dubié, Paul. Christianisme, Islam, et Animisme chez les Bamoun (Cameroun). BIFAN, t. 19, juil./oct. 1957: 337–381. DT1.I5123, v. 19

In the Bamoun region, located in the southwestern part of the United Republic of Cameroon, the Animist substratum was subjected to Fulbe and Hausa Islam, while the colonial period ushered in the Christian faith. Dubié traces the history of both religious penetrations and the balance they have achieved to the detriment of a fading Animism. Appended is a translation from Bamoun of *Nouot Nkweté* [Pursue and Reach], a 21-precept doctrine of Sultan Ibrahima Njoya (1888–1923).

1076
Hugot, P. Tchad et Soudan. A&A, no 37, 1. trimestre, 1957: 3–10. DT1.A85, 1957

1077
Ismā'īl Ḥāmid. La civilisation arabe en Afrique Centrale. RMM, t. 14, janv.? 1911: 1–35. DS36.R4, v. 14

1078
Jest, C. Décoration des calebasses foulbées. NA, no 72, oct. 1956: 113–116. DT1.I513, 1956

1079
Noye, D. Les coutumes du mariage chez les Foulbé du Nord-Cameroun. Camelang, v. 3, 1971: 59–70. DLC

EASTERN REGION

Archival Material

1080
Abū Salīm, Muḥammad Ibrāhīm. al-Murshid ilā wathā'iq al-Mahdī. [Guide to the Mahdi's archives] [Khartoum] Dār al-Wathā'iq al-Markazīyah, 1969. 575 p. DT108.3.A64

"ṣudira al-murshid fī awwal marrah ma'a risālah qaddamtuha li-jāmi'at al-Kharṭūm li-nayl al-dukturah . . . wa qad ra'aytu an udkhila fīhi ta'dīlāt. [The guide was published initially as part of a dissertation I presented to the University of Khartoum as a requirement for the Ph.D. . . . I also saw fit to introduce certain modifications]"

Abū Salīm, director of the Sudan National Archives, was faced, when cataloging the Mahdist epistolary material, with the problem of classification. He tried to arrange it by subject, then by author, but finally decided to organize it according to the initial sentence. Each entry includes the recipient of the letter, its initial sentence, a note on content, and source. Some entries also include a short commentary.

1081
Allen, J. W. T. The Swahili and Arabic manuscripts and tapes in the library of the University

College Dar-es-Salaam; a catalogue. Leiden, Brill, 1970. 116 p. Z6605.S85A4

1082
Cerulli, Enrico. Iscrizioni e documenti arabi per la storia della Somalia. Rivista degli studi orientali, v. 11, 1926: 1–25. PJ6.R4, v. 11

1083
Dāghir, Yūsuf As'ad. al-'Uṣūl al-'Arabīyah lil-dirāsāt al-Sūdānīyah, Jam' wa i'dād wa tansīq Yūsuf As'ad Dāghir. [Beirut, Librairie orientale] 1968. 262 p. Z3665.D34

Cover title: *Sudanese Bibliography, Arabic Sources (1875–1967)* by Joseph Assaad Dagher.

Includes a section on religion; p. 20–32.

1084
East African Swahili Committee. List of manuscripts in the East African Swahili Committee Collection, University College Library, Dar es Salaam, compiled and edited by Jan Knappert and H. Ball [of the] East African Swahili Committee. [Dar es Salaam] 1964. 25 p. (Dar es Salaam. University College. Library. Library bulletin and accessions list, no. 24). CSt–H

1085
Faublée, Jacques. Les manuscrits arabico-malgaches du Sud-Est, leur importance historique. Revue français d'histoire d'outre-mer, v. 57, no 208, 1970: 268–287. N1801.R4, v. 57

From the earliest European records on, members of a *Zafiraminia* lineage are shown writing in an Arabic script and treasuring their ancestral manuscripts. Notwithstanding such a respect towards these old books, copies, by native hands, are known to be kept in several Western libraries. Also, tradition concerning them is getting somewhat blurred.

The study of Arabico-Malagasy manuscripts can be of some profit for students of the history of Madagascar: their hand-made paper was circulating from the Xth century A.C. onwards; the mode of writing used shows that the ancestors of the *Temuru* copyists did not come by way of East Africa or the Comoro Islands. The oldest manuscripts were not written by Arabs but by Malagasy who had learnt the Arabic script. They put Islamic or Arabic features on the traditions brought by Indo-Javanese immigrants. While a few Malagasy month names are Indo-Javanese, the Antemuru astrologers maintain a lunar and astral calendar.

A few of these manuscript records do have some historical significance, as far as a certain period is concerned; they throw light upon these family ties which made up the social structure, before the war between noble clans and commoners brought an end to the traditional society.—(Abstract supplied)

1086
Ferrand, Gabriel. Un chapitre d'astrologie arabico-malgache, d'après le manuscrit 8 du fonds arabico-malgache de la Bibliothèque Nationale de Paris. Journal asiatique, 10. série, v. 5, sept./oct. 1905: 193–273. PJ4.J5, 10th ser., v. 5

1087
———Un texte arabico-malgache du seizième siècle, transcrit, traduit et annoté d'après les manuscrits 7 et 8 du Fonds Malgache de la Bibliothèque Nationale. Paris. Bibliothèque nationale. Notices et extraits des manuscrits de la Bibliothèque nationale et autres bibliothèques, v. 38, 1906: 449–576. Z6620.F8P2, v. 38

1088
Grandidier, Alfred. Collection des ouvrages anciens concernant Madagascar, publiée sous la direction de MM. A. Grandidier . . . Charles Roux, Cl. Delhorbe, H. Froidevaux et G. Grandidier. Paris, Comité de Madagascar, 1903–20. 9 v. illus., ports., maps (part fold.), plans. DT469.M22G7

Subtitle varies.

1089
Holt, Peter M. The archives of the Mahdia. SNR, v. 36, June 1955: 71–80. DT118.S85, v. 36

The archives of the Mahdist movement fell into British hands after the battle of Omdurman in 1898. These archives "which are now in the possession of the Ministry of the Interior form a collection of thousands of documents, written almost entirely in Arabic, illustrating every aspect of the political and administrative history of the Sudan between 1885–1898."

1090
———Mahdist archives and related documents. *In* British Records Association. Archives, v. 5, Sept. 1962: 193–200. CD1.B7, v. 5

1090a
———The source materials of the Sudanese Mahdia. Middle Eastern affairs, no. 1, 1958: 107–118. (Saint Anthony's papers, no. 4) DS42.4.M5 1958

1091
Mirghanī Ḥamzah, Maymūnah. Bīblyūghrāfiyā al-Mahdīyah bi-al-'Arabīyah. [Bibliography of the

Mahdist movement in Arabic] Khartoum. University. Sudan Research Unit. Bulletin of Sudanese studies, v. 1, July 1968: 121–130. DLC

Included are 100 books, periodical articles and manuscripts related to this period of Sudan's history. The compiler is a research assistant in the Sudan Research Unit.

1092

Molet, Louis. Les manuscrits arabico-malgaches. Revue de Madagascar, no. 30, 1. trimestre, 1957: 53–61. DT469.M21R43, 1957

1093

Mondain, G. Note historique sur les manuscrits arabico-malgaches. *In* Académie malgache. Bulletin, v. 30, nouv. sér., 1951–52: 162–170. DT469.M21A35, n.s., v. 30

1094

Mu'nis, Ḥusayn. Wathā'iq 'an Mahdī al-Sūdān. [Documents on the Sudanese Mahdi] *In* Cairo. Jāmi'at 'Ayn Shams. Kullīyat al-Ādāb. Ḥawliyyāt Kullīyat al-Ādāb, m. 2, May 1953: 139–197. AS693.C36, v. 2 Orien Arab

Translation of a manuscript in the collection of the American Oriental Society at Yale (Landberg 543) containing 19 letters of the Mahdi to his followers. The translator suggests that these letters "are of great importance in elucidating the personality of the Mahdi and the nature of his relationship with his entourage."

1095

Qāsim, Jamāl Zakarīyā. al-Maṣādir al-'Arabīyah li-Tārīkh Sharq Ifrīqiya. [Arabic sources for the study of East Africa] *In* Cairo. al-Jām'iyah al-Miṣrīyah lil-dirāsāt al-tārīkhīyah. al-Majallah al-tārīkhīyah al-Miṣriyah, m. 14, 1968: 169–230. DT77.J28, v. 14 Orien Arab

Detailed study of Arabic sources on East Africa, defined as the region from the gulf of Delgado to Cape Guardafi. Qāsim divides the material into general and local Arabic sources. The periods covered include the ancient, Islamic, Portuguese, and Omani eras. The final section encompasses the era of European colonization. Some less known sources are included, such as the Urjūzah Sufālīyah [Sofala Iambic poem], a 700–verse poem mentioning the arrival of the Portuguese in East Africa.

1096

Ramaḍān, Muḥammad Rif'at. Maḥfūḍhāt al-Khartūm. [The Khartoum Public Record Office.] *In* Cairo. Jāmi'at 'Ayn Shams. Kullīyat al-Adāb. Majallat Kullīyat al-Adāb, m. 8, 1963: 286–313. AS693.C36, v. 8 Orien Arab

After an introduction on the historical development of the Khartoum Public Record Office, the author—who teaches in Khartoum—describes the organization of the agency, analyzes its collections, and suggests possible topics of research.

1097

Rehfisch, F. A note on the contemporary source materials on the Sudanese Mahdia. SNR, v. 44, 1963: 143. DT118.S85, v. 44

Comment on Holt's article on Mahdist primary sources (*see* 1090a).

1098

Sudan Government Archives. A calendar of the correspondence of the Khalifa Abdallahi and Mahmud Ahmad, A.H. 1315/1897–8 A.D. Edited by P. M. Holt. Khartoum, Printed for the Sudan Govt. Ministry of the Interior, by the Publications Bureau, 1950. 141 p. DT108.5.A43

"The originals of the letters are in the archives of the Sudan Government at Khartoum."

Biography

1099

'Abbas *Bey*. The Diary of 'Abbas Bey. SNR, v. 32, Dec. 1951: 179–196. DT118.S85, v. 32

Diary of 'Abbās Bey, secretary of 'Alā' al-Dīn Pasha, the Governor-General of the Sudan who was killed with Hicks Pasha's army in Kordofan in 1883. The diary begins on September 10, 1883, and ends on November 1, 1883, four days after the army was annihilated by Mahdist forces.

1100

Abdallah, Hemed. Utenzi wa Seyyidna Huseni bin Ali. The history of Prince Hussein son of Ali. Dar es Salaam, East African Literature Bureau, 1965. 131 p. (Johari za Kiswahili no. 6) DLC

Swahili text in Arabic script, with English translation, of the history of Ḥusayn ibn 'Alī.

1101

'Āmir, al-Tijānī. al-Sulālāt al-'Arabīyah al-Sūdānīyah fī al-Nīl al-Abyaḍ. [Families of Arab Sudanese stock in the White Nile region] [Khartoum] Dāar al-Fikr [1970] 150 p. col. map. DT132.A67 Orien Arab

1102

Badrī, Bābakr. Tārīkh Ḥayātī. [My Life's history] [Khartoum 1959–61] 3 v. LA2389.B3A3 Orien Arab

Memoirs of a distinguished Sudanese educator (1864–1954) intimately involved in the history of modern Sudan. See also the English version of the memoirs (LA2389.B3A313).

1103
al-Bakrī, Tawfīq Aḥmad. Muḥammad Aḥmad al-Mahdī. [Cairo] Lajnat tarjamat dā'irat al-Ma'ārif al-Islāmīyah [1944] 128 p. (A'lām al-Islām, 7)
DT108.05.M8B3 Orien Arab
Biography of the Sudanese Mahdi (1848–1885).

1104
Barclay, Harold B. Muslim "Prophets" in the modern Sudan. MW, v. 54, Oct. 1964: 250–255.
DS36.M7, v. 54
Biographies of two self-proclaimed prophets who maintained that they were good Orthodox Muslims.

1105
Bell, G. W. Suleiman Hariga. SNR, v. 20, pt. 2 1937: 296–299. DT118.S85, v. 20
Short note on Alexander Inger, an Austrian officer who served in the armies of the Mahdi. Inger was "governor" of an Ethiopian province during the period of Mahdist hegemony in Ethiopia. *See also* 1137.

1106
Bennett, Norman R., *ed.* Leadership in Eastern Africa; six political biographies. [Boston, Mass.] Boston University Press, 1968. 260 p. geneal. table, maps, ports. (Boston University. African research studies, no. 9) DT365.A1B4
Biographies of Menelik II, Muḥammad A'bd Allāh Ḥasan, Shaykh Mabruk bin Rashid bin Salim el Mazrui, Mweni Kheri, Gungunhana, and Lobengula.

1107
Bermann, Richard A. The Mahdi of Allah; the story of the dervish, Mohammad Ahmed; with an introduction by the Rt. Hon. Winston S. Churchill. New York, Macmillan, 1932. 317 p. front., maps, plates, ports. DT108.3.B43 1932
"Translated from the German by Robin John."—p. [iv]
A paternalistic biography of the Mahdi as seen through European eyes. Bermann says, "I resolve to tell this tale once more, with every detail, without inventing anything. And, if I can, I want to be fair to the Mahdi."

1108
Bredin, G. F. R. The life of Yuzbashi 'Abdullah Adlan. SNR, v. 42, 1961: 37–52.
DT118.S85, v. 42
Bredin, who was Deputy Governor at El Obeid in 1933, met on an inspection tour a much decorated Yūzbāshī [captain] named 'Adlān who intrigued him. Here he presents the man's biography. 'Adlān was the son of a Fung leader. He enrolled in the Khedive's army and was among Gordon's troops at the siege of Khartoum. Drafted into the Mahdist troops, he deserted to join in the "reconquest" of the Sudan.

1109
Crummey, Donald. Shaikh Zäkaryas: an Ethiopian prophet. Journal of Ethiopian studies, v. 10, Jan. 1972: 55–66. DT371.J67, v. 10
Shaykh Zakariyyā (1845–1912) was born of Amhara Muslim parents. After a solid koranic education, he had a "series of visions which first nearly drove him mad, and then led him to be the most powerful agent of voluntary Muslim conversion in recent Ethiopian history. Until 1895 he preached Muslim reform and often clashed with Muslim religious leaders. After 1895 his teaching was increasingly influenced by Christian ideas culminating in his baptism in 1910." Crummey investigates the man and his ideas and closes with a host of still unanswered questions requiring further research.

1110
Dekmejian, R. H., *and* M. J. Wiszomirski. Charismatic leadership in Islam: the Mahdi of the Sudan. Comparative studies in society and history, v. 14, Mar. 1972: 193–214. illus.
H1.C73, v. 14

1111
Dunbar, A. R. Kabarega, king of the Bunyoro-Kitara. Baessler-Archiv, Bd. 15, Jun. 1967: 153–168. GN1.B3, v. 15

1112
Ekemode, G. O. Kimweri the great: Kilindi king of Vuga. Tarikh, v. 2, no. 2, 1968: 41–51. DLC

1113
Fouquer, Roger. Mirambo, un chef de guerre dans l'Est Africain vers 1830–1884. Paris, Nouvelles éditions latines, 1967. 191 p. maps, plates.
DT445.F6

1114
Gavin, R. J. Sayyid Sa'id. Tarikh, v. 1, Nov. 1965: 16–29. DLC

1115
Ghulam Mustafa, M. Muḥammad Aḥmad Mahdī Sūdānī; najāt dihandah-i Sūḍān, bai tīg͟h laṛne vālā mujāhid jis ne Angrezo͟n ko Sūdān se nikāldīyā. [Muhammad Ahmad, Mahdi of Sudan; the liberation of the Sudan by the fighter and mujahid who threw the British out of the Sudan] Peshawar, Yūnīvarsiṭī Buk Ejansī [1965?] 72 p. (Bi-silsilah-yi tavārīkhī Kutab, 2) DT108.M8G5
In Urdu.
Text partially vocalized.

1116
Hamid ibn Muhammad, *called Tipoo Tib.* Maisha ya Hamed bin Muhammad el Murjebi, yaani Tippu Tip, kwa maneno yake mwenyewe. [The life of Hamed bin Muhammed el-Murjebi, also known as Tippu Tip, as told in his own words] Kimefasiriwa na W. H. Whiteley. [Translated by W. H. Whiteley] Nairobi, East African Literature Bureau [1966] 141 p. maps. (Johari za Kiswahili 8) DT361.H33
"First published as a supplement to the East African Swahili Committee *Journals* no. 28/2, July 1958, and no. 29/1, January 1959."
"The text . . . is that originally collected by Brode and published by him in the *Mitteilungen des Seminars für Orientalische Sprache* 1902–3."

1117
Hess, R. L. The "Mad Mullah" and northern Somalia. JAH, v. 5, no. 3, 1964: 415–433.
DT1.J65, v. 5

1118
Hill, Richard L. A biographical dictionary of the Sudan. 2d ed. London, Cass, 1967. 409 p.
DT108.05.A2H5 1967
Previous edition published as *A Biographical Dictionary of the Anglo-Egyptian Sudan* (Oxford, Clarendon Press, 1951).

1119
———Rulers of Sudan, 1820–1885. SNR, v. 32, June 1951: 85–95. DT118.S85, v. 32
List of governors-general and provincial governors of the Sudan during the Egyptian regime.

1120
Hillelson, Sigmar. Tabaqât Wad Dayf Allah; studies in the lives of the scholars and saints. SNR, v. 6, Dec. 1923: 191–230. DT118.S85, v. 6
The biographical dictionary or collection of biographies has, since early times, been one of the recognized literary forms of Islam. The *Ṭabaqāt* by Muhammad al Nūr Ibn Ḍayf Allāh, of Halfāyat al-Mulūk near Khartoum, contains notices on about 260 men, roughly arranged in alphabetical order. The period covered extends from 1500 to 1800, from the founding of the Fung Kingdom to the author's own time. The men cited are theologians, lawyers, mystics, and saints (ṣāliḥ or wālī).

1121
Holt, Peter M. Holy families and Islam in the Sudan. *In his* Studies in the history of the Near East. London, Cass, 1973. p. 121–134.
DT108.1.H6 1973

1122
———The sons of Jabir and their kin: a clan of Sudanese religious notables. BSOAS, v. 30, pt. 1, 1967: 142–157. PJ3.L6, v. 30

1123
Jackson, Henry C. Osman Digna . . . with an introduction by General Sir Reginald Wingate, bt. . . . London, Methuen [1926] 232 p. front. (port.), fold. map. DT108.15.J3

1124
Jardine, Douglas J. The Mad Mullah of Somaliland. With a foreword by the Right Honourable the Viscount Milner. New York, Negro Universities Press [1969] 336 p. illus., maps.
DT406.J3 1969
Reprint of the 1923 ed.

1125
Kindy, Hyder. Life and politics in Mombasa. Nairobi, East African Pub. House, 1972. 236 p.
DLC
Autobiography of a local political leader in Mombasa, Kenya. Offers glimpses of Muslim life there.

1126
Martin, Bradford G. Notes on some members of the learned classes of Zanzibar and East Africa in the nineteenth century. African historical studies, v. 4, no. 3, 1971: 525–545. DT1.A226, v. 4
By probing into the lives of seven prominent members of the ulema class, Martin has focused effectively on a major sector of the intellectual dominant minority of East Africa.

1127
Mutahaba, G. R. Portrait of a nationalist: the life of Ali Migeyo, as told to G. R. Mutahaba. [Nairobi] East African Pub. House [c1969] 27 p. map. (Historical Association of Tanzania. Paper no. 6)
DT446.M5M8

1128
Nūr al-Dīn, 'Abd al-Maḥmūd. Azāhīr al-riyāḍ fī manāqib quṭb al-zamān wa-shams al-'irfān wa-tāj al-'ārifīn wa-'umdat al-muqarrabīn al-ustādh al-Shaykh Aḥmad al-Ṭayyib ibn al-Bashīr raḍiya Allāh 'anhu. [The flowers of the gardens on the virtues of the pole of his time, the sun of knowledge, the crown of those knowledgeable, the chief of those close [to God], Professor Shaykh Aḥmad al-Ṭayyib ibn Bashīr may God be pleased with him] [al-ṭab'ah 3.] Cairo, Marba'at al-Qāhirah [1973] 284 p. DLC
A biography of a Sudanese Sufi.

1129
Reid, J. A. R. The death of Gordon; an eye-witness account. SNR, v. 20, pt. 2, 1937: 172–173. DT118.S85, v. 20
Short description of the last moments of Gordon in Khartoum by Ibrāhīm Ṣābir, an eye-witness.

1130
———The Mahdi's Emirs. SNR, v. 20, pt 2, 1937: 308–312. DT118.S85, v. 20
The administration of the Mahdist state in the Sudan relied heavily on the emirs who were both commanders of the army as well as governors and executive officers. The emirs were grouped under three Khalīfah, each with his own army and special flag. Reid describes the various emirs and their fates.

1131
———Reminiscences of the Sudan Mahdi, Sheikh Mohammed Ahmed by his personal servant Mohammed el-Mekki Ghuleib, who is still living in the Sudan. *In* Royal African society. Journal, v. 35, Jan. 1936: 71–75. DT1.R62, v. 35

1132
———Some notes on the Khalifa Abdullahi from contemporary Sudanese sources. SNR, v. 21, pt 2, 1938: 207–211. DT118.S85, v. 21
Biographical notes on the successor of the Mahdī and the administrative organization of the state devised by the Khalīfah.

1133
Roberts, Andrew. The history of Abdullah ibn Suliman. Africa social research, v. 4, Dec. 1967: 241–270. DLC
Comment on a probable Swahili text relating the life of a trader who was the leader of the Swahili community in the Kingdom of Tabwa at the end of the 19th century. It shows the social dynamics of contacts between foreigners and the Tabwa, Bemba, and Lunda of Kazemba.

1134
Robinson, Arthur E. Nimr, the last king of Shendi. SNR, v. 8, 1925: 105–118. DT118.S85, v. 8
History of the Nimrab dynasty of the Ja'lī of Shendi, founded in the 16th century and surviving until the arrival of Kitchener after the Mahdist movement. The sources used by Robinson are oral traditions and some written documents.

1135
Rondot, Pierre. Quelques remarques sur le personnage et le rôle historique de Mohammed Abdillé Hassan. Pount, no 8, 1969: 7–14. DLC

1136
Salmon, R. The story of Sheikh Abdullahi Ahmed ben Gelaha, a Sudanese Vicar of Bray. SNR, v. 21, 1938: 79–103. DT118.S85, v. 21
Autobiography of a former 'ālim (scholar) who participated in the Mahdist movement, as told to an official of the Sudan government. Shaykh 'Abdullahi was present at the major battles of the period.

1137
Sanderson, G. N. "Emir Suleyman Ibn Inger Abdullah." An episode in the Anglo-French conflict on the Upper Nile, 1896–1898. SNR, v. 34, June 1954: 22–74. DT118.S85, v. 34
Alexander Inger is one of those obscure characters suddenly thrown into the limelight of the political scene, who then disappears as suddenly, to the puzzlement of historians trying to piece together the history of the period. Sanderson sifts all the information available on the Austrian former "general" of the Sudanese Mahdi, showing his utopian efforts to bring about a rapprochement between the Mahdi and the Sublime Porte and his involvement with the French during the Marchand episode. *See also* 1105.

1138
Sayyid, Muḥammad al-Mu'taṣim. Mahdī al-Ṣūmāl, baṭal al-thawrah ḍud al-isti'mār. [The Somali Mahdi, hero of the revolt against imperialism] [Cairo, al-Dār al-qawmīyah lil-ṭibā'ah wa-al-nashr, 1963?] 71 p. (Madhāhib wa-shakhsīyat, 63) DT416.S37

1139
Shaked, Haim. A manuscript biography of the Sudanese Mahdi. BSOAS, v. 32, pt. 3, 1969: 527–

540. PJ3.L6, v. 32
Ismā'īl ibn 'Abd al-Qādir (ca. 1820's–1897) was a chronicler of the Mahdist movement. After a biographical introduction showing the vicissitudes of the man's personal life, Shaked presents a critical analysis of 'Abd al-Qādir's work, *Kitāb Sa'ādat al-mustahdī bi-sīrat al-Imām al-Mahdī* [The Book of the Bliss of Him Who Seeks Guidance by the Life of the Imam the Mahdi] *See also* 1320, 1391.

1140
Theobold, Alan B. The Khalifa Abdallahi. SNR, v. 31, Dec. 1950: 254–273. DT118.S85, v. 31
The Khalifah Abdullahi succeeded the Mahdi in June 1885 and ruled the Sudan until his death in 1898. Theobold presents the history of the Mahdist movement from June 1885 to the beginning of the "reconquest" in March 1896.

Christian Missions

1141
Allen, Roland. Islam and Christianity in the Sudan. The International review of missions, v. 9, Oct. 1920: 531–543 BV2351.I6, v. 9
Alarmist description of the expansion of Islam and the apparent failure of Christianity to win animist Africans to Christ. Allen cites Blyden's work on Islam in which he shows the advance of the faith (*see* 586).

1142
Anderson, William B. The role of religion in the Sudan's search for unity. *In* Workshop in Religious Research, University College, Nairobi, 1967–1968. African initiatives in religion. Edited by David B. Barrett. Nairobi, East African Pub. House, 1971. p. 73–87. BL2464.W67
Analysis of the religious aspect of the Southern Sudan question. A missionary there from 1952 until he was expelled in 1959, Anderson provides the background of the problem, explains the policy of Arabization and Islamization under Ali Baldo which led to the expulsion of the missionaries in 1964, points out the dilemma of the Church within the context of the Anyanya movement, and suggests a more militant position: "Perhaps Southern Sudanese Church leaders could render far better service by saying openly 'We are all Anyanya.' "

1143
André, Marie. La véridique histoire des martyrs de l'Ouganda. [Paris] Spes [1965] 188 p. map. BR1608.U45A7
Story of the Uganda martyrs and the religious conflicts during the last quarter of the 19th century as seen through Catholic missionary eyes.

1144
Anglars, H. P. Wana wa Ibrahimu. [The children of Abraham] Tabora [Tanzania] T. M. P. Book Dept. [1971] 200 p. illus. BP172.A53
Sympathetic presentation of the similarities between Islam and Christianity.

1145
Bernander, Gustav A. The rising tide; Christianity challenged in East Africa. Translated by H. Daniel Friberg. Rock Island, Ill., Augustana Press [1957] 70 p. BV3530.B452
Study of East African Islam published by the Institute of Missionary Research, Uppsala, Sweden. The author sees Islam as both a danger and a challenge to missionary efforts.

1146
Bruen, S. Tristam. The Arab and the African; experiences in eastern equatorial Africa during a residence of three years. London, Seely, 1891. 338 p. illus., plates. DT365.P97
During his three years of missionary work in the region, Bruen came in contact with a number of Muslim traders. His approach to Islam and its adherents reflects the attitudes of the period.

1147
Cederquist, K. Islam and Christianity in Abyssinia. MW, v. 2, Apr. 1912: 152–159. DS36.M7, v. 2
After a historical account of the conflict between the two faiths, Cederquist concludes, "If the Abyssinian Church is not awakened, and if liberty is not given to the Word of God, the doom of Abyssinia is sealed and the whole country will fall to Islam."

1148
Courtois, V. The progress of Islam in Central Africa. Notes on Islam, v. 10, Mar. 15, 1957: 2–12. BP1.N6, v. 10
Progress report on the advance of Islam in Central Africa by the Jesuit editor of the periodical. He urges that missionary work and competition be kept apolitical and includes with the article a page of statistics from the 1954 *Annuaire du Monde Musulman* on the Muslim population of Africa.

1149
Holway, James D. C.M.S. contact with Islam in East Africa before 1914. Journal of religion in Africa/Religion en Afrique, v. 4, fasc. 3, 1972: 200–212.

BL2400.J68, v. 4

After surveying the missionary activities of the Anglican Church Missionary Society since 1844, when Johann Ludwig Krapf arrived in Mombasa, and its relationship with Islam, Holway concludes on a note of amazement as to the lack of coordination between the C.M.S. in East Africa and in both India and Egypt and its failure to seek the help of the Christian communities in the Arab world.

1150

———Islam and Christianity in East Africa. *In* Workshop in Religious Research, University College, Nairobi, 1967–1968. African initiatives in religion. Edited by David B. Barrett. [Nairobi] East African Pub. House [1971] p. 262–273.
BL2464.W67

Results of an investigation into the degree of interconversion between the Muslim and Christian communities in East Africa.

1151

Ja'far, 'Alī al-Sayyid. Ḥawla mu'āmarāt al-mubashshirīn bi-janūb al-Sūdān. [On the plots of missionaries in the Southern Sudan]. Cairo. al-Jāmi' al-Azhar. Majallat al-Azhar, m. 29, Apr. 1958: 936–939. BP1.C3, v. 29 Orien Arab

Brief note on the problem of the missionaries in the Southern Sudan as seen from an Azhari point of view. Ja'far, who visited the region and observed missionary activities, suggests the creation of Muslim institutions of learning to counter the influence of the missions he equates with colonial power.

1152

Kesby, John D. Warangi: Muslim traditionalists, Catholic progressives. *In* Kampala, Uganda. Makerere University College. *East African Institute of Social Research.* Conference papers, pt. C, no. 359, 1966: 1–8. HN792.K3, 1966

1153

Kumm, H. K. W. The Sudan United Mission in Islam. MW, v. 8, Oct. 1918: 294–298.
DS36.M7, v. 8

Short essay in which the mission is seen as a dam against Muslim infiltration into Africa south of the Sahara.

1154

Massaja, *Cardinal* Gugliemo. Note sur l'Abyssinie. Nouvelles annales des voyages, v. 134, 1852: 109–111. G161.A6. v. 134

Pessimistic report on the decline of Christianity and the great advance of Islam in Ethiopia.

1155

Soseleje, M. D. The Church's encounter with Islam in East Africa. Ministry (Morija, Lesotho), v. 8, Oct. 1968: 177–184. BR1.M46, v. 8

1156

Trimingham, J. Spencer. The Christian approach to Islam in the Sudan. London, New York, Oxford University Press, 1948. 73 p. BV3625.S8T7

By analyzing missionary activities in the Sudan, the author hopes to stimulate what he terms "creative thought in missionary thinking," in an effort to encourage the development of a Christian community in the Sudan that will be truly indigenous.

1157

Trowbridge, Stephen. Beyond Khartum. MW, v. 7, Oct. 1917: 372–389. DS36.M7, v. 7

Trowbridge saw Islam rapidly progressing in the southern Sudan. Analyzing the routes and extent of Muslim inroads, he concludes, "What then is able to block the advance of Islam? Nothing short of Christianization. And in order that that great experience may be accomplished the sooner, every branch and brotherhood of the Christian Church must put forth a united and undaunted effort."

1158

Uganda Museum, *Kampala, Uganda.* Islam and the early Christian missions in Uganda, 1844–1910. Compiled by Merrick Posnansky, Valerie Vowles [and] C. M. Sekintu, as a guide to the Islam and the Early Christian Missions in Uganda Exhibition held at the Uganda Museum in August, 1960. 2d ed. [Kampala] 1966. 15 leaves. (Uganda Museum, Kampala, Uganda. Occasional paper no. 9) DLC

Cities

1159

Berg, Fred J., *and* B. J. Walter. Mosques, population and urban development in Mombasa. Hadith, v. 1, 1968: 47–100. illus., maps.
DT434.E2A25, v. 1

No. 1 issued as the proceedings of the annual conference of the Historical Association of Kenya.

1160

Caulk, Richard A. Harrar town in the 19th century and its neighbours. Paper presented to the International Congress of Africanists, third session, Dec. 9–19, 1973. Addis Ababa. 19 p. DLC

1161
Chittick, H. Neville. Kilwa: a preliminary report. Azania, v. 1, 1966: 1–36. DT365.3.A94, v. 1

1162
———Kilwa and the Arab settlement of the East African coast. JAH, v. 4, no. 2, 1963: 170–190. DT1.J65, v. 4

1163
———Kisimani Mafia; excavation at an Islamic settlement on the East African coast. [Dar es Salaam, Printed by the Govt. Printer, 1961] 33 p. illus. (Tanganyika. Ministry of Education. Antiquities Division. Occasional papers, no. 1) IEN

1164
———The Mosque at Mbuamaji and the Nabahani. Azania, v. 4, 1969: 159–160. DT365.3.A94, v. 4

Mbuamaji is a village situated on the coast some 15 kilometers southeast of Dar es Salaam.

1165
———A new look at the history of Pate. JAH, v. 10, no. 3, 1969: 375–391. illus., map. DT1.J65, v. 10

Based on a critical examination of the Pate Chronicle in the light of new archeological and external historical evidence, this article presents a case for the revision of the early history of the town. It maintains that Pate was the latest of the settlements to rise to importance in the region, being of little importance before the 16th century—(Abstract supplied, modified)

1166
———Notes on Kilwa. TNR, no. 53, Oct. 1959: 179–203. DT436.T3, 1959

1167
Craster, John E. E. Pemba, the spice island of Zanzibar. London, T. Fisher Unwin [1913] 358 p. front. (port. group) fold. maps, plates. DT469.P4C7

Report on the survey of Pemba at the request of the Zanzibar government. Includes a number of references to Islam on the island.

1168
Dafalla, Hassan. Notes on the history of Wadi Halfa Town. SNR, v. 46, 1965: 8–26. illus. DT118.S85, v. 46

Wadi Halfa, a frontier town between Egypt and the Sudan, was built in the second half of the 19th century. Dafallah describes the city's vicissitudes during the Mahdist period.

1169
Engeström, Tor. Notes sur les modes de construction au Soudan. [La traduction en français en a été affectuée avec le concours de Marguerite Borch] Stockholm, 1957. 41 p. illus., map. (Statens etnografiska museum. Smärre meddelanden, nr. 26) GN4.S7, no. 26

1170
Gray, *Sir* John Milner. Dar es Salaam under the sultans of Zanzibar. TNR, no. 33, July 1952: 1–21. DT436.T3, no. 33

1171
Harries, Lyndon. Swahili traditions of Mombasa. Afrika und Ubersee, Bd. 43, Jul. 1959: 81–105. PL8000.Z4, v. 43

1172
Heepe, M., *tr. and ed.* Suaheli-chronik von Pate. *In* Berlin. Universität. Seminar für orientalische sprachen. Mitteilungen, Bd. 31, 3, 1928: 145–192. PJ25.B5, v. 31

1173
Hichens, William. Khabar al-Lamu—A chronicle of Lamu by Shaibu Faraji bin Hamed al-Bakariy al-Lamuy. Bantu studies, v. 12, Mar. 1938: 1–33. DT764.B2B3, v. 12

Lamu was a trade center and point of contact between the inhibitants of the East African coast and the Arabs for many centuries.

1174
Ibn Salīm, *Prof.* Jazīrat Lāmū (Markaz al-thaqāfah al-Islāmīyah fī Sharq Ifrīqīyah). [The Island of Lamu (Center of Islamic culture in East Africa)] Cairo. al-Jāmiʻ al-Azhar. Majallat al-Azhar, m. 32, June 1960: 87–89. BP1.C3, v. 32 Orien Arab

Focusing on the religious life of the island, Ibn Salīm describes its activities and sanctuaries. Among the prominent families of the city are "the Ommayads who were sent by the Caliph ʻAbd al-Malik ibn Marwān, and it is said that his own son, Ḥamzah, propagated Islam [in the region]." The descendants of these families are the religious leaders of the town, where they are the custodians of the mosque and officiate at the public prayers and sacrifices related to the rain ceremonies. One of them, Ḥabīb Ṣāliḥ, established a religious school in 1885 which at his death came under the direction of his son Ḥabīb Aḥmad Badawī.

1175
Kirkman, James S. Kinuni—an Arab manor on the coast of Kenya. *In* Royal Asiatic Society. Journal, 1957, pt. 2: 145–150. AS122.L72, 1957

1176
———Mnarari of Kilifi: the mosques and tombs. Ars orientalis, v. 3, 1959: 95–111. N7260.A7, v. 3

1177
———Takwa—the mosque of the Pillar. Ars orientalis, v. 2, 1957: 175–182. N7260.A7, v. 2

1178
Lienhardt, Peter. The Mosque College of Lamu and its social background. TNR, no. 53, 1959: 228–242. MBU

1179
Martin, Chryssee M. P., *and* Bradley B. Martin. Quest for the past; an historical guide to Lamu. Nairobi, Woolworths, 1970. 40 p. illus., maps. DT434.E29L27

1180
Martin, Esmond B. The history of Malindi: a geographical analysis of an East African coastal town from the Portuguese period to the present. Nairobi, East African Literature Bureau [1973] 301 p. illus. DLC

1181
———Malindi, past and present. Nairobi, National Museum of Kenya, 1970. 28 p. maps. DT434.E29M34

1182
Paul, H. G. Balfour. Islam at Uri. SNR, v. 35, June 1954: 139–140. DT118.S85, v. 35

Brief description of a mosque at Uri, northwest of Kutum in the Sudan.

1183
Rehfisch, F. A sketch of the early history of Omdurman. SNR, v. 45, 1964: 35–47. illus. DT118.S85, v. 45

History of the city of Omdurman from its beginnings to the end of the Mahdist era in 1898, covering the prehistoric, Christian, Fung, Egyptian, and Mahdist periods.

1184
Schneider, Karl-Günther. Dar es Salaam. Stadtentwicklung unter dem Einfluss der Araber und Inder. Mit 8 Karten, 6 Abbildungen, 20 Bildern, 11 Tabellen und English summary. Wiesbaden, Steiner, 1965. 87 p. (Beiträge zur Länderkunde Afrikas, Heft 2) DT449.D3S3

1185
Strong, S. Arthur. The history of Kilwa. Edited from an Arabic manuscript. *In* Royal Asiatic Society. Journal, Apr. 1895: 385–430. AS122.L72, 1895

1186
Werner, A., *tr.* A Swahili history of Pate. *In* African Society. Journal, v. 14, Jan. 1915: 148–161; v. 14, Apr. 1915: 278–297; v. 14, July 1915: 392–413. DT1.R62, v. 14

This history of the island was given in manuscript to Werner by A. C. Hollis, then secretary for native affairs in the East African Protectorate. It was said "to have been copied out in 1903 by order of the then Wali of Lamu, Abed bin Hamad, from a MS. written by Muhammad bin Fumo Omar en-Nabhani, commonly called Bwana Kitini." Includes lists of the sultans of Pate and the imams and Sayyids of Oman.

1186a
el-Zein, Abdul Hamid M. The sacred meadows: a structural analysis of religious symbolism in an east African town. [Evanston, Ill.] Northwestern University Press, 1974. xxiii, 365 p. illus. BP64.K462L358

Education

1187
al-Amīn, ʻAbd Allāh ʻAbd al-Raḥmān. Kitāb al-ʻArabīyah fī al-Sūdān. [Book on the Arabic language in the Sudan] [al-ṭabʻah 2.] Beirut, Dār al-kitāb al-Lubnānī [1967] 2 v. in 1. port. PJ8302.A4 Orien Arab

1188
al-ʻAmmārī, ʻAlī. al-Taʻlīm al-dīnī fī al-Sūdān. Cairo. al-Jāmiʻ al-Azhar. Majallat al-Azhar, m. 30, March 1959: 727–731; v. 30, Apr. 1959: 894–899. BP1.C3, m. 30

Two-part essay on the Islamization of the Sudan and its religious educational system. The author shows the Sudanese to be a very religious people centered around Islam and its multitudinous manifestations. He also notes the efforts of the colonial powers to undermine both Islam and the Arabic language and describes the Koranic schools, jurisprudence centers, and exalted position of the religious learned men in the society.

1189
al-Biyalī, Aḥmad Muḥammad Ismā'īl. al-Ta'līm fī al-Khalwah. [Education in the Koranic School] Khartoum [al-Maṭba'ah al-Ḥukūmīyah] 1974. 14 p. DLC

At head of title: al-Amānah al-'āmmah lil-shu'ūn al-dīnīyah wa-al-'awqāf. Maṣlaḥat al-dirāsāt al-dīnīyah.

1190
Carter, Felice. The education of African Muslims in Uganda. Uganda journal, v. 29, pt. 2, 1965: 193–199. DT434.U2U3, v. 29

Analysis of the Muslim educational system in Uganda where education was mainly in the hands of Protestant and Catholic missionaries. *See also* 2454.

1191
Conference on Muslim Education, *Dar es Salaam, 1958.* Proceedings of the Conference . . . on 20th–22nd November, 1958. [Nairobi, Printed by the Govt. Printer, 1959] 40 p. DLC

At head of title: East Africa High Commission.

1192
Fahmī, Muṣṭafā, *and* 'Abd al-Laṭīf Fu'ād Ibrāhīm. Dirāsāt Ijtimā'īyah nafsīyah tarbawīyah fī janūb al-Sūdān. [Social, psychological, and educational studies in Southern Sudan] [Cairo] Dār Miṣr lil-Ṭibā'ah [195–?] 180 p. map, plates. HN831.S82F3

Study of the Shilluk and suggestions to improve their educational system.

1193
Gt. Brit. *Fact-Finding Mission to Study Muslim Education in East Africa.* Report by the fact-finding mission to study Muslim education in East Africa. Nairobi, Govt. Printer, 1958. 23 p. MBU

At head of title: East Africa High Commission.
Signed by: V. L. Griffiths and R. B. Serjeant.

1194
Harlow, Frederick J. Observations on the Mombasa Institute of Muslim Education (visited November 8, 9 and 10, 1950). [n.p., 1951] 8 p.

Source: Col. Off. Lib. Cat.

1195
Jahadmy, Ali Ahmed. A note on Arab schooling and the Arab role in East Africa. African affairs, v. 51, Apr. 1952: 150–152. DT1.R62, v. 51

1196
Kenya. Mombasa's Institute of Muslim Education. Nairobi, 1949.

Source: London. Univ. Inst. of Educ. Cat.

1197
Mombasa. Institute of Muslim Education. Prospectus. [Mombasa, 1952] 17, [5] p.

Source: Col. Off. Lib. Cat.

History

1198
'Abd al-Jalīl, al-Shāṭir al-Buṣaylī. al-Salṭanah al-Fūnjīyah al-Islāmīyah fī Sūdān wādī al-Nīl. [The Muslim Funj sultanate in the Nile Valley Sudan]. *In* Cairo. al-Jam'īyah al-Miṣrīyah lil-dirāsāt al-tārīkhīyah. al-Majallah al-tārīkhīyah al-Miṣrīyah, m. 18, 1971: 179–192. DT77.J28, v. 18 Orien Arab

"What is the origin of the Funj? What were the beginnings of the Sultanate? Was the dynasty really founded by escaping Ummayids?" Such are the questions asked by the author in his attempt to elucidate the origins of the sultanate and to devise a chronology of the reigning dynasty.

1199
———Sūdān wādī al-Nīl wa-al-Islām. [The Nile valley Sudan and Islam] *In* Cairo. al-Jam'iyah al-Miṣrīyah lil-dirāsāt al-tārīkhīyah. al-Majallah al-tārīkhīyah al-Miṣrīyah, 2, Oct. 1949: 39–53. DT77.J28, v. 2 Orien Arab

An investigation of the many views, opinions, and theories regarding the origins of the Fung Sultanate.

1200
Abdel-Rahim, Muddathir. The development of British policy in the southern Sudan, 1899–1947. [Khartoum, Published for] the School of Extra-Mural Studies, University of Khartoum [Khartoum University Press, 1968] 58 p. DT108.6.A63

Compilation of and commentaries on six documents providing background information on the problem of the Southern Sudan. These are: Civil Secretary's circular letter to Governors of Southern Provinces (Main features of Southern Policy Restated); Governor Bahr El Ghazal Province to District Commissioner, Raja (Administration of Districts);

Governor Bahr El Ghazal to District Commissioners, circular letter (Pay of Locally Recruited Staff); Governor Bahr El Ghazal to District Commissioners, circular letter (Rate of Pay of Locally Recruited Staff); Civil Secretary's Circular Letter to Governors of Southern Provinces and Directors of Departments (Revision of Southern Policy); Inaugural Address Delivered by Prime Minister Sayed Sir El Khatim El Khalifa at the Round Table Conference on the Southern Sudan (Nature and Development of Southern Problem—Africanism, Arabism, the October Revolution and the New Policy).

1201
Abel, Armand. Un drapeau magique musulman provenant de la campagne contre Rumaliza (note presentée par G. Smets). *In* Académie royale des sciences coloniales. Bulletin des séances. Nouv. ser., t. 3, no 3; 1957. Bruxelles, 1957. p. 578–587. JV2802.A3, n.s., v. 3

1202
Abū Salīm, Muḥammad Ibrāhīm. al-Ḥarakah al-fikrīyah fī al-Mahdīyah. [The intellectual life in the Mahdist movement] Khartoum, Jāmiʻat al-Kharṭūm, qism al-taʼlīf wa-al-nashr [1970]. 209 p.
DT108.3.M84A63 Orien Arab

Based on part I of the author's doctoral dissertation (University of Khartoum, 1966), this study investigates the intellectual foundations of the Mahdist movement and the writings of the Mahdi. It also provides an analysis of the manuscripts pertaining to this period of Sudanese history.

1203
Abū Sinn, ʻAlī ʻAbd Allāh. Mudhakkirāt Abī Sinn ʻan Mudīrīyat Dārfūr. [Memorandum of Abū Sinn on the Darfur Province] [Khartoum] Ṭubiʻa bi-Dār al-Wathāʼiq. [Printed at the National Archives] 1968. 208 p. DT135.D2A64 Orien Arab

First Sudanese governor of Darfur Province (1955–59), Abū Sinn presents a general introduction to Darfur and its multitudinous tribal groups.

1204
Adeleye, R. Aderemi. Rābiḥ b. Faḍlallāh and the diplomacy of European imperial invasion in the Central Sudan, 1893–1902. JHSN, v. 5, Dec. 1970: 399–418. DT515.A2H5, v. 5

Rabāḥ's misfortune as an empire builder was "that the imperial expansion which he led directly impinged on vital European imperialist interests, most notably the conflicting interests of the British and French." The clash of views on the very area he tried to secure for himself led to European "arrangements" culminating in his defeat and death at Kousseri (April 21, 1900) and that of his son Faḍl Allāh at Gujba (August 23, 1901). Adeleye, who has concentrated his research on this period, untangles the politico-military web of this episode of colonial history.

1205
Afawarq Gabra ʼIyasus. Ṭobiyā [Tobiya] leb walad tārik kaʼAfawarq Gabra ʼIyasus yaTemehertenā šena tebab ministér bašerʻāta temehertenā maṣāḥef zegejet wānā diréksiyon ʼAdis ʻAbabā banego mātamiyā bét tātama. [Reprinted 1964, i.e. 1971–72, c 1919–27] 80 p. DLC

Text in Amharic.

Love story with a background of the slave trade and the war between Muslims and Christians.

1206
Aglen, E. F. Sheikan battlefield. SNR, v. 20, 1937: 138–145. illus., maps. DT118.S85, v. 20

An Egyptian army was sent under Hicks Pasha in 1883 to recapture El-Obeid from Mahdist troops. The whole army of about 10,000 men except for two or three hundred who escaped, was ambushed and annihilated at Sheikhan (November 5, 1883). Piecing various sources together, Aglen reconstructs the event.

1207
Aḥmad, Yūsuf. al-Islām fī al-Ḥabashah, wathāʼiq ṣaḥīḥah qayyimah ʻan aḥwāl al-Muslimīn fī mamlakat Athyūbyā, min shuruq shams al-Islām ilā hadhihi al-ayyām. [Islam in Ethiopia; true and valuable documents on the conditions of Muslims in the Kingdom of Ethiopia, from the dawn of the sun of Islam to the present] Cairo, Maṭbaʻat Ḥijāzī, 1935. 111 p. BP64.E8A7 Orien Arab

This critical study recounts the fate of Islam in Ethiopia since the migration of the Prophet's followers before the Islamic era. The author describes the plight of Muslims and calls upon emperor Haile Selassie to do them justice.

1208
Akinjola, G. A. The Mazrui of Mombasa. Tarikh, v. 2, no. 3, 1968: 26–40. DLC

1209
———Slavery and slave revolts in the Sultanate of Zanzibar in the nineteenth century. JHSN, v. 6, June 1972: 215–228. DT515.A2H5, v. 6

"This article is . . . an attempt to describe the institution of slavery in the sultanate and to assess the role of the servile class in the social, economic, and political life of that state."

1210
Ali, Abbas Ibrahim Muhammad. The British, the slave trade and slavery in the Sudan, 1820–1881. Khartoum, Khartoum University Press, 1972. 137 p. HT1162.A75

"Nineteenth century British writers associated the slave trade and slavery in the Sudan with Islam and the Muslims," concludes Professor Ali after describing the ambivalent position of such men as Charles G. Gordon and Samuel W. Baker. His well-documented book corrects many commonly accepted views regarding the Anti-Slavery Society.

1211
Alpers, Edward A. The East African slave trade. Nairobi, Published for the Historical Association of Tanzania by the East African Pub. House, 1967. 27 p. (Historical Association of Tanzania. Paper no. 3) HT1326.A64

Alpers, writing in 1967, refutes the older interpretations regarding the Arab role in the slave trade. He states, "It should be clear by now that the old stereotyped idea that most slaves were seized by marauding bands of Arab and Swahili traders is just another one of the myths which have grown up around the East African slave trade. But we must not make a mistake by underestimating the role which these individuals played in this business."

1212
———Towards a history of the expansion of Islam in East Africa: the matrilineal peoples of the southern interior. *In* The Historical study of African religion. Edited by T. O. Ranger and I. N. Kimambo. Berkeley, University of California Press, 1972. p. 172–201. BL2400.H153 1972

The Islamization of the southern interior area of East Africa (Southern Tanzania, Northern Mozambique, and Southern Malawi) is examined from the viewpoint of Islamic expansion rather than the nature of Islamic practice. Alpers looks at the precolonial and colonial stages of Muslim development then presents the external agents of proselytization, such as Arab traders and resident Muslim Waalimu. He also examines the vehicles of expansion, such as ceremonies for the installation of chiefs and magical practices. One thread that runs through the whole process of Islamization is the "historical relationship between the long islamized Swahili coast and those parts of the interior with which it had become intimately involved through either long-distance international or regional trade."

1213
———Trade, state, and society among the Yao in the nineteenth century. JAH, v. 10, no. 3, 1969: 405–420. DT1.J65, v. 10

Through their deep involvement in the long-distance trade of eastern central Africa, the Yao were increasingly exposed to the impact of Swahili traders and their culture. During the nineteenth century the increased volume of trade, and the ever growing importance of slaves in that trade, combined to produce a marked growth in the scale of Yao political units. This paper begins by outlining the growth of Yao trade before the nineteenth century. It then considers the nature of Yao political organization and the way in which the slave trade, in particular, facilitated the rise of large territorial chiefdoms. The last section deals with related social and cultural changes, including the growth of towns and the introduction of Islam.—(Abstract supplied)

1214
'Arab faqīh. Shihāb al-Dīn Aḥmad ibn 'Abd al-Qādir. Futūḥ al-Ḥabashah [The Conquest of Ethiopia] 1898. MH

See also 1226.

1215
Arkell, Anthony J. Fung origins. SNR, v. 15, pt. 2, 1932: 201–250. plates. DT118.S85, v. 15

Arkell, who studied the Sudan extensively, suggests that the Fung represent the northernmost expansion of the Shilluk wave that reached the Blue Nile at the time the Arabs were beginning to overrun the Kingdom of Aloa. He describes their Islamization and Arabization and their claim to be descendants of the Prophet, suggesting that their ancestors came from the Hejaz via Ethiopia. *See also* 1217, 1245, 1289, 1371.

1216
———The history of Darfur. pts. 1–4. SNR, v. 32, June/Dec. 1951: 37–70, 207–238; v. 33, June/Dec. 1952: 129–155, 244–275. DT118.S85, v. 32, 33

Thorough, comprehensive investigation of the Darfur region and its historical development from the 12th century to the 18th. The major periods discussed are the Daju, Tungur, Darfur as part of the Bornu Empire, and the Fur (Keira) Dynasty.

1217
———More about Fung origins. SNR, v. 27, 1946: 87–98. DT118.S85, v. 27

A reevaluation of the origins of the Fung as presented by the author in an article in 1932.

Arkell's subsequent research for a thesis on medieval Darfur provided him with added information for this latest presentation on the subject. He concludes "a Bornu origin for the Fung dynasty is not unreasonable as it seems to some people today."

1218
Atiya, Samuel. Senin and 'Àlî Dinâr. SNR, v. 7, Dec. 1924: 63–70. DT118.S85, v. 7.

Sanīn Wād Ḥusayn of Kebkabiya in western Darfur was a strong supporter of the Mahdist movement. With the collapse of the Mahdist resistance, 'Alī Dīnār was recognized as a tributary sultan of Darfur by the Sudan Government. After many unsuccessful attempts, he defeated and killed Sanīn in 1907. Included is a letter from Sanīn to the Sudan Government affirming his allegiance to the government and complaining about 'Alī Dīnār.

1219
Aujas, L. Notes historiques et ethnographiques sur les Comores. *In* Académie malgache. Bulletin, v. 9, 1911: 125–141; v. 10, 1912: 183–200. MiU

1220
al-'Awwām, Aḥmad. Naṣīḥat Aḥmad al-'Awwām; wa-al-'ilāqah bayn al-'Urābīyah wa-al-Mahdīyah. [The advice of Ahmad al-'Awwām; and the relationship between the Urabi and Mahdist movements] Edited by Muḥammad Rushdī Ḥasan. [Khartoum] al-Dār al-Sūdānīyah [1971] 80 p.
DT108.2.A9 Orien Arab

al-'Awwām was an Egyptian nationalist deported by the British to Khartoum in 1882 after the suppression of the Urabi revolt in Egypt. His book about the Mahdist movement described both the Urabi and Mahdist movements as revolts against imperialism and Western influences. He called for Muslim unity and a return to the true caliphate.

1221
al-'Aydarūs ibn 'Alī. Hādhā kitāb bughyat al-āmāl fī tārīkh al-Ṣūmāl. [This is the book: the aim of hopes on the history of Somalia] [Mogadishu, Maṭba'at al-idārah al-Iṭālīyah al-qā'imah. cover 1955] 1954. 291 p. illus., map, ports.
DT410.A9 Orien Arab

Cover title: Bughyat al-āmāl fī tārīkh al-Ṣūmāl liba'ḍ mulūkihā wa-sukkānihā wa 'umrānihā wa-al-dīn al-ladhī ya'taniqūnahu qabl al-Islām bi-thamāniyat qurūn ilā al-ān. [The aim of hopes on the history of Somalia; of some of its kings, inhabitants, cities, and the religion they hold to eight century before Islam to the present] Trattato di storia somala; notizie di alcuni re della Somalia, delle sue populazioni, della sua civitá e della religione professata otto secoli prima dell'Islam ad oggi.

History of Somalia by the head of the Islamic community presented in a traditional format, beginning with the Prophet Muhammad and concluding with the Italian administration under U.N. auspices in 1950.

1222
al-Badrī, 'Abd al-Saṭṭār. Janūb al-Sūdān al-Wathanī bayn al-Islām wa-l-Masīḥīyah. [Pagan Southern Sudan between Islam and Christianity] *In* Cairo. al-Jāmi' al-Azhar. Majallat al-Azhar, m. 41, Apr. 1969: 128–132. BP1.C3, m. 41 Orien Arab

With its "southern policy" (1902–1948), Britain tried to uproot and prevent the diffusion of Arab-Islamic influence in the Southern Sudan. Christian missions were given a free hand and every support to convert the southern Animists, thus damming the flood of Islam from the heart of black Africa. The policy of Christianization failed, according to al-Badrī, because only six percent of three million southerners converted to Christianity. Discussing the causes for the success of Islam in Africa, he adds, "It is known that the disturbances which took place in Southern Sudan were apparently political while they are essentially religious," offering practical suggestions for the propagation of Islam. He advocates such methods as providing religious teachers to the refugee camps in neighboring African countries where southerners are located, spreading the teaching of Arabic in the south, linking the two regions of the Sudan by a transportation network, answering the various accusations against Islam in simple studies to be spread by print or audio-visual means. The author concludes that "it is possible to state that the future of civilization in the Southern Sudan and the political stability of the Sudan as a whole—North and South—hinge upon the efforts made to spread the teachings of Islam in the Southern Sudan."

1223
Baker, E. C. *tr.* An early history of Mombasa and Tanga (by Sheikh Omari bin Stanboul). TNR, v. 31, July 1951: 32–36. DT436.T3, v. 31

1224
———A history of Africa, recorded by Sheikh Hemedi bin Abdullah of Dargube, Tangata. TNR, v. 32, Jan. 1952: 65–82. DT436.T3, v. 32

1225
Bardey, Alfred. Notes sur le Harar. *In* France. *Comité des travaux historiques et scientifiques. Section de*

géographie. Bulletin, 1897: 130–180. G11.F8, 1897

Bardey, a merchant from Aden, had commercial agents and intricate trade relations in Harar. He describes his route from Zeila to the walled city and provides a detailed analysis of the Galla stronghold and its people during the Egyptian interlude. Included are letters and political reports from his commercial agents.

1226

Basset, René. Histoire de la conquête de l'Abyssinie [XVIe siècle] par Chihab el-din Ahmed Ben Abd el-Qadr surnommé Arab-Faqih. Paris, 1897–99. 2 v.

Source: Marcus 233.

1227

Becker, Carl H. Materials for the understanding of Islam in German East Africa. Edited and translated by B. G. Martin. TNR, no. 68, Feb. 1968: 31–61. DT436.T3, 1968

Translation and commentaries on an article first printed in 1911 by a leading German islamicist. Though dated, the article "shows many of the views and attitudes of an 'establishment' German orientalist towards the 'problem of Islam' in what was then a German colony." The translation is greatly enhanced by extensive footnotes by Martin.

1228

Bennett, Norman R. The Arab impact. *In* Ogot, Bethwell A., *and* J. A. Kieran, *eds.* Zamani; a survey of East African history. [Nairobi] EAPH [1968] p. 216–237. maps. DT431.O37

Arab contacts with East Africa have a long and continuous history. Bennett investigates the various routes of Arab penetration into the hinterland at the beginning of the 19th century, suggesting that it had been a movement of individuals who were unable to resist European encroachments since they had no support among the indigenous African groups.

1229

———The slave trade in East Central Africa. Paper presented at the 8th annual meeting of the African Studies Association, Philadelphia, 1965. DLC–Micro 03782

Collation of the original: 10 p.

1230

Beshir, Mohamed Omer. Abdel Rahman ibn Hussein el Jabri and his book "History of the Mahdi." SNR, v. 44, 1963: 136–139. DT118.S85, v. 44

Comment on a book by a Yemenite from San a' on the Mahdist movement. The book was confiscated in the Sudan and S. Hillelson, who was then acting director of intelligence, summarized and analyzed it. Besides a number of details unknown about the movement, the "main value of the book . . . is that it is a history of the Mahdia as the Mahdists told it, explained it and believed in it." Beshir also notes the resemblance between this manuscript and *Naṣīḥat al-'Awwām (see* 1220).

1231

———Nasihat al Awam. [Advice of al-'Awwām] SNR, v. 41, 1960: 59–65. DT118.S85, v. 41

Analysis of the book by al-'Awwām on the Mahdist movement and his attempt to draw the attention of the Muslim world "to the illegal character of the war against the Mahdi from a Muslim point of view." A photostat reproduction of the text is in the Archives of the Sudan Government.

1232

Bouvat, Lucien. L'Islam dans l'Afrique nègre: La civilisation souahilie. RMM, t. 2, mars 1907: 10–27. DS36.R4, v. 2

Africans from the East Coast of Africa have served in Muslim armies from the beginning of Islam. Two Muslim currents influenced the coast. Omani and Persian Islam competed for supremacy until the European takeover. In addition to the historical narrative, Bouvat describes the customs and traditions of Swahili-speaking Muslims.

1233

Brown, L. Carl. The Sudanese Mahdiya. *In* Rotberg, Robert I., *and* Ali M. Mazrui, *eds.* Protest and power in black Africa. New York, Oxford University Press, 1970. p. 45–212. maps. DT353.R6

1234

Burton, *Sir* Richard F. Zanzibar; city, island and coast. New York, Johnson Reprint Corp. [1967] 2 v. illus., maps. (Landmarks in anthropology) DT435.B9 1967

Title pages include original imprint: London, Tinsley Bros., 1872.

1235

Caroselli, Francesco S. Ferro e fuoco in Somalia; con lettera introduttiva del gen. Emilio de Bono. Roma, Sindicato italiano Arti grafiche, 1931. 333 p. facsims., maps (1 fold.), plans, plates. (Collezione di opere e di monografie a cura del Ministero delle colonie, no 13) DT406.C3

Quasi-official contemporary Italian version of the

movement of Muhammad 'Abd Allāh Ḥasan, the so-called Mad Mullah.

1236
Caulk, Richard A. Yohannes IV, the Mahdists, and the colonial partition of northeast Africa. Transafrican journal of history, v. 1, July 1971: 23–42.
DLC

European powers "stumbled in the north-east" in their scramble for colonies. They were, however, faced by what Caulk calls "religious nationalism," which delayed and checked European advances. With the death of Yohannes while fighting the Mahdists in March 1889, Menelik II became the sole defender of Ethiopia as the geopolitical epicenter shifted from Tigre to Shoa. The author analyzes the role of the many actors of this complex play and provides a clear image of a confused period.

1237
Cerulli, Enrico. L'Islam en Ethiopie: sa signification historique et ses méthodes. *In* Colloque sur la sociologie musulmane, *Brussels, 1961.* Actes, 11–14 septembre 1961. Bruxelles, Centre pour l'étude des problèmes du monde musulman contemporain [1962] p. 315–329. (Correspondance d'Orient, no 5) HC498.C6, no. 5

Ethiopia, "a Christian isle in an ocean of non-Christian," has often been studied from the viewpoint of Ethiopian Christianity. Cerulli, in this presentation, relates the role and historical problems of Ethiopian Islam.

1238
———L'Islam nell'Africa Orientale. *In* Accademia d'Italia, *Rome. Centro Studi per il Vicino Oriente.* Conferenze e letture, anno 1, 1941. p. 74–93.
DS41.A3, v. 1

1239
———Islam w Etiopi. [Islam in Ethiopia] Przegląd orientalistyczny (Warsaw), 1(65), 1968: 3–13. PJ9.P7, 1968

1240
———La fine dell'Emirato di Harar in nuovi documenti storici. *In* Naples. Istituto orientali. Annali, n.s., v. 14, 1964: 75–82
PJ6.N32, n.s., v. 14

1241
———Note sul movimento musulmano Somalia. Rivista degli studi orientali, v. 10, 1923–1925: 1–36.
PJ6.R4, v. 10

1242
———Nuovi documenti arabi per la storia della Somalia. *In* Accademia nazionale dei Lencei (Rome). Rendiconti, ser. 6, v. 3, 1927: 392–410.
AS222.R65, ser. 6, v. 3

1243
———Somalia, scritti vari editi e inediti. A cursa dell'Amministrazione fiduciaria italiana della Somalia. [Roma, Istituto poligrafico dello Stato P.V., 1957–59] 2 v. illus. (part col.), col. map.
DT401.C4

Italian, English, and/or Arabic.

An anthology of writings on Somalia. The work is divided into sections dealing with: the history of Somalia; Islam in Somalia; the text and translation of *Kitāb al-Zunūj,* a chronicle of the East Coast; law and ethnography; linguistics; and "How lives a Hāwīyah tribe," an ethnographic study of a Somali group.

1244
Chaker, Eunice A. Early Arab and European contacts with Ukerewe. TNR, no. 68, Feb. 1968: 75–86. DT436.T3, 1968

1245
Chataway, J. D. P. Fung origins. SNR, v. 17, pt. 1, 1934: 111–117. DT118.S85, v. 17

Short critique of Arkell's lengthy article on the origin of the Fung (*see* 1215).

1246
Chittick, H. Neville. An archaeological reconnaissance of the Southern Somali coast. Azania, v. 4, 1969: 115–130. illus. DT365.3.A94, v. 4

Includes digs of mosques and other buildings showing a Muslim influence.

1247
———Discoveries in the Lamu archipelago. Azania, v. 2, 1967: 37–67. DT365.3.A94, v. 2

1248
———Ibn Battuta and East Africa. JOSAF, t. 38, fasc. 2, 1968: 239–241. DT1.S65, v. 38

1249
———Kisimani Mafia; excavations at an Islamic settlement on the East African coast. [Dar es Salaam, Printed by the Govt. Printer, 1961] 33 p. illus., map. (Tanganyika. Ministry of Education. Antiquities Division. Occasional paper, no. 1)
MiEM

1250
Collins, Robert O. British policy in the Southern Sudan, 1898–1953. Paper presented at the 4th annual meeting of the African Studies Association, New York, 1961. DLC–Micro 03782
Collation of the original: 15 p.

1251
———Land beyond the rivers; the southern Sudan, 1898–1918. New Haven, Yale University Press, 1971. 368 p. maps. DT108.6.C62 1971
Deals in some sections with the problem of Islam as perceived by the missions and the British administration.

1252
Crawford, Osbert G. S. The Fung kingdom of Sennar; with a geographical account of the middle Nile region. Gloucester [Eng.] J. Bellows, 1951. 359 p. geneal. tables, maps, plates, ports. DT135.S4C7

1253
Cunnison, Ian. Kazembe and the Arabs to 1870. *In* Stokes, Eric, *and* Richard Brown. The Zambezian past; studies in Central African history. Manchester, Manchester University Press, 1966. p. 226–237. DT854.S8

1254
Cuyler Young, T. East Africa and Classical Islam: some remaining research problems in relationships. Transafrican journal of history, v. 2, no. 2, 1972: 3–10. DLC
Assigned to organize a course on "East Africa and the Orient" for the History Department of University College, Nairobi, and realizing the vastness of the subject, the author limited the project to a "diagnostic research," namely to delineate the areas needing investigation. His thrust was in the direction of trade between the coast and the Muslim world. He concludes that the most important problem in East African-Islamic relations is "the time and space depth for the Islamization of the East African coast."

1255
Dale, Godfrey. The peoples of Zanzibar; their customs and religious beliefs. New York, Negro Universities Press, 1969. 124 p. BL2470.Z35D3 1969
Reprint of the 1920 ed.

1256
Dar es Salaam. University College. *History Dept.* Maji Maji research project, 1968; collected papers. [Dar es Salaam, 1969?] 1 v. (various pagings) maps. DT447.D37
Text in English or Swahili.

1257
Davies, R. The Masalit Sultanate. SNR, v. 7, Dec. 1924: 49–62. fold. map. DT118.S85, v. 7
The Masalit Sultanate was located in the center of the western border of Darfur. It included Dar Masalit proper in the south, Dar Erenga to the north, and Dar Jebel to the north of Dar Erenga. The sultanate was established at the outbreak of the Mahdist movement and fought against the Sultan of Darfur and the French, only to be absorbed eventually into the Anglo-Egyptian Sudan. This narrative, based on the account of an eyewitness, is interspersed with war songs by the women of the Gernyang sect of the Masalit.

1258
Deschamps, Hubert. Histoire de Madagascar. Paris, Berger-Levrault, 1960. 348 p. illus., maps. (Mondes d'outre-mer. Série histoire) DT469.M27D4

1259
Dias Farinha, António. Un exemple de la présence de la langue arabe sur la côte occidentale de l'Afrique: L'Histoire de 'Abd Al-Qadir. *In* Congrès d'études arabes et islamiques, *5th Brussels, 1970.* Ve [i.e. Cinquième] Congrès international d'arabisants et d'islamisants. Bruxelles, 31 août-6 septembre 1970; actes. Bruxelles, Publications du Centre pour l'étude des problèmes du monde musulman contemporain [1971] p. 171–174. (Correspondance d'Orient, no 11) HC498.C6, no. 11
Conference organized by the Union européenne des arabisants et islamisants. Comment on *Kitāb 'Abd al-Qādir Bitwātr* [?] *fī qiṣat ahl qāb* [The Book of 'Abd al-Qādir Bitwātr on the Story of the People of Cabo], an anonymous history of the populations of Cabo, near Bafatá at the meeting point of the borders of Guinea-Bissau, Guinea, and Senegal. The probable date of writing is toward the end of the 19th century. The chronicle relates political developments among the Mandingo of the area and their conflict with the Fulbe. The original text, found by Avelino Teixera da Mota in the 1950's, was destroyed during a fire at the Bigine Mosque where it had been kept.

1260
Dujarric, Gaston. L'état mahdiste du Soudan. Paris, Librairie orientale et américaine, 1901. 312 p. 4DT.424

1261
Dye, William M. Moslem Egypt and Christian Abyssinia, or military service under the Khedive, in his provinces and beyond their borders, as experienced by the American staff. New York, Negro Universities Press [1969] 500 p. illus., map. DT106.D96 1969

Reprint of 1880 ed.

1262
Frölich, W. G. Islam in Nubia. MW, v. 6, Apr. 1916: 155–169. DS36.M7, v. 6

Description by a Swiss medical doctor, who lived nine years among the Nubians, of the life of a Nubian from the village of Dabod in Upper Egypt.

1263
Eipperle. Mittheilungen aus Galabat (Abessinien). Ausland, v. 36, 1863: 1181–1185.

Source: Marcus 1611.

1264
Ekemode, G. O. Arab influence in 19th century Usambara. The African historian, v. 2, May 1968: 14–20. DLC

1265
L'Emiro de Harrar. L'Esplorazione commerciale, v. 1, 1886: 154–155.

Source: Marcus 870.

1266
Emrith, Moomtaz. The Muslims in Mauritius. With an introduction by Sir Seewoosagur Ramgoolam. [Port Louis, Printed by P. Mackay] 1967. 150 p. DLC

1267
Farwell, Byron. Prisoners of the Mahdi: the story of the Mahdist Revolt from the fall of Khartoum to the reconquest of the Sudan by Kitchener fourteen years later, and of the daily lives and suffering in captivity of three European prisoners, a soldier, a merchant and a priest. London, Longmans, 1967. 356 p. illus., map, 12 plates (incl. ports.) DT108.3.F34

The story of the captivity of the three prisoners of the Mahdists—Rudolf Slatin, a governor of Darfur; Father Joseph Ohrwalder, a missionary priest; and Charles Neufeld, a merchant—provides a myriad of details on everyday life in the camp of the Mahdi, although the perspective of the observers is, for obvious reasons, somewhat biased. *See also* 1351 and 1396.

1268
Faublée, Jacques. L'Islam chez les Antemuru (Sud-Est de Madagascar). Revue des études islamiques, t. 26, 1958: 65–71. BP1.R53, v. 26

1269
Ferrand, Gabriel. Les musulmans à Madagascar et aux îles Comores. Paris, E. Leroux, 1891. 3 pts. in 1 v. (Publications de l'Ecole des lettres d'Alger. Bulletin de correspondance africaine, v. 9) AS651.A6, v. 9

Partial contents: Les Antaimoro.—Zafindraminia, Antambahoaka, Onjatsy, Antaiony, Zafikazimambo, Antaivandrika et Sahatavy.—Antakarana, Sakalava, migrations arabes.

1270
———Le pilote arabe de Vasco de Gama et les instructions nautiques arabes au XVe. Annales de géographie, v. 31, no 172, 1922. G1.A6, no. 172

1271
Fetha nagast. English. The Fetha nagast—The Law of the kings. Translated from the Ge'ez by Paulus Tzadua. Edited by Peter L. Strauss. Addis Ababa, Faculty of Law, Haile Sellassie I University [1968] 339 p. DLC–LL

"A collection of laws . . . originally written in Arabic by the Coptic Egyptian writer Abu-l Fada'il Ibn al-Assal (commonly known as Ibn al-Assal)."

1272
al-Fikī, 'Abd al-Raḥmān. Ḥurūb al-Imām al-Mahdī Ibtidā' min awwal wāqi'at al-Jazīrah Abā ilā nihāyat wāqi'at Shīkān. [Wars of the Imam al-Mahdi from the battle of Aba Island to the end of the battle of Sheikan]. [Cairo, Maktabat al-Kāmalābī, 1966] 63 p. maps, ports. DT108.3.F3

At head of title: Jihād fī sabīl Allāh wa al-Waṭan (Jihad for God and country).

1273
Freeman-Grenville, G. S. P. Historiography of the East African coast. TNR, no. 55, Sept. 1960: 279–289. DT436.T3, 1960

1274
Gassita, R. N. L'Islam à l'île Maurice. RMM, t. 21, déc. 1912: 290–329. illus. DS36.R4, v. 21

Status report on Islam in Mauritius. A short historical note shows that Muslims were living on the island as early as 1791, but the great influx of Indian Muslims began in 1834. Gassita provides statistical data on the four groups of Muslims settled on the island: traders, farmers, manufacturers, and white collar workers. He gives the names of Muslims in trade and the administration, as well as detailed information on religious organizations such as mosques, schools, newspapers, and associations. Appended are "The Religious Meetings Ordinances, 1898" and "Standards of Examinations in Primary and State Aided Schools."

1274a
Gaudefroy-Demombynes, Maurice. Les tribus musulmanes de Madagascar. Revue de géographie, 2. semestre, 1894: 416–420. G1.R43, 1894

1275
Gee, T. W. A century of Muhammadan influence in Buganda, 1852–1951. Uganda journal, v. 22, Sept. 1958: 139–150. DT434.U2U3, v. 22

1276
General report on the seige [sic] and fall of Khartoum, by Mohd. Nushi and others. Printed in C. R. O., 1885. [n. p., 19–] 160 p. DT154.K63G4

"In June 1885 . . . a board of officers under the presidency of Muhammad Nushi Pasha compiled a report on the siege of Khartoum. . . . The report was originally written in Arabic and it is said to be deposited in the Cairo Archives. All attempts to get hold of a copy were fruitless. The report was probably written on the officers' own in[i]tiative." (From introduction by Maymona Marghani Hamza.) The report was translated by N. Shuqayr in 1891. *See also* 1284, 1417.

1277
Ghayth, Fatḥī. al-Islām wa-al-Ḥabashah 'abra al-tārīkh. [Islam and Ethiopia throughout history] [Cairo, Maktabat al-Nahḍah, 1967] 391 p. 2 maps. BP64.E8G35 Orien Arab

Historical analysis of Ethiopian political developments in the context of Muslim-Christian relations. The author concludes: "We request for the Muslims of Ethiopia justice and fairness, not pity and generosity," stressing the fact that solidarity of its various elements is the only way for Ethiopia to be part of the modern age.

1278
Grandidier, Alfred, *ed.* Histoire physique, naturelle et politique de Madagascar. Paris, Impr. nationale, 1875–1958. 30 v. in 56. plates. QH195.M2G7

1279
Grandidier, G. Fouilles dans les ruines arabes de Mahanara (Côte Nord-East). *In* Comité de Madagascar. Bulletin, v. 5, mai 1899: 230–232. DT469.M21R38, v. 5

1280
Gray, Richard. A history of the Southern Sudan, 1839–1889. [London] Oxford University Press, 1961. 219 p. maps. DT108.G7 1961

1281
Greenfield, Richard. Ethiopa: a new political history. African paperback ed. London, Pall Mall Press, 1969. 515 p. illus., maps (Pall Mall library of African affairs) DT381.G7 1969

1282
Guérinot, A. L'Islam et l'Abyssinie. RMM, t. 34, 1917–1918: 1–67. DS36.R4, v. 34

Muslims had taken refuge in Ethiopia before the Hijrah, but Islamization began in earnest in 800 with the conversion of the Beja tribe. Guérinot presents a report on the Muslim communities of Ethiopia, including the Mansa, Habab, Beja, Bogo, Banū, Amīr, Maria, and Baria, located in the northeastern corner of the country.

1283
Gulla, Sheikh Ali. The defeat of Hicks Pasha. SNR, v. 8, 1925: 119–123. DT118.S85, v. 8

Description of the defeat of the Hicks Relief Expedition by a former member of the Mahdist forces, as related to L. F. Nalder. Shaykh 'Alī, who later became a guide to both Kitchener and Gordon, provides a candid picture of the three men.

1284
Ḥamzah, Maymūnah Mīrghanī. Ḥiṣār wa-suqūṭ al-Kharṭūm Yanāyir 1884–1885. [The siege and fall of Khartoum January 1884–1885] [Khartoum] Jāmi'at al-Kharṭūm, Dār al-ta'līf wa-al-tarjamah wa-al-nashr] 1972. 194 p. DLC

See also 1276 and 1417.

1285
Harries, Lyndon. The Arabs and Swahili culture. Africa (London), v. 34, July 1964: 224–229. PL8000.I6, v. 34

The Arab influx on the east coast of Africa occurred in two waves. The first wave of Perso-Arabians reached the coast from the 8th to the 15th century. This group was assimilated by the African majority. The second wave of Hadrami and Omani Arabs arrived during the 18th and 19th centuries and "moulded the development and character of the Swahili language and of Swahili culture." The last is closely associated with Islam and its future, Harries suggests, "rests or falls upon the continuance of Islam among the coastal people."

1286
———Islam in East Africa. London, Universities' Mission to Central Africa, 1954. 92 p. BP64.E3H3

1287
Ḥasan, Sa'd Muḥammad. al-Mahdīyah fī al-Islām mundhu aqdam al-'uṣūr ḥattā al-yawm: dirāsah wāfiyah li-tārīkhihā al-'aqadī wa-al-siyāsī. [The Mahdiyah in Islam from the remote past to the present: comprehensive study of its ideological, political and literary history] Cairo, Dār al-kitāb al-'Arabī, 1953. 304 p. facsim. BP166.93.H37

At head of title: Jamā'at al-Azhar lil-ta'līf wa-al-tarjamah wa-al-nashr.

1288
Ḥasan, Yūsuf Faḍl. The Umayyad genealogy of the Funj. SNR, v. 46, double issue, 1965: 27–32. DT118.S85, v. 46

With the fall of Dongola, capital of the Christian kingdom of Nubia, in the middle of the 14th century, Arab immigrants poured into the Sudan. Ḥasan, a noted Sudanese historian, traces the origin of the Fung who claim to be, "and are classed in Sudanese genealogies as," Umayyads. He critically reviews several traditions making that claim.

1289
Henderson, K. D. D. Fung origins. SNR, v. 18, no. 1, 1935: 149–152. DT118.S85, v. 18

Critique of Arkell's article on the Fung origins (*see* 1215).

1290
al Ḥifnī, Aḥmad ibn Muḥammad. Kitāb al-jawāhir al-ḥisān fī tārīkh al-Ḥubshān. [The book of beautiful gems in the history of the Abyssinians] Būlāq [Cairo] al-maṭba'ah al-kubrā al-amīrīyah 1321 [1903]. 16, 24, 324 p. BP64.E8H5 1903

1291
Hill, Richard L. Egypt in the Sudan, 1820–1881. London, New York, Oxford University Press, 1959. 188 p. fold. map. (Middle Eastern monographs, 2) DT108.2.H5

In this study, Hill analyzes the Egyptian occupation of the Sudan beginning in 1820 and ending with the final Egyptian withdrawal in 1885 under pressure from both the Mahdist troops and the British. The administrative, political, social, and economic aspects of the Egyptians' presence is presented with a wealth of details based on many sources, the latter presented in a seven-page bibliographic essay.

1292
———*comp.* On the frontiers of Islam: two manuscripts concerning the Sudan under Turco-Egyptian rule, 1822–1845; translated from the Italian and French, with introduction and notes by Richard Hill. Oxford, Clarendon, 1970. 234 p. map, fold. plate. (Oxford studies in African affairs) DT108.1.H5 1970

Translations of two anonymous manuscripts: *A History of the Sudan, 1822–1841* (originally written in Italian), and *Journal fait durant un voyage au Sennar et à l'Hédjaz, 1837–1840.*

1293
Hillelson, Sigmar. Historical poems and traditions of the Shukriya. SNR, v. 3, Jan. 1920: 33–75. DT118.S85, v. 3

The Shukriyah are a camel-owning nomadic group located in the southern Butana region of the Sudan in a quadrilateral area bounded by the main Nile, the Atbara, the Blue Nile, and the Abyssinian foothills. Their leading family, the Abū Sinn, has provided governors and cavalry irregulars to the Turkīyah regime. Hillelson presents the history of the Shukriyah through historical poems and traditions.

1294
Hinawi, Mbarak Ali. Al-Akida and Fort Jesus, Mombasa. [2d ed.] Nairobi, East African Literature Bureau [1970] 79 p. illus. DT432.H56 1970

"Utenzi wa al-Akida (a Swahili poem)" by Abdallah bin Mas'ud bin Salim al-Mazrui: p. [67]–79.

English or Swahili.

Muhammad bin Abdallah (ca. 1837/38–1894/6), better known as al-Akida, played an important role in Zanzibar politics at the end of the 19th century. Hinawi—a major figure in the Clove Island's politics in the first part of the 20th century—provides a narrative leading to a better understanding of the epic poem about the life and feats of al-Akida.

1295
Hollingworth, Lawrence W., *ed.* Historia fupi ya pwani ya Afrika ya Mashariki. [A short history of the east coast of Africa] Translated in the East African Literature Bureau. London, Macmillan, 1966. 183 p. illus., map, port. IEN

1296
———Milango ya historia. [Gateways to history] Translated from Swahili by A. A. Seif. London, Macmillan, 1965. 3 v. illus. IEN

Reprint of the 1943 ed.

1297
Holt, Peter M. The Mahdist state in the Sudan, 1881–1898; a study of its origins, development and overthrow. 2d ed. Oxford, Clarendon Press, 1970. 264 p. illus. DT108.3.H6 1970

1298
———A modern history of the Sudan; from the Funj Sultanate to the present day. London, Weidenfelt and Nicolson [1965, c1961] 247 p. illus., facsim., maps, ports. (Asia-Africa series) DT108.H72 1965

1299
———The place in history of the Ṣudanese Mahdia. SNR, v. 40, 1959: 107–112.
DT118.S85, v. 40

1300
———A Sudanese historical legend: The Funj conquest of Sūba. BSOAS, v. 23, pt. 1, 1960: 1–12. PJ3.L6, v. 23

Holt analyzes the main sources of Funj history and critically evaluates a chronicle of rulers of the Sudan and the conquest of Sūba. He concludes that the work is a fabrication of the chronicler, suggesting a political parable directed against the Egyptian conquest.

1301
———The Sudanese Mahdia and the outside world. 1881–9. BSOAS, v. 21, pt. 2, 1958: 276–290. PJ3.L6, v. 21

The Expected Mahdi came to the Sudan with the goal and duty to achieve the ideals of the Muslim faith. "The outside world," Holt writes, "was a theological rather than a geographical concept. All those who did not accept the divine mission of their leader were unbelievers, even though they might profess Islam." He investigates the Mahdist movement's contacts with the outside world and the clash of the religious reform movement with the realities of foreign relations with Sudan's neighbors.

1302
———Sultan Selim I and the Sudan. JAH, v. 8, no. 1, 1967: 19–24. DT1.J65, v. 8

1302a
———Two traditional Sudanese historical works. *In* Ibadan, Nigeria. University. *Centre of Arabic Documentation.* Research bulletin, v. 5, Dec. 1969: 1–20. DT352.4.I2a, v. 5

Comments on the background of *Kitāb ṭabaqāt Wād Ḍayf Allāh fī awliyā' wa-ṣāliḥīn wa-'ulamā' wa-shu'arā' al-Sūdān* [The Book on the Classes of Wad Dayf Allah of the Sudan's Beloved Ones [of God], Men of Good Will, Erudites and Poets] and the *Funj Chronicle.*

1303
Hourani, George F. Arab seafaring in the Indian Ocean in ancient and early medieval times. Princeton, Princeton University Press, 1951. 131 p. illus., maps. (Princeton Oriental studies, v. 13)
V45.H68
PJ25.P7, v. 13 Orien Arab

1304
Ḥusayn, 'Abd Allāh. al-Sūdān, min al-tārīkh al-qadīm ilā riḥlat al-bi'thah al-miṣrīyah. [Sudan, from ancient history to the campaign of the Egyptian expedition] Cairo, al-maṭba'ah al-rīḥānīyah, 1935. 3 v. in 1. illus., maps, ports. DT108.H8

Vol. 3 has imprint: Miṣr, Maṭba'at wādī al-mulūk.

1305
Ibrahim, 'Abd Allāh 'Alī. The Mahdi-'Ulema conflict. Khartoum, Sudan Research Unit, University of Khartoum, 1968. 64 p. (Occasional papers, 3)
DLC

English and Arabic text.

1306
Ingham, Kenneth. A history of East Africa. Rev. ed. New York, Praeger [1965] 462 p. illus., maps, ports. DT365.I5 1965

1307
Ingrams, William H. Zanzibar: its history and its people. London, Cass, 1967. 527 p. front., illus., 14 plates (incl. 2 maps), tables.
DT435.I5 1967

Originally published, London, H. F. Witherby, 1931.

1308
Iwarson, J. Islam in Eritrea and Abyssinia. MW, v. 18, Oct. 1928: 356–364. DS36.M7, v. 18

1309
Jackson, Henry C. The Mahas of Eilafun. SNR, v. 2, Dec. 1919: 285–292. DT118.S85, v. 2

Eilafun ['Aylah Fung?], situated 20 miles southeast of Khartoum on the east bank of the Nile, was the center of the activities of a religious notable,

Shaykh Idrī Wād Muḥammad al-Arbāb. Founded in 1600, the city drew Mahas tribesmen from Dongola and elsewhere in northern Sudan. The shrine located in the town has attracted many Muslims and is considered, by Jackson, one of the early centers of Islam in the Sudan.

1310
Katumba, Ahmed, *and* F. B. Welbourne. Muslim martyrs in Buganda. Uganda journal, v. 28, Sept. 1964: 151–163. DT434.U2U3, v. 28

1311
Kenrick, J. W. The kingdom of Tegali, 1921–46. SNR, v. 29, pt. 2, 1948: 143–150. DT118.S85, v. 29

1312
Khazanov, A. M. Antikolonial'noe dvizhenie v Somali pod predvoditel'stvom Mukhammeda Bin Abdullahi. [The anti-colonial movement in Somaliland under the leadership of Muḥammad ibn 'Abd Allāh] Narody Azii i Afriki, 2, 1960: 113–122. DS1.P7, 1960

Tables of contents also in English and Chinese; summaries in English.

1313
King, Noel, *and others*. Islam and the confluence of religions in Uganda, 1840–1966. Tallahassee, Florida State University Press, 1973. 60 p. (American Academy of Religion. Studies in religion, 6) DLC

Brief introduction to the beginnings and development of Islam in Uganda partially based on interviews with persons involved in some of the events reported.

1314
Kirkman, James S. The Kenya littoral. Current anthropology, v. 7, June 1966: 347–348. GN1.C8, v. 7

1315
———Men and monuments on the East African coast. London, Lutterworth Press [1964] 224 p. illus., maps, plans. DT365.K5

1316
Kirunda-Kivejinja, 'Ally M. Muslims in Uganda and their problems. The Islamic review, v. 47, Dec. 1959: 33–35. BP1.I7, v. 47

Islam was introduced into Uganda over a century ago. It first appeared in the palace of the Kabaka Mutesa I in 1845. Having survived many tribulations, Muslims in Uganda today are a minority. Kirunda-Kivejinja gives a brief account of the present problems facing the Islamic community and the efforts made through a Muslim educational system to alleviate them.

1317
Klamorth, M. Der Islam in Deutschostafrika. Berlin, Buchlandlung der Berliner evangel. Missionsgesellschaft, 1912.

Source: Dar es Salaam lib. bull. no. 23.

1318
Knappert, Jan. Islam in Mombasa. *In* Oosters Genootschap in Nederland. Acta Orientalia Neerlandica. Proceedings of the congress of the Dutch Oriental Society, held in Leiden on the occasion of its 50th anniversary, 8th–9th May 1970. Ed. by P. W. Pestman. Leiden, Brill, 1971 [1972] p. 75–81. DS1.5.O67

1319
al-Kurdufānī, Ismā'īl 'Abd al-Qādir. al-Ḥarb al-Ḥabashīyah al-Sūdānīyah 1885–1888; al-Ṭirāz al-manqūsh bi-bushrā qatl Yūḥannā malik al-Ḥubūsh. [The Ethiopian-Sudanese war (1885–1888); the embroidery decorated with the good omen of the killing of Johannes king of the Ethiopians] Edited by Muḥammad Ibrāhīm Abū Salīm [and] Muḥammad Sa'īd al-Qaddāl. [Khartoum, Shirkat al-ṭābi' al-Sūdānī, 1972] 125 p. maps (Jāmi'at al-Khartūm. Ma'had al-Dirāsāt al-Ifrīqīyah al-Asyawīyah. Shu'bat abḥāth al-Sūdān. al-Kurrās no. 8) DLC

1320
———Sa'ādat al-mustahdī bi-sīrat al-Imām al-Mahdī. [The Bliss of him who seeks guidance by the life of the Imam al-Mahdi] Edited by Muḥammad Ibrāhīm Abū Salīm. [Khartoum, al-Majlis al-qawmī li-ri'āyat al-ādāb wa-al-funūn, 1972] 406 p. DLC

See also 1139, 1391.

1321
Labrousse, Henri. Le Mad Mullah du Somaliland; (vingt ans de guerre et de révoltes). Pount, 2. année, 3. trimestre 1969: 17–37; 3. année, 3. trimestre 1970: 15–28. maps. DLC

Labrousse, a naval officer, presents a much-detailed narrative of Muhammad ibn Abd 'Allah Ḥasan's revolt. Illustrated with maps.

1322
Lambert, H. E., *tr.* Habari za Mrima (Document attributed to Sheikh Ali Hemedi el-Buhry, with tr. and notes). Swahili, n.s., v. 1, pt. 3, 1961: 34–59. PL8701.E2, n.s., v. 1

1323
Lampen, G. D. History of Darfur. SNR, v. 31, Dec. 1950: 177–209. DT118.S85, v. 31

Lampen spent many years in the Sudan Political Service in Darfur until he reached the position of governor of the province. Here he presents a geographical description, the history of the region, and an outline of the administrative system during each of the periods described.

1324
Leclerc, Max. L'influence arabe et mahométane à Madagascar. Revue de géographie, t. 21, juil./déc. 1887: 334–346. G1.R43, v. 21

1325
Le Tourneau, Roger. Aperçu sur les musulmans des territoires de la communauté dans l'Océan indien. A&A, no 49, 1960: 10–25. DT1.A85, 1960

1326
Lewicki, Tadeuz. Z Przeszłosci Nubii. [Out of Nubia's past]. Przegląd Orientalistyczny, Nr 3 (55), 1965: 215–228. PJ9.P7, 1965

1327
Lewis, I. M. Shaikhs and warriors in Somaliland. *In* International African Seminar. *3d, Salisbury, Southern Rhodesia, 1960.* African systems of thought; studies presented and discussed at the third International African Seminar in Salisbury, December 1960. London, New York, Published for the International African Institute by the Oxford University Press, 1965. p. 204–223. BL2400.I5 1960

1328
Lighton, G. The numerical strength of Islam in the Sudan. MW, v. 26, July 1936: 253–273. DS36.M7, v. 26

A colony-by-colony study of Muslim populations in British West Africa, Portuguese Guinea, Liberia, French West Africa, Togoland, and the Cameroons.

1329
Littman, Enno. Hemerkungen über den Islam in Nordabessinien. Der Islam, Bd. 1, 1910: 68–71. DS36.I7, v. 1

Translated as "Notes on Islam in North Abyssinia" (MW, v. 1, Apr. 1911: 183–184. (DS36.M7)).

1330
Lorimer, F. C. S. The Rubatab. SNR, v. 19, pt. 2, 1936: 162–167. geneal. tables, map. DT118.S85, v. 19

Short note on the Rubātāb tribe which is located "along both sides of the River Nile from Khor Singeir . . . to Shamkhia." The Rubātāb claim descent from al-'Abbās, the uncle of the Prophet.

1331
McElroy, Paul S. Ethiopia: Moslem or Christian? MW, v. 28, Apr. 1938: 125–137. DS36.M7, v. 28

1332
MacGaffey, Wyatt. The history of Negro migrations in the northern Sudan. Southwestern journal of anthropology, v. 17, summer 1961: 187–197. GN1.S64, v. 17

1333
MacMichael, *Sir* Harold A. A history of the Arabs in the Sudan and some account of the people who preceded them and of the tribes inhabiting Darfur. New York, Barnes & Noble [1967] 2 v. geneal. tables. GN652.A7M3 1967b

Reprint of the 1922 ed.

1334
el-Mahdi, *el-Sayed Sir* Abdel Rahman. The Mahdi's last letter to General Gordon. SNR, v. 24, 1941: 229–232. DT118.S85, v. 24

Note by the posthumous son of the Mahdi to the editor of *Sudan Notes and Records,* enclosing a copy of the last letter of the Mahdi to Gordon under siege in Khartoum. The Arabic text of the letter, dated January 12, 1885, is accompanied by a translation.

1335
Marchand, *Interprète.* La religion musulmane au Soudan français, d'aprés le texte du sergent Benezis. *In* L'Afrique française; bulletin du Comité de l'Afrique française. Renseignements coloniaux et documents, 1897: 91–111. DLC–Micro 03878

1336
Martin, Bradford G. Migration of Hadramis to East Africa and Indonesia: 1300–1900.

Source: ASA, Program, 15th, 1972.

1337
———Shaykh Uways bin Muhammad al-Barawi and Muslim resistance to German rule. Paper presented at the 12th annual meeting of the African Studies Association, Montreal, 1969. DLC–Micro 03782

Collation of the original: 16 p.

1338
Marzūq, 'Abd al-Ṣabūr. Adwā' 'alā al-Ṣūmāl. [Lights on Somalia] Cairo, Dār Sa'd Miṣr [1957] 203 p. tables.   DT401.M3

1339
Middleton, John, *and* Jane Campbell. Zanzibar, its society and its politics. London, New York, Oxford University Press, 1965. 71 p. maps. DT435.M5
"Issued under the auspices of the Institute of Race Relations, London."
Social conditions and political development in the island up to the time of independence.

1340
Misiugin, V. M. Suakhiliĭskaia khronika srednevekovogo gosudarstva Pate. [The Swahili chronicle of the medieval state of Pate]. *In* Akademiiă nauk SSSR. *Institut etnografii.* Trudy. Novaiă seriiă, t. 90. Moskva, 1966. (Afrikanskii etnograficheskii sbornik, 6) p. 52–83.   GN2.A2142, v. 90
English summary.

1341
Mohammedanism in Darfur. MW, v. 7, July 1917: 278–282.   DS36.M7, v. 7
Note by a "correspondent" on Islam in Darfur.
Appended is a brief report by the *Sudan Times'* correspondent in Darfur on trade relations between Darfur and Wadai.

1342
Muḥammad, Muḥammad 'Awad. al-Sūdān al-shimālī, sukkānuhu wa-qabā'iluhu. [Northern Sudan; its peoples and tribes] Cairo, Lanjat al-ta'līf wa-al-tarjamah wa-al-nashr [1951] 316 p. illus., maps (part fold.), plates, ports.   DT132.M8

1343
Muḥammad Aḥmad, *calling himself* al-Mahdī. Manshūrāt al-Mahdīyah. [Edicts of the Mahdiyah] Edited by Muḥammad Ibrāhīm Abū Salīm. [Beirut?] 1969. 375 p. facsims., ports.
DT108.2.M8
Third edition published in Khartoum, 1964, in the Idārat al-Maḥfūẓāt al-Markazīyah series no. 11–14.

1344
Munzinger, Werner. Auszüge aus Werner Munzinger's Tagebuch, angefangen den 13. Juli 1861 bei der Abreise von Mocullu (Om Kullu), vollendet den 15. October 1861 in Keren. Mitgetheilt von Dr. H. Barth. *In* Zeitschrift für Allgemeine erd-

kunde, n. F. Bd. 12, 1962:   162–174; 356–363.
G13.G5, v. 12
Touches upon the Islamization of the groups in the Anseba River region in Ethiopia.

1345
Mus'ad, Muṣṭafā Muḥammad. Ba'ḍ Mulāhaḍhāt jadīdah fī tārīkh mamlakat al-Funj al-Islāmīyah. [New comments on the history of the Islamic Fung Kingdom] *In* Khartoum. Jāmi'at al-Qāhirah fī al-Kharṭūm. Majallat Jām'at al-Qāhirah fī al-Kharṭūm, m. 3, 1972: 1–40.   DLC
The history of the Fung Sultanate has been drawn, according to the author, from many sources, including oral traditions, which were later recorded in such works as *Ṭabaqāt Wad Ḍayf Allah* and the *Makhṭūṭāt Kātib al-Shūnah*, and the writing of foreign travelers and missionaries. In this article, Mus'ad deals specifically with certain aspects of Fung history now the subject of debate among researchers: "The rise of the Fung kingdom, the origin of the Fung people and their place of origin development of the system of government, relations between the central government and local tribe groups in addition to relations between the Sultanate and its neighbors."

1346
——Salṭanat Dārfūr, tārīkhuha wa ba'ḍ maḍhāhir ḥaḍāratihā. [The Darfur sultanate, its history and some aspects of its civilization] *In* Cairo. al-Jam'īyah al-Miṣrīyah lil-dirāsāt al-tārīkhīyah. al-Majallah al-tārīkhīyah al-Miṣrīyah, m. 11, 1963: 215–253.
DT77.J28, v. 11   Orien Arab
The sultanate of Darfur played a major role in the early history of the Sudan. Located in the northwestern corner of the country, it was in contact with both the Nile Valley and the kingdoms and states to the west. Though recognizing that very little is known of its early history, Mus'ad draws dynastic tables for the sultanate, examines its history under Egyptian administration (1875–1883), and explores its political structure. One author he has drawn upon extensively is Muḥammad ibn 'Umar al-Tūnisī, who had a thorough knowledge of the region.

1347
Les musulmans chaféites de l'archipel des Comores. Bulletin de Madagascar, no 34, 1951: 30–34.   NN

1348
Nachtigal, Gustav. Saharâ und Sûdân. Ergebnisse sechs-jähriger reisen in Afrika. Berlin, Weidmann,

1879–81. 2 v. illus., facsims., 6 maps in pocket, plates, tables. DT351.N12

Maps wanting.

Chapter 4 of this book, about Wadai and Darfur, was published as *Sahara and Sudan,* translated from the original German, with new introduction and notes, by Allan G. B. Fisher and Humphrey J. Fisher with Rex S. O'Fahey (Berkeley, University of California Press, 1971. DT351.N1413).

1349

Nahabu, H. Activities of Muslims in Mauritius. The Islamic review, v. 35, Mar. 1947: 190–196. BP1.I7, v. 35

Islam came to Mauritius in 1835 with the first Indians brought in as laborers. Muslim teaching was neglected until the 1920's when Mawlānā 'Abdullah Rashīd Nawāb founded the Muslim Educational Society and the Muslim High School, which revived the faith in Mauritius.

1350

Naṣr, Aḥmad 'Abd al-Raḥīm, *comp.* Tārīkh al-'Abdulāb, min khilāl riwāyātihim al-sama'īyah. [History of the Abdilab according to their oral traditions] [Khartoum] Jāmi'at al-Khartūm, Kulliyat al-Ādāb, shu'bat abḥāth al-Sūdān, 1969. 170 leaves, maps. (Silsilat dirāsāt fī al-turāth al-Sūdānī, 7) GR360.S78N3

In the Sudanese dialect.

1351

Neufeld, Charles. A prisoner of the Khaleefa, twelve years' captivity at Omdurman. 3d ed. London, Chapman & Hall, 1899. 365 p. front., maps, plans, plates, ports. DT108.3.N4 1899

Appeared in the *Wide World Magazine,* June 1899 to March 1900, under title "In the Khalifa's Clutches."

The entourage of the Khalīfah as seen by a Christian prisoner, who flaunted his beliefs in the face of his captors and bitterly complained about the consequences. *See also* 1267 and 1396.

1352

Noirot, Ernest. A travers le Fouta-Diallon et le Bambouc (Soudan occidental). Paris, E. Flammarion [1885?]

Source: Brasseur, 2580.

1353

Oded, Arye. Islam in Uganda; Islamization through a centralized state in pre-colonial Africa. New York, Wiley [1974] 381 p. illus. BP64.U3503

"A Halsted Press book."

In his preface the author delineates the perimeter of his study: "The kingdom of Buganda provides an instructive case history for the study of Islamic penetration into a centralized state in East Africa. This volume investigates the penetration and expansion of Islam in Buganda, examines the patterns of Islamization in the kingdom in comparison with other regions, analyzes the causes which facilitated and enhanced the diffusion of Islam, and indicates the factors which hindered its progress. Special attention has been given to the contact and conflict between the Muslim traders and the Christian missionaries. Finally, an attempt has been made to evaluate the influence of the Muslims on the history and development of Buganda, which was the centre for the diffusion of Islam throughout the area that later became known as Uganda."

1354

O'Fahey, R. Sean. Slavery and the slave trade in Dar Fur. JAH, v. 14, no. 1, 1973: 29–43. map. DT1.J65, v. 14

The institutions of slavery, slave raiding and the slave trade were fundamental in the rise and expansion of the Keira Sultanate of Dār Fūr. The development of a long-distance trade in slaves may be due to immigrants from the Nile, who probably provided the impetus to state formation. This process may be remembered in the 'Wise Stranger' traditions current in the area. The slave raid or *ghazwa,* penetrating into the Baḥr al-Ghazāl and what is now the Central African Republic, marked the triumph of Sudanic state organization over the acephalous societies to the south.

The slaves, who were carefully classified, were not only exported to Egypt and North Africa, but also served the sultans and the title-holding elite as soldiers, labourers and bureaucrats. In the latter role, the slaves began to encroach on the power of traditional ruling groups within the state; the conflict between the slave bureaucrats and the traditional ruling elite lasted until the end of the first Keira Sultanate in 1874.—(Abstract supplied)

1355

———al-Tunisi's travels in Darfur. *In* Ibadan, Nigeria. University. *Centre of Arabic Documentation.* Research bulletin, v. 5, Dec. 1969: 66–74. DT352.4.I2a, v. 2

Commentaries and historical sketch on al-Tunisi's *Tashḥīdh al-Adhhān bi-sīrat bilād al-'Arab wa-al-Sūdān* [The Whetting of Minds With the Story of Arab Countries and the Sudan]. *See also* 263, 1409.

1356
Omar, C. A. Sharif. Kisiwa cha Pemba; historia na masimulizi. [History and traditions of the island of Pemba] Nairobi, Eagle Press [1951] 27 p. illus., map. DHU

1357
Owen, T. R. H. The Hadendowa. SNR, v. 20, pt. 2, 1937: 183–208. DT118.S85, v. 20

Historical note on the Hadendowa tribe—the Fuzzy-Wuzzy of Kipling's days—located north of Khashm el-Girba in the hinterland of Suakin in the Sudan. Owen deals with the early history and the Turkīyah period, the Mahdist era, and the 20th century.

1358
Pankhurst, Richard K. P. State and land in Ethiopian history. Addis Ababa, Institute of Ethiopian Studies, 1966. 211 p. facsims., maps. (Monographs in Ethiopian land tenure, no. 3) HD1021.E8M6 no. 3

1359
Pearce, Francis B. Zanzibar, the island metropolis of eastern Africa. New York, Barnes & Noble [1967] 431 p. illus., maps (1 fold.), ports. DT435.P4 1967b

Reprint of the 1920 ed.

1360
Penn, A. E. D. Traditional stories of the 'Abdullab tribe. SNR, v. 17, pt. 1, 1934: 59–82. DT118.S85, v. 17

Translation of an Arabic manuscript regarding the origins and history of the 'Abdullāb tribe of the Sudan. The tradition relates the peregrinations and tribulations of the tribe from the 16th century, when it settled in the Sudan, to 1912, when Shaykh Muḥammad al-Shaykh Jammā', the 'Abdullāb leader, was decorated by King George V on his visit to Port Sudan.

1361
Perrot, G. L'Islamisme chez les Gallas dans la province du Harrar. L'Afrique française; bulletin du Comité de l'Afrique française et du Comité du Maroc. Renseignements coloniaux et documents, 1913: 121–124. DLC–Micro 03878

1362
Pleticha, Heinrich. Der Mahdiaufstand in Augenzeugenberichten. Hrsg. und eingeleitet von Heinrich Pleticha. [Düsseldorf] Rauch [1967] 429 p. several leaves of illustration. ([In Augenzeugenberichten]) DT108.15.P55

1363
Prins, Adriaan H. J. The Swahili-speaking peoples of Zanzibar and the East African Coast: Arabs, Shirazi, and Swahili. London, International African Institute, 1967. 146 p. illus., fold. map. (Ethnographic survey of Africa: East Central Africa, pt. 12) GN659.Z3P7 1967

Reprint of 1961 ed.

1364
al-Qaddāl, Muḥammad Sa'īd. al-Mahdīyah wa-al-Ḥabashah, dirāsah fī al-siyāsah al-dākhilīyah wa-al-khārijīyah li-dawlat al-Mahdīyah, 1881–1898. [The Mahdist movement and Ethiopia, a study in internal politics and foreign affairs of the Mahdist state, 1881–1898] [Khartoum] Jāmi'at al-Kharṭūm, Dār al-ta'līf wa-al-tarjamah wa-al-nashr [1937] 167 p. illus. DLC

1365
Qandīl, Ḥasan. Fatḥ Darfūr sanat 1916 M., wa-nubdhah min tārīkh sulṭānihā 'Alī Dīnār. [The conquest of Darfur in 1916 A. D., and a brief note on the story of its sultan 'Alī Dīnār] Alexandria, Maṭba'at al-'Adl, 1937. 49 p. DT135.D2Q2

'Alī Dīnār ibn Zakariyā became Sultan of Darfur after the collapse of Mahdist forces in 1898. During World War I he allied himself with the Germans and Turks and joined the Senussi of Cyrenaica against the British, who subsequently defeated and killed him at El-Fasher (May 22, 1916). Qandīl describes the campaign and provides a brief biography of 'Alī Dīnār.

1366
Qāsim, 'Awn al-Sharīf. al-Masjid fī ḥayātinā. [The mosque in our lives] [Khartoum, al-Maṭba'ah al-ḥukūmīyah, 1973] 39 p. DLC

At head of title: al-Amānah al-'āmmah lil-shu'ūn al-dīnīyah wa-al-awqāf. Maṣlaḥat al-masājid wa-al-awqāf.

1367
Qāsim, Jamāl Zakarīyā. Dawlat Bū Sa'īd fī 'Umān wa-sharq Afrīqiyā. [The state of Bū Sa'īd in Oman and East Africa] [Cairo] Maktabat al-Qāhirah al-ḥadīthah [1968] 295 p. DS247.O67Q3

Risālat al-Mājistīr—Jāmi'at 'Ayn Shams.

1368
———al-Khalīj al 'Arabī, dirāsah li-tārīkh al-imārāt al-'Arabīyah, 1840–1914. [The Arab Gulf, study of the history of the Arab emirates, 1840–1914] Cairo, Maṭba'at jāmi'at 'Ayn Shams, 1966.

522 p. maps (3 fold.) DS326.Q37 Orien Arab
Risālat al-Duktūrāh—Jāmi'at 'Ayn Shams.

1369
Rabī', Ṣidqī. al-Nūbah bayna al-qadīm wa-al-jadīd. [Nubia between past and present] [Cairo, al-Dār al-qawmīyah lil-ṭibā'ah wa-al-nashr, 1965] 110 p. illus., maps. DT135.N8R3

1370
Raux, M. Pénétration musulmane dans l'Est africain. Grands lacs; revue générale des missions d'Afrique, no 3, 15 déc. 1947: 5–8, 149–152.
BV3500.A35, 1947

1371
Reusch, Richard. Der Islam in Ost-Afrika; mit besonderer Berücksichtigung der muhammedanischen Geheim-Orden. Leipzig, A. Klein, 1931. 360 p. 4BP.2

1371a
Riyāḍ, Zāhir. al-Islām fī Atyūbyā (Ta'līq). [Islam in Ethiopia (A comment)] *In* Cairo. Jāmi'at al-Qāhirah. Kulliyat al-ādāb. Majallat Kulliyat al-ādāb, m. 18, Dec. 1956: 121–142.
AS693.C25, v. 18 Orien Arab
Critical review of J. Spencer Trimingham's *Islam in Ethiopia (see* 1407).

1372
Rizq, Yūnān. Qiyām wa suqūṭ al-Mahdīyah fī al-Sūdān al-ḥadīth. [Rise and fall of the Mahdist movement in contemporary Sudan] al-Siyāsah al-duwalīyah, m. 6, July 1970: 8–25.
D839.S55, v. 6 Orien Arab
"To this day, most writers and researchers who have studied the Mahdiyah have dealt with it as a historical study and not a political question," says Rizq, who studies it from its inception, investigating its religious, social, and political bases, and analyzes its attempts to return to power (1899–1919), the period of consolidation (1919–45), the search for authority (1945–56), its political zenith (1956–69) when the Ansār were either in power or behind those in power, and finally its fall, with the revolt on the Aba island and the execution of the successor of Muḥammad Aḥmad.

1373
Robertson, J. W. Fung origins. SNR, v. 17, pt. 2, 1934: 260–266. DT118.S85, v. 17
Critique of Arkell's article on the origins of the Fung (*see* 1215).

1374
Robinson, Arthur E. "Abu el-Kaylik," the king-maker of the Fung of Sennar. American anthropologist, new ser., v. 31, Apr./June 1929: 232–264.
GN1.A5, n.s., v. 31

1375
———The Tekruri sheikhs of Gallabat (S.E. Sudan) *In* African Society. Journal, v. 26, Oct. 1926: 47–53. DT1.R62, v. 26
Gallabat, a frontier town between Gedaref and Gondor, was founded by Ja'li merchants from Metemmeh in Berber Province. Robinson reports the occupation of the city by a group of Kungara from Jebel Marra and the reigns of their rulers during a 200-year period when the "Tekruri" preserved a distinct identity although surrounded by Arabs, Gallas, Amhara, and other ethnic groups.

1376
Robinson, Charles H. Mohammedanism in the Central Sudan. Liberia, no. 7, Nov. 1896: 57–63.
E448.L68, 1896
Issued by the American Colonization Society.

1377
Ruini, Meuccio. L'Islam e le nostre colonie. Città di Castello, Il Solco, 1922. IEN

1378
Rusillon, Henry. Islam in Madagascar. MW, v. 12, Oct. 1922: 386–389. DS36.M7, v. 12
Brief note on the history of Islam in the Great Isle and practical suggestions to lure Gujarati Muslims away from the Path. Rusillon concludes, "The task is very limited. It could permit of experiences of which the results could be used elsewhere. It would bring, we are certain, encouragement, and would at the same time cause indigenous Islam to disappear, which would no longer have support."

1379
Saadi, Amur Omar, *Kadhi.* Mafia: History and traditions. Transl. by D. W. I. Piggott. TNR, no. 12/13, 1941. MBU

1380
Sabry, Mohammed. Miṣr fī Ifrīqiyā al-Sharqīyah, Harar wa-Zayla' wa Barbarah. [Egypt in East Africa, Harar, Zeila and Berbera] [Cairo] Maṭba' at Miṣr wa-maktabatuhā, 1939. 79 p. illus., map, ports. DT82.5.S6S22

1381
Sadik el-Müeyyed Paşa. Riḥlat al-Ḥabashah. [Voyage to Ethiopia] Ta'rīb Rafāq Bey al-'Aẓm wa Ḥiqqī Bey al-'Azm. [Cairo] Ṭubi'a bi-maṭba'at al-Jarīdah, 1908. 335 p. col. maps, plates, ports. DT378.S212

Translation of *Habeş seyahatnamesi.*

A diary covering the period April 15–July 16, 1896.

1382
Said, Beshir Mohammed. The Sudan: crossroads of Africa. With an introd. by Colin Legum. London, Bodley Head [1965] 238 p. illus., map. DT108.6.S3 1965

The Sudan is part of the Sudanic belt stretching from Nouakchott to Khartoum where two modes of life, mentality, and, often, religion meet. The countries and states within this belt are in the process of nation building, with all the resulting strains and passions. Due to historical, ethnic, and religious differences, northern and southern Sudan were split in a civil war which began in 1955. Beshir Said, a northerner, focuses all his erudition, patience, and sense of fair play on presenting the northern viewpoint about a delicate and difficult problem. The missionaries are harshly treated, but with some historical justification. The author ends his book stating, "While the South should not give in to emotion and allow its fate to be cast by misguided elements, the North should be more realistic in its approach to the problem. Let us hope that very soon a wise counsel will prevail." A number of appendixes are provided, including the Condominium Agreement of 1899 and other official documents.

1383
Salīl ibn Ruzaik. History of the imâms and seyyids of 'Oman, by Salîl-ibn-Razîk, from A.D. 661–1856. Translated from the original Arabic and edited, with notes, appendices, and an intro., continuing the history down to 1870, by George Percy Badger. New York, B. Franklin [1963?] 435 p. fold. map (works issued by the Hakluyt Society, 1st ser., no. 44) G161.H22 no. 44

Though centered on the history of the rulers of Oman, Salil ibn Ruzayk's work provides useful information on the relationship between the Peninsula and the East Coast of Africa.

1384
Sánchez, Juan. Persecucion religio-racial en el Sudan. Africa, anõ 21, mayo 1964: 16–20. illus. DT137.A1A4, 1964

1385
Sanders, G. E. R. The Amarar. SNR, v. 18, no. 2, 1935: 195–200. geneal. table, map. DT118.S85, v. 18

The Amarar tribe, in the hinterland of Port-Sudan, played an active role during the Mahdist period. Sanders presents the organization of the tribe and its history up to the British occupation.

1386
Sanderson, G. N. Conflict and cooperation between Ethiopia and the Mahdist state, 1884–1898. SNR, v. 50, 1969: 15–40. DT118.S85, v. 50

1387
Sayyid, Muḥammad al-Mu'taṣim. Janūb al-Sūdān fī mi'at 'ām. [Southern Sudan in the last 100 years] [al-ṭab'ah 2. Cairo, Maṭba'at nahḍat miṣr, 1972] 243 p. maps. (Malāmiḥ sūdānīyah, 1) DT108.6.S39

1388
Schacht, Joseph. Notes on Islam in East Africa. Studia Islamica, v. 23, 1965: 91–136. illus. BP1.S8, v. 23

Report on visits to East Africa made in 1953, 1963, and 1964, discussing Islam in Uganda, Kenya, Tanganyika, and Zanzibar separately. Schacht examines the comparatively recent Islamization of Uganda (1860) and the special characteristics, problems, and facets of Ugandan Islam. He looks into the Aḥmadīyah in the region as a whole and its confrontation with orthodox Islam. In Kenya, the Muslim communities are concentrated in the coastal strip, while they live in a diaspora in the interior. It seemed to the author that a large part of the Muslim population in Tanganyika is only nominally orthodox, in spite of a strong tradition of high learning, and that Zanzibar "is the most completely Islamic part of East Africa." He describes its society and educational and juridical systems. Includes eight pages of illustrations of mosques and related buildings.

1389
Schippel, *Dr.* Vom Islam im westlichen Teile von Deutsch-Ostafrika. Die Welt des Islams. Bd. 2, 1964: 6–10. DS36.W4, v. 2

1390
Schmidt, Rochus. Geschichte des Araberaufstandes in Ost-Afrika: seine Entstehung, seine Niderwerfüg und seine Folgen. Frankfurt am Oder, Trowitzsch [1892] 360 p. fold. col. map. IEN

1391
Shaked, Haim. The presentation of the Sudanese Mahdi in a unique Arabic manuscript biography. Abr-Nahrain, v. 13, 1972/1973: 24–32.
PJ3001.A2, v. 13

Discussion of a manuscript biography of the Sudanese Mahdi written by a Muslim religious scholar who presents a sympathetic view of the reformer. Ismā'īl 'Abd al-Qādir al-Kurdufānī's *Kitāb sa'ādat al-mustahdī bi-sīrat al-Imām al-Mahdī* [The Book of the Bliss of Him Who Seeks Guidance by the Life of the Imam al-Mahdi] provides researchers with a justification and rationale of the Mahdist movement and its leader. *See also* 1139, 1320.

1392
Shaw, George A. The Arab element in South East Madagascar: as seen in the customs and traditions of the Taimoro tribe. Antananarivo annual, 1892: 99–109; 1893: 205–210. DT469.M21A6

1393
———Arab migrations into southeast Madagascar, an important paper. *In* Victoria Institute, or Philosophy Society of Great Britain, *London.* Journal of the transactions. v. 33; 1901. London, 1901. p. 334–361. AS122.L9, v. 33

Presentation of the origins and life style of the Taimòro group in Madagascar. Shaw discusses the extent of their Islamization and its manifestations.

1394
Shibeika, Mekki. Mamlakat al-Fūnj al-Islāmīyah, muḥāḍarāt alqāhā Makkī Shubaykah 'alā ṭalabat qism al-dirāsāt al-tārīkhīyah wa-al-Jughrāfīyah, 1963. [The Islamic kingdom of Funj, lectures delivered by Mekki Shibeika to the students of the historical and geographical studies section, 1963] [Cairo] Jāmi'at al-duwal al-'Arabīyah, Ma'had al-dirāsāt al-'Arabīyah al-'āliyah, 1964. 127 p.
DT135.N8S45

1395
Shuqayr, Na'ūm. Jughrāfīyat wa-tārīkh al-Sūdan. [Geography and history of the Sudan] Beirut, Dār al-Thaqāfah [1967] 3 v. in 1 (1395 p.) illus., maps, ports. DLC

Shuqayr worked for the Sudan government under British administration. He accompanied Kitchener in his campaign againt the Mahdi and translated captured Mahdist documents for the British expeditionary forces. His book is based on a large number of primary sources including Mahdist manuscripts.

1396
Slatin, Rudolf Carl, *Freiherr* von. Fire and sword in the Sudan; a personal narrative of fighting and serving the dervishes, 1879–1895. Translated by F. R. Wingate. Illustrated by R. Talbot Kelly. 2d ed. New York, Negro Universities Press [1969] 636 p. illus., maps, ports. DT108.S63 1969

Reprint of the 1896 ed.

See also 1267.

1397
Smirnov, S. R. Vosstanie Makhdistov v Sudane. [The Mahdist uprising in the Sudan] *In* Akademiîa nauk SSSR. *Institut etnografii.* Trudy. Novaîa seriîa, t. 6. Moskva, 1950. p. 1–100. illus.
GN2.A2142, v. 6

1398
Spaulding, Jay. The Funj: a reconsideration. JAH, v. 13, no. 1, 1972: 39–53. DT1.J65, v. 13

Three lines of evidence regarding the Funj prior to the rise of the Sinnār Sultanate about 1500 have been considered. Shilluk tradition remembers the Funj as the previous inhabitants of the present Shilluk homeland, while many of the eighteenth- and nineteenth-century visitors to Sinnār were told that the Funj came from the White Nile. While neither set of traditions should be accepted without question, the fact that they tend to confirm each other lends weight to both.

Archaeological evidence derived from pottery finds on the White Nile mounds may be interpreted to imply that the Funj were a southern Nubian people, an hypothesis that must be weighed against alternatives that would suggest an unknown or even Meroitic cultural identity. The presence of red brick structures along the White Nile south of the generally accepted borders of the Sultanate, as well as in the capital itself, tends to support the 'Nubian' hypothesis. Further research concerning the Funj language and the archaeological cultures south of the latitude of Sinnār should help resolve these ambiguities; many aspects of government and society in the Sinnār Sultanate are clarified by considering the era a Nubian Renaissance.—(Abstract supplied, modified)

1399
Stevenson, Roland C. Some aspects of the spread of Islam in the Nuba Mountains. SNR, v. 44, 1963: 9–20. DT118.S85, v. 44

See also 150.

1400
Stigand, Chauncy H. The land of Zinj: being an account of British East Africa, its ancient history and present inhabitants. London, Cass, 1966. 351 p. front., plan, 20 plates. DT423.S7 1966a

1401
Sudan in Africa; studies presented to the first international conference sponsored by the Sudan Research Unit, 7–12 February, 1968. Edited with a special introduction by Yūsūf Faḍl Ḥasan. [Khartoum] Khartoum University Press [1971] 316 p. maps (Sudanese studies library, 2) DT118.S83

"The main objective of the conference, 'The Sudan in Africa', was to emphasize points of contacts, similarities and contrast between the Sudan and neighbouring African countries from a linguistic, archaeological, historical, social anthropological, and political point of view." Only the following contributions were included in the volume "owing to the high cost of production": R. C. Stevenson, The Significance of the Sudan in Linguistic Research, Past, Present and Future; B. G. Haycock, The Place of the Napata-Meroitic Culture in the History of the Sudan and Africa; P. L. Shinnie, The Culture of Medieval Nubia and its Impact on Africa; M. Posnansky, East Africa and the Nile Valley in Early Times; Merid Wolde Aregay and Sergew Hable Selassie, Sudano-Ethiopian Relations Before the Nineteenth Century; Yūsūf Faḍl Ḥasan, External Islamic Influences and the Progress of Islamization in the Eastern Sudan Between the Fifteenth and Eighteenth Centuries; R. S. O'Fahey, Religion and Trade in the Kayra Sultanate of Dar Fur; 'Umar A. al-Naqar, The Historical Background for 'The Sudan Road'; T. Hodgkin, Mahdism, Messianism and Marxism in the African Setting (*see also* 350); Muḥammad A. al-Hājj, Hayātū b. Sa'īd: a Revolutionary Mahdist in the Western Sudan; Mekki Shibeika, The Expansionist Movement of Khedive Ismā'īl to the Lakes; R. O. Collins, Sudanese Factors in the History of the Congo and Central West Africa in the Nineteenth Century; G. N. Sanderson, Sudanese Factors in the History of Ethiopia in the Nineteenth Century; I. Cunnison, Classification by Genealogy: a Problem of the Baqqara Belt; W. R. James, Social Assimilation and Changing Identity in the Southern Funj; I. M. Lewis, Spirit Possession in North-East Africa; Muddathir, Abdel Rahim, Arabism, Africanism, and Self-Identification in the Sudan (*see also* Journal of Modern African Studies, v. 8, July 1970: 233–250); Ali A. Mazrui, The Multiple Marginality in the Sudan; Ja 'far M. A. Bakheit, Native Administration in the Sudan and its Significance to Africa; Natale O. Akolawin, Islamic and Customary Law in the Sudan.

1402
Tādrus, Ramzī. Kitāb ḥāḍir al-Ḥabashah wa-mustaqbaluhā. [Book on the present of Ethiopia and its future] Cairo, Maḥba'at Miṣr [190–?] 171 p. illus. DT386.T3 1900z

1403
Ṭarkhān, Ibrāhīm 'Alī. al-Islām wa al-mamālik al-Islāmīyah bi-al-Ḥabashah. Islam and the Muslim Kingdoms in Ethiopia] *In* Cairo. al-Jam'iyah al-Miṣrīyah lil-dirāsāt al-tārīkhīyah. al-Majallah al-tārīkhīyah al-Miṣrīyah, m. 8, 1959: 1–68. DT77.J28, v. 8 Orien Arab

Following a historical note on the Ethiopian kingdom, its conversion to Christianity, and its relations with the Arabian Peninsula before and after Islam, Ṭarkhān analyzes the Islamic political entities, their conflicts with Ethiopia, their appeal to Egypt for support, and the latter's role in the dispute. He closes with the Ottoman Empire taking over from Egypt the responsibility of protecting Islam in Ethiopia.

1404
al-Tayyib, Mudaththar 'Abd al-Raḥīm. Mushkilat janūb al-Sūdān, ṭabī'atuhā wa tatawwuruhā wa-athar al-siyāsah al-Brīṭānīyah fī takwīnihā. [The problem of the southern Sudan; its nature, development and the impact of British policy on its creation] al-Khartoum, al-Dār al-Sūdānīyah [1970] 224 p. map. DT108.7.T38 Orien Arab

General analysis of the southern Sudan question.

1405
Theobold, Alan. Darfur and its neighbours under Sultan 'Ali Dīnar, 1898–1916. SNR, v. 40, 1959: 113–120. DT118.S85, v. 40

1406
———The Mahdiya; a history of the Anglo-Egyptian Sudan, 1881–1899. London, New York, Longmans, Green [1951] 273 p. maps, ports. DT108.T48

1407
Trimingham, J. Spencer. Islam in Ethiopia. New York, Barnes & Noble [1965] xv, 299 p. maps (part fold. col.) BP64.E8T7 1965

1408
———Islam in the Sudan. New York, Barnes & Noble [1965] 280 p. illus., 2 maps.

BP64.S8T7

"The Sudanese received Islam whole-heartedly, but, through their unique capacity of assimilation, moulded it to their own particular mentality; escaping the formulae of theologians, they sang in it, danced in it, wept in it, brought their own customs, their own festivals into it, paganized it a good deal, but always kept the vivid reality of its inherent unity under the rule of the one God." The thorough investigation of Sudanese Islam is divided into the following chapters: The Land and the People; Historical Outline: The Christian Kingdoms to the Arab Conquest; History of the Sudan Under Muslim Rule; Orthodox Islam; Beliefs and Practices of Popular Islam; The Religious Orders; Islam and Pagan Sudan; Influence of Westernization on the Sudan.

1409

al-Tūnisī, Muḥammad ibn 'Umar. Voyage au Ouadây, par le Cheykh Mohammad ibn-Omar el-Tounsy ... tr. de l'arabe par le Dr. Perron ... ouvrage accompagné de cartes et de planches et du portrait du cheykh, pub. par le Dr. Perron et M. Jomard ... ouvrage précédé d'une préface de ce dernier, contenant des remarques historiques et géographiques, et faisant suite au Voyage au Dârfour. Paris, Chez B. Duprat [etc] 1851. 756 p. front. (port.), map, plan, plate (part fold.). DT354.M6

"Planches" have special t.p.

Half-title: Voyage au Soudan oriental. Le Ouadây.

L.C. has preface only.

See also 263,1381.

1409a

Turton, E. R. The impact of Mohammad Abdille Hassan in East African Protectorate. JAH, v. 10, no. 4, 1969: 641–657. DT1.J65, v. 10

1410

Twaddle, Michael. The Muslim revolution in Buganda. African affairs, v. 71, Jan. 1972: 54–72. DT1.R62, v. 71.

Tracing the events in the ouster of Mwanga II from the Ganda throne in September 1888 by the Christians and then the counter-coup by the Muslims, who were in turn finally defeated in October 1889, Twaddle suggests a model to show that the revolutionaries were the Muslims, not the Christians, as has been argued by authors in the past.

1411

Utenzi wa vita vya Uhud; the epic of the battle of Uhud. Collected and compiled by Haji Chum. Edited, with a translation and notes, by H. E. Lambert. Dar Es Salaam, East African Literature Bureau, 1962. 97 p. (Johari za Kiswahili, 3) PL8704.U8

1412

Verin, P. Les Arabes dans l'Océan indien et à Madagascar. Revue de Madagascar, v. 34, 2. trimestre, 1966: 16–18. DT469.M21R34, v. 34

1413

al-Walīlī, Ibrāhīm Muṣṭafā. Mā warā'a khazzān aṣwān, aw bilād al-nūbah. [Beyond the Aswan Dam, or Nubia] Cairo, Maṭba'at jarīdāt al-ṣabāḥ, [cover 1927] 1924. 114 p. illus., ports. DT135.N8W3

1414

Walker, J. Islam in Madagascar. MW, v. 22, Oct. 1932: 393–397. DS36.M7, v. 22

1415

Westermann, Diedrich H. Islam in the eastern Sudan. International review of missions, v. 2, July 1913: 454–485. BV2351.I6, v. 2

1416

Wingate, *Sir* F. Reginald, *bart.* Mahdism and the Egyptian Sudan: being an account of the rise and progress of Mahdism, and of subsequent events in the Sudan to the present time. 2d ed. with a new introduction by P. M. Hold. London, Cass, 1968. 617 p. illus., 25 maps (9 col.), 3 plans, 30 plates (10 fold.) (Cass library of African studies, General studies, no. 44) DT108.3.W5 1968

Originally published in 1891.

Wingate, who was director of military intelligence, based his work on captured Mahdist documents.

1417

———The siege of Khartum. SNR, v. 13, pt. 1, 1930: 1–82. maps. DT118.S85, v. 13

Translation and annotations on an extensive report on the siege and fall of Khartoum by a committee of Egyptian officers, presenting a non-Western viewpoint. *See also* 1276, 1284.

1418

Yūnus, Muḥammad 'Abd al-Mun'im. al-Ṣūmāl, waṭanan ... wa sha'ban ... [Somalia, Fatherland ... and people] Cairo, Dār al-Nahḍah al-'Arabīyah [1962] 236 p. maps. DT410.Y8

1419
Yūsuf, 'Umar 'Abd Allāh Aḥmad. Mawqi'at Abī Ḥamd. [The battle of AbūḤ amd] [Khartoum, Maṭba'at Miṣr-Sūdān, 1972?] 17 p. DLC
Modern Arabic poem on a battle between the British Army and the Sudanese during the conquest campaign, late 19th century.—(Abstract supplied)

1420
Ẓabyān, Muḥammad Taysīr. al-Ḥabashah al-Muslimah. [Muslim Ethiopia] Damascus, Yuṭlab miṇ idārat jarīdat al-jazīrah, wa min maktabat 'Urfah, 1937. 150 p. illus., ports. (*His* 1, Mushāhadātī fī diyār al-Islām) DT378.Z27
Cover title: *L'Ethiopie musulmane,* par M. Taissir Zabian Kaylanie.

1421
Zahrān, 'Umar Ṭal'at. al-Islām fi Madaghashqar. [Islam in Madagascar] *In* Cairo. al-Jāmi' al-Azhar. Majallat al-Jāmi' al-Azhar, m. 22, 1951: 555–559. BP1.C3, v. 22 Orien Arab
Muslim influence reached Madagascar in four waves beginning in the 7th or 8th century. As a result, Arabic script was used until recently to transliterate Malagasy and many Arabic words were adopted, especially in astronomy, greetings, coins, and musical instruments. A new Muslim trend taking root is the Ahmadi movement introduced by Indians in 1934. According to Zahrān, Catholic missions have repeatedly tried to convert Muslims to Christianity. In his conclusion, the author appeals to the rector of the Azhar and reminds him that the jurisdiction of the Azhar extends to wherever Muslims are found.

1422
al-Zayn, Ādam, *comp. and ed.* al-Turāth al-Sha'bī liqabīlat al-Musabba'āt (Sharq madīnat al-Fāshir). [Popular heritage of the Musabba'āt tribe (East of El Fasher)] [Khartoum] Jāmi'at al-Kharṭūm, Kuliyyat al-Ādāb, Shu'bat Abḥāth al-Sūdān, 1970. 131 p. map. (Silsilat dirāsat fā al-Turath al-Sūdānī, 10) GR360.S78Z3 Orien Arab

1423
al-Zubayr Bāshā. Black ivory; or, The story of El Zubeir Pasha, slaver and sultan, as told by himself. Translated and put on record by H. C. Jackson. New York, Negro Universities Press [1970] 118 p. DT108.15.Z83 1970
Reprint of the edition published in 1913 under title: *Black Ivory and White.*
"The story of [El Zubeir's] life as he recounted it, in the year 1900, to Naoum Bey Shoucair. This story I have supplemented and annotated from other sources." The original account appeared in *Tārīkh al-Sūdān al-qadīm wa-alḥadīth wa jughrāfiyatuh,* by Na'ūm Shuqayr (Cairo, 1903). *See also* 1395.

1424
Zwemer, Samuel M. Islam in Ethiopia and Eritrea. MW, v. 26, Jan. 1936: 5–15. DS36.M7, v. 26
Ethiopia was one of the early refuges of persecuted Muslims during the fifth year of the Hijrah. Islam began its penetration and conquests during the 13th and 14th centuries. Sporadic fighting started about 1521 with Muhammad Gran's invasion of Ethiopia and continued until the 19th century. Zwemer, editor of *The Muslim World,* provides an analysis of missionary activities among the Muslim populations of the Horn of Africa.

1425
———Islam in Madagascar: a blind spot. MW, v. 30, Apr. 1940: 151–167. DS36.M7, v. 30

Languages & Linguistics

1426
Bell, G. W. Some examples of Arabic slang used in the Sudan. SNR, v. 34, Dec. 1953: 299–308. DT118.S85, v. 34
Study of European terms incorporated in Sudanese colloquial Arabic. Appended are "some comments by a Sudanese reader" providing a corrective to some of the explanations.

1427
Berthier, Hugues J. De l'usage de l'arabico-malgache en Imerina au début du XIXe siècle. Le cahier d'écriture de Radama I. Tananarive, Imprimerie G. Pitot, 1934. 134 p. (Mémoires de l'Académie malgache. fasc. 16) DT469.M21A4 fasc. 16
Text, translation, and comments on a notebook belonging to King Radama between 1810 and 1828 where he kept personal notes and dates of events both in Latin and Malagasy in Arabic script. The booklet is of value because of its relative age and because it provides information on the Imerana dialect at the onset of the 19th century and the use of Arabic script.

1428
Bertin, F. Quelques signes de l'arabisation des noms propres portés par les Issa. Pount, 1. année,

3. trimestre, 1967: 29–30. DLC

Brief investigation of the trend among the Issa of the French Territory of the Afars and Issas to adopt Arabic names and abandon Issa ones. Bertin wonders whether it is an attempt to be integrated into the Muslim collectivity or a need to get away from names which seem incongruous today.

1429
Cepollaro, Armando. I Swahili e la loro lingua. Africa, v. 17, marzo/aprile 1962: 67–82.
DT1.A843, v. 17

1430
Colançon. A propos d'une note sur l'emploi de l'écriture arabe à Madagascar. *In* Académie malgache. Bulletin, nouv. sér., v. 6, 1922/1923: 77–84. DT469.M21A35, n.s., v. 6

See also 1455.

1431
Dahle, L. The influence of the Arabs on the Malagasy language as a test of their contribution to Malagasy civilisation and superstition. The Antananarivo annual and Madagascar magazine, 1876: 203–218. DT469.M21A6, 1876

1432
Dale, Godfrey, A Swahili translation of the Koran. MW, v. 14, Jan. 1924: 5–9. DS36.M7, v. 14

Commentary on a Swahili translation of the Koran published for the Universities Mission to Central Africa by the Society for Promoting Christian Knowledge. Of interest is the rationale for the translation which can be used in a confrontation between the Christian missionary and the Muslim Koranic teacher.

1433
Dez, Jacques. De l'influence arabe à Madagascar à l'aide de faits linguistique. Revue de Madagascar, nouv. sér., no 34, 1966: 19–38.
DT469.M21R34, n.s., no. 34

Study of the impact of Arabic on the Malagasy island. At the level of phonology, Dez looks at the adaptation of the Arabic script to the Antaimoro and Antambahoaka variants of Malagasy. He then investigates loan words in the two major dialects. Includes a useful glossary of loan words. *See also* 1543.

1434
Ferrand, Gabriel, Note sur l'alphabet arabico-malgache. Anthropos, v. 4, janv./fév. 1909: 190–206.
GN1.A7, v. 4

1435
———Note sur la transcription arabico-malgache, d'aprés les manuscrits Antaimorono. *In* Société de linguistique de Paris. Mémoires, v. 12, 3. fasc., 1902: 141–175. P12.S45, v. 12

1436
Gautier, Emile-Félix. Notes sur l'écriture antaimoro. Paris, E. Leroux, 1902. 83 p. (Publications de l'Ecole des lettres d'Alger. Bulletin de correspondance africaine, v. 25) AS651.A6, v. 25

Study of the use of Arabic to write Malagasy. This usage is more widespread among the Antaimoro tribe. Included is the Arabic text, transliteration, and translation of an Antaimoro manuscript.

1437
Holt, Peter M. Three Mahdist letter-books. BSOAS, v. 18, pt. 2, 1956: 227–238. PJ3.L6, v. 18

1438
Huntingford, G. W. B. Arabic inscriptions in Southern Ethiopia. Antiquity, v. 29, Dec. 1955: 230–233. CC1.A7, v. 29

1439
Jeffreys, M. D. W. The impact of the Arab language on East Africa. Muslim digest (Durban), v. 5, May 1955: 209–212. BP1.I553, v. 5

1440
Knappert, Jan. The discovery of a lost Swahili ms. from the 18th century. African language studies, v. 10, 1969: 1–30. PL8003.A34, v. 10

1441
———Swahili religious terms. Journal of religion in Africa/Religion en Afrique, v. 3, no. 1, 1970: 67–80. BL2400.J68, v. 3

"More than two centuries of literary tradition have established a fixed terminology of Swahili words for religious concepts. Most of these concepts are virtually identical with those found in other parts of the Islamic world, but some have developed along their own lines within the boundaries of the Swahili culture. The following is a list of some of the most important Swahili religious terms. They are important for one of two reasons: either they are extremely frequent in Swahili literary or colloquial usage, or else their meaning is a special one and requires some explanation in order to be properly appreciated."

1442
Krumm, Bernhard. Words of Oriental origin in Swahili. London, Sheldon Press, 1940. 102 p.
PL8703.K78

1443
Leslau, Wolf. An analysis of the Harari vocabulary. [Arabic loanwords] Annales d'Ethiopie, v. 3, 1959: 275–298. DT379.A6, v. 3

1444
———Arabic loanwords in Amharic. BSOAS, v. 19, pt. 2, 1957: 221–244. PJ3.L6, v. 19

1445
———Arabic loanwords in Argobba (South Ethiopia). *In* American Oriental Society. Journal, v. 77, Jan./Mar. 1957: 36–39. PJ2.A6, v. 77

1446
———Arabic loan-words in Ge'ez. Journal of Semitic studies, v. 3, Apr. 1958: 146–168.
PJ3001.J6, v. 3

1447
———Arabic loanwords in Gurage (Southern Ethiopia). Arabica; revue d'études arabes, t. 3, Sept. 1956: 266–284. PJ6001.A7, v. 3

1448
———Arabic loanwords in Harari. *In* Studi orientalistici in onore di Giorgio Levi Della Vida. Roma, Istituto per l'Oriente, 1956. p. 14–25.
DS42.4.S78

1449
———Arabic loanwords in Tigre. Word, v. 12, Apr. 1956: 125–141. P1.W65, v. 12

1450
———Arabic loanwords in Tigrinya. *In* American Oriental society. Journal, v. 76, Oct./Dec. 1956: 204–213. PJ2.A6, v. 76

1451
———The meaning of "Arab" in Ethiopia. MW, v. 39, Oct. 1949: 307–308. DS36.M7, v. 39

1452
———The phonetic treatment of the Arabic loanwords in Ethiopia. Word, v. 13, Apr. 1957: 100–123. P1.W65, v. 13

1453
Małecka, A. Quelques emprunts arabes de la langue Souaheli. Folia orientalia, v. 1, 1959: 141–143.
PJ9.F6, v. 1

According to an analysis of three dictionaries, Małecka suggests that 30 percent of Swahili words are of Arabic origin. Although the etymology of most of the words under consideration is established, the author concentrates on six items, providing new or corrective interpretations. The six words are: bushuti, kekee, kikuku, kuta, m-nafiki, and m-wali.

1454
Molet, Louis. Presentation du manuscrit arabo-malgache offert à l'Académie malgache par le Gouverneur Lavau. *In* Académie malgache. Bulletin, nouv. sér., v. 30, 1951–52: 130–132. DT469.M21A35, n.s., v. 30

1455
Mondain, G. Complément à la note sur l'emploi de l'écriture arabico-malgache. *In* Académie malgache. Bulletin, nouv. sér., v. 6, 1922/23: 85–89.
DT469.M21A35, n.s., v. 6

See also his "Note sur l'écriture arabe à Madagascar, *in* "Académie malgache. Bulletin, v. 13, 1913 (held by the New York Public Library). And *see also* 1430.

1456
Pain, G. Un manuscrit arabico-malgache inédit. *In* Académie malgache. Bulletin, nouv. sér., v. 34, 1956: 77–79.
DT469.M21A35, n. s., v. 34

Description of a Malagasy manuscript written in Arabic script.

1457
Struck, Bernhard. An unpublished vocabulary of the Comoro language. *In* African Society. Journal, v. 8, July 1909: 412–421. DT1.R62, v. 8

1458
Waterlot, G. Quatre stèles arabes d'Anorotsangana (Madagascar). RMM, t. 58, 1924 (2. section): 268–273. plates. DS36.R4, v. 58

1459
Williamson, John. The use of Arabic script in Swahili. TNR, v. 6, no. 4, 1947: supplement, 1–7.
DT436.T3, suppl. to v. 6

Law

1460
Anderson, James N. D. Muslim marriages and the courts in East Africa. Journal of African law, v. 1, spring 1957: 14–22. DLC–LL

Case study of two decisions of the Court of Appeal for Eastern Africa, one concerning Isma'ili Khojas and the other pertaining to divorce and what constitutes a valid marriage between two members of the Isma'ili community.

1461
———Recent developments in Shari'a Law in the Sudan. SNR, v. 31, June 190: 82–104. DT118.S85, v. 31

In this substantial essay, Anderson attempts to review in detail reforms introduced in the judicial system which parallel those taking place in Egypt under the influence of the modernist ulemas.

1462
———*Waqfs* in East Africa. Journal of African law, v. 3, autumn 1959: 152–164. DLC–LL

Critical analysis of the problems related to Waqf law and its application to East Africa. Anderson concludes, "It would surely be infinitely preferable to introduce legislation explicitly prohibiting the creation of family perpetuities through the medium of a *waqf* . . . than to exasperate and bewilder the Muslim communities concerned by invalidating some of these *waqfs*, but not others, either through a misapplication of English principles or through giving a rigid doctrinaire interpretation to Ordinances which were introduced to remedy similarly unhappy judicial decisions of the past."

1463
el-Buhriy, Hemedi bin Ali. Mirathi, a handbook of the Mahomedan law of inheritance, with appendices on wills and gifts and an introduction, translation and notes, by Sheik Ali bin Hemedi el Buhuri, *Kathi* of Tanga. Translation and notes by P. E. Mitchell, Administrative Officer, Tanganyika Territory. [Nairobi, Reprinted for the Govt. Printer by D. L. Patel Press, pref. 1923, 1949] 65, 59 p. DLC–LL

English and Swahili.

1464
———Nikahi: a handbook of the law of marriage in Islam, by Sheikh Ali Hemedi El Buhriy. [Translated by J.W.T. Allen] Dar es Salaam, 1959. 42 p.

Source: Royal Comm. Soc. Cat.

1465
Farran, Charles d'Olivier. The relationship between civil law, custom and Sharia. Sudan law journal and reports, 1959: 103–111. DLC–LL

1466
Guy, Paul. Islam comorien. *In* Charnay, Jean Paul, *ed.* Normes et valeurs dans l'Islam contemporain. Paris, Payot, 1966. p. 145–158. (Bibliothèque scientifique) BP165.C5

Analysis of the conflicts of law and social change among the Muslims of the Comoro Islands. Muslim intellectuals steeped in the Islamic tradition argue in favor of a revival of traditional Islam, while the new middle class shaped in the mold of French culture call for a modernization of the Shari'a.

1467
———Les musulmans chafeites de l'Archipel des Comores et leur droit. Revue algérienne, pt. 1, 1951: 59–64. AP27.R4, 1951

1468
Maiorani, Angelo. Lezioni di diritto musulmano, tenute nella Scuola di giurisprudenza di Asmara. Asmara, Tip. Fioretti, 1954. 142 p. DLC–LL

Cover title: *Isti tuzioni di diritto musulmano.*

1469
Singer, Norman J. Islamic law and the development of the Ethiopian legal system. Howard law journal, v. 17, no. 1, 1971: 130–168. DLC–LL

1470
el-Tahir Omer, el-Fahal. The administration of justice during the Mahdiya. Sudan law journal and reports, 1964: 167–170. DLC–LL

1471
Vaughan, John H. The dual jurisdiction in Zanzibar. Zanzibar, Govt. printer; London, Crown Agents for the Colonies, 1935. 123 p. NNSc

Literature

1472
Abdallah ibn Ali ibn Nasir. al-Inkishafi. The soul's awakening. Translated from the Swahili texts and edited by William Hichens. Nairobi, Oxford University Press, 1972. 190 p. illus. PL8704.A33I5 1972

English and Swahili.

The Soul's Awakening is "a work which the Swahili rightly regard as one of the flowers of their national literature." The poem was composed ca. 1810–20 and remains unfinished at verse 76. The Swahili text is reproduced in both Arabic and Latin scripts.

1473
Ahmad Nassir bin Juma Bhalo. Malenga wa Mvita; diwani ya Ustadh Bhalo, tungo za Ahmad Nassir. Zimehaririwa na Shihabuddin Chiraghdin. [The bard from Mombasa; anthology of Master Bhalo. Edited by Shihabuddin Chiraghdin] Nairobi, Oxford University Press, 1971. 195 p. PL8704.A45M3

1474
———Poems from Kenya; gnomic verses in Swahili. Translated and edited by Lyndon Harries. Madison, University of Wisconsin Press, 1966. 244 p. PL8704.A45

English and Swahili.

1475
'Alī, Muḥammad Muḥammad. al-Shi'r al-Sūdānīfī al-ma'ārik al-siyāsīyah, 1821–1924. [Sudanese poetry and the political struggle, 1821–1924] [Cairo] Maktabāt al-Kulliyāt al-Azharīyah [1969] 416 p.
PJ8310.A35 Orien Arab

Risālat al-Mājistīr—Jāmi'at al-Qāhirah.

Includes a section on the use of poetry as a political instrument during the Mahdist era.

1476
Allen, J. W.T., *comp.* Tendi; six examples of a Swahili classical verse form with translation and notes. New York, Africana Pub. Corp. [1971] 504 p. facsim., music. PL8704.A2A4

After a scholarly introduction to Swahili prosody, Allen, who has a long familiarity with Swahili, presents six poems. "Utendi wa Mwana Kupona" (Mwana Kupona's poem), written in Pate in 1858, is an admonition by the author to her daughter to lead a virtuous life. "Utendi wa Ngamia na Paa" (The Camel and the Gazelle) is a moral fable, the story of two animals who complained about their plight to the Prophet. The author of the poem states that the original version of the poem was in Arabic and he translated it into Swahili. "Utendi wa Masahibu" (Adversity) shows the defeat of vice by virtue. "Utendi wa Mikidadi na Mayasa" (Miqdad and Mayasa) is "typical of tales of the heroes of the time of the Prophet and shortly after his death." "Utenda wa Ayubu" (Job) relates the story of Job. "Utenda wa Qiyama" (The Last Judgement) is a vivid description of supernatural joys and pains requiring a symbolic interpretation.

1477
Badri, Babakr. al-Amthāl al-Sūdānīyah. [Sudanese proverbs] [Khartoum?, 1963?] 416 p.
PN6519.S8B3 Orien Arab

Collection of 2,004 Sudanese colloquial proverbs.

1478
al-Bashīr, al-Ṭāhir Muḥammad 'Alī. al-Adab al-Ṣūfī al-Sūdānī. [Sudanese Sufi literature] [Khartoum?] al-Dār al-Sūdānīyah [1970] 270 p.
PJ8310.B3 1970 Orien Arab

Originally presented as the author's thesis (M.A.), University of Cairo, 1965.

Through a detailed study of Sufi poetry, al-Bashīr provides a sure thread to the cultural and religious history of the Sudan. After a general introduction to Sufism in the Sudan and the three stages of Sufi poetry—colloquial, semicolloquial, and classical—the author investigates the Simmānīyah fraternity of al-Shaykh Muḥammad ibn 'Abd al-Karīm al-Qirshī al-Madanī, better known as al-Simmānī, and four of its most prominent poets, namely Muḥammad Sharīf Nūr al-Dā'im, 'Abd al-Maḥmūd Nūr al-Dā'im, Qarīb Allāh Abū Ṣāliḥ, and Muḥammad Sa'īd al-'Abbāsī, and their impact on Sudanese society.

1479
el-Buhriy, Hemedi bin Abdallah. Utenzi wa Kutawafu Nabii. [The release of the Prophet] With translation by Roland Allen. Edited by J.W.T. Allen. *In* East African Swahili Committee. Journal, no. 26, June 1956: supplement, 1–72.
PL8701.E2, suppl. to no. 26

Text and translation of a poem portraying the death of the Prophet Muḥammad. Appended is a variant of the poem as reported by C.B. Büttner in *Anthologie aus der Suaheli-literatur* (Berlin, Emil Faber, 1894) that he acquired from Daniel J. Rankin, formerly British consul in Mozambique. Also included are a short vocabulary list and an analysis and indexes of the two versions.

1480
D. R. *and* S. H. Two texts from Kordofan. SNR, v. 13, pt. 2, 1930: 117–122. DT118.S85, v. 13

Text and translation of two letters in Sudanese colloquial Arabic written in Arabic script. The letters are part of the tradition of oral feud between the Kabābīsh and the Ḥamar of the Sudan. They are messages to be recited by the envoy using saj', or rhymed prose, as a rhetorical embellishment.

1481

Dammann, Ernst. The tradition of Swahili islamic poetry. *In* Ibadan, Nigeria. University. *Centre of Arabic Documentation.* Research bulletin, v. 5, no 1-b, 1969: 21–46. DLC

1482

Demoz, Abraham. Moslems and Islam in Ethiopic literature. Journal of Ethiopian studies, v. 10, Jan. 1972: 1–11. DT371.J67, v. 10

"The expansion of Islam into Ethiopia differed from its expansion into much of the rest of Africa in that in Ethiopia Islam was challenged by one of the 'higher' religions of the world which had entrenched itself in the country," states Demoz, introducing his topic. The impact of the struggle between the two religions on Ethiopic, namely Ge'ez, literature is shown in religious and secular writings. Examples of religious writings are *Anqäṣä Amin* [The Gate of Faith] written by "a former Muslim who was converted to Christianity and became so learned and devout in his new faith that he rose to the rank of *Eččagé* [abbot] of the monastery of Däbrä Libanos," and *Mäṣhafä Qéder* [Book of Impurity], about special rites and prayers for those returning to the Christian faith. In the secular field, the chronicles of the emperors reflect the bitter antagonism and the appearance of a Christian Jihad syndrome in such works as the exhortations of Emperor 'Amda Ṣeyon and the "lamentations" composed on the death of Emperor Gälawdéwos.

1483

Farsi, Shaaban Saleh. Swahili sayings from Zanzibar. Dar es Salaam, East African Literature Bureau, 1958. 2 v. in 1. PN6519.S9F3

In Swahili and English.

Contents: book 1. Proverbs.—book 2. Riddles and superstitions.

1484

Harries, Lyndon, *ed. and tr.* Swahili poetry. Oxford, Clarendon Press, 1962. 326 p. facsim. PL8704.A2H3

Texts in Swahili-Arabic script are transliterated and translated into English.

1485

Ḥasan, Qurashī Muḥammad. Qaṣā'id min shu'arā' al-Mahdīyah. [Poems by poets of the Mahdis era] [Khartoum] al-Majlis al-qawmī li-ri'āyat al-ādāb wa-al-funūn [1974] 311 p. DLC

Anthology of modern Arabic poetry in the Sudanese dialect related to the Mahdi Muḥammad Aḥmad.

1486

Hasani bin Ismail. The medicine man: Swifa ya Nguvumali; edited and translated by Peter Lienhardt. Oxford, Clarendon Press, 1968. 208 p. (Oxford library of African literature) PL8704.H3

Introduction and appendix in English; poem in English and Swahili.

1487

Jackson, Henry C. Sudan proverbs. SNR, v. 2, Apr. 1919: 105–111. DT118.S85, v. 2

Collection of 25 Sudanese colloquial Arabic proverbs with Arabic text, English translation, and comments.

1488

Klamorth, M. Der literarische charakter des ostafrikanisschen Islams. Die welt des Islams, Bd. 1, 1913: 21–31. DS36.W4, v. 1

1489

Knappert, Jan. Het epos van Heraklios; een proeve van Swahili poëzie. Tekst en vertaling, voorzien van inleiding, kritisch commentar en aantekeningen. Alkmaar, Druk, N.J. Hofman [1958] 326 p. PL8704.K53K5

Text, translation, and commentary on a long poem (1150 verses) on the Prophet Muḥammad and his early wars against Rome and Byzantium as recorded from the version of Shaykh Muhammed Abubekr bin Omar Kijumwa Masihii.

1490

———Miiraji—The Swahili legend of Mohammed's ascension. Swahili, v. 36, Sept. 1966: 105–156. PL8701.E2, v. 36

1491

———Notes on Swahili literature. African language studies, v. 7, 1966: 126–159. PL8003.A34, v. 7

1492

———Rhyming Swahili proverbs. Afrika and Übersee, Jahrg. 49, Jun. 1966: 59–68. PL8000.Z4, v. 49

1493

———Social and moral concepts in Swahili Islamic literature. Africa, v. 40, Apr. 1970: 123–136. PL8000.I6, v. 40

1494

———Swahili Islamic poetry. Leiden, Brill, 1971. 3 v. PL8704.A2K57

Texts in Swahili with parallel English translations.

Contents: v. 1. Introduction, The celebration of Mohammed's birthday, Swahili Islamic cosmology.—v. 2. The two burdas.—v. 3. Mieraj and Maulid.

1495
———Traditional Swahili poetry. An investigation into the concepts of East African Islam as reflected in the Utenzi literature. Leiden, E. J. Brill, 1967. 272 p. PL8704.K6

1496
———, *ed.* Wilada Nabii: a praise poem on the prophet Mohammed. Afrika and Übersee, Jahrg. 50, pt. 1-b, 1967: 34–40. PL8000.Z4, v. 50

1497
al-Madā'iḥ al-Ṣadafīyah. [The mother-of-pearl praises] [Khartoum, Idārat al-Maḥfūẓāt al-Markazīyah, 1969] 222 p. PJ7632.M75M3
A collection of prose and poetry in praise of the Prophet Muḥammad, in the Sudanese dialect.

1498
Werner, A. Moslem literature in Swahili. MW, v. 10, Jan. 1920: 25–29. DS36.M7, v. 10
Short study of religious poems in Swahili. The tenzi, which Werner compares to the chansons de geste, deal with Muslim theology and traditions.

1499
Yagi, Viviane Amina. Contes et légendes du Soudan. Correspondance d'Orient; études, no 1/2, 1962: 17–66; no 3, 1963: 67–98. DS36.C65, 1962–63
Introduction to the folklore of the Sudan. The author focuses her attention on the Arab urban sector and particularly on the Omdurman/Khartoum area.

Numismatics

1500
Arkell, Anthony J. The coinage of 'Alī Dīnār, Sultan of Darfur, 1898-1916. SNR, v. 23, no. 1, 1940: 151–160. illus. DT118.S85, v. 23
Substantial study of the currency of 'Alī Dīnār collected by Arkell at El-Fasher, the former capital of the sultanate. Arkell also interviewed the surviving smiths and overseers of the royal workshops, as well as former court officials. *See also* 1508.

1501
———Forged Mahdi pounds. SNR, v. 26, pt. 1 1954: 43–49. DT118.S85, v. 26
Brief article on the authenticity of some alleged Mahdist currency.

1502
Artin, Yacoub. Monnaies de Mehdy Mouhammed Ahmed du Soudan. *In* Institut Egyptien. Bulletin. 2. sér., no 8, 1887: 231–246. DT43.I61, 2d ser., 1887
Description of one gold and two silver pieces minted by the Sudanese Mahdi in the 1880's.

1503
Chittick, H. Neville. A coin hoard from near Kilwa Azania, v. 2, 1967: 194–198. DT365.3.A94, v. 2

1504
———Six early coins from near Tanga. Azania, v. 1, 1966: 156–157. DT365.3.A94, v. 1
Two of the coins are Ummayad and one is probably Fatimid.

1505
Freeman-Grenville, G. S. P. East African coin finds and their historical significance. JAH, v. 1, no. 1, 1960: 31–43. MBU

1506
Job, H. S. The coinage of the Mahdi and the Khalifa. SNR, v. 3, July 1920: 163–196. plates. DT118.S85, v. 3
Thorough presentation of the coinage of the Mahdist period, 1885–98, in the Sudan. Included are descriptions and photographs of various coins.

1507
Smith, Samuel, Jr. Some notes on the coins struck at Omdurman by the Mahdi and the Khalifa. Numismatic chronicle, 4th series, pt. 1, 1902: 62–73. CJ1.N6, 4th ser., 1902

1508
Walker, J. The coinage of Ali Dinar. SNR, v. 19, pt. 2, 1936: 147–149. illus. DT118.S85, v. 19
Short note on the currency of the Darfur sultanate with line drawings of various coins.

1509
Walker, J., *and* G. S. P. Freeman-Grenville. The history and coinage of the Sultans of Kilwa. TNR, no. 45, Dec. 1956: 33–65. DT436.T3, 1956

Politics

1510
Aguda, Oluwadare. Arabism and Pan-Arabism in Sudanese politics. Journal of modern African studies, v. 11, June 1973: 177–200. D1.J68, v. 11

Introducing his study by stating that "the greatest achievement of Arabism in the Sudan has been that unquestioned acceptance by the whole world that this is an Arab state, in spite of the fact that only about 40 per cent of the population is Arab," Aguda then proceeds to investigate the "Arabness" of the Sudanese, the historical background of the regional dichotomy, external influences, and the results of the agreement signed in March 1972 between the Central Government and the Southern Resistance Movement.

1511
Beshir, Mohamed Omer. The Southern Sudan; background to conflict. New York, Praeger [1968] 192 p. maps. DT108.B4 1968b

Writing at a time of intense emotions regarding the political problems of the Sudan, Beshir provides a factual historical analysis and pleads for a quick solution, as "the present deadlock in North-South relations has to be broken. The longer the present state of affairs and the small war are allowed to continue, the more people are likely to be killed. And they will die, not for the sake of any basic political principle, but through a simple failure in communications between the political leaders." He then discusses the chances of federalism, calling for a united Sudan.

See also his translation in Arabic (DT108.B412).

1512
Coupland, *Sir* Reginald. The exploitation of East Africa, 1856–1890: the slave trade and the scramble; with an introduction by Jack Simmons. 2d ed. London, Faber, 1968. 508 p. illus., col. map, 5 plates, ports., table. DT365.C6 1968

Portrays the situation on the coast and the contacts of the colonial powers with the centers of Arab influence and control.

1513
Depraetere, Marguerite. Le conflit entre la République du Soudan et ses provinces méridionales: élément d'explication. Bruxelles [Centre d'étude et de documentation africaine] CEDAF, 1972. 70 leaves. maps. (Les Cahiers du CEDAF, 7/1972. Série 2: Histoire) DT1.C45 no. 7, 1972

1514
Diamond, Stanley, *and* Fred G. Burke, *eds.* The transformation of East Africa; studies in political anthropology. New York, Basic Books [1967, c1966] 623 p. maps. DT365.D5

Papers written for a faculty-student seminar on problems of nation building in East Africa of the Program of East African Studies, Syracuse University.

The problems of Islam in relation to both Christianity and the colonial administration are marginally discussed in many studies of this compilation.

1515
Eilts, Hermann F. Ahmad bin Na'man's mission to the United States in 1840, the voyage of al-Sultanah to New York City. *In* Essex Institute. Historical collections, v. 98, oct. 1962: 219–277. F72.E7E81, v. 98

1516
Ferrand, Gabriel. Notes sur la situation politique, commerciale et religieuse du Pachalik de Harar et de ses dependences. *In* Société de géographie de l'est. Bulletin, t. 8, 1886: [1]–17; 231–244. G11.S56, v. 8

1517
Garang, Joseph U. The dilemma of the southern intellectual. Is it justified? Khartoum, Ministry of Southern Affairs, 1971. 30 p. DT108.7.G37

1518
al-Ḥasan, Mūsā al-Mubārak. Tārīkh Dārfūr al-siyāsī, 1882–1898. [The political history of Darfur, 1882–1898] [Khartoum] Jāmi'at al-Kharṭūm, Qism al-ta'līf wa-al-nashr [1970] 256 p. maps. DT135.D2H38

1519
Howell, John, *and* M. Beshir Hamid. Sudan and the outside world. African affairs, v. 68, Oct. 1969: 299–315. DT1.R62, v. 68

1520
'Ifārah, Jamīl Ilyās. Mashākil al-Sūdān al-siyāsīyah wa-al-dawāfi 'al-bārizah warā' al-inqilāb al-'askarī al-akhīr. [The political problems of the Sudan and the apparent motives behind the latest military coup] [Beirut? Sharikat al-ṭab' wa-al-nashr al-Lubnānīyah] 1958. 183 p. illus., map, ports. DT108.6.I34

1521
Ismā'īl, 'Uthmān Sayyid Aḥmad. al-Dīn wa-al-siyāsah wa-nash'at wa taṭawwur al-Khatmīyah wa-al-Anṣār [Religion, politics and the rise and development of the Khatmīyah and the Anṣār] [Khartoum, al-Sharikah al-Sūdānīyah lil-tawzī' al maḥdūd, 1972?] 32 p. DLC

1522
McClintock, David W. The Southern Sudan problem: evolution of an Arab-African confrontation. The Middle East journal, v. 24, autumn 1970: 466–478. DS1.M5, v. 24

A Foreign Service officer, McClintock concludes, "In the context of time, it appears that the Sudan's Muslim North set out to consolidate and lead a new nation at precisely the moment the mostly pagan, partly Christian South was searching for its own identity."

1523
Mahjub, Ahmed Ahmad. Democracy on trial; reflections on Arab and African politics. London, André Deutch, 1974. 318 p. illus. DT108.7.M33

Memoirs of a prominent Sudanese figure who was intimately linked to a number of political developments in both the Near East and Africa.

1524
Martin, Bradford G. Muslim politics and resistance to colonial rule: Shaykh Uways B. Muḥammad al-Barāwī and the Qādirīya Brotherhood in East Africa. JAH, v. 10, no. 3, 1969: 471–486. DT1.J65, v. 10

Shaykh Uways b. Muḥammad al-Barāwī (1847–1909) was an important leader of the Qādirīya brotherhood in southern Somalia, on Zanzibar, and along the East African coast from Kenya to Mozambique, and founded his own branch of Qādirīya, the Uwaysīya. Before his death in 1909 when he was assassinated by representatives of the rival Sālihīya brotherhood (under the leadership of Muḥammad Abdallāh Ḥasan, the 'Mad Mullah'), Uways' missionary activities were very considerable.

Uways' branch of the Qādirīya was probably behind certain episodes of Muslim resistance to European penetration into Buganda in the late 1880's, at the behest of Sayyid Barghash of Zanzibar. Indeed, the relations between Shaykh Uways and successive rulers of Zanzibar, Barghash, Khalīfa, and Ḥamid b. Thuwaynī were very close. In 90's, certain Muslim elements in Tanganyika, in conjunction with the *ṭarīqa,* made trouble for the Germans in SE Tanganyika during the 'Mecca Letters affair' at Lindi in 1908. This episode revealed a division in the Tanganyika Muslim community.

The Uwaysīya was responsible for massive conversions to Islam in the coastal region, in inner Tanganyika, and on the Eastern fringes of the Congo at the end of the 19th and the beginning decades of the 20th centuries.—(Abstract supplied)

See also 1337.

1525
Nimitz, August. Traditional Shirazi political systems.

Source: ASA, Program, 14th, 1971.

1526
Padmore, George. The background of the Sudan crisis. The Islamic review, v. 43, Sept. 1955: 15–17. BP1.I7, v. 43

Brief historical presentation of the legacy of British rule in Southern Sudan and the eruption of the mutiny among southern elements of the Sudan Defence Force in 1955.

1527
Pozdniakov, N. A. Problema natsional'nogo edinstva Sudane. [The problem of Sudan's national unity] Narody Azii i Afriki, 4, 1970: 27–44. DS1.P7, 1970

Tables of contents also in English and Chinese; summaries in English.

1528
Warburg, Gabriel. Religious policy in the Northern Sudan: 'Ulama' and Sufism, 1899–1919. Asian and African studies, v. 7, 1971: 89–120. DS1.A4734, v. 7

1529
Welbourn, Frederick B. Religion and politics in Uganda, 1952–1962. [Nairobi] East African Pub. House, 1965. 78 p. map. (EAPH historical studies, 1) BL2470.U3W4

Although primarily about Catholics and Protestants, this work provides a useful analysis of the problems connected with the concept of national identity in Uganda.

1530
Wilmington, Martin W. The Zande Scheme in the Sudan: a test case of Arab-African economic cooperation. Paper presented at the 3rd annual meeting of the African Studies Association, Hartford, Conn., 1960. DLC–Micro 03782

Collation of the original: 17 p.

Sects

1531
Abū Salīm, Muhhammad Ibrāhīm. Makhṭūṭ fī tārīkh mu'assis al-Khatmīyah; al-Ijābah al-Ibānah al-Nūrīyah fī sha'n ṣāḥib al-ṭarīqah al-Khatmīyah mawlānā al-Sayyid Muḥammad 'Uthmān al-Khatm. [Manuscript on the history of the founder of the Khatmiyah; the enlightening answer and proof concerning the founder of the Khatmiyah sect Mawlana al-Sayyid Muhammad Uthman al-Khatm] *In* Khartoum. University. *Sudan Research Unit.* Bulletin of Sudanese studies, v. 1, July 1968: 36–44. DLC

The Khatmīyah sect played a great historical role in the life of the Sudan. Its founder was born in al-Ṭā'if, Saudi Arabia; after a long period of initiation and travel he established his sect in the Sudan. Abū Salīm describes a manuscript, found in Suakin in 1890, that gives valuable information on al-Sayyid Muḥammad, including an introduction and 12 chapters on the life, description, genealogy, and predictions about the founder, as well as his relations with the Mek of Kordofan, the sultan of Sennar, and the Ethiopian rulers.

1532
Dammann, Ernst. Ahmadistische propaganda in O. Afrika. Neue Allgemeine missionszeitschrift, Bd. 14, Nr. 5, 1937: 148–153. CtY–D

1533
al-Ḍawī, Tāj al-anbiyā' 'Alī. al-Ṭarīqah al-Ismā'īlīyah fī madīnat al-Ubayyid. [The Ismā'īlī sect in el-Obeid] Sudan society, 1969: 132–118 [pagination follows Arabic format] HN831.S8A6, 1969

The Ismā'īli sect was created in the 1820's in El-Obeid (Kordofan Province) by Ismā'īl ibn 'Abd Allāh, better known as al-Sayyid Ismā'īl al-Waliy. al-Ḍawī presents the history of the sect, its evolution, and development. He also examines the movement as a religious as well as social system and the bonds it creates between individuals from different areas, races, and professions as a result of their participation in group Sufi practices.

1534
Ḥusayn, Muḥammad Kāmil. Ṭā'ifat al-Ismā'īlīyah, tārīkhuha, nudhumuhā, 'aqāiduhā. [The Ismaili sect, its history, organization, and beliefs] Cairo, Maktabat al-nahḍah al-Miṣrīyah [1959] 190 p. (al-Maktabah al-tārīkhīyah, 4) BP195.I8H8

1535
Lewis, I. M. Sufism in Somaliland: a study in tribal Islam. BSOAS, v. 27, pt. 3, 1955: 581–602; v. 28, pt. 1, 1956: 145–160. PJ3.L6, v. 27, 28

Detailed analysis of Sufism among the Somali. After examining the role of the religious movement and its interaction with the Somali traditions, Lewis concludes, "In tribal societies where stress is placed upon the power of lineage ancestors to mediate between man and God, Sufism provides an interpretation of Islam which, while preserving the supreme absoluteness of *Allāh,* mitigates the uniqueness of the Prophet in favour of more accessible and more immediate intercessors."

1536
Maḥmūd, 'Abd al-Qādir. al-Fikr al-Ṣūfī fī al-Sūdān, maṣādiruhu, wa-tayārātuhu wa-alwānuhu. Sufi thought in the Sudan; its sources, trends and aspects] [Cairo] Dār al-fikr al-'Arabī 1968–69 [i.e. 1968] 229 p. geneal. tables. BP189.M282

1537
Monteil, Vincent. Un Coran ahmadi en swahili. BIFAN, t. 29, juil./oct. 1967: 479–495. DT1.I5123, v. 29

The Aḥmadīyah sect was established in Kashmir in 1889 by Mirza Ghulam Ahmad Qadiyani (1835–1908). It differs from Orthodox Islam on a number of points, including the recognition of prophets not mentioned in the Koran, such as Krishna and Buddha; the Prophet Muhammad is not the "Seal of Prophets"; no verses of the Holy Book can be abrogated by later verses; Jesus did not die but escaped, lived in Kashmir, and was buried in Shrinagar. Though English is commonly used, Swahili is widely used in East Africa for proselytism. Monteil discusses an Ahmadi Koran (Kurani Tufuku; Pamoja na Tafsiri na Maelezo Kaw Kiswahili) published in Nairobi in 1953 by the Ahmadiyya Muslim Mission. He compares it with an Orthodox version on three points: polygamy, the crucifixion, and the ascension of Jesus.

1538
Morris, H. S. The divine kingship of the Agha Khan: a study of theocracy in East Africa. Southwestern journal of anthropology, v. 14, winter 1958: 454–472. GN1.S64, v. 14

1539
Rebelo, Domingos J. S. Breves apontamentos sobre um grupo de Indianos em Moçambique a communidade ismaília moametana. *In* Sociedade de estudos de Moçambique. Boletim, ano 30, jul./set. 1961: 83–89. DT451.S6, v. 30

1540
Rizvi, Seyyid Saeed Akhtar, *and* Noël Q. King. Some East African Ithna Asheri *Jamaats* (1840–1967). Journal of religion in Africa/Religion en Afrique, v. 5, fasc. 1, 1973: 12–22. BL2400.J68, v. 5

The Ithnā ʻasharī of East Africa, a small Shiite group, consists largely of descendants of the Khoja Muslims of India. The authors describe the various jamāʻah, or congregations, in Zanzibar, Pemba, Lamu, Mombasa, Pangani, Arusha, Moshi, Bagamoyo, Dar es Salaam, Kilwa, Lindi, Singida, Bukoba, Mwanza, Tabora, and Kampala.

1541
Willis, C. Armine. Religious confraternities of the Sudan. SNR, v. 4, Dec. 1921: 175–194. DT118.S85, v. 4

Description of the various religious fraternities as they existed in the Sudan in 1921. These included the Qādirīyah, Khilwatīyah, Shādhilīyah, Aḥmadīyah, (or Idrīsīyah), Mīrghānīyah (or Khatmīyah), Rashīdīyah, Naqshabandīyah, and Shahwardīyah.

Society & Culture

1541a
Ahmed, Ahmed Dini. Un fait social 'Afar: La *Fi'ma*. La *Fi'ma:* différent types, organisation, fonctionnement. Pount; bulletin de la Société d'études de l'Afrique orientale, no 3, 3. trim. 1967: 31–36. DLC

Description of the Fiʻmah phenomenon by the T.F.A.I. Minister of the Interior. The Fiʻmah is an organization striving to harmonize and regulate social relations; the author presents its various types and their structures and procedures.

1542
Amiji, Hatim. An aspect of Islam and social change in East Africa.
Source: ASA, Program, 15th, 1972.

1543
Arabes et islamisés à Madagascar et dans l'océan Indien. Documents présentés par le Service général de l'information de la République Malagasy (Revue de Madagascar no 34, 35, 36, 37) et le Centre d'archéologie de la Faculté des lettres et des sciences humaines de l'Université de Madagascar. [Tananarive, Revue de Madagascar; distribué par Hachette—Madagascar, 1967] 57 p. illus. DT356.4.A7

Summary in English and Malagasy.

Published jointly by the Revue de Madagascar and Taloha as an irregular series issued by the University of Madagascar, this compilation includes: Pierre Vérin, Introduction: les Arabes dans l'océan Indien et à Madagascar; Jacques Dez, De l'influence arabe à Madagascar à l'aide de faits de linguistique; Neville Chittick, L'archéologie de la côte orientale africaine; Claude Robineau, l'Islam au Commores; une étude d'histoire culturelle de l'île d'Anjouan; Raymond Deval, (Présentation de l'étude de): Les musulmans à Madagascar; problèmes contemporains, résumé et situation; James Kirkman, Les importations de céramiques sur la côte du Kenya; W. G. N. van Der Sleen, Observations sur les perles de Madagascar et de l'Afrique orientale; R. Battistini and Pierre Vérin, Irodo et la tradition vohémarienne; Jean-Claude Hebert, Essai d'interprétation de la stèle indéchiffrée d'Ambilobe.

1544
Ardant du Picq, Charles P. L'influence islamique sur une population malayo-polynésienne de Madagascar. Paris, Charles-Lavauzelle, 1933. 70 p., double geneal. table, tables. NN

1545
Auber, J. A propos de la formule "Voa salamou haza" qui clôt les écrits et les sentences arabico-madécasses. *In* Académie malgache. Bulletin, nouv. sér., t. 32, 1954: 47–50. DT469.M21A35, v. 32

1546
Cerbella, Gino. La diffusione in Eritrea della casa musulmana typica. Africa (Rome), anno. 17, nov./dic. 1962: 291–299. DT1.A843, v. 17

1547
Cerulli, Enrico. Canti amarici dei musulmani di Abissinia. *In* Accademia nazionale dei Lencei (Rome). Rendiconti, ser. 6, v. 2, 1926: 433–447. AS222.R65, ser. 6, v. 2

1548
Davies, R. A system of sand divination. SNR, v. 3, July 1920: 157–162. DT118.S85, v. 3

Description of a method of foretelling the future as practiced by Arabs in northern Sudan, particularly by the Maḥāmīd and Ṭaʻāyshah of northern and central Kordofan.

1549
Fawzi, Saʻad ed'din. Social aspects of urban housing in the Northern Sudan. SNR, v. 35, June 1954: 91–109. DT118.S85, v. 35

Social mores of a society are often best reflected in its architecture and its use of space. Fawzī, who was head of the Department of Economics at the university in Khartoum, bases his study "around the all-important question of how to provide adequately for the requirements of family life and the family's social commitments within the limitations imposed by the need for economy in low-cost housing."

1550
Garlake, Peter, *and* Margaret Garlake. Early ship engravings of the East African coast. TNR, no. 63, Sept. 1964: 197–206. DT436.T3, no. 63

1551
Hillelson, Sigmar. Aspects of Muhammadanism in the Eastern Sudan. *In* Royal Asiatic Society. Journal, Oct. 1937: 657–677. AS122.L72, 1937

1552
Holt, Peter M. Four Funj land-charters. SNR, v. 50, 1969: 2–14. illus. DT118.S85, v. 50

Text, translation of, and commentary on four Funj land charters presented by A. J. Arkell to the School of Oriental and African Studies in 1967. "The land charters of the late Funj period (i.e. the reigns of Badi IV and his successors) fall into two categories: those which originate, and those which confirm, a grant of land and exemptions. . . . The four documents . . . form two pairs, each consisting of one originating and one confirmatory charter."

1553
Hussey, E. J. R. A fiki's clinic. SNR, v. 6, July 1923: 35–39. DT118.S85, v. 6.

Description of a faqīh (religious scholar) and his treatment of cases of madness. Hussey describes the clinic as well as the cures used by the holy man.

1554
Kamil, Abdallah Mohamed. Un fait social Afar: la *Fi'ma;* aspects sociologiques de la *Fi'ma.* Pount, no 3, 3. trimestre 1967: 36–40. DLC

Analytical essay on the Fiʻmah. The institution, according to the author, "a été créée pour proteger l'Afar: 1° contre ses semblables; 2° contre les aléas de la vie; 3° contre le sentiment de solitude qui s'empare de lui, quand il est privé de l'encadrement, du contact des autres hommes." He is pessimistic as to the future of the Fiʻmah and believes that urbanization will result in its eventual disappearance. "Et la disparition de la *fi'ma* signifiera celle du célèbre "communnisme des revenus", tel qu'il existe chez les 'Afar. Chacun devra compter seulement sur soi. Alors, l'Afar sera devenu vraiment citadin, avec toutes les conséquences qui en découlent et, en particulier, le développement d'un *lumpenproletariat.*"

1555
Kennedy, J. G. Nubian Zar ceremonies as psychotherapy. Human organization, v. 26, winter 1967: 185–194. GN1.H83, v. 26

1556
Knappert, Jan. Une culture en voie de disparition. *In* International Congress of Anthropological and Ethnological Sciences, *6th, Paris, 1960.* VIᵉ [i.e. Sixième] Congrès international des sciences anthropologiques et ethnologiques, Paris, 30 juillet-6 août 1960. Paris, Musée de l'homme [1962]–64. p. 225–227. GN3.I39 1960c

1557
———The function of Arabic in the Islamic ritual on the East African Coast. *In* Congrés d'études arabes et islamiques, *5th, Brussels, 1970.* Vᵉ [i.e. Cinquième] Congrès international d'arabisants et d'islamisants, Bruxelles, 31 août-6 septembre 1970. Actes. Bruxelles, Publications du Centre pour l'étude des problèmes du monde musulman contemporain [1971] p. 185–296. (Correspondance d'Orient, no 11) HC498.C6, no. 11

Study of the impact of Arabic among East African Muslims. The language of the Koran is still the medium of "ritual, liturgy and magic, of the calendar of festivities, as well as in the realm of courtesy and civil manners." However, with the spread of Swahili the influence of Arabic outside the realm of religion is bound to diminish, although the latter has left an indelible mark on Swahili and the cultures of East Africa.

1558
Laurioz, Jacques. Notes sur les pratiques relatives aux génies "zar" en T.F.A.I. Pount, 2. année, 3. trimestre 1969: 5–11. DLC

Description of the zār rites in Djibouti. Laurioz states "nous nous efforcerons successivement de définir un type de cérémonie *zār* plus généralement attesté, puis de dresser la liste des autres rites, en usage dans le Territoire Français des Afars et des Issas." In his conclusion he suggests "nous pouvens donc conclure à une double et contradictoire évolution de cette superstition importée d'Ethiopie. D'une part, une dégénérescence en milieu traditionnel, concrétisée souvent par l'entrée des hommes dans l'assemblée. De prêtresses, les *alaka* tendent à devenir de vulgaires sorcières ou des guérisseuses souvent redoutées, tandis que le cérémonial est vidé de son contenu mythologique et rituel."

1559
Lewis, I. M. Marriage and the family in Northern Somalia. Kampala, East African Institute of Social Research, 1962. 51 p. illus. (East African studies, no. 15) HQ700.S62L4

1560
Low, Donald A. Religion and society in Buganda, 1875–1900. Kampala, Uganda, East African Institute of Social Research [1957] 16 p. (East African studies, no. 8) DLC

1561
Mahmoud Abdi Hirad. Somali marriage custom in outline. Somaliland journal, v. 1, Dec. 1955: 92–93. MBU

1562
Mazrui, Ali A. Islam and the English language in East and West Africa. *In* International African Seminar, 9th, University College, Dar es Salaam, 1968. Language use and social change: problems of multilingualism with special reference to Eastern Africa: studies presented and discussed at the ninth International African Seminar at University College, Dar es Salaam, December 1968, edited with an introduction by W. H. Whiteley. London, Published for the International African Institute by Oxford University Press, 1971. p. 179–197. PL8016.I5 1968

A Muslim and master in the use of the English verb, Mazrui shows the "interplay between language and religion in Africa's political experience." Suggesting two main themes, he analyzes Islamic attitudes toward English, which was identified with missionary activities, then points out that the strongest rivals of metropolitan languages have been African languages with Islamic associations (Arabic, Hausa, Swahili). In spite of cultural blocks to English, he concludes that "among the best articulators of English sounds in African societies, are precisely people who grew up speaking Swahili, Hausa, and perhaps Arabic."

1563
Mkabarah, J. Salum Abdallah; mwanamuziki wa Tanzania. [Salum Abdallah; musician of Tanzania] [Dar es Salaam Chuo cha Uchanguzi wa Lugha ya Kiswahili, 1972] 91 p. ports. ML410.Y42M6

1564
Pankhurst, E. Sylvia. Ethiopia, a cultural history. With a foreword by Canon John A. Douglas. Essex [Eng.] Lalibela House [1955] 747 p. illus. (part col.), facsims., music, plans, ports. DT381.P35

1565
Paul, H. G. Balfour. A prehistoric cult still practised in Muslim Darfur (by the Zaghawa). *In* Royal Anthropological Institute of Great Britain and Ireland. Journal, v. 86, Jan./June 1956: 77–86. GN2.A3, v. 86

1566
Prins, Adriaan H. J. Sailing from Lamu; a study of maritime culture in Islamic East Africa. Assen, Van Gorcum, 1965. 320 p. illus., maps. DT434.E29L3

On label mounted on t.p.: Humanities Press, New York.

1567
Pruen, S. Tristram. The Arab and the African; experiences in Eastern Equatorial Africa during a residence of three years. London, Seeley, 1891. 338 p. illus., front. (port.), plates. DT365.P97

1568
Skene, Ralph R. F. H. Arab and Swahili dances and ceremonies. *In* Royal Anthropological Institute of Great Britain and Ireland. Journal, v. 47, 1917: 413–434. GN2.A3, v. 47

1569
Tanner, R. E. S. The relationships between the sexes in a coastal Islamic society: Pangani district, Tanganyika. African studies, v. 21, no. 2, 1962: 70–82. DT751.A4, v. 21

1570
Zenkovsky, S. *Zar* and *Tambura* as practised by the women of Omdurman. (Paper read before the Philosophical Society of the Sudan in 1948). SNR, v. 31, June 1950: 65–81. DT118.S85, v. 31

Theology

1571
Ĕnbāqom. Anqaṣa Amin (La porte de la Foi); apologie éthiopienne du Christianisme contre l'Islam à partir du Coran. Introduction, texte critique, traduction par E. J. van Donzel. Leiden, E. J. Brill, 1969. 303 p. plate. BT1170.E5

Ĕnbāqom, a Coptic monk whose origins are still shrouded in mystery, became an active religious personality in his country of adoption. The *Anqaṣa Amin* [The Gate to Faith] was written primarily as a theological argument addressed to Imam Grāñ, urging him to change his attitude toward Christian Ethiopia. It is a work of apologetics attempting to put an end to a bloody religious war.

1572
Holway, James D. Quran in Swahili. MW, v. 61, Apr. 1971: 102–110. DS36.M7, v. 61

1573
Kayfa Taḥujj? [How to accomplish the pilgrimage?] [Khartoum] Jumhurīyat al-Sūdān al-Dīmūqrātīyah. al-Amānah al-'Āmmah lil-Shu'ūn al-Dīnīyah [1973] 24 p. illus. DLC

1574
Knappert, Jan. The divine names. Swahili, n.s., v. 1, [no. 31], Sept. 1960: 180–199. PL8701.E2, n.s., v. 1

Arabic and Swahili.

1575
———Swahili theological terms. African language studies, v. 8, 1967: 82–92. PL8003.A34, v. 8

1576
Lewis, I. M. The names of God in northern Somali. BSOAS, v. 22, pt. 1, 1959: 134–140. PJ3.L6, v. 22

God is universally known in Somali by the names *Allaah* and *Rabbi.* Lewis presents a partial list of purely Somali terms for God compiled by his former assistant, Yuusuf Maygaag.

1577
Masomo ya Ki-Islamu. [A reader on Islam]. Dar es Salaam, Bilal Muslim Mission of Tanzania [1971?] 16 p. (Kitabu cha Kwanza) DLC

Trade

1578
Beachey, R. W. The East African ivory trade in the nineteenth century. JAH, v. 8, no. 2, 1967: 269–290. DT1.J65, v. 8

1579
Bell, G. W. Shaibun gold. SNR, v. 20, pt. 1, 1937: 125–137. DT118.S85, v. 20

Brief discussion of gold in the Sudan.

1580
Brown, Beverly. Muslim influence on trade and politics in the Lake Tanganyika region. African historical studies, v. 4, no. 3, 1971: 617–629. DT1.A226, v. 4

Investigation of the interaction of trade activities and political developments and the role of both among the Muslim traders around Ujiji during the last part of the 19th century.

1581
Casati, Gaetano. Dopo Cassala. Explorazione commerciale, v. 9, 1894: 265–70. HF3872.E7, v. 9

1582
Guillan, Charles. Documents sur l'histoire, la géographie et le commerce de l'Afrique orientale. Paris, A. Bertrand [1856] 3 v. in 2. fold geneal. table, map. DT365.G9

1583
Triulzi, Alessandro. Trade, Islam, and the Mahdia in northwestern Wallaga, Ethiopia. Paper presented to the International Congress of Africanists, third session, Dec. 9–19, 1973. Addis Ababa. 19 p. DLC

SOUTHERN REGION

History

1584
Du Plessis, Izak D. The Cape Malays. Libertas, v. 4, July 1944: 40–45. AP9.L5, v. 4

1585
———The Cape Malays: history, religion, traditions, folk tales, the Malay quarter. [3d ed.] Cape Town, A. A. Balkema, 1972. 97 p. illus. (part col.) DT764.M3D82 1972

1586
Garabedian, S. Mohammedanism in Cape Town. MW, v. 5, Jan. 1915: 30–37. DS36.M7, v. 5

Observations on the spread of Islam in Cape Town, followed by a short note by "A Churchman" on the threat of Islam there.

1587
Hagel, F. G. Der Islam in Südafrika. Zeitschrift für Missionswissensschaft und Religionswissenschaft, 36. Jahrg, no. 1, 1952: 28–36. BV2130.Z4, v. 36

1588
Hampson, A. R. The mission to Moslems in Capetown. MW, v. 24, July 1934: 271–177. DS36.M7 v. 24

After Shaykh Yūsūf, a convict from Batavia, was brought to South Africa by the Dutch East India Company in 1694, Islam developed rapidly among the Cape Muslims called "Malays." Hampson discusses the methods and approaches of converting these Muslims to Christianity.

1589
Hampson, Ruth M. Islam in South Africa, a bibliography compiled by Ruth M. Hampson. [Cape Town] University of Cape Town, School of Librarianship, 1964. 55 p. (University of Cape Town. School of Librarianship. Bibliographical series) Z7835.M6H27

1590
Hetherwick, A. Islam and Christianity in Nyasaland. MW, v. 17, Apr. 1927: 184–186. DS36.M7, v. 17

1591
Hofmeyr, A. L. Islam in Nyasaland. MW, v. 2, Jan. 1912: 3–8. DS36.M7, v. 2

Investigation of the reasons for the success of Islam in Nyasaland and the dangers it constitutes for Christianity. Islam developed among the populations of the area because of the Arabs and the Yao, who have been Muslims for a long time. One of the reasons given by the author for Muslim successes is that "Islam may be particularly acceptable to the natives because it is a black man's religion and not one acquired from the whites. Undoubtedly there is already among the natives a dislike and distrust of the white man as such. And the more this feeling grows—and grow it will—the more will anything that is totally apart from the white man appeal to the native."

1592
Islam at the Cape. The Cape monthly magazine, v. 10, July/Dec. 1861: 353–363. NN

1593
Islamic mission to South Africa—Khwaja Kamal-ud-Din and Lord Headley at Cape Town. The Islamic review, v. 14, May 1926: 163–167. BP1.I7, v. 14

Report on a visit by Lord Headley, who had converted to Islam, and the editor of *The Islamic Review* and leader of the Muslim community in England.

1594
Muḥammad 'Alī. Riḥlat sumuww al-amīr Muḥammad 'Alī Bāshā fī Janūb Ifrīqiyā, sannat 1342 H./sannat 1924 M. [The voyage of H. H. Emir Muhammad Ali to South Africa in 1342 A.H./1924 A.D.] By Aḥmad Mukhtār. [Cairo] Maṭba'at al-I'timād [1924?] 98 p. DT757.M8

1595
Rochlin, Samuel A. Aspects of Islam in 19th century South Africa. BSOAS, v. 10, pt. 1, July 1939: 213–221. PJ3.L6, v. 10

1596
———Early Arabic printing at the Cape of Good Hope. BSOAS, v. 7, pt. 1, 1933: 49–54. PJ3.L6, v. 7

The first Arabic printed material at the Cape seems to have appeared about the first quarter of the 19th century.

1597
Stephenson, John E. Muhammedan early days in the copperbelt of Northern Rhodesia. Compiled and arranged by N. Namushi and M. L. Mwewa. Lusaka, National Archives of Zambia, 1972. 41 p. (National Archives. Occasional paper, no. 1) DLC

1598
Van de Merwe, W. J. Missions to Moslems in South Africa. MW, v. 26, July 1936: 287–290. DS36.M7, v. 26

Report on the difficulty of converting South African Muslims to Christianity.

1599
Van Wyk, A. C. Mohammedanism in Nyasaland today. MW, v. 24, Apr. 1934: 191–192. DS36.M7, v. 24

1600
Zwemer, Samuel Marinus. Islam at Cape town. MW, v. 15, Oct. 1925: 327–333. DS36.M7, v. 15
Editorial on the Muslim populations of Cape Town and the impact on the Malays of those returning from the Pilgrimage to the Holy Places of Islam.

Theology

1601
Abu Bakr Effendi. The religious duties of Islam as taught and explained by Abu Bakr Effendi. A translation from the original Arabic and Afrikaans, edited with an introduction by Mia Brandel-Syrier. Photomechanical reprint with additions and corrections. Leiden, Brill, 1971. 205 p. (Pretoria oriental series, v. 2) BP184.A2313 1971
"A close copy of the Multaqā l-abḥur of Muhammad b. Ibrahīm ul-Ḥalabī." Translation of Bayān al-Dīn.
In 1862 Queen Victoria wrote to Sultan 'Abd al-Azīz that her Muslim subjects in the Cape Colony were arguing about Muslim Islamic law and requested a Muslim scholar to settle their disputes. Abu Bakr ibn 'Umar al-Khashnāwī was sent to Cape Town and taught there. He published in 1874 a book of instruction entitled *Bayān al-Dīn*, written in Afrikaans but transliterated in Arabic script. In this edition, Mia Brandel-Syrier provides an English translation with ample commentaries.

1601a
Adams, Charles C. Muhammad Abduh and the Transvaal fatwa. *In* The Macdonald presentation volume; a tribute to Duncan Black Macdonald, consisting of articles by former students, presented to him on his seventieth birthday, April 9, 1933. Princeton, N.J., Princeton University Press, 1933. p. 11–30. BP20.M25
Muhammad Abduh (1849–1905) was "a zealous reformer of the religion of Islam and one of the leading modern advocates of the adaptation of Islam to the conditions of modern civilization." One of his best known fatwā, or official juridical decisions in matters pertaining to the faith, is what became known as the Transvaal Fatwā, which consists of three questions submitted by a Muslim from Transvaal. The questions read as follows: "1. There are individuals [Muslims] in this country who wear the hat in order to carry on their business and secure the return of profit to themselves. Is this permissible or not? 2. The manner in which they [i.e., Christians of the Transvaal] slaughter animals intended for food differs [from the manner prescribed for Muslims] because they strike cows with an axe and after that they slaughter [i.e., cut their throats], without repeating the *basmalah* ["In the name of God"]; and small cattle they also slaughter without repeating the *basmalah*. Is this permissible or not? 3. The Shaf'ites perform the public prayers standing behind the Ḥanafites, without repeating the *basmalah*, and they perform the prayers behind them on the occasion of the two feasts. It is well known that there is a difference of opinion between the Shafi'ites and the Ḥanafites, whether repeating the *basmalah* of the two feasts is obligatory or not. Is it permissible to perform the prayers, the one behind the other, or not?"

1602
"Die Heilige Qur'an" in Arfikaans. The Islamic review, v. 49, Aug. 1961: 21. BP1.I7, v. 49
Brief note on the translation of the Holy Koran into Afrikaans.

1603
Koran. Afrikaans. Dit is 'n vertaling van die dertig dele van die Heilige Qur'an beeengebring in een band en oorgesit in Afrikaans deur Imam M. A. Baker. [This is a translation of the 30 parts of the Holy Koran collected in one volume and translated into Afrikaans by Imam M. A. Baker] Kaapstad, Nasionale Boekhandel, 1961. 464 p. BP127.A33B34
Imam Baker was principal of the Simonstown Muslim School at Cape Town.

1604
al-Shubrā Bukhūmī, Yūsuf Shalabī. al-Ta'ādīl al-Islāmīyah fī takhṭi'at ḥizb al-fatāwī al-transfālīyah. [Islamic rectifications in confounding the Transvaal fatwa party] Cairo, 1904, 96 p. BP174.M793S58 Orien Arab
In 1321 A. H. (1902–1903), a Ḥājj Muṣṭafā from Transvaal wrote to Shaykh Muḥammad 'Abduh, Mufti of Egypt, requesting clarification on three points of Islamic jurisprudence. The answer of 'Abduh elicited a number of objections by some ulemas. al-Shubrā Bukhūmī takes the former Mufti to task in this polemical work and criticizes him bitterly for his fatwā (*see* 1601a).

1605
Smith, G. R. A Muslim saint in South Africa. African studies, v. 28, no. 4, 1969: 267–278. port. DT751.A4, v. 28

Many aspects of South African Islam still need to be studied. Smith, senior lecturer in Arabic at the University College, Durban, concentrates on Shāh Ghulām Muḥammad Ḥabībī, a Muslim Sūfī leader from India who catered to the Indian population in South Africa. Ḥabībī arrived in Durban in about 1895 and established his own Tarīqah—the Ḥabībīyah—but, although he lived and taught there, he left no writings. Included in the article is a translation of the text of the Chishtī deed of succession by which Ḥabībī passed the leadership of the sect to his nephew.

WESTERN REGION

Architecture

1606
Brasseur, Gérard. Les établissements humains au Mali. Dakar, IFAN, 1968. 549 p. illus., maps (part col., 2 fold. col. in pocket), plans. (Mémoire de l'Institut fondamental d'Afrique noire, no 83)
GN413.B7

Summaries in English and German.

Dwellings often reflect the attitudes, beliefs, and world views of their owners. In this thoroughly researched and amply illustrated work, Brasseur presents settlements in Mali, including the dwelling configurations of Muslim populations.

1607
Creac'h, Paul. Notes sur l'art décoratif architectural foula du Haut Fouta-Djallon. *In* International West African Conference. Comptes rendus. v. 2; 1945. Dakar, I.F.A.N., 1951. p. 300–312. illus.
DT471.I58 1945

At head of cover title: Gouvernement général de l'Afrique occidentale française. Institut français d'Afrique noire.

Various languages.

Profusely illustrated study of architectural decoration, from rock painting to house ornamentation, in the upper Fouta Djallon Fulbe region.

1608
Crowder, Michael. The decorative architecture of Northern Nigeria: indigenous culture expressed in Hausa craftsmanship. African world, Feb. 1956: 9–10.
DT1.A24, 1956

1609
Duchemin, Georges J. A propos de décorations murales des habitants de Oualata (Mauritanie). BIFAN, t. 12, oct. 1950: 1095–1110. illus.
Q89.I5, v. 12

Visiting Walātah, a qsar in southeastern Mauritania, Duchemin was struck by the originality of its mural decorations. He analyzed them and tentatively classified the designs into various categories according to the explanations given by the only two women-servants still capable of decorating the houses.

1610
Du Puigaudeau, Odette. L'architecture maure. BIFAN, t. 22, janv./avril 1960: 92–133. illus.
DT1.I5123, v. 22

The Berber tribes—Kuntah, Idaw 'Ali, and others—descendants of the Almoravids, have exchanged the sword for the prayer beads and found in religion and commerce a compensation for their more martial days. They settled in villages (*qṣar/qṣur* from Arabic *qaṣr/qūṣūr,* "palace") where they developed an architecture reflecting their glorious days in the great cities of North Africa, Andalusia, and the Arab East. Du Puigaudeau investigates this Moorish architecture and describes the general characteristics of the village, giving detailed descriptions of the houses illustrated by photographs and drawings.

1611
———Contribution à l'étude du symbolisme dans le décor mural et l'artisanat de Walâta. BIFAN, t 19, janv./avril 1957: 137–183. illus.
DT1.I5123, v. 19

Odette du Puigaudeau has traveled extensively in Mauritania and has come in close contact with its people and cultures. In this detailed study she attempts to trace the origin of the mural decoration and artifacts of the city of Walātah in southeastern Mauritania. Unlike the other qṣur due to the puritanical attitudes of its men and the seclusion of its women, it developed a particular architecture and decoration patterns, to the extent of becoming a Maghrabi island on the southern shores of the desert. The symbolism of the decoration is attributed, hesitantly, by the author to a maternity cult. Profusely illustrated with both photographs and line drawings.

1612
Fontanière, J. de. L'habitat peul en Guinée française. Geographia, t. 6, mars 1952: 43–48.
G1.G319, v. 6

1613
Foyle, Arthur M. Architecture in West Africa. Africa south, v. 3, Apr./June 1959: 97–105. illus.
DT751.A28, v. 3

1614
———The house of a merchant in Kofarmata Street, Kano. Nigeria magazine, no. 37, 1951:29–35. illus. DT515.N47, 1951
Well-illustrated article on a typical Muslim house in Kano.

1615
Gouilly, Alphonse. Les mosquées du Sénégal. Revue juridique et politique; indépendance et coopération, v. 19, oct./déc. 1966: 531–576.
DLC–LL

1616
Haselberger, Herta. Essai de classification des differents styles du décor mural en Afrique occidentale. NA, no 106, avril 1965: 47–49.
DT1.I513, 1965

1617
———Wandmalerein und plastischer banschmuck in Guinea. *In* Leipzig. Museum für völkerkunde. Jahrbuch, Bd. 19; 1962. Leipzig, 1962. p. 138–166.
GN37.L4233, v. 19

1618
Kirk-Greene, Anthony H. M. Decorated houses in a northern city. Kaduna, Printed by Baraka Press, 1963. CtY

1619
———Decorated houses in Zaria. Nigeria magazine, no. 68, Mar. 1961: 53–78. illus.
DT515.N47, 1961
Profusely illustrated article about traditional house wall decorations, or *zanen gida* as they are known in Hausa.

1620
Mercier Marcel. Notes sur une architecture berbère saharienne. Hespéris, t. 8, 3./4. trimestres, 1928: 413–429. DT181.H4, v. 8

1621
Moughtin, J. C. The traditional settlements of the Hausa people. Town planning review, v. 35, Apr.1964: 21–34. NA9000.T6, v. 35

1622
Moughtin, J. C., *and* A. H. Leaf. Hausa mud mosque. Architectural review, v. 137, Feb. 1965: 155–158. NA1.A67, v. 137

1623
Prussin, Labelle. Architecture in Northern Ghana; a study of forms and functions. Berkeley, University of California Press, 1969. 120 p. illus., maps.
GN414.A1P7

1624
———The architecture of Islam in West Africa. African arts, v. 1, winter 1968: 32–35, 70–74.
NX587.A6, v. 1

1625
———The impact of Islam architecture in West Africa. Paper presented at the 10th annual meeting of the African Studies Association, New York, 1967. illus. DLC–Micro 03782
Collation of the original: 21 p.

1626
———Sudanese architecture and the Manding. African arts, v. 3, summer 1970: 12–19, 64–67.
NX587.A6, v. 3

1627
Schacht, Joseph. Sur la diffusion des formes d'architecture religieuse musulmane à travers le Sahara. *In* Algiers (city). Université. *Institut de recherches sahariennes.* Travaux, t. 2, 1. semestre, 1954: 11–27. illus. DT331.A4, v. 2

Archival Material

1628
Barbier de Meynard, A. Note sur un fragment de manuscrit arabe copié à Araouan par le lieutenant M. Cortier. La Géographie, v. 14, 2. sem., 1906: 342.
Source: Brasseur, 1.
Madame Brasseur considers this notice "Apocryphe sans intérêt."

1629
Bouvat, Lucien. Une collection de manuscrits arabes provenant des Touareg Oulliminden (Niger). Journal asiatique, t. 209, juil./sept. 1926: 119–125.
PJ4.J5, v. 209
Review of 31 manuscripts "collected" by Dr. A. Richer, "médecin-major de 1ère classe des Troupes Coloniales" in the Niger region. Bequeathed to the Société asiatique, the collection includes works on theology, the occult sciences, grammar and rhetoric, and history. Two of the works are in the mashriqi, while the rest is in the maghribi script. The dates of the manuscript are unknown.

1630
Brown, William A. The Bakka'iyya books of Timbuktu [Kunta]. Ibadan, Nigeria University. *Centre of Arabic Documentation.* Research bulletin, v. 3, Jan. 1967: 40–44. DT352.I2a, v. 3

1631
———A new bibliographical aid: The izālat al-raib of Aḥmad Abū'l-I'rāf al-Tinbuktī. The Northern (Nigerian) history research scheme: second interim report (Zaria, 1967). *In* Ibadan, Nigeria. University. *Centre of Arabic Documentation.* Research bulletin, v. 3, July 1967: 128–138. DT352.I2a, v. 3

1632
Delafosse, Maurice. Note sur les manuscrits arabes acquis en 1911 et 1912 par M. Bonnel de Mézières dans la région de Tombouctou-Oualata (Haut-Sénégal et Niger). *In* Comité d'études historiques et scientifiques de l'Afrique occidentale française. Annuaire et mémoire, 1916: 120–129.
Source: Brasseur, 5.

1633
Gironcourt, G. de. Missions de Gironcourt en Afrique occidentale, 1908–1919—1911–1912. Documents scientifiques. Paris, Société de géographie, 1920. 623 p. illus., plates, maps.
Source: Brasseur, 58.
Includes "Répertoire des manuscrits rapportés du Soudan par la Mission de Gironcourt," p. 357–369.
"Il s'agit d'environ 200 manuscrits déposés sous le no 417 à la Bibliothèque de l'Institut de France, et dont aucun n'a été traduit (sauf toutefois un essai de D.-P. de Pedrals . . .) Rouch signale que certains donnent des listes genéalogiques perdues aujourd'hui."

1634
Gray, J. Richard. The archives of the Vatican and the Propaganda Fide as a source for the history of West Africa. *In* Society for African Church History. Bulletin, v. 1, Apr. 1963: 2–8. DLC

1635
Gwarzo, Ḥasan Ibrāhīm. Seven letters from the Tripoli archives. Kano studies, v. 1, pt. 4, 1968: 50–60. DLC
These letters are part of a group of 14 letters discovered in the Libyan Government Archives at the Red Castle in Tripoli. All dated from the 19th century, they can be classified into two groups: "Letters originating from Bornu directed to the Mutasarrifs or to the Walis of Tripoli, and letters from Fezzan to Tripoli on matters concerning either Bornu or Kano." The form of the script is transitional, between the maghribi and mashriqi script. Included are:
"I. From the Qaimmaqam Fezzan Umar to the Governor (Wali) of Tripoli Mustapha Nuri Basha. One folio of 16 lines per page. Dated 29th Dhu al-Qaada 1269 (3rd September, 1853). Dar al Mahfuzat al-Tarikhiyya, Tripoli.
II. From the Wakil Qaimmaqam Fezzan, Ahmad to Mustapha Nuri Basha of Tripoli (1852–1855). Dated 7th Jumada 'l-Ula 1271 (26th January, 1885). One folio in 16 lines, dar al-Mahfuzat al-tarikhiyya, Tripoli.
III. From al-Sharif Abd al-Rahman Burkan, the Wasir of Bornu to Muhammad Effendi Bashala, dated 2nd Muharram 1286 (14th April 1869). This letter is only available in Arabic translation from the Turkish. Dar al-Mahfuzat al-Tarikhiyya, Tripoli.
IV. From the Wazir of the Kingdom of Bornu Abd-al-Rahman b al-Sharif Muhammad Burkan to the Mutasarrif of Fezzan. Dated 15th Jumada 'l-Awwal 1286 A. H. (23rd August, 1869). Available in translation from the Turkish original text, Dar al-Mahfuzat al-Tarikhiyya, Tripoli.
V. From Abu Bakr b. Umar al-Kanami (1881–4) to the Wali of Tripoli Muhammad Nazif Basha (1880–1882). Dated 20th Muharram 1299 (12th December 1881). One folio of 16 lines. Dar al-Mahfuzat al-Tarikhiyya, Tripoli.
VI. From Mukhtar Hassan to Alhajj Muhammad. Dated 10th Sha'ban 1299 (27th June, 1882). One folio of 14 lines. Dar al-Mahfuzat al-Tarikhiyya, Tripoli.
VII. From the Wakil of the Mutasarrif of Fezzan to the Wali of Tripoli Kamal-Basha (1893–98) One folio of eight lines in Mashriqi Script. Dated 29th April, 1893. Dar-al-Mahfuzat al-Tarikhiyya."

1636
Houdas, Octave V. Recueil de lettres arabes manuscrites publiées par O. Houdas et G. Delphin. 2. ed. Alger, A. Joudan, 1891. 168, 110 p. 4PJ.360

1637
Hunwick, J. O., *and* H. I. Gwarzo. Another look at the Gironcourt papers. *In* Ibadan, Nigeria. University. *Centre of Arabic Documentation.* Research bulletin, v. 3, July 1967: 74–99. DT352.4.I2a, v. 3

1638
nstitut fondamental d'Afrique noire. Catalogue les manuscrits de l'I.F.A.N., par Thierno Diallo [et l.] Fonds Vieillard, Gaden, Brevié, Figaret, Shaykh Mousa Kamara et Cremer en langues arabe, peule t voltaïque. Dakar, 1966. 154 p. (*Its* Catalogues et locuments, 20) Z6621.I582

In the introduction, Vincent Monteil notes that 'avec la création du Département 'Islam' l'IFAN, u 1er janvier 1965, une section des manuscrits a té organisée, à part, pour regrouper, inventorier t classer les manuscrits concernant la langue rabe, le peul et différentes langues voltaïques." The guide is divided according to the original wners and subdivided by area and subject.

1639
ohnson, James, *and* David Robinson. Deux fonds l'histoire orale sur le Fouta Toro. BIFAN, t. 31, anv. 1969: 120–127. DT1.I5123. v. 31

1640
l-Kettani, Mohammed. Les manuscrits de 'Occident africain dans les bibliothèques du Maroc. Hespéris-Tamuda (Rabat), t. 9, fasc. 1, 1958: 57–3. DT301.H45, v. 9

1641
Klein-Franke, F. Notes sur les textes arabes dans es carnets de route de H. Barth. *In* Société de géographie de Paris. Acta geographica, fasc. pécial 69/70, 4. trimestre, 1967: 15–18. G1.S553, 1967

1642
Leriche, Albert. Deux lettres du temps de la pacification (Mauritanie). BIFAN, t. 14, avril 1952: 27–635. illus. Q89.I5, v. 14

Partial text and translation of letters found in amily archives in the Trarza region of eastern Mauritania. The first, dated 1856, is addressed to General Faidherbe from Shaykh Ibn al-Mukhtār bn al-Haybah, known as Shaykh Sīdiyyā al-Kabīr, ounder of the ṭarīqah bearing his name, in which e urges Faidherbe to become a Muslim. The econd one, dated 1860, is from Sultan Mawlāy Muḥammad ibn Mawlāy 'Abd al-Raḥmān, ruler of Morocco, in answer to a letter by Shaykh Sīdiyyā ecognizing Mawlāy Muḥammad as his suzerain.

1643
Levtzion, Nehemia. Early 19th century Arabic nanuscripts from Kumasi. *In* Historical Society of Ghana. Transactions, v. 8; 1965. Legon, 1965. p. 9–119. DT515.A1H5, v. 8

Investigation of Arabic manuscripts at the Royal Swedish Library. The author has located 15 letters, dated from 1808 to 1818, between Kumasi and Mamprusi, Dagomba and Gonja. Besides showing relations between the Ashanti and the hinterland, they make it possible to identify a number of Muslim leaders and underline the importance of the Qadiri sect among the Muslims of Kumasi.

1644
Martin, Bradford G. Arabic materials for Ghanaian history. *In* Ghana. University, *Legon. Institute of African studies.* Research review, v. 2, no. 1, 1965: 74–83. DT1.G48, v. 2

1645
———A Mahdist document from Futa Jallon. BIFAN, t. 25, janv/avril 1963: 47–65. DT1.I5123, v. 25

Documentation on al-Ḥājj 'Umar ibn Sa'īd, the third of the great West African Muslim reformers, is not easily available in Western languages. "So far, . . . Arabic sources, which are voluminous, but scattered and poorly known, have been exploited only superficially." One of these sources is "a two-folio document in poor Arabic, undated, and seeming to be a statement from 'Abd al-Muṭṭalib ibn Ghālib, Sharīf of Makka, concerning the coming of the Mahdī, and the part to be played by al-Ḥājj 'Umar in preparing this event." The document was found by Gilbert Vieillard in 1942 in the Fouta Djallon. Martin provides a modern Arabic script version and translation, including the interpretation of a number of obscure points of this difficult and elusive text.

1646
———Turkish archival sources for West African history. African studies bulletin, v. 10, Dec. 1967: 59–65. DT1.A2793, v. 10

1647
Mission Tilho. Documents scientifiques de la Mission Tilho, 1906–1909. Paris, Impr. nationale, 1910–11. 2 v. illus. (1 col.), geneal. tables, group port., maps (part fold., 1 col.), and case (7 fold. col. maps) DT527.M58

At head of title: République française. Ministère des colonies.

Of interest in volume 2 is "Onzième partie. Du Tchad au Niger; notice historique," including a number of genealogies and chronicles.

1648
Mokhtar ould Hamidoun, *and* Albert Leriche. Curiosités et bibliothèques de Chinguetti. NA, no 48, oct. 1950: 109–112. DT1.I513, 1950

Survey of Arabic tombstone inscriptions and libraries in Shinqīt (Chinguetti) in Mauritania. Appended is a list of family libraries, noting the number of books and manuscripts held, names of authors, and origins, whether Moorish, Egyptian, or Maghrib.

1649
Mokhtar ould Hamidoun, *and* Adam Heymowski. Catalogue provisoire des manuscrits mauritaniens en langue arabe préservés en Mauritanie. Stockholm, 1965–66 [i.e. 1966?] 274 p. Z6605.A6M6

"Répertoire confectionné à Bibliothèque nationale de Mauritanie, déc. 1964–févr. 1965; xérographié à la Bibliothèque royale de Suède."

A list of about 2,200 Arabic manuscripts located in Mauritania in various private libraries belonging to eminent families. The majority of the documents pertain to religion, including theology, Shari'a, and the Koran. Another significant part of the compilation consists of poems and treatises on grammar and literature.

1650
Monteil, Vincent. Sur quelques textes arabes provenant du Soudan (région de Tombouctou). BCAOF, v. 21, oct./déc. 1938: 499–517. DT521.C6, v. 21

Translation by Monteil of three short Arabic manuscripts, including a letter from Shaykh Aḥmad al-Bakkā'ī defending Barth (September 1853) and two short histories—*Tarikh Abī Jibīhā* and *Tarikh al-Barābīsh.* The *Tarikhs* have genealogical tables, the listing in the first being similar to the ones in Paul Marty's "Chronique de Oualata et de Nema" (*see* 1739).

1651
Odoom, K. O., *and* J. J. Holden. Arabic collection. *In* Ghana. University, *Legon. Institute of African Studies.* Research review, v. 4, no. 1, 1967: 30–73; v. 4, no. 2, 1968: 66–102. DT1.G48, v. 4

1652
Paris. *Bibliothèque nationale. Département des manuscrits.* Catalogue des manuscrits arabes des nouvelles acquisitions (1884–1924). Edited by E. Blochet. Paris, Editions Ernest Leroux, 1925. 424 p. Z6621.P22A6 1924

In his introduction, Blochet reports on the Collection Archinard (no. 5256, 5259, 5260–5750, 6101–6113, 6130, 6135, 6136, 6249, 6637 and 6638), which consists of material brought back by Archinard when his troops stormed the tata of Ahmadu, ruler of the Masima, in 1894.

1653
Smith, H. F. C. Arabic manuscript material bearing on the history of the Western Sudan: the archives of Segu. *In* Historical Society of Nigeria. Bulletin of news, v. 4, 1959: supplement. IEN

1654
———Nineteenth century Arabic archives of West Africa. JAH, v. 3, no. 2, 1962: 333–336. DT1.J65, v. 3

1655
———Source material for the history of the Western Sudan. JHSN, v. 1, Dec. 1958: 238–248. DT515.A2H5, v. 1

The importance of Arabic manuscripts for the study of history of the Western Sudan is underlined by Smith, who is concerned about their preservation. He also notes the most outstanding works in the collection gathered by Georges de Gironcourt in the Niger Bend region in 1911.

1656
Sölken, Heinz. AfrikanischeDokumente zur Frage der Entstehung der Hausanischen Diaspora in Oberguinea. Sonderabdruck [Berlin, Druck J. J. Augustin, 1939] 127 p. (Mitteilungen der Ausland-Hochschule an der Universität Berlin, Jahrg. 42. Abt. 3: Afrikanische Studien) PJ25.B5, v. 42

1657
Toupet, Charles. Orientation bibliographique sur la Mauritanie. BIFAN, t. 21, janv./avril 1959: 201–238. DT1.I5123, v. 21

A 408–entry bibliography on Mauritania covering the whole spectrum of physical and social sciences divided into 20 headings. History includes 70 entries, and Islam 14.

1658
Vajda, Georges. Contribution à la connaissance de la littérature arabe en Afrique occidentale. JOSAF t. 20, fasc. 2, 1950: 230–237. DT1.S65, v. 20

Annotated list of signed texts and historical documents from among the 511 Arabic manuscripts taken by Col. Louis Archinard as booty after his defeat of Aḥmadū, ruler of the Masina in 1894. The list includes works of Usuman dan Fodyo, Muhammad Bello, and 'Umar Sa'īd al-Fūtī, as well as historical documents related to these leaders.

1659
el-Wakkad, Mahmoud. Arabic manuscripts in Ghana. Ghana notes and queries, no. 2, May/Aug. 1961: 11. DT510.A1H553, 1961
Introduction to the wealth of Arabic material located in Ghana.

1660
Wilks, Ivor. Arabic manuscript collection. *In* Ghana. University, *Legon. Institute of African Studies.* Research bulletin, v. 2, no. 1, 1965: 17–31. DT1.G48, v. 2
Preliminary descriptive list of 31 Arabic and seven Hausa manuscripts in the university's collection.

1661
———A note on the Arabic MS IASAR/298, and others from Wa. *In* Ghana. University, *Legon. Institute of African Studies.* Research bulletin, v. 2, no. 2, 1966: 63–68. DT1.G48, v. 2
Comments on *Akhbār Salṭanat Bilād Wā* [History of the Wa Sultanate] and other appended manuscripts on the northern Ghanaian city. *See also* 2001, 2002.

Biography

1662
Bâ, Amadou-Hampâté, *and* Marcel Cardaire. Tierno Bokar, le sage de Bandiagara. Paris, Présence africaine [1957] 124 p. illus., geneal. table, ports. BP80.T54B3
Amadou-Hampâté Bâ, the Malian erudite, writes about a man in whose tradition he is steeped. Tierno Bokar Salif (1875–1940), who taught that work was as important as meditation, lived his teachings in the daily round of his life, traveling from his house to his field, to the mosque. Bâ and Cardaire attempt to present, in an empathic way reminiscent of the writings of Louis Massignon, the teachings of the wise man of Bandiagara, in Central Mali.

1663
Baba *of Karo*. Baba of Karo, a woman of the Muslim Hausa. [Autobiography recorded] by M. F. Smith. With an introduction and notes by M. G. Smith; preface by Daryll Forde. London, Faber and Faber [1954] 299 p. illus. DT515.B115 1954
Baba of Karo (1877–1951)—not unlike Shaihu Umar of Abubakar Tafawa Balewa (*see* 2622)—witnessed the passing of one era and the dawn of another. With patience and skill, Mary Smith gathered the threads of the remarkable Hausa woman's life story and wrote a narrative preserving a style that carries the reader into the bustle of the Zaria compound.

1664
Behrman, Lucy C. Ahmadou Bamba (1850–1927).
Source: ASA, Program, 9th, 1966.

1665
Besson, M. Le pélerinage d'un marabout soudanais (El Hadj Boubeker). *In* Vieux papiers du temps des Isles, 2. sér. Paris, Editions de géographie maritime et coloniale, 1930. p. 183–188.
Source: Joucla, 848.

1666
Bouvat, Lucien. Cheikh Saadibout et son entourage. RMM, t. 18, mars 1912: 185–199. DS36.R4, v. 18

1667
Brenner, Louis. The Shehus of Kukuwa; a history of the al-Kanemi dynasty of Bornu. Oxford, Clarendon Press, 1973. 145 p. illus. (Oxford studies in African affairs) DR515.9.B6B7
A revision of the author's thesis, Columbia University.

1668
Charles, Eunice A. Ouali N'dao: the exile of Alboury N'Diaye. African historical studies, v. 4, no. 2, 1971: 373–382. DT1.A226, v. 4
Alboury N'Diaye ruled the Djolof state from 1875 to 1890, fighting the penetration of both French influence and presence. When he could resist no more, he left Djolof and fought with Aḥmadu, son of al-Hajj 'Umar, against French encroachments and was presumably killed in a battle near Dogondoutchi, in Southern Niger. This account of Alboury and his exile were told in Wolof by Ouali N'Dao, a Djolof who accompanied Alboury in 1890. The text was translated into French and subsequently into English.

1669
De Goeje, Michael J. Note sur "Mohammad Mahmoud es-Chingîti." Journal asiatique, 8. sér., v. 1, 1883, note 1: 537. PJ4.J5, 8th ser., v. 1

1670
Désiré-Vuillemin, Genevieve-M. Cheikh Ma El Aïnin et le Maroc, ou l'echec d'un moderne Almoravide. Revue d'histoire des colonies, v. 45,

nov. 1958: 29–52. JV1801.R4, v. 45

Shaykh Mā' al-'Aynayn al-Qalqamī tried to oppose the French advance in Mauritania and by his able leadership united the religious fraternities of the area in an effort to repeat the Almoravid hegemony of an earlier period. After an initial success, he was defeated by the troops of General Moinier, June 23, 1910. With the collapse of his dream, the Quṭb [Pole of Islam], as the ulemas of Fès called him, died in October 1910 at Tiznit. Désiré-Vuillemin presents a lively narrative of the period.

1671
Doi, A. R. I. The Yoruba Mahdi. Journal of religion in Africa/Religion en Afrique, v. 4, fasc. 2, 1971: 119–136. illus. BL2400.J68, v. 4

Muhammad Jumat Adesina (1896–1959) was born in Ijebu-Ode in Western Nigeria, where he traded in Arabic books and taught the language. On December 20, 1941, he declared himself Mahdi and started a campaign of proselytization among the Yoruba, after sending a number of letters to prominent Muslim leaders urging them to follow him. Doi, who visited the city and met the successor of the Mahdi, provides the history of the movement.

1672
Dumont, Fernand. Amadou Bamba, apôtre de la non-violence (1850–1927). NA, no 21, jan. 1969: 20–24. DT1.I513, 1969

Short study of Amadu Bamba, founder of the Murid sect in Senegal, and his basic beliefs. One characteristic of the Murid leader is that he is the product of a strictly sub-Saharan Islam, trained and formed by local teachers. He was a mystic who opted for action rather than retreat, and was, as Dumont puts it, "the example of the ascetic who preferred the desert of the mob to that of silence."

1673
Fisher, Humphrey J. The early life and pilgrimage of al-Hajj Muhammad al-Amin the Soninke (d. 1887). JAH, v. 11, no. 1, 1970: 51–69. DT1.J65, v. 11

Investigation of the early period of Muḥammad al-Amīn's life, his education, and pilgrimage, up to his return home in 1885. Fisher uses both oral traditions gathered in the Gambia and Mali and published French sources.

1674
Fofana, Kalil. Almamy Samori; l'homme et son oeuvre. Recherches africaines; études guinéennes, nouv. sér. no 1, janv./mars 1963: 3–27. DT543.A3R4, n.s., 1963

Biography of Samory Toure based on oral traditions. In his introduction, Fofana points out that "le contenu émotionel de ces récits n'est pas non plus d'un moindre intérêt. En effet chaque conteur a ses épisodes favoris et vous les rabâche volontier comme un refrain obsédant: ce qui en somme, nous assure une gamme variée de récits pathétiques."

1675
Holas, Bohumil. Un document authentique sur Samory. NA, no 74, avril 1957: 52–57. DT1.I513, 1957

Excerpts from an oral tradition regarding Samory. The story was dictated by Mamadou Sulayman Dem, a contemporary and member of the court of the Almamy, to his son Tidiane Dem. This represents one of the few African interpretations of that turbulent period leading to the capture of Samory at Guélémou.

1676
Ismā'il Hāmid. Littérature arabe saharienne. RMM, t. 12, oct. 1910: 194–213; t. 12, nov. 1910: 380–405. DS36.R4, v.12

Ismā'īl Ḥāmid was a scholar attached to the French administration in West Africa. From the fragments of writings he discovered, he was convinced of the presence in both the Sahara and Sudan of a large body of old Arabic literature. In these two contributions, he analyzes *Kitāb al-tarā'if wa-al-talā'id fī karamāt al-Shaykhān al-Wālidah wa-al-Wālid* [Book of New and Old Stories on the Virtues of the Two Sheikhs, My Mother and Father] by Muḥammad ibn al-Mukhtār Aḥmad ibn Abī Bakr al-Kuntī (d. 1826). The father was Sīdī al-Mukhtār al-Kabīr (1729–30—1811), leader of the Kuntah. The biographer discusses at length his father's life, education, and teachers of sufism. The manuscript ends with chapter five. Two chapters dealing with the death of Sīdī al-Mukhtār and the life of the biographer's mother are missing.

1677
Kirk-Greene, Anthony H. M., *comp.* West African travels and adventures; two autobiographical narratives from Northern Nigeria. Translated and annotated by Anthony Kirk-Greene and Paul Newman. New Haven, Yale University Press, 1971. 255 p. illus., facsim., map, ports. DT472.K57 1971

Includes selections from the original Hausa texts. Partial contents: The life and travels of Dorugu.—The story of Maimaina of Jega, Chief of Askira.

1678
Kouroubari, Amadou. Histoire de l'Imam Samori. BIFAN, t. 21, juil./oct. 1959: 544–571. DT1.I5123, v. 21

Translation of a Mande history of Samory related by Maurice Delafosse in his *Essai de manuel pratique de langue mandée ou mandingue* (Paris, E. Leroux, 1901) and given to him by a Mande who witnessed part of the events related. The story is divided, by Delafosse, into 12 sections beginning with the early life of Samory and ending with his capture on September 29, 1898, at Guélémou.

1679
Lavers, John E. Jibril Gaini: a preliminary account of the career of a Mahdist leader in north-eastern Nigeria. *In* Ibadan, Nigeria. University. *Centre of Arabic Documentation.* Research bulletin, v. 3, Jan. 1967:16–39. map. DT352.I2a, v. 3

1680
Le Coeur, Charles. Un Toubou conciliateur de l'Islam et du Christianisme. Revue des études islamiques, cahier 1, 1948: 85–88. BP1.R53, 1948

Report on the ecumenical ideas of Aba Musa, a Muslim Tubu from around Zinder (Niger) who, after meeting Christian missionaries, "considers himself a Christian without, however, rejecting Islam."

1681
Lô, Mahtar, *Shaykh.* La vie de Seydina Mouhamadou Limamou Laye. BIFAN, t. 34, juil. 1972: 497–524. DT1.I5123, v. 34

Translation, by al-Hajj Mouhamadou Sakhir Gaye and Assane Silla, of the biography of a Senegalese Muslim erudite written by one of his close collaborators.

1682
Mademba, Bendaoud. La dernière étape d'un conquérant; (Odysée des dernières années du Sultan Ahmadou de Ségou, racontés par son cousin et compagnon d'infortune Hassmiou Tall). BCAOF, [v. 4] juil./sept. 1921: 473–480. DT521.C6, [v. 4]

Translated from the Bambara by Bakar Diko.

1683
Mévil, André. Samory. Paris, Flammarion [1899?] 267 p. illus.

Source: Brasseur, 3104.

1684
Mohammed, Abdullahi. A Hausa scholar-trader: a case study of Umar Falke. Paper presented at the 16th annual meeting of the African Studies Association, Syracuse, N.Y., 1973. DLC–Micro 02782

Collation of the original: 15 p.

1685
Monteil, Vincent. Lat Dior, Damel du Kayor, et l'islamisation des Wolofs. Archives de sociologie des religions, 8. année, juil./déc. 1963: 77–104. BL60.A7, v. 8

In order to gain the support of Ma Dyakhu Ba the Tukulor, Lat Dior had to convert to Islam, thus leading the way for the conversion of the Wolof.

1686
al-Moutabassir. Mâ el 'Aïnîn ech Changuîty. RMM, t. 1, 1907: 343–351. DS36.R4, v. 1

Anonymous refutation of the once commonly accepted allegation that Mā' al-'Aynayn, the Mauritanian leader, was a "thaumaturge, un sorcier vulgaire ignorant et grossier."

1687
N'Diaye, Saki Olal. The story of Malik Sy; translated and edited by A. Neil Skinner and Philip D. Curtin with the assistance of Hannady Amadou Sy. CEA, v. 11, 3. cahier, 1971: 467–487. DT1.C3, v. 3

Transcription and translation, with ample annotations, of a tradition relating the history of the Bundu kingdom in the present-day Department of Bakel in Senegal.

1688
Norris, H. T. Shaykh Mā'al-'Aynayn al-Qalqamī in the folk-literature of the Spanish Sahara. BSOAS, v. 31, pt. 1, 1968: 113–136; v. 31, pt. 2, 1968: 347–376. PJ3.L6, v. 31

Shaykh Mā' al-'Aynayn al-Qalqamī, "the last of the warrior saints," began before 1900 to build a center of Koranic studies at Semara in the Saguia al Hamra. However, he clashed with French interests, was defeated by General Moinier (July 23, 1910) near Marrakech, and retired to Tiznit where he died on October 29, 1910. The Shaykh had acquired a great reputation of saintliness and erudition. Yet, his enemies accused him of fostering his fame as a wonder-worker. "For a truer picture of Shaykh Mā' al-'Aynayn, as he appeared to his followers," says Norris, "panegyrics in Ḥassānīya and other poems in the vernacular, are the spontaneous indication of popular belief in his miraculous personality. An example is a *dīwān* of poems in Ḥassānīya by a poet of the Spanish Sahara, or the Adrār, Sīdī Sālim. The *dīwān* includes at least 51 poems in different metres." Norris transliterates, translates, and comments on this literary monument in praise of the venerable Shaykh.

1689
Nyambarza, Daniel. Le marabout el-Hadj Mamadou Lamine d'aprés les archives françaises. CEA, v. 9, 1. cahier, 1967: 124–145. DT1.C3, 1967
Portrait of al-Ḥājj Mamadū Lamine Dramé, a marabout who tried to establish a Saratole state between the Niger and Senegal rivers between 1885 and 1888. The author's aim is to "cerner la personnalité du marabout, de définir son activité et de préciser autant que possible ses rapports avec les puissances qui dominaient la région au moment de son intervention." The sources are mainly drawn from reports located at the Archives nationales (ANSOM) of French military operations. Noteworthy is his analysis of the qasidah called *La vie d'el Hadj Omar* in Fulfulde by Mohammadou Aliou Tyam (*see* 812).

1690
Odoom, K. O. A document on pioneers of the Muslim community in Accra. *In* Ghana. University, *Legon. Institute of African studies.* Research review, v. 7, no. 1, 1969: 1–31. DT1.G48, v. 7
Malam Muḥammad Baako, who died on January 21, 1938, combined the two offices of Sarkin Zongo and Friday Imām of Accra for some 30 years. Odoom presents the text, translation, and commentaries on the eulogy of the Muslim leader. A xeroxed copy of the manuscript, entitled *al-Lāmīyah al-Sughrā*, is in the institute under no. IASAR/195.

1691
Ọlọruntimẹhin, B. Ọlatunji. Muhammad Lamine in Franco-Tukulor relations, 1885–1887. JHSN, v. 4, Dec. 1968: 375–396. DT515.A2H5, v. 4
The Tuḳulor Empire of al-Ḥājj 'Umar clashed with advancing French imperialism from the beginning of the empire to its collapse. The interests of the two protagonists coincided for a short period, however, with the rise of Muḥammad Lamine between 1885 and 1887. By the local populations—Bambara, Sarakole, and Mandingo—both the French and the Tukulor were regarded as imperialists. With the defeat of Lamine, Franco-Tukulor relations returned to their original antagonism until France completed its "pacification." *See also* 1689.

1692
Person, Yves. Les ancêtres de Samori. CEA, v. 4, 1. cahier, 1963: 125–256. DT1.C3, v. 4
Thorough investigation of the origins of the Toure Dyamu [clan] and the ancestors of Samory Toure. The greatest density of the clan appears to be in the Middle Niger region between Timbuktu and Bamako. The "Wagadou Chronicle" reported it to be of Soninke origin. Person discusses the Islamization of the clan and its absorption into the animist Konyanke before their eventual re-Islamization by al-Ḥājj 'Umar in the middle of the 19th century.

1693
———Samori; une révolution Dyula. Dakar, I.F.A.N., 1968–70. 2 v. (Mémoires de l'Institut fondamental d'Afrique noire, no 80) DLC
Major contribution toward a definitive work on Samory. Person has produced a monumental work of 1,217 pages on the ancestor of Sékou Touré who attempted to stop the flood of colonial conquest in West Africa.

1694
Questions and answers with H. E. Alhaji Sir Ahmadu Bello, Prime Minister of Northern Nigeria. al-Muslimūn, no. 4, Nov. 1961: 2–6. BP1.M86 Orien Arab 1961.
Interview with the late Sardauno in which he expresses his views on Islam in Africa.

1695
Quinn, Charlotte A. Maba Diakhou Ba: scholar-warrior of the Senegambia. Tarikh, v. 2, no. 3, 1968: 1–12. DLC

1696
Saint-Martin, Yves J. Un fils d'El-Hadj Omar: Aguibou, roi du Dinguiray et du Macina. CEA, v. 8, 1. cahier, 1968: 144–178. DT1.C3, v. 8
Detailed biography of 'Ajībū, the son of al-Ḥājj 'Umar, ruler of Dinguiray and Masina during the early period of French colonization.

1697
Salenc, J., *ed and tr.* La vie d'Al Hadj Omar. Traduction d'un manuscrit arabe de la Zaouia tidjaniya de Fez. BCAOF, v. 3, 1918: 405–431.
Source: Joucla 8381

1698
Salifou, André. Malam Yaroh, un grand négotiant du Soudan Central à la fin du XIXe siècle. JOSAF, t. 42, 1. cahier, 1972: 7–27. DT1.S65, v. 42

Though trans-Saharan international trade was generally in the hands of Arab traders, Malam Yaroh, a trader established in Zinder and belonging to a family of marabouts, was one of the exceptions in the 19th century. Yaroh had his main office in Zinder and branches in Kano and Tripoli. It is reported that his business connections stretched all the way to London. Salifou shows the extent of his enterprise, his relations with the French colonial authorities, and his involvement in an anti-French plot. The sad end and bankruptcy of Malam Yaroh reflect the changing commercial patterns in the Sudanic belt in the 19th century.

1699
Ṣāliḥ, 'Abd al-Raḥmān. Aḥmadū Billu; za'īm min Nayjīryā. [Ahmadu Bello; a leader from Nigeria] [Cairo, al-Dār al-qawmīyah lil-ṭibā'ah wa-al-nashr, 1963] 96 p. (Madhāhib wa shakhṣīyat)
DT515.6.B4S2 Orien Arab

Biography of the late Sardauna of Sokoto.

1700
Samb, Amar, *tr. and ed.* La vie d'El-Hadj Omar par Cheikh Moussa Kamara. BIFAN, t. 32, janv. 1970: 44–135. DT1.I5123, v. 32

1701
Suret-Canale, Jean. L'Almamy Samory Touré. Recherches africaines; études guinéennes, nouv. sér., no 1/4, janv./déc. 1959: 18–22.
DT543.A3R4, n.s., 1959

Sympathetic note on Samory Touré with an explanatory statement by Mamadou Traore Ray Autra explaining Samory's attempted suicide.

1702
Sylla, Assane. Les persécutions de Seydina Mouhamadou Limâmou Laye par les autorités coloniales. BIFAN, t. 33, juil. 1971: 590–641.
DT1.I5123, v. 33

1703
Verdat, Marguerite. Le Ouali de Goumba. *In* Institut français d'Afrique noire, *Centre de Guinée.* Etudes guinéennes, no 3, 1949: 3–18.
DT543.A3R4, 1949

Essay on the attempt of Karamoko "Sekkan Aliou," known as the Wālī of Goumba, near Kindia in Guinea, to establish his authority in an area where France was consolidating its own authority and control. "Pièce annexe no 2" is a "note sur l'Islam en A.O.F. Les Chadelyia" by "Mariani, Inspecteur de l'enseignement musulman en A.O.F." dated Dakar, August 8, 1909.

1704
Wane, Yaya. De Halwaar à Degenbere, ou l'itinéraire islamique de Shaykh Umar Taal. BIFAN, t. 31, avril 1969: 445–451.
DT1.I5123, v. 31

After a long visit to Mecca where he was named Muqaddim of the Tijani Order, Shaykh 'Umar Tall went back to his native Fouta Toro and began his political career. Drawing on the Fulfulde qaṣīdah on the life of the Shehu by M. A. Tyam (*see* 812) Yaya Wane presents the intellectual and political itinerary of the Tijani reformer.

Christian Missions

1705
Ajayi, W. O. Aspects of Protestant missionary work in Northern Nigeria, 1887–1910. Odu, no. 3, July 1966: 40–55. DT515.A2O32, no. 3

Ajayi investigates the conflict between missionary efforts and the policy of indirect rule. The raison d'état ultimately won, under Sir Percy Girouard, over the religious factor.

1706
Ayandele, E. A. The missionary factor in Northern Nigeria, 1870–1918. JHSN, v. 3, Dec. 1966: 503–522. DT515.A2H5, v. 5

1707
Blyden, Edward W. Black spokesman; selected published writings of Edward Wilmot Blyden. Edited by Hollis R. Lynch. New York, Humanities Press, 1971. 354 p. DT4.B538 1971

"In much of his writings after 1870," states Lynch, "Blyden harshly criticized European sectarian missionary influences which he regarded as dividing Africans and creating a sense of inferiority among them. On the other hand, Blyden was highly sympathetic to Islam in West Africa because he saw it as an elevating influence bringing the Arabic language and literature to Africans, and a unifying one cutting across ethnic lines. He greatly deplored the fact that many Europeans, particularly missionaries, and their African protégés, tended to despise and belittle Muslims. It was one of his goals in West Africa to eliminate the traditional hostility between Muslims and Christians and to build a bridge of communications between them." In this series of articles published between 1871 and 1902, Blyden shows his sympathy for and understanding of Islam.

1708
Campbell, Dugald. The Scriptures in the Sahara. MW, v. 24, Jan. 1934: 53–57. DS36.M7, v. 24

Like a Muslim trader buying his wares in North Africa and selling them in the Sudanic belt after a trans-Saharan trip, Campbell loaded "fourteen well-chosen and fine fat camels from Tripoli" with Bibles in Arabic and medical supplies, and traveled from Tripoli to Marzūq, the Kufrah oasis, and to Egypt and returned to Marrakech via Kano. This missionary carpetbagger gave copies of the Scriptures to his numerous hosts including the Amanoukal of the Azger Tuareg, a Fezzani qadi, as well as Egyptian frontier officials in the oasis of Farafra.

1709
——Timbuctoo. MW, V. 20, Apr. 1930: 169—173. DS36.M7, v. 20

The image of a Christian missionary selling Bibles to the Tuareg is indeed foreign to today's Africanists. Yet, Campbell did precisely that with four missionaries who settled in Timbuktu and where, he reported, "they are doing a splendid and efficient evangelistic work."

1710
Farrant, H. G. Northern Nigerian opportunity; an entrance of Mohammedan Emirates and how it was secured. MW, v. 27, Oct. 1937: 337–347. DS36.M7, v. 27

Reaction to Marais' article, "Northern Nigeria as a Mission Field" (*see* 1712). Farrant shows how Christian missions were able to persuade the government to lift restrictions on missionary work in the northern emirates.

1711
Hughes, Kenneth. Christianity and Islam in West Africa. I: Concern for frontier theology. II: The approach confrontation. Christian century, v. 81, Feb. 1964: 264–267; v. 81, Mar. 1964: 298–302. BR1.C45, v. 81

1712
Marais, Benjamin J. Northern Nigeria as a mission field. MW, v. 27, April 1937: 173–185. DS36.M7, v. 27

Islam was used in Northern Nigeria during the period of indirect rule as a unifying force. Missionary work was not permitted in the Northern Province in an effort to strengthen the traditional leadership. Rebuking this policy, Marais concludes, "If Northern Nigeria is to be won for Christ at all, the British Government must withdraw its restrictions which at present withhold Christian work and favor Islam."

1713
Sadler, George W. Mohammedanism in Nigeria. MW, v. 35, Apr. 1945: 133–137. DS36.M7, v. 35

Report on Christian missions in Nigeria and the efforts of proselytization among the Muslims.

1714
Walker, F. Deaville. Islam and Christianity in West Africa. MW, v. 19, Apr. 1929: 129–133. DS36.M7, v. 19

Articles in the *Muslim World* up to the 1950's likened the "progress of Islam in West Africa to a prairie fire sweeping all before it." Walker suggests that "the advance of Islam is being definitely checked, and that today we are winning far more Africans to the faith of Christ than the Moslems are winning for their Prophet."

Cities

1715
Bernus, Edmond. Kong et sa région. Etudes eburnéennes, no 8, 1960: 242–322. illus., fold. maps. DT545.E8, 1960

Located south of Ferkéssédougou in northern Ivory Coast, Kong was a thriving trade center and entrepôt until it was caught in the struggle between Samory and the advancing French. Accusing its residents of collaborating with the French, the Malinke leader destroyed the city in July 1897, and it never regained its former fame and wealth. Bernus investigates the historical, social, political, religious, and agricultural life of the city and its canton. His description of the household of al-Hajj Abu Sananogo, the imam of the mosque, provides an insight into the life of a Muslim family in a Muslim environment.

1716
——Notes sur l'histoire de Korhogo. BIFAN, t. 23, janv./avril 1961: 284–290. DT1.I5123, v. 23

Report on the history of Korhogo in northern Ivory Coast, as reported by two brothers of a reigning chief. The city was established during the 18th century and witnessed the defeat of Samory's armies.

1717
Bivar, A. D. H., *and* P. L. Shinnie. Old Kanuri capitals. JAH, v. 3, no. 1, 1962: 1–10. DT1.J65

1718
Bonnel de Mézières, A. Reconnaissance à Tendirma et dans la région de Fati. *In*

France. *Comité des travaux historique et scientifiques.* Bulletin de la section de géographie, v. 29, 1914: 128–131. G11.F8, v. 29

Investigation of the cemetery of the Banū-Isra'il and the wells dug in Tendirma by the Jewish community.

1719
Bonnier, Gaëtan. L'occupation de Tombouctou. Paris, Editions du monde moderne [1926] 288 p. plates, maps. DT553.T6B6

1720
Boulègue, Jean. Mosquées de style soudanais au Fuuta Tooro (Sénégal). NA, no 136, oct. 1972: 117–119. DT1.I5123, 1972

1721
Boutillier, Jean-Louis. La ville de Bouna: de l'époque précoloniale à aujourd'hui. Cahiers O.R.S.T.O.M. Sciences humaines, v. 6, no 2, 1969: 3–20. DT521.C3, v. 6

Bouna, located in the northeastern corner of the Ivory Coast, was an important trade center during the precolonial period, as well as the capital of the Koulango Kingdom. The city was sacked and destroyed by Samory's troops under the command of his nephew, Sarankola Mory, and never recovered its pristine importance. Boutillier explores the history of the city before, during, and after the colonial period.

1722
Bryant, K. J. Kano; gateway to Northern Nigeria, a guide-book. [Zaria, Nigeria, Gaskiya Corp., 196-] 38 p. DLC

1723
Cherbonneau, Auguste. Gadamès et le commerce soudanais. Revue de géographie, t. 8, janv./juin 1881: 412–419. G1.R43, v. 8

1724
Chirot, Daniel. Urban and rural economies in the Western Sudan: Birni N'konni and its hinterland. CEA, v. 8, 1968: 547–565. DT1.C3, v. 8

The collapse of the major cities of the Western Sudan empires has long puzzled Africanists. In his study of one of these centers—Birni N'Konni, located on the border between Nigeria and Niger north of Sokoto—Chirot investigates the economic basis for the growth of the city and its relations with its rural surroundings. He concludes that Birni N'Konni and likewise the ancient capitals must have lacked two essentials: "sufficient peace in the countryside to let the peasant population rise beyond a certain point, and a place to buy possible cash crops and supply cheap goods to sell to the peasantry in order to stimulate production." Because they never initiated a process of self-sustaining economic growth, the collapse of the trade led to the collapse of the metropolises.

1725
Clapier Valladon, M. Les ksouriens de Nema. Ethnopsychologie, t. 26, mars 1971: 43–72. BF732.R48, v. 26

1726
Delmond, P. Dans la boucle du Niger: Dori, ville peule. *In* Institut français d'Afrique noire. Mélanges ethnologiques. Dakar, IFAN, 1953. p. 9–110. illus., maps. (*Its* Mémoires, no 23) GN643.I5

In this descriptive essay, a short introduction to the history of the Fulbe city of Dori (Upper Volta) precedes an account of its environment, demography, and political and social organization, as well as its cultural and religious activities.

1727
Du Puigaudeau, Odette. La tessett de Jean Léon l'Africain. NA, no 96, oct. 1962: 123–126. DT1.I513, 1962

Historical investigations by an old Saharan hand on the location of the "Tessett" of Leo Africanus. Instead of locating the town in Tichît, in Central Mauritania, like a number of writers did, Puigaudeau believes it to be the oasis of Assa, about 100 miles south of Goulimine.

1728
Dupuis, Auguste V. Notes sur la population de Tombouctou (castes et associations). Revue d'ethnographie et sociologie, t. 1, 1910: 233–236. GN1.R5, v. 1

1729
———Industries et principales professions des habitants de la région de Tombouctou, par Dupuis-Yakouba. Paris, E. Larose, 1921. 193 p. illus. DT553.T6D88

1730
———Les ruines de Bokar et de Kama dans la région de Bankor. BCAOF, v. 7, juil./oct. 1922: 400–410. illus., plate. DT521.C6, v. 7

Preliminary investigation of a site in the Bankor region, near Lake Faguibine (Mali). Dupuis-Yacouba noticed the ruins of a mosque which have remained unexplained.

1731
Granderye, *Capt.* Notes et souvenirs sur l'occupation de Tombouctou. Revue d'histoire des colonies, t. 34, 1947: 87–131. JV1801.R4, v. 34
In these notes on events in the "Soudan" at the end of the 19th century, Granderye provides detailed information on political and military activities and a description of the area.

1732
Hacquard, Augustin. Monographie de Tombouctou. Accompagnée de nombreuses illustrations et d'une carte de la région de Tombouctou dressée d'après les documents les plus récents. Paris, Société des études coloniales & maritimes, 1900. 119 p. illus., ports., fold. map. DT558.T6H2

1733
Hallam, W. R. K. The great emporium. Nigeria magazine, no. 81, June 1964: 84–97. illus. DT515.N47, 1964
Short history of Kano.

1734
Halle, Claude. Notes sur Koly Tenguella, Olivier de Sanderval et les ruines de Guémé-Sangan. Recherches africaines; études guinéennes (nouv. sér.), no. 1, janv./mars, 1960: 37–41. DT543.A3R4, n.s., 1960
Travelogue report on a visit to the village of Guémé-Sangan, one of the strongholds of Koly Tenguella, the Denianke conqueror. Halle cites briefly Olivier de Sanderval who lived in the city and wrote about Koly Tenguella's treasure. He also relates his visit to the village outer walls and the house of the ruler where a treasure is presumed to be hidden.

1735
Hassan, *Alhaji.* A Chronicle of Abuja. Translated and arranged from the Hausa of Alhaji Hassan and Mallam Shuaibu Na'ibi by Frank Heath. [Rev. and enl. ed. Lagos, African Universities Press, 1962] 91 p. illus., map, ports. DT515.9.A2H33 1962

1736
Ismāʿīl Ḥāmid. Ville sahariennes. RMM, t. 19, juil. 1910: 260–279. DS36.R4, v. 19

1737
Leriche, Albert. Petite note pour servir à l'histoire d'Atar (Mauritanie). BIFAN, t. 14, avril 1952: 623–626. Q89.I5, v. 14
This short history of the mausoleum of Shaykh al-Imām al-Ḥaḍramī (d. 1087) was drawn from a three-volume work by al-Imām Majdhūb, who is said to have been inspired by al-Ḥaḍramī to discover the latter's tomb. The story was pieced together from fragments of the Arabic manuscript by the Mauritanian scholar Mokhtar Ould Hamidoun.

1738
Levtzion, Nehemia. Salaga—a 19th century trade town in Ghana. Asian and African Studies, v. 2, 1966: 207–244. DS1.A4733, v. 2
This article is based on the author's Ph.D. dissertation (*see* 627).

1739
Marty, Paul. La chronique de Oualata et de Néma (Soudan français). Revue des études islamiques, no 3, 1927: 255–426; no 4, 1927: 531–575. BP1.R53, 1927
Chronicles of Walātah and Nema [Niʿmah], located in the southwestern corner of present-day Mauritania, by Muḥammadi Ūld Sīdī ʿUthmān, a learned man from Walātah. The chronicles begin with the reign of Askiya Dāwūd (1549), relating intertribal conflicts and developments through the French occupation. The narrations end with 1335 A.H. (1916/1917).

1740
Mauny, Raymond. Notes d'archéologie sur Tombouctou. BIFAN, t. 14, juil 1952: 899–918. illus. Q89.I5, v. 14
Timbuktu, which fired the imagination of men like Caillé, Laing, and Barth, is now a sedate city. Mauny gives a description of the historic city based on "Arab authors, ancient local traditions, travel relations and some modern works," and his own research on the spot. There are photographs and diagrams of the mosques of Jingereber, Sankore, and Sīdī Yaḥyā, and the Madugu (palace of the Mandingo kings), and the Moroccan Kasbah.

1741
———La tour et la mosquée de l'Askia Mohammed à Gao. NA, no 47, juil. 1950: 66–67. DT1.I513, 1950
Note on the mausoleum of Askiya Muḥammad, the oldest standing monument in Gao, and the tower and the mosque which Mauny believes to be the actual tomb of the Songhay ruler.

1742
Meillassoux, Claude. Histoire et institution du Kafo de Bamako d'après la tradition de Niaré. CEA, v. 4, 2. cahier, 1963: 187–227. DT1.C3, v. 2

1743
———Urbanization of an African community; voluntary association in Bamako. Seattle, University of Washington Press [1968] 165 p. illus., maps (American Ethnological Society. Monograph 45)
E51.A556, v. 45 1968
HN810.M33B35

Includes references to Muslim associations such as the Hajj societies for sending members to Mecca.

1744
Meunié, Dj. Jacques. Cités anciennes de Mauritanie, provinces du Tagannt et du Hodh. Préface de Henri Terrasse. Paris, Librairie C. Klincksieck, 1961. 194, [82] p. illus., maps, plans.
N7388.M38M4

1745
———Cités anciennes de Mauritanie: Tichitt et Oualata. *In* Académie des inscriptions et belles-lettres. Comptes rendus des séances, avril/juin 1954: 217–226. AS162.P315, 1954

1746
———Cités caravanières de Mauritanie, Tichite et Oualata. JOSAF, t. 27, fasc. 1, 1957: 19–35.
DT1.S65, v. 27

Both Walatah and Tichît were part of the trans-Saharan network of cities that flourished from the 10th to the 16th century. Walatah, established about 1224, became a major trade center on the threshold of the Sahara, while Tichît, whose foundation could be as old as the eighth century, was an important stop along the salt trail. The author presents a complete analysis of these two cities including their geography, demography, social structures, and a detailed description of their Saharan architecture.

1747
Miner, Horace M. The primitive city of Timbuctoo. [Princeton] Published for the American Philosophical Society by Princeton University Press, 1953. 297 p. illus., map. (Memoirs of the American Philosophical Society, v. 32) DT553.T6M53

1748
Mokhtar ould Hamidoun, *and* Cyr Deschamps. Que veut dire Nouakchott? NA, no 118, avril 1968: 62–64. DT1.I513, no. 118

In this interpretation of the name of the capital the authors see four possibilities. The most plausible is *Inwakshudh,* or the place of the shudh: "la couche aquifère d'un puit, s'il contient des coquilles."

1749
Monod, Théodore. Découverte archéologique à Djenné. NA, no 20, oct. 1943: 10.
DT1.I513, 1943

1750
Monteil, Charles V. Une cité soudanaise: Djenné, métropole du delta central du Niger. Préf. de Vincent Monteil. Paris, Editions Anthropos [1971] 301 p. illus., maps, plates.
DT551.9.D35M6 1971

"Réimpression anastatique de l'édition originale publiée en 1932."

Monograph on the city of Jenné. Monteil presents a total picture of the city including the physical background and social, economic, and historical and religious developments.

1751
———Fin de siècle à Médine (1897–1899). BIFAN, t. 28, janv./avril 1966: 82–172. DT1.I5123, v. 28

Review of the social structure of Médine, a small town southwest of Kayes in Mali, based on Charles Monteil's diary, as edited by Vincent Monteil. It is divided into seven parts: the family, personal property, the chiefs, justice, beliefs and customs, Islam, and history and traditions. The section on Islam is subdivided into: Africanized Koranic traditions, circumcision, Koran and prayers, mosques, and marabouts.

1752
———Goundiourou. NA, no 12, 1941: 63–64. WU

Translation of two texts on the history of the city located near Kayes in southwestern Mali.

1753
———Le Tekrour et la Guinée. Outre-mer, v. 1, 1929: 387–405. NN

1754
Monteil, Vincent. Chronique de Tichit (Sahara occidental). BIFAN, t. 1, janv. 1939: 282–312.
Q89.I5, v. 1

Annotated translation of the chronicle of Tichît in the Tagant region in central Mauritania compiled from four versions. The work covers the period 1153–1909. A list of place names and tribes is annexed.

1755
———Le dyolof et Al-Bouri Ndiaye. BIFAN, t. 28, juil./oct. 1966: 595–636. DT1.I5123, v. 28

"The popular hero is the one in whom the people recognize themselves because he embodies their aspirations and hopes," says Monteil. He investigates the life of Alboury N'diaye (1842–1902) within the broader context of the development of the Dyolof state.

1756
Moody, H. L. B. Ganuwa: the walls of Kano city. Nigeria magazine, no. 92, Mar. 1967: 19–38. illus. DT515.N47, 1967

1757
———A Kano mystery. Nigeria magazine, no. 97, June/Aug. 1968: 62–67. DT515.N47, 1968
Brief article on the Waika tablet, a small iron plate in the form of a Muslim writing board bearing an Arabic inscription.

1758
———The walls and gates of Kano city: historical and documentary references; a preliminary review. Kano studies, no. 3, June 1967: 12–26. DLC

1759
Muggs, Jonathan W., *Capt.* Voyage à Tombouctou. Journal des voyages, t. 24, 1824: 283–298. G161.J86, v. 24
Report of a voyage to Timbuktu and description of the city by a Captain Muggs from Georgia, who is the son of an American father and a woman from Timbuktu. The report also describes his encounter with a sea serpent that let go of his ship only after "avoir reçu dans l'oeil gauche un boulet de canon bien ajusté, et qui fut obligé d'aller chercher un collyre au sein des eaux."

1760
Norris, H. T. The history of Shinqīṭ, according to the Idaw 'ali tradition. BIFAN, t. 24, juil./oct. 1962: 393–413. DT1.I5123, v. 24
Shinqīṭ, the Chinguetti of French texts, is famous for its scholars and religious men. Yet, unlike Tichit, Oulâta, and Nema, no local chronicle of the city has been discovered. The story of the qṣār is found in a short chronicle on the Idaw 'Ali tribe by Sīdī 'Abd Allāh ibn al-Ḥājj Ibrāhīm. A genealogy of the Idaw 'Ali and Aghāl of Mauritania is appended.

1761
Ottenberg, Simon. A Moslem Igbo village. CEA, v. 11, 2. cahier, 1971: 231–260. DT1.C3, v. 11
Analysis of Anohia Itim, an Igbo village of the Akikpo group. Between 1951/53 and 1959/60 the major portion of the village had become Muslim. Ottenberg shows the process of Islamization under the direction of a son of the village who had become Muslim and a successful business man, and the dynamics of the conflict between traditional beliefs and the new adopted faith.

1762
Pageard, Robert. Une tradition musulmane relative à l'histoire de Ségou. NA, no 101, janv. 1964: 24–26. DT1.I513, 1964
Translation of an oral tradition recorded in 1960 from 'Abd al-Raḥmān Djire, Imam of Ségou, on the history of the city. The tradition reports that the founder came from Damascus. A chronological note compares the similar genealogies of Djire and L. Tauxier.

1763
Palmer, *Sir* Herbert R. History of Katsina. *In* African Society. Journal, v. 26, Apr. 1927: 216–236. DT1.R62, v. 26

1764
———, *trans. and ed.* The Kano chronicle. *In* Royal Anthropological Institute of Great Britain and Ireland. Journal, v. 38, Jan./June 1908: 58–98. illus. GN2.A3, v. 38

1765
Péfontan, *Commandant.* Araouan. BCAOF, v. 16, juil/sept. 1933: 411–442. DT521.C6, v. 16
Arawan, located 300 kilometers north of Timbuktu, has always been a watering stop for travelers crossing the Azwad desert. Péfontan, who was personally acquainted with the area, relates the history of this transit point, from the 12th century to the 1930's, as told by the learned men of this once prosperous city.

1766
———Histoire de Tombouctou de sa fondation à l'occupation française (XIIe siècle–1893). BCAOF, v. 5, janv./mars 1922: 81–113. DT521.C6, v. 5
A history of Timbuktu from its founding during the 12th century to the French occupation in 1893. The author, in a footnote, cites his sources as "*Tarich es Soudan; Tarich es Fettachi; Haut-Sénégal et Niger* (Delafosse); légendes; récits; tarich personnels des indigènes, principalement, ceux de Ahmed Baba, Ahmadi Sidi Alouata, Amadon San Sirfi (representants de vieilles familles ayant joué un grand rôle dans l'histoire de la ville), et Cheikh Sidi Bekaï." An appendix includes lists of the rulers and notables of Timbuktu. Also included are copies of

six letters in Arabic pertaining to the administration of the city.

1767

Rougier, F. Les salines de Taodeni. BCAOF, v. 12, juil./déc. 1929: 476–483. DT521.C6, v. 12

Short history of the salt mine which replaced Teghaza in 1558 after the Moroccans devastated it. Provides price indices for 1901–1923.

1768

Samb, Amar. Touba et son "Magal." BIFAN, t. 31, juil. 1969: 733–753. DT1.I5123, v. 31

Touba, in Senegal, is the "capital" of the essentially Wolof Murid sect. It is the residence of the caliph-general of the Murids; the location of the mausoleum of Shaykh Amadu Bamba, the founder of the movement, and his successors; and the site of the gigantic mosque built by the Murid community as a living testimony to their faith and secular success. Amar Samb, director of IFAN, describes both the city and the "magal," or annual pilgrimage to the venerated town.

1769

Savonnet, Georges. La ville de Thiès, étude de géographie urbaine. Saint Louis, Sénégal, Centre IFAN, 1955. 179 p. illus., maps (part fold.) (Etudes sénégalaises, no 6) HN810.T5S3

1770

Szumowski, Georges. Fouilles au nord du Macina et dans la région de Ségou. BIFAN, t. 19, janv./avril 1957: 224–258. DT1.I5123, v. 19

1771

Urvoy, Yves F. M. A. Chronique d'Agadés. JOSAF, t. 4, fascicule 2, 1934: 145–178. DT1.S65, v. 4

Translation of 10 manuscripts held by the Sultan of Aïr relating the history of Adagez and the dynasties of the Aïr sultanate.

Education

1772

Anderson, E. Christian. Early Muslim education and British policy in Sierra Leone. West African journal of education, v. 14, Oct. 1970: 177–179. L81.W4, v. 14

"From the early days of British colonial development the Union Jack was accompanied by merchants, civil servants, and missionaries who watched warily as the heritage of Mohammed became something to be reckoned with in serious terms. Islamic influence affected the merchandising of shopkeepers, worked upon the policies of public officials, and worried Christian Evangelists," says Anderson in his introductory paragraph. In Sierra Leone, where Muslim proselytization was rife, education proved to be a problem until a Muslim school was established about 1890 in Freetown and the Department of Mohammedan Education was organized in 1902. Government aid for specifically Muslim education in the period after 1924 was negligible. Mission objection, uncertainty about the value of the madrasas, insufficient funds, and the demands of other programs all contrived ultimately to assure the end of this experiment in education in Sierra Leone.

1773

Armer, J. Michael. Psychological impact of education in Northern Nigeria. Paper presented at the 10th annual meeting of the African Studies Association, New York, 1967. DLC-Micro 03782

Collation of the original: 12 p. tables.

1774

Bala Abuja, J. Koranic and Moslem law teaching in Hausa Land. Nigeria magazine, no. 37, 1951: 25–28. DT515.N47, 1951

One of the graduates describes the Koranic school system in northern Nigeria. This cycle of learning the Koran by rote takes about 12 years.

1775

Balogun, I. A. B. Training of Arabic teachers for schools and colleges. West African journal of education, v. 13, Feb. 1969: 33–39 L81.W4, v. 14

Showing the historical and contemporary importance of Arabic to Africa, the author suggests ways and means to increase the number of teachers of Arabic in the secondary school system.

1776

Beyries, Jean-Louis. Questions mauritaniennes: 1. Note sur l'enseignement et les moeurs scolaires indigènes en Mauritanie. 2. Note sur les Ghoudf de Mauritanie. Revue des études islamiques, t. 9, 1. cahier, 1935: 39–73. BP1.R53, v. 9

The first note details traditional Muslim education in Mauritania. After describing school material, Beyries presents the curriculum and daily routines of both the Koranic schools and higher education institutions. The second note investigates the organization, doctrines, and rituals of the Ghudf fraternity founded in the first half of the 19th century by Shaykh al-Mukhtār Ūld Ṭālib 'Amr Ūld Nūḥ.

1777
Bittinger, Desmond W. An educational experiment in northern Nigeria in its cultural setting. Elgin, Ill., Brethren Pub. House, 1941. 343 p. illus., diagrs., tables. LA1611.N5B5

Dissertation on the educational system in northern Nigeria and the problems related to its modernization.

1778
Burns, *Sir* Alan C. History of Nigeria. 7th ed. London, Allen & Unwin, 1969. 366 p. maps (1 col.), 9 plates, ports., 2 tables. DT515.B8 1969

Includes a chapter on religion and education dealing in part with Islam.

1779
Doi, A. R. I. Influence of Islam and the spread of Islamic learning in West Africa Contributions of E. W. Blyden to the Islamic Studies, 1. The Islamic Review, v. 54, Nov. 1966: 31–34. BP1.I7, v. 54

After a brief introduction on the spread of Islam in Africa, Doi examines the contribution of Edward W. Blyden to the education of Muslims in West Africa, his striving for a better understanding between Christianity and Islam, and his interest in the language and manuscripts.

1780
Donald, Leland. Arabic literacy among the Yulanka of Sierra Leone. Africa, v. 44, Jan. 1974: 71–81. PL8000.I6, v. 44

1781
Fisher, Humphrey J. Early Muslim-Western education in West Africa. MW, v. 51, Oct. 1961: 288–298. DS36.M7, v. 51

Islam was preached among the Fante of southern Ghana about 1885 by a former Fante Wesleyan. The small group of converts tried to blend Muslim traditional learning with Western education. A logbook of a Muslim primary school located at Ekrofol was shown to Fisher in 1959. It was begun in 1896 and ends with scattered entries for 1920. The manuscript provides a rare glimpse, from an African perspective, of the vagaries of Muslims "on the furthest fringes of Islam at the turn of the century."

1782
Gbadamosi, G. O. The establishment of Western education among Muslims in Nigeria 1896–1926. JHSN, v. 4, Dec. 1967: 89–115. DT515.A2H5, v. 4

The initial attitude of Northern Nigeria's leaders towards Western education was one of aversion if not scorn. This sentiment soon changed to one of acceptance, bringing about "the impressive education record of today," says the author.

1782a
Hiskett, Mervyn. The teaching of Islamic history in Northern Nigeria: Problems and approaches. JHSN, v. 1, Dec. 1957: 130–137. DT515.A2H5, v. 1

Examination of the problems, syllabus, and methods of teaching Islamic history. Hiskett suggests that Islamic history in Northern Nigeria should be taught by Muslims especially when dealing with the life of the Prophet, and also since "few expatriate teachers know Arabic."

1783
Jones, V. The content of history syllabuses in Northern Nigeria in the early colonial period. West African journal of education, v. 9, Oct. 1965: 145–148. L81.W4, v. 9

1784
Legendre, P. Politique et pédagogie: texte d'une enquête sur l'enseignement traditionnel en A.O.F. (1907). Paedagogica historica, v. 13, no 1, 1973: 57–65. L10.P24, v. 13

1785
Leriche, Albert. De l'enseignement arabe féminin en Mauritanie. BIFAN, t. 14, juil. 1952: 975–983. Q89.I5, v. 14

Leriche believes that the "education of women in Islam, instead of evolving has generally deteriorated." He describes the type of religious education girls receive in Mauritania. This curriculum includes the Koran, the biography of the Prophet—*al-Sīrah al-Nabawīyah*—some fiqh, poetry, and Arabic grammar.

1786
Lesourd, Michel. Dessins géométriques composés par les élèves des écoles coraniques d'In Çalah. JOSAF, t. 6, fasc. 2, 1936: 213–216. DT1.S65, v. 6

Investigation of the significance of geometrical patterns found on the "writing boards" of students at the Koranic schools of In Salah in central Algeria.

1787
Mahmud, Khalil. The influence of the Holy Koran on the development of libraries. Nigeria journal of Islam, v. 1, Jan./June 1971: 11–22. DLC

1788
Orr, *Sir* Charles W. J. The making of Northern Nigeria; with a new introduction by A. H. M. Kirk-Greene. 2d ed. London, Cass, 1965. 306 p. 3 plates (maps). DT515.O8 1965
Chapter 26 is about "Religion and Education."

1789
Proudfoot, L., *and* H. S. Wilson. Muslim attitudes to education in Sierra Leone. MW, v. 50, Jan. 1960: 86–98. DS36.M7, v. 50
Since the days of E. W. Blyden's appeal for Muslim education, Sierra Leone had followed a policy of separate educational systems which survived until a unified system was adopted in 1927. Proudfoot and Wilson investigate the September 1958 conference on Muslim education held at Fourah Bay College. Its main themes were: "The need for a blending of Eastern and Western education; the injustices of the past and the unfairness of the Christians; the lack of reward and status for men of good Islamic education; the need for special help from government to the Muslim Community; self-help and the need for organization; and the position of women." The recommendations of the conference—which are addended—reflect the apprehensions of the Muslim community regarding traditional Islamic education once independence is achieved.

1790
Samb, Amar. Essai sur la contribution du Sénégal à la littérature d'expression arabe. Dakar, IFAN, 1972. 531 p. illus. (Mémoire de l'Institut fondamental d'Afrique noire, no 87) PJ8390.S4S2
An eminent Arabist, Samb has undertaken a herculean task. Through the study of the various schools of Arabic learning in Senegal, he has successfully delineated the extent of Senegalese contribution to Arabic scholarship. After a general introduction defining the physical and historical background, the perimeter of Senegalese culture, Arabization, the literary schools, and the dominant traits of Arabic literature in Senegal, Samb examines the following schools: St. Louis (Bū al-Mughdād); Gauguel (Shaykh Mūsā Kamara); N'Guiguilone (Thierno Yoro Bal); Louga (al-Ḥājj 'Abbās Sall); Thiès (Dhū al-Nūn Ly); Kolda (Ibn Zubayr); Kaolock (Muḥammadū Khalīfah Niasse); Dār al-Khayr (Shams al-Dīn); Sokone (Aḥmad Deme); Ainoumane (Khālī Madiakhate Kala); Tivaouane (al-Ḥājj Mālik Sy); Dakar (Limāmū Laye); Touba (Aḥmadū Bambā).

1791
Smith, H. F. C. An early 18th century school text. *In* Historical Society of Nigeria. Bulletin of news, v. 4, June 1959. DLC

1792
[Schieffelin, Henry M.] *ed.* The people of Africa; a series of papers on their character, condition, and future prospects, by Edward W. Blyden, D.D., Tayler Lewis, D.D., Theodore Dwight, Esq. New York, A. D. F. Randolph, 1871. 157 p. plates, facsims (part fold.) DT15.S4
Collection of essays by several scholars, dealing with Islam and the state of learning, primarily among the Muslims of Liberia. It is one of the earliest collections of studies concerned with the influence of Arabic learning upon the peoples of West Africa. Included are photographic reproductions of Arabic manuscripts.

1793
Wilks, Ivor. The growth of Islamic learning in Ghana. JHSN, v. 2, Dec. 1963: 409–417. DT515.A2H5, v. 2

1794
———The transmission of Islamic learning in the western Sudan. *In* Goody, John R. Literacy in traditional societies, edited by Jack Goody. Cambridge [Eng.] Cambridge University Press, 1968: 161–197. LC149.G6
Extensive study of Islamic learning in the Dyula-dominated areas of Mali, Guinea, Upper Volta, Ivory Coast, and Ghana. "Wilks writes about the Western Sudan, but he is concerned not so much with a specific 'culture' or 'society' in the usual sense as with the specialized trading groups of the Dyula, which also constituted a major channel of Muslim learning throughout a large part of the Western Sudan. . . . [He also] examines the way in which learning is handed down over the generations, the relationship between trade and learning . . . and refers to the role of a universalistic written code in helping to establish the conditions for a flourishing long-distance trade crossing ethnic and linguistic frontiers."—(Abstract supplied, modified)

History

1795
Abu Bakr. *Imam of Zaria.* Tarihim annabi. [An introduction to Islamic history, Hausa text] Zaria, North Regional Literature Agency, 1957. IEN

1796
Adam, G. Légendes historiques du Pays de Nioro (Sahel). Paris, Challamel, 1904.
Source: Joucla, 41.

1797
Adamu, Muhammad Uba. Some notes on the influence of North African traders in Kano. Kano studies, v. 1, pt. 4, 1968: 43–49. DLC
Drawing on oral evidence "with footnotes by J. E. Lavers," Adamu describes the development of Arab influence in Kano. So many of these traders were from Ghadames and Ghat that a consul was appointed about 1846 for the Ghadames traders to look after their interests. These Arabs introduced leather work in Kano and played a not unimportant political and religious role in the life of the northern metropolis. The author concludes, "Today the Arab community of Kano has been largely assimilated but they have left many traces of their presence."

1798
Adeleye, R. A. The dilemma of the Wazir: the place of the Risālat al-Wazir 'ila ahl al-'ilm wa'l-tadabbur. [Treatise of the Wazir to the people of knowledge and reflection] JHSN, v. 4, June 1968: 285–298. DT515.A2H5, v. 4
Text, translation, and commentaries on the *Risalah* of the Wazir of Sokoto, Muhammad al-Bukhari ibn Ahmad (1886–1910). "It is an apologia for the role he played in working with the British conquerors after the conquest of Sokoto on the morning of Sunday, 15 March 1903." The significance of the *Risalah,* according to the author, is the Islamic character of the Caliphate's resistance.

1799
———Power and diplomacy in Northern Nigeria, 1804–1906; the Sokoto Caliphate and its enemies. [New York] Humanities Press [1971] 387 p. illus. maps. (Ibadan history series)
DT515.9.F8A64 1971
The study of Northern Nigeria is now undertaken with the help of the very substantive manuscript material that has been brought together recently. The detailed investigation of Adeleye represents the approach of a new generation of scholars at home with the wealth of documents now available. The author looks at the Sokoto Caliphate during the 19th century and analyzes the various foci of power and their interaction. The three parts of the study are: the Caliphate in the 19th century; relations with Europeans during the scramble era; and the overthrow of the Caliphate. Substantial bibliography.

1800
———Mahdist triumph and British revenge in Northern Nigeria: Satiru 1906. JHSN, v. 6, June 1972: 193–214. DT515.A2H5, v. 6
Adeleye's article represents a well-established trend of writing African history as seen by Africans, in which Africans are at the center of the stage and not in some obscure wing. The Satiru "rebellion" in 1906 embodied anticolonial resistance in Nigeria and "the reaction to the establishment of European infidel rule in the overthrown Caliphate."

1801
Ajayi, J. F. Ade. Milestones in Nigerian history. Ibadan, Nigeria, University College [1962] 47 p. illus., map. DT515.5.A64
Studies of four significant periods in Nigerian history: the Fulani Jihad (1804), the age of Bishop Crowther (1864), Amalgamation (1914), and the Richards Constitution (1947).

1802
Ajayi, J. F. Ade, *and* Ian Espies, *eds.* A thousand years of West African history: a handbook for teachers and students. Ibadan, Ibadan University Press, 1965. 543 p. DT471.A4
In this general introduction to West African history, a strong thread of Islamic influence runs through most of the volume.

1803
Alis, H. Nos africains. Paris, Hachette, 1894. 568 p. illus.
Source: Brasseur, 3059.

1804
Allen, Edmund W. The travels of Abdul Karim in Hausaland and Bornu. Illustrated by Caroline Sassoon. Zaria [Nigeria] N.R.L.A., 1958. 80 p. illus. DT515.2.A75
Popularization of Henry Barth's travels in Nigeria, 1821–65.

1805
Amilhat, P. Petite chronique des Ida ou Aich, héritiers guerriers des Almoravides sahariens. Revue des études islamiques, v. 11, no. 1, 1937: 41–130. BP1.R53, v. 11
Detailed and elaborate study of the Idaw 'Aish of the Tagant region in Mauritania from the 11th century to their submission to French authorities in 1908. Included are eight indices on genealogies and special notes. The work was also published in monograph form by Geuthner in 1937.

1806
Arcin, André. La Guinée française; races, religions, coutumes, production, commerce. Paris, A. Challamel, 1907. 659 p. DT543.A7

Exhaustive study of Guinea from a colonial viewpoint. The chapter on Islam (p. 481–527) describes its propagation and activities and contains a brief section on the political importance of the faith in the colony.

1807
Ardant du Picq, Charles P. Une population africaine: les Djerma. BCAOF, v. 14, oct./déc. 1931: 471–704. DT521.C6, v. 14

A monograph on the Djerma based on field notes and research undertaken in 1905–06 in Dosso, Niger. The author examines, in detail, the history, geography, ethnic origins, language, and folklore of the group. A Djerma-French and French-Djerma dictionary is appended.

1808
Arlabosse, Louis. Une phase de la lutte contre Samory (1890–1892)—Souvenirs du Général Arlabosse. Revue d'histoire des colonies, t. 20, sept./oct. 1932: 385–432; nov./déc. 1932: 465–514. JV1801.R4, v. 20

When Archinard arrived in West Africa (1890), he was faced by two centers of resistance: in the Kaarta region, Ahmadu at Nioro and Samory in Sanankoro. Arlabosse participated for two years in the "pacification" during which he kept a logbook describing the vicissitudes of the French forces in their fight against the two Muslim leaders.

1809
Arnaud, Robert. Un chérif marocain enterré à Sansanding. *In* Société de géographie l'A.O.F. Bulletin, v. 1, 1907: 223–226.

Source: Brasseur 1761.

1810
———Précis de politique musulmane. Alger, Jourdan, 1906.

Source: Joucla 324.

v. 1: Pays maure de la rive droite du Sénégal.

1811
Arnaud, Robert, *and* Pasquier, *Capt.* La situation politique musulmane chez les Oulliminden. L'Afrique française, t. 17, 1907: 122–123. DLC-Micro 03878

1812
Aubert, A. Légendes historiques et traditions orales recueillies dans la Haute-Gambie. BCAOF. v. 6, juil./sept. 1923: 384–428. map. DT521.C6, v. 6

Aubert, who spent 51 months in the region as "administrateur adjoint des colonies," reports the traditions of the Malinke, Sarokole, Bassari, and other groups of the area as told by various griots. Appended are "Notes sur la langue bassari."

1813
Bâ, Amadou Hampâté. Des Foulbe du Mali et de leur culture. Abbia, no 14/15, juil./déc. 1966: 23–54. AP9.A24, 1966

1814
——— Jaawambe. Traditions historiques des Peuls Jaawambe; présentées Amadou Hampâté Bâ. Niamey, Regional Documentation Centre for Oral Tradition [1973?] 89 p. DT530.B23

1815
Ba, Amadou Hampâté, *and* Jacques Daget. L'empire peul du Macina. Paris, Mouton, 1962+ maps. (Le Monde d'outre-mer, passé et présent 1. sér.: Etudes, 15) L.C. has v. 1. DT551.9.M3B3

In an effort to show that oral traditions are as valid a source of historical knowledge as any other source, the authors present a well-researched history of the empire founded by Shaykh Aḥmadū, based primarily on the oral traditions of the Masina region. The first volume covers the period 1818–53.

1816
Ba, Mahmadou Ahmadou. Contribution à l'histoire des Régueibat. BCAOF, v. 16, juil./sept. 1933: 333–359. DT521.C6, v. 16

Political, social, economic, and religious history of the Rujaybāt who nomadize between Mauritania and the Spanish Sahara, disdainful of international boundaries.

1817
———Notice sur Maghama; et le canton du Littama. BIFAN, t. 1, oct. 1939: 743–761. Q89.I5, v. 1

The story of the Maghama region, located near the Senegal River between Kaedi and Bakel, which was a no man's land at the end of the 19th century, separating the turbulent Moors and the settled populations. The story, told by the "Chef de canton" of Littama, is based on oral traditions and provides a description of the area, its people, and social structures, as well as a narrative of the history of the early contacts with the French administration.

1818
Ba, Oumar. Les peuls Bouméyâbé et Rangâbé (Sénégal et Mauritanie). BIFAN, t. 33, oct. 1971: 747–763. DT1.I5123, v. 33

Oumar Ba, a noted researcher at IFAN, traces family ties of the Fulbe Diallo clan in the Masina and the Fouta Toro and the role played by the Senegal River as a link between the two communities regardless of colonization and independence.

1819
Backwell, H. F. The occupation of Hausaland 1900–1904; being a translation of Arabic letters found in the house of the Wazir of Sokoto, Bohari, in 1903, edited with an introduction by H. F. Backwell. 1st ed. reprinted with an introductory note by M. Hiskett. London, Cass, 1969. 90 p. (Cass library of African studies. General studies, no. 79) DT515.9.N5B3 1969

Reprint, with new introduction, of 1927 ed.

Translation of 131 letters "collected" when the British occupied Sokoto in 1903.

1820
Balogun, I. A. B. The introduction of Islam into the Etsako Division of the Mid-Western State of Nigeria. Orita, v. 6, June 1972: 27–38. DLC

Etsako is heavily populated with Muslims. Balogun reviews the history of the Islamization of the division, a result of Nupe invasions during the second half of the 19th century, as reported by 12 local informants.

1821
Barrows, David P. Berbers and blacks; impressions of Morocco, Timbuktu and the Western Sudan. New York, Century Co., [c 1927] 251 p. illus., front, maps (part. fold.), plans, plates. DT310.B25

1822
Basset, René. Mission au Sénégal; étude sur le dialecte Zénaga, notes sur le Hassania, recherches historiques sur les maures. Paris, E. Leroux, 1909. 661 p. (Publications de l'École des lettres d'Alger. Bulletin de correspondance africaine, v. 39) AS651.A6, v. 39

1823
Bathily, Abdoulaye. Mamadou Lamine Dramé et la résistance anti-impérialiste dans le Haut-Sénégal (1885–1887). NA, no 125, janv. 1970: 20–32. DT1.I513, 1970

1824
Binger, Louis G. Esclavage, islamisme et christianisme. Paris, Société d'éditions scientifiques, 1891. 112 p. HT919.B4

Binger learned to respect Muslims through close contacts with them, especially in Kong in the Ivory Coast, and he presents a sympathetic analysis of the two monotheistic religions and slavery. He foresaw Islam's gaining the upper hand over Christian missionaries and suggests that France should collaborate with Muslims to win the support of the indigenous populations and use it as a conduit for French influence. It is interesting to note the empathy with which Binger talks about Islam at a period when, as he says, people believed that "the Muslim destroys everything, plunders, sacks, spoils and dirties all he touches. . . ."

1825
———Du Niger au Golfe de Guinée par le pays de Kong et le Mossi. Paris, Hachette, 1892. 2 v. front., illus., plates, ports, maps (part fold.) DT527.B6

In 1887 Binger traveled from Bamako through the Niger Bend to Grand Bassam, on the coast, via Ouagadougou. His logbook contains a number of useful observations on Islam in the area he visited.

1826
———Le péril de l'Islam. Paris, Comité de l'Afrique française, 1906. 118 p. 4JQ31

1827
Boisnard, Magali. Sultans de Touggourt; histoire d'une dynastie et d'un royaume sahariens, d'aprés le folklore et les documents contemporains. Paris, Geuthner, 1933. NjP

1828
Bou Hagg. Noirs et blancs aux confins du désert. BCAOF, v. 21, oct./déc. 1938: 480–488. DT521.C6, v. 21

Historical note on social relations between blacks and whites on the periphery of the desert.

1829
Bowdich, Thomas Edward. Mission from Cape Coast Castle to Ashantee. 3d., edited with notes and an introduction by W. E. F. Ward. London, Cass, 1966. [597] p. plates (incl. music, maps) tables. DT507.B78 1966

Originally published in 1819.

Though primarily about the Ashanti, Bowdich's classic work includes a number of leads on Islam and trade connections with the northern area.

Includes itineraries of trade routes as reported by Arabic manuscripts.

1830
Boyer, Gaston. Un peuple de l'Ouest soudanais, les Diawara [par] G. Boyer. Contribution à l'histoire des Songhay [par] J. Rouch. Dakar, IFAN, 1953. 259 p. illus., plates, maps, tables (Mémoires de l'Institut français d'Afrique noire, no 29) DT356.B76

1831
Braimah, J. A., *and* John R. Goody. Salaga: the struggle for power. London, Longmans, 1967 [i.e. 1968] 222 p. DT510.42.B69

1832
Brown, William A. Towards a chronology for the caliphate of Hamdullahi. CEA, v. 8, 3. cahier, 1968: 428–434. DT1.C3, v. 8

Analysis of two versions of *Tārīkh Fittūgah* "a region on the right bank of the Niger, dominated by the Fittobé Pulo clan" written by al-Mukhtār ibn Ismā'īl Wadī'at Allāh (d. 1863/64). Using the chronicle as his main source, Brown proposes a tentative chronology of the caliphate of Hamdullahi (1816/17–1863/64) which developed in the Masina region.

1833
Butler, Jeffrey, *ed.* Boston University papers on Africa. African history. v. 2. Boston, Boston University Press, 1966. 335 p. maps. DT1.B8

The following articles in this compilation are relevant to Islam: Ronald Cohen, The Bornu King Lists, and The Dynamics of Feudalism in Bornu; John D. Hargreaves, The Tokolor Empire of Segou and Its Relations with the French.

1834
Caillé, René. Travels through Central Africa to Timbuctoo, and across the Great Desert, to Morocco, performed in the years 1824–1828. London, Cass, 1968. 2 v. plates (incl. 2 fold.), illus., maps, plans, port. (Cass library of African studies. Travels and narratives, no. 36) DT356.C13 1830b

Facsimile reprint of first English edition, London, Calburn & Bentley, 1830; originally published as *Journal d'un voyage à Temboctou et à Jenné,* Paris, Imp. royale, 1830 (DT356.C12 1965).

René Caillé, the first European to visit Timbuktu and return to tell about it, started his long journey at St. Louis in August 1824 and arrived in Rabat, exhausted and sick, in August 1828. His description of his itinerary and of Timbuktu and Jenné contains valuable raw material for research on Islam in the area during the 19th century.

1835
Carreira, António. Duas cartas topograficas de Graça Falcão (1894–1897) e a expansão do islamismo no rio Farim. Garcia de Orta, v. 11, no 2, 1963: 191–212. JV4201.G3, v. 11

1836
Chapelle, Jean. Les nomades noirs du Sahara. Paris, Plon [1958, c. 1957] 449 p. illus., maps (1 fold. col.), plates (part col.) (Recherches en sciences humaines, 10) IEN

1837
Charbonneau, Jean. Sur les traces du Pacha de Tombouctou. La pacification du Sud-Marocain et du Sahara occidental. Préf. de M. le général Gouraud. Illus. de Théophile-Jean Delaye. Paris, Charles-Lavauzelle, 1936. 166 p. illus., plates, fold. maps, tables. NN

1838
Cissé, Bocar. Les peulhs du Soudan Occidental: origine et fractionnnement—chronologie des chefs du Macina. *In* Bamako. Institut des sciences humaines du Mali. Etudes Maliennes, no 5, avril 1973: 18–34. DLC

Essay on the Masina Fulbe including a discussion of the various *'Uqbah* cited in Fulbe traditions of origins, a summary of a Fulbe *Tārīkh* written down by "Alfa Ismaïla – Kou Wadia," former qadi of Tindirma, and a chronology of the "Ardo and Amirou" of the Masina.

1839
Clozel, Marie François J., *ed.* Haut-Sénégal-Niger. Paris, E. Larose, 1919: G. P. Maisonneuve et Larose, 1972. 3 v. maps (part fold.), fold. col. map in pocket of v. 3. DT551.C62

At head of title: Maurice Delafosse.

Contents: t. 1. Le pays, les peuples, les langues. —t. 2. L'histoire.—t. 3. Les civilisations.

Monumental study based on administrative reports and the vast knowledge of its author, Maurice Delafosse. In spite of its age and some obvious lacunae and dated interpretations, the work is still a mine of information on the area.

1840
Cohen, Ronald. From empire to colony: Bornu in the nineteenth and twentieth centuries. *In* Gann, Lewis H., *ed.* Colonialism in Africa, 1870–1960. Vol. 3: Profile of change: African society and

colonial rule. Edited by Victor Turner. Cambridge [Eng.] Cambridge University Press, 1971. p. 74–126. DT31.G3

1841
Collieaux, Alfred. Détails rétrospectifs sur l'histoire des dernières opérations contre Samory et la prise de l'Almamy (1897–1898). BCAOF, v. 21, avril/juin 1938: 290–303. DT521.C6, v. 21
Collieaux has personally known all the characters of the cast involved in the capture of Samory. Drawing on interviews and French documents, he narrates the events leading to the capitulation of the Almamy and his *sofa.* The relationship between Gouraud and Samory is highly reminiscent of that between Gordon and the Mahdi of the other Sudan.

1842
Colombani, François-Marie. Le Guidimaka; étude géographique, historique et religieuse. BCAOF, v. 14, juil./sept. 1931: 365–432. DT521.C6, v. 14
Exhaustive study of the Guidimaka region, located in southern Mauritania, by the man who "pacified" the country. A geographical description is followed by a detailed historical narrative gathered from various griots describing the political and religious organization of the Moors and the Sarakole of the Shammāmah.

1843
Crozals, J. de. Trois états foulbés du Soudan occidental et central: le Fouta, le Macina, l'Adamaoua. *In* Grenoble. Université. Annales, v. 8, no 2, 1896: 257–309. AS162.G8, v. 8

1844
Crozier, Frank P. Five years hard. New York, J. Cape & R. Ballou [1932] 2 p. l., 7–221 p. illus. maps, plates. DA69.3.C7A35
Memoirs of a British officer during the occupation of northern Nigeria. Reflects the attitudes of his time.

1845
Curtin, Philip D., *ed.* Africa remembered; narratives by West Africans from the era of the slave trade. With introductions and annotations by Philip D. Curtin [and others] Madison, University of Wisconsin Press, 1967. 363 p. illus., facsims., geneal. table, maps, ports. DT471.C8

1846
Dankoussou, Issaka. Katsina; traditions historiques des Katsinaawaa après la Jihad. Niamey, Centre régional de documentation pour la tradition orale [1970] 214 p. DT515.9.K35D35
In Hausa.

1847
Debrunner, Hans W., *and others.* Early Fante Islam. [1913 report by A. J. Lochman] Ghana bulletin of theology, v. 1, Dec. 1959: 23–33; v. 1, June 1960: 13–28. CtY-D

1848
Delafosse, Maurice. Chroniques du Foûta sénégalais. RMM, t. 24, sept. 1913: 1–114. maps. DS36.R4, v. 24
Siré 'Abbās Sow was a learned man of the village of Dyaba in the Cercle of Saldé who was an authority on genealogy. He wrote two manuscripts on the history of the Senegalese Fouta, which Delafosse condensed in one version. In addition to various documents found in the area, the major source of information was a now lost *Tafsīn Boggel* by a marabout named Aḥmadū Samb who wrote in the 19th century. The chronicle begins with the origins of the Fulbe and goes up to the arrival of the French about 1877. Included are a list of imams of the region and two maps showing the places cited in the text.
Published separately in Paris by E. Leroux (1913. 328 p. ports., geneal. tables, tables. Collection de la Revue du monde musulman) IEN

1849
——— Traditions historique et légendaires au Soudan occidental. *In* L'Afrique française; bulletin du Comité de l'Afrique française et du Comité du Maroc. Renseignements coloniaux et documents, 1913: 293–306, 325–329, 355. DLC-Micro 03878

1850
——— Traditions musulmanes relatives à l'origine des Peuls. RMM, t. 20, sept. 1912: 242–267. DS36.R4, v. 20
The enigma of Fulbe origins is yet to be solved. Delafosse attempts to unravel the many leads about their origin. He presents translations of Arabic documentation on the subject ranging from oral traditions gathered in Cairo in 1855 to the writings of Muḥammad Bello, Sultan of Sokoto.

1851
Delafosse, Maurice, *and* Henri Gaden, *eds.* Chronique du Fouta sénégalais, traduites de deux manuscrits arabes inédits de Siré Abbas Soh et accompagné de notes, documents, annexes et commentaire, d'un glossaire et de cartes. Paris, E.

Leroux, 1914. 328 p. (Collection de la Revue du monde musulman)
Source: Joucla 4017.
See also 1848.

1852
Désiré-Vuillemin, Geneviève M. Contribution à l'histoire de la Mauritanie de 1900 à 1934. Dakar, Editions Clairafrique [1962] 412 p. fold. map.
DT553.M2D4, v. 33

Mme Désiré-Vuillemin is the daughter of E.-B. Vuillemin, who participated in the Tagant-Adrar mission of 1905. This history of Mauritania during its formative years covers the role of Coppolani, his "divide and rule" policy between Shaykh Sidiyā and Shaykh Mā' al-'Aynayn, and the problem of Mauritania as seen by the French authorities in Morocco. She concludes, "La Mauritanie tient les commandes de l'Islam en Afrique occidentale. Malgré les progrès du matérialisme, le desert reste encore le lieu où souffle l'esprit."

1853
Diakité, Mamadou Aïssa Kaba, *comp.* Livre renfermant la généalogie des diverses tribus noires du Soudan et l'histoire des rois aprés Mahomet, suivant les renseignements fournis par certaines personnes et ceux recueillis dans les anciens livres. *In* Académie des sciences coloniales. Annales, v. 3, 1929: 189–225.
Source: Brasseur 2953.

1854
Diop, Amadou-Bamba M'Bakhane. Lat-Dior et l'Islam, suivi de la doctrine sociale de Mouhamadou Bamba. [Bruxelles, Les arts graphiques, 1973?] 111 p. BP64.S4D56

The author, a grandson of Lat-Dyor, Damel of Cayor (1842–86), presents the impact of Islam in the region and analyzes the social doctrine of Shaykh Bamba.

1855
——— Lat-Dior et le problème musulman. BIFAN, t. 28, janv./avril 1966: 493–539. DT1.I5123, v. 28

Diop traces the development of Islam before Lat-Dyor and the conflicts between the Damel and his Thiedo and the marabouts, culminating in the battle of Louga in 1863. The narrative of Lat-Dyor's reign begins with the conversion of the Diop family and the "conversion" of Lat-Dyor. The third section, "Islam after Lat-Dior," describes the Muslim sects, such as the Murid, Qadiri, and Tijani, and the genesis of the Bamba movement, as well as the ensuing political, social, economic, and cultural revolution. The fervor of Islam is best illustrated by the construction of the mosque at Touba, a spirit not unlike that of the medieval European cathedral builders.

1856
Doucouré, Boubou. Notice sur l'origine des habitants de Goumbou, subdivision de Nara, Cercle de Nema. BIFAN, t. 2, juil./oct. 1940: 350–357.
Q89.I5, v. 2

Doucouré has written down the traditional history of his family, founders of the village of Goumbou in central Mali. The history begins with the origin of the family in Canaan and proceeds to the first part of the 20th century. Based on oral traditions as reported by the village griots. *See also* 714.

1857
Doutressoulle, Georges. Le cheval au Soudan Français et ses origines. BIFAN, t. 2, juil./oct. 1940: 342–346. illus., map. Q89.I5, v. 2

Though the theory about migrations to West Africa presented in this article is outdated, its value resides in the map showing the distribution of the two prevalent types of horses in West Africa, namely the Barb and Dongolawi. The author is a military veterinarian.

1858
Duffield, Ian. The business activities of Duse Mohammed Ali: an example of the economic dimension of Pan-Africanism, 1912–1945. JHSN, v. 4, June 1969: 571–600. DT515.A2H5, v. 4

1859
Duveyrier, Henri. Exploration du Sahara: les Touâreg du Nord. Paris, Challamel aîné, 1864. 499 p. illus., port., fold. map. DT346.T7D9
Half title: Exploration du Sahara, tome premier. No more published.

1860
Eagleton, William. The Islamic Republic of Mauritania. Middle East journal, v. 19, winter 1965: 45–53. DS1.M5, v. 19

1861
Escayrac de Lauture, Stanislas, *comte* d'. Mémoire sur le Soudan, géographie naturelle et politique, histoire et ethnographie, moeurs et institutions de l'empire des Fellatas, du Bornou, du Baguermi, du Waday, du Darfour d'après des renseignements entièrement nouveaux et accompagné d'une es-

quisse du Soudan oriental. Paris, A. Bertrand, 1853–56. 184 p. fold. map. DT351.E74

1862
Fage, J. D. An introduction to the history of West Africa. [3d ed.] Cambridge [Eng.] Cambridge University Press, 1962. 232 p. DT471.F15 1962

1863
Fall, Cheilch. La randonnée de Birima Fatma Thioubé. NA, no 116, oct. 1967: 124–132.
DT1.I513, 1967

1864
Fashole-Luke, E. Christianity and Islam in Freetown. Sierra Leone bulletin of religion, v. 9, June 1967: 1–16. DLC

1865
Forde, C. Daryll, *and* P. M. Kaberry, *eds.* West African kingdoms in the nineteenth century. London, Oxford University Press, for the International African Institute, 1967. 289 p. front., maps, diagrs. DT471.F69

The following articles are relevant to Islam: M. G. Smith, A Hausa Kingdom: Maradi Under Dan Baskore, 1854–75; Jack Goody, The Overkingdom of Gonja; Kenneth Little, The Mende Chiefdoms of Sierra Leone; Vincent Monteil, The Wolof Kingdom of Kayor.

1866
Freeman, Richard A. Travels and life in Ashanti and Jaman. [1st ed. reprinted]. London, Cass, 1967. 559 p. front., illus. (incl. ports., music), 2 col. plates, facsims., diagrs. (Cass library of African studies. Travels and narratives, no. 17).
DT507.F85 1967

First ed. originally published, London, A. Constable, 1898.

1867
Fuglestad, Finn. Les révoltes des Touaregs du Niger (1916–17). CEA, v. 13, 1. cahier 1973: 82–120. DT1.J65, v. 13

Analysis of the causes and circumstances of these rebellions. French colonisation and its administrative methods were strongly grievous to Twareg interests and ways of life. Not only did the onset of World War I result in the French losing the support of the sedentary, non-Twareg tribes, due to conscription and requisition, but it also facilitated the spread of Senusiya propaganda which was successful among the Twareg for political rather than religious reasons. The western rebellion was crushed to a large extent due to the fact that the Twareg of *amenokal* Firhun were not supported by the sedentary tribes. In the North-East and in Aïr the situation was much more difficult for the French who were besieged more than 3 months on Agades. The pacification went on till 1931.—(Abstract supplied)

1868
The Fulani creation story. Recorded by Amadou Hampaté Bâ. Black Orpheus, no. 19, Mar. 1966: 7.
PL8000.B6, 1966

1869
Gaden, Henri. Ta'rîkh Peul de Douentza (1895). BIFAN, t. 30, avril 1968: 682–690.
DT1.I5123, v. 30

Translation of an Arabic manuscript belonging to the Emir of Douentza (northeast of Bandiagara in Mali) found by Gaden, who sent it to Charles Monteil. The *Tārīkh* is one version of chapter 26 of *Tārīkh al-Sūdān,* translated and annotated by Oscar Houdas in 1900. The document also contains clarifications, especially concerning the transliteration of African names in Arabic, which is a thorny problem when retranslating them into Western languages. Gades has added some notes on information he gathered from local informants during his visit to Bandiagara in 1895.

1870
Genevière, J. Les Kounta et leur activités commerciales. BIFAN, t. 12, oct. 1950: 1111–1127.
Q89.I5, v. 12

The nomadic Kuntah, an Arab bedouin tribe, are found from Ghardaïa (Algeria) to Sokoto (Nigeria) and from Goundam (Mali) to Tahoua (Niger), monopolizing commercial distribution within that large area of the Sahara. Genevière describes the goods involved, both those produced by the Kuntah and those acquired, the intricate commercial organization, and the various sectors where they concentrate their commercial activities.

1871
Gerbeau, H. La région de l-'Issa-Ber. Ancienne route d'invasions, zone marginale des grands empires soudanais, trait d'union entre le Macina et Tombouctou. Etudes d'outre-mer, 1959: 51–58; 91–108. illus.

Source: Brasseur 158.

1872
Gidley, C. G. B. Mantanfas: a study in oral

tradition. African language studies, v. 6, 1965: 32–51. map. PL8003.A34, v. 6

1873
Golbéry, Sylvain M. X. de. Travels in Africa, performed by Silvester Meinrad Xavier Golberry, in the western parts of that vast continent: containing various important discoveries with a particular account of . . . the internal government, both civil and military, of the various kingdoms and nations; together with an account of the discovery of extensive gold mines. Translated from the French, by W. Mudford, esq. 2d ed. London, Jones and Bumford, 1808. 2 v. fronts (1 fold.), fold. map, fold. plan, plates. DT356.G61 1808

1874
Goloubinow, Rotislaw. L'or en Guinée française. *In* Congrès international des mines, de la métallurgie et de la géologie appliquée. *7th, Paris, 1935.* Compte rendus. Paris [1936] p. 31–40. TN5.C7, 1935

1875
Goody, John R. The Akan and the North. Ghana notes and queries, v. 9, Nov. 1966: 18–24. DT510.A1H553, v. 9

1876
——— A note on the penetration of Islam into the West of the Northern Territories of the Gold Coast. *In* Historical Society of the Gold Coast and Togoland. Transactions, v. 1, no. 2, 1953: 45–46. DT510.A1H55, v. 1

Brief note on the Dyula traders who carried Islam into the Voltaic area. Goody disagrees with "Rattray's expression of doubt as to the provenance of the core of Muslim inhabitants of Wa from 'Mende' [as Rattray] fails to appreciate the role of the Mande-speaking peoples in the expansion of Islam and of trade in the Voltaic area." Goody believes that the latter formed the link between the Akan states and the empires of the Niger bend.

1877
——— Salaga in 1876. Ghana notes and queries, v. 8, Jan. 1966: 1–5. DT510.A1H553, v. 8

1878
Gonçalves, José J. O islamismo na Guiné portuguesa; ensaio sociomissionelógico. Lisboa, 1961. 222 p. illus. BP64.G8G6

1879
Gouilly, Alphonse. L'Islam dans l'Afrique occidentale française. Paris, Larose, 1952. 318 p. illus. BP65.A4G6

1880
——— L'Islam devant le monde moderne. Paris, La Nouvelle édition [1945] 295 p. fold. map. (Collection diplomatique & politique internationale) DS38.G6

1881
Grant, Norman K. Some oral traditions from Sabon Birnin Gwari. JHSN, v. 4, Dec. 1967: 135–139. DT515.A2H5, v. 4

1882
Griffin, Donald W. African resistance and local history in French West Africa. Paper presented at the 8th annual meeting of the African Studies Association, Philadelphia, 1965. DLC-Micro 03782

Collation of the original: 12 p.

1883
Guebhard, P. L'Histoire du Fouta Djallon et des Almamys. L'Afrique française; bulletin du Comité de l'Afrique française et du Comité du Maroc. Renseignements coloniaux et documents, 1909: 49–56, 81–82. DLC-Micro 03878

1884
Guinée. *Archives nationales.* Traités avec les chefs du Fouta Djallon. Recherches africaines; études guinéennes, nouv. sér., no 1, jan./mars 1969: 160–167. DT543.A3R4, n.s., 1969

The French colonial authorities, according to the author, prevailed in Africa through cunning and the sword, "lorsque la ruse prévalait, on faisait signer aux chefs 'indigènes' de prétendus traités qui sont autant de chef-d'oeuvre de fourberie et de perfidie." Included are the treaty of July 5, 1881, between France and the Fouta Djallon leaders; ratification by the chiefs of the 1881 treaty Convention of Timbo between the Almamys of the city and Dr. Bayol, the French representative, May 23, 1893; and the treaty of February 6, 1897, between France and the chiefs.

1885
Hallam, W. K. R. An introduction to the history of Hausaland. Nigerian field, v. 31, Oct. 1966: 164–177. QH195.N5A15, v. 31

1886
Hama, Boubou. Contribution à la connaissance de l'histoire des Peuls. Publication de la République du Niger. Paris, Présence africaine, 1968. 306 p. plate. DT530.H35

1887
——— Histoire des Songhay. Publication de la République du Niger. Paris, Présence africaine, 1968. 372 p. plate. DT530.H353

1888
——— L'histoire traditionnelle d'un peuple, les Zarma-Songhay. Publication de la République du Niger. Paris, Présence africaine, 1967. 280 p. illus., maps, plates, ports. DT530.H3

1889
——— Recherches sur l'histoire des Touareg sahariens et soudanais. Paris, Présence africaine, 1967. 559 p. maps, plates. DT346.T7H3

1890
Hargreaves, John D., *comp.* France and West Africa: an anthology of historical documents. London, Macmillan, 1969. 278 p. map. DT534.H3

1891
Harris, Joseph E. The Foula of Fouta Diallon: their origin, migration and religion. Paper presented to the International Congress of Africanists, second session, December 11–20, 1967. Dakar. 14 p. DLC

1892
——— Les précurseurs de la domination coloniale au Fouta Djallon. Présence africaine, no 60, 4. trimestre, 1966: 54–66. GN645.P74

1893
——— Protest and resistance to the French in Fouta Diallon. Genève-Afrique. Geneva-Africa, v. 8, 1969: 3–18. map. DT1.G44, v. 8

Attracted by reports of commercial prosperity, the French occupied Fouta Djallon in 1896. The stronghold of the Fulbe was "an established center for commerce and for Muslim learning and proselytization." Harris, using a spectrum of sources, analyzes the revolts of Thierno Shehu 'Aliyyū (1911) and Ala Yaya (1905 and 1911). With the elimination of the early leaders, Muslim leaders and the French administration developed a symbiotic relation which was apparent as late as the 1958 "non."

1894
Hébert, P. Samory en Haute Volta. Etudes voltaïques (nouv. sér.), no 2, 1961 [1963]: 5–55. DLC

1895
Hickin, L. The advance of Islam in Nigeria. MW, v. 26, July 1936: 400–403. DS36.M7, v. 26

Alarmist note on the advance of Islam in Nigeria. Included is reference to the quotes from a lecture "given by a Professor Nnamdi Azikiwe to members of the Young Ansar-ud-Deen Society." Hickin concludes, "Why worry about the spread of Islam in Nigeria? Because we are convinced that *only the best is good enough for Africa.*"

1896
Hiskett, Mervyn. The 'Song of Bagauda': a Hausa king list and homily in verse. BSOAS, v. 27, pt. 3, 1964: 540–568; v. 28, pt. 1, 1965: 112–135; v. 28, pt. 2, 1965: 363–385. PJ3.L6, v. 27, 28

Text, translation of, and ample commentaries on a long poem in Hausa. The *Song* is divided into four major sections: a prelude, including a doxology and eulogy of the Prophet Muhammad; a king list; a homily on the frailty of the world; and finally a section on fatāwī, or rulings on points of Muslim law.

1897
Hodgkin, Thomas L. Nigerian perspectives, an historical anthology. London, Oxford University Press, 1960. 340 p. illus. (West African history series) DT515.A3H6

1898
Hodgson, William B. The Foulahs of Central Africa, and the African slave trade. [New York?] 1843. 24 p. GN652.F9H6

An early essay on the Fulbe, their culture, and their proselytizing efforts for Islam. The author suggests that they are "destined to be the great instrument in the future civilization of Africa, and the consequent suppression of the external Atlantic slave trade."

1899
Hogben, Sidney J., *and* A. H. M. Kirk-Greene. The emirates of Northern Nigeria; a preliminary survey of their historical traditions. London, Oxford University Press, 1966. 638 p. illus., maps (1 fold. col.) DT515.65.H6

"This book is virtually a new one . . . that has grown . . . out of its predecessor, *The Muhammadan Emirates of Nigeria.*"

Recasting of an old and valuable classic. Hogben rewrote the first part, while both authors collaborated in updating the second part dealing with the various emirates. *See also* two other works by Hogben: *An Introduction to the History of the Islamic*

Emirates of Northern Nigeria (Ibadan, Oxford University Press, 1967. 351 p. DT515.65.H63), and *The Muhammadan Emirates of Nigeria* (London, Oxford University Press, H. Milford, 1930. 351 p. DT515.H65).

1900
Holden, H. H. The Zabarima conquest of North-West Ghana. *In* Historical Society of Ghana. Transactions. v. 8, pt. 2; 1965. Legon, 1965. p. 60–86. DT510.A1H55, v. 8

1901
Hopen, C. Edward. The pastoral Fulbe family in Gwandu. London, Published for the International African Institute by the Oxford University Press, 1958. 165 p. illus., maps. GN652.F9H66

1902
Hubert, Lucien. Avec ou sans l'Islam? Paris, Edition de la Correspondance d'Orient, 1913.
Source: Joucla, 5822.

1903
Hunwick, J. O. A little known episode in the history of Kebbi. JHSN, v. 5, June 1971: 575–581. DT515.A2H5, v. 5

1904
Ismā'īl Ḥāmid. Les Kounta. RMM, t. 15, sept. 1911: 302–318. DS36.R4, v. 15
The Kuntah are a well-known Saharan tribe of religious learned men and traders. They claim to be of Zenata stock, pushed south by the Ṣanhājah. Ḥāmid translates the entire *Tārīkh Kuntah,* a manuscript given to Captain Cortier in 1909 by Bā Ūld Shaykh Sīd 'Umar, marabout of Etelia in the Adrar des Iforas. A genealogy is appended.

1905
Jackson, James G. An account of Timbuctoo and Housa, territories in the interior of Africa, by El Hage Abd Salam Shabeeny; with notes, critical and explanatory. [1st ed. reprint]. London, Cass, 1967. 547 p. 2 plates (col. maps) (Cass library of African studies. Travels and narratives, no. 25) DT198.J13 1820a
Facsimile reprint of 1st ed., London, Longmans, 1820.

1906
Jeffreys, M. D. W. Arab knowledge of the Niger's course. Africa, v. 25, Jan. 1955:84–90. PL8000.I6, v. 25
The course of the Niger was almost unknown to Europe until the 19th century. It became better known through Mungo Park and the Lander brothers who traveled from Busa to the Ocean. Jeffreys suggests that the course of the river was known to Arab geographers such as al-Bakrī and al-Idrīsī as early as the 11th century.

1907
———.Bahr Sudan-Black Sea-Niger. African studies, v. 27, no. 2, 1968: 95–97. DT751.A4, v. 27

1908
———.The Niger and the Arabs. Muslim Digest, v. 5, Jan. 1955: 3–8. BP1.I553, v. 5

1909
Jones, D. H. Jakpa and the foundation of Gonja. *In* Historical Society of Ghana. Transactions. v. 7, pt. 1; 1964. Legon, 1964. p. 24–41. DT510.A1H55, v. 7

1910
Junaidu, *Malam, Waziri of Sokoto.* Tarihin Fulani. [History of the Fulbe] Zaria, Gaskiya Corporation, 1970. 86 p.
In Hausa.
Source: Gaskiya 1970, p. 6.

1911
Kaké, Ibrahima Baba. L'aventure des Bukhara (prétoriens noirs) au Maroc au XVIIIe siècle. Présence africaine, no 70, 2. trimestre, 1969: 67–74. GN645.P74, 1969

1912
Kane, Issa. Histoire et origine des familles du Fouta Toro. *In* Comité d'études historiques et scientifiques de l'Afrique occidentale française. Annales et mémoires, v. 1, 1916: 325–344. MnU

1913
Kane, Oumar. Samba Gelajo-Jegi. BIFAN, t. 32, oct. 1970: 911–926. DT1.I5123, v. 32

1914
Kanya-Forster, Alexander S. The conquest of the Western Sudan: a study in French military imperialism. London, Cambridge University Press, 1969. 297 p. 2 maps. DT532.K35

1915
Khaṭṭāb, Maḥmūd Shīt. Qādat fatḥ al-Maghrib al-'Arabī. [The leaders of the conquest of the Arab Maghrib] Beirut, Dār al-fatḥ lil-ṭibā 'ah wa-al-nashr [1966] 2 v. illus., maps (3 fold.), ports. (*His* Qādat al-fatḥ al-Islāmī) DT199.K43 Orien Arab

1916
al-Khūrī, Fu'ād I. al-Islām 'inda qabīlat al-Timniy. [Islam among the Temne tribe] al-Abḥāth, m. 18, Sept./Dec. 1965: 339–372.
AS595.A6A36, v. 18 Orien Arab

Islam reached the Temne of Sierra Leone through Muslim traders and then via Islamic reformers. al-Khūrī investigates its encounter with traditional beliefs and secret societies such as the Poro. In order to show the syncretism of Temne Islam, the author presents translations of three poems on their Islamization, on Alfa Brahima (the Prophet Abraham), and the creation of man. He then examines the Temne's world view and the division of the universe into the worlds of angels, man, and the spirits.

1917
Kirk-Greene, Anthony H. M. The kingdom of Sukur: a Northern Nigerian *Ichabod*. Nigerian field, v. 25, 2, Apr. 1960: 67–96.
QH195.N5A15, v. 25

1918
Klein, Martin A. Processes of Islamization in late 19th century Senegambia. Paper presented to the International Congress of Africanists, second session, December 11–20, 1967. Dakar. 23 p. DLC

1919
Kozlov, S. Iă. Osnovnye etapy sotsial'noi gvineiskikh Ful'be. [The major stages of the social history of Guinea's Fulbe] Sovetskaîa etnografiîa, 4, 1965: 94–105. GN1.S65, 1965

Tables of contents also in French; summaries in French.

1920
———.Zagatka proiskhozhdeniia Ful'be naroda. [The enigma of the origin of the Fulbe people] Sovetskaîa etnografiîa; 1, 1967: 117–129.
GN1.S65, 1967

Tables of contents also in French; summaries in French.

1921
Kraemer, H. A Moslem "Missionary" in Mendeland, Sierra Leone. Man, v. 46, Sept./Oct. 1946: 111–113. GN1.M25, v. 46

1922
La Chapelle, F. de. Esquisse d'une histoire du Sahara occidental. Hespéris, t. 11, 1930: 35–95.
DT181.H4, v. 11

1923
Lartigue, R. de. Notice sur les Maures du Sénégal et du Soudan. *In* L'Afrique française; bulletin du Comité de l'Afrique française. Renseignements coloniaux et documents, 1897: 41–72.
DLC-Micro 03878

1924
Lavers, John E. The adventures of a Kano pilgrim, 1892–1893. Kano studies, v. 1, pt. 4, 1968: 69–78.
DLC

"The account that follows was given to Major Wingate in 1892 when he was collecting material on Rabih b. Fadlallah for the Intelligence Department of the Egyptian War Office. Little is known of his informant, al-Hajj Isa Hassan Sulaiman al-Kanami . . . [who] gives what must be a typical account of the trials and tribulations of a pilgrimage, although it is more detailed than most, and it is particularly interesting for its description of Rabih."

1925
Legassick, Martin. Firearms, horses, and Samorian army organization. JAH, v. 7, no. 1, 1966: 95–115.
DT1.J65, v. 7

1926
Le Grip, A. Aspects actuels de l'Islam en A. O. F.: 1. Mouvements et influences anti-traditionalistes. 2. L'Islam traditionnel et ses moyens défense. A&A, no 24, 4. trimestre 1953: 6–20; no 25, 1. trimestre 1954: 43–61. DT1.A85, 1953, 1954

The first part is concerned with the various threats facing traditional Islam: the Wahhabi movement, modernism, French education, and political and social reforms. Le Grip suggests that the Wahhabi movement is an instrument both of religious and cultural reforms and of social and political struggles. The second part deals with the reaction of the conservative element to the threats. Traditional religious education, which is declining everywhere except possibly Mauritania, and such religious fraternities as the Qadiri, Tijani, and Shadihli sects, are the tools at the disposal of the traditional structures in facing up to the Middle Eastern and Western assault on traditionalism in West Africa. He concludes that two channels are open to Muslims: the masses would follow the call of a new Mahdi, and the intellectuals would follow a progressive reform movement not unlike the Salafiyah trend in Egypt.

1927
Leriche, Albert. l'Islam en Mauritanie. BIFAN, t 11, juil./oct. 1949: 458–470. Q89.I5, v. 11

In the 15th century Islam took hold in what is today Mauritania. Leriche, who deeply and empathically knew Mauritania, analyzes Islam through the four religious fraternities: Ṣūfīyah, Qādirīyah, Shādhilīyah, and Tījānīyah. The Ṣūfīyah, with almost no adepts, and the Shādhilīyah, with only a few, were of no great significance. The Qādirīyah, to which most Moors Muslims of North Africa belong, is the most important, followed by the Tījānīyah, which is centered in the Tagant central region. A chronology of the two important sects is given with a genealogy of its most representative leaders.

1928

Leriche, Albert, *and* Mokhtar Ould Hamidoun. Note pour servir à l'histoire maure (notes sur les forgerons, les Kunta, et les Maures du Hod). BIFAN, t. 15, avril 1953: 737–750.
Q89.I5, v. 15

In collaboration with Moukhtar Ould Hamidoun, Leriche gives a historical analysis of the origin of the blacksmiths in Moorish society and the fluctuations of their status with the vagaries of conquest. Another group briefly studied is the Kuntah of the Tuat who, forced to migrate southward, proselytzed the people of the Sahara and the blacks on the periphery of the desert.

1929

————.Notes sur le Trârza, essai de géographie historique. BIFAN, t. 10, 1948: 461–538.
Q89.I5, v. 10

A historical geography in the tradition of Yāqūt al-Hamawī, the 13th-century Arab geographer. Mokhtar Ould Hamidoun describes the various regions of the Trarza, in southwestern Mauritania centered around Boutilimit and Nouakchott, and gives the history of its tribes and wells. A chronological table and detailed indexes on place names, tribes and their subdivisions, and family names are included.

1930

Le Rumeur, Guy. Le Sahara avant le pétrole. Paris, Société continentale d'éditions modernes illustrés [1960] 332 p. illus. (Connaissance de l'Afrique)
DT333.L49

1931

Le Sourd, Michel. Tarikh el Kawar. BIFAN, t. 8, no 1/4 1946: 1–54.
Q89.I5, v. 8

History of the Kawar, located in the northeastern part of Niger, based on oral traditions. Includes sections on the Senussi zāwiyah established at "Chemidom" in 1879 and on the Qadiri and Tijani sects. Also included are lists of marabouts settled in various cities of the region.

1932

Levtzion, Nehemia. Notes sur l'origine de l'Islam militant au Fouta-Djalon. NA, no 132, oct. 1971: 107–110.
DT1.I513, 1971

1933

Low, Victor N. Three Nigerian emirates; a study in oral history. Evanston, Ill., Northwestern University Press, 1972. 296 p. illus.
DT515.65.L68

Part of illustrative matter in pocket.

Substantial study of the emirates of Gombe, Katagum, and Hadejia. Low provides a methodological framework for the study of traditional structures through their oral traditions.

1934

Lugard, Flora L. S., *Lady*. A tropical dependency; an outline of the ancient history of the western Sudan with an account of the modern settlement of northern Nigeria. New York, Barnes & Noble [1965] 508 p. 2 fold. maps.
DT502.L82   1965

1935

Maiden, Robert L. B. Historical sketches; studies in exploration and history, African and Islamic. Zaria, N.R.L.A., 1965. 115 p. illus., ports.
IEN

1936

Makulski, Krzystof. Historia badań etnograf icznych Sahary na tle historii. [History of ethnographic research on the Sahara in the light of the history of the penetration of the Sahara] Etnografia polska, t. 9, 1965: 347–387.   GN585.P6E8, v. 9

1937

Markov, W., *and* P. Sebald. The treaty between Germany and the sultan of Gwandu. JHSN, v. 4, Dec. 1967: 141–153.
DT515.A2H5, v. 4

Fearing to be left without a place in the imperial sun, the supporters of the Pan-Germanic Union and such organizations pushed for a German expedition in West Africa to establish German legal rights in the hinterland of Togo. Treaties were signed by several rulers claiming that their territories belonged to the Sultanate of Gwandu. The expedition then signed a treaty with the sultan of Gwandu in 1895. The authors provide a critical analysis of the treaties and attempt to untangle the *quid pro quo*. The Arabic texts are reproduced with an English translation of the original German. Also included is a note on the documents by Abdullahi Smith and F. H. El Masri.

1938
Martin, Bradford G. A new Arabic history of Ilorin. *In* Ibadan, Nigeria. University. *Centre of Arabic Documentation.* Research bulletin, v. 1, Jan. 1965: 20–27. DT352.4.I2a, v. 1

Descriptive analysis of *Ta'līf akhbār al-qurūn min Umarā' bilād Ilūrūn* [Work on the News of the Centuries on the Princes of Ilorin] by Ibn Kūkūra, reporting on the political developments in Ilorin from the beginning of the 19th century to the 1890's and the arrival of the British.

1939
Martin, H. Les tribus du Sahel et du Rio de Oro; les Oulad Bou Sba. BIFAN, t. 1, avril/juil. 1939: 587–629. Q89.I5, v. 1

The Awlād Bū Sbā' migrated from Morocco to Mauritania during the 19th century. They settled in the region of Akjoujt and fought the Kuntah, the Adrar warriors, the Awlād Dalīm, and the Rujaybāt. They were used by the French colonial forces in the first decade of the 20th century and are considered in this study as a potential buffer tribe against the turbulent Bīdān of Mauritania.

1940
Marty, Paul. Etudes sur l'Islam au Dahomey. RMM, t. 60, 2. trimestre, 1925: 109–188; t. 61, 3. trimestre, 1925: 75–162. DS36.R4, v. 60–61

The first Muslims to venture into southern Dahomey in 1704 were probably Hausa merchants who were killed for their inquisitiveness. In this two-part study, Marty provides, in his usual thorough fashion, a detailed analysis of Islam in Dahomey. He divides his investigation into Northern (above the 10th degree north) and Southern Dahomey. Describing first the history of the southern part of the country and its Islamization by the liberated slaves coming from Brazil, and the infiltration, via the north, by the Hausa and Yoruba traders, he includes the World War I period and relations with Northern Nigeria. The last part presents a detailed description, by "cercles" of the Muslim communities and their leaders in both regions.

1941
———Etudes sur l'Islam au Sénégal. Paris, E. Leroux, 1917. 2 v. illus. maps, plates, facsims. (Collection de la Revue du monde musulman) BP65.S35M3

Contents: 1. v. 1. Les personnes.—2. v. 2. Les doctrines et les traditions. L.C. has v. 1.

Marty conceives of Islam as affiliation to a religious fraternity and following a Thierno or marabout. In the 410-page first volume, the author explores the religious impact of the Mauritanian Moorish religious leaders; investigates the Tukulor Tijani groups, the Kunyah, and the Casamance Mandingo; and concludes with a study of Shaykh Yūnus (b. 1850) who first settled in Sandiniery and then moved to Banghère. Included are a number of appendixes as diverse as a list of Moorish marabouts in Wolof country from 1670 to 1690, a genealogy of the M'Bake family, a list of Murids in the Siné-Saloum cercle, and a partial bibliography of Amadū Bamba's works.

1942
———Etudes sur l'Islam en Côte d'Ivoire. Paris, E. Leroux, 1922. 495 p. facsims., maps, plates, ports. (Collection de la Revue du monde musulman, v. 12) BP64.I9M

1943
———Etudes sur l'Islam et les tribus du Soudan. Paris, E. Leroux, 1920–21 [v. 3, '21] 4 v. facsims. geneal. tables, maps (part fold.), plates, ports. (Collection de la Revue du monde musulman [v. 6–9]) DT551.M3

Contents: t. 1 Les Kounta de l'Est. Les Berabich. Les Iguellad.—t. 2 La région de Tombouctou (Islam songhaï). Dienné, le Macina et dépendances (Islam peul).—t. 3 Les tribus maures du Sahel et du Hodh.—t. 4 La région de Kayes. Le pays mambara. Le Sahel de Nioro.

1944
———Etudes sur l'Islam et les tribus maures; les Brakna. Paris, E. Leroux, 1921. 398 p. facsims., maps, plates, ports. (Collection de la Revue du monde musulman) DT530.M

"Annexes" (p. [347]–[393]) include texts of treaties and other documents in French and/or Arabic.

The Brakna are descendants of the Hassānīyah Arab tribes who reached Mauritania in the 14th century in the wake of the great Hilalian invasion of North Africa in the 11th century. Marty presents their history from the domination of the Awlād Rizg in the 15th century to the French occupation in the first quarter of the 20th. He also provides a chronicle of the various fractions of the tribe and their subdivisions. Appended is a genealogy of the Kuntah's Ahl Shaykh.

1945
———Etudes sur l'Islam maure; Cheikh Sidïa—le Fadelïa, les Ida Ou Ali. Paris, E. Leroux, 1916. 25 p. facsims, plates. (Collection de la Revue du monde musulman) BP65.M3M

Study of the Shaykh Sīdiyā sect, its origin and impact in Mauritania; the Fāḍilīyah, who are a branch of the Qadiri sect; and the Idaw 'Alī adherents of the Tijani sect. The appendixes include a number of rare and interesting documents.

1946
———L'histoire des puits de M'hammed Ould Ahmed Youra. BCAOF, v. 3, juil./oct. 1920: 311–345. DT521.C6, v. 3

Translation of a long poem written in 1910 by a Mauritanian scholar, Muḥammad ūld Aḥmad Yūrā, at the request of Commandant Gaden, who was then "Adjoint au Commissaire du Gouvernement Général" in Mauritania. The poem describes the various wells in the region, including the etymology of each name and the tribes gravitating to it, thus providing a general history of the Banū Ḥasan of Mauritania.

1947
———L'Islam en Guinee; Fouta Diallon. Paris, E. Leroux, 1921. 588 p. illus., facsims., geneal. tables, maps, ports. (Collection de la Revue du monde musulman) BP64.A4F8

Exhaustive study on Islam in Fouta Djallon, Guinea, which reflects the spirit of an era. In the final paragraph, Marty expresses the hope that "les coloniaux français seront mieux documentés et plus avertis que leur ancêtre romain pour mener à bien, quels que soient les facteurs religieux, la double tâche du maintien de l'imperium français et du progrés des indigènes." The author divides his work into the following chapters: L'ancien régime; Les groupements Chadelïa; Les Diakanké Qadrïa de Touba; Les Tidianïa Toucouleurs de Dinguiraye; Les Tidianïa Foula; L'influence maure; La doctrine et le culte; L'enseignement musulman; L'Islam dans les institutions juridiques; L'Islam dans les coutumes sociales; Rites, pratiques et survivances du passé.

Attached are 28 appendixes including genealogies, correspondence, treaties, catalogs of private libraries, *silsila,* autographs, charms, etc.

1948
———L'Islam en Mauritanie et au Sénégal. RMM, t. 31, 1915/1916: 1–280. DS36.R4, v. 31

Contents: La politique indigène du Gouveneur Général Ponty en Afrique occidentale française.—Cheikh Sidïa et sa "voie" (Mauritanie).—Les Fadelïa.—Les Ida ou Ạli, Chorfa Tidianïa de Mauritanie.—Les groupements Tidianïa dérivés d'al-Hadj Ọmar (Tidianïa Toucouleurs).—Le groupement Tidiani d'al-Hadj Malik (Tidianïa Ouolofs).—Le groupement des Bou Kounta.—Les Mandingues, élément islamisé de Casamance.—Chérif Younous de Casamance.

1949
———L'Islam et les tribus dans la colonie du Niger (2. série). Revue des études islamiques, v. 5, cahier 2, 1931: 139–240. BP1.R53, v. 5

After a historical introduction to the Kaouar and Tibesti subdivisions, noting the various centers—Bilma, Fachi, Djado, Yat, and Zouar—and the personalities involved, Marty describes the Islamic doctrines and legal obligations, the educational system, and the impact of Islam on the social and juridical fields in the region. Annexed are notes on Koranic schools, marabouts, the text of the Niamey Convention (June 20, 1909) between Colonel Laperrine and Lieutenant-Colonel Venel to delineate the jurisdictions of Algeria and the A.O.F., a Senussi genealogy, and a short bibliography.

1950
———Poème historique d'Abou Bakr Ibn Hejab, le Dimani. BCAOF, v. 4, avril/juin 1921: 252–263. DT521.C6, v. 4

A 147-verse poem (rajaz meter) on the history of Mauritania's tribes. The work is patterned after a famous poem by Walīd ūld Khalīnah, the Dimānī poet. A footnote states that the original text is "en dépôt au 'Service des affaires musulmanes du Gouvernement général'."

1951
Mason, Michael. The *Jihad* in the South: an outline of the nineteenth century Nupe hegemony in north-eastern Yorubaland and Afenmay. JHSN, v. 5, June 1970: 193–209. map. DT515.A2H5, v. 5

1952
Mauny, Raymond. Note historique autour des principales plantes cultivées d'Afrique occidentale. BIFAN, t. 15, avril 1953: 684–730. Q89.I5, v. 15

Examination of the major plants cultivated in West Africa. Mauny traces the origin of each and the period it was introduced in the region with citations of many Arab authors regarding these plants, including a section on cotton and its spread following the expansion of Islam. Bibliography.

1953
———La photographie aérienne et les recherches archéologiques en A.O.F. NA, no 53, janv. 1952: 6–9. illus. DT1.I513, 1952

Aerial photography has opened still another avenue for the study of African history. In this article, with a number of references to aerial photography applied to Africa, Mauny reports on several medieval sites photographed by the French Air Force. There is also a list of sites to be photographed.

1954
———Tableau géographique de l'Ouest africain au Moyen Age, d'après les sources écrites, la tradition et l'archéologie. Dakar, I.F.A.N., 1961. 587 p. illus., maps (part fold.), plans. (Mémoires de l'Institut français d'Afrique noire, no 61) DT471.M35

Mauny's magnum opus. This work of great erudition and love for Africa has inspired a number of Africanist vocations.

1955
Meillassoux, Claude. Les origines de Gumbu (Mali). BIFAN, t. 34, avril 1972: 269–298.
DT1.I5123, v. 34

Goumbou is a village in the "Cercle" of Nara in Mali along the line separating the sedentary from the nomadic populations. Meillassoux reports the foundation and early history of the settlement and its people, the Kusu, based on legends kept by the griots, two short chronicles "conservées par les deux fractions de la famille chorfa des Koreishi de Gumbu," and oral traditions. *See also* 1856.

1956
Méniaud, Jacques. Sikasso; ou, l'histoire dramatique d'un royaume noir au XIXe siècle. Paris, F. Bouchy, 1935. 208 p. illus., facsims. maps (1 fold.), plates (2 col.), ports. DT553.S5M4

1957
Miske, Ahmed. Une tribu maraboutique du Sahel: les Ahel Barikalla. BCAOF, v. 20, oct./déc. 1937: 482–506. DT521.C6, v. 20

History of the Ahl Bārik Allāh marabout tribe of Mauritania by one of its learned descendants. Provides genealogical lists and a glossary of Moorish terms.

1958
Miské, Ahmed Bâba. al-Wasīt; tableau de la Mauritanie au début du XXe siècle. Présenté par Ahmed-Bâba Miské. Paris, C. Klincksieck, 1970. 128 p. illus. PJ8390.M3S535

Anthology of Ḥassānīyah poetry augmented by a small section describing the Bīḍān society at the end of the 19th century. Aḥmad Bābā ūld Miskih, former Mauritanian ambassador to Washington, an editor of *Africasia,* and a poet himself, describes the social organization of the "Moorish society of the 19th century both glorious and decadent, living in an amazing intellectual luxury, but politically in full decay." He then relates the ethnic origin of the Bīḍān and describes their society through an analysis of their poetry, classical (Shi'r) and dialectical (lᵊ-ghna, from classical Arabic, *al-Ghinā',* meaning "singing"). *See* 2038 for the original Arabic version.

1959
Modat, *Colonel.* Portugais, Arabes et Français dans l'Adrar mauritanien. BCAOF, v. 5, oct./déc. 1922: 550–582. DT521.C6, v. 5

The Mauritanian Adrar has been a point of contact between the northern invaders from the time of the first Portuguese incursions into Wadān from Arguin about 1455. The Banī Ḥasan followed the Portuguese and last came the French, who established firm control in 1913 after a difficult period of "pacification."

1960
Mokhtar ould Hamidoun. Précis sur la Mauritanie. Saint-Louis, Sénégal, Centre IFAN-Mauritanie, 1952. 69 p. illus. (Etudes mauritaniennes, no 4)
DT553.M2M6

1961
Monnier, Marcel. Mission Binger. France noire (Côte d'Ivoire et Soudan). Paris, E. Plon, Nourrit, 1894 [1893] 298 p. front. (port.), map, plates.
DT527.B7

1962
Monteil, Charles V. Les Bambara du Ségou et du Kaarta. Etude historique, ethnographique et littéraire d'une peuplade du Soudan français. Paris, Larose, 1924. 404 p. map, plates.

Source: Brasseur, 1082.

1963
———Les Khassonké, monographie d'une peuplade du Soudan français. Paris, E. Leroux, 1915. 528 p. (Collection de la Revue du monde musulman) 4DT.869

Includes a section on the Islamization of the group.

1964
Monteil, Vincent. Essai sur le chameau au Sahara occidental. Saint-Louis du Sénégal, Centre IFAN-Mauritanie, 1952. 132 p. illus., plates. (Etudes mauritaniennes, no 2) SF249.M6

1965
———Esquisses sénégalaises: Wâlo, Kayor, Dyolof, Mourides, un visionnaire. Dakar, IFAN, 1966. 243 p. illus., maps (part fold.), ports. (Université de Dakar. Institut fondamental d'Afrique noire. Initiation et études africaines no 21) DT549.42.M65

Includes the following studies: Chronique du Wâlo sénégalais; Lat Dior, damel du Kayor (1842–1886) et l'islamisation des Wolofs; Le Dyolof et Al-Bouri Ndiaye; Une confrérie musulmane: les Mourides du Sénégal; Un visionnaire musulman sénégalais (1946–1965).

1966
Moody, Johanna E. Paul Staudinger: an early traveller to Kano. Kano studies, no. 3, June 1967: 38–53. DLC

1967
Muffet, D. J. M. Concerning brave captains; being a history of the British occupation of Kano and Sokoto and of the last stand of the Fulani forces. With a foreword by Alhaji Sir Ahmadu Bello. [London] A. Deutsch [1964] 224 p. illus., geneal. tables, fold. maps, ports. DT515.9.N5M8

1968
Muhammad, Akhbar. The origins and rise of Muslim authority in Bondoukou.
Source: ASA, Program, 15th, 1972.

1969
Muḥammad, Muḥammad Ismā'īl. Nayjīrīyah wa-Dāhūmī wa-al-Kāmīrūn. [Nigeria, Dahomey and Cameroon] [Cairo] Mu'assasat Rūz al-Yūsuf, 1961. 253 p. illus. (al-Alf kitāb, 338. al-Majmū'ah al-Ifrīqīyah) DT471.M94

1970
———Sīrāliyūn wa-Laybīryā. [Sierra Leone and Liberia] [Cairo] Mu'assasat sijil al-'Arab, 1963. 251 p. illus., maps, ports. (al-alf kitāb, 449) DT516.2.M8

1971
Muqlid, Muḥammad Yūsuf. Mūrītāniyā al-ḥadīthah: ghābiruha, ḥādiruha; aw al-'Arab albīḍ fī Ifrīqiyā al-sawdā': tārīkhuhum, aṣluhum, 'Urūbatuhum, aḥwāluhum. [Contemporary Mauritania: her remote past, present; or the White Arabs in black Africa: their history, origin, Arabness, and situation] [Beirut] Dār al-kitāh al-Lubnānī [1960] 386 p. illus., facsims., ports. DT553.M25M85

1972
Nadel, Siegfried F. A black Byzantium: the kingdom of Nupe in Nigeria. With a foreword by the Right Hon. Lord Lugard. London, New York [etc.] Published for the International Institute of African Languages and Cultures by the Oxford University Press, 1942. 420 p. illus., diagrs., front., maps (part fold.), plates, tables. DT515.N27

1973
al-Naqar, 'Umar. The pilgrimage tradition in West Africa; an historical study with special reference to the nineteenth century [Khartoum] Khartoum University Press, [1972] 160 p. illus. BP64.A4W363

The pilgrimage to Mecca, which every Muslim should perform at least once in his lifetime if possible, is a unique experience for the Islamic Ummah, or community, where Muslims from every corner of the world congregate to partake in an intense religious experience. al-Naqar, who wrote his dissertation on the subject, presents a well-documented investigation of the history of the Hajj, including the pilgrimage of some of the rulers of West Africa during the "medieval" period; he then concentrates on the 19th century and concludes with an analysis of "attitudes to the Pilgrimage." Substantial bibliography.

1974
———Takrur the history of a name. JAH, v. 10, no. 3, 1969: 365–374. DT1.J65, v. 10

Study of the origin of the term *Takrūr,* which in Arabic writings has come to refer to all Muslims from West Africa. The author also attempts to delineate the territory included in the geographical area called Takrūr.

1975
———West Africa and the pilgrimage to the Holy Places of Islam. Ibadan, Nigeria. University. *Centre of Arabic Documentation.* Research bulletin, v. 2, Jan. 1966: 37–38. DT352.4.I2a, v. 2

1976
Niane, Djibril Tamsir. Mise en place des populations de la Haute-Guinée. Recherches africaines; études guinéennes, nouv. sér., no. 2, avril-juin 1960: 40–53. DT543.A3R4, n.s. 1960

"Là ou s'arrête le 'So' [type of savanna bush] là s'arrête le Manding" says the Mandingo dictum. Niane attempts in this study to delineate the territory of the Mande-Tan, those who say "N'Ko" for "I say." Based on the local traditions of villages forming the core of Mandingo territory, namely the region between Siguiri and Bamako, he traces the migrations and political vagaries of this enterprising ethnic group.

1977
Niane, Djibril Tamsir, *and* J. Suret-Canale. Histoire de l'Afrique occidentale. [Paris] Présence africaine [1961] 223 p. illus. (part col.), ports. DT532.N5
"La présente edition du 'Manuel d'histoire de l'Afrique occidentale' reprends, pour l'essentiel, le texte de l'ouvrage publié en octobre 1960 à Conakry par le Ministère de l'éducation nationale de la République de Guinée. Cet ouvrage, exclusivement destiné aux écoles, n'avait pas été mis en vente dans le public."

1978
Norris, H. T. Yemenis in the western Sahara. JAH, v. 3, no. 2, 1964: 317–322. DT1.J65, v. 3

1979
Northern history research scheme (Project). First interim report. Zaria, 1966. 55 p. DT515.9.N5N66
Issued by the Ahmadu Bello University and the Ibadan University.
Includes lists of Arabic manuscripts held on microfilm at Ahmadu Bello University, Zaria.

1980
Notes et études sur l'islam en Afrique noire. By Marcel Chailley [and others] Paris, Peyronnet, 1962. 195 p. illus., map. IEN
Contents: Marcel Chailley, Aspects de l'islam au Mali.—A. Bourlon, Mourides et mouridisme, 1953.—B. Bichon, Les musulmans de la subdivision de Kombissiry (Haute-Volta).—F. J. Amon d'Aby, Attitude de l'animisme face à l'islam et au christianisme.—F. Quesnot, Influence du Mouridisme sur le Tidjanisme et les cadres maraboutiques de l'Islam.

1981
al-Nuwayy, Ibrāhīm Ṣāliḥ. Tārīkh al-Islām wa-ḥayāt al- 'Arab fī Imbirāṭūrīyat Kānim burnū. [History of Islam and the life of Arabs in the Kanem-Bornu Empire] By Ibrāhīm Ṣāliḥ ibn Yūnis ibn Muḥammad al-awwal ibn Yūnis ibn Ibrāḥīm ibn Muḥammad al-Makkī ibn 'Amrū al-Ḥusaynī al-Nuwayy. [Khartoum, Jāmi 'at al-Khartūm, kulliyat al-ādāb, shu'bat abḥāth al-Sūdān, 1970] 285 leaves (Silsilat dirāsāt fī al-turāth al-Sūdānī, 14)
DT515.9.B6N89

1982
Ọlọruntimehin, B. Ọlatunji. 'Abd al-Qadir's mission as a factor in Franco-Tukulor relations, 1885–1887. Genève-Afrique/Africa-Geneva, v. 7, no 2, 1968: 33–50. DT1.G44, v. 7

1983
———Resistance movements in the Tukulor empire. CEA, v. 8, 1968: 123–143. DT1.C3, v. 8
Study of the resistance to the Tukulor empire of al-Hajj 'Umar ibn Sa'īd Tall (1852–64) by populations of the Senegambia who consistently refused to grant the Tukulor rule any legitimacy. The history is divided into two phases: the first witnessed the establishment of the empire and the clash between the Tijānīyah and the Qādirīyah; the second phase culminated in a military confrontation between al-Ḥājj 'Umar and the local populations who, eventually, collaborated with the French forces to bring about the collapse of the state.

1984
———The Segu Tukulor Empire. [London] Longmans [1972] 357 p. illus., maps, ports. (Ibadan history series) DT532.3.O44
Comprehensive study of the Segou Empire. The author proposes to "deal with the process of political unification, administration and politics in the Western Sudan under the leadership of the Tukulor."

1985
———The treaty of Niagassola, 1886: an episode in Franco-Samori relations in the era of the scramble. JHSN, v. 4, June 1969: 601–614.
DT515.A2H5, v. 4

1986
L'opinion musulmane au Soudan et les évènements de Turquie. L'Afrique française, 1915: 90–94.
DLC-Micro 03878
"Récit de troubles provoqués par quelques éléments islamisés. Addresses de loyalisme de Cheikh Sidi El Kheïr (un des chefs des Tâleb Mokhtar), des notables de Oualata et de Tombouctou."—(abstract by Brasseur, 1766)

1987
Otton Loyewski, d', *Lt.* Coppolani et la Mauritanie. Revue d'histoire des colonies, t. 26, 2. trimestre, 1938: 1–70. JV1801.R4, v. 26
Xavier Coppolani initiated, in 1901, the conquest of Mauritania, which was not "pacified" until 1934. Coppolani relied upon tribal rivalries. Using a politics of divide and rule—"Je m'applique à maintenir les divisions, à les acentuer"—he saw the need to draw religious leaders and maraboutic tribes to the French cause, "ce qu'il faut c'est . . . les attirer et les annexer, en faire des agents de

notre politique." The success of his policy was cut short by his death at the age of 39 in 1905. Otton Loweski recalls nostalgically, "Ce qui aurait pu être fait par Coppolani en 1905 avec quelques goumiers nécessitera en 1908 une véritable éxpédition d'un millier d'hommes et de multiples combats."

1988
Ouane, Ibrahima Mamadou. L'énigme du Macina. Monte-Carlo, Regain [1952] 187 p. DT551.O8
'Ajībū, son of al-Ḥājj 'Umar, was named ruler of Masina and Dinguiraye by Colonel Archinard on May 4, 1893. Ouane, a great-grandson of al-Ḥājj 'Umar, provides the history of his family and shows the great friendship it harbored for France.

1989
Pageard, Robert. Notes sur l'histoire des Bambaras de Ségou. Clichy [France] 1957. 32 p.
Source: Brasseur, 3028.

1990
Palmer, *Sir* Herbert Richmond. The girgam. *In* African Society. Journal, v. 12, Oct. 1912: 71–83. DT1.R62, v. 12
According to Palmer, this *girgam,* or list of ancestors, translated by Mallan 'Umar of "Kazauri," was written in Kanuri and not Arabic as were those procured by Barth and Nachtigal. The Kanuri text is provided with an English translation.

1991
———The Bornu Sahara and Sudan. New York, Negro Universities Press [1970] 296 p. illus., facsims., maps (part fold.) DT515.9.B6P3 1970
Reprint of the 1936 ed.
One of the earliest attempts to write the history of a region on the basis of local African sources. Palmer, who was a resident of the Bornu Province and spent 26 years in the area, presents the political development of Bornu using various mahram and girgam as his main sources of information.

1992
Panikkar, Kavalam Madhusudan. The serpent and the crescent; a history of the Negro empires of western Africa. New York, Asia Publication House [1964, c1963] 286 p. map (on lining-papers), geneal. table. DT471.P3

1993
Paris. Université. *Centre des hautes études administratives sur l'Afrique et l'Asie.* Carte des religions de l'Afrique. République de la Côte d'Ivoire. 1957. 1 v. (various pagings) BL2470.I8P3

1994
———Carte des religions de l'Afrique de l'ouest; notice et statistiques. [Paris, Documentation française, 1966] 135 p. BL2465.P26

1995
Paris-Teynac, E.J. Notes sur les puits de l'Azaouad (Soudan). NA, no 53, 1952 janv. 1952: 24–29. illus. DT1.I513
The Azwad region north of the Niger bend and Timbuktu was a transit region for the trans-Saharan trade. Wells were of great importance and formed a chain of "coaling stations." Paris discusses the wells of the area and the building techniques employed.

1996
Parrinder, Edward G. The story of Ketu, an ancient Yoruba kingdom. 2d [rev.] ed. Edited by I. A. Akinjogbin. [Ibadan] Ibadan University Press, 1967. 106 p. fold. map. DT513.P3 1967
Includes references to conflicts with Muslim populations.

1997
Périé, J. Notes historiques sur la région de Maradi (Niger). BIFAN, t. 1, avril/juil. 1939: 377–400. Q89.I5, v. 1
Historical study of the Maradi region in southern Niger bordering on northern Nigeria. Based on local traditions gathered by the Tilho Mission (1906–09), it investigates the origin of the Hausa, Gobirawa, Tuareg, and Fulbe of the area and presents a history of the sultanates of Gobir and Maradi in the 19th century. Five genealogical tables are annexed.

1998
Peroz, E. L'empire de l'Almamy Emir Samory. Besançon, 1888.
Source: Joucla, 7755.

1999
Person, Yves. Samori et la Sierra Leone. CEA, v. 7, 1. cahier 1967: 5–26. DT1.C3, v. 7
Historical analysis of contacts in Sierra Leone between Samory and European traders settled on the Atlantic coast. Person traces the conflict between Dyula traders and the advancing colonial powers that culminated in the collapse of the Samory empire.

2000
Philibert, [Charles] La conquête pacifique de l'intérieur africain; nègres, musulmans et chrétiens; par le Général Philibert. Paris, E. Leroux, 1889. 376 p. illus., maps (part. fold.), plates, port. DT527.P54

2001
Piaszewicz, Stanislas. A story of the Wala people; a Hausa text from the IASAR/152 manuscript. Africana bulletin, nr 10, 1969: 53–76. DT19.9.P6A65

The Institute of African Studies, University of Legon (Ghana), holds a significant collection of historical records on Africa. "The Story of the Wala People," a Hausa manuscript in Ajami script, was translated and commented on by Piaszewicz as a doctoral dissertation. The Wala, who are centered around Wa in northern Ghana, are a Muslim people. Included are the Hausa text and its transliteration in addition to an English translation. *See also* 1661.

2002
———The story of Wala, our country. Africana bulletin, nr 11, 1969: 59–78. DT199.P6A65, 1969

Another version of the preceding history based on the manuscript IASAR/45. *See also* 1661.

2003
Pol-Pagès. La Mahométisme dans le "Hombori" en 1922 (Région de Tombouctou—Soudan Français). BCAOF, v. 16, juil./sept. 1933: 360–410. DT521.C6, v. 16

Pol-Pagès, who was "Administrateur des Colonies, commandant le Bas Sénégal," presents Islam in the Hombori, as described by the "Chef de canton" and the qadi of the city. After a general introduction, he explores the people, institutions, doctrines and cults, religious fraternities, Shari'a and local customs, the social action of Islam on the indigenous populations, the impact of Islam in the economic field, and French policies toward Islam in the area. Pol-Pagès concludes that "le programme de notre politique vis-à-vis de l'Islam peut à notre avis, dans ce pays, se résumer en quelques lignes: appel à nous par une confiance absolue de tous les indigènes, developpement de leurs intérêts agricoles, commerciaux et industriels, respect de leurs coutumes tant qu'elles ne lèsent point nos droits et leur dispenser sans réserve les bienfaits de l'assistance médicale et de l'enseignement de la langue française."

2004
Pottier, René. Histoire du Sahara. Paris, Nouvelles editions latines [1947] 334 p. (L'Histoire vivante) DT333.P68

2005
Poulet, Georges. Les Maures de l'Afrique occidentale française. Préf. de Binger. Paris, A. Challamel, 1904. 172 p. 4DT.982

2006
Prost, André. L'Islam en Afrique occidentale. Grands lacs; revue générale des missions d'Afrique, v. 63, oct. 15, 1947: 11–19. BV3500.A35, v. 63

2007
Quenum, Maximilien. Légendes africaines, Côte-d'Ivoire, Soudan, Dahomey. Rochefort-Sur-Mer, Impr. A. Thoynon, 1946. 10 p. illus. 4PQ.Fr306

Includes a section on "Fama Soundiata," p. 45–72.

2008
Quinn, Charlotte A. Mandingo kingdoms of the Senegambia; traditionalism, Islam, and European expansion. Evanston, Ill., Northwestern University Press, 1972. 211 p. maps. DT509.42.Q56

The three-cornered conflict in the Senegambia between the animistic Mandingo kingdoms, the supratribal Muslim grouping, and the European intruders form the basis of this thoroughly researched work. Charlotte Quinn has based her study on oral traditions, British official documents, and a plethora of other sources to document her analysis of the Soninke-Marabout wars and Ma Diakhu Ba (1809–1867), the leader of the Islamic revivalist movement.

2009
———A nineteenth century Fulbe state. JAH, v. 12, no. 3, 1971: 427–440. DT1.J65, v. 12

About 1867 Fulbe living in the Mandingo kingdoms of Tomani and Jimara on the south bank of the Gambia river revolted against their Mandingo landlords. Under their leader, Alfa Molo, the Fulbe went on to destroy the decadent Mandingo state system over much of the Gambia's south bank, and south into Portuguese Guinea, in one of the few determinative conquests in Gambia history. A new state emerged from this revolution which was based on the political dissatisfactions and ethnic consciousness of the Fulbe, its institutions moulded by the political skills and vigorous personality of Alfa's son, Musa Molo.

Hostility towards the old Mandingo ruling classes which unified Musa's following in the early years of the Fulbe revolt dissipated with their continuous victories. For the following decade the marabouts leading a Muslim *jihād* in the Senegambia fulfilled the role of the enemy without, as by edict and assassination Musa worked to stabilize his kingdom.

Although both Fuladu and its Muslim neighbour states were superseded by European colonial rule at the beginning of the twentieth century, Musa Molo had made a brilliant attempt to unify the Gambia valley during the chaotic last years of the pre-colonial period.—(Abstract supplied, modified)

2010

———Niumi: a nineteenth-century Mandingo kingdom. Africa, v. 38, Oct. 1968: 443–455.
PL8000.I6, v. 38

2011

Quiquandon, F. Histoire de la puissance mandingue d'après la légende et la tradition. Les Traouré dans le Kénédougou jusqu'au moment de l'arrivée de la mission Quinquandon. *In* Société de géographie commerciale de Bordeaux. Bulletin, t. 15, 1892: 305–318; t. 15, 1892: 400–429.
DLC-Micro 38304

A history of the Mandingo people based on oral tradition, including the reigns of Sundiata, Kanku Mūsā, the Traoré in Sikasso, and the 19th century.

2012

Reeve, Henry F. The Gambia; its history, ancient, mediaeval, and modern, together with its geographical, geological, and ethnographical conditions, and a description of the birds, beasts, and fishes found therein. New York, Negro Universities Press [1969] 287 p. illus., maps, port.
DT509.R4 1969

Reprint of the 1912 ed.

2013

Richer, A. Les Touareg du Niger (Région de Tombouctou, Gao): les Oulliminden. Paris, Larose, 1924. 359 p.

"Une première partie (pages 13 à 112) traite des Touareg nigériens avant la conquête française, et elle est interessante; mais la deuxième partie, de beaucoup la plus importante (pages 113 à 340)—'Les Oulliminden depuis la conquête française'—constitue la portion principale et véritablement originale du volume. . . . Il [Richer] a surtout compulsé et utilisé les archives inédites des postes de Tombouctou, Gao, Bamba, Bourem, Ménaka, Kidal, Dori, Tillabéry, Ansongon, etc., postes dont plusieurs n'existent plus à l'heure actuelle."—(from a review by Maurice Delafosse in *Revue de l'histoire des colonies françaises,* t. 13, 2. trimestre, 1925: 297–301. JV1801.R4, v. 13).

Source: Brasseur, 1969.

2014

Richet, Etienne. En Mauritanie. La tribu maraboutique des Oulad Biri. La Réforme sociale, 8. sér., v. 7, janv./juin 1919: 405–427.
H3.R3, 1919

Investigation of the Awlād Bīrī, a tribe located in the Trarza region of Mauritania. They are a maraboutic group that has not renounced the right to carry weapons. The author provides information on their history and their political, social, religious, and material life.

2015

Rivière, Claude. Bilan de l'islamisation de la Guinée. Afrique documents, no 105/106, 1969: 319–359.
DT1.A479, 1969

2016

Robinson, Charles H. Hausaland, or, Fifteen hundred miles through the central Soudan. London, S. Low, Marston, 1896. 304 p. front., illus., facsim., plates, ports., fold. map.
DT518.H3R6

Appendix II: The Hausa Association: p. 286–292. Appendix IV: List of Books Published on the Hausa People or Language During the Last Half Century: p. 293–295.

2017

Robinson, David. The impact of al-Hajj 'Umar on the historical traditions of the Fulbe. *In* Folklore Institute. Journal, v. 8, Aug./Dec. 1971: 101–113.

Source: International African bibliography, v. 3, July 1973.

2018

Rougier, F. L'Islam à Banamba. BCAOF, v. 13, avril/juin 1930: 217–263.
DT521.C6, v. 13

Study of Islam in Banamba, located in what was then the "Cercle" of Bamako, encompassing the people, institutions, doctrine and cult, religious orders, Muslim law, impact of Islam on the local populations, and Islam's influence in the political and economic fields. The concluding paragraph suggests that Koranic schools be expropriated by the government in order to control the evolution of Islam in Banamba.

2019

Rousseau, R. Le Sénégal d'autrefois. Etude sur le Cayor; cahiers de Yoro Dyâo. BCAOF, v. 26, avril/juin 1933: 237–298.
DT521.C6, v. 26

2020
———Le Sénégal d'autrefois. Etude sur le Oualo; cahiers de Yoro Dyâo. BCAOF, v. 12, janv./juin 1929: 133–211. DT521.C6, v. 12

2021
———Le Sénégal d'autrefois: Etude sur le Toubé; papiers Rawane Boy. BCAOF, v. 14, juil./sept. 1931: 334–364. DT521.C6, v. 14

2022
———Le Sénégal d'autrefois. Seconde étude sur le Cayor (Compléments tirés des manuscrits de Yoro Dyâo) BIFAN, t. 3, janv./oct. 1941: 79–144. Q89.I5, v. 3

2023
Saïd, Mohamed. Les Touareg de la région de Tombouctou; leur exode vers le nord-est. Revue tunisienne, v. 10, janv. 1903: 34–49; v. 10, mars 1903: 116–123; v. 10, mai 1903: 209–214. DT241.R45, v. 10

2024
———Les tribus arabes de la région de Tombouctou. Revue tunisienne, v. 11, nov. 1904: 479–488. DT241.R45, v. 11

2025
Saint Croix, F. W. de. The Fulani of Northern Nigeria: some general notes. Farnborough, Gregg, 1972. 74 p. DT515.42.S25 1972

First published in 1945.

2026
Saint-Martin, Yves J. La volonté de paix d'El Hadj Omar et d'Ahmadou dans leurs relations avec la France. BIFAN, t. 30, juil. 1968: 785–802. DT1.I5123, v. 30

European historians of the colonial period and "certain African writers and journalists" have held opposite views on al-Ḥājj 'Umar and his son Aḥmadū, but according to Saint-Martin both views have contributed to the image of the men as "exemplary resistants to colonization."

Saint-Martin's thesis is that both al-Ḥājj 'Umar and his son "desired to retain peaceful relations with the French." His sources for this belief are a number of oral traditions, official reports, and correspondence, as well as published monographs. *See also* 2031.

2027
Saint-Père, J. H. Création du Royaume du Fouta Djallon. BCAOF, v. 12, juil./déc. 1929: 484–555. DT521.C6, v. 12

Story of the Fouta Djallon Kingdom based on oral traditions as told by the old "Karamokobe, Tiernobe, Dielibe, Hodobe, and Kikakabe" and on old manuscripts lent to the author by the learned men of Koïne.

2028
———Les Sarakollé du Guidimaka. Paris, E. Larose, 1925. 188 p. (Publications du Comité d'études historiques et scientifiques)

Source: Brasseur 1076.

2029
Salifou, André. Le Damagaram, ou Sultanat de Zinder au 19e siècle. Niamey, Centre nigérien de recherche en sciences humaines, 1971. 318 p. (Etudes nigériennes, 27) DLC

2030
Samb, Amar. L'Islam et l'histoire du Sénégal. BIFAN, t. 33, juil. 1971: 461–507. DT1.I5123, v. 33

2031
———Sur el Hadj Omar (à propos d'un article d'Yves Saint-Martin). BIFAN, t. 30, juil. 1968: 803–805. DT1.I5123, v. 30

Comment on an article by Saint-Martin (*see* 2026) suggesting that al-Ḥājj 'Umar and his son Aḥmadū wanted to retain peaceful relations with the French. Samb, basing his case on political and religious arguments, flatly denies and rejects Saint-Martin's thesis. *See also* 2247.

2032
Sanderval, A. Oliver. De l'Atlantique au Niger par le Foutah-Djallon; carnet de voyage. Paris, P. Ducrocq, 1882. 407 p. illus. IEN

2033
Ṣaqr, 'Aṭīyah. al-Islām fī Nayjiryā. [Islam in Nigeria] Cairo. al-Jāmi' al-Azhar. Majallat al-Azhar, m. 32, Dec. 1960: 730–735. BP1.C3, v. 32

After a short historical note on the introduction of Islam by the Almoravids in the 10th and 11th centuries and on the Sokoto Empire, Ṣaqr suggests that Muslims in Nigeria are very religious though their beliefs are sometimes "mixed with legends, sorcery and jugglery." He then describes the various Islamic associations, such as the Anṣār al-Dīn and Anwār al-Dīn societies, and the only Muslim periodical, *al-Ḥaqīqah,* published in Lagos. The essay ends with a note on the struggle between Islam and Christianity for the conversion of the Animist populations of the Bauchi plateau.

2034
Schacht, Joseph. Islam in Northern Nigeria. Studia Islamica, v. 8, 1957: 123–146. BP1.S8, v. 8

The development of the study of Islam in northern Nigeria is best illustrated by Schacht's statement in 1950: "I do not know of a single publication that treats of Islam in Northern Nigeria as such." In this essay on his visit to the region under the auspices of the Colonial Office to report on the position of Islamic law, he discusses the propagation of Islam, the development of Muslim education, and the judicial system. He concludes that "the nearest parallel I know to the present state of Islam in Northern Nigeria, in more than one respect, is the form it took, many centuries ago, under the Almoravids."

2035
Schultze, A. The sultanate of Bornu. Translated with additions and appendices by P. A. Benton. London, Cass, 1968. 401 p. (Cass library of African studies; general studies, no. 50)
DT515.9.B6S3 1968

First published in 1913.

2036
Séré de Rivières, Edmond. Histoire du Niger. Paris, Berger-Levrault, 1965. 311 p. illus., plates. (Mondes d'outre-mer. Série histoire) DT547.S38

2037
Shākir, Maḥmūd. Ghīniyā. [Guinea]. Damascus, Dār al-Fikr [196–?] 79 p. maps. (Mawāṭin al-Shu'ūb al-Islāmīyah fī Ifrīqiyā, 1) DLC

2038
al-Shinqīṭī, Aḥmad ibn al-Amīn. al-Wasīṭ fī tarājim udabā' shinqīṭ wa-al-kalām 'alā tilka al-bilād taḥdīdan wa takhṭīṭan wa- 'ādātihim wa-akhlāqihim wa-ma yata'allaq bi-dhālika. [The mediator in the lives of the Shinqit scholars, and discourse on the country, locationally and descriptively; their habits and manners and all that pertains to these] al-ṭab'ah 2. bi-'ināyat Fu'ād Sayyid. Cairo, Maktabat al-Khankā, 1961. 582 p. PJ8390.M3S5

See also 1958 for a French translation of the work.

2039
Skinner, Elliott P. Christianity and Islam among the Mossi. American anthropologist, v. 60, Dec. 1958: 1102–1119. GN1.A5, v. 60

2040
Smith, H. F. C. A neglected theme of West African history: the Islamic revolution of the 19th century. JHSN, v. 2, Dec. 1961: 169–185.
DT515.A2H5, v. 2

2041
Smith, Pierre. Les Diakhanké: Histoire d'une dispersion. *In* Société d'anthropologie de Paris. Bulletin et mémoires, t. 8, fasc. 3/4, 1965: 231–262.
GN2.S61, v. 8

2042
Sölken Heinz. Die Geschichte von Kabi nach Imamu Umari. *In* Akademie der Wissenschaften, *Berlin.* Institut für Orientforschung. Mitteilungen, Bd. 7, Heft 1, 1959: 129–162; Bd. 9, Hefte 1, 1963: 30–163. PJ5.A5A25, v. 7, 9

2043
———Reise in Wangara. *In* Wort und Religion; studien zur Afrikanistik, Missionswissenschaft, Religionswissenschaft, Ernest Dammann zum 65. Geburtstag. Hrsg. Hans-Jürgen Greschat und Hermann Junggraithmayr. Stuttgart, Evangelischer Missionsverlag [1969] p. 127–132. PL8003.W6

2044
Sow, Alfâ Ibrahîm. Chroniques et récits du Foûta Djalon. Paris, C. Klincksieck, 1968. 262 p. plates. (Langues et littératures de l'Afrique noire, 3)
DT553.F8S6

French and Fulfulde.

2045
Staude, Wilhelm. La légende royale des Kouroumba. JOSAF, t. 31, fasc. 2, 1961: 209–260.
DT1.S65, v. 31

2046
Stewart, Charles C. A new document concerning the origins of the Awalad Ibiri and the N'Tishait. BIFĀN, t. 31, janv. 1969: 309–319.
DT1.I5123, v. 31

Reproduction and translation of an Arabic manuscript discovered in 1966 beneath the tomb of Maryam al-Madhkurah, the grandmother of the wife of Shaykh Sīdiyā al-Kabīr (1782–1868), near the well of Bir Allah, 100 kilometers northwest of Boutilimit in southern Mauritania. The body of the document, written in Maghribi style, comprises a genealogy of the Awlād Ibīrī of the eastern Trarza region. Stewart, through internal criticism and circumstantial evidence, tends to doubt the authenticity of the work which, nevertheless, sheds new light on this period of Mauritanian history.

2047
Tardivet, R. Les sultans de l'Aïr. BCAOF, v. 11, oct./déc. 1928: 689–694. DT521.C6, v. 11

Free translation of an Arabic manuscript on the history of the sultans of Agadez from the reign of Yūnus (15th century) to Sultan 'Umarū.

2048
Tauxier, Louis. Un dernier chapitre de l'histoire de Bondoukou. Revue d'ethnographie et des traditions populaires, 8. année, no 31/32, 1927: 213–226. NNC

2049
———Histoire des Bambara. Paris, P. Geuthner, 1942. 226 p. front. (port.), illus. (map) GN652.B2T3

After presenting the sources for Bambara (Bamana) history, Tauxier traces their history under Mamari Coulibali, and describes the Kaarta Bambara, the settlement of the Tukulor in Segou, and the French period starting in 1890.

2050
———Moeurs et histoire des Peuls. I. Origines, II. Les Peuls de l'Issa-ber et du Macina, III. Les Peuls du Fouta-Djallon. Avec 23 gravures et 1 carte. Paris, Payot, 1937. 419 p. illus. (map), xvi plates on 8 leaves. (Bibliothèque scientifique) GN652.F9T3

With an introduction of 116 pages, Tauxier investigates the various theories regarding the origin of the Fulbe. He then describes the material life, customs, and history of the Fulbe before and after the Tukulor conquest.

2051
———Le noir de Bondoukou, Koulangos, Dyoulas, Abrons, etc. Paris, Editions E. Leroux, 1921. 770 p. (Etudes soudanaises) 4DT.1011

See the review by Delafosse in BCAOF, v. 4, oct./déc. 1921: 702–705 (DT521.C6).

2052
Temple, Olive S. M. M. Notes on the tribes, provinces, emirates, and states of the northern provinces of Nigeria, compiled from official reports. Edited by C. L. Temple. New York, Barnes & Noble [1967] 595 p. geneal. tables. DT515.T45 1967

Reprint of the 2d ed., 1922, with bibliography and index added.

2053
Tidjani, Ahmed. al-Islām fī al-Sinighāl, abḥāth wa-dirāsāt ḥawla intishār al-Islām wa-al-fikr al-Islāmī fī Ifrīqiyā, wa taṣwīr ḥāl al-Muslimīn fī Ifrīqiyā al-Gharbīyah. [Islam in Senegal, research and studies on the spread of Islam and Muslim thought in Africa, and description of the status of Muslims in West Africa] Beirut, Dār Maktabat al-Ḥayāt [1970?] 130 p. BP88.T47I8

2054
Tordoff, William. A note on the relations between Samory and king Prempeh of Ashanti. Ghana notes and queries, No. 3, Sept./Dec. 1961: 5–7. DT510.A1H553, 1961

2055
Traoré, Dominique. Les relations de Samory et de l'état de Kong. NA, no 47, juil. 1950: 96–97. DT1.I513, 1950

2056
Trimingham, J. Spencer. The Christian church and Islam in West Africa. London, SCM Press [1955] 55 p. illus., map. (I.M.C. research pamphlets, no. 3) BV3540.T7

Based on material collected under the sponsorship of the Church Missionary Society and the Methodist Missionary Society.

2057
———Islam in West Africa. Oxford, Clarendon Press, 1959. 262 p. diagr., fold. map. BP64.A4W4

Analytical study of Islam, its fraternities and development, and its impact on the social and cultural manifestations of the region.

2058
Trimingham, J. Spencer, *and* Christopher Fyfe. The early expansion of Islam in Sierra Leone. Sierra Leone bulletin of religion, v. 2, Dec. 1960: 33–40. DLC

2059
al-Tuwaṭī, 'Abd al-Qādir ibn Abī Bakr. Le Sahara et le Soudan: Documents historiques. Revue de l'Orient, v. 13, 1853: 73–91. DS1.R4, v. 13

Translated by J. Bargés.

2060
Urvoy, Yves F. M. A. Chronologie de Bornou. JOSAF, t. 11, 1941: 21–31. DT1.S65, v. 11

The chronology of Bornu rulers was first given by H. Barth, then modified by H. R. Palmer in his *Sudanese Memoirs* (*see* 730). Urvoy, using both dynastic lists—Girgam—and Arabic authors, proposes a modified chronology of 72 rulers beginning with the mythical Sayf to Dunama IX (1810–17). A genealogical chart is included.

2061
———Histoire de l'empire du Bornou. Paris, Larose, 1949. 166 p. maps (part fold.) (Mémoires de l'Institut français d'Afrique noire, no 7) DT515.U7

Study of the Bornu Empire covering Kanem (700-1224), the loss of Kanem (1224–1507), the New Empire (1507–1819), and the Kanemi Bornu (19th century). The introduction of Islam in the 12th century and its development is traced up to the Rabāḥ interlude and the French occupation. The appendix includes a section on correspondence between Muḥammad Bello and Shaykh al-Amīn al-Kānimī and another on the development of commerce in the area. The style is somewhat uneven as Urvoy died before revising his first draft.

2062
———Histoire des Oulliminden de l'Est. BCAOF, v. 16, janv./mars 1933: 66–97. DT521.C6, v. 16

Historical analysis of the eastern Oulliminden Tuaregs. Refers to a translation of a "History of Ader" written on 1907 by "Mallam-Be-Detchoukou," marabout of the Sultan of Agadez, and included in *Monographie du Cercle de Tahoua* by Lieutenant Peignot (1912). An interesting inclusion is the text of the surrender document of the Oulliminden.

2063
———Petit atlas ethno-démographique du Soudan entre Sénégal et Tchad. Paris, Larose, 1942. 46 p. illus., 3 fold. maps, 4 plates. GN651.U7

Thèse complémentaire—Université de Paris.

Concise study of the Sudan between Senegal and Chad, including pictures and drawings of dwelling types and tribal scarifications. Maps show population density, distribution of ethnic groups, and Muslim and Animist areas of concentration. The last is of interest for comparative purposes as it was compiled about 1939.

2064
Vieillard, Gilbert P. Notes sur les Peuls du Fouta-Djallon. BIFAN, t. 2, janv./avril 1940: 85–210. Q89.I5, v. 2

A comprehensive study of the Fulbe populations of the Fouta Djallon "Cercles" of Labé, Makou, and Kindia. Annexed are translations of a poem by Tierno Mohammadou Tierno Sâdou on "God and Work in the Fields" and another incantation to the Lord.

2065
Wade, Amadou. Chronique du Wâlo sénégalais (1186?–1885). Translated by Bassirou Cissé and annotated by Vincent Monteil. BIFAN, t. 26, juil./oct. 1964: 440–498. DT1.I5123, v. 26

Translation and annotation of a chronicle on the Senegalese Walo—centered in Dagana—dictated by Amadou Wade in Wolof from Arabic notes he had prepared. Contains valuable information regarding Walo relations with the surrounding Muslim groups and the efforts of the Berbers to convert the Walo populations. Included is a dynastic list of the 52 brak of Walo (1186–1855).

2066
Wane, Yaya. Etat actuel de la documentation au sujet des Toucouleurs. BIFAN, t. 25, juil./oct. 1963: 457–477. DT1.I5123, v. 25

Survey of present documentation on the Tukulor. The bibliography has four major sections: history, ethnology-anthropology, economics, and archival materials. A subsection on ethnology includes six titles on Islam.

2067
Westermann, Diedrich. Islam in the West and Central Sudan. International review of missions, v. 1, Oct. 1912: 618–653. BV2351.I6, v. 1

2068
Wilks, Ivor. Islam in Ghana history: an outline. Ghana bulletin of theology, v. 2, Dec. 1962: 20–28. CtY-D

2069
———The Northern factor in Ashanti history. [Legon] Institute of African Studies, University College of Ghana, 1961. 46 p. illus. DT507.W5

See also his "The Northern factor in Ashanti history: Begho and the Mande" (JAH, v. 2, no. 1 1961: 25–34. DT1.J65) in which he concludes that "from its inception the Ashanti kingdom was in commercial contact not only with the European trading companies on the coast to the south, but also with the great towns of the Niger bend to the north," providing a new dimension to the trans-Saharan trade linking the Sahel with North Africa and Europe. Wilks shows the role of the urban centers in present-day Ghana in the trade network.

2070
Zahrān, 'Umar Ṭal'at. al-Islām fī Sīrālīyūn. [Islam in Sierra Leone]. *In* Cairo. al-Jāmi' al-Azhar. Majallat al-Azhar, v. 21, 1949: 281–285.

BP1.C3, v. 21

Islam was brought to Sierra Leone by Fulbe and Mandingo traders as early as the 1700's. Zahrān relates the opposition of Col. R. Doherty, governor of Sierra Leone, and relations between the Muslims of Fourah Bay and Dinguiraye, in central Guinea, where children received a solid religious education.

2071

Zakī, ʻAbd al-Raḥmān. al-Islām wa-al-Muslimūn fi Gharb Ifrīqiyā. [Islam and Muslims in West Africa] *In* Majallat al-dirāsāt al-Islāmīyah, m. 2, Oct. 1969: 138–182. DS36.M24, v. 2

Substantial study on the spread of Islam in West Africa from a traditional Muslim viewpoint. The author presents the beginnings of Islam in Africa; the Islamization of the various ethnic groups; the Sufi sects of West Africa; and Islam today in Nigeria, and Chad. Noteworthy is a section on Aḥmad Bābā al-Tinbuqtī (1553–1627) with a partial list of his writings.

2072

Zemp, Hugo. La légende des griots malinke. CEA, v. 6, 4. cahier, 1966: 611–642. DT1.C3, v. 6

Investigation of the Malinke griots based upon their oral traditions. Zemp traces back Sourakata, their ancestor, to Surāqah ibn Mālik ibn Juʻshum, who is mentioned by the Arab historian Ibn Isḥāq. Zemp also reports the cosmogonic myth referred to by the griots, concluding that more research is needed to settle the question of their origins.

Languages & Linguistics

2073

Ba, Oumar. Vocabulaire de base. Introduction à l'étude du poular du Fouta sénégalais. BIFAN, t. 30, juil. 1968: 1271–1282. DT1.I5123, v. 30

List of basic vocabulary of Senegalese Fouta Fulfulde by a Fula scholar attached to IFAN. The work, divided into 27 sections, is of interest insofar as it shows the impact of Arabic on Fulfulde.

2074

Bivar, A. D. H. The Arabic calligraphy of West Africa. African language review, v. 7, 1968: 3–15. plates. DLC

The discussion is based largely on Nigerian material. A heavy, angular Kufic script found in early (16th-17th centuries) Korans from Bornu, and in the derived form known as Ajami in many later Nigerian Korans, as well as on the Gao tombstones (1100 A.D.), would appear to derive from a primitive Ifrīquī style general in North Africa until Almoravid times. But Almoravid rule in Spain, and the emigration from Spain in later centuries, led to the acceptance of a more delicate Andalusian style throughout North Africa, and this spread to West Africa, but probably only after the Moroccan conquest of 1590. In the 18th century, elements from current Egyptian book-hands influenced the devolved Andalusian, and produced a style employed for the literature of the Fulani jihad, which may be termed Jihādī. A later more flowing style produced in the learned circles of Sokoto may be termed Tābiʻī. The lateness of Egyptian and Eastern, as opposed to Maghribī and Andalusian, influences is to be noted.—(From the synopsis in *African abstracts*, v. 20, July 1969: 112)

2075

———A dated Qur'an from Bornu. Nigeria magazine, no. 65, June 1960: 199–203. DT515.N47, 1960

2076

Canu, Gaston. Remarques sur quelques emprunts lexicaux en Mò:re (dialecte de Ouagadougou). The Journal of West African languages, v. 5, Jan. 1968: 25–34. PL8017.J65, v. 5

Investigation of loan words in Mò:re. Most of these borrowings are from Arabic, either directly or via another language such as Songhay, Mandingo, Bamana, or Fulfulde. Canu, who worked on a lexical corpus of 1,296 words, divides the borrowings into assimilated and nonassimilated. He found that 52.5 percent of the borrowed words came from Arabic.

2077

Charlton, Lionel E. O. A Hausa reading book containing a collection of texts reproduced in facsimile from native manuscripts. London, New York, Oxford University Press, 1908. 83 p. 45 facsims. IEN

2078

Davidson, Basil. West African Arabic scripts. West Africa, no. 2433, Jan. 18, 1964: 59. DT491.W4, 1964

2079

Delafosse, Maurice. Les noms des noirs musulmans du Soudan occidental. RMM, t. 12, oct. 1910: 257–261. DS36.R4, v. 12

Short notice on the Africanization of Arab names as a result of the Islamization of the Sudanic belt.

2080
Dianoux, H.-J. de. Les mots d'emprunt d'origine arabe dans la langue songhay. BIFAN, t. 23, juil./oct. 1961: 596–606. DT1.I5123, v. 23

Arabic, as the vehicle of Islamic teachings, started to spread in the region of the Niger Bend in the 13th century. It was reinforced with the Moroccan conquest of 1591 and remains of considerable importance in this transit region. De Dianoux studies the impact of Arabic on the Gao dialect of Songhay. Most of the terms, as expected, refer to the cultural, religious, and commercial spheres where Arab influence was predominant. Thorough treatment of the linguistic assimilation and transformation of Arabic phonemes when transferred into Songhay.

2081
Dupuis, Auguste V. Essai de méthode pratique pour l'étude de la langue songoi, ou songaï, langue commerciale et politique de Tombouctou et du Moyen-Niger. Suivie d'une légende en songoï avec traduction et d'un dictionnaire songoï-français. Paris, E. Leroux, 1917. 210 p. PL8685.D8

2082
Féral, G. Notes sur la morphologie du verbe dans le dialecte Hassane (Mauritanie). BIFAN, t. 13, janv. 1951: 214–250. Q89.I5, v. 13

Analysis of the morphology of the Ḥassānīyah dialect of Arabic spoken in Mauritania. Both the triliteral and quadriliteral forms of the verb, as well as the irregular verbs, are presented with a profusion of examples.

2083
Gaden, Henri. Un chant de guerre Toucouleur. BCAOF [v. 25?] 1916: 349; [v. 26?] 1917: 497. MH

2084
Goerner, Margaret, Youssef Salman, *and* Peter Armitage. Two essays on Arabic loan words in Hausa. [Zaria, Northern Nigeria] Dept. of Languages, Ahmadu Bello University, 1966. 32 leaves. (Ahmadu Bello University. Dept. of Languages. Occasional paper no. 7) P25.A34 no. 7

Contents: Foreword, by A. H. M. Kirk-Greene.—Arabic Loan Words in Hausa, by M. Goerner and Y. Salman.—Some Common Arabic Loan Words in Hausa and Swahili, by P. B. Armitage.

2085
Gouffé, Claude. Problème de toponymie haoussa: les noms de villages de la région de Maradi (République du Niger). Revue internationale d'onomastique, v. 19, juin 1967: 95–127. CS2300.R4, v. 19

2086
Greenberg, Joseph H. Arabic loan words in Hausa. Word, v. 3, Apr. 1947: 85–97. P1.W65, v. 3

2087
Gregersen, Edgar. The dating of loanwords in the Western Sudan. Paper presented at the 10th annual meeting of the African Studies Association, New York, 1967. DLC-Micro 03782

Collation of the original: 3 p.

2088
———Linguistic seriation as a dating device for loanwords with special reference to West Africa. African language review, v. 6, 1967: 102–108. MH

2089
Hiskett, Mervyn. The historical background to the naturalization of Arabic loan-words in Hausa. African language studies, v. 6, 1965: 18–26. PL8003.A34, v. 6

The impact of Islam on Hausa is apparent in both Muslim religious terms and cavalry-related terms adopted by Hausa-phone peoples between 1350 and 1450. Mystic religious poetry has also infiltrated Hausa vocabulary with Shari'a terminology.

2090
Hunwick, J. O. The influence of Arabic in West Africa. *In* Historical society of Ghana. Transactions. v. 7, pt. 1; 1964. Legon, 1964. p. 24–41. DT510.A1H55, v. 7

"It is hardly surprising that Islam, being the religion of a book, not of a man, should have placed such a high degree of importance on the ability to read." As a result of the primordial importance of Arabic, whenever Islam spread, Arabic and Arabic schools trailed not far behind. Hunwick, discussing the impact of the "language of God," shows its influence in West Africa as early as the Ghana Empire. He also examines the "main uses to which the language was put during the 19th century in Nigeria" such as correspondence, political books and pamphlets, treatises of advice to emirs, biographical literature, histories, ethnography and sociology, and education.

2091
Jacobs, J. Les épopées de Soundjata et de Chaka: une étude comparée. Aequatoria, v. 25, no 4, 1962: 121–124. MH–P

2092
Kirk-Greene, Anthony H. M. The meaning of place names in Hausaland. BIFAN, t. 31, janv. 1969: 264–278. DT1.I5123, v. 31

The study of African history relies upon a cluster of disciplines, one of which is toponymy. Kirk-Greene, who is fluent in Hausa, provides a detailed analysis of Hausa history as seen through its names. The study is divided into traditional territorial terms and classes of toponymic origin which includes topographic features, personal names and derivations, ethnic derivations, and derivations from flora and fauna. Two other sections deal with the spelling of Hausa place names and town praise names, Kíráarì.

2093
———A preliminary inquiry into Hausa onomatology; three studies in the origins of personal, title and place names. Zaria, Institute of Administration, 1964. 56 leaves. DLC

In the foreword the author states: "This is an exploratory enquiry into the derivation of certain basic functional terms in Hausa: personal name (*suna*), title (*sarauta*), and place (*wari*). A study of these nominal origins is not only of practical value to the newcomer to Northern Nigeria, but can also lead to a deeper understanding of some of the phenomena of Hausa society with which he comes into immediate contact." Three appendixes provide a list of titles current in a typical pre-Fulani (pre-1804) Hausa emirate, the titles of the first and second-class chiefs of Northern Nigeria in order of precedence, and a historical note on the name "Nigeria."

2094
Labouret, Henri. La langue des Peuls ou Foulbé. Dakar, IFAN, 1952. 286 p. (Mémoires de l'Institut français d'Afrique noire, n 16) PL8181.L3

"Léxique peul-français. Léxique français-peul": p. [245]–286.

2095
Lacroix, Pierre F. Remarques préliminaires à une étude des emprunts arabes en Peul. Africa, v. 37, Apr. 1967: 188–202. PL8000.I6, v. 37

The peripatetic Fulbe have been in contact with a large number of societies, with one result that Fulfulde is characterized by numerous cultural borrowings. Lacroix believes that the main channel of borrowing from Arabic has been through the written word, whether the Koran, religious treatises, or literary works. He also proposes an elaborate schema to show the various avenues of borrowing: direct from written Arabic; direct from an Arabic dialect; indirect from written Arabic via a relay language; indirect from an Arabic dialect via a relay language; indirect from written Arabic via two relay languages; and indirect from an Arabic dialect via two relay languages. He analyzes the structure of the loanwords and their precise meaning in Fulfulde, comparing it to the meaning of the original Arabic term.

2096
Leriche, Albert. Anthroponymie Toucouleur. BIFAN, t. 18, janv./avril 1956: 169–188. DT1.I5123, v. 18

Investigation of Tukulor names. Leriche describes the individual name *'indé,* the clan name *yettôdé,* and diminutives *sowâré,* and provides an extensive list of Tukulor names of Arabic origin followed by a list of names based on religious events.

2097
———Toponymie et histoire maure. BIFAN, t. 14, janv. 1952: 337–343. Q89.I5, v. 14

One of the difficulties in reading the works of early explorers and writers on Africa is deciphering the distortions of the place names. In this article, Leriche takes four sites—Ydamen, Synguyty, Tynygumhy, and Marzy and Emersey—from Duerta Pacheco Pereira's *Esmeraldo de Situ Orbis* and locates them with the aid of Arabic writings and oral traditions. There are ample notes.

2098
Lukas, Johannes. A study of the Kanuri language: Grammar and vocabulary. London, Dawsons of Pall Mall for International African Institute, 1967. PL8361.L8 1967

"First published . . . 1937."

2099
Monteil, Vincent. La cryptographie chez les maures; notes sur quelques alphabets secrets du Ḥodh. BIFAN, t. 13, oct. 1951: 1257–1264. Q89.I5, v. 13

Brief sketch on nine cryptographic systems derived from Arabic. These were prevalent in the Ḥodh region in southeastern Mauritania.

2100
Mouradian, Jacques. Notes sur les altérations du nom de Mohammad chez les Noirs islamisés de l'Afrique occidentale. BCAOF, v. 21, juil./sept. 1938: 459–462. DT521.C6, v. 21

Essay on the adaptations, in West Africa, of the Prophet Muḥammad's name.

2101
———Notes sur quelques emprunts de la langue wolof à l'arabe. BIFAN, t. 2, juil./oct. 1940: 269–284. Q89.I5, v. 2

Arabic, the language of Islam and the Koran, influenced Wolof Islam to the extent that it incorporated many Arabic names. Mouradian lists about 100 Wolof terms which he traced to Arabic, showing the patterns of linguistic assimilation.

2102
N'Diaye, Aïssatou. Complement à une note sur les emprunts de la langue wolof à l'arabe. NA, no 41, janv. 1949: 26–29. DT1.I513, 1949

Further information on Arabic loan-words in Wolof, to be added to an article by Jacques Mouradian on the same topic (*see* 2101).

2103
Poussibet, F. Répertoire des termes géographiques maures de la région de Tombouctou. BIFAN, t. 24, janv./avril 1962: 199–262. DT1.I5123, v. 24

Index of 509 terms related to Ḥassānīyah geographical terminology, including hydrology, pluviometry, and botany.

2104
———Vocabulaire maure relatif à la météorologie. BIFAN, t. 24, janv./avril 1962: 263–264. DT1.I5123, v. 24

2105
Prost, André. Mots mossi empruntés au songhay. BIFAN, t. 28, janv./avril 1966: 470–475. DT1.I5123, v. 28

Investigates Mò:re linguistic borrowings from Songhay, mainly in the religious and cavalry-related fields.

2106
Samb, Amar. Les langues africaines et leurs emprunts à l'arabe. NA, no 138, avril 1973: 41–45. DT1.I513, 1973

2107
Taylor, Frank W. A Fulani-Hausa vocabulary. Oxford, Clarendon Press, 1927. 136 p. (Taylor's Fulani-Hausa series, IV) PL8183.T33

Useful in tracing Hausa and Fulfulde terms of Arabic origin.

2108
Vincent, B. Acte de vente passé à Tombouctou; manuscrit arabe venue de Tombouctou. Journal asiatique, 3 sér., t. 9, 1840: 375–389. PJ4.J5, 3d ser. 1840

Manuscripts from North Africa were an important trade item after the Islamization of the Sudanic belt. The author presents the text, translation, and commentaries on the bill of sale of a manuscript from Morocco.

2109
Vohsen, Ernest. Proben der Fulah-sprache. Zeitschrift für Afrikanische, ozeanische und ostasiatische sprachen, Jahrg. 1, ockt. 1887/juli 1888: 217–237; Jahrg. 3, okt. 1889/juli 1890: 298–315. PL8000.Z36, v. 1, 3

Transliteration and translation of a Fulbe manuscript in Arabic from the Fouta Djallon region in Guinea.

Law

2110
Afrika-Instituut (*Netherlands*) The future of customary law in Africa. L'avenir du droit coutumier en Afrique. Symposium-colloque, Amsterdam, 1955. Organized by the Afrika Instituut, Studiecentrum, Leiden, in collaboration with the Royal Tropical Institute, Amsterdam. Leiden, Universitaire Pers Leiden, 1956. xvii, 305 p. DLC–LL

2111
Anderson, James N. D. Conflict of law in Northern Nigeria. Journal of African law, v. 1, summer 1957: 87–98. DLC–LL

Examination of two recent judgments in Northern Nigeria dealing with homicide, illustrating the conflict between Islamic and statutory laws.

2112
Brito, Eduíno. O direito islâmico dos Fulas e Mandingas da Guiné. Boletim cultural de Guiné Portuguesa, v. 22, jul./obro 1967: 269–291. DT613.B6, v. 22

2113
Brown, William A. A monument of legal scholarship: the Nawâzil al-Takrûr of al-Mustafa b. Ahmad al-Ghalâwî. *In* Ibadan, Nigeria. University. *Centre of Arabic Documentation.* Research bulletin, v. 3, July 1967: 137–138. DT352.4.I2a, v. 3

2114
Chabas, Jean. Le droit des successions chez les Ouolofs. Annales africaines, v. 1, 1956: 75–119. DLC–LL

2115
Da Silva, Artur A. O direito penal entre os Fulas da Guiné. Boletim cultural da Guiné Portuguesa, v. 9, julho 1954: 481–495; v. 10, jan. 1955: 1–22.
DT613.B6, v. 9, 10

2116
Guèye, Youssouf. Essai sur les causes et les conséquences de la micropropriété au Fouta Toro. BIFAN, t. 19, janv/avril 1957: 28–42.
DT1.I5123, v. 19

The reason for the fragmentation of arable land in the Fouta Toro is attributed by Guèye to the Muslim law of inheritance. The continuing division of land to satisfy such tenets led to an exodus of the rural population to the overcrowded urban centers. The article closes on a pessimistic note on the fragmentation trend in view of continued intensive cultivation methods.

2117
Hill, D. J. Comparative aspects of the Maliki law and common law of agency. *In* Zaria. Abdullahi Bayero College. *Centre of Islamic Legal Studies.* Journal, v. 1, no. 2 [1967?]: 53–69.
K1.H5, v. 1

2118
Hopen, C. Edward. A note on *Alkali Fulfulde;* a reformation movement among the nomadic Fulbe (Fulani) of Sokoto Province. Africa, v. 34, Jan. 1964: 21–27. PL8000.I6, v. 34

In order to stand up to Hausa economic and cultural encroachments and adapt their own culture to northern conditions, the Fulbe youth of northwestern Nigeria instituted a creative innovation—the *Alkali Fulfulde* (Judge of the Fulbe way)—to serve as a quasi-tribunal to implement the Fulbe "way of life." Hopen considers the institution to be typologically marginal to "revitalization movements."

2119
Joubert, *Lt.* Les coutumes et le droit chez les Kel Tdélé. BIFAN, t. 1, janv. 1939: 245–281.
Q89.I5, v. 1

General examination of the Kel Tdélé, nomads of the Aïr region, including their physical characteristics and way of life, family structure, religion, and Islamic law.

2120
Kozlov, S. Ia. Pozemel'nye otnoshenii͡a na Futa-Dzhallone (XVIII–XX vv). [Land tenure relations in the Fouta Djallon (18th–20th century)] Sovetskii͡a etnografii͡a, 6, 1965: 50–60. GN1.S65, 1965

2121
Leriche, Albert. Des châtiments prévus par la loi musulmane et leur application en Mauritanie. BIFAN, t. 19, juil./oct. 1957: 446–463.
DT1.I5123, v. 19

Analysis of the application of punishments as set in the Shari'a in Mauritania. Islam provides four types of penalties: retaliation, blood price, cases defined by the law, and arbitrary decisions taken by a qadi or imam if not determined explicitly by the law. The conclusion reached by Leriche is that the Ḥassānīyah society is less rigorous in the application of the letter of the law than other Muslim societies.

2122
McDowell, C. M. The breakdown of traditional land tenure in Northern Nigeria. *In* International African Seminar, *8th, Haile Sellassie I University, 1966.* Ideas and procedures in African customary law; studies presented and discussed at the Eighth International African Seminar at the Haile Sellassie I University, Addis Ababa, January 1966. Edited by Max Gluckman, with an introduction by A. N. Allott, A. L. Epstein, and M. Gluckman. London, Published for the International African Institute by the Oxford University Press, 1969. p. 266–278.
DLC–LL

2123
Meek, Charles K. Land tenure and land administration in Nigeria and the Cameroons. London, H. M. Stationery Off., 1957. 420 p. 5 fold. maps (in pocket) ([Gt. Britain] Colonial Office. Colonial research studies, no. 22) JV33.G7A48 no. 22

Deals with problems of land tenure, especially when complicated by Islamic inheritance laws in the Muslim areas.

2124
Pautrat, René. La justice locale et la justice musulmane en A. O. F. Rufisque, Impr. du Haut Commissariat de la république en Afrique occidentale française, 1957. 267 p. forms, tables.
DLC–LL

At head of title: Haut Commissariat de la république en Afrique occidentale française.

2125
Prothero, R. Mansell. Land use, land holdings and land tenure at Soba, Zaria Province, Northern Nigeria. BIFAN, t. 19, juil./oct. 1957: 558–563.
DT1.I5123, v. 19

Analysis of the conflict between customary law and Muslim law regarding land tenure at a time of land hunger and scarcity.

2126
Smith, David N. Native courts of Northern Nigeria: techniques for institutional development. Boston University law review, v. 48, winter 1968: 49–82. DLC–LL

2127
Verdier, R. Problèmes fonciers nigeriens. Recueil Penant, v. 74, oct./nov./déc. 1964: 587–593. K18.E5, v. 74

Investigation of the conflict between traditional land tenure and Islam as well as European concepts introduced by the colonial authorities.

2128
Wilks, Ivor. The Saghanughu and the spread of Māliki law: a provisional note. *In* Ghana. University, *Legon. Institute of African Studies.* Research review, v. 2, no. 3, 1966: 67–73. DT1.G48, v. 2

Report on the problems related to the Maliki isnad delivered by the Shaghanughu, a Dyula lineage of learned men in northern and western Ivory Coast and in western Upper Volta. Includes a manuscript example of a sanad of Mallam 'Abd al-Raḥmān ibn Ḥāmid Tarawirī, of Wa.

2129
Williams, T. H. The criminal procedure code of Northern Nigeria: the first five years. Modern law review, v. 29, May 1966: 248–272. DLC–LL

Literature

2130
Bâ, Amadou-Hampâté, *and* G. Dieterlen. Koumen: Texte initiatique des pasteurs peuls. Paris, Mouton, 1961. 196 p. IEN

2131
Bâ, Amadou-Hampâté, *and* L. Kesteloot. Une épopée peule: "Silamaka." L'Homme, v. 8, janv./mars 1968: 5–36. GN1.H68, v. 8

2132
Bâ, Amadou Oumar. Les mystères du Bani; roman folklorique soudanais. Monte-Carlo, Editions regain [1960] IEN

2133
Bâ, Thierno. Lat Dior, le chemin de l'honneur; drame historique en huit tableaux. [Dakar, Imp. A. Diop, 1970] 98 p. illus. PQ3989.2.B24L3

2134
Beyries, Jean-Louis. Proverbes et dictons mauritaniens. Revue des études islamiques, v. 4, 1. cahier, 1930: 1–15. BP1.R53, v. 4

Text, translations, and comments on 198 Mauritanian proverbs and sayings.

2135
Cherbonneau, M. A. Histoire de la littérature au Soudan. Journal asiatique, sér. 5, v. 6, déc. 1855: 391–407. PJ4.J5, v. 6

2136
Cissé, Bassirou. "Ma dyêma burati . . ." "Je vais essayer de m'élever encore une fois . . ." Poème de Moussa Ka (1883–1967). Transcribed and translated by Bassirou Cissé. Edited and annotated by Amar Samb. BIFAN, t. 30, juil. 1968: 847–860. DT1.I5123, v. 30

Text, translation of, and commentaries on an 80-verse poem on God, life, and the afterlife. Cissé notes that the poem "nous fait songer à la Divine Comédie de Dante et à l'Apocalypse de Saint-Jean par l'évocation saisissante des faits eschatologiques, par les fresques grandioses et les tableaux terrifiants"

2137
Clair, Andrée. Bakari, enfant du Mali. Paris, Présence africaine [1960] [18] p. illus. IEN

2138
Colin, Roland. Les contes noirs de l'Ouest africain; témoins majeurs d'un humanisme. Préf. de Léopold S. Senghor. Paris, Présence africaine [1957] 206 p. IU

2139
Dembo, Coly. Poème d'un lettré mandingue de Casamance. NA, no 36, oct. 1947: 3. DT1.I513, 1947

2140
Diagne, Amadou Matapé. Les trois volontés de Malic. Paris, Larousse, 1920.

Source: Jahn, 330.

2141
Diop, Birago. Contes choisis. Edited Joyce A. Hutchinson. Cambridge [Eng.] Cambridge University Press, 1967. 176 p. GR350.D512

French text, introduction in English.

The stories in this selection are from *Les contes d'Amadou-Koumba* (1947) and *Les nouveaux contes d'Amadou-Koumba* (1958).

2142
———Les contes d'Amadou-Koumba. 3. edition. Paris, Présence africaine, 1969. 191 p. (Collection Contes africains) GR350.D5 1969
See also English translation by Dorothy S. Blair (GR350.D513).

2143
———Les nouveaux contes d'Amadou-Koumba. Préf. de Léopold Senghor. Paris, Présence africaine [1958] 173 p. 4Pq Fr. 4797

2144
Diop, Ousmane Socé. Karim, roman sénégalais, suivi de Contes et légendes d'Afrique noire. 3. ed. Paris, Nouvelles éditions latines, 1966. 240 p. (Bibliothèque de l'Union française) PQ3989.D56K3 1966

2145
Ekwensi, Cyprian. Burning grass; a story of the Fulani of Northern Nigeria. London, Heinemann [1962] 150 p. illus., map. (African writers series, 2) PZ4.E349Bu

2146
Erickson, John D. Kane's *L'Aventure ambiguë*.
Source: ASA, Program, 15th, 1972.

2147
Gaden, Henri. Proverbes et maximes peuls et toucouleurs, traduits, expliqués et annotés. Institut d'ethnologie, 1931. 368 p. (Université de Paris. Travaux et mémoires de l'Université d'ethnologie-16) PN6519.F8G3

2148
Gueye, Youssouf Aliou. Le légende de Oumarel. Présence africaine (nouv. sér.), no 6, fév./mars 1956: 126–142; no 7, avril/mai 1956: 102–119. GN645.P74, 1956

2149
Gwandu, Umaru. Wakokin Wa'azi. [Zaria, Gaskiya Corporation, 1959] 3 v. in 1. PL8234.G9W3
Religious poem by a blind man.

2150
Innes, Gordon. Stability and change in griots' narrations. African language studies, v. 14, 1973: 104–118. PL8003.A34, v. 14
Study of variations in *griots* performances. Taking the Sundiata epic as an example, Innes studies the versions of two brothers, Banna and Dembo Kounate, who have studied under their father, and proceeds to analyze the process by which major changes have taken place in the lifetime of the performers.

2151
Hiskett, Mervyn. The Arab star-calendar and planetary system in Hausa verse. BSOAS, v. 30, pt. 1, 1967: 158–176. PJ3.L6, v. 30

2152
———Mamman Konni: An eccentric poet and holy man from Boddinga. African language studies, v. 11, 1970. 211–229. DLC
"In honor of Malcolm Guthrie."
Text and translation of a Hausa poem written by a holy man castigating his wife for telling tales about him to her Gobir kinsfolk. The poem is unusual in that, in addition to its stinging wit, it reflects a profound erudition in Islamic culture.

2153
Kaïdara. Kaïdara, récit initiatique peul, rapporté par Amadou-Hampâté Bâ. Edité par Amadou-Hampâté Bâ et Lilyan Kesteloot. [Paris] Julliard, 1969. 183 p. (Classiques africains, 7) PL8184.K3 1969
Fulfulde text and French translation on opposite pages.
Initiatory poem of Fulbe learned men extolling knowledge over fortune and power.

2154
Kane, Hamidou. Ambiguous adventure; translated from the French by Katherine Woods. London, Heinemann, 1972. 178 p. (African writers series, 119) PZ4.K163 Am8
Translation of *L'aventure ambiguë*.

2155
———L'aventure ambiguë; récit. Préface de Vincent Monteil. [Paris] Julliard [1966, c1961] 209 p. PQ3989.2.K3A98 1966

2156
Kane, Mohamadou. Les contes d'Amadou Coumba; du conte traditionnel au conte moderne d'expression française. Dakar, 1968. 243 p. (Université de Dakar. Publications de la Faculté des lettres et des sciences humaines. Langues et littérature, no 16) GR350.K27

2157
Kesteloot, Lilyan. The West African epics. Présence africaine, no 58, 2. quarterly, 1966: 165–169. GN645.P74, 1966

2158
Kesteloot, Lilyan, *and others.* Une épopée malienne: Da monzon de Ségou. Abbia, no 14/15, juil./déc. 1966: 171–229. AP9.A24, 1966

2159
Kirk-Greene, Anthony H. M. Hausa ba dabo ba ne: a collection of 500 proverbs. Translated and annotated by A. H. M. Kirk-Greene. Ibadan [Nigeria] Oxford University Press, 1966. 84 p. PN6519.H35K5

Text in English and Hausa.

2160
Koelle, Sigismund W. African native literature [; or Proverbs, tales, fables, and historical fragments in the Kanuri or Bornu language, to which are added a translation of the above and a Kanuri-English vocabulary]. Introduction: David Dalby. Published in association with the African Language Review. (Um eine Einleitung verm. Nachdruck der 1854 in London erschienenen Ausg. Photomechanischer Nachdruck) Graz, Akademische Druck- u. Verlagsanstalt, 1968. 434 p. PL8361.Z77 1968

2161
Kouyaté, Seydou Badian. Sous l'orage. Avignon, Presses universitaires, 1957.

Source: Jahn, 178.

2162
Laye, Camara. The dark child. With an introduction by Philippe Thoby-Marcellin. [Translated from the French by James Kirkup and Ernest Jones] New York, Farrar, Strauss and Giroux [1969, c1954] 188 p. DT543.4.L313 1969

Translation of *L'enfant noir.*

Autobiographical.

2163
———Dramouss, roman. [Paris] Plon, 1966. 251 p. PQ3989.L37D7

2164
———A dream of Africa. Translated from the French by James Kirkup. With an introduction by Emile Snyder. New Collier Books [1971] 190 p. (African/American library) PQ3989.L37

Translation of *Dramouss.*

2165
———L'enfant noir. Edited by Joyce A. Huchinson. Cambridge [Eng.] Cambridge University Press, 1966. 189 p. map. PQ3989.L37E6 1966

Autobiographical.

Introduction and notes in English.

2166
———Le regard du roi, roman. Paris, Plon [1954] 254 p. IU

2167
Louis-Marie de Saint-Joseph, *Frère.* Fables et contes maures: Les histoires du chacal. BIFAN, t. 10, 1948: 560–594. Q89.I5, v. 10

Free translation of 20 fables and tales gathered from a goumier (camel corps soldier) from the Trarza by a former commanding officer of the Goum of Akjoujt.

2168
Ly, Djibril. Coutumes et contes des Toucouleurs du Fouta Toro. BCAOF, v. 21, avril/juin 1938: 304–326. DT521.C6, v. 21

Short introduction to Tukulor customs followed by 13 tales gathered from wandering minstrels in the Fouta Toro in Senegal.

2169
Marty, Paul. Poème de Mohammed al-Yadâli à la louange de l'Emir des Brakna Ahmad ould Heïba. BCAOF, v. 4, avril/juin 1921: 264–267. DT521.C6, v. 4

2169a
Molin, Paul Marie, *Bp.* Recueil de proverbes bambaras et malinkés. Issy-les-Moulineaux, Impr. Saint-Paul [1960] 315 p. PN6519.B3M6

2170
Monteil, Charles V. Soudan français: Contes soudanais. Paris, E. Leroux, 1905. 205 p. (Collection de contes et chansons populaires, t. 28) GR15.C6, v. 28

2171
Muhammad, Liman. Comments on John N. Paden's 'A Survey of Kano Hausa poetry.' Kano studies, no. 2, July 1966: 44–52. DLC

2172
Muqlid, Muḥammad Yūsuf. Shu'arā' Mūrītāniyā al-qudamā' wa-al-muhdathīn. [The old and modern poets of Mauritania] Casablanca, Maktabat al-wiḥdah al-'Arabīyah [1962] 752 p. illus., facsims., ports. PJ8390.M3M8

2173
Ndao, Aliou. L'Exil d'Albouri. Suivi de La décision. Honfleur, P. J. Oswald, 1967. 134 p. (Théâtre africain, 1) PQ3989.2.N4E9

2174

———Le fils de l'Almamy. Suivi de La case de l'homme; théâtre. [Paris] P. J. Oswald [1973] 76 p. (Théâtre africain, 20) PQ3989.2.N4F5

2175

Nicolas, François-J. Folklore Twareg, poésies et chansons de l'Azawarh. BIFAN, t. 6, no 1/4, 1944: 1–463. Q89.I5, v. 6

Issue devoted to a compilation of 86 Tuareg poems. Each poem is given in phonetic transliteration followed by its translation. The author is a graduate of the Ecole des langues orientales.

2176

Norris, H. T. Saharan myth and saga. Oxford, Clarendon Press, 1972. 240 p. illus., 2 facsims., geneal. tables, map. (Oxford library of African literature) PJ8390.S2N58

With mentors such as Mukhtār Ūld Ḥāmidūn and Muḥammad Ūld Mawlūd Ūld Dāddah, Norris was bound to produce a thorough work on Saharan literature. He states in his introduction that "the aim of this book is to present typical examples of perennial Saharan saga and tribal chronicles as they have survived in their Arabic, and not their Berber form. A wide selection of Maghribi—North African and Spanish-Arab—literature has been introduced to delineate recurrent motifs in these sagas and to show that many of them are variations on themes found in ancient Semitic, Yemenite, and late-medieval Oriental romances."

2177

———Shinqiti folk literature and song. Oxford, Clarendon Press, 1968. xiv, 200 p. illus., facsims., map, 2 plates, port. (Oxford library of African literature) PJ8390.S2N6

Thorough study of Arabic classical and vernacular literature and music in Mauritania. The author, who has worked under the guidance of Mukhtār ūld Ḥāmidūn, divides his work into two major parts. In the first, he analyzes West Saharan society, its various dialects, the historical development of Ḥassānīyah poetical forms, its musicians and poets, musical instruments, recitals, and dances. The second part deals with Ḥassānīyah Zwāghah poetry as well as folk tales of the Trarza. Norris translates and analyzes a large body of literature, thus providing a clear picture of the Weltaunschaung of a great nomadic society. Appended are two manuscripts on Mauritanian music and Saharan folk poetry.

2178

Ouane, Ibrahima Mamadouï. Fadimata, la princesse du desert *and* Drame de Deguembéré. Avignon, Presses Universitaires, 1956.

Source: Jahn, 921.

2179

Paddon, E. M. Hausa proverbs and Hausa character. MW, v. 5, Oct. 1915: 409–412. DS36.M7, v. 5

2180

Paden, John N. A survey of Kano Hausa poetry. Kano studies, no. 1, Sept. 1965: 33–39. DLC

Wáakàa (poetry) is an integral part of the daily lives of the people of Kano. With a wealth of examples, Paden illustrates the various styles and trends of Hausa poetry. In addition to the traditionalists who use Ajami (Arabic script, from *'Ajamī*, foreigner) and Arabic meters, he provides samples by modernist writers who use Boko (Roman script) and Latin meter.

2181

Prost, André. Légendes songhay. BIFAN, t. 18, janv./avril 1956: 188–201. DT1.I5123, v. 18

2182

Rattray, Robert S., *ed. and tr.* Hausa folk-lore, customs, proverbs, etc., collected and transliterated with English translation and notes. Oxford, Clarendon Press. 1913. 2 v. illus., fronts. 2 plates. PL8234.A1R3

Transliterated text with English translation and Hausa text on opposite pages.

2183

Samb, Amar. Influence de l'Islam sur la littérature <<wolof.>> BIFAN, t. 30, avril 1968: 628–641. DT1.I5123, v. 30

Exploring the impact of Islam on both Wolof vocabulary and poetry, the author shows the influence of Arabic prosody in the adoption of the meter, the traditional qaṣīdah form, as well as the classical themes of Arabic poetry. Samb also indicates how, through vocabulary and poetry, Islam has pervaded the Wolof world view.

2184

Seydou, Christiane. Essai d'études stylistiques de poèmes peuls du Fouta-Djallon. BIFAN, t. 29, janv./avril 1967: 192–233. DT1.I5123, v. 29

Stylistic review of Fulbe poems of the Fouta Djallon region in Guinea, an area noted for its Fulbe erudites and scholars. In this study, Madame Seydou investigates the techniques of prosody indicating strong Islamic influences and similarity with those of the classical forms in Arabic.

2185
———<<Majaaɗo Alla gaynaali>> poème en langue peule du Foûta-Djalon. CEA, v. 6, 4. cahier, 1966: 643–681. DT1.C3, v. 6

Substantial analysis of a religious poem by Rahmatullahi, a woman from Telikoo in the Fouta Djallon. The poem is a "sermon on death" which, according to Madame Seydou, is characterized by "the fascinating power of evocation brought about by the regularity of the rhythm; the stubborn dance of language engulfing the audience in the hallucinating whirlwind of the verb, and the quasi magical invocation of the Image, ending by the spell of an inspired trance. And yet, at no time, does the author let herself be dominated by the unbridled force of words: her art and faith have always remained firmly in control."

2186
———Note sur le <<mot-date>> (Procédé mnémotechnique et littérature utilisé par les écrivains peul et hausa). JOSAF, t. 38, fasc. 1, 1968: 15–18. DT1.S65, v. 38

Dating of Hausa and Fulfulde manuscripts is not an easy task. Sometimes the scribe closes his work with a religious formula in which he includes the date of completion. Another method is the inclusion of a "date-word" in which a numerical value is attributed to each letter, the sum of which gives the date. Seydou, using a table provided by Shaykh Hampâté Bâ, shows the working of the mnemonic system.

2187
———Panorama de la littérature peule. BIFAN, t. 35, janv. 1973: 176–218. DT1.I5123, v. 35

Includes two oral traditions and two written poems. The last poem is an elaborate funeral oration.

2188
———Trois poèmes mystiques peuls du Foûta-Djalon. Revue des études islamiques, v. 40, 1972: 141–185. BP1.R53, v. 40

The translations of the three poems are accompanied by commentaries. Seydou discusses the Tijani sect and al-Hajj Alfā ʻUmar Saydū, the author of two of the poems. The third poem is an anonymous funeral oration on the occasion of the death of ʻAliyyū Būbā N'Jan, a well-known Fouta Djallon poet.

2189
Sissoko, Fily Dabo. La passion de Djimé. Paris, Editions de la Tour de guet [1956] 113 p. PQ3989.S52P3

2190
———Sagesse noire (sentences et proverbes malinkés) Paris, Editions de la Tour du guet [1955] xviii, 62 p. IU

2191
Sow, Alfâ Ibrâhîm, *ed.* La Femme, la vache, la foi, écrivains et poètes du Foûta-Djalon. [Paris] Julliard, 1966. 376 p. plates. (Classiques africains, 5) PL8184.A2S6

French and Fulfulde.

When converted to Islam, the Fulbe modibbe became what Amadou-Hampâté Bâ calls "the aristocracy of the Book." They produced a vast literature in Fulfulde pertaining to Islam and the "Straight Path." Sow, a Fulbe who teaches Fulfulde at the Paris Ecole des langues orientales, is eminently qualified to present his people's literature, which is divided into two broad categories—aristocratic and popular. The former is essentially religious, from the great masters of the 18th century to the modern writers in social criticism. The author traces the history of literary movements using poems which have been translated and annotated. A small Fulfulde-French dictionary and a helpful index of names are appended.

2192
———Notes sur les procédés poétiques dans la littérature des peuls du Fouta-Djalon. CEA, v. 5, 3. cahier, 1965: 370–387. DT1.C3, v. 5

Fulbe learned men (modibbo/modibbe) have successfully emulated traditional Arabic poetry. With the democratization of Fulbe Islam and its spread during the 18th and 19th centuries, poetry in Fulfulde slowly developed to reach the non-Arabic-speaking faithful. Sow analyzes in great detail the whole range of Fulfulde prosody.

2193
Teffahi, M. Introduction à la littérature maure. NA, no 59, juil. 1953: 87–88. DT1.I513, 1953

Ḥassānīyah literature may be divided between classical Arabic poetry, Shiʻr, and vernacular Arabic in the form of gāf and talʻat, which are sung accompanied by the tidimit, a four-string guitar, and ardine, a Mauritanian flute. Included is a poem by a Hassani poet translated by Teffahi.

2194
———La poésie populaire maure; les tal'at et les guifen. NA, no 60, oct. 1953: 116–117.

DT1.I513, 1953

Second part of an article on Mauritanian poetry (*see* 2193), concentrating on the vernacular poetry in Ḥassānīyah. These short poems show, by the delicate choice of words, the wealth of vocabulary of the poet in describing the loved one, satirizing an ugly action, or describing a historical episode.

2195

Tinguidji, Boûbacar, *and* Christaine Seydou, *eds.* Silâmaka et Poullôri: récit épique peul. Paris, Colin, 1972. 227 p. illus., map, records. (Classiques africains, 13) PL8184.T5S5

2195a

Travélé, Moussa. Proverbes et contes Bambara. Paris, Librairie orientale Paul Geuthner, 1923. 240 p. DHU

2196

Usuman dan Fodio. Nour-el-eulbab (Lumière des coeurs) de Cheïkh Otmane ben Mohammed ben Otmane dit Ibn-Foudiou. Revue africaine, no 227, 4. trimestre, 1897: 297–321.
DT271.R4, 1897

Translated and commented on by Ismā'īl Ḥāmid.

2197

Vieillard, Gilbert P. Poèmes peuls du Fouta Djallon. BCAOF, v. 20, juil./sept. 1937: 225–311.
DT521.C6, v. 20

Collection of eight poems in Fulfulde gathered in the Fouta Djallon. Four poems deal with the French occupation and the other four describe the women of the region. Text is in Fulfulde with a French translation.

2198

———Récits peuls du Macina et du Kounari. BCAOF, v. 14, janv./juin 1931: 137–156.
DT521.C6, v. 14

Collection of four oral traditions on the exploits of the Fulbe chiefs of the Masina and Kounari (Mopti region) from the eighth century to the beginning of the 19th century. The accounts were taken from itinerant Fulbe merchants and griots.

Music

2199

Balandier, Georges, *and* Paul Mercier. Notes sur les théories musicales maures à propos de chants enregistrés. *In* International West African Conference. Comptes rendus. v. 5; 1947. Lisboa, 1952. p. 137–191. illus. DT471.I58, 1947

At head of title: [Portugal] Ministério das Colónias. Junta de Investigações Colónias.

Proceedings issued without title.

Various languages.

2200

Krieger, Kurt. Musikinstrumente der Hausa. Baessler-Archiv, neue folge, Bd. 16, Dec. 1968: 373–430. GN1.B3, n.s., v. 16

2201

Leriche, Albert. Instruments de musique maure et griots. BIFAN, t. 12, juil. 1950: 744–750.
Q89.I5, v. 12

2202

———Poésie et musique maure. BIFAN, t. 12, juil. 1950: 710–743. Q89.I5, v. 12

Leriche, who spoke Hassānīyah, presents an analysis of the various poetical forms used by the poets, such as the gāf and Tal'at. The author also analyzes the various types of songs and the structured occasions for each type.

2203

MacKay, Mercedes. The Shantu music of the harims of Nigeria. African music, v. 1, no. 2, 1955: 56–57. ML5.A26, v. 1

2204

———The traditional musical instruments of Nigeria. The Nigerian field, v. 15, July 1950: 112–133. QH195.N5A15, v. 15

2205

Nikiprowetzky, Tolia. Les griots du Sénégal et leurs instruments, communication présentée au XVe Congrès du Conseil International de la Musique populaire, Gottwaldov, Tchécoslovaquie, 1962. [Paris, 1962?] 1 v. (unpaged) illus. ML3760.N53

2206

———The music of Mauritania. *In* International Folk Music Council. Journal, v. 14, Jan. 1962: 53–55. ML3760.N543, v. 14

2207

———L'ornementation dans la musique des Touareg de l'Aïr. *In* International Folk Music Council. Journal, v. 16, Jan. 1964: 81–83.
ML26.I544, v. 16

2208
———Trois aspects de la musique africaine, Mauritanie, Sénégal, Niger. Paris, Office de coopération radiophonique [1966?] 93 p. illus. ML3760.N543
French and English.

2209
Rabeh, S., *tr.* Four Hausa songs. Black Orpheus, no. 19, Mar. 1966: 5–7. PL8000.B6, 1966

Numismatics

2210
Delafosse, Maurice. Sur l'origine des noms de monnaies usités au Soudan. Journal asiatique, v. 208, janv./mars 1926: 177–184. PJ4.J5, v. 208

2211
Hiskett, Mervyn. Materials relating to the cowry currency of the Western Sudan. A late nineteenth-century schedule of inheritance from Kano. 2. Reflections on the provenance and diffusion of the cowry in the Sahara and the Sudan. BSOAS, v. 29, pt. 1, 1966: 122–142; v. 29, pt. 2, 1966: 339–366. PJ3.L6, v. 29

2212
Kirk-Greene, Anthony H. M. The major currencies in Nigerian history. JHSN, v. 2, Dec. 1960: 132–150. DT515.A2H5, v. 2

2213
Mauny, Raymond. Anciens ateliers monétaires ouest-africaine. NA, no 78, avril 1958: 34–35. DT1.I513, 1958
The minting of gold currency, both mithqal and dinar, in Tademekka, present-day Es-Souk, was reported by al-Bakrī. However, after a close reading of Joseph Dupuis' *Journal of a Residence in Ashantee* (*see* 854), Mauny has concluded that the major minting centers were Bornu and Nikki, the capital of Borgho.

Politics

2213a
Arnaud, Robert. L'Islam et la politique musulmane française en Afrique occidentale française. L'Afrique française; bulletin du Comité de l'Afrique française et du Comité du Maroc. Renseignements coloniaux et documents, 1912: 2–30; 115–127; 142–154. DLC-Micro 02878

2214
Benquey. Considérations sur l'Islam africain (Haute-Côte d'Ivoire). BCAOF, [v.] 4 oct./déc. 1921: 678–688. DT521.C6, v. 4
Arguing against the notion that Islam should be encouraged in the colonies, the author invalidates, to his satisfaction, all the arguments in favor of the spread of Islam as a buttress of the colonial administration.

2215
Borgnis-Desbordes, A. Un cinquantenaire. L'arrivée des Français au Niger. 1. février 1883- 1. février 1933. Revue militaire de l'A.O.F., avril 1933: 33–41. map.
Source: Brasseur, 3139.
Includes references to the 1882 Kéniéran battle against Samory.

2216
British policy and Islam in Nigeria. MW, v. 1, July 1911: 296–300. DS36.M7, v. 1
Remarks by a former staff officer of the West African Frontier Force in answer to a previous article on Nigeria. He concludes, "The recognition of Hausa as the future Hindustani of our West African colonies and the gradual substitution of Roman characters in writing for the Arabic alphabet, which is taking place under Government auspices and for which the language is well adapted, should prove a considerable aid in the spread of Christian literature and ideas."

2217
Chailley, Marcel. Quelques aspects de l'Islam sénégalais. *In* Académie des sciences d'outre-mer. Comptes rendus mensuels des séances, t. 22, juin 1962: 249–262. JV1802.A314, v. 22
Chailley stresses the ecumenical tendency of the faith in Senegal and concludes: "Je ne pense pas, sauf manoeuvres politiques, toujours possible en Islam, que le Sénégal musulman puisse s'aligner dans le cadre d'une Umma arabisée. Il a été trop formé à nos idées. Il n'est plus à ses yeux un danger dans le monde qui puisse heurter ses idéologies religieuses. Il s'est vraiment occidentalisé."

2218
Champagny, Aymar de. Négro-africanité de l'Islam malien. Vivant univers, no 267, mars/avril 1970: 14–21. G1.V57, 1970

2219
Charles, Eunice A. French West African policy and Muslim resistance in Senegal, 1880–1890. Paper presented at the 16th annual meeting of the African Studies Association, Syracuse, N.Y., 1973. DLC-Micro 03782
Collation of the original: 5 p.

2220
Clozel, J. Lettres de Korbous; politique musulmane au Soudan; pacification du Sahara soudanais. L'Afrique française; bulletin du Comité de l'Afrique française et du Comité du Maroc. Renseignements coloniaux et documents, 1913: 60–61; 106–108; 149–152; 182–186. DLC-Micro 03878

2221
Connant, F. P. The manipulation of ritual: an indigenous political technique in Northern Nigeria. Paper presented at the 3rd annual meeting of the African Studies Association, Hartford, Conn., 1960. DLC-Micro 03782
Collation of the original: 10 p.

2222
The contribution of Islam to national life in West Africa; a talk given in August 1955 at an orientation course for teachers appointed for service in West Africa. Overseas education, v. 28, Oct. 1956: 99–105. LC2601.O8, v. 28

2223
Crowder, Michael. West Africa under colonial rule. Evanston, Ill., Northwestern University Press, 1968. 540 p. maps (1 fold.) DT476.2.C76 1968b
Investigation of the colonial period (1885–1960). Though not primarily dealing with Islam, a Muslim thread runs through the work covering the rise of militant Islam, the French encounter with the Tukulor and Samory, and the confrontation of Islam vs. Christianity under colonial rule.

2224
———, *ed.* West African resistance: the military response to colonial occupation. London, Hutchinson, 1971. 314 p. 8 plates, illus., maps, ports. DT476.2.C77
This study of African resistance to the colonial powers includes the following articles: J. K. Fynn, Ghana-Asante (Ashanti); A. S. Kanya-Forstner, Mali-Tukulor; B. Oloruntimehin, Senegambia-Mahmadou Lamine; Yves Person, Guinea-Samori; David Ross, Dahomey; Robert Smith, Nigeria-Ijebu; Obaro Ikime, Nigeria-Ebrohimi; La Ray Denzer, Sierra Leone-Bai Bureh; D. J. M. Muffett, Nigeria-Sokoto Caliphate.

2225
Curtin, Philip D. Jihad in West Africa: Early phases and inter-relations in Mauritania and Senegal. JAH, v. 12, no. 1, 1971: 11–24. DT1.J65, v. 12
The tradition of religious revolution directed against partially Muslim rulers is traced to the religious reform movement among the *zwāya* of Mauritania in the 1660s, and to the jihad that brought them briefly into control of Futa Toro, Cayor, Walo, and Jolof in the 1670s. In spite of the reconquest of these states by their secular rulers and the re-establishment of Hassānī control in southwestern Mauritania, the tradition of religious revolt and the aim of establishing an imamate under religious leadership lived on, to reappear in other Fulbe states. It came a generation later, with the jihad of Malik Sy in Bundu during the 1690s, and direct connexions can be traced between the leadership in Bundu and the leadership in the later jihad in Futa Jallon. The jihad in Futa Toro in the 1770s and 1780s followed in the same tradition. This evidence suggests that the external influence of the mid-eighteenth-century revival of Islam in Arabia and the Middle East has been overemphasized in West African religious history. Forces working for the reform of Islam based in Africa itself were already at work—(Abstract supplied)

2226
Delafosse, Maurice. L'état actuel de l'Islam dans l'Afrique occidentale française. RMM, t. 11, mai 1910: 32–53. DS36.R4, v. 11
Status report on Islam in French West Africa, including: expansion, "cette marche paraît bien être aujourd'hui stationnaire"; statistics and distribution; impact of Islam on traditional civilizations; and attitudes of Muslims. Delafosse concludes that "l'intérêt de la domination européenne, comme aussi l'intérêt bien entendu des indigènes, nous fait donc un devoir de désirer le maintien du *statu quo* et de garder une neutralité absolue vis-a-vis de tous les cultes."

2227
———Une lettre du Cheikh sénégalais Moussa Kamara. Revue des études islamiques, v. 1, 1. cahier, 1927: 140–144. BP1.R53, v. 1
Text and translation of a pro-French letter accompanying a contribution toward the payment of the French Public Debt. It is interesting to note in the preface the mention of an *Histoire des peuples soudanais* by Shaykh Mūsā Kamara, which Delafosse had undertaken to translate.

2228
Dent, M. J. Elections in Northern Nigeria. Journal of local administration overseas, v. 1, Oct. 1962: 213–224. JS40.J6, v. 1

2229
Diallo, Thierno. Les institutions politiques du Fouta Dyalon au XIXe siècle. (Fii Laamu alsilaamaaku Fuuta Jaloo). [Paris] Université de Paris, Faculté des lettres et sciences humaines [196-] 337 leaves. 3 fold. maps. DT553.F8D5

Doctoral dissertation on Fulbe political institutions of the Fouta Djallon. After a survey of the geography and history of the region, the author analyzes its social and economic structures. The second part of the study investigates the political intricacies of the system, namely the Almami's role and the division of power between the Alfaya and the Soriya groups. The last part deals with the councils and assemblies, including the village council, provincial council, the "permanent" council of Timbo, Grand Council of Elders, also known as the federal assembly of freemen, and the believers' assemblies. Includes also genealogies, a lexicon of Fulbe terms, an index of proper names, and a substantial bibliography.

2230
Dudley, B. J. O. Traditionalism and politics: a case study of Northern Nigeria. Government and opposition, v. 2, July/Oct. 1967: 509–524. JA8.G6, v. 2

2231
Du Plessis, Johannes. Government and Islam in Africa. MW, v. 11, Jan. 1921: 2–22. DS36.M7, v. 11

The adoption of a policy of indirect rule in Northern Nigeria greatly disturbed missionaries in Africa. Lugard's statement that "government will in no way interfere with the Mohammedan religion" curtailed missionary activity. Du Plessis criticizes three arguments presented against proselytization: "1. Christian missionaries in Mohammedan areas are a menace to peace and quiet; 2. Christian schools and Christian missions generally exercise a denationalizing influence on the native and 'destroy racial identity' . . .; 3. experience proves that Islam is better adapted to the African than Christianity, and, in point of fact, it is making much more rapid headway."

2232
Echenberg, Myron J. Jihad and state building in late nineteenth century Upper Volta: The rise and fall of the Marka state of al-Kari of Bousse. Canadian journal of African studies, v. 3, no. 3, 1969: 531–561. DLC

2233
Hodgkin, Thomas L. Islam and national movements in West Africa. JAH, v. 3, no. 2, 1962: 323–327. DT1.J65, v. 3

2234
Kaba, Lansiné. Islam, society and politics in pre-colonial Baté, Guinea. BIFAN, t. 35, avr. 1973: 323–344. DT1.I5123, v. 35

This study reflects the transition in African history from the study of large political units to the lesser-known smaller ones, which, nevertheless, played an important role in the political continuum of West Africa. Baté—meaning between rivers—was a Maninka-Mori state that developed in about the 17th century around Kankan. The author, drawing on oral traditions and the writings of early travelers and French administrators, reconstructs the history of this small but significant piece of the West African historical puzzle.

2235
Klein, Martin A. Islam and imperialism in Senegal; Sine-Saloum, 1847–1914. Stanford, Calif., Published for the Hoover Institution on War, Revolution, and Peace by Stanford University Press, 1968. 285 p. maps. DT549.7.K55

2236
Laizé. L'Islam dans le territoire militaire du Niger. BCAOF, v. 2, avril/juin 1919: 177–183. DT521.C6, v. 2

2237
Markovitz, Irving L. Traditional social structure, the Islamic brotherhood, and political development in Senegal. The Journal of modern African studies, v. 8, 1970: 73–96. DT1.J68, v. 8

"Traditional social structures in new African states have not withered away according to the plans of modernising African leaders or the projections of Western social scientists. Leaders and social interests of long ancestry continue to count, and often determine the policies of so-called modern governments. Many chiefs and religious figures have succeeded in maintaining their relative power *vis-a-vis* their former subjects." On the basis of this premise, Markovitz analyzes the situation in Senegal. He looks at the ancient reigning families, the marabouts and Murid Order, French policies toward the latter, and the ability of the conservative classes to change. As a result of the interaction of these separate variables, he shows how relationships have been transformed and adapted to meet the demands of the modern period.

2238
O'Brien, Donal C. [Cruise O'Brien, Donal] Towards an "Islamic policy" in French West Africa, 1854–1914. JAH, v. 8, no. 2, 1967: 303–316. DT1.J65, v. 8

2239
Ọlọruntimẹhin, B. Ọlatunji. Franco-Samori relations 1886–1889: Diplomacy as War. JHSN, v. 6, Dec. 1971: 67–92. DT515.A2H5, v. 6

After introducing his essay with a section on the nature of diplomacy, Ọlọruntimẹhin states, "This essay is a case study in the use of diplomacy as a form of war. In the period covered by the study the French were concerned with diplomacy solely as an alternative means of attaining the same goals which had eluded them earlier on when they had engaged in open war." He examines the Treaty of Keniebakoura (1886), the Bissandougou Convention (1887), and the Treaty of Niako (1889) and suggests, "In Franco-Samori relations, especially in the period from 1886 to 1889, and thereafter, the only distinction between one episode and another was one between the disguised and the open war."

2240
———The idea of Islamic revolution and Tukulor constitutional evolution. BIFAN, t. 33, oct. 1971: 675–692. DT1.I5123, v. 33

Starting with the premise that "the concept of 'Islamic revolution' and the studies based on it are unsatisfactory largely because they lead to a projection of situations in a way that tends to merge the idea with the fact, and the ideal as instituted for the adherents of the religion with the concrete social reality," Ọlọruntimẹhin shows the symbiosis of the Islamic aspirations of the Tukulor as expressed by al-Ḥājj 'Umar and the forces representing the ideas and attitudes indigenous to Tukulor society, such as the caste and clan systems. These two factors manifesting themselves "in the decentralized structure of the empire and the fraticidal strife that was a feature of its politics contributed in a large measure to its fall."

2241
La propagande islamique au Soudan. L'Afrique française; bulletin de l'Afrique française et du Comité du Maroc. Renseignements coloniaux et documents, 1906: 288–289. DLC-Micro 03878

2242
Quellien. La politique musulmane dans l'Afrique occidentale française. Paris, E. Larose, 1910.

Source: Joucla, 7993.

2243
Quinquand, J. La pacification du Fouta-Djallon. Revue d'histoire des colonies, v. 26, no 4, 1938: 49–134. JV1801.R4, v. 26

Under the pretext of securing trade lines, between 1881 and 1886, France prepared the path for the ultimate occupation of the Fouta Djallon and the defeat of Almamy Bokar of Timbo. Quinquand reports the French side of the story, showing the various efforts of Beckmann and his reliance upon the rivalries between the Fouta leaders to complete the conquest and occupation of the region.

2244
Robinson, David. Indigenous and external legitimation in 18th century Fouta Toro.

Source: ASA, Program, 15th, 1972.

2245
Saint-Martin, Yves J. L'empire toucouleur et la France; un demi-siècle de relations diplomatiques, 1846–1893. Dakar, 1967. 482 p. illus., facsims., maps, plans, ports. (Université de Dakar. Publications de la Faculté des lettres et sciences humaines. Histoire, no 11) DT549.42.S3

Substantial study of Tukulor-French relations. The empire of al-Ḥājj 'Umar, resting on a religious basis, conditioned to a great extent the attitudes of its leaders toward the conquering French representing a Kāfir encroachment on a segment of Dār al-Islām. Saint-Martin attempts to put to rest the stereotype of al-Ḥājj 'Umar as "le fanatique prophète noir" in contradiction to Faidherbe, Gallieni, and Archinard, "les bâtisseurs d'empire," and looks at the period as an exercise in diplomatic relations and military operations.

2246
———Les relations diplomatiques entre la France et l'Empire toucouleur de 1860 à 1887. BIFAN, t. 27, janv./avril 1965: 183–222. DT1.I5123, v. 27

Analysis of peace negotiations between France and al-Ḥājj 'Umar and then his son Aḥmadū, beginning in 1864 and concerning territorial concessions and protection rights. Study of the various treaties, including the last one signed at Gouri in 1887 between Aḥmadū and Gallieni. The text of this treaty is appended.

2247
———L'artillerie d'El Hadj Omar et d'Ahmadou. BIFAN, t. 27, juil./oct. 1965: 560–572.
DT1.I5123, v. 27

Relates the efforts of the two leaders to secure artillery to resist the French conquest.

Roads & Itineraries

2248
Abbadie, A. d'. Itinéraire de pélerin maure au XIXe siècle. NA, no 78, avril 1958: 40–41.
DT1.I513, 1958

A short excerpt from the report of a pilgrimage to Mecca by a Mauritanian from the Hawd region. He went via Tangiers by sea to Egypt and returned by land via Sennar, Kordofan, Darfur, Bornu, Hausaland, and Timbuktu.

2249
'Abd Allāh ibn Qāsim al-Tilimsānī. Itinéraire de Tlemsen à Timbectou donné par Abdallah ben Cassem de Tlemsen et suivi par lui jusqu'à Saglia Hamra; communiqué par M. Ch. Cournault. Revue de l'Orient, nouv. ser., t. 4, 1856: 331–33.
DS1.R4, 1856

2250
Cherbonneau, Auguste. Indication sur la route de Touggourt à Timbouctou. Revue de géographie, v. 6, janv./juin 1880: 31–39. G1.R43, v. 6

2251
Cortier, M. De Tombouctou à Taoudenni, suivi de: note sur un fragment de manuscrits arabes recopiés à Araouane. La géographie, v. 14, déc. 1906: 317–341. G11.S4, v. 14

2252
Denis, P. A propos des salines et des pistes caravanières du Sahara occidental. Bulletin de liaison saharienne, v. 3, oct. 1952: 26–32.
DT331.B83, v. 3

Sects

2253
Alexandre, Pierre. A West African Islamic movement: Hamallism in French West Africa. *In* Rotberg, Robert I., *and* Ali M. Mazrui. Protest and power in Black Africa. New York, Oxford University Press, 1970. p. 497–512. maps. DT353.R6

In 1900 Sī Muḥammad ūld 'Abd Allāh al-Akhḍar, a Sharif from Touat who settled in Nioro du Sahel, differed with the established Tijani order over a prayer formality. The dispute grew and his disciple, Ḥamāhu Allāh ibn Sharīf Muḥammad ibn Sīdnā 'Umar, broke away from the Tijani and established what became known as the Ḥamālīyah, reformed Tijani, or sometimes Tidjanisme-onze-grains. Alexandre presents the history of the fraternity and its relations with the colonial administration and its close collaboration, if not integration, with the Rassemblement démocratique africain.

2254
André, Pierre J. L'Islam noir, contribution à l'étude des confréries religieuses islamiques en Afrique Occidentale, suivie d'une étude sur l'Islam au Dahomey. Paris, P. Geuthner, 1924. 129 p. fold. table. BP65.A4A6

In the introduction, J. Carde, Governor-General of French West Africa, shows the concern of the authorities for the spread of Islam in the coastal zones when he states that "le marabout ne prend plus place dans la caravane qui s'enfonçait naguère dans le désert vers les rives nigeriennes, il arrive par le paquebot." The fact that André went originally to French West Africa to head the intelligence apparatus provides the framework for the investigation. After a historical sketch of the Islamization of the region, the author analyzes the various sects, such as the Qadiri, Tijani, Senussi, and Ahmadi groups. The conclusion points out the threat of Islam in providing a cover for nationalist tendencies and calls attention to Communist indoctrination of the "tirailleurs indigènes." Appended is a short study of Islam in Dahomey and the Porto-Novo complex in particular.

2255
Behrman, Lucy. The political significance of the Wolof adherence to Muslim brotherhoods in the 19th century. African historical studies, v. 1, Jan./June, 1968: 60–78. DT1.A226, v. 1

This paper has proposed that the reasons for the political power of the Marabouts among the Wolof can be found in the nature of the brotherhoods and in the general insecurity of the ethnic group at the time at which it joined the Muslim orders. The brotherhoods had developed by the twelfth century into tight hierarchical organizations whose leaders had unquestioned authority over their followers. The orders attracted followers in Senegal because they symbolized opposition to the colonialists, expressed the desire of various parts of the population for social reform, and provided a framework of security for the Wolof whose social and political system was disintegrating. The Wolof joined the Muslim orders whose leaders replaced the traditional kings and nobles as social, economic, and political rulers.—(Abstract supplied)

2256
Bergmann, M. Die bruderschaft der Muriden, funktionale analyse. Sociale welt, v. 19, no. 2, 1968: 150–171. IEN

2257
Bourlon, Abel. Actualités des mourides et du Mouridisme. A&A, no 46, 2. trimestre, 1959: 10–30. DT1.A85, 1959

Muridism is a Wolof adaptation of the Qadiri fraternity. Boulon, who had close contacts with the sect, describes Touba, the holy city of the Murids, its mosque and pilgrimage. He also presents the great leaders of the group, their influence, rivalries, and relations with the French Administration, and analyzes the importance of the movement in the economic, social, and political life of Senegal.

2258
Cole, J. Augustus. A revelation of the secret orders of West Africa. Dayton, United Brethren Pub. House, 1886. 99 p. HS317.C65

2259
Cruise O'Brien, Donal B. Le Talibé mouride: étude d'un cas de dépendance sociale. CEA, v. 9, 3. cahier, 1969: 502–507. DT1.C3, v. 9

In a substantial issue devoted to "relations of personal dependence in Black Africa," the role of the Murid movement appears as a clear case of social dependency. After the collapse of the Wolof state system, the Murid sect, a branch of the Qadiri fraternity, provided a substitute for the traditional system of allegiance and client relationships. The talibé (Arabic *Ṭālib,* student) owes his Shaykh absolute allegiance after the rite of submission, Njebbel. He works in his fields and makes regular payments. In return, the talibé receives religious instruction and certain material benefits in times of crisis.

2260
———The Mourides of Senegal: the political and economic organization of an Islamic brotherhood. Oxford, Clarendon Press, 1971. 321 p. 8 plates, illus., maps, ports. (Oxford studies in African affairs) DT549.42.C76

Substantial study of the Murid sect. The author divides his analysis into three major sections: origins and growth, the structure of religious authority, and from agrarian settlement to urban politics, concluding on a pessimistic note regarding the future of the fraternity.

2261
Delafosse, Maurice. L'Ahmadisme et son action en Afrique occidentale française. L'Afrique française; bulletin du Comité de l'Afrique française et du Comité du Maroc. Renseignements coloniaux et documents, 1924: 32–36. DLC-Micro 03878

2262
———Les confréries musulmanes et le maraboutisme dans les pays du Sénégal et du Niger. L'Afrique française; bulletin du Comité de l'Afrique française et du Maroc. Rensiegnements coloniaux et documents, 1911: 81–90. DLC-Micro 03878

2263
Diarra, Thiam Médoune. Cheikh Ahmadou Bamba, fondateur du Mouridisme (1850–1927). [Conakry, Impr. nationale Patrice Lumumba, 1964] 32 p. illus. BP195.M67B357

2264
Fisher, Humphrey J. Ahmadiyyah; a study in contemporary Islam on the West African coast. [London] Published for the Nigerian Institute of Social and Economic Research [by] Oxford University Press, 1963. 206 p. BP64.A4W35

Detailed analysis of the Aḥmadīyah movement in Nigeria, Ghana, Sierra Leone, the Gambia, the French-speaking areas, and Liberia.

2265
———Ahmadiyya in the Gambia, French territories and Liberia. West Africa, no. 2330, Jan. 27, 1962: 93. DT491.W4, 1962

2266
———The Aḥmadiyya movement in Nigeria. African affairs. no. 1: p. 60–88. (St. Anthony papers, no. 10) DT1.A185, no. 1

Issued also in Carbondale, Ill., by Southern Illinois University Press. DT1.A16.

The Aḥmadīyah movement was introduced in Nigeria by Nigerian Muslims, mainly from Lagos, who were concerned "to find a more modern expression of Islam." Fisher's report, based on a 1958–59 visit to West Africa, provides a historical analysis of the movement. In spite of its original impetus, directed mainly to education, Fisher feels that "the maintenance and remoulding of Islam there [Nigeria] seem now decisively the responsibility of the non-Aḥmadī Muslims."

2267
———Ahmadiyya in Sierra Leone. Sierra Leone bulletin of religion, v. 2, June 1960: 1–10. DLC

2268
———Ahmadiyya in West Africa. West Africa, no. 2216, Nov. 21, 1959: 1000. DT491.W4, 1959

2269
———Independency and Islam: the Nigerian Aladuras and some Muslim comparisons: review article. JAH, v. 11, no. 2, 1970: 269–277. DT1.J65, v. 11

Critical review of two works: J. D. Y. Peel's *Aladura: A Religious Movement Among the Yoruba* (London, Published for the International African Institute by the Oxford University Press, 1968. 300 p.) and H. W. Turner's *History of an African Independent Church* (Oxford, Clarendon Press, 1967. 2 v.). Fisher compares these separatist churches with their Muslim equivalent regarding three features: prayer, healing, and revelation.

2270
———Planting Ahmadiyya in Ghana. West Africa, no. 2226, Jan. 30, 1960: 121. DT491.W4, 1960

2271
———Some novelties introduced into West African Islam by Ahmadiya. *In* Nigerian Institute of Social and Economic Research (Ibadan). Proceedings of the annual conference. v. 6; 1958. Ibadan, 1958. p. 220–231. HN792.W43, 1958

2272
———Some reflexions on Islam in independent West Africa. Clergy review, v. 53, Mar. 1968: 178–190. BX801.C6, v. 53

2273
Halpern, J. La confrérie des Mourides et le développement au Sénégal. Cultures et développement, v. 4, no 1, 1972: 99–125. HD83.C85, v. 4

2274
Holas, Bohumil. La Goumbée: une association de jeunesse musulmane en basse Côte d'Ivoire. Kongo-overzee, v. 19, no. 2/3, 1953: 116–131. map. DT641.K57, v. 19

2275
Kaba, Lansiné. The Wahhabiyya; Islamic reform and politics in French West Africa. Evanston, Ill., Northwestern Press, 1974. xv, 285 p. map (Studies in African religion) DLC

2276
Kesby, John D. Muslims of Senegal. West African review, v. 33, Sept. 1962: 37–44. DT491.W47, v. 33

Brief article on the Murids.

2277
Laforgue, Pierre. Une secte hérésiarque en Mauritanie: Les Ghoudf. BCAOF, v. 11, oct./déc. 1928: 647–653. DT521.C6, v. 11

A small religious sect in Mauritania, the Ghudfiyah, was centered around Atar and spread among the "Ideïboussat." The original sufism of the founder, Muḥammad Maḥmūd al-Khalīfah, was later mixed with various non-sufi practices, thus inspiring the scorn of the orthodox ulemas.

2278
Maintenance sociale et changement économique au Sénégal [par] J. Copans [et al.] Paris, O.R.S.T.O.M., 1972 illus. (Travaux et documents de l'O.R.S.T.O.M., no 15) HN810.S4M34

Table of contents in English (2 leaves) inserted. L.C. has v. 1, Doctrine économique et pratique du travail chez les Mourides.

2279
Marone, Ibrahima. Le Tidjanisme au Sénégal. BIFAN, t. 32, janv. 1970: 136–215. DT1.I5123, v. 32

Substantial study. After providing a historical analysis, Marone describes the organization and structure of the fraternity and concludes with a section on the dynamics of the Tijani sect and the evolution of the Senegalese society. Appended are various religious poems and incantations.

2280
Martin, Bradford G. Notes sur l'origine de la *tariqa* de Tiğaniyya et sur les débuts d'al-Hağğ 'Umar. Revue des études islamiques, v. 37, 2. cahier, 1969: 267–290. BP1.R53, v. 37

2281
Martin, V. Le mouvement mouride et l'arachide. *In* Mission Roland Portères. Aménagement de l'économie agricole et rurale au Sénégal; mission d'étude 15 mars-30 avril 1952. [Dakar, 1952] p. 102–112. HD2135.S42M5

2282
Marty, Paul. Les Mourides d'Amadou Bamba. Paris, E. Leroux, 1913. (Collection de la Revue du monde musulman)
Source: Joucla 6992

2283
al-Maṣrī, Imām. Minbar al-Islām tushārik al-ṭā'ifah al-Tījānīyah iḥtifālihā bil-mawlid al-nabawī al-sharīf. [Minbar al-Islam participates with the Tijani community in its celebration of the Holy Prophet's birthday] Minbar al-Islām, v. 29, July 1971: 212–220. DS36.M53, v. 29 Orien Arab
Report on the celebrations in Kaolack, Senegal, which—according to al-Maṣrī—brought together about 200,000 persons from all of West Africa. Included is an interview with a new convert to Islam from the midwest region of Nigeria.

2284
Monteil, Vincent. Chronique de la Zaouïa d'Assa. *In* Mutanawwi'āt Muḥammad al-Fāsī. [Rabat? 1969?] p. 81–89. AC105.M87 Orien Arab
At head of title: al-Mamlakah al-Maghribīyah: Jāmi'at Muḥammad al-Khāmis.

2285
———Une confrérie musulmane: Les Mourides du Sénégal. Archives de sociologie des religions, 7. année, juil./déc. 1962: 77–104. BL60.A7, v. 7
Historical analysis of the Murid sect, the tribulations of its leader Amadu Bamba, and the impact of the sect on the economy of Senegal.

2286
Rossie, Jean-Pierre. Influence occidentale dans la structure religieuse musulmane (confréries) en Afrique Ouest Francophone pendant la première moitié du XIXe siècle. Correspondance d'Orient; Etudes, no 11/12, 1967: 35–48. DS36.C65, 1967
Analysis of the Hamalli and Murid movements during the early part of the 19th century. The author isolates two variables—namely the role and influence of the French administration, and the feelings and values upon which the latter based its policy—and shows their historical evolution and dynamics.

2287
Stewart, Charles C. Notes on North and West African manuscript material relating to the West African Qadiriyya *tariqa. In* Ibadan, Nigeria. University. *Centre of Arabic Documentation.* Research bulletin, v. 4, Dec. 1968: 1–25. DT352.4.I2a, v. 4

2288
Sy, Cheikh Tidiane. Ahmadou Bamba et l'islamisation des Wolof. BIFAN, t. 32, avril 1970: 412–433. DT1.I5123, v. 32

2289
———La confrérie sénégalaise des Mourides, un essai sur l'Islam au Sénégal. [Paris] Présence africaine, 1969. 354 p. plates. BP195.M66S9
Study of one of the major religious fraternities in Senegal. The author—a Senegalese—has divided his work into two main parts. In the first part, he studies the Islamization of West Africa and the Wolof and analyzes the development of the Murid movement by Aḥmadū Bamba (1850–1927), its doctrine and expansion. In the second part, Sy looks at Muridism in the light of the conjuncture of the political and economic aspects of Senegalese society. Extensive bibliography.

2290
Triaud, Jean-Louis. La lutte entre la Tidjaniya et la Qadriya dans le Macina au 19e siècle. In Abidjan, Ivory Coast. Université. Annales, v. 1, no 1, 1969: 149–171. DLC

2291
Villeneuve, Michel. Une société musulmane d'Afrique noire: la confrérie des mourides. IBLA [revue de l'Institut des belles lettres arabes] 28. année, no 110, 2. trimestre, 1965: 127–163.
AS653.I5, v. 28

2292
Wade, A. La doctrine économique du mouridisme. Annales africaines, 1967: 175–206. DLC–LL
Analysis of the Murid doctrine. Wade believes it to be a unique example of a blend of religious beliefs and economic development in Islam. He shows the originality of the formula: learning, prayer, and work, and the impact of the economic tenets of the fraternity on the Senegalese economy.

Society & Culture

2293
Abdul, M. O. A. Yoruba divination and Islam. Orita, v. 4, July 1970: 17–26. DLC
As an example of the adaptability of Islam to the African environment, Abdul presents divination as one of the important traditional practices that have assimilated Islamic elements and are accommo-

dated by the latter. The Ifā of the Yoruba and its Muslim counterpart, the Hati, are analyzed to show the similarities and interaction between the two practices and two religions.

2294
Abimbola, Wande. Ifa divination poetry and the coming of Islam in Yoruba: a preliminary investigation. Paper presented at the 14th annual meeting of the African Studies Association, Denver, 1971.
DLC-Micro 03782

Collation of the original: 16 p.

2295
Anawati, Georges C. Trois talismans musulmans en arabe provenant du Mali (Marché de Mopti) Annales islamologiques, v. 11, 1972: 287–339.
BP1.A65, v. 11

"Volume dédié à la mémoire de Gaston Wiet."

2296
Appia, Béatrice. Les forgerons du Fouta-Djallon. JOSAF, t. 35, fasc. 2, 1965: 317–352.
DT1.S65, v. 35

Description of the smith caste in the Fouta Djallon region of Guinea. This study, revised by Germaine Dieterlen and annotated by A. Hampâté Bâ, examines in detail the smiths, their religious and social organizations, including the various spirits (iron, trees, wind, mountains, and mosques), the training period, initiation, and techniques. Appia quotes various prayers and incantations, including a number of Muslim terms, showing the growing influence of Islam on that group.

2297
Arnaud, Robert. Croyances relatives aux éclipses de lune à Tombouctou. Revue d'ethnographie et des traditions populaires, v. 3, 2. trimestre, 1922: 154.
GN1.R53, v. 3

2298
Ba, Oumar. Notes sur la démocratie en pays toucouleur. [n.p., Imp. A. Diop, 1966] 52 p. (Etudes mauritaniennes) IEN

2299
———La polygamie en pays toucouleur. Afrique documents, no 64, juil./oct. 1962: 165–179.
DT1.A479, 1962

Critique of the practice of polygamy by the Tukulor of the Foto Toro region. Ba dissects the "Nialigou" institution and, though polygamous himself, declares himself opposed to it.

2300
Balewa, Sir. Abubakar Tafawa. The city of language. The Nigerian teacher, v. 1, no. 4, 1935: 52. illus. DT515.N47, v. 1

The former Prime Minister of Nigeria began his career as a teacher. In this article he imaginatively explains the parts of speech and their interrelations in English by comparing them to a "Hausa city, with its hierarchy of officials, dependent one on the other." By reversing the process, the intricacies of Hausa social relations are schematically presented to the student of Northern Nigeria.

2301
Bivar, A. D. H. Nigerian panoply: arms and armour of the Northern Region [Nigeria] [Lagos, Nigeria] Dept. of Antiquities, 1964. IEN

2302
Bouillié, Robert. Les coutumes familiales au Kanem. Paris, Domat-Montchrestien, 1937. 359 p. fold. geneal., fold. maps., plates, ports.
DT553.K2B6

Doctoral dissertation on social structures of the Kanem region population of Chad. Bouillié, who was "capitaine d'Infanterie Coloniale," spent two years in Mao studying these populations. Though not directly dealing with Islam, the essay contains a large section (40 pages) on Islam in Kanem. The rest of the work is concerned with the various aspects of the society which is greatly influenced by Islam. The attitude of the writer toward his wards is best expressed by the following colonial *dictum*: "Il est en effet, en matière de colonisation, un principe absolu et indiscutable qu'il convient de ne jamais oublier: lorsque l'indigène se croit suffisament puissant pour se libérer de la tutelle dont il est l'objet, il n'hésite pas à se retourner contre l'autorité dominante s'il juge celle-ci dépouillée de son prestige et de sa force, quels que soient les bienfaits dont il ait pu profiter."

2303
Boutillier, Jean-Louis. Les rapports du système foncier Toucouleur et de l'organisation sociale et économique traditionnelle. Leur évolution actuelle. *In* International African Seminar. *2d, Leopoldville, Congo, 1960.* African agrarian systems; studies presented and discussed. Edited with an introduction by Daniel Biebuyck. Foreword by Daryll Forde. [London] Published for the International African Institute by the Oxford University Press, 1963. p. 116–136. HD966.I5 1960

2304
Bravmann, René A. Islam and tribal art in West Africa. [London, New York] Cambridge University Press [1974] 189 p. illus. (African studies series no. 11) N7398.B72

2305
Brenner, Louis. Concepts of legitimacy in Bornu as manifested in various forms of literary expression and behavior.
Source: ASA, Program, 15th, 1972.

2306
Brévié, Jules. Islamisme contre "le Naturalisme" au Soudan français; essai de psychologie de politique coloniale. Paris, Leroux, 1923. 320 p.
"Préoccupé spécialement d'exposer les éléments mystiques et sociaux sur lesquels repose la civilisation indigène des populations du Soudan occidental et de montrer en quoi l'islamisme contrecarre ces éléments et quelle réaction résulte de l'opposition de deux tendances distinctes. . . . La troisième partie du volume contient, sur les rapports de la colonisation française avec l'islamisme soudanais et sur les conséquences variées et parfois contradictories des méthodes de politique indigène successivement adoptées, des aperçus originaux fort instructifs pour ceux qui voudraient écrire l'histoire de l'intervention européenne en Afrique Occidentale."—(From a review by Maurice Delafosse in *Revue de l'histoire des colonies françaises,* v. 15, 2. trimestre. 1923: 310–313. JV1801.R4)
Source: Joucla, 1253.

2307
Brito, Eduino. Festas religiosas do Islamismo Fula. Boletim Cultural da Guiné Portuguesa, v. 11, jan. 1956: 91–105. DT613.B6, v. 11

2308
Brouin, M. Un îlot de vieille civilisation africaine; le pays de Ouacha (Niger français). BCAOF, v. 21, oct./déc. 1938: 469–479. DT521.C6, v. 21
Description of the country southwest of Zinder which was part of the "Sosébaki" empire of the Darnikawa. The empire flourished until the advent of Usuman dan Fodyo. Brouin describes its social structure and religious beliefs, as well as a former ribāt near the "Illela" mountain where is located the shrine of a marabout named Wālī dan Ṣadaqah, who lived there in the 17th century.

2309
Burness, Helen N. The position of women in Gwandu and Yauri. Overseas education, v. 26, Jan. 1955: 143–152. LC2601.O8, v. 26
Notes on the position of women in the Gwandu and Yauri emirates of Northern Nigeria.

2310
Cardaire, Marcel P. L'Islam et la cellule sociale africaine. A&A, no 29, 1955: 20–28. DT1.A85, 1955
Cardaire believes that while Islam was the religion of "Princes" in West Africa for about 10 centuries, it has become in the recent past an Islam of religious fraternities. The conquering chiefs did not impose their beliefs on the traditional social structure, which remained impervious to Islam. With the weakening of these structures and a resulting feeling of alienation, Cardaire argues, the impact of the modern world created a spiritual void. Islam provided people separated from the traditional groups with a refuge in a new all-embracing socio-religious membership. He believes that African Muslim scholars are beginning to rethink African Islam to adapt it to African traditional realities.

2311
Coutouly, François de. La famille, les fiançailles et le mariage chez les Peuls du Liptako (Haute-Volta). Revue d'ethnographie et des traditions populaires, v. 4, 3. trimestre 1923: 259–270. GN1.R53, v. 4

2312
Daniel, F. de F. The regalia of Katsina, Northern Provinces, Nigeria. *In* African Society. Journal, v. 31, Jan. 1932: 80–83. DT1.R62, v. 31
Description of the regalia consisting of "two swords, a large camel drum of bronze and a bronze pot of overlapping plates riveted together." The information was given Daniel by Mallam Zayara, Wazirin, Katsina.

2313
Delafosse, Maurice. Le clergé musulman de l'Afrique occidentale. RMM, t. 11, juin 1910: 177–206. DS36.R4, v. 11
Description of the religious men in West Africa. Delafosse examines the composition, recruitment, functions, hierarchy, insignia, income, doctrine, training, teaching, and "intellectual and moral values" of this group. He also describes their public prayers. His investigation concentrates on the "almami, modibbo" including the "alfa, karamoko, moriba, tyerno" better known as marabout, and the "alkali."

2314
———Coutumes et fêtes matrimoniales chez les musulmans du Soudan occidental. RMM, t. 11, juil./août 1910: 405–421. DS36.R4, v. 11

After pointing out pre-Islamic residues among the Islamized Mande, Delafosse examines the wedding ceremonies, or "fourou-ba-don"; the "water feast," or "dyi-sou," taking place on the full moon preceding the fast of Ramaḍān; and the "virgins' feast," or "soungouroudon," celebrated on the last day of Ramaḍān.

2315
Dieterlen, Germaine, *and* Z. Ligers. Notes sur un talisman bambara. NA, no 83, juil. 1959: 89–90. DT1.I513, 1959

Comments on and reproduction of a Bambara talisman from the Ségou region.

2316
Dubot, B. Nouvelles notes sur la croix d'Agadés. NA, no 111, juil. 1966: 100–103. DT1.I513, 1966

Contribution on the complex question of the origin of the Agadez cross.

2317
———Notes sur la croix d'Agadés. NA, no 68, oct. 1955: 106–108. illus. DT1.I513, 1955

2318
Dupire, Marguerite. Organisation sociale des Peul: étude d'ethnographie comparée. Paris, Plon [1970] 624 p. illus., maps, plates. (Recherches en sciences humaines, 32. Serie jaune.) GN652.F9D79

Monumental study on the social structure of the Fulbe covering an area from Dakar to Lake Chad. Marguerite Dupire shared the life of the still-enigmatic Fulbe and throws a welcome light on the elements that make these communities, both herders and farmers, one people in spite of the relative degree of assimilation in the host societies.

2319
———Peuls nomades; étude descriptive des Woḍaaɓe du Sahel nigerien. Paris, Institut d'ethnologie, Musée de l'homme, 1962. 336 p. illus., maps (part fold., part col.) GN652.F9D8

2320
Dupuch, Charles. Essai sur l'emprise religieuse chez les Peulh du Fouta-Djallon. *In* Comité d'études historiques et scientifiques de l'Afrique occidentale française. Annuaire et mémoire, 1917: 290–309.

Source: Joucla 4368.

2321
Du Puigaudeau, Odette. La Ziâra de Cheikh Mohammed Fadel. BIFAN, t. 13, oct. 1951: 1218–1226. illus. Q89.I5, v. 13

Description of the mausoleum of Shaykh Muḥammad Fāḍil ūld 'Ubayd, one of the most venerated religious leaders in the Adrar region of Mauritania. The author visited the site as early as 1937 and describes the mausoleum in great detail with drawings and photographs.

2322
Dupuis, Anne, *and* Nicole Echard. La poteirie traditionnelle hausa de l'Ader (Rép. du Niger). JOSAF, t. 41, fasc. 1, 1971: 7–34. illus. DT1.S65, v. 41

Study of traditional Hausa pottery of the Ader region in Niger, carried out in Bakin Dabagi, a village in the Tahoua "Prefecture." Included are various techniques used by women potters.

2323
Durand, O. Moeurs et institutions d'une famille Peule du cercle de Pita. BCAOF, v. 12, janv./juin 1929: 1–85. DT521.C6, v. 12

Exhaustive investigation of Fulbe family life in the village of Timbi-Touni, located south of Labe in Guinea. The study focuses on an Elayanke Fulbe family under the leadership of Thierno Muḥammadu Mukhtār Ba, the "Chef de Canton" of the village. With an unmistakably Gallic wit, Durand presents the setting, including the village, dwellings, and furniture; he then describes in great detail marriage, conjugal life, sexual mores, prostitution, death, funerals, and the many facets of everyday life.

2324
Earthy, E. Dora. The impact of Mohammedanism on paganism in the Liberian hinterland. Numen; international review for the history of religions, v. 2, Sept. 1955: 206–216. BL1.N8, v. 2

2325
Echard, Nicole. Note sur les forgerons de l'Ader (pays hausa, République du Niger). JOSAF, t. 35, fasc. 2, 1965: 353–372. DT1.S65, v. 35

2326
Ferguson, Phyllis. Islamization in Dagbon: a study of the alfanema of Yendi. [Cambridge, Eng.] 1972. 381 p. illus., maps. IEN

2327
Gabus, Jean. Au Sahara. Neuchâtel, La Baconnière [1954, c1955-(1958)] 2 v. illus., maps. DT337.G3

Contents: [1] Les hommes et leurs outils.—[2] Arts et symboles.

2328
Gaden, Henri. Légendes et coutumes sénégalaises; cahiers de Yoro Dyao. Revue d'ethnographie et de sociologie, no 3/4, mars/avril 1912: 119–137; no 5/6, mai/août 1912: 191–202. GN1.R5, 1912

2329
———Du nom chez les toucouleurs et peuls islamisés du Fouta sénégalais. Revue d'ethnographie et de sociologie, v. 3, janv./fév. 1912: 50–56. GN1.R5, v. 3

2330
Gbadamọsi, G. O. The imamate question among the Yoruba Muslims. JHSN, v. 6, June 1972: 229–237. DT515.A2H5, v. 6

With the development of Islam among the Yoruba, the organizational problems of the Muslim community crystallized around the position of the Imam. Gbadamọsi examines the question and divides it into three main phases: "The first phase was primarily a period of rough and ready improvization. The second phase covered the period when there was only a single Imam for the Muslim community. During this period, the community was still small, and the knowledge of Islam and Arabic was generally scanty. Much more important was the fact that new ideas and systems were introduced, albeit in growing synthesis, with old established customs and practices. In the third phase, there was a Chief Imam with other local Imams (Imam Ratib) for the community. The community has grown large, and general knowledge had increased considerably. The conventions of the past which had become established in many areas were now being boldly challenged."

2331
Goody, John R. The impact of Islamic writing on the oral cultures of West Africa. CEA, v. 11, 3. cahier, 1971: 455–466. DT1.C3, v. 11

After investigating the impact of Arabic writing on non-literate West African cultures, Goody concludes "by suggesting that the initial appeal of Islam to outsiders was frequently magical (or magico-religious) and that writing was at first valued for its role in superhuman rather than human communication." This appeal, in turn, paved the way for the conversion of non-Islamic elements, while at the same time introducing novel practices and beliefs, thus creating a unique brand of Islam.

2332
Greenberg, Joseph H. The influence of Islam on a Sudanese religion. New York, J. J. Augustin [1947, c1946] 73 p. diagrs., map. (Monographs of the American Ethnological Society, 10) E51.A556 no. 10

2333
———Islam and clan organization among the Hausa. Southwestern journal of anthropology, v. 3, autumn 1947: 193–211. GN1.S64, v. 3

2334
———Some aspects of Negro-Mohammedan culture-contact among the Hausa. American anthropologist, v. 43, Jan./Mar. 1941: 51–61. GN1.A5, v. 43

2335
Grindal, Bruce T. Islamic affiliations and urban adaptation: The Sisala migrant in Accra, Ghana. Africa, v. 43, Oct. 1973: 333–346. PL8000.I6, v. 43

Study of the Sisala migrant traders, a group from northwestern Ghana, in Accra, particularly the relatively high incidence of Islamic affiliation among traditionally non-Muslim migrants. He believes that the attraction stems from insecurities resulting from migration and that Islam provides the instruments and channels to facilitate adjustment to urban life.

2336
Hill, Polly. Rural Hausa; a village and a setting. Cambridge [Eng.] Cambridge University Press, 1972. 368 p. illus. DT515.42.H54

2337
Hiskett, Mervyn. Some historical and Islamic influences in Hausa folklore. *In* Indiana. University. *Folklore Institute.* Journal, v. 4, June/Dec. 1967: 145–161. GR1.I5, v. 4

2338
Holas, Bohumil. La clef des songes des musulmans sénégalais. NA, no 42, avril 1949: 45–49. DT1.I513, 1949

Key to the interpretation of dreams as used by the Wolof of Senegal. The main source of information for Holas was his students at the Ecole normale William Ponty.

2339
Honeyman, A. M. A Muslim charm from West Africa. *In* Glasgow. University. *Oriental Society.* Transactions. v. 13; 1947–49. Glasgow, 1949. p. 53–56. MH

2340
Institut français d'Afrique noire. Mélanges ethnologiques. Dakar. IFAN, 1953. 408 p. illus., geneal. tables, maps (part fold., 1 col.), 23 plates, tables. (*Its* Mémoires, no 23) GN643.I5

Contents: Dans la boucle du Niger: Dori, ville peule, par P. Delmond.—La vie matérielle des Maures, par P. Dubié.—Catalogues des scarifications en usage chez certaines populations du Dahomey et du Nord-Togo, par J.-C. Froelich.—Phytothérapie maure, par A. Leriche.—Les noms individuels chez les Dogon (Soudan Français), par D. Lifchitz et D. Paulme.—La légende du Ouagadou et l'origine des Soninké, par C. Monteil.

2341
Kane, Elimane. La polygamie musulmane au Sénégal. Revue indigène, v. 15, janv./mars 1920: 26. JV1835.R6, v. 15

2342
Kane, Issa. La circoncision chez les Toucouleurs. L'Education africaine, v. 29, janv./juin 1937: 42–47. L81.E42, v. 29

2343
Kangiwa, *Mallam Shehu, and al-Haji* A. K. Metteden. Leatherwork in Northern Nigeria. Nigeria magazine, no. 74, Sept. 1962: 2–9. DT515.N47, 1962

2344
al-Khūrī, Fu'ād I. The African-Lebanese mulattoes of West Africa: a racial frontier. Anthropological quarterly, v. 41, Apr. 1968: 90–103. GN1.P7, v. 41

2345
———'Ayn 'alā Lubnān. [An eye on Lebanon] Beirut [Dār majallat Shi'r] 1963. 184 p. illus. DT471.K45

History of the Lebanese community in West Africa.

2346
Klein, Martin A. Social and economic factors in the Muslim revolution in Senegambia. JAH, v. 13, no. 3, 1972: 419–441. DT1.J65, v. 13

2347
Kozlov, S. ÎA. Polozhenie zavisimykh grupi naseliniîa na Futa-Dzhallone v b. 19—pervoĭ polovine 20 b. [Status of dependent groups of the Fouta-Djallon population (19th-first part of the 20th c.)] *In* Akademiîa nauk SSSR. *Institut etnografii.* Trudy. Novaia seriîa, t. 90. Moskva, 1966. (Afrikanskii etnograficheskii sbornik, 6) p. 11–24. GN2.A2142, v. 90

English summary.

2348
Laforgue, Pierre. Les Djenoun de la Mauritanie saharienne. BCAOF, v. 14, juil./sept. 1931: 433–452; v. 15, avril/sept. 1932: 400–424. DT521.C6, v. 14, 15

Islam in Mauritania, writes Laforgue, has not obliterated the old substratum of animistic religious beliefs. In this study on magic, he shows the old beliefs and their relationship with Muslim folklore regarding the meddlesome jinns.

2349
Leriche, Albert. Notes sur les classes sociales et sur quelques tribus de Mauritanie. BIFAN, t. 17, janv./avril 1955: 173–202. DT1.I5123, v. 17

Mauritanian society consists of two traditional groups: the warriors, carriers of rifles, and the marabouts, carriers of the prayer beads. Leriche presents the various divisions of the Mauritanian social structure which includes marabouts, warriors, tributaries, servants, and blacksmiths. He then delves into the origins of the tribes, whether Arab or Berber, concluding with a note on the numerous confederations of tribes.

2350
Leroux, Henri. Animism et Islam dans la subdivision de Maradi (Niger). BIFAN, t. 10, 1948: 595–695. Q89.I5, v. 10

The interaction of the local form of Animism with Maradi Islam is thoroughly investigated in this study. Leroux emphasizes animistic beliefs gravitating around the family and the land, including a number of rites and rituals. The spread of Islam is studied in terms of such agents of propagation as Muslim traders and Islamic law, the special status of Islam, and its own rituals with the local population. The result of the interaction reflects the plasticity of the Prophet Muhammad's message.

2351
Lunning, H. A. The impact of socio-economic factors on the land tenure pattern in Northern

Nigeria. Journal of local administration overseas, v. 4, July 1965: 173–182. JS40.J6, v. 4

2352
MacMichael, Harold A. Sudan Arabs in Nigeria. SNR, v. 6, July 1923: 109–110. DT118.S85, v. 6

2353
Maḥmūd, Ḥasan Aḥmad. Dawr al-'Arab fī nashr al-ḥaḍārah fī gharb Ifrīqiyah. [The role of the Arabs in the propagation of civilization in West Africa] Cairo. al-Jam'īyah al-Miṣrīyah lil-dirāsāt al-tārīkhīyah. al-Majallah al-tārīkhīyah al-Miṣrīyah, m. 14, 1968: 40–107. DT77.J28, v. 14 Orien Arab

The propagation of Islamic Arab culture in West Africa faced the same problem it faced in other regions, i.e., the encounter with indigenous cultures. "Islam," as Mahmūd puts it, "both took and gave," resulting in a symbiosis, and "local cultural environments developed as a result of this cultural encounter, each with its own particular characteristics but all encompassed within one frame of shared Islamic characteristics of a common language, religion and ideals." Mahmūd studies the spread of Islamic culture in West Africa from the first contacts with the Tuareg to the rise of the Islamic empires during the medieval period and then presents a detailed view of the system of government, Arab culture, and its centers during that period. He concludes with the confrontation, during the 19th century, between Islam and the West and the many forms resistance to the encroachment of Western culture took, such as Wahhabi trends, Sufi orders, and Mahdist movements.

2354
Marty, Paul. Les amulettes musulmanes au Sénégal. RMM, t. 27, juin 1914: 319–368. DS36.R4, v. 27

The flexibility of Islam is best illustrated in its adaptability in Africa. Taking religious amulets as an example, Marty shows their role in the Islamization of the Animist populations of black Africa. In a detailed presentation of the religious charms, gri-gri, he reviews the type of marabouts selling the amulets, describes the talisman and its content, and explains the meaning given to the various numbers and letters in the texts. Appended are texts and translations of some talismans examined.

2355
———Nos programmes de dessins et la reproduction des êtres animés dans l'Islam. L'Education africaine; bulletin de l'enseignement en A.O.F., no 34, nov. 1917: 18. PU–Mu

2356
Mauny, Raymond. Autour de la croix d'Agadés. NA, no 65, janv. 1955: 15. illus. DT1.I513, 1955

Excerpts from a letter by Lord Rennel of Rodd to Mauny on an article regarding the origin of the Agadez cross (*see* the following entry). Lord Rennell believes that the cross is derived from the ancient Egyptian Ankh symbol of life. Also included are photographs of crosses given to IFAN by Col. R. Thiriet.

2357
———Une énigme non résolue: origine et symbolique de la croix d'Agadés. NA, no 63, juil. 1954: 70–79. illus. DT1.I513, 1954

Substantive study of the enigmatic Agadez cross. Mauny analyzes the various shapes of the cross and the symbolism behind it. After reviewing its hypothetical Egyptian, Carthaginian, and Greek origins, he concludes "... nous ne savons encore rien de certain à ce sujet." Extensive bibliography.

2358
Maupoil, Bernard. Contribution à l'étude de l'origine musulmane de la géomancie dans le Bas-Dahomey. JOSAF, t. 13, fasc. 1, 1943: 1–94. DT1.S65, v. 13

2359
Miner, Horace M. Culture change under pressure: a Hausa case. Human organization, v. 19, fall 1960: 164–167. GN1.H83, v. 19

2360
Modat, *Colonel.* Aperçu sur la société maure de l'Adrar. BCAOF, v. 5, avril/juin, 1922: 264–276. DT521.C6, v. 5

Brief introduction to traditional Mauritanian society of the Adrar region. A study of the social structure and sources and focuses of authority, as well as the centers of religious activities.

2361
Monteil, Charles V. La divination chez les noirs de l'Afrique occidentale française. BCAOF, v. 14, janv./juin 1931: 27–137. DT521.C6, v. 14

Detailed study of divination in former French West Africa. The senior Monteil, after consulting a number of marabouts, among whom was Ahmadu Gano from Djenne who referred him to a book by Shaykh Muḥammad al-Zanātī, presents a substantial analysis of divination and geomancy in the area.

2362
Monteil, Vincent. Contribution à la sociologie des Peuls (Le Fonds Vieillard de l'IFAN). BIFAN, t. 25, juil./oct. 1963: 351–414. DT1.I5123, v. 25

Gilbert Vieillard died on the battlefield in 1940. He was fascinated by Africa and the Fulbe in particular. His notes gathered at IFAN in Dakar in a "Fonds Vieillard" are a valuable source of information on the peripatetic Fulbe. In this study, Monteil, former director of the IFAN, presents an element of Fulbe sociology based on Vieillard's papers. Of special interest are the sections on the religious texts, Fulbe Islam, and social structure.

2363
———Un visionnaire musulman sénégalais (1946–1965). Archives de sociologie des religions, 10. année, janv./déc. 1965: 69–98. BL60.A7, v. 10

Report on a Tukulor who kept a diary of his dreams and visions, and their interpretations. After the pilgrimage to the Holy Places, the man began to heal people and perform miracles. Monteil reports on the whole episode.

2364
Murūwah, Kāmil. Naḥnu fī Ifrīqīyah, al-hijrah al-Lubnānīyah al-Sūrīyah ilā Ifrīqīyah al-Gharbīyah: Māḍīhā, ḥādiruhā, musṭaqbaluhā. [We in Africa, Lebano-Syrian immigration in West Africa: its past, present, future] Beirut, al-Makshūf, 1938 [cover 1939] 323 p. illus., maps (1 col.), ports. DT530.M8

2365
Nadel, Siegfried F. Nupe religion; traditional beliefs and the influence of Islam in a West African chiefdom. New York, Schocken Books [1970] 288 p. illus. BL2480.N8N3 1970

"Intended as a sequel to . . . [the author's] first monograph on the Nupe people, *A Black Byzantium*" (*see* 1972).

2366
Noye, Dominique, *comp.* Humour et sagesse peuls; contes, devinettes et proverbes foulbé du Nord-Cameroun, traduits et annotés, suivis d'un lexique foulfoulde-français. Maroua, Mission catholique, 1968. 118 p. PL8184.A2N6

Texte in Fulfulde and French.

2367
Olusanya, G. O. The Sabon-gari system in northern states of Nigeria. Nigeria magazine, no. 94, Sept. 1967: 242–248. DT515.N47, 1967

Investigation of the system of urban segregation imposed by the colonial authorities.

2368
Paden, John N. Religion and political culture in Kano. Berkeley, University of California Press, 1973. 461 p. maps, tables. BP173.P3 1973

Paden, who came to know Kano and its people intimately, provides an analytical study of the interaction between social and political systems in the famed city. He looks at Islam and its impact on religious leadership and political authority in the community. Paden concludes his substantial work stating that: "When political and religious authority roles are embodied in the same actors, the question of a political-culture zone becomes redundant to some extent, depending on the degree to which the actors can establish distinctive boundaries between these two sets of roles. If the political or religious authorities are of the charismatic variety, role boundaries tend to be blurred. This may facilitate community consolidation for a particular time period but seems to set up reactions in the community by those, particularly the bureaucracy, who are adversely affected by the fusion of all authority into a single source. The evidence from Kano would suggest that, despite the pressures for bureaucratic routinization and differentiation, the periods of community crisis (and in a plural society this is related primarily to interethnic tensions) can only be resolved by authority figures with fused roles (especially religious and political). The subsequent differentiation of these roles allows for bureaucratic consolidation of the new-scale community."

2369
Parrinder, E. Geoffrey. Islam and West African indigenous religions. Numen; international review for the history of religions, v. 6, Dec. 1959: 130–141. BL1.N8, v. 6

2370
———Religion in an African city. London, New York, Oxford University Press, 1953. 211 p. illus. BL2465.P29

The Yoruba of Nigeria have begun to accept Islam since the early part of the 19th century, and yet Islam, says Parrinder, "is the most considerable factor today in the religious life of Ibadan." In this study of religion in the Yoruba city, Parrinder, who has a missionary background, examines both Christianity and Islam, their manifestations, and impact on an African urban society.

2371
Péfontan, *Commandant.* Les Armas. BCAOF, v. 9, janv./mars 1926: 153–179. DT521.C6, v. 9

An ethno-historical study of the Arma group of the Niger Bend. The origin and the culture of these men, who first arrived with the Juder expedition of 1590, is amply studied. Arma, according to the author, comes from *Rumi,* which in Arabic means "Greek" or Westerner in general. It is believed that this elite commando of arquebusiers was formed of Spanish renegades.

2372
Pokrovskii, V. S. K voprosu o sotsialno ekonomicheskoi kharakteristiki gosudarstva Zapadnogo Sudana v 19 v. [Social and economic features of West African states during the 19th century] Narody Azii i Afriki, 2, 1963: 86–98.
DS1.P7, 1963
Tables of contents also in English and Chinese; summaries in English.

2373
Proudfoot, L. Mosque-building and tribal separatism in Freetown East. Africa, v. 29, Oct. 1959: 405–416. PL8000.I6, v. 29
There were few mosques at the beginning of the 20th century in Freetown, Sierra Leone. Interest gradually developed among the various ethnic groups, and an elaborate mosque was considered a status symbol for the Muslims of that city. As a result, the Mandingo, Temne, Fulbe, and Limba have built their own mosques where tribal languages are used rather than Krio, which is considered the *lingua franca* of Sierra Leone. According to Proudfoot, the mosque, originally a religious focus, is slowly drawn into the vortex of the political life of Freetown.

2374
———Towards solidarity in Freetown. Africa, v. 31, Apr. 1961: 142–157. PL8000.I6, v. 31
After discussing, in the preceding entry, the centrifugal forces at work on the Muslim community of Freetown, Proudfoot analyzes the centripetal forces which have led Muslims to strive to unite in the face of the Christian challenge. The organizations instrumental in developing these efforts are the Muslim Association, the Ahmadi sect, and the Muslim Reformation Society.

2375
al-Qaddāḥ, Na'īm. Afrīqiyā al-gharbīyah fī ẓill al-Islām. [West Africa under the shade of Islam] Reviewed by 'Umar al-Ḥakīm. [Damascus, Maktabat Aṭlas, 1961?] 168 p. illus., maps. (Dirāsāt Afrīqīyah) DT471.Q2
Silsilat al-thaqāfah al-Sha'bīyah, 6.
At head of title: Wizārat al-thaqāfah wa-al-irshād al-qawmī. Mudīriyyat al-ta'līf wa-al-tarjamah.

2376
———Ḥaḍārat al-Islām wa-ḥadārat Ūrūbbā fī Ifrīqiqiyā al-Gharbīyah. [The civilization of Islam and Western civilization in West Africa] Damascus, Maktabat Aṭlas, 1965. 294 p. illus., maps, ports.
BP64.A4W365 Orien Arab

2377
———al-Ta'thīr al-'Arabī al-Islāmī fī Mujtama' Ifrīqiyā al-Gharbīyah. [The Arab Muslim impact on the society of West Africa] al-Ma'rifah, no. 11, Apr. 1963: 48–58. AP95.A6M3, 1963 Orien Arab

2378
Raulin, H. Un aspect historique des rapports de l'animisme et de l'Islam au Niger. JOSAF, t. 32, fasc. 2, 1962: 249–274. DT1.S65, v. 32
With the spread of Islam in the Niger Valley, earth belonged to the Animist masters of the land while political authority was the realm of the Muslim conquerors. In this study focusing on land tenure, socio-economic family groups, and Animism based essentially on the concept of Mother Earth, Raulin looks at the Islamization of the Niger Valley and the interaction between Islam and Animism and the resulting relationship after centuries of contact.

2379
Reed, L. N. Notes on some Fulani tribes and customs. Africa, v. 5, Oct. 1932: 422–454.
PL8000.I6, v. 5

2380
Revol, *Lt.* Etude sur les fractions d'Imraguem de la Côte mauritanienne. BCAOF, v. 20, janv./juin 1937: 179–224. DT521.C6, v. 20

2381
Robin, J. L'évolution du mariage coutumier chez les musulmans du Sénégal. Africa, v. 17, July 1947: 192–201. PL8000.I6, v. 17

2382
Rodney, Walter. Jihad and social revolution in Futa Djalon in the eighteenth century. JHSN, v. 4, June 1968: 269–284. DT515.A2H5, v. 4

2383
Rouch, Jean. Migrations au Ghana (Gold Coast); (Enquête 1953–1955). JOSAF, t. 26, fasc. 1/2, 1956: 33–196. DT1.S65, v. 26
Includes a section on Islam among the migrants.

2384
———Problèmes relatifs à l'étude des migrations traditionnelles et des migrations actuelles en Afrique occidentale. BIFAN, t. 22, juil./oct. 1960: 369–378. DT1.I5123, v. 22
By describing present migrational patterns, Rouch raises the problem of migrations during the era of Western Sudanic empires.

2385
Scott Macfie, J. W. A jeweller in Northern Nigeria. Revue d'ethnographie et de sociologie, no 9/10, sept./oct. 1912: 281–286. GN1.R5, 1912

2386
Silla, Ousmane. Les Arabes et le Sénégal: Arabisme sans Arabisation. NA, no 121, janv. 1969: 24–30. DT1.I513, 1969
In the spread of Islam two processes took place: Islamization, which extended to China and Spain, and Arabization, which was halted whenever met by a strong indigenous culture such as that of Iran and the Indian subcontinent. Ousmane Silla, who is attached to IFAN, looks at the impact of Islam on Senegal and analyzes its social, religious, and cultural influences, concluding that the Muslim population of Senegal has been Islamized but not Arabized in the sense of feeling part of the Arab nation stretching from the Atlantic Ocean to the Persian Gulf. This seems to be due to French colonial policies, as well as to Senegalese attitudes towards Arabs caused by historical residues or economic factors.

2387
Siossat, J. Les coutumes des orpailleurs indigènes du Maramandougou. BCAOF, v. 20, juil./sept. 1937: 336–349. DT521.C6, v. 20
A technician, Siossat lived with the gold diggers of the Maramandougou, near Bamako, for a long time. He spoke Malinke and, as a result of this daily contact, gives a thorough description of gold-panning in the 1930's which had not changed considerably since older times and therefore provides valuable information about gold-panning operations at the time of the great Sudanic empires.

2388
Skinner, Elliott P. The diffusion of Islam in an African society. *In* New York Academy of Sciences. Annals. v. 96, article 2; 1962. New York, 1962. p. 659–669. Q11.N5, v. 96
This issue is devoted to the papers of a conference entitled "Anthropology and Africa Today" held by the New York Academy of Sciences on May 1–3, 1961.

In this investigation of the expansion of Islam in West Africa, Skinner concludes with a study of Islam in Kombissiri in the "cercle" of Ouagadougou based on his field notes for 1941–54.

2389
Smith, M. G. The Hausa system of social status. Africa, v. 29, July 1959: 239–252. PL8000.I6, v. 29
The Hausa provides an excellent example of the sociological importance of distinctions based upon status. In this article Smith looks into the status of the Hausa which is determined by such factors as ethnic origin (whether Fulbe or Habe), descent and lineage, kinship and social position, distinction between rulers and ruled, and the system of occupational class. Smith also devotes a section to the "Social Placement of Women" where the distinction between child and adult overrides all other status considerations.

2390
Stewart, Charles C., *and* E. K. Stewart. Islam and social order in Mauritania; a case study from the nineteenth century. Oxford, Clarendon Press, 1973. 204 p. (Oxford studies in African affairs) BP64.M3573 1973
Through the life of Shaykh Sīdiyā al-Kabīr (1775–1868) Stewart expertly traces the impact of the Kuntah on the religious, social, political, and economic life of Mauritania.

2391
Ṭarkhān, Ibrāhīm 'Alī. al-Islām wa-al-lughah al-'Arabīyah fī Gharb Ifrīqiyā. [Islam and the Arabic language in West Africa] Cairo. Jāmi'at al-Qāhirah. Kuliyyat al-ādāb. Majallat Kuliyyat al-ādāb, m. 27, pt. 1–2, May/Dec. 1965: 51–92. AS693.C25 Orien Arab
Substantial analysis of Islam in West Africa. Professor Tarkhān, who teaches at the Khartoum branch of Cairo University, has divided his study into two sections, Islam and the Arabic language. In the first section, he shows the various phases of Islam: the beginnings in the seventh century, followed by the Almoravid, Mali, Songhay, and Fulbe phases. The second part of the study examines the impact of Arabic on the region, the changes it has undertaken, and the indigenous literature written in that language.

2392
Taylor, Frank W., *and* A. G. G. Webb. Labarun al'adun Hausawa da zantatukansu; accounts and conversations describing certain customs of the Hausas. With a foreword by Henry Balfour. Lon-

don, Oxford University Press, H. Milford, 1932. 225 p. diagrs. (Taylor's Fulani-Hausa series, VII) PJ8234.A1T3

The accounts were written by "natives but they have been edited as regards orthography, and expressed in the standard Kano dialect."

2393
Telli, Diallo. Le divorce chez les Peuls. Présence africaine, nouv. sér., no 22, oct./nov. 1958: 29–47. GN645.P74, n.s., 1958

2394
Thomas, Louis-Vincent. Les Diola; essai d'analyse fonctionnelle sur une population de Basse-Casamance. Dakar, I.F.A.N., 1969. 2 v. music, plates. (Mémoires de l'Institut français d'Afrique noire, no 55) DT549.T48

2395
Touré, Soualou. Notes sur une communauté "Nigerienne" ancienne en Côte d'Ivoire: Maradadiassa. Edited by Jean Rouch and Edmond Bernus. NA, no 84, oct. 1959: 107–110. DT1.I513, 1959

Transcription and translation of an oral tradition regarding the origin of the village of Marabadiassa ("the Hausa palissade" in Mande), located about 50 miles northwest of Bouake. The village was a Muslim center that retained friendly relations with its Animist neighbors.

2396
Tremearne, Arthur J. N. Hausa superstitions and customs; an introduction to the folk-lore and the folk. [London] Cass, 1970. 548 p. illus., fold. map. (Cass library of African studies. General studies no. 90) GN653.T7 1970

Hausa folklore "is part of the general Islamic heritage and contains a wealth of evidence to enable us to explain and understand the nature of the Islamic presence in Africa," writes Mervyn Hiskett in his introductory note to this new edition. Tremearne has gathered a wealth of tales, parables, and legends such as *Kalīlah wa Dimnah* which show clearly both the impact of Islamic lore on Hausa traditional literature and its coexistence and accommodation with a pre-Islamic substratum.

2397
Vermel, P. L'influence du Mahdisme au Nigeria. A&A, no 93–94, 1./2. trimestres, 1971: 47–60. DT1.A85, 1971

Exploring the impact of Mahdism, from Usuman dan Fodyo in Northern Nigeria and Ḥayātū ibn Sa'īd in the Adamawa region, to Muḥammad ibn 'Abd Allāh Ḥasan in the Sudan and their many imitators, Vermel concludes that the movement brought about religious reforms which marked the intellectual life of the Sahel from Senegal to the Sudan.

2398
Vieillard, Gilbert P. Notes sur les coutumes des Peuls au Fouta Djallon. Paris, Larose, 1939. 127, [1] p. (Publications du Comité d'études historiques et scientifiques de l'Afrique occidentale française. Sér. A. No 11) DLC–LL

2399
Wane, Yaya. Les Toucouleurs du Fouta Tooro (Sénégal); stratification sociale et structure familiale. Dakar, Institut fondamental d'Afrique noire, 1969. 250 p. illus. (Initiations et études africaines, 25) DT549.42.W36

Detailed and thorough study of social change among the Tukulor. Wane investigates Tukulor social stratification, kinship structures, and concludes with a section on the Tukulor family and social dynamics. In his closing remarks he points to the heavy responsibility of African leadership in creating a viable modern nation by conciliating ethnic particularisms and the colonial legacy. Included is a sobering "Avertissement" on methodology in which he states, "Et, semble-t-il, rien n'est autant nocif que ce savoir plus apparent que réel, que chacun croit naturellement posséder sur sa civilisation ancestrale." Substantial bibliography and a useful glossary of Tukulor terminology.

2400
Watt, W. Montgomery. Islam and the integration of society. London, Routledge & Paul [1961] 293 p. (International library of sociology and social reconstruction) HN40.M6W3 1961a

Includes a section on Islamization of West Africa.

2401
———Some problems before West African Islam. The Islamic quarterly, v. 4, Apr./July 1957: 43–51. D198.I8, v. 4

Watt, a well-known student of Islam, looks at West African Islam and the problems it is facing. Regarding the symbiotic relationship between certain animistic practices and Islam, Watt asks, "Should the Islamic norms of social life be adapted to the West African environment? Or must one wait patiently for the slow moulding of the West African outlook by the Islamic norms?" Another problem cited by Watt is that of Westernization, also faced by all Islamic countries. Watt suggests that "some solutions found in the 'heartlands' will prove applicable to the 'frontiers'. That is the best hope of a 'frontier' like West Africa, and that Muslims belonging to the 'heartlands' should have some awareness of the problems of the 'frontiers'."

2402
Winder, R. B. The Lebanese in West Africa. *In* Lloyd A. Fallers, *comp.* Immigrants and associations. The Hague, Paris, Mouton. 1967 [1968] p. 103–153. HV3199.C6F3

History of the Syrian-Lebanese immigrants in West Africa, who lived apart, in turn, from both the white colonialists and the African nationalists and rarely identified with their country of residence.

2403
Yeld, E. R. Islam and social stratification in Northern Nigeria. British journal of sociology, v. 11, June 1960: 112–128. HM1.B75, v. 11

Theology

2404
al-Ḥā'irī, 'Alī ibn Zayn al-'Ābidīn. Ilzām al-nāṣib fī ithbāt al-hujjah al-ghā'ib. [Coercion of he who exerts himself in proving the absent eminence]. Karbala', al-Maktabah al-Islāmīyah, 1968. 2 v. DT108.3.H32 1963

"Kitāb al-bayān fī akhbār ṣāḥib al-zamān, imlā' Ibn 'Abd Allāh Muḥammad ibn Yūsuf ibn Muḥammad al-Qarashī al-Kanjī," v. 2, p. [1]–59 (2d group).

2405
Khane, E. R. Le "Guibla" et l'Islam soudanais. Revue indigène, v. 14, nov./déc. 1919: 260–263. JV1835.R5, v. 14

2406
Samb, Amar, *trans. and ed.* L'Islam et le Christianisme, par Cheikh Moussa Kamara. BIFAN, t. 35, avr. 1973: 269–322. DT1.I5123, v. 35

Amar Samb translates and presents an ecumenical work by Shaykh Musa Kamara (1864–1943), a Senegalese religious teacher. Entitled *Kāda al-ittifāq wa-al-ilti'ām an yakūn bayn dīn al-Naṣārā wa-al-Islām* (The Quasi-agreement and Harmony Between Christianity and Islam) shows the many points of agreement between the two monotheistic faiths and calls for greater understanding.

2407
Tall, Bokar Salif *Thierno.* Jésus et Hasdu; conte initiatique de la mystique peule, enseigné à la Zaouia de Bandiagara. Translated by Amadou Hampâté Bâ. BIFAN, t. 31, juil. 1969: 754–786. DT1.I5123, v. 31

2408
Willis, John R. *Jihād fī sabīl Allāh:* its doctrinal basis in Islam and some aspects of its evolution in nineteenth-century west Africa. JAH, v. 8, no. 3, 1967: 395–415. DT1.J65, v. 8

Trade

2409
Arhin, Kwame. Aspects of the Ashanti northern trade in the nineteenth century. Africa, v. 40, Oct. 1970: 363–373. PL8000.I6, v. 40

Nineteenth-century Ashanti trade with Hausa, Mande, and Mossi caravans at "transit" markets in the Ashanti hinterland was based on the exchange of kola, a forest product, for savannah, natural, and craft products. This forest vs. savannah exchange was the center of secondary exchanges involving European trade goods entering the trade system from the Gold Coast and the entrepôts of the middle Niger and other goods, including slaves, from the regions traversed by the northern caravans. Ashanti traders consisted of three groups: 'target', state, and professional traders. These differed in the scale and continuity of their operations and in the types of labor used. The goods brought by these traders into Ashanti can be classified on the basis of the groups of traders and the use they made of their acquisitions into consumer, prestige, and capital goods: the third is further classifiable into trading or working capital. An explanation of the successful development of cocoa growing in Ashanti must take into account the capitalistic outlook and methods and resources developed through the trade in kola.—(Abstract supplied)

2410
Baier, Stephen. The trade of the Hausa of Damerghou, 1900–1930. Paper presented at the 16th annual meeting of the African Studies Association, Syracuse, N.Y., 1973. DLC-Micro 03782

Collation of the original: 19 p.

2411
Bargès, *Abbé* J. J. L. Mémoire sur les relations commerciales de Tlemcen avec le Soudan sous le

règne des Beni Zeyan. Revue de l'Orient, de l'Algérie et des Colonies, v. 12, 1853: 337–348.

Histoire des relations d'une famille commerçante de Tlemcen avec le Tekrour par l'intermédiaire de Sidjilmassa (Tafilelt).—(Abstract supplied)

Source: Brasseur 3044.

2412

———Le Sahara et le Soudan; documents historiques et géographiques recueillis par le Cid el-Hadj Abd'-El-Kader-Ben Abou-Bakr-et-Touaty. Revue de l'Orient et de l'Algérie et des colonies, v. 13, 1853: 73–91. DS1.R4, v. 13

Translation of a report prepared in 1851 by al-Ḥājj 'Abd al-Qādir ibn Abī Bakr al-Ṭuwātī. He provides a detailed description of the road from the northern oasis to Timbuktu and Jenne and their populations, as well as a description of the ores found in the region. Included is a Tifinagh alphabet.

2413

Boahen, A. Adu. The caravan trade in the 19th century. JAH, v. 3, no. 2, 1962: 349–359. DT1.J65, v. 3

2414

———The Ghana kola trade. Ghana notes and queries, no. 1, Jan./Apr. 1961: 8–10. DT510.A1H553, 1961

Brief historical note on the trade between the forest region and the savanna where the kola nut was, and still is, greatly appreciated by the Muslim populations.

2415

Brulard, M. Aperçu sur le commerce caravanier Tripolitaine-Ghat-Niger vers la fin du XIXe siècle. Bulletin de liaison saharienne, no 31, sept. 1958: 202–215. DT331.B83, 1958

2416

Cohen, Ronald. Some aspects of institutionalized exchange: a Kanuri example. CEA, v. 5, 3. cahier, 1965: 353–369. DT1.C3, v. 5

Examination of the applicability of various approaches to the study of the relationship of the economy to other aspects of social relations in different societies. Cohen studies the Kanuri of Bornu in northeastern Nigeria and concludes that "each approach has something to contribute" and that "a proper theory of comparative economics will not become available until we have a well-tested and documented body of data and theory on the evolution of human societies and their cultures."

2417

Constantin, P. Alger et Timbocktou. Etude sur le commerce transsaharien. Paris, Challamel, 1885. 36 p.

Source: Joucla 3673.

2418

Goody, John R., *and* T. M. Mustapha. The caravan trade from Kano to Salaga. JHSN, v. 3, June 1967: 611–616. DT515.A2H5, v. 3

2419

Grandin, *Capt.* Notes sur l'industrie et le commerce du sel au Kawar et en Agram. BIFAN, t. 13, avril 1951: 488–533. Q89.I5, v. 13

Salt was one of the major commodities in the trans-Saharan trade. The exploitation of the Bilma site reflects, but palely, the once prosperous trade. This study shows present-day production and trade patterns of the salt and provides an insight into the role played by Bilma in the trade. A Kanuri, Hausa, and Tamashek glossary on salt is appended.

2420

International African Seminar, *10th Fourah Bay College, 1969.* The development of indigenous trade and markets in West Africa; studies presented and discussed at the Tenth International African Seminar at Fourah Bay College, Freetown, December 1969; edited with an introduction by Calude Meillassoux; foreword by Daryll Forde. London, Oxford University Press for the International African Institute, 1971. 444 p. illus., maps. HF3872.I55

Title also in French: L'Evolution du commerce africain depuis le XIXe siècle en Afrique de l'ouest.

French or English with summaries in either language.

Includes the following articles: Colin W. Newbury, Prices and Profitability in Early 19th Century West African Trade; Catherine Coquery-Vidrovitch, De la traite des esclaves à l'exportation de l'huile de palme et des palmistes au Dahomey: 19e siècle; Ivor Wilks, Asante Policy Towards the Hausa Trade in the 19th Century; Emmanuel Terray, Commerce pré-colonial et organisation sociale chez les Dida de Côte d'Ivoire; Marc Augé, L'organisation du commerce pré-colonial en Basse-Côte d'Ivoire et ses effets sur l'organisation sociale des populations côtières; Kwame Y. Daaku, Trade and Trading Patterns of the Akan in the 17th and 18th Centuries; Claude Meillassoux, Le commerce pré-colonial et le développement de l'esclavage à Gūbu du Sahel (Mali) (*see also* 714); Kwame Arhin, Atebubu Markets: ca. 1884–1930; Michel Izard,

Les Yarse et le commerce dans le Yatênga pré-colonial; Philip D. Curtin, Pre-colonial Trading Networks and Traders: the Diakhanké; Jean-Louis Boutillier, La cité marchande de Bouna dans l'ensemble économique Ouest-Africain pré-colonial; Jean-Loup Amselle, Parenté et commerce chez les Kooroko; Abner Cohen, Cultural Strategies in the Organization of Trading Diasporas; Marc Piault, Cycles de marchés et "espaces" socio-politique; Polly Hill, Two Types of West African House Trade; Robert H. T. Smith, West African Market-Places: Temporal Periodicity and Locational Spacing; B. W. Hodder, Periodic and Daily Markets in West Africa; Samir Amin, La politique coloniale française à l'égard de la bourgeoisie commerçante sénégalaise (1820–1960); Rowena M. Lawson, The Supply Response of Retail Trading Services to Urban Population Growth in Ghana; Marvin P. Miracle, Capitalism, Capital Markets, and Competition in West African Trade.

2421
Johnson, Marion. The ounce in 18th century West African trade. JAH, v. 7, no. 2, 1966: 197–214.
DT1.J65, v. 7

2422
———The 19th century gold 'mithqal' in West and North Africa. JAH, v. 9, no. 4, 1968: 547–569.
DT1.J65, v. 9

2423
Kaba, Lansiné. Islam, trade, and politics in Bate (Upper Guinea) before 1890.
Source: ASA, Program, 14th, 1971.

2424
Le Coeur, Charles. Le commerce de la noix de kola en Afrique occidentale. Annales de géographie, v. 37, 15 janv. 1927: 143–149.
G1.A6, v. 37

2425
Leriche, Albert. Mesures maures; notes préliminaires. BIFAN, t. 13, oct. 1951: 1227–1256.
Q89.I5, v. 13

Leriche's daily contacts with a people he respected opened many doors and hearts. This detailed study of the measuring system, which he modestly calls "preliminary notes," is divided into five parts. The first deals with measures of capacity for grains, drugs and gunpowder, tea and flour, salt, and liquids. A substantial subsection is devoted to the quantity of milk produced by a camel. The second section deals with measures of length, depth, height, and width for cloth, tent material, land and distances, and wells. The remaining three sections deal with weight measures, currency, and the parts of the day and night.

2426
Levtzion, Nehemia. Commerce et Islam chez les Dagomba du Nord-Ghana. Annales; économies, sociétés, civilisations, 23. année, juil./août 1968: 723–743.
AP20.A58, v. 23

2427
Lovejoy, Paul E. The Kambarin Beriberi: the formation of a specialized group of Hausa traders in the nineteenth century. JAH, v. 14, no. 4, 1973: 633–651. map.
DT1.J65, v. 14

Lovejoy, who wrote his Ph.D. dissertation on the origins, development, and commercial organization of the Hausa Kola traders, examines here a specific group of traders who, though descendants of Kanuri immigrants who settled at Gummi in the Zamfara River Valley, had absorbed Hausa culture and become specialists in Kola marketing. "Islam provided a unifying ideology which has helped overcome the problems of long-distance trade . . . [and] buttressed the common economic interests of dispersed settlements along trade routes."

2428
———Long-distance trade and Islam: the case of the nineteenth century Hausa kola trade. JHSN, v. 5, June 1971: 537–548.
DT515.A2H5, v. 5

Study of the relationship between Islam and the 19th-century kola trade between Asante and the Sokoto Caliphate, the role of Islam in the Hausa trade centers, and the impact of Islam on the major commercial communities.

2429
Mathews, Felix A. Trade of Morocco with Timbuctoo and the Soudan, across the Great Desert. *In* U.S. *Bureau of Manufactures.* Reports from the consuls of the United States on the commerce, manufactures, etc., of their consular districts. no. 8, 1881. Washington, Govt. Print. Off. p. 792–797.
HC1.R2 1881

Issued by the U.S. Bureau of Foreign Commerce.

2430
Newbury, Colin W. North African and Western Sudan trade in the 19th century: a re-evaluation. JAH, v. 7, no. 2, 1966: 233–246.
DT1.J65, v. 7

2431
Perinbaum, Marie B. Trade and society in the Western Sahara and the Western Sudan: an overview [since 1000 A.D.] BIFAN, t. 34, oct. 1972: 778–801. DT1.I5123, v. 34

2432
Prax. Tembouctou; Son commerce avec l'Algérie. Revue orientale, 1852: 129–135.
Source: Brasseur, 3010.

2433
Relations commerciales entre le Maroc-Algérie et le Sénégal-Soudan. Revue franco-musulmane et Saharienne, v. 1, juil./août, 1902. NNC

2434
Sundström, Lars. The trade of Guinea. [Uppsala] 1965. 262 p. (Studia ethnographica Upsaliensa, 24) HF3909.G8S8

Akademisk avhandling—Uppsala.

Without thesis statement.

Investigation of precolonial trade on the coast of West Africa from the Senegal to the Congo rivers, particularly during the 18th and 19th centuries.

2435
Traoré, Dominique. Mesures locales soudanaises. NA, no 43, juil. 1949: 81–82. DT1.I513, 1949

2436
Trumelet, Charles. Itinéraire de Touggourt au Djebel el Qamar (montagne de la Lune). Traduit de l'arabe. *In* Société languedocienne de géographie. Bulletin, v. 3, 1880: 97–115. G11.S84, v. 3

Logbook of a voyage in 1953 from Touggourt to "the moon mountain" by a Chaamba from the Atlas Mountains. His itinerary takes him via Timbuktu, Djenne, "Nouni," and "Sebkhet Ech-Chanâqt'a" [Chinguetti?], on to his unknown final destination.

1960–1974

CENTRAL REGION

History

2437
al-As'ad, Rashīd Jabr. al-Thawrah al-Musallaḥah fī Tshād wa ab'ād al-taghalghul al-Isrā'īlī. [The armed revolution in Chad and the extent of Israeli penetration] Rāja'ahu [Revised by] 'abd al-Raḥmān Maḥmūd. Baghdād, Mu'assasat al-Ṣahāfah al-'Arabīyah, 1970. 103 p. (Silsilat al-madār al-siyāsī, 3) DT546.48.A85 Orien Arab

The armed struggle of FROLINAT [Front de libération nationale] and Israeli penetration are probed within the context of an Islamic revolt against the present government.

2438
Martin, Jean-Yves. L'école et les sociétés traditionnelles au Cameroun septentrional. *In* France. *Office de la recherche scientifique et technique outre-mer.* Cahiers O.R.S.T.O.M. Série sciences humaines, t. 8, no 3, 1971: 295–335. DLC

Martin, a sociologist attached to the Yaounde O.R.S.T.O.M. office, looks at problems related to education in Northern Cameroon. He examines the impact of a foreign variable—in this case Western education—on northern organic social systems. He concludes that "the effort to be exerted in education in the North cannot be dissociated of efforts to be made in all the other fields of development, particularly the field of economics: one institution cannot change a whole environment."

2439
al-Sammān, Muḥammad 'Abd Allāh. Mādhā yurād bil-Islām fī Ifrīqiyā [What are they doing to Islam in Africa?] *In* Cairo. al-Jāmi' al-Azhar. Majallat al-Azhar, m. 33, Jan. 1962: 992–995. BP1.C3, v. 33

Excerpts from and comments on a letter from a Muslim from Abéché, Chad, complaining about discrimination against Muslims. He states that France, with the help of the Catholic Church, fights the teaching of Arabic, tries to convert Muslims to Christianity and failing to do so, attempts to corrupt the moral fiber of the youth. al-Sammān calls for help from the Azhar, which is considered the bastion and champion of Islam by the African Muslim minorities.

2440
Santerre, Renaud. Pédagogie musulmane d'Afrique noire: l'école coranique peule du Cameroun. Montréal, Presses de l'Université de Montréal, 1973. 169 p. illus. DLC

2441
al-Ṭaḥḥāwī, 'Ināyāt. Jumhūrīyat Ifrīqiyah al-Wusṭā. [The Central African Republic] Minbar al-Islām, m. 27, July 1969: 92–95.
DS36.M53, v. 27 Orien Arab

———Jumhūrīyat Tshād. [The Republic of Chad] Minbar al-Islām, m. 26, May 1968: 112–120
DS36.M53, v. 26 Orien Arab

———Kunghū Kinshāsā wa-al-Kunghū Brāzāfīl. [Congo (Kinshasa) and Congo (Brazzaville)] Minbar al-Islām, m. 27, May 1969: 170–178.
DS36.M53, v. 27 Orien Arab

Brief presentations of these. Part of a series of articles entitled "What Do You Know About the Muslim World, Its States, and Peoples?" Each includes a section on Islam in that country.

Society & Culture

2442
Adler, Alfred. Les Day de Bouna; notes sur la vie sociale et religieuse d'une population du Moyen-Chari. Fascicule publié avec le concours du Secrétariat à la Coopération. Fort Lamy, I.N.T.S.H. [1966] 78 p. illus. (Etudes et documents tchadiens. Série A, 1) DT546.442.A45

Issued by the Institut national tchadien pour les sciences humaines.

2443
Eguchi, M. J. Aspects of the life style and culture of women in the Fulbe districts of Maroua. *In* Kyoto Daigaku. *Committee of the Kyoto University*

Africa Primatological Expedition. Kyoto University African studies, v. 8, 1973: 17–92. illus. DLC

2444
Eguchi, P. K. The chants of the Fulbe rites of circumcision. *In* Kyoto Daigaku. *Committee of the Kyoto University Africa Primatological Expedition.* Kyoto University African studies, v. 8, 1973: 205–231. illus. DLC

2445
Mayssal, Henriette. Poèmes Foulbé de la Bénoué. Abbia, no 9–10, juil./août 1965: 47–90. illus. AP9.A24, 1965

Eleven Fulbe poems with translations collected by the students of the Lycée of Garoua in 1963–64. They cover a number of such topics as rain, initiations, rituals, invectives, marriage, and love.

2446
———Poèsie Massa. Abbia, no 17/18, juin/sept. 1967: 93–130. AP9.A24, 1967

2447
Roth-Laly, Arlette. Lexique des parlers arabes tchado-soudanais. An Arabic-English-French lexicon of the dialects spoken in the Chad-Sudan area. Paris, Editions du Centre national de la recherche scientifique, 1969–72. 4 v. map. PJ6901.S8R6

2448
Santerre, Renaud. Linguistique et politique au Cameroun. Paper presented at the 12th annual meeting of the African Studies Association, Montreal, 1969. DLC-Micro 03782

Collation of the original: 16 p.

2449
Seid, Joseph Brahim. Coutumes successorales traditionnelles au Tchad islamisé. Revue juridique et politique, indépendance et coopération, v. 26, oct./déc. 1972: 811–818. K21.J85, v. 26

2450
Tanner, R. E. S. The *Jamaa* movement in the Congo: a sociological comment on some religious interpretations. The Heythrop journal, v. 9, Apr. 1968: 164–178. BX801.H4, v. 9

EASTERN REGION

Education

2451
Abdulla, Ahmed. The ambivalence of Muslim education. East Africa journal, Feb. 1965: 7–11. DT421.E28, 1965

Focusing on East Africa, the author discusses the resistance of Muslims to an educational system provided by the Christian Church and suggests that "the crucial problem today is how to adjust into one system old and new educational aims."

2452
Ahmad, Khurshid. There is no god but Allah and Muhammad is the messenger of Allah. 2d ed. [Port Louis] Le Cercle islamique de l'Ile Maurice, 1972 18 p. DLC

Short introduction to Islamic teachings.

2453
Byrne, Hubert J. Muslim education in Uganda; great strides made in last five years. African world, Apr. 1960: 11–12. DT1.A24, 1960

2454
Sykes, J. A further note on the education of African Muslims. Uganda journal, v. 30, pt. 2, 1966: 227–228. DT434.U2U3, v. 30

Comment on an article on Muslim education (*see* 1190).

2455
el-Tayib, Griselda. Women's education in the Sudan. Kano studies, no. 1, Sept. 1965: 43–46. DLC

2456
Williams, Denis. A Sudanese calligraphy. Transition, v. 9, June 1963: 19–20. DLC

History

2457
Abdallah bin Hemedi 'lAjjemy. The Kilindi. Edited by J. W. T. Allen and William Kimweri bin Mbago bin Kibwana bin Maiwe wa Kwekalo (Mlungui) bin Kimweri Zanyumbai. Nairobi, East African Literature Bureau, 1963. 238 p. illus. DT443.A5813

Translation of *Habari za Wakilindi.*

2458
Adatia, A. K., *and* N. Q. King. Some East African *Firmans* of H. H. Agha Khan III. Journal of religion in Africa/religion en Afrique, v. 2, no. 3, 1969: 179–191. BL2400.J68, v. 2

Commentary on the advice of Muhammad Shah, Agha Khan III (1885–1957), to his East African community as embodied in his Firmans.

2459

Allen, J. Muslims in East Africa. African ecclesiastical review, v. 7, July 1965: 255–262. IEN

2460

Anderson, William B. The role of religion in the Sudan's search for unity. *In* Workshop in Religious Research, Nairobi, 1967–68. African initiatives in religion; 21 studies from Eastern and Central Africa. David B. Barrett, editor. [Nairobi] East African Pub. House [1971] p. 73–87. DLC

2461

Bayok, Job. The Southern Sudan problem: a test in Afro-Arab relations. The Cuttington review, v. 12, July 1968: 11–17. DLC

2462

Beegun, Goolhamid. Problems of Muslims in Mauritius. Port Louis, Printed by Alpha Printing; [the Mauritius Urdu Academy, 1968] 36 p. illus., ports. BP63.M3B4

Of a population of about 800,000 persons, Mauritius has approximately 140,000 Muslims, according to the author, who is secretary of the Mauritius Urdu Academy. In this call for unity, he admits the fault of the Muslim community and urges its members to carry out reforms in the economic, social, and educational fields.

2463

Bilfaqīh, Ahmad ibn Zayn ibn Ḥasan. al-Islām fī Zinjibār. [Islam in Zanzibar] al-Muslimūn, no. 10, Feb. 1963: 90–96. BP1.M86, 1963 Orien Arab

2464

Bunger, Robert L., Jr. Islamization among the Upper Pokomo. [Syracuse, N.Y.] Program of Eastern African Studies, Syracuse University, 1973. 166 p. (Eastern African studies, 11) DT433.542.B86

The Pokomo, who live on the banks of the Tana River from Kipini and up to and including the Mbalamba Location in Kenya, have been Islamized only in the last 80 years. Bunger states in his introduction that "the nature of a regional variety of Islam is a function of the contact situation between the groups which accept Islam and those persons and groups who introduced Islam to them." He then studies Pokomo Islam in relation to the four following variables: "1. The pre-Islamic culture of the group which becomes Muslim. 2. The culture of the group which introduces Islam. 3. The particular variety of Islam. 4. The precise nature of the contact."

2465

Carreira, António. Aspectos históricos da evolução do Islamismo na Guiné Portuguesa. Boletim cultural da Guiné Portuguesa, t. 21, no 84, 1966: 405–456. DT613.B6, 1966

2466

el-Dessuky, M. A. Ebyafaayo ebitonotono ku bulamu bwa Nnabbi Muhammad. [A brief history of the Prophet Muhammad] Kampala, Uganda Pub. House, 1971. 49 p. illus. DLC

In Ganda.

2467

Gil Benumeya, R. Lo arabigo y lo africano en el Sudán después del gulpe de Estato. Revista de política internacional, no 104, julio/agosto 1969: 97–104. D839.C85, no. 104

2468

Islam in Mozambique (East Africa). Islamic literature, v. 15, Sept. 1969: 45–53. BP1.I68, v. 15

Islam reached Mozambique in the eighth century. Arab seamen and traders had probably been in contact with the area at a much earlier period. Sofala, which was the southern-most reach of Islam on the coast, was described in glowing terms by al-Mas'ūdī who visited the metropolis in 922. The arrival of the Portuguese in the 16th century put an end to Arab hegemony. Portuguese Catholic influence is best described by the Concordat of 1940 which "gave to the Portuguese Catholic Church the legal monopoly of all education of Africans in Mozambique." Muslim resistance crystallized in 1960 with the creation of the Mozambique African National Union (MANU) under the leadership of A. Kibriti Diwani. MANU clashed with FRELIMO which the author accuses of being under the influence of the U.S., Israel, and "a puppet government under the control of President Nyerere's government." The Muslim League of Mozambique is striving to protect the Muslim heritage of the Islamic community and prepare them to play a significant role in an independent Mozambique.

2469

Ismael, Tareq Y. The United Arab Republic and the Sudan. The Middle East journal, v. 23, winter 1969: 14–28. DS1.M5, v. 23

Introducing his essay by stating that the "primary objective of Egypt's policy in the Sudan is to safeguard strategic interests," Ismael shows the importance of the Nile River sources to Egyptian leadership. Besides control of the water sources, the Sudan also represents an economic outlet and a window on sub-Saharan Africa. Ismael divides his study into three parts: rationalization of the policy, 1952–55, with intensification of Egyptian efforts for union; relations in crisis, which witnessed the independence of the Sudan, a cooling off period, and a territorial dispute; and the military rule, 1958–64, of General ʻAbbūd, who brought about a rapprochement with Egypt.

2470
Jawhar, Hasan Muhammad, Ḥusayn Ahmad Shalabī, *and* ʻAbd al-Fattāḥ Shalabī. al-Ṣumāl. [Somalia] Cairo, Dār al-Maʻārif, 1965. 112 p. illus., map. (Shuʻūb al-ʻālam, 17) DT401.J34

2471
Kjellberg, Eva. The Ismailis in Tanzania. Dar es Salaam, Institute of Public Administration, University College, 1967. 66 leaves. illus. fold. map. BP195.I8K53

"The purpose of my study is (a) to present as much information as possible about the Islamilis in Tanzania—their religion, organisation, and way of life—and (b) to try to analyse their problem in the national context," states Miss Kjellberg, a student at the Department of Anthropology, University of Stockholm. After a general introduction to Asians in East Africa and Ismaili beliefs, she then concentrates on the community in Tanzania, analyzing its structure and organization, way of life, economic and political problems, as well as a short attitudunal study. Includes a 71-entry bibliography.

2472
Lewis, I. M. The modern history of Somaliland, from nation to state. New York, Praeger [1965] 234 p. illus., maps, ports. (The Praeger Asia-Africa series) DT410.L4

2473
Lofchie, Michael F. Zanzibar: background to revolution. Princeton, N.J., Princeton University Press, 1965. 316 p. maps. DT435.5.L6 1965

Zanzibar, the stronghold of an Arab oligarchy originally from Muscat and Oman, witnessed a violent revolution on January 12, 1964. The author analyzes the political development of the island, the emergence of political parties, and party politics leading to the conflagration ignited by the quixotic John Okello.

2474
Martin, J. Les notions de clans, nobles et notables. Leur impact dans la vie comorienne aujour'dhui. A&A, no 81/82, 1968: 39–63. DT1.A85, 1968

2474a
Mendes Pedro, Albano. Atitudes perante o maometismo na Africa Portuguesa. Estudos ultramarinos, no 1, 1961: 43–56. JV4201.E8, 1961

2475
Mtume Muhammad, S. A. W. Tarehe yake kwa ufupi. [Brief history of the life of the Prophet] Mombasa, Bilal Muslim Mission of Kenya [1973?] 14 p. DLC

Text in Swahili.

2476
al-Najjār, ʻAbd al-Raḥmān. al-Islām fī al-Ṣūmāl. [Islam in Somalia] [Cairo, Maṭābiʻ al-Ahrām al-Tijārīyah] 1973. 118 p. illus. (Jumhūrīyat Miṣr al-ʻArabīyah. al-Majlis al-Aʻlā lil-Shuʼūn al-Islāmīyah. Lajnat al-Taʻrīf bi-al-Islām, 79) BP64.S6N34

2477
Nichols, Woodrow W., Jr. The Ismaili sect in East Africa. Ufahamu, v. 1, spring 1970: 34–51. DT1.U4, v. 1

2478
Riyāḍ, Zāhir, *and* ʻAbd al-ʻAlīm al-Sayyid Mansī. Athyūbiyā. [Ethiopia] [Cairo] Markaz kutub al-Sharq al-Awsaṭ, 1963. 77 p. illus., map, port. DT373.R58

2478a
Salim, I. A. The Swahili-speaking peoples of Kenya's coast, 1895–1965. Nairobi, East African Pub. House, 1973. 272 p. illus. (Peoples of East Africa, no. 4) DT433.542.S24 1973

2479
Ṣaqr, ʻAtīyah. al-Islām fī Ūghandah. [Islam in Uganda] *In* Cairo. al-Jāmiʻ al-Azhar Majallat al-Azhar, m. 33, June 1961: 39–44. BP1.C3, v. 33

According to missionary estimates there were in 1961 about a quarter of a million Muslims in Uganda. The Ismaili sect, Ṣaqr reports, is very active, while the Orthodox group is divided on minor points of jurisprudence. Britain is undermining Muslim influence and there is a great need for Islamic missions to strengthen the Muslim community and provide a meaningful religious education to resist Christian proselytism.

2480
———al-Islām fī Zinjibār. [Islam in Zanzibar] *In* Cairo. al-Jāmiʻ al-Azhar. Majallat al-Azhar, m. 34, Nov. 1962: 472–478. BP1.C3, v. 34

Ṣaqr paints a sad picture of Islam in Zanzibar.

The various Muslim communities are divided among themselves, religious education is neglected, and the colonial authorities are preaching disunity. Concluding his remarks, Ṣaqr calls upon the Azhar to be more energetic in its religious mission in the island.

2481
al-Ṭaḥḥāwī, 'Ināyāt. Jumhūriyat Kīnyā. [The Republic of Kenya] Minbar al-Islām, m. 26, Sept. 1968: 146–151. DS36.M53, v. 26 Orien Arab

———al-Muslimūn fī Ithyūbyā. [Muslims in Ethiopia] Minbar al-Islām, m. 26, July 1968: 146–152. DS36.M53, v. 26 Orien Arab

———al-Muslimūn fī Ūghandah. [Muslims in Uganda] Minbar al-Islām, m. 26, Nov. 1968: 114–119. DS36.M53, v. 26 Orien Arab

Brief presentations on Kenya, Ethiopia, and Uganda. Part of a series entitled "What Do You Know About the Muslim World, Its States and Peoples?" Includes a section on Islam in each country.

2482
Trimingham, John Spencer. Islam in East Africa; the report of a survey undertaken in 1961. [London] Published for the World Council of Churches Commission on World Mission and Evangelism by Edinburgh House Press, 1962. 47 p. map. (C. W. M. E. research pamphlets, no. 9) BP64.A4E28

2483
Voll, John. Islam and its future in the Sudan.
Source: ASA, Program, 15th, 1972.

Law

2484
Abu Rannat, Sayyid Muhammad. The relationship between Islamic and customary law in the Sudan. Journal of African Law, v. 4, spring 1960: 9–16. DLC–LL

Address by the Chief Justice of the Sudan on the complexity of the Sudanese legal system. At the time the lecture was delivered the judiciary was "split into two quite separate hierarchies: The Sharia Division of which the Grand Kadi is the head, and the Civil Division over which I have the honor to preside. Within the Civil Division there are three main types of courts: 'Civil Courts' as established under the Civil Justice Ordinance, Native Courts set up under the Native Courts Ordinance in the six Northern Provinces, and Chiefs Courts set up by the Chiefs' Courts Ordinance in the three Southern Provinces." In spite of these categorizations, problems did arise where more than one system were involved, thus taxing the perspicacity of the judges.

2485
Anderson, James N. D. The Isma'ili Khojas of East Africa: A new constitution and personal law for the community. Middle Eastern studies, v. 1, Oct. 1964: 21–39. DS41.M535, v. 1

Commentaries on the "Constitution of the Shia Imami Ismailis in Africa" dated August 11, 1962.

2486
———The modernization of Islamic law in the Sudan. Sudan law journal and reports, 1960: 292–312. DLC–LL

2487
el-Busaidy, Hamed bin Saleh. Ndoa no talaka. [Marriage and divorce] Nairobi, East African Literature Bureau, 1968. 45 p. DLC–LL

2488
Farran, Charles d'Olivier. Matrimonial laws of the Sudan, being a study of the divergent religious and civil laws in an African society. London, Butterworths, 1963. 325 p. (Butterworth's African law series, no. 7) DLC–LL

2489
Rarijaona, René. Le Concept de propriété en droit foncier de Madagascar étude de sociologie juridique. Paris, Editions Cujas, 1967. 306 p. (Etudes malgaches, 18) DLC–LL

2490
Rassool Sheik, Andrée. Etude sur quelques secteurs réformistes de l'Islam. Revue juridique et politique, no 3, juil./sept. 1966: 489–512. DLC–LL

Languages & Linguistics

2491
Crewe, W. J. The place of Sudanese Arabic: A study in comparative Arabic dialectology. Khartoum, University of Khartoum, Institute of African and Asian studies, 1973. 18 leaves (African and Asian studies seminar series, no. 20) DLC

2492
Ferguson, Charles A. The role of Arabic in Ethiopia: A sociolinguistic perspective. *In his* Language structure and language use; essays. Selected and introduced by Anwar S. Dil. Stanford, Calif., Stanford University Press, 1971. p. 293–312. P27.F4

2493
Gasim, A. A.-S. Some aspects of Sudanese colloquial Arabic. SNR, v. 46, pt. 1, 1965: 40–49. DT118.S85, v. 46

2494
Munawwar, Muhammad. A lively discussion . . . between Sumi [sic] and Ahmadi Muslims about Swahili translations of the Holy Koran: continuation of prophethood in Islam: death and second advent of Jesus Christ: founder of the Ahmadiyya Movement in Islam. [Ed. by Sheikh Muhammad Munawwar. Dar es Salaam, Tanganyika Ahmadiyya Muslim Mission, 1967] 79 p.

Source: Dar es Salaam Lib. Bull. no. 86.

2495
Pirone, M. La lingua somala e i suoi problemi. Africa, 22, giugno 1967: 198–209. DT1.A843, v. 22

Discussion of the various attempts since the 1930's to establish an alphabet for the Somali language.

2496
Slavíková, M., *and* Margaret A. Bryan. Comparative Bantu: the case of two Swahili dialects. African language studies, v. 14, 1973: 53–81. PL8003.A34, v. 14

Comparison of the Unguja and Mviṭa dialects.

2497
Zaborski, Andrzej. Arabic loan-words in Somali: Preliminary survey. Folia Orientalia, v. 8, 1966: 125–167. PJ9.F6, v. 8

Preliminary compilation of 1,200 Arabic words in the various Somali dialects, showing the magnitude of cultural interaction. Included are some morphological peculiarities which have entered the Somali language, and phonetic alterations introduced by the borrowings.

Literature

2498
Andrzejewski, B. W. The *roobdóon* of Sheikh Aqib Abdullahi Jama: a Somali prayer for rain. African language studies, no. 11, 1970: 21–34. PL8003.A34, v. 11

A special issue in honor of Prof. Malcolm Guthrie.

Text, translation, and commentaries on a prayer for rain by a prominent Somali Shaykh known for his advocacy of using Somali for religious purposes rather than classical Arabic.

2499
Farsy, Muhammad Saleh. Kurwa na Doto; maelezo ya makazi katika kijiji cha Unguja yaani Zanzibar. Dar es Salaam, East African Literature Bureau, 1960. 62 p. PL8704.F3

Added t.p.: *Kurwa and Doto; a Novel Depicting Life in a Typical Zanzibar Village.*

2500
Shalabī, Ḥusayn Aḥmad. Aqāṣīṣ min al-Ṣūmāl. [Tales from Somalia] Cairo, Dār al-Ma'ārif, 1962. 152 p. illus. GR360.S57S5

2501
al-Ṭayyib, al-Ṭayyib Muḥammad, *comp.* al-Turāth al-Sha'bī li-qabīlat al-Ḥamrān. [The popular heritage of the Ḥamrān tribe] [Khartoum] Jāmi'at al-Kharṭūm, Kulliyat al-Ādāb, Shu'bat abḥāth al-Sūdān, 1970. 90 leaves (Silsilat dirāsāt fī al-turāth al-Sūdānī, 12) GR360.S78T3 Orien Arab

Partially vocalized.

In the Sudanese dialect.

Politics

2502
'Abd al-Raḥmān, Muḥammad Fawzī Muṣṭafā. al-Thaqāfah al-'Arabīyah wa-atharuhā fī tamāsuk al-wahdah al-qawmīyah fī al-Sūdān al Mu'āṣir. [Arabic culture and its influence on national cohesion in Modern Sudan] Khartoum, al-Dār al-Sūdānīyah [1972] 251 p. DT131.A6 Orien Arab

2503
Ahmad, Abdel Ghaffar Muhammad. Shaykhs and followers: political struggle in the Rufa'a al-hoi Nazirate in the Sudan. Bergen, University of Bergen, Dept. of Social Anthropology, 1973. 228 leaves, illus. DT133.R8A49

Thesis—Bergen.

2504
Albino, Oliver. The Sudan: a southern viewpoint; with a foreword by Arnold Toynbee. London,

Published for the Institute of Race Relations by Oxford University Press, 1970. 132 p.
DT108.7.A63 1970

Though the Southern Sudan problem was a political one, a religious dimension was ever present. Albino states in his introduction that he has refrained from setting aside a chapter on the religious aspect of the question, yet feels that "any exposition of the Southern problem that does not mention religious persecution is incomplete." The conflict between the two faiths is evenly discussed throughout the book.

2505
al-As'ad, Rashīd Jabr. Aḍwā' 'alā al-qadīyah al-Īrītrīyah. [Lights on the Eritrean problem] Baghdad, Dār al-nadhīr lil-ṭibā'ah wa-al-nashr, 1969. 63 p.
DT397.A8 Orien Arab

The question of Eritrea as seen from a Muslim viewpoint in which Islam plays a catalytic role in the armed resistance against Ethiopia and its supporters.

2505a
The Black Book of the Sudan on the expulsion of the missionaries from Southern Sudan: an answer. [Milano?, 1964?] 217 p.
DLC

Rebuttal by the Catholic Church of the charges made by the Government of Sudan against the Verona Missions, expelled from the Southern Sudan in 1964.

2506
Ethiopia. Yamāstāwaqiyā ministėr. Religious freedom in Ethiopia. [Addis Ababa, Publications of the Foreign Languages Press Dept., Ministry of Information, 1965] 91 p. illus. (part col.), ports.
BR1370.A46

Statements by Emperor Haile Selassie and other Ethiopian responsibles. *See also* the Arabic edition, BP64.A4E83.

2507
Ingrams, H. Islam and Africanism in Zanzibar. New commonwealth, v. 40, July 1962: 427–430.
JX1901.N3, v. 40

2508
Jibi Dima, Scopas A. Political troubles in the Southern Sudan: A southern student's experience. African forum, v. 3, fall 1967/winter 1968: 58–74.
DT1.A225, v. 3

Historical analysis of problems in Southern Sudan by a southerner. Jibi Dima begins with the Juba Conference of 1947 and closes with the creation of a Southern Sudan Provincial Government. He describes the various steps taken by the Khartoum Government to suppress Southern resistance and concludes with a section on the "Africaness" of Northern Sudan, calling for a compromise within the context of African unity.

2509
Mazrui, Ali A. Religion and democracy in the first republic of the Sudan. Makerere journal, v. 11, Dec. 1965: 39–50.
AS25.K33, v. 11

2510
Mazzoldi, Sixte. Notes sur la situation politique et religieuse dans les régions méridioniales du Soudan et l'expulsion en masses des missionnaires chrétiens. [n. p.] 1964.
Cst-H

2511
McClure, Bryan. Religion and nationalism in southern Ethiopia. A current bibliography on African affairs, v. 5, Sept./Nov. 1972: 497–508.
Z3501.C87, v. 5

Taking as examples the Somali, Oromo, and Gurage of the southern part of Ethiopia, "south of the present provincial boundaries of Shoa," McClure shows that "the religious orientation of the various peoples of southern Ethiopia seem to have definite political ramifications. Nationalist pride in ethnic identity is often channeled through religious expression."

2512
Mrozek, Anna. Islam a naród w Afryce: Somalia, Sudan, Libia. [Islam and Nation in Africa: Somalia, Sudan, Libya] Warszawa, Państowowe Wydawn. Naukowe, 1973. 260 p.
BP173.7.M76

Summary in English.

The book comprises an attempt of the analysis of the range and forms of influence of Islam on the process of formation of the African nations.—(Abstract supplied, modified)

2513
———Rola i funkcje Islamu w kształtowaniu więzi narodowej Somalijczyków. [The role and functions of Islam in the formation of national bounds among the Somali] Przegląd socjologiczny, t. 25, 1972: 167–222.
HM7.P7, v. 25

2514
———Wzajemne stosunki polnocnych poludniowych plemion Sudanu: mozliwoso a rzeczywistoso. [Relations between the southern and north-

ern tribes in the Sudan: possibilities and reality] Przeglad socjologiczny, tom 21, 1967: 125–151. HM7.P7, v. 21

2515
al-Numayrī, Ja'far Muhammad. al-Hukm al-dhātī al-iqlīmī lil-janūb. [Regional autonomy for the South] [Khartoum] al-qism al-thaqāfī bi-wizārat al-irshād al-qawmī al-muqaddimah 1969] 3 p. DT108.7.N83

At head of title: Jumhūriyat al-Sūdān al-Dīmūqrātīyah. Wizārat al-irshād al-qawmī. Added t. p.: Policy Statement on the Southern Question.

Arabic and English.

2516
Oduho, Joseph, *and* William Deng. The problem of the Southern Sudan. With an introd. by Richard Gray. Issued under the auspices of the Institute of Race Relations, London. London, Oxford University Press, 1963. 60 p. illus. DT108.7.O3 1963

In an era of continental Pan-Africanism, the civil war in the Sudan was an anachronism. The authors, formerly active members of Southern resistance to Khartoum, present the viewpoint of the South on a major problem and the challenges facing the revolutionary government in the Sudan.

2517
Ritchie, James M. East Africa. MW, v. 56, Oct. 1966: 296–303. DS36.M7, v. 56

Issue devoted to Islam in Politics: a Symposium. "The Muslims of East Africa could perhaps be described as a colonial group, demoted from its position as ruler, and yet unable to 'withdraw' as powers such as Britain and France have from their former colonies. The Muslims are in the area, and they are there to stay for they have nowhere to go . . . Two major problems face the community. The first is to find a secure place in the modern world with the fast tempo, competition, complexity and challenge which comes with it. This they have in common with the world of Islam as a whole. The second, their own special problem, is to find their proper place in the new East Africa, a political East Africa in revolution, and in a state of rapid change and advancement."

2518
Shaffer, N. M. The Sudan: Arab-African confrontation. Current history, v. 50, Mar. 1966: 142–146. D410.C82, v. 50

2519
Sudan. *Wizārat al-Dākhilīyah.* Memorandum on reasons that lead to the expulsion of foreign missionaries and priests from the southern provinces of the Sudan. [Khartoum] Republic of the Sudan, Ministry of the Interior, 1964. 1 v. (various pagings) facsims. DT108.7.S85 1964

Cover title: *Expulsion of Foreign Missionaries and Priests From the Southern Provinces.*

2520
The Sudan: a new era. Africa today, v. 20, summer 1973. DT1.A22, v. 20

Special issue devoted to the post-Regional Autonomy Agreement period. Included are: J. Bowyer Bell, The Sudan's African Policy: Problems and Prospects; Bona M. M. Ring, Political Relationships Between Northerner and Southerner Blacks in the Sudan; Francis M. Deng, The Dynamics of Identification: a Basis for National Integration in the Sudan; Philip Abbas Ghabashi, The Growth of Black Political Consciousness in Northern Sudan; Special correspondent, Sudan: Joy of Peace, Burden of Pioneering; Robert E. Gribbin, Two Relief Crises: Biafra and Sudan.

2521
Urfer, Sylvain. Etats islamiques et régimes militaires en Afrique: I, Le Soudan. Cahiers d'action religieuse et sociale, no 511, 1. fév. 1970: 87–92. BX802.C3, 1970

2522
'Uthmān, Muḥammad Khayr. al-Sūdān bayna al-'Urūbah wa-al-Ifrīqīyah. [Sudan between Arabism and Africanism] al-Kharṭūm: majallah fikrīyah jāmi'ah, no. 5, Feb. 1966: 16–22. DLC

2523
Vermont, René. Le problème du Soudan nilotique. Orient, v. 9, 4. trimestre 1965: 33–47. DS1.O44, v. 9

2524
Wai, Dunstan, M., *ed.* The Southern Sudan: the problem of national integration. London, Cass, 1973. 255 p. maps. DT108.7.W33 1973

Contents: Dunstan M. Wai, The Southern Sudan: the Country and the People.—Abel Alier, The Southern Sudan Question.—Muddathir Abdel Rahim, Arabism, Africanism, and Self-Identification in the Sudan (*see also* 1401).—Ali A. Mazrui, The Black Arabs in Comparative Perspective: the Political Sociology of Race Mixture.—Joseph U. Garang, On Economics and Regional Autonomy.—

Peter Russell and Storrs McCall, Can Secession Be Justified?—A. G. G. Gingyera-Pinycwa, The Border Implication of the Sudan Civil War.—Donald Denoon, The Education of Southern Sudanese Refugees.—Dunstan M. Wai, Political Trends in the Sudan and the Future of the South.

A number of important related documents are appended.

2525
Watt, W. Montgomery. The political relevance of Islam in East Africa. International affairs, v. 42, Jan. 1966: 35–44. JX1.I53, v. 42

2526
Wol Wol, L. The place of South Sudan in the new Arab federation. Grass Curtain, v. 2, Oct. 1971: 9–12. DLC

2527
Yangu, Alexis Mbali. The Nile turns red; Azanians chose freedom against Arab bondage. Edited by A. G. Mondini. [New York] Pageant Press [c1966] 184 p. map. DT108.7.Y3

Society & Culture

2528
'Ābidīn, 'Abd al-Majīd. Ḥawla al-thaqāfah al-'Arabīyah al-Islāmīyah fī al-Sūdān. [On Arab Islamic culture in the Sudan] [Cairo, Maṭba'at Mukhaymar, 1968?] 15 p. map. (Jāmi'at Umm Durmān al-Islāmīyah. Muḥāḍarāt al-mawsim al-thaqāfī al-thānī lil-'ām al-jāmi'ī 1967–1968) DT131.A62 Orien Arab

Text of a lecture by the dean of the Faculty of Arts of the Omdurman Islamic University, delivered at the cultural center of El Obeid.

2529
Barclay, Harold B. Muslim religious practice in a village suburb of Khartoum. MW, v. 53, July 1963: 205–211. DS36.M7, v. 53

Description of religious behavior in Būrri al-Lamāb, a village located near Khartoum, on the banks of the Blue Nile. Barclay compares the evolution and resistance of both the little and the great traditions in Islam to modernization.

2530
Bayne, E. A. A religious nationalist in Somalia; a comment on modern nationalism allied with Islam as a unifying dynamic. *In* American Universities Field Staff. Reports service. Northeast Africa series, v. 13, no. 3, 1966. 7 p. DLC

Sympathetic report on the problems of "church" and state as seen by the leading imam of Mogadiscio.

2531
Bonfanti, Adriano. Soudan: Noirs et blancs, dixième parallèle. Le mois en Afrique, v. 1, janv. 1966: 24–42. map. DT1.R4, v. 1

2532
Farsy, Muhammad Saleh. Ada za harusi katika Unguja. [Marriage customs in Unguja] [Rev.] Nairobi, East African Literature Bureau [1967] 50 p. illus. (Custom and tradition in East Africa) GT2789.Z3F3 1967

First published in 1956.

2533
Fitzgerald, M. L. Factors influencing the spread of Islam in East Africa. Orita: journal of religious studies, v. 5, Dec. 1971: 93–104. DLC

2534
Guillotte, J. V., III. Attitudes towards *Ujamaa* in a multi-ethnic rural community in Northern Tanzania. Paper presented at the 16th annual meeting of the African Studies Association, Syracuse, N.Y., 1973. DLC-Micro 03782

Collation of the original: 14 p.

2535
Hale, Sondra. Arts in a changing society: Northern Sudan. Ufahamu, v. 1, spring 1970: 64–79. DT1.U4, v. 1

2536
Ibn Ruschd, *comp.* Kitab al-Salawat; Kitab-us-Salat. Lourenço Marques, [Minerva Central] h. 1387 [1967] 45 p. DLC

Muslim prayer book in Portuguese with Arabic citations from the Koran, followed by a section on "meditação."

2537
Langlands, B. W., *and* G. Namirembe. Studies on the geography of religion in Uganda. Kampala, Uganda, Dept. of Geography, Makerere University College [1967] 65 p. illus., maps. ([Kampala, Uganda. Makerere University College. Dept. of Geography] Occasional paper, no. 4) BL2470.U3L3

Includes a short section on Muslims.

2538
Mrozek, Anna. Wybrane aspekty Islamu Sudanskiego. [Certain aspects of Islam in the Sudan] Etnografia polska, t. 13, Zesz. 2, 1969: 133–169.
GN585.P6E8, v. 13

2539
Muḥammad, ʻAbbās Aḥmad. Al-Zār aw (al-Rīḥ al-Aḥmar) ʻind al-Shayqīyah. [The *Zar* (or Red Wind) among the Shayqīyah] Sudan society, 1969: 117–99 [pagination follows Arabic format]
HN831.S8A6, 1969

"My aim . . . is to strictly register some of the fundamental facts about the *zār* in the Shayqiyyah region," states the author of this descriptive article. After defining the zār, he describes the qualifications of the Shaykhah, the woman leader of the ceremony, and her income; the zār implements; the types of spirits, "Red Wind" and the more malefic "Black Wind" and their nature; the diagnosis of the sickness; the type of zār and the appropriate incantations for each occasion; and the relation of the zār to the more orthodox religious beliefs. Muhammad then describes, in detail, an actual zār ceremony.

2540
Muḥammad, ʻAwad Maḥmūd. Azhār al-Nūbah, majmūʻah min al-Aghānī al-Kinzīyah. [The flowers of Nubia, a collection of Kenuz songs] Translated into Arabic by ʻAwad Maḥmūd Muḥammad. [Alexandria, Matḅaʻat al-Kunūz 1968–] port.
PL8575.M8

L.C. has v. 1.
Nubian and Arabic.

2541
Nordenstam, Tore. Descriptive ethics in the Sudan: An example. SNR, v. 48, 1967: 90–98.
DT118.S85, v. 48

After an "introductory survey of some of the problems and possible lines of research" in the field of ethical beliefs, Nordenstam focuses his analysis on the concept of dignity, or Karāmah, among the Muslim population of northern Sudan.

2542
Parkin, David. Politics of ritual syncretism: Islam among the non-Muslim Giriama of Kenya. Africa, v. 40, July 1970: 217–233. PL8000.I6, v. 40

The Giriama "distinguish by word and deed the peripheral adoption of Islamic elements from the centrality of their traditional ritual and belief system," suggests Parkin who provides an anthropological analysis of the use of Islam as both a shield and intensifier of certain skills without abandoning traditional beliefs.

2543
Peirone, Frederico J. A tribo ajaua do alto Niassa (Moçambique) e alguns aspectos da sua problemática neo-islâmica. Lisboa, 1967. 203 p. illus., facsims., plans, ports. (Religiões e missões, 1. Estudos missionários, no. 1) BP64.A3Y3

At head of title: Junta de Investogações de Ultramar. Centro de Estudos Missionarios.

2544
Prins, Adriaan H. J. Didemic Lamu: social stratification and spatial structure in a Muslim maritime town. Groningen, Instituut voor Culturele Antropologie der Rijksuniversiteit, 1971. 74 leaves. illus.
HN800.K42L345

2545
———Islamic maritime magic: a ship's charm from Lamu. *In* Wort und Religion; Studien zur Afrikanistik, Missionswissenschaft, Religionswissenschaft, Ernest Dammann zum 65. Geburtstag. Hrsg. von Hans-Jûrgen Greschat und Hermann Junggraithmayr. Stuttgart, Evangelisher Missionsverlag [1969] p. 294–304. PL8003.W6

2546
Solzbacher, Regina M. Continuity through change in the social history of Kibuli. Uganda journal, v. 33, pt. 2, 1969: 163–174. DT434.U2U3, v. 33

Study of social change in Kibuli, a Muslim area located south of Kampala.

2547
Suleiman, S. M. Women in the Sudan public service. Sudan journal of administration and development, v. 2, Jan. 1966: 37–53. DLC

2548
Tanner, R. E. S. Cousin marriage in the Afro-Arab community of Mombasa, Kenya. Africa, v. 34, Apr. 1964: 127–138. PL8000.I6, v. 34

The Afro-Arab community of Kenya and Tanzania includes people of Arab origin who have retained their language and others who have intermarried with indigenous groups and have adopted Swahili. This study of a sample of 630 persons from Mombasa shows six categories of cousin marriage in a society that has retained its cultural identity, strengthened by strict application of Islamic law regarding marriage and inheritance and by steering clear of non-Muslim Bantu groups among whom they live.

2549
Thomas, H. B. Fakih Ibrahim, Muslim ulema. Uganda journal, v. 30, pt. 1, 1966: 97
DT434.U2U3, v. 30

SOUTHERN REGION

Society & Culture

2550
Higgins, Edward. The sociology of religion in South Africa. Archives de sociologie des religions, v. 16, juil./déc. 1971: 143–164. BL60.A7, v. 16
Includes some statistics on Islam.

2551
Kähler, Hans. Studien über die Kultur, die Sprache und die arabisch-afrikaanse Literatur der Kap-Malaien. Berlin, D. Reimer, 1971. 205 p. (Veröffentlichungen des Seminars für Indonesische und Südseesprachen der Universität Hamburg, Bd. 7) PJ6901.S68K2

2552
Mamede, Suleiman Valy. Movimentos reformistas no Islão. Boletim geral do ultramar, ano 44, jan./fev. 1968: 85–90. JV4201.M62, v. 44
Study of the two reformist tendencies in Islam, modernism and the Salafiyah movement, and their role in sub-Saharan Africa.

WESTERN REGION

Archival Material

2553
Arif, Aida S., *and* Ahmad M. Abu-Hakima. Descriptive catalogue of Arabic manuscripts in Nigeria in the Jos Museum and Lugard Hall Library, Kaduna. London, Luzac, 1965 [i.e. 1966] 216 p.
Z6620.N6A7
Includes more than 1,000 manuscripts.

2554
Freeman-Grenville, G. S. P. Summary of a report on a conference on Arabic documents, held at the University of Ghana, 26th and 27th February, 1965. *In* Ibadan, Nigeria. University. *Centre of Arabic Documentation.* Research bulletin, v. 1, July 1965: 8–39. DT352.4.I2a, v. 1

2555
Ghana. University, *Legon. Institute of African Studies.* Report on a conference on Arabic documents, organised by the Institute of African Studies and held at Akuafo Hall, University of Ghana, February 26 and 27th, 1965. Legon, 1965. 25 p. DLC

2556
Report of the UNESCO meeting of experts on the utilisation of written sources for the history of Africa held at Timbuktu, December 1967. *In* Ibadan, Nigeria. University. *Centre of Arabic Documentation.* Research bulletin, v. 4, Dec. 1968: 52–69.
DT352.4.I2a, v. 4

2557
Réunion d'experts sur l'utilisation des sources écrites pour l'histoire de l'Afrique. Rapport final; Tombouctou, 30 novembre–7 décembre 1967. BIFAN, t. 30, avril 1968: 769–780.
DT1.I5123, v. 30

2558
Wilks, Ivor, *and* J. J. Holden. Arabic collection. *In* Ghana. University, *Legon. Institute of African studies.* Research review, v. 2, no. 2, 1966: 8–23.
DT1.G48, v. 2
Preliminary descriptive list of 40 Arabic manuscripts of the university collection.

2559
———Arabic collection. *In* Ghana. University, *Legon. Institute of African studies.* Research review, v. 2, no. 3, 1966: 9–19. DT1.G48, v. 2
Preliminary descriptive list of 29 Arabic and two Hausa manuscripts of the university collection.

Biography

2560
Alkali, Hamidu, *al-Hajj.* The "Mahdi" of Toranke. Kano studies, v. 1, pt. 4, 1968: 92–95. DLC
Account of a religious uprising in Toranke in March and April 1965 headed by Abubakar Bawande, who declared himself a Mahdi and established his own brand of Tijānīyah. He was later arrested and sentenced to a prison term.

2561
Bello, *Sir* Ahmadu. My life. Cambridge [Eng.] Cambridge University Press, 1962. 245 p. illus.
DT515.6.B4A3
Like the golden threads of an elaborate Hausa tobe (man's gown), many facets of Islamic life are

interwoven in the autobiography of the late Sardauna of Sokoto (1910–66).

2562
Froelich, Jean-Claude. Visite à El-Hadj Ibrahima Niasse. A&A, no 83–84, 2.–3. trimestres 1968: 37–41. DT1.A85, 1968

Interview of al-Ḥājj Ibrahima Niasse, Khalīfah of the Tijani sect, who lives in Kaolack, Senegal. The leader of the ṭarīqah relates the history of the sect and its basic tenets.

2563
Sölken, Heinz. Zur biographie des Imam Umaru von Kete-Kratyi. Africana Marburgensia, Bd 3, Heft 2, 1970: 24–30. DT1.A255, 1970

2564
West African chiefs; their changing status under colonial rule and independence. Edited by Michael Crowder and Obaro Ikime. New York, Africana Pub. Corp., 1970. 453 p. JV246.W4413

Includes the following contributions pertaining to Islam: Jean Suret-Canale, The Fouta-Djalon Chieftaincy; John N. Paden, Aspects of Emirship in Kano; Ronald Cohen, The Kingship in Bornu.

Cities

2565
Addo, N. O. Demographic and socio-economic aspects of Madina, an Accra suburb. Ghana journal of sociology, v. 2, Oct. 1966: 1–7. CU

2566
el-Masri, Fathi Hasan. Islam. *In* The City of Ibadan. Edited by Peter C. Lloyd, A. L. Mabogunje, B. Awe. London, Cambridge University Press in association with the Institute of African Studies, University of Ibadan, 1967. p. 249–257. DT515.9.I2C5

2567
Monteil, Vincent. Les religions: L'Islam. *In* Groupe d'études dakaroises. Dakar en devenir. Sous la direction de M. Sankalé, L. V. Thomas, P. Fougeyrollas. [Paris] Présence africaine, 1968. p. 199–210. HN810.S42D33

2568
Moughtin, J. C. The Juma'a (Friday) mosque, Zaria city. Savanna, v. 1, Dec. 1972: 143–163. HC517.N48S29

2569
Villien-Rossi, M. L. Bamako, capitale du Mali. BIFAN, t. 28, janv./avril 1966: 249–380. DT1.I5123, v. 28

Education

2570
Diallo, Cheikh Amalla. Contribution à une étude de l'enseignement privé coranique au Sénégal. Revue française d'études politiques africaines, no 76, avril 1972: 34–48. DT1.R4, 1972

2571
Gwarzo, H. I. Arabic teacher training in Nigeria. *In* Seminar on the teaching of Arabic in Nigeria, *University of Ibadan, 1965.* Report. Ibadan, 1965. p. 18–20. DLC

2572
Fafuwa, A. B. Islamic concept of education with particular reference to modern Nigeria. Nigerian journal of Islam, v. 1, Jan./June 1970: 15–20. DLC

2573
Galadanci, S. A. Arabic in secondary schools. *In* Seminar on the Teaching of Arabic in Nigeria, University of Ibadan, 1965. Report. Compiled by J. O. Hunwick. Ibadan, 1965. p. 20–22. DLC

2574
———Education of women in Islam with reference to Nigeria. Nigerian journal of Islam, v. 1, Jan./June 1970: 5–10. DLC

2575
Ḥakīm, Salīm. Ta'līm al-Lughah al-'Arabīyah fī Nayjīryā. [The teaching of Arabic in Nigeria] Baghdad, Wizārat al-thaqāfah wa-al-irshād, 1966. 131 p. illus., facsims., maps, ports. (al-Silsilah al-thaqāfīyah, 12) PJ6068.N5H3

2576
Monteil, Vincent. Educational problems in Nigeria. Présence africaine, no. 40, 1. quarter, 1962: 122–129. GN645.P74, 1962

Monteil stresses the importance of Arabic and deals with three basic problems: the teaching of Arabic; African languages used in schools; and higher education (universities).

2577
Portères, Roland. Encres et tablettes à écrire de fabrication et d'utilisation locale à Dalaba (Fouta-

Djalon, République de Guinée). NA, no 101, janv. 1964: 28–29. DT1.I513, 1964

2578
Samb, Amar. L'education islamique au Sénégal. NA, no 136, oct. 1972: 97–102. DT1.I513, 1972

2579
Sesay, S. I. Koranic schools in the Provinces [Sierra Leone] Journal of education, v. 1, Apr. 1966: 24–26. L81.J68, v. 1

2580
el-Tayib, Abdallah. The teaching of Arabic in Nigeria (Ibadan Arabic Seminar, 1965) Kano studies, no. 2, July 1966: 11–14. DLC

After discussing the problems of Arabic teaching in general, al-Ṭayyib focuses on language training in Nigeria. He feels that the major handicap is the coexistence of two educational systems, namely the modern secular and the Koranic traditional. The problem is compounded by the shortage of teachers and books. He concludes that "Arabic is in many respects the classical language of Western Africa."

2581
Weiler, Hans N., *ed.* Erziehung und Politik in Nigeria. Education and politics in Nigeria. Freiburg im Breisgau, Rombach [1964] 294 p. (Freiburger Studien zu Politik und Soziologie) LA1611.N5W4

"Eine Veröffentlichung des Arnold-Bergstraesser-Instituts für kulturwissenschaftliche Forschung, Freiburg im Breisgau."

German or English with summary in the other language.

History

2581a
'Abd al-'Azīz, Nādiyah. Ghānah fī al-Tirāth al-'Arabī al-qadīm. [Ghana in the old Arab heritage] al-Majallah, no. 9, Sept. 1957: 104–108.
AP95.A6M25, 1957 Orien Arab

Writing at the time Ghana gained its independence, the author suggests that the new Ghana is the Ghana of Arab geographers and travelers. She quotes extensively from Ibn al-Faqīh, al-Iṣṭakhrī, Ibn Ḥawqal, al-Idrīsī, Yāqūt al-Ḥamawī, and concludes with Ibn Baṭṭūṭah and his description of Mali to show Arab knowledge of the medieval empires.

2582
'Abd al-Ẓāhir, Ḥasan 'Īsā. Nayjīryā; al-waṭan al-Islāmī al-kabīr fī gharb Ifrīqiyā. [Nigeria; the great Islamic nation in West Africa] al-Wa'y al-Islāmī, v. 5, Jan. 8, 1970: 58–69.
BP1.W3, v. 5 Orien Arab

A description of Nigeria with emphasis on its geography, population, and political developments. The article concentrates on the spread and expansion of Islam in Nigeria, noting that Animism is a fertile ground for the spread of Islam and urging that a vigorous effort of proselytization be undertaken. The author concludes with a warning against the danger of Christian missions in the field of education.

2583
Abdur Rehman. Muslims in Senegal. Islamic literature, v. 15, Nov. 1969: 59–62. BP1.I68, v. 15

An introduction to Islam in Senegal. The author suggests that the clash between President Senghor and former Prime Minister Mamadou Dia in 1962 was "a clash of Christian-Muslim interests in which Leopold Senghor, with the help of police and army (which are dominated by Christian elements), emerged as victorious." He also sees the traditional religious leaders as subservient tools of the presidency.

2584
Aderibigbe, A. B. Trends and patterns in recent historical research in Nigeria. Paper presented at the International Congress of Africanists, third session, Dec. 9–19, 1973. Addis Ababa. 23 p. DLC

2585
al-Alūrī, Ādam 'Abd Allāh. Mūjaz tārīkh Nayjiryā, qāmūs ṣaghīr yalqī al-ḍaw' 'alā tārīkh ḥadhihi al-bilād qadimih wa hadithih. [Summary of the history of Nigeria; small dictionary that throws light on the old and new history of this country] Beirut, Dar maktabat al-ḥayāt [1965] 173 p. illus., maps. DT515.5.A7 Orien Arab

Includes one page on scarification.

2586
Baḥrī, Yūnus. Hādhihi jumhūriyat Mūrītāniyā al-Islāmīyah. [This is the Islamic Republic of Mauritania] Ceci: La République islamique de Mauritanie. [Bayrūt, Mu'assasat dār al-ḥayāt lil-ṭibā'ah wa-al-nashr, 1961] 288 p. illus., maps, ports.
DT553.M28B3 Orien Arab

At head of title: Yunus Bahri yuqadimm. [Yunus Bahri presents]

History of Mauritania by the former Radio Berlin speaker of World War II fame.

2587
Barīr, Maḥjūb. Nayjiryā bayna al-ams wa-al-yawm. [Nigeria between yesterday and today] [Khartoum, Jāmi'at al-Khartūm, Dār al-ta'līf wa-al-tarjamah wa-al-nashr, 1971] 107 p. illus. (*His* 1, Silsilat al-Kutub al-ta'rīfīyah bi-duwal wa-shu'ūb al-qārah al-Ifrīqīyah) DT515.75.B37 Orien Arab

2588
Bijlefeld, W. Anmerkungen zur Begegnung zwischen Christentun und Islam in Westafrika. Evangelische missionzeitschrift, Bd. 22, no. 2, 1965: 49–57. NjPT

2589
De Rachewiltz, Boris. Missione etno-archeologica nel Sahara maghrebino. Rapporto preliminari. Prima campagna (29 maggio-3 luglio 1971). Seconda campagna (28 marzo-7 maggio 1972). Africa, v. 27, Dec. 1972: 519–568. illus. DT1.A843, v. 27

Preliminary report on two missions undertaken in the Tafilelt region of Morocco. The team also investigated the ruins of Sijilmāsah, the gate to the Sudan in the medieval period.

2590
Garnier, Christine, *and* Philippe Ermont. Désert fertile, un nouvel état la Mauritanie. [Paris] Hachette [1960] 230 p. illus. DT553.M2G3

2591
Gerteiny, Alfred G. Mauritania. New York, Praeger [1967] 243 p. map. (Praeger library of African affairs) DT553.M2G4

2592
Ibrāhīm, Muḥammad 'Abd al-Fattāh. Jumhūrīyat Mālī. [The Mali Republic] [Cairo, 1961] 35 p. map. (Kutub qawmīyah, 116) DT551.8.M35I35

2593
Maliki, A. A. Islam in Nigeria. Islamic quarterly, v. 9, Jan./June, 1965: 30–36. D198.I8, v. 9

2594
Moreau, R. L. Note sur le pèlerinage à la Mecque vécu au Sénégal aujourd'hui. *In* Cairo. Institut dominicain d'études orientales. Mélanges, no. 9, 1967: 215–220. PJ9.C3, 1967

Pilgrimage to the Holy Places of Islam (hajj) is urged for all Muslims. Before the independence of Senegal the pilgrimage was on a small scale due to both economic and political factors as the former colonial administration attempted to isolate Muslims in Senegal from the mainstream of Islam. To facilitate the hajj, mutual aid pilgrimage associations were developed, which were often mutated into "amicale de pèlerins" after the return of the pilgrims who developed a strong bond of friendship through shared religious experiences. Pilgrimages in Senegal today are under government supervision in order to avoid abuses and to insure health measures.

2595
al-Najm, 'Abd al-Bārī 'Abd al-Razzāq. Jumhūrīyat Mūrītāniyah al-Islāmīyah, dirāsāt fi awḍā' Mūrītāniyah al-ṭabī'īyah wa-al-basharīyah wa-al-siyāsīyah. [The Islamic Republic of Mauritania, studies in physical, human, economic and political aspects of Mauritania] Beirut, Dār al-Andalus [1966] 196 p. map. DT553.M2N3

2596
Rato, Bernabé. Los Hausas y su Islam. Africa, año 23, septiembre 1966: 15–19. DT37.A1A4, v. 23

2597
Ṣawwār, Aḥmad. Jumhurīyat al-Nayjar. [The Niger Republic] [Cairo, al-Dār al-qawmīyah lil-ṭibā'ah wa-al-nashr, 1962] 74 p. map. (Kutub siyāsīyah) DT547.8.S2

2598
Shākir, Maḥmūd. Nayjīriyā. [Nigeria] [al-Ṭab'ah 2. Beirut] Mu'assasat al-Risālah lil-Ṭibā'ah wa-al-nashr [multazim al-tawzī': al-Shirkah al-muttaḥidah lil-tawzī', 1971] 128 p. maps. (Mawāṭin al-Shu'ūb al-Islāmīyah fī Ifrīqiyā, 2) DT515.S48 1971

2599
———al-Sinighāl. [Senegal] Damascus, Maktabat Dār al-Fatḥ [1971] 106 p. maps. (Mawāṭin al-Shu'ūb al-Islāmīyah fī Ifrīqiyā, 8) DT549.S47

2600
Sharābī, Maḥabbāt Imām Aḥmad. Nayjīriyā al-jadīdah, kunūzuhā wa-iqtiṣādiyātuhā. [The new Nigeria, its wealth and economy] [Cairo] al-Mu'assasah al-Miṣrīyah al-'āmmah lil-ta'līf wa-al-tarjamah wa-al-nashr [1964] 324 p. maps. DT515.S49

2601
Smith, H. F. C. The Northern [Nigeria] history research scheme: Second interim report; extracts. *In* Ibadan, Nigeria. University. *Centre of Arabic Documentation.* Research bulletin, v. 3, July 1967: 129–134. DLC

2602
Stenning, Derrick J. Savannah nomads; a study of the Woḍaaɓe pastoral Fulani of Western Bornu Province, Northern Region, Nigeria. With a foreword by Daryll Forde. London, Published for the International African Institute by Oxford University Press, 1969. 266 p. illus., maps (part fold.)
GN652.F9S8 1959

2603
al-Ṭahḥāwī, 'Ināyāt. Jumhūrīyat Sīrāliyūn. [The Republic of Sierra Leone] Minbar al-Islām, m. 26, Aug. 1968: 156–163.
DS36.M53, v. 26 Orien Arab

———al-Muslimūn fī Ghānā. [Muslims in Ghana] Minbar al-Islām, m. 26, Oct. 1968: 150–156.
DS36.M53, v. 26 Orien Arab

Brief presentations of Sierra Leone and Ghana. Part of series entitled "What Do You Know About the Muslim World, Its States and Peoples?" Includes a section on Islam in each country.

2604
Traoré, El-Hadj Sadia. Note sur le Dâdougou. NA, no 126, avril 1970: 33–42. DT1.I513, 1970

2605
'Ubayd, Jamīl. al-Mudīrīyah al-Istiwā'īyah. [The Equatorial province] Cairo, Dār al-Kitāb al-'Arabī, 1967. 583 p. maps. (al-Maktabah al-'Arabīyah, 56. al-ta'līf, 39. al-tārīkh, 5) DT137.M84U2

At head of title: al-Jumhūrīyah al-'Arabīyah al-Muttaḥidah. Wizārat al-Thaqāfah. Risālat al-Duktūrāh.

Languages & Linguistics

2606
Berque, Jacques. Un arabisant chez les Diola. *In* Mutanawwi'āt Muhammad al-Fāsī. [Rabat? 1969?] p. 5–14. AC105.M87 Orien Arab

At head of title: al-Mamlakah al-Maghribīyah: Jāmi'at Muḥammad al-Khāmis.

Added cover title: Mélanges Mohammed el Fasi.

2607
Bukhārī, Aḥmad al-Maḥallī. Ḥādir al-lughah al-'Arabīyah wa-al-dīn al-Islāmī fī gharb Nayjiryā, nidā' ilā zu'amā' al-'Arab wa-man yahummuhu amr al-Islām [Present status of the Arabic language and Islam in western Nigeria; a call to Arab leaders and all those concerned about Islam] [Beirut?196–] 15 p. illus. NjP

2608
Cohen, David. Le dialecte arabe Ḥassānīya de Mauritanie (parler de la Gəbla), par David Cohen avec la collaboration de Mohammed el Chennafi. Paris, C. Klincksieck, 1963. 293 p. illus. (Etudes arabes et islamiques. Etudes et documents, 5)
PJ6770.M3C6

2609
Oduyoye, Modupe. Yoruba and Semitic languages. Nigeria magazine, no. 99, Dec. 1968: 304–308.
DT515.N47, 1968

A study of Yoruba vocabulary of Semitic origin. The analysis attempts to show that lexical items have a genetic relationship to the Semitic family, implying a link which predates cultural contacts during the period of Islamic-Arabic infusion.

2610
Skinner, A. Neil. The Hausa particle ammā: an etymological note. Journal of African languages, v. 6, pt. 2, 1967: 146–152. PL8000.J6, v. 6

Investigation of the use of the Arabic term *ammā* (but) to mark the change of theme in the discourse, rather than its original adversative meaning.

2611
Wilks, Ivor. The Mande loan element in Twi. Ghana notes and queries, no. 4, Jan./Dec. 1962: 26–28. DT510.A1H553, 1962

Law

2612
Anderson, James N. D. Law and custom in Muslim areas in Africa: recent developments in Nigeria. Civilisations, v. 7, no. 1, 1957: 17–31.
AP1.C55, v. 7

Commenting on the 1956 "Moslem Court of Appeal Law" and "Native Courts Law," Anderson suggests that "the creation of the Moslem Court of Appeal, however inevitable it may have been on political grounds, can only be regarded as a step in the wrong direction. It would have been preferable, on every count, to have set up a special section of the High Court to hear appeals in all cases decided under native law and custom—as has, indeed, been suggested as a possible development in other territories also. All that can now be hoped for in the next few years is that the progressive unification of Nigeria as a whole, and increasing familiarity with developments in other Muslim countries, will eventually lead to the restriction of Islamic law to matters of personal status and family law. . . ."

2613
Diop, M. A. La dévolution successorale musulmane: détermination des héritiers dans le code sénégalais de la famille. Revue juridique et politique, indépendance et coopération, v. 26, oct./déc. 1972: 799–810. K21.J85, v. 26

2614
Mohamed Fall, O. A. Les successions en droit mauritanien. Revue juridique et politique; indépendance et coopération, v. 26, oct./déc. 1972: 754–757. DLC–LL

2615
Mortimore, M. J., *and* J. Wilson. Land and people in the Kano close-settled zone; a survey of some aspects of rural economy in the Ungogo District, Kano Province. [Zaria, Nigeria] Ahmadu Bello University, Dept. of Geography, 1965. 119 p. illus., maps. (Ahmadu Bello University. Dept. of Geography occasional paper no. 1) HC517.N482K375

"A report to the Greater Kano Planning Authority."

Of interest is the land distribution and its related problems of land tenure as well as the structure of settlements in a predominantly Muslim area.

2616
Muhammad, Yahaya. The legal status of Muslim women in the northern states of Nigeria. *In* Ahmadu Bello University, Zaria, Nigeria. *Centre of Islamic Legal Studies.* Journal, v. 1, no. 2, 1967: 1–28. K1.H5, v. 1

2617
Richardson, S. S. "Opting out": an experiment with jurisdiction in Northern Nigeria. Journal of African law, v. 8, no. 1, 1964: 20–28. DLC–LL

2618
Salacuse, Jeswald W. Selective survey of family law in Northern Nigeria. Zaria, Northern Nigeria, Institute of Administration, 1965. 113 leaves. (Ahmadu Bello University, Zaria, Nigeria. Institute of Administration. Research memorandum.) DLC–LL

Literature

2619
Arnott, D. W., *ed.* 'The song of rains': a Hausa poem by Na'ibi S. Wali. African language studies, v. 9, 1968: 120–147. PL8003.A34, v. 9

2620
Ba, Oumar, *and* Pierre-Francis Lacroix. Dix-huit poèmes peuls modernes. CEA, v. 2, 4. cahier, 1962: 536–550. DT1.C3, v. 2

Fulfulde poetry is traditionally restricted to epic poems and religious themes. In Senegal, students often gather in the evening for giri sessions, where they recite classical Arabic and Fulfulde poetry as well as their own poems. In this collection of 18 poems, Oumar Ba presents a lighter aspect of versification dealing with social aspects in a humorous vein, not unlike the satirical verses of the Ḥassānīyah bards of Mauritania.

2621
Baejou, R. Over Arabische litterate in West-Afrika. Kroniek van Afrika, v. 4, 1972: 173–186. DT1.K76, v. 4

2622
Balewa, *Sir* Abubakar Tafawa. Shaihu Umar: A novel. Translated and with an introduction and notes by Mervyn Hiskett. London, Longmans, 1967. 80 p. PZ4.B182Sh

Novel by the late federal Prime Minister providing a clear image of Hausa society at the end of the 19th century. The story revolves around three important Hausa institutions: the court, slavery, and the traditional Muslim system of education. Shaihu Umar represents the ideal type of the Hausa. He embodies, as Hiskett states, "the devotion to learning, the piety and patience in adversity [which] are part of the Hausa concept of a malam."

2623
King, A. V., *and Malam* Rashid Ibrahim. 'The song of rains': metric values in performance. African language studies, v. 9, 1968: 148–155. PL8003.A34, v. 9

See also 2619.

2624
Mabendy, Guissé. Devinettes recueillies au Mali. NA, no 112, oct. 1966: 133–135. DT1.I513, 1966

2625
———Sentences et expressions populaires au Mali. NA, no 109, janv. 1966: 19–21. DT1.I513, 1966

A list of 47 sayings from Mali containing "the wisdom of the ancestors and transmitted orally from generation to generation." The impact of Islam and its influence give these sayings a Muslim overtone.

2626
Mohammed Aliyun, Wada. A Hausa folktale. Kano studies, v. 1, June 1967: 54–61. DLC

2627
Scharfe, Don, *and* Yahaya Aliyu. Hausa poetry. Black Orpheus, no. 21, Apr. 1967: 31–36.
PL8000.B6, 1967

After reviewing the state of the art, the authors conclude, "The tradition of Hausa poetry is a live one, and the pattern of Hausa poetry is varied, from the oral traditions of the street to the learned works of the literate. In the range of its influence may lie its strength."

2628
Terrisse, André. Contes et légendes du Sénégal. Illustrations de Papa Ibra Tall. Paris, F. Nathan, 1965. 251 p. illus., col. plates. (Collections des contes et légendes de tous les pays) GR360.S4T4

2629
Thomas, Louis-Vincent. Récits Filham. NA, no 122, avril 1969: 41–54. DT1.I513, 1969

First of a series of articles relating fables from the Fogny region of lower Casamance in Senegal. This region has been greatly influenced by Islam and by one of its most representative groups, the Dyula, often labeled the "carpetbaggers of Islam." From this installment of 12 fables, Thomas concludes that Dyula flexibility has permitted it to weave Islam into the very fabric of traditional Dyula cultural heritage.

2630
Touré, Aïssata Kane, Ely Ould Allaf, *and* Maries Delarozière, *comps.* Il était une fois . . . en Mauritanie. Contes. Préface de Hamid Ould Mouknass. Paris, Ligel [1968] 104 p. illus. (part col.)
GR360.M342T6

2631
Traoré, Issa. Contes et récits du terroir. Bamako, Editions populaires [1970] 223 p. (Collection "Hier") PQ3989.2.T68C6

Politics

2632
Gerteiny, Alfred G. Race and politics in the Islamic Republic of Mauritania. Paper presented at the 8th annual meeting of the African Studies Association, Philadelphia, 1965. DLC-Micro 03782

Collation of the original: 13 p.

2633
———The racial factor and politics in the Islamic Republic of Mauritania. Race, v. 8, jan. 1967: 263–275. HT1501.R25

2634
Kamil, al-Sharif. The challenge of Nigeria. Middle East forum, v. 37, Jan. 1961: 9, 36.
DS41.M45, v. 37

Report on a visit to Nigeria by the deputy secretary general of the Islamic Congress in Jerusalem and his views regarding Islam as a variable in the Arab-Israeli conflict.

2635
Moore, C. M. One partyism in Mauritania. Journal of modern African studies, v. 3, Oct. 1965: 409–420. DT1.J68, v. 3

Study of the cleavage in Mauritanian politics between the Bīḍān and the blacks of the Fleuve region.

2636
Nicolas, Guy. Fondements magico-religieux du pouvoir politique au sein de la principauté hausa du Gobir. JOSAF, fasc. 39, 1969: 199–231.
DT1.S65, v. 39

"Sultan et prêtre, médiateur entre la 'terre' dont il est l''époux' et les puissances surnaturelles, le souverain du Gobir est également considéré par ses sujets comme un magicien maniant des forces numineuses en vue d'accroître et de défendre sa 'fortune' (*nasara*) et, partant, celle de sa principauté." Nicolas has studied the Gobir political structure in the Maradi region of Niger. Here he shows the complexity of political power in the principality and the delicate balance between Islamic tenets and the magico-religious substratum of political authority where "la stabilité du *Gobir* repose avant tout sur les alliances séculaires unissant la dynastie et les forces numineuses ou les groupes liés aux puissances surnaturelles."

2637
Schildkrout, Enid. Islam and politics in Kumasi: an analysis of disputes over the Kumasi Central Mosque. New York, American Museum of Natural History, 1974. p. 113–137. illus. (Anthropological papers of the American Museum of Natural History; v. 52, pt. 2) GN2.A27 vol. 52, pt. 2
DT512.9.K8

2638
———The Kumasi mosque dispute.

Source: ASA, Program, 15th, 1972.

Sects

2639
Abun-Nasr, Jamil M. The Tijaniyya, a Sufi order in the modern world. London, New York, Oxford University Press, 1965. 204 p. (Middle Eastern monographs, 7) BP189.7.T5A3 1965

Abū al-Naṣr, who wrote the work as a dissertation under Albert Hourani, provides a general history of the movement both in the Arab world and in West Africa. In the introduction, he states that "the story of the Tijaniyya presented below offers an example . . . of the dilemma which faced the Sufi orders during the French period: desirous of preserving their hold over their followers they needed to curry favour with the French, who were the political masters of the society. But association with the 'infidel' authorities was detrimental to their prestige in society, and gave their religious opponents, the Salafi fundamentalists, the opportunity to condemn them on both religious and political grounds."

2640
Behrman, Lucy C. Muslim brotherhoods and politics in Senegal. Cambridge [Mass.] Harvard University Press, 1970. 224 p. illus., map, ports. JQ3396.A3 1970.B43

Based on the author's thesis, Boston University, 1967.

2641
Cruise O'Brien, Donal B. Mouride studies. Africa, v. 40, July 1970: 257–260. PL8000.I6, v. 40

Review article.

2642
Doi, A. R. I. The Bamidele movement in Yorubaland. Orita, v. 3, Dec. 1969: 101–118. DLC

2643
Roch, J. Les mourides du vieux bassin arachidier sénégalais: entretiens recueillis dans la region du Baol. Dakar, Centre O.R.S.T.O.M., 1971. 113 p. DLC

2644
Rocheteau, Guy. Système mouride et rapports sociaux traditionnels. Le travail collectif agricole dans une communauté pionnière du Ferlo Occidental (Sénégal). Dakar, Centre O.R.S.T.O.M., 1969. 40 p. plans, plates.

Source: Senegal. Archives nationales. Bibliographie du Sénégal, no 40, 1972: no 167.

Society & Culture

2645
Barkow, J. H. Hausa women and Islam. Canadian journal of African studies, v. 6, no. 2, 1972: 317–328. CU

2646
——— Muslims and Magazawa in North Central State, Nigeria: an ethnographic comparison. Canadian journal of African studies: v. 7, no. 1, 1973: 59–76. CU

2647
Besmer, Fremont E. Kídan dárán sállà: music for the eve of the Muslim festivals of Id al-fitr and Id al-kabir in Kano, Nigeria. Bloomington, African Studies Program, Indiana University, 1974. 84 p. illus. ML350.B48

2648
Cohen, Abner. Custom & politics in urban Africa; a study of Hausa migrants in Yoruba towns. Berkeley, University of California Press, 1969. 252 p. map. HN800.N5C6 1969

"This monograph is a study in the role of customs in politics within some contemporary urban settings in Africa. It discusses the process by which, under certain circumstances, an ethnic group manipulates some values, norms, beliefs, symbols, and ceremonials from its traditional culture in order to develop an informal political organization which it uses as a weapon in its struggle for power with other groups, within the contemporary situation." The author shows how, in the process, Islam and the Tijani tariqah gained a commanding influence in the Hausa quarter of Ibadan and created a network of relationships strengthening ties between its members, leading to their control of long distance trade. One element undermining the cohesiveness of the community was the rapid growth of Yoruba Islam which "swallowed" the Hausa of Sabon who became no longer distinct as a religious group.

2649
Cohen, Ronald. Dominance and defiance; a study of marital instability in an Islamic society. [Washington, American Anthropological Association, 1971] 213 p. illus. (Anthropological studies, no. 6) DT515.42.C597

Detailed anthropological investigation of marriage and its instability in Kanuri society.

2650
Dawodu, S. A. Youth and Islam in Nigeria. Nigerian journal of Islam, v. 1, Jan./June 1971: 29–32. DLC

2651
Deniel, Raymond. Croyances religieuses et vie quotidienne, Islam et christianisme à Ouagadougou. Paris. Collège de France. Laboratoire d'anthropologie sociale, 1970. 360 p. fold. plan. (Recherches voltaïques, 14) DLC

Attitudinal study of Christianity and Islam Ouagadougou (February 1968–February 1969). Deniel, who interviewed both adults and school age children, tried to find answers to three basic questions: how do urban dwellers see their religion and other religions? What is the place of religion in their everyday life? and, What is the influence of their religious affiliation on the way they envision both religion and everyday life?

2652
Doi, A. R. I. An aspect of Islamic syncretism in Yorubaland. Orita, v. 5, June 1971: 36–45. DLC

2653
———Islamic thought and culture: Their impact on Africa with special reference to Nigeria. The Islamic review and Arab affairs, v. 57, Oct. 1969: 18–23. BP1.I7, v. 57

Looking at the long history of Islam in Africa, Doi attempts to show that Islam and Africa have been closely connected since the dawn of Islam. He then proceeds to look at Islam in northern Nigeria and its social impact. Included are a list of Hausa and Yoruba loan words from Arabic and a list of Arab names and their "Nigerianized" equivalents.

2654
Gallais, J. Signification du groupe ethnique au Mali. L'homme, t. 2, mai/août 1962: 106–129. GN1.H68, v. 2

2655
Gast, Marceau. Evolution de la vie économique et structures sociales en Ahaggar de 1660 à 1965. *In* Algiers. Université. *Institut de recherches sahariennes.* Travaux, v. 24, 1./2. semestres, 1965: 129–143. DT331.A4, v. 24

2656
———Mesures de capacité et de poids en Ahaggar. JOSAF, t. 33, fasc. 2, 1963: 209–230. DT1.S65, v. 33

2657
Ghazali, Abdul Karim. Sierra Leone Muslims and sacrificial rituals. Sierra Leone bulletin of religion, v. 2, June 1960: 27–32. DLC

2658
Griffeth, Robert R. The Dyula as guests in West Voltaïc societies.

Source: ASA, Program, 14th, 1971.

2659
Hallam, W. K. R. The men behind traditions. Nigeria magazine, no. 91, Dec. 1966: 271–278. illus. DT515.N47, 1966

2660
———The Shehu's installation, eventual Bornu ceremony. Nigeria magazine, no. 30, Dec. 1968: 280–290. illus. DT515.N47, 1968

A concise narrative of the Bornu Emirate and a report on the installation of Shehu Umar Ibn Abubakr Gaibai al-Kanemi as the new Shehu. The detailed description of the ceremony is of interest for comparative studies of earlier ceremonies reported by travelers.

2661
Joliot, Catherine. Entretien avec Ibra N'Diaye, peintre et sculpteur sénégalais. L'Afrique littéraire et artistique, no 11, 1970: 25–32. DT1.A54, no. 11

2662
Jones, William I. Tradition and agricultural development in the Republic of Mali. Paper presented at the 8th annual meeting of the African Studies Association, Philadelphia, 1965. DLC-Micro 03782

Collation of the original: 11 p.

2663
King, A. V. A Bòorîi liturgy from Katsina. African language studies, v. 7, 1967: 105–125; supplement to v. 7, 1967. 157 p. PL8003.A34, v. 7 and suppl.

Supernatural possession is termed *Bòorìi* in Hausa. Such practice, though frowned upon, is tolerated in some Muslim urban areas. "The state of possession," suggests King, "is induced with the aid of music which, depending on circumstances, may vary from a simple rhythmic hand-clap to an elaborate performance where the *wáakàa* (song) and the *kíráarìi* (identifying praise-epithets) of the *ìskàa* (supernatural spirit) invoked are accompanied by a suitable musical ensemble." The study is divided into two parts. The first part includes the introduction and kíráarìi and the second part the wáakàa with transliteration and translations of the various epithets and songs.

2664
Leighton, Neil O. The Lebanese community in Sierra Leone.
Source: ASA, Program, 15th, 1972.

2665
Lloyd, Peter C. Sallah at Ilorin. Nigerian magazine, no. 70, Sept. 1961: 266–278. DT515.N47, 1961
Description of the 'Id al-Kabīr in Ilorin. The Sallah ceremony shows the blend of Islamic and residual Yoruba practices.

2666
Ly, Boubacar. L'honneur dans les sociétés ouolof et toucouleur du Sénégal. Présence africaine, no 61, 1. trimestre, 1967: 32–67. GN645.P74, 1967

2667
Mabendy, Guissé. Salutations et voeux du Mali. NA, no 108, oct. 1965: 124–128. DT1.I513, 1965
Compilation of greetings and salutations in Mali. The influence of Islam is clear from the large number of references to God (Allāh).

2668
Madauci, Ibrahim, Yahya Isa, *and* Bello Daura. Hausa customs. [Zaria] Northern Nigerian Pub. Co., 1968. 96 p. DT518.H3M3

2669
el-Masri, Fathi Hassan. The role of Imams in the new Nigeria. Nigerian journal of Islam, v. 1, June 1970: 21–24. DLC

2670
Mathin, Céline. Pour une sémiologie du geste en Afrique occidentale. Semiotica, v. 3, no 3, 1969: 245–255. B820.S45, v. 3

2671
Miner, Horace H. Urban influences on the rural Hausa. *In* California. University. *University at Los Angeles. African Studies Center.* Urbanization and migration in West Africa, edited by Hilda Kuper. Berkeley, University of California Press, 1965. p. 110–130. HB2331.C33

2672
Moreau, R. L. Les marabouts de Dori. Archives de sociologie des religions, 9. année, janv./déc. 1964: 113–134. BL60.A7, v. 9
Detailed study of the marabout group in Dori in northern Upper Volta. After describing the various aspects and functions of the marabout, the author concludes that because of those who returned from the pilgrimage, Islam in Dori is slowly becoming closer to the Sunnah and orthodoxy.

2673
Muffet, D. J. M. Legitimacy and deference in a tradition oriented society: observations arising from a case study in Kano, 1962–63. Paper presented at the 16th annual meeting of the African Studies Association, Syracuse, N.Y., 1973. DLC-Micro 03782
Collation of the original: 14 p.

2674
Paden, John N. Situational ethnicity in Urban Africa with special reference to the Hausa. Paper presented at the 10th annual meeting of the African Studies Association, New York, 1967. illus. DLC-Micro 03782
Collation of the original: 17 p.

2675
Paul, P. Le système des référentiels personnels en wolof. BIFAN, t. 34, juil. 1972: 607–616. DT1.I5123, v. 34

2676
Quéchon, Martine. Réflexions sur certains aspects du syncrétisme de l'Islam ouest-Africain. CEA, t. 11, 2. cahier, 1971: 206–230. DT1.C3, v. 11
After reviewing the various theories regarding syncretism in West African Islam, such as those of P. Marty, A. Gouilly, and J.-C. Froelich, Quéchon looks into the more recent interpretative writings, including those of J. S. Trimingham, I. M. Lewis, and Vittorio Lanternari. According to the author, Lanternari "préfère une classification diachronique et dynamique qui a le mérite de privilégier non plus la forme des mouvements mais leur fonction, leur rapport à une société globale donnée." She studies how Islam has been influenced by local syncretism (Bambara, Nupe, and Songhay), animistic survivals and their reinterpretation, and possession cults (Hausa, Lebu). In conclusion, she applies Lanternari's theories by examining three socio-historical factors: a long contact with a foreign religion, the disintegration or upsetting of local culture, and the emergence of one or more charismatic leaders.

2677
Shani, Ma'aji A. The status of Muslim women in the Northern States of Nigeria. *In* Ahmadu Bello University, Zaria, Nigeria. *Centre of Islamic Legal Studies.* Journal, v. 1, no. 2, 1967: 39–52. K1.H5, v. 1

2678
Skinner, Elliott P. African urban life. The transformation of Ouagadougou. Princeton, N.J., Princeton University Press, 1974. 487 p. illus., tables.
HN810.U63O97
Includes a section on Islam and its interactions with modernization and with other religions.

2679
Smith, Michael G. Historical and cultural conditions of political corruption among the Hausa. Comparative studies in society and history, v. 6, Jan. 1964: 164–195. H1.C73, v. 6

2680
——The social functions and meaning of Hausa praise-singing. Africa, v. 27, Jan. 1967: 26–45.
PL8000.I6, v. 27

2681
Wane, Yaya. Les Toucouleurs du Sénégal et la modernisation. BIFAN, t. 32, juil. 1970: 888–900.
DT1.I5123, v. 32
Wane considers the religious factor a definite element of resistance to the acculturation process spreading like wild fire among the more or less Islamized ethnic groups.

2682
Whitaker, C. S., Jr. Three perspectives on hierarchy. Journal of commonwealth political studies, v. 3, Mar. 1965: 1–19. JN248.J65, v. 3
Analyzing the views of three Northern Nigerian leaders, namely Alhaji Sir Ahmadu Bello, the late Sardauno of Sokoto, Alhaji Sir Abubakar Tafawa Balewa, the late Prime Minister of the former Federal Government, and Malam Aminu Kano, who comes from a patrician family of erudites, the author attempts "1) to show that on a central issue of speculative political thought, namely the proper basis and structure of political participation, the three leading Northern Nigerian political figures take three different positions, each compatible with the practice of government within a democratic framework; 2) to contend that the ideological differences between these men may be explained, in part at least, by the fact that each occupies a different position within a common traditional political culture, the structure of which is hierarchical."

Glossary*

Ahmadi sect (Aḥmadīyah, Ahmadism)
A Muslim un-Orthodox reform movement founded in Kashmir in 1889 by Mirza Ghulam Ahmad Qadiyani. It was introduced in Nigeria about 1934 and has spread to a number of other African states.

Alfa
Fulbe title of a learned religious man.

Almamy
Title of the Tukulor ruler.

al-Anṣār
Originally used to identify the "helpers" of the Prophet Muḥammad after his flight from Mecca to Medina. Adopted by the supporters of the Khatmīyah sect in the Sudan.

Ardo
Among the nomadic Fulbe, a camp leader whose function is one of advice and representation of the group rather than command.

Bīḍān
Arabic term meaning "whites" referring to the Moors (Maures) of Mauritania as opposed to the darker populations of the Fleuve region.

Damel
Ruler of the Cayor state which was established in the 16th century on the coast of Senegal north of Cape Vert and lasted until the French intervention in the 19th century.

Dhimmī
"People of Scripture"—Christians, Jews, and Sabeans—have a special status in territories conquered by Muslims and where the Shari'ah is the law of the land. Each community of *Ahl al-Dhimmah*, or "People of the Covenant and Obligation," governed itself under its responsible head who was its link with the Muslim authorities.

Diwān
A collection of the works of a poet.

Fiqh
Muslim jurisprudence. Islam regulates all aspects of public and private life and the science of these laws is called fiqh.

Faqīh (colloquial Arabic: Fiqi/Fi'i)
A teacher versed in jurisprudence and canon law. Sometimes refers to a casuist.

Griots
Member of a caste found in many ethnic groups in West Africa. They are historically the repository of tradition and function now as musicians, genealogists, and praise singers.

Girgam (Mahram)
Traditional histories of Kanuri mais (rulers) usually written in Arabic or preserved orally in Kanuri verse form.

Hajj (Hadji, Hajji)
Arabic title, meaning pilgrim, bestowed on one who has made the pilgrimage to Mecca.

al-Ḥisbah
A term in administrative law for the office of the *Muḥtasib*, or functionary in charge of weights and measures in the market place, the registration of births and deaths, and a number of other responsibilities.

Jihad
Arabic term, meaning to strive or struggle, connoting the duty of every Muslim adult when possible (Fard 'ala al-kifayah) to fight for the expansion of Dar al-Islam. Lately, the meaning has been interpreted by reformers to mean the striving to be a better Muslim and to improve the lot of the Islamic community.

Karamoko
Title of a Dyula religious teacher.

Laamido (Pl. Laamibe)
Fulbe ruler. His jurisdiction can encompass from a small group of a few hundred persons to a large kingdom.

al-Mahdī.
"The Guided One." Refers to the last Imam, or Redeemer, who will appear at the End of Time to restore the true faith and conquer the world for Islam. The concept is more fundamental to the Shi'ite creed than to that of the Orthodox Sunnites. Generally used, in the bibliography, with reference to Muḥammad Aḥmad, the Sudanese leader.

Magal
The annual pilgrimage to Touba in Senegal, seat of the Murid sect, in celebration of the return from exile of its founder Amadu Bamba.

*Most of the definitions of the glossary were drawn from *The Encyclopedia of Islam; a Dictionary of the Geography, Ethnography and Biography of the Muhammadan Peoples, Prepared by a Number of Leading Orientalists*, published under the patronage of the International Association of the Academies (Leyden, E. J. Brill; London, Luzac, 1913–34. 4 v. illus. DS37.E5).

Mai
Traditional ruler of the Kanuri people.

Malikite School of Law
One of the four major schools of jurisprudence named after Mālik ibn Anas (d. 795), a theologian and jurist from Medina.

Mallam
A Hausa learned man. Derived from Arabic *Mu'allim,* teacher, or master.

Marabout
French appelation for a Muslim holy man or ascetic in West Africa. Derived from Arabic *Murābit*, or Muslim "Templar."

Modibbo
Fulbe term for a religious erudite. Derived from Arabic *Mu'addib,* teacher, or educator.

Muqaddim
Arabic term for chief or commander of a body of troops or a ship. Also a Sufi term designating a leader in a religious sect, or brotherhood. The Murid leaders holding this title are divided into three grades with various powers of consecration.

Murid sect (Murīdīyah, Mouridism, Muridism)
A Sufi sect founded by Amadu Bamba (ca. 1850–1927) and centered mainly in Senegal, which has played a significant role in Senegalese politics.

Qaṣīdah
Arabic ode with no less than seven or 10 verses.

Ribāṭ
A fortified monastery, usually found at the frontiers of Islam, and occupied by soldier-"monks." Provided the root for terms such as Almoravids and marabout.

Sahel
Arabic term derived from *Sāḥil* (shore) and referring to the climatological zone stretching across West and Central Africa between the Sahara desert and the Savannah areas.

Saj'
A particular form of rhetoric where rhymed words occur at short intervals. The absence of regular rhythm or meter distinguishes it from poetry.

Salafīyah
An Egyptian religious modernist reform movement begun at the end of the 19th century and early in the 20th century by Shaykh Muḥammad 'Abduh (1849–1905) under the influence of Shaykh Jamāl al-Dīn al-Afghānī with whom he later published al-*'Urwah al-Wuthqā* in Paris, which had a profound influence on the development of nationalism in the Arab world.

Sarkin Zongo
Hausa term referring to the chief of the Hausa ward in urban areas outside Hausaland.

Senussi sect (Sanūsīyah)
A Muslim military sect founded by Sayyid Muḥammad ibn 'Alī al-Sanūsī (1791–1859) centered in Cyrenaica, Libya.

Shī 'ah (Shi'ism, Shi'ites)
General name for a large number of very different Muslim sects, all of which do agree on the recognition of 'Alī ibn Abī Ṭālib as the legitimate caliph after the death of the Prophet Muhammad. Considered the second major division of Islam as opposed to Sunnah.

Sunnah (Sunnism, Sunnites)
Arabic for custom, use, or wont. Also the Orthodox "People of the Sunnah and the Community" in Islam, as opposed to the *Shī-'ah*, the other major division in the Muslim world. The Sunnites are divided into the four schools of jurisprudence, namely Hanafites, Hanbalites, Malikites, and Shafi'ites.

Taṣawwuf (Sufi)
The act of devoting oneself to the ascetic mystical life on becoming a Sufi. The term *Sufi* is thought by some to be derived from *ṣūf*, or wool, and to refer to the penitents' practice of wearing the woolen robe, *labs al-Ṣūf*.

Thierno
Tukulor teacher and religious leader.

Tyeddo
Warrior class in the Wolof pagan states. They were opposed to the marabout forces who labeled them as irreligious "bad Muslims." Amadu Bamba recruited them in the Murid sect during its formative period.

Waqf
Arabic legal term for a pious endowment to be used only for a permitted charitable purpose.

Zār
Amharic word for genii or spirits, adopted by the Muslim world. Also for exorcistic rites, under the leadership of a shaykhah accompanied by drums, gyrations, and sacrifices of fowls, to summon the evil spirit to "tell his name" and thus deprive him of his power and hold on the victim.

Zāwiyah
Literally, corner of a building, and by extension a small mosque or monastery to which a holy man has retired to live and devote his time to meditation, learning, and mysticism surrounded by his pupils and followers.

Zikr
Sufi ritual consisting of the repetition of words in praise of God, usually with music and gyrating dancing.

List of Periodicals

Abbia. Yaounde. AP9.A24
al-Abḥāth. Beirut. AS595.A6A36 Orien Arab
Abr-Nahrain. Leiden, E. J. Brill. PJ3001.A2
Académie des inscriptions et belles-lettres, Paris. Comptes rendus des séances. Paris, C. Klincksieck. AS162.P315
Académie des sciences d'outre-mer. Comptes rendus mensuels des séances. Paris. JV1802.A314
Académie malgache. Bulletin. Tananarive. DT469.M21A35
Académie royale des sciences d'outre-mer. *Classe des sciences morales et politiques.* Mémoires. Verhandelingen. Bruxelles. DT641.A27
Académie royale des sciences d'outre-mer. Bulletin des séances. Mededelingen der zittingen. Bruxelles. JV2802.A3
Acta ethnographica. Budapest. GN1.A25
Acta geographica. Paris. G1.S553
Aequatoria; mission catholique. Coquilhatville. MH-P
Affari esteri. [Roma, Associazione italiana per gli studi di politica estera] D839.E812
Africa. London, Oxford University Press. PL8000.I6
Africa [revista de acción española] Madrid [Instituto de Estudios Políticos] DT37.A1A4
Africa; rivista bimestrale di studi e documentazione. [Roma] DT1.A843
Africa Institute. Bulletin. [Pretoria] DT1.A2146
Africa quarterly. [New Delhi] DT1.A216
African affairs; journal of the Royal African Society. [London] DT1.R62
African arts. Arts d'Afrique. [Los Angeles] NX587.A6
African ecclesiastical review. Masaka, Uganda. IEN
African forum. [New York, American Society of African Culture] DT1.A225
The African historian. Ile-Ife, Nigeria. DLC
African historical studies. Brookline, Mass., African Studies Center of Boston University. DT1.A226
African language studies. London, University of London, School of Oriental and African Studies. PL8003.A34
African music. Roodepoort, South Africa. ML5.A26
African Society, *London.* Journal.
See African affairs.
African studies. Johannesburg, Witwatersrand University Press. DT751.A4
African studies bulletin. Stanford, Calif. DT1.A2293
African studies review. Cairo.
See Majallat al-dirāsāt al-Ifrīqīyah.
African studies review. East Lansing, Mich., African Studies Center, Michigan State University. DT1.A2293
African world. [London, African Publications] DT1.A24
Africana bulletin. [Warsaw] DT19.9.P6A65
Africana Marburgensia. [Marburg] DT1.A255
The Africanist. Washington. DLC
Afrika heute. Bonn, L. Röhrscheid. DT1.A27
Afrika und Ubersee; Sprachen, Kulturen. Berlin, D. Reimer. PL8000.Z4
Afrique documents. Dakar. DT1.A479
L'Afrique et l'Asie. [Paris] DT1.A85
L'Afrique française; bulletin mensuel du Comité de l'Afrique française et du Comité du Maroc. Paris, Comité de l'Afrique. JV14.C67
L'Afrique littéraire et artistique. Paris. DT1.A54
Afrique nouvelle. Dakar. AP27.A58
Afro-Asia. Bahia, Universidade Federal da Bahia, Centro de Estudos Afro-Orientais. DLC
Ahmadu Bello University, *Zaria, Nigeria. Centre of Islamic Legal Studies.* Journal. [Zaria] K1.H5
Akademie der Wissenschaften, *Berlin. Istitut für Orientforschung.* Mitteilungen. Berlin, Akademie-Verlag. PJ5.A5A25
Akademia nauk SSSR. *Institut etnografii.* Trudy. Moskva. GN2.A2142
Algiers (City) Université. *Institut de recherches sahariennes.* Travaux. DT331.A4
American anthropologist. Menasha, Wisc. American Anthropological Association. GN1.A5
American Oriental Society. Journal. New Haven. PJ2.A6
American Universities Field Staff. Reports service: Central & Southern Africa series. New York. DT751.A54
al-Andalus. Madrid-Granada. DP102.A6
Annales africaines. Paris, A. Pedone. DLC-Law
Annales d'Ethiopie. Paris, C. Klincksieck. DT379.A6
Annales d'histoire économique et sociale. Paris, A. Colin. HB3.A5
Annales de géographie. Paris, A. Colin. G1.A6
Annales; économies, sociétés, civilisations. [Paris] A. Colin. AP20.A58
Annales islamologiques. Le Caire, Impr. de l'Institut français d'archéologie orientale. BP1.A65

Année africaine. Paris, Editions A. Pedone. DT30.A56
Anthropological quarterly. Washington, Catholic University of America Press. GN1.P7
L'Anthropologie. Paris. GN1.A68
Anthropos. Fribourg. GN1.A7
Antiquity; a quarterly review of archaeology. [Gloucester, Eng.] CC1.A7
Arabica; revue d'études arabes. Leiden, E. J. Brill. PJ6001.A7
Archaeologia Polona. Warszawa, Zaklad Narodowy im. Ossolińskich. GN845.P7A75
The Architectural review. New York. NA1.A67
Archiv für Völkerkunde. Wien. GR1.A59
Archives de sociologie des religions. Paris, Editions du Centre national de la recherche scientifique. BL60.A7
Ars orientalis; the arts of Islam and the East. [Washington] N7260.A7
Asian and African studies. Bratislava, Vydavateľstvo Slovenskej akadémie vied. DS1.A4733
Asian and African studies. Jerusalem. DS1.A4734
Association de géographes français, Paris. [Paris] G11.A8
Aussenpolitik. Stuttgart, Deutsches Verlags-Anstalt. D839.A885
Azania. Nairobi, Oxford University Press. DT365.3.A94

B

Baessler-Archiv; Beiträge zur Völkerkunde. Berlin, D. Reimer. GN1.B3
Bantu studies. Johannesburg, Witwatersrand University Press. DT764.B2B3
Berlin. Universität. *Seminar für Orientalische Sprachen.* Mittheilungen. PJ25.B5
Black Orpheus. [Ikeja, Longmans of Nigeria] PL8000.B6
Boletim cultural de Guiné Portuguesa. [Bissau] DT613.B6
Boston University law review. Boston, Boston University Law School. DLC-LL
The British journal of sociology. London, Routledge and Kegan Paul. HM1.B75
Bulletin de jurisprudence des tribunaux indigènes du Ruanda-Urundi. Astrida. DLC-LL
Bulletin de liaison saharienne. Algiers. DT331.B83
Bulletin de Madagascar. [Tananarive, Service général de l'information] DT469.M21B8
Bustan. Vienna. DS35.3.B87

C

Cahiers d'action religieuse et sociale. [Paris] Editions Spes. BX802.C3
Cahiers d'études africaines. Paris. DT1.C3
Les Cahiers d'outre-mer. Revue de géographie de Bordeaux et de l'Atlantique. Bordeaux. G1.C15
Cairo. Institut dominicain d'études orientales. Mélanges. [Le Caire] PJ9.C3
Cairo. al-Jāmi'al-Azhar. Majallat al-Azhar. BP1.C3 Orien Arab
Cairo. Jāmi'at'Ayn Shams. *Kullīyat al-Ādāb.* Ḥawlīyāt Kullīyat al-Ādāb. AS693.C36 Orien Arab
Cairo. Jāmi'at al-Qāhirah. *Kullīyat al-Ādāb.* Majallat Kullīyat al-Ādāb. AS693.C25 Orien Arab
Cairo. al-Jam'iyah al-Miṣrīyah lil-'Ulūm. al-Majallah al-Miṣrīyah lil-'ulūm al-siyāsīyah. JA26.M2 Orien Arab
Cairo. al-Jam'iyah al-Miṣrīyah lil-Dirāsāt al-Tārīkhīyah. al-Majallah al tārīkhīyah al-Miṣrīyah. DT77.J28 Orien Arab
Cairo. Ma'had al-Buḥūth wa-al-Dirāsāt al-Ifrīqīyah. DLC
Camelang. Université du Cameroun. DLC
Canadian journal of African studies. [Montreal] DT19.9.C3B82
The Cape monthly magazine. Cape Town. NN
The Catholic digest. [St. Paul, Minn.] BX801.C34
Cauris. Strasbourg. NN
Centre d'étude et de documentation africaines. Les cahiers. DT1.C45
Centre of Islamic Legal Studies. Journal. Zaria. ICU
The Christian century. [Chicago] Christian Century Press. BR1.C45
Civilisations. [Bruxelles] AP1.C55
The Clergy review; a magazine for the clergy. London. BX801.C6
Comité d'études historiques et scientifiques de l'Afrique Occidentale française. Annales et mémoires. MnU
———Bulletin. Paris. DT521.C6
Comparative studies in society and history. The Hague, Mouton. H1.C73
The Contemporary review. London. AP4.C7
Core. [Rangely, Me., Orgone Institute] RZ999.C8
Corona. London. JV1001.C77
Correspondance d'Orient. Etudes. Bruxelles, Centre pour l'étude des problèmes du monde musulman contemporain. DS36.C65
Cultures et développement. Louvain. HD83.C85
Current anthropology. [Utrecht] GN1.C8
A Current bibliography on African affairs. Washington. Z3501.C89
Current history. [Philadelphia] D410.C82
The Cuttington review. Guaranga, Liberia. DLC

D

Dakar. Université. *Faculté des lettres et sciences humaines.* Annales. AS659.S4D35

E

East Africa journal. [Nairobi, East African Institute of Social and Cultural Affairs] DT421.E28
East African law journal. Nairobi. DLC-LL
Economies et sociétés. MH
L'Education africaine. Bulletin officiel de l'enseignement en A.O.F. [Dakar] L81.E42
Encyclopédie mensuelle d'outre-mer. [Paris] JV1801.E5
Estudos ultramarinos; revista. Lisboa. JV4201.E8
Ethnohistory. [Bloomington, Indiana University] E51.E8
Ethnopsychologie. Le Havre. BF732.R48
Etnografia polska. Wrocław, Zaklad Narodowy im Ossolińskich. GN585.P6E8
Etudes congolaises. Léopoldville. DT658.E8
Etudes éburnéennes. [Mâcon, France] DT545.E8
Etudes maliennes. Bamako. DLC
Etudes soudaniennes. [Koulouba, Bamako] DT551.E83
Euhemer; przegląd religioznawczy. Warszawa, Państwowe Wydawn. Naukowe. BL9.P6E8
Europe, France outre-mer. [Paris] JV1801.E65

F

Fei-chou yen chiu [African studies] [Taipei] DLC
Folia orientalia. Kraków [Państwowe Wydawn. Naukowe] PJ9.F6
France. *Comité des travaux historiques et scientifiques.* Bulletin. Paris. G11.F8
France. *Office de la recherche scientifique et technique outre-mer.* Cahiers O.R.S.T.O.M. Série sciences humaines. Paris. DT521.C3
Frankfurter Hefte; Zeitschrift für Kultur und Politik. Frankfurt am Main. AP30.F555

G

Garcia de Orta. Lisboa. JV4201.G3
Genève-Afrique. Geneva-Africa. Geneva. DT1.G44
The Geographical journal. London, Royal Geographical Society. G7.R91
Gesellschaft für Erdkunde zu Berlin. Zeitschrift. Berlin, D. Reimer. G13.G5
Ghana. University, *Legon. Institute of African Studies.* Research review. DT1.G48
Ghana bulletin of theology. Achimota. DLC
Ghana notes and queries. Accra. DT510.A1H553
Glasgow. University. *Oriental Society.* Transactions. MH
Grands lacs; revue générale des missions d'Afrique. Namur. BV3500.A35

H

Hadith. [Nairobi] East African Pub. House. DT434.E2A25
al-Hady al-Islāmī. al-Bayḍā'. BP1.H33 Orien Arab
The Harvard review. [Cambridge, Mass.] AS36.H23
Hespéris, archives berbères et bulletin de l'Institut des hautes-études marocaines. Paris, Librairie Larose. DT181.H4
Hespéris-Tamuda. Rabat, Editions techniques nord-africaines. DT301.H45
The Heythrop journal. Oxford, Heythrop College. BX801.H4
Historical Society of Ghana. Transactions. Legon. DT510.A1H55
Historical Society of Nigeria. Journal [Ibadan] DT515.A2H5
———Bulletin of news. Ibadan. DLC
Hochland. München. AP30.H67
L'Homme. Paris, Mouton. GN1.H68
L'Homme et la société. [Paris, Editions Anthropos] HM3.H6
Howard law journal. Washington. DLC-LL
Human organization. [New York] GN1.H83

I

IBLA [revue de l'Institut des belles lettres arabes] Tunis. AS653.I5
Ibadan. University. *Centre of Arabic Documentation.* Research bulletin. DT352.4.I2a
Indiana. University. *Folklore Institute.* Journal. [The Hague] Mouton. GR1.I5
The Indiana law journal. Buffalo. K9.N37
Institut égyptien, *Cairo.* Bulletin. DT43.I61
Institut français d'Afrique noire. Bulletin. Dakar. DT1.I5123
Institut français d'Afrique noire. *Centre du Cameroun.* Etudes camerounaises. [Douala] DT561.I5
International affairs. [London] JX1.I53
International development review. Washington, Society for International Development. HC60.I546
International Folk Music Council. Journal. Cambridge, Eng. ML26.I544
International journal of African historical studies. [New York] Africana Pub. Corp. DT1.A226
International journal of Middle East studies. [London] Cambridge University Press. DS41.I55
International review of missions. Edinburgh. BV2351.I6
Internationales Afrika Forum. München, Europäische Institut für politische, wirtschaftliche und soziale Fragen. DLC
Der Islam. Strassbourg, K. J. Trübner. DS36.I7
Islamic culture; an English quarterly. Hyderabad, Deccan, Islamic Culture Board. DS36.I74

Islamic literature. [Lahore, Sh. Muhammad Ashraf] BP1.I68
The Islamic quarterly. London, Islamic Cultural Centre. D198.I8
The Islamic review. Woking, Eng., The Mosque. BP1.I7

J

Jāmi'at al-Qāhirah bi-al-Kharṭūm. Majallah. DLC
Journal asiatique. Paris. PJ4.J5
Journal des voyages, découvertes et navigations modernes. Paris. G161.J86
Journal of administration overseas. [London] H. M. Stationery Off. JS40.J6
Journal of African history. [London, New York] DT1.J65
Journal of African languages. London, Macmillan. PL8000.J6
Journal of African law. London. DLC-LL
Journal of Commonwealth political studies. [Leicester] Leicester University Press. JN248.J65
Journal of Ethiopian studies. Addis Ababa. DT371.J67
Journal of human relations. Wilberforce, Ohio, Central State College. H1.J55
The Journal of modern African studies. [London] Cambridge University Press. DT1.J68
The Journal of Negro history. Washington, Association for the Study of Negro Life and History. E185.J86
Journal of religion in Africa. Leiden. BL2400.J68
Journal of Semitic studies. Manchester, Manchester University Press. PJ3001.J6
The Journal of West African languages. [London] PL8017.J65

K

Kano studies. Dirāsāt Kānū. Kano, Nigeria. DLC
Kenya education journal. Nairobi. DLC
Kongo-overzee. Antwerpen, De Sikkel. DT641.K57
Kontynenty. Warsaw. G464.K685
Kush; journal of the Sudan Antiquities Service. Khartoum. DT129.K8
Kutub Islāmīyah. Cairo. BP20.K8 Orien Arab
Kyklos. Bern, A. Francke A. G. H1.A15

L

Leipzig. Museum für Volkerkunde. Jahrbuch. Berlin, Akademie-Verlag. GN37.L4233
Liberia. Washington. E448.L68
Libri; international library review and communications. Copenhagen, Munksgaard. Z671.L74
London. University. *School of Oriental and African studies*. Bulletin. [London] PJ3.L6

M

Madrid. Ma'had al-dirāsāt al-Islāmīyah. Sahifah. DP103.M32 Orien Arab
Maghreb digest. Los Angeles. DT181.M34
al-Majallah. Cairo. AP95.A6M25 Orien Arab
Majallat al-dirāsāt al-Ifrīqīyah. [Cairo] L71.N337 Orien Arab
Majallat al-dirāsāt al-Islāmīyah. Cairo. DS36.M24 Orien Arab
Majallat al-dirāsāt al-Sūdānīyah. Khartoum. DLC
Makerere journal. [Kampala] AS625.K33
Man. London. GN1.M252
al-Ma'rifah. Damascus. AP95.A6M3 Orien Arab
Materialy zachodnio-pomorskie. Szezecin. DD491.P745M3
Michigan Academy of Science, Arts and Letters. Papers. New York, Macmillan. Q11.M56
Middle East forum. [Beirut] DS41.M45
The Middle East journal. Washington. DS1.M5
Middle Eastern affairs. New York, Praeger. DS42.4.M5
Middle Eastern studies. London. DS41.M535
Minbar al-Islām. Cairo. DS36.M53 Orien Arab
ha-Mizraḥ he-ḥadash. Jerusalem. DS41.M56 Orien Hebr
The Modern law review. London, Modern Law Review Ltd. DLC-LL
Monde non-chrétien. Paris. NjPT
The Muslim world. Hartford, Conn. DS36.M7
The Muslim's digest. [Durban, Natal] Makki Publications. BP1.I553
al-Muslimūn. Geneva. BP1.M86 Orien Arab

N

Naples. Istituto orientale. Annali dell'Istituto superiore orientale. Roma. PJ6.N32
Narody Azii i Afriki. Moscow. DS1.P7
New Orient. [Prague, Czechoslovak Society for Eastern Studies] DS1.N43
New York Academy of Sciences. Annals. Q11.N5
Nigeria magazine. [Lagos] DT515.N47
The Nigerian field; the journal of the Nigerian Field Society. London. QH195.N5A15
Nigerian geographical journal. [Ibadan, Nigerian Geographical Association] DT515.A2N5
Nigerian journal of Islam. Ile-Ife, Nigeria. DLC
Nigrizia. Verona. BV3500.A43
Notes africaines. [Dakar] DT1.I513
Notes et documents voltaïques. Ouagadougou. DT553.U7A25
Notes on Islam. Calcutta, Oriental Institute (Islamic Section), St. Xavier's College. BP1.N6
Notices et extraits des manuscrits de la Bibliothèque nationale et autres bibliothèques. Paris, Impr. nationale. Z6620.F8P2

La Nouvelle revue française d'outre-mer. [Paris] JV1801.N6
Nový orient; kulturne-politicky mesicnik. Prague. DS1.N6
Numen; international review for the history of religions. Leiden, Brill. BL1.N8
The Numismatic chronicle, and journal of the Royal Numismatic Society. London. CJ1.N6
The Nyasaland journal. Blantyre, Nyasaland. DT858.N9

O

Odu. Ife, Nigeria. DT515.A2O32
Orbis. [Philadelphia] Foreign Policy Research Institute. D839.O68
Orient. [Paris] DS1.O44
Oriental art. [London] N8.O75
Orita. Ibadan. DLC
Osiris; studies on the history and philosophy of science, and on the history of learning and culture. Bruges. Q1.O7
Oversea education. London. LC2601.O8

P

Paedagogica historica. Gent. L10.P24
Paideuma, Mitteilungen zur Kulturkunde. [Frankfurt am Main] CB3.P3
Past & present; a journal of historical studies. [Oxford] D1.P37
Patterns of prejudice. London. DS145.P34
Portugal. *Agencia Geral do Ultramar*. Boletim geral do ultramar. Lisboa. JV4201.A33
Pount; bulletin de la Société d'études de l'Afrique orientale. Djibouti. DLC
Présence africaine. [Paris] GN645.P74
Przegląd historyczny. Warszawa, Państwowe Wydawn. Naukowe. DK401.P915
Przegląd orientalistyczny. Warszawa, Państwowe Wydawn. Naukowe. PJ9.P7
Przegląd sojologiczny. Łodz. HM7.P7

R

Race. London, Oxford University Press. HT1501.R25
Rassegna di studi etiopici. Roma, La Libreria dello stato. DT371.R3
Recherches africaines. [Conakry] DT543.A3R4
La Réforme sociale. Paris. H3.R3
Remarques africaines. Bruxelles. DT1.R34
Réunion d'études algériennes. Bulletin. Paris. *Source*: Brasseur
The Review of nations; an organ for pan-humanism and spiritual freedom. Geneva. AP4.R38
The Review of politics. Notre Dame, Ind. JA1.R4
Revue africaine; journal des travaux de la Société historique algérienne. Algiers, Bastide. DT271.R4
Revue anthropologique. Paris, E. Nourry. GN2.P25
Revue camerounaise d'histoire. Cameroon historical review. Yaounde. DLC
Revue d'ethnographie et de sociologie. Paris, E. Leroux. GN1.R5
Revue d'ethnographie et des traditions populaires. Paris, Société française d'ethnographie. GN1.R53
Revue d'histoire des colonies.
See Revue française d'histoire d'outre-mer.
Revue de défense nationale. [Paris] Berger-Levrault. D410.R45
Revue de géographie. Paris, C. Delagrave. G1.R43
La Revue de géographie humaine et d'ethnologie. Paris, Gallimard. GN1.R54
Revue de l'histoire des colonies françaises.
See Revue française d'histoire d'outre-mer.
Revue de l'Orient, de l'Algérie et des colonies. Bulletin de la Société orientale de France. Paris, Delavigne. DS1.R4
La Revue de Madagascar. Tananarive, Impr. officielle. DT469.M21R43
Revue de Paris. Bruxelles. AP20.R268
Revue des deux mondes. Paris. AP20.R3
Revue des études islamiques. Paris, P. Geuthner. BP1.R53
Revue des questions de défense nationale.
See Revue de défense nationale.
Revue des troupes coloniales.
See Tropiques.
Revue du monde musulman. Paris, E. Leroux. DS36.R4
Revue française d'études politiques africaines. [Paris, Société africaine d'édition] DT1.R4
Revue française d'histoire d'outre-mer. Paris. JV1801.R4
Revue franco-musulmane et saharienne. Paris. NNC
La Revue indigène; organe des intérêts des indigènes aux colonies et pays de protectorat. Paris. JV1835.R5
Revue internationale d'onomastique. Paris, Editions d'Artrey. CS2300.R4
Revue juridique et politique, indépendance et coopération. Paris. DLC
Revue militaire générale. Paris, Editions Berger-Levrault. U2.R48
Revue politique et parlementaire. Paris, A. Colin. H3.R4
Revue tunisienne; organe de l'Institut de Carthage. Tunis. DT241.R45
al-Risālah. Cairo. AP95.A6R5 Orien Arab
Rocznik orientalistyczny. Warszawa. PJ9.R6

Royal African Society. Journal.
See African affairs.
Royal Anthropological Institute of Great Britain and Ireland. The journal. London. GN2.A3
Royal Asiatic Society of Great Britain and Ireland. The journal. AS122.L72

S

Saeculum. Jahrbuch für Universalgeschichte. Freiburg, K. Alber. D2.S3
Savanna. Zaria, Nigeria, Ahmadu Bello University. HC517.N48S29
Semiotica. The Hague. B820.S45
Seychelles Society. Journal. [Victoria, Seychelles] DT469.S4S43
The Sierra Leone bulletin of religion. Freetown. DLC
Sierra Leone studies. [Freetown] DT516.A1S5
al-Siyāsah al-Duwalīyah. [Cairo, Mu'assasat al-Ahrām] D839.S55
Sociedade de Estudos de Moçambique. Boletim. Lourenço Marques. DT451.S6
Société d'anthropologie de Paris. Bulletins et mémoires. Paris. GN2.S61
Société d'études camerounaises. Bulletin. Douala. DT561.S6
Société de géographie, *Paris*. Bulletin. Paris. G11.S4
———Recueil de voyages et de mémoires. Paris. G161.S67
Société de géographie commerciale de Bordeaux. Bulletin. DLC-Micro 38304
Société de géographie de l'AOF. Bulletin. *Source:* Brasseur
Société de géographie et d'archéologie de la province d'Oran. Bulletin trimestriel de géographie et d'archéologie. Oran. DT298.O8S622
Société de linguistique de Paris. Mémoires. Paris. P12.S45
Société des africanistes, *Paris*. Journal. DT1.S65
Société Jean Bodin pour l'histoire comparative des institutions. Recueils. Bruxelles. H13.S622
Société languedocienne de géographie, *Montpellier*. Bulletin. Montpellier. G11.S84
Society of Malawi journal. [Blantyre] DT858.N9
Somaliland journal. Hargeisa. MBU
Southwestern journal of anthropology. Albuquerque. GN1.S64
Sovetskaia etnografiía. Moscow. GN1.S65
Spain. *Consejo Superior de Investigaciones Cientificas. Instituto de Estudios Africanos.* Archivos. Madrid. DT1.S75
Studia Islamica. Paris, Larose. BP1.S8
Sudan law journal & reports. Khartoum. DLC-LL
Sudan notes and records. Khartoum. DT118.S85
Sudan society. Khartoum. HN831.S8A6
Swahili. Dar es Salaam. PL8701.E2

T

La Table ronde. [Paris] AP20.T3
Tanzania notes and records. Dar es Salaam. DT436.T3
Tarikh. Ikeja, Nigeria. DLC
al-Ṭarīq. Beirut. DLC
Togo-Cameroun; magazine mensuel. Paris [Libraire Larose] HC557.T6T6
The Town planning review. Liverpool, University Press. NA9000.T6
Transafrican journal of history. [Nairobi, East African Pub. House] DT1.T7
Transition. Kampala. AP9.T7
Tropiques; revue des Troupes coloniales. [Paris, Pouzet] UA709.A6T7

U

Ufahamu. [Los Angeles] DT1.U4
The Uganda journal. London, Oxford University Press. DT434.U2U3
Ultramar. [Lisboa] JV4201.M62
United Nations Educational, Scientific and Cultural Organization. Le courrier. Paris. AS4.U8A23

V

Victoria Institute, or Philosophical Society of Great Britain, *London*. Journal of the transactions. London. AS122.L9
Vieux papiers du temps des Isles. Paris. *Source:* Joucla
Visages d'Afrique. Ouagadougou. NX589.6.U6V55

W

WALA news. [Ibadan] Z674.W25
al-Wa'y al-Islāmī. al-Kuwayt. BP1.W3 Orien Arab
Die Welt des Islams. Leiden, E. J. Brill. DS36.W4
West Africa. London. DT491.W4
West African journal of education. [Ibadan] L81.W4
The West African review. [Liverpool] DT491.W47
Word. New York. P1.W65

Index

Numbers refer to items. An "n" following the number indicates reference is not in the entry but in the annotation. An "R" following "Sudan" refers to the western region of the continent as opposed to the Republic of Sudan. Whenever available, Library of Congress form has been followed for personal names; otherwise they are given as reported by the author.

A

A.O.F. *See* French West Africa
Aba Island Battle, 1272
Aba Musa, an ecumenical Tubu, 1680
al-'Abbādī, 'Abd al-Ḥamīd, 389
al- 'Abbādī, Aḥmad Mukhtār, 579
Abbadie, A. d', 2248
'Abbās, *Bey*, 1099
'Abbās, Muḥammed Jalāl, 41, 47, 284, 390, 391
'Abbās Sall, *al-Hajj*, 1790n
Abbasids, 102n, 502n, 949n
  Islam under, 190
Abbo, Mohamadou, 990, 991
'Abbūd, Ibrāhīm, *Gen.*, 2469n
'Abd Allāh ibn al-Ḥājj Ibrāhīm, 1760n
'Abd Allāh ibn Muḥammed Fūdī. *See* Abdullahi dan Fodyo
'Abd Allāh ibn Yāsīn, 525
'Abd Allāh Thīkah al-Fallātī al-Baghāwī, 778
'Abd al-'Azīz, *Sultan*, 1601n
'Abd al- 'Azīz, Nādiyah, 2581a
'Abd al-Hamīd, Sa'd Zaghlūl, 622
'Abd al-Jalīl, al-Shātir Busaylī, 738, 1198
'Abd al-Mahmūd Nūr al-Dā 'im, 1478n
'Abd al-Majīd, Amīn 'Abd al-Majīd, 739
'Abd al-Malik ibn Marwān and Lamu, 1174n
'Abd al-Muṭṭalin ibn Ghālib, 1645n
'Abd al-Nabī, 'Abd al-Ḥamīd, 15
'Abd al-Qādir, Ḥāmid, 65
'Abd al-Qādir ibn Abū Bakr al-Tuwatī, *al-Hajj*, 2412
'Abd al-Qādir's mission and Franco-Tukulor relations (1885–1887), 1982
'Abd al-Raḥmān, Muṣhammad Fawzī Muṭafā, 2502
'Abd al-Raḥmān Djire, 1762
'Abd al-Raḥmān ibn Hāmid Tarawīrī, 2128n
'Abd al-Tahmān ibn Husayn al-Jabrī, 1230
'Abd al-Wahāb, Ḥasan Ḥusnī, 452
'Abd al-Wāḥid al-Marrākuskī, 580
'Abd al-Zāhir, Ḥasan 'Īsā, 2582
Abdallah, Hemed, 1100
Abdallah bin Hemedi 'LAjjemy, 2457
Abdallah ibn Ali ibn Nasir, 1472
Abdel Rahim, Muddathir, 1200, 1401, 1404
'Ābdīn, 'Abd al-Majīd, 479, 480, 2528
'Abduh, Muḥammad, *Shaykh*, 47n, 1604n
Abdul, M. O. A., 2293
Abdul, Raoul, 314n
Abdul Basit, 66
Abdul Haye, Muhammad, 437
Abdul Karim, *See* Barth, Heinrich
Abdulla, Ahmed, 2451
'Abdullāb origins and history, 1350, 1360
Abdullah ibn Suliman of Tabwa, biography, 1133
'Abdullahi, Khalifah of the Mahdi, 1098, 1132, 1140
Abdullahi dan Fodyo Arabic manuscripts, 781, 825, 970
Abdur Rehman, 2583
Abéché, 2439
Abed bin Hamad Wali of Lamu, 1186n
Abedi, Kaluta Amri, 438
Abel, Armand, 992, 993, 1074, 1201
Abemba, Bulaimu, 994
Abimola, Wande, 2294
Abir, Mordechai, 740, 772
Abraham, 1144
Abrahamowicz, Marianna, 184, 706
Abron, 2051
Abū 'Abd Allāh Muḥammad ibn Masānih ibn Ghumāhu ibn Muḥammad ibn 'Abd Allāh ibn Nūḥ al-Barnāwī al-Kashināwī, 778
Abū al- 'Arab Muḥammad ibn Aḥmad al-Tamīmī, 67
Abū Bakr, *Imam* of Zaria, 1795
Abū Bakr al-Bārikum, 778
Abū Bakr ibn Ḥijāb al-Dimānī, 1950
Abū Bakr ibn 'Umar, 596
Abū Bakr ibn 'Umar al-Khashmāwī, *Effendi*, 1601
Abū Fadl 'Iyyad ibn Mūsā, 979n
Abū al-Fidā'. *See* Abulfeda
Abū Ḥabl, 487n
Abu Hakima, Ahmad M., 2553
Abū Ḥamd Battle, 1419
Abū al-Kaylik, 1372
Abū Rannāt, Sayyid Muḥammad, 2484
Abū al-Rūs, Khālid, 741
Abu Salīm, Muḥammad Ibrāhīm, 1080, 1202, 1320, 1343, 1531
Abu Sananogo, *al-Hajj*, 1715n
Abu Sinn, 'Alī 'Abd Allāh, 1203
Abū Sinn family, 1293n
Abubakar, S., 995
Abubakar Bawande, 2560n
Abuja Chronicle, 1735
Abulfeda, 68
Abun-Nasr, Jamil M., 2639
Abyssinia. *See* Ethiopia
Accounting, 163
Accra Muslim community, 1690
Acculturation, 91, 97, 199, 402, 419, 433–35, 1556
  Adamawa, 998
  Boran, 150
  Comoro Islands, 1466n
  Gogo, 150
  Hausa, 885n
  Kanuri, 885n
  Kilwa Kivinje, 150

H

J

L

M

South Africa (*continued*)
19th cent., 1597
statistics, 2550
a Sufi from, 1605
visit of Prince Muḥammad ʻAlī, 1594
Southern Sudan. *See* Sudan, Southern
Sow, Alfâ Ibrahîm, 9, 939, 2044, 2191, 2192
Sowâré, 2096n
Spain, 102n
possible origin of Sané stelae, 569a
Spain, David, 396
Spaulding, Jay, 1398
Spillman, Georges, 386
Spirit possession in northeastern region, 1401
Stafford, A. O., 23
Stanley, Henry M., 989n
lecture in Cairo (1890), 1036n
Stanleyville, 989
Staude, Wilhelm, 2045
Staudinger, Paul, early traveler to Kano, 1966
Star calendar, Arab planetary system, Hausa poem, 2151
Stelae
Anorotsangana, 1458
Bentia, 531a, 534a, 541, 541a, 577a, 577b
El-Kreib, 577a
Kumbi Ṣāiḥ, 577a
Qiha, 505a
Sané, 560n, 561n, 562, 569a, 577a, 577b, 937
Sudanic regions, 577a
Tilemsi, 541b
undeciphered in Ambilobe, 1543
Stenning, Derrick J., 150, 2602
Stephenson, John E., 1597
Stępniewska, Barbara, 662, 663, 708
Stevenson, Roland C., 150, 1399, 1401
Stewart, Charles C., 2046, 2287, 2390
Stewart, E. K., 2390
Stigand, Chauncy H., 1400
Stones, precious and semiprecious, 331
Strabo, 496n
Strandes, Justus, 769
Strauss, Peter L., 1271
Strelcyn, Stefan, 62, 770
Strong, S. Arthur, 1185
Strong, Tracy, 255
Struck, Bernhard, 1457
Students from Africa at Azhar University, 64n
Suakin, 1355n
Sūbā
destruction, 741
Fung conquest, 1300
Ṣub al-Aʻshā fī Ṣinā ʻat al-Inshā', 234
Sublime Porte, Inger and the Mahdi, 1137n
Sudan, 261n, 1298, 1302, 1304
in Africa, 1401, 2508
African policy, 2520
Arab
African confrontation, 2518
culture in, 495
Islamic culture, 2528
Arabic language
dialect, 2491, 2493
slang, 1426
sources on, 1083
Arabism
and Africanism, 2522
Africanism and self-identification, 2524
and Pan-Arabism, 1510

Sudan (*continued*)
Arabization, 479
and Arabs (7th-16th cent.), 493
Arabs in, 1333
and Africans, 2467
Arabs in Nigeria, 2352
biographical dictionary, 1118
governors-general and provincial governors, 1119
saints and scholars (16th-19th cent.), 1120
blacks and whites, 2531
borders and civil war, 2524
Britain and the slave (19th cent.), 1210
building methods, 1169
central region
history and civilization (17th-19th cent.), 738
and Chad, 1076
Christian kingdoms (500–1500), 497
civil war, 260, 2524, 2526
civilization (4th-20th cent.), 742
clan of religious notables, 1122
Congo and Central West Africa (19th cent.), 1401
Conquest of Sūbā Chronicle, 1300
eastern region, 96n
history and civilization (17th-19th cent.), 738
Islam in, 1415
Islamization (15th-18th cent.), 1401
economics and regional autonomy, 2524
education (6th-19th cent.), 739
and Egypt (1820–1881), 1291
Equatorial Province, 2605
Ethics, concept of dignity, 2541
Ethiopia
relations (pre-19th cent.), 1401
war (1885–1888), 1391
geography, 1395
history
medieval sources, 493n
to 1821, 743
identification and national integration, 2520
Islam in, 172, 1408, 2538
and Christianity, 1141
and its future, 2483
and holy families, 1121
and nation building, 2512
politics and the sects, 1521
Islamic law
and customary law, 1401, 2484
reforms, 1461, 2486
Islamic state and military regime, 2521
linguistics, 1401
Mahdi's emirs, 1130
marriage and conflict of laws, 2488
in medieval writings, 484, 500
multiple marginality, 1401
Muslim
poetry, 1497
states (1450–1821), 494
nationalism and independence, 421
Native Administration and Africa, 1401
Nilotic region
and Darfur, 483
Islamization, 421
problem, 2523
northern region, 1342
Arabization, 493n
arts, 2535
Islamization, 493n

T

Library of Congress Publications on Africa Since 1960

Africa south of the Sahara; a selected, annotated list of writings. 1963. 354 p.
Out of print.

Africa south of the Sahara; index to periodical literature, 1900–1970. 1971. 4 v.
Available from G. K. Hall and Co., 70 Lincoln St., Boston, Mass. 02111; $325 in the U.S., $357 elsewhere

Africa south of the Sahara; index to periodical literature. First supplement. 1973. 521 p.
Available from G. K. Hall and Co.; $65 in the U.S., $71.50 elsewhere.

African libraries, book production, and archives; a list of references. 1962. 64 p.
Out of print.

African music; a brief annotated bibliography. 1964. 55 p.
L

African names and naming practices; a selected list of references in English. 1977. [2] p.
Reprinted from the Library of Congress *Information Bulletin*, v. 36, Mar. 25, 1977.
D

African newspapers in selected American libraries. 3d ed. 1965. 135 p.
L

The African Section in the Library of Congress. [1975] folder ([5] p.)
D
Also available in French.

Africana acquisitions; a report of a publication survey trip to Nigeria, southern Africa, and Europe, 1972. 1973. 122 p.
L

Agricultural development schemes in sub-Saharan Africa; a bibliography, 1963. 189 p.
Out of print.

American doctoral dissertations on the Arab world, 1883–1974. 2d ed. 1976. 173 p.
SuDocs (LC1.12/2:Arl/883–974) $4.60.

Arab-African relations, 1973–75. 1976. 26 p. (Maktaba Afrikana series).
D

Botswana, Lesotho, and Swaziland; a guide to official publications, 1868–1968. 1971. 84 p.
L

East African Community; subject guide to official publications. 1976. 272 p.
SuDocs (LC2.2:Af8/13) $6.65.

Folklore from Africa to the United States: an annotated bibliography. 1976. 161 p.
SuDocs (LC2.2:F71) $4.50.

French-speaking Central Africa; a guide to official publications in American Libraries. 1973. 314 p.
L

French-speaking West Africa; a guide to official publications. 1967. 201 p.
L

Ghana; a guide to official publications, 1872–1968. 1969. 110 p.
L

A list of American doctoral dissertations on Africa. 1962. 69 p.
Out of print.

Madagascar and adjacent islands; a guide to official publications. 1965. 58 p.
L

Nigeria; a guide to official publications. 1966. 166 p.
L

Official publications of British East Africa
Part 1. The East African High Commission and other regional documents. 1960. 67 p.
Out of print.
Part 2. Tanganyika. 1962. 134 p.
Out of print.
Part 3. Kenya and Zanzibar. 1962. 162 p.
L
Part 4. Uganda. 1963. 100 p.
L

Official publications of French Equatorial Africa, French Cameroons, and Togo, 1946–1958; a guide. 1964. 78 p.
Out of print.

Official publications of Sierra Leone and Gambia. 1963. 92 p.
L

Official publications of Somaliland, 1941–1959. 1960. 41 p.
Out of print.

Portuguese Africa; a guide to official publications. 1967. 217 p.
L

The Rhodesias and Nyasaland; a guide to official publications. 1965. 285 p.
L

Serials for African studies. 1961. 163 p.
Out of print.

Spanish-speaking Africa; a guide to official publications. 1973. 66 p.
Out of print.

Sub-Saharan Africa; a guide to serials. 1970. 409 p.
L

Tanganyika African National Union; a guide to publications by and about TANU. 1976. 52 p. (Maktaba Afrikana series)
D

Uganda; subject guide to official publications, 1977. 271 p.
SuDocs

United States and Canadian publications on Africa in 1960. 1962. 98 p.
SuDocs (LC2.2:Af8/7)

Key to Abbreviations:

D Distributed free by the Library of Congress, African Section, Washington, D.C. 20540

L Available to U.S. libraries and institutions upon request to the Library of Congress, Central Services Division, Washington, D.C. 20540. Foreign libraries may apply to the Exchange and Gift Division.

SuDocs For sale by the Superintendent of Documents, U.S. Government Printing Office, Washington, D.C. 20402. When ordering, cite the GPO catalog number; it appears in parentheses after the symbol "SuDocs." Add 25% for foreign postage. Increases in costs make it necessary for the Superintendent of Documents to increase the selling price of many publications offered. As it is not feasible for the Superintendent of Documents to correct the prices manually in all publications stocked, the prices charged on your order may differ from the prices printed in the publications.

Out of print Copies of out of print publications may be ordered from the Library of Congress, Photoduplication Service, Washington, D.C. 20540.

Guides in Preparation or Under Consideration

Bibliographic guides on the following subjects are in preparation or under consideration in the Library's African Section; when published, each will be announced in the Library's *Information Bulletin.*

Eastern African university publications (Kenya, Malawi, Tanzania, Uganda, and Zambia)
Kenya, official publications
Nigerian petroleum industry
Tanzania, official publications
United States Government publications on Africa, and supplement

☆ U.S. GOVERNMENT PRINTING OFFICE: 1978 O—588-332